HANDBO

SOCIAL CO

Second I

Volum

Basic Pro

HANDBOOK OF SOCIAL COGNITION
Second Edition

Volume 1
Basic Processes

Edited by

ROBERT S. WYER, JR.
THOMAS K. SRULL
University of Illinois, Urbana-Champaign

LEA LAWRENCE ERLBAUM ASSOCIATES, PUBLISHERS
1994   Hillsdale, New Jersey   Hove, U K

Lawrence Erlbaum Associates, Inc., Publishers
365 Broadway
Hillsdale, New Jersey 07642

Library of Congress Cataloging-in-Publication Data

Handbook of social cognition / edited by Robert S. Wyer, Thomas K.
Srull. — 2nd ed.
p.   cm.
Includes bibliographical references and indexes.
Contents: v. 1. Basic processes — v. 2. Applications.
ISBN 0-8058-1057-9 (vol. 1, cloth). — ISBN 0-8058-1056-0 (set)
ISBN 0-8058-1058-7 (vol. 2, cloth)
1. Social perception. 2. Cognition. 3. Cognition—Handbooks.
4. Social perception—Handbooks. I. Wyer, Robert S., Jr. II. Srull,
Thomas K.
HM132.H333 1994
302'.12—dc20   93-29484
                                                         CIP

Books published by Lawrence Erlbaum Associates are printed on acid-free
paper, and their bindings are chosen for strength and durability.

Printed in the United States of America
10 9 8 7 6 5 4 3 2 1

Contents

Foreword

The first edition of the *Handbook of Social Cognition* was a revolutionary manifesto. It was both a challenge to traditional ways of social psychological theorizing and a statement from the rabble that "we are here and we mean to stay." It was confrontational and passionate. It was fists and sinew demanding recognition and acceptance.

THE GROWTH OF SOCIAL COGNITION

That first edition was published only a decade ago, in 1984. This is an unusually short interval of time between editions for volumes of this sort. For example, the *Handbook of Social Psychology* has averaged over 15 years between editions, and yet, there clearly was a need for this revised edition. The need was motivated not by discontent with the coverage or scholarship of the first edition, but rather by the enormous outpouring of new research and theory on the topic in the past 10 years. The field of social cognition has changed substantially since the appearance of the first edition.

The rapid expansion of social cognition also can be seen in the large number of edited volumes that have been published in the past 10 years, including the *Advances in Social Cognition* series, edited by Wyer and Srull, which focus on specialized topics in the field. In addition, the first comprehensive text on social cognition, authored by Fiske and Taylor, was published in the same year as the first edition of this *Handbook*. The second edition of that text, involving revisions ranging from 40% to 80% of each chapter, was published in 1991. Those authors, like the editors of this *Handbook*, recognized and responded promptly to the fast-paced dynamism of the field.

The table of contents of the present edition of the *Handbook* reveals several clues as to the nature of the changes in this field. Of the 15 chapters in this second edition, only four involve authors who had contributed to the first edition. This illustrates several points. First, it displays the rapid growth in the number of scholars entering the field of social cognition. Second, it shows the increased acceptance of social cognition concepts as relevant to understanding traditionally important social psychological processes (see Volume 1) and domain-specific applications of those processes (see Volume 2).

Further comparison of contributors shows that, although 7 of the 17 chapters in the first edition were authored or coauthored by cognitive psychologists, no authors in the present edition are identified primarily with cognitive psychology. In assembling the first edition, the editors apparently believed it necessary to recruit cognitive psychologists for the purpose of educating social psychologists about many of the basic principles and issues in cognitive psychology. In contrast, the present edition reflects a confidence that most readers come to the volume with such understandings well in hand. It correctly takes for granted that the current generation of readers will have already completed their basic training in cognitive psychology through undergraduate and graduate course work. The present edition displays a comfortable self-acceptance with the role that social cognition has come to play in the field.

THE SOVEREIGNTY OF SOCIAL COGNITION

The first edition of this *Handbook* led off with a chapter entitled "The Sovereignty of Social Cognition." No other chapter conveyed the revolutionary manifesto of that edition more forcefully than did this one. The chapter, and especially its zealous title, proved offensive to some scholars in the field. It was viewed as being, in part, naive and, in part, delusional. Many of those skeptics felt that social cognition would prove to be only a minor (and slightly offensive) digression in the history of social psychology.

Perhaps the title of that chapter was ill chosen. It certainly led some of the chapter's critics to not even bother reading the chapter. Rather, those scholars condemned the whole field on the basis of the presumptuousness of the chapter's title. Yet the substance of the chapter was intended to be self-critical and conciliatory, rather than arrogant and confrontational. It was intended to embrace diverse traditional perspectives rather than to reject or condemn them.

The editors of this second edition suggested to me that I prepare a new updated introductory chapter. After some thought, I declined. It seemed to me that the basic points made in the earlier chapter were still valid and that, although the exposition of those ideas could be improved, the issues raised there are still the ones most fundamental to the field of social cognition. To obtain a sense of the scope and integrative potential of social cognition, contemporary readers may find it beneficial to include that chapter as part of their readings in the field.

Three topics received special emphasis in that chapter. I offer some commentary on each in the remainder of this Foreword.

DEFINING SOCIAL COGNITION

When that chapter was written, there had been 22 separate attempts to define the term *social cognition*. That number probably has increased to over 100 by now, given the number of papers, chapters, and textbooks that have been published in the interim on the subject. An analytic synthesis of this extensive list would prove overwhelming and probably would yield little of value even if the required time and effort were devoted to the task. After all, the real goal of the field is to improve one's understanding of social psychological phenomena. There is no reason to be distracted by definitional squabbles that dwell only on the label given to the new research and theory.

I regard single-sentence definitions of social cognition to be slightly offensive, despite their necessity for textbooks and despite the fact that I have done so in my own writings. It is impossible to convey past history and future aspirations in a single sentence, it is impossible to capture the creative richness of the ideas in a single sentence, and it is impossible to portray the enthusiasms of its scholars in a single sentence. I stated in the earlier chapter that my definition of the field was the entire chapter. It would be more accurate to say that my preferred definition is the entire *Handbook of Social Cognition*, both this and the first edition combined.

At the heart of social cognition is the conceptual orientation that has emerged from the information-processing perspective in cognitive psychology, a perspective that recently has expanded to include cognitive science. The social cognition approach is based on the conviction that constructs relevant to cognitive representation and process are fundamental to understanding all human responses, regardless of whether those responses are social or nonsocial in nature. Cognitive psychologists have applied these concepts to the analysis of a wide range of phenomena, such as text comprehension, recall, recognition, classification, reasoning, vision, and audition. Social cognition researchers share this theoretical perspective, differing solely in the phenomena to be understood. Those social phenomena are, of course, the focus of the two volumes in this *Handbook*.

ACTION IS THE CORE OF SOCIAL BEHAVIOR

The single most important theme of my earlier chapter was that cognitive activity was in the service of interpersonal action. Thinking, along with its more mindless cognitive companions, has evolved to allow persons to act on and react to a world that is first and foremost social in nature. Lamentably, it seems that this theme was poorly understood and widely ignored by the field. Despite this neglect, I believe the analyses offered in that chapter remain valid today.

The chapter presented a fourfold analysis of the difference between social and nonsocial knowledge and their attendant cognitive processes. Much of the research covered in the first two editions of the *Handbook* falls in the first three categories of that classification system. Unfortunately, these three categories are the least social of the system. They describe characteristics of persons as stimulus objects (Category One), characteristics of the perceiver (Category Two), and contingencies in human interaction (Category Three). The nature of these categories, and their relation to earlier attempts at defining social cognition, were discussed at some length in that chapter.

Category Four highlights the perceiver as an interaction participant. It includes the processes of the first three categories, but goes beyond them. In doing so, it aspires to understand cognitive representations and cognitive processes as they operate on-line while the person engages in meaningful congress with one or more other persons.

Category Four information processing has several important features. Most notably, it involves a heavy processing load on the perceiver's cognitive capacities. As perceivers, we have personal goals to form and modify on-line. We have to be selectively attentive to the other person's responses, and to draw inferences from those responses regarding the other person's beliefs, intentions, and affective dispositions. We must be able to access memory for past encounters with that person as well as earlier transactions in the current encounter. We must be able to anticipate the partner's reaction to alternative personal initiatives and to select for display the one judged to be most effective.

Not only do social exchanges have multiple sources of demand on our cognitive system, but they also possess a number of very distracting features. Distractions come from the inherent unpredictability of our partner's responses, from the fact that concurrent verbal and nonverbal behavior of the partner may be inconsistent with one another, and, in the case of multiple interaction partners, from the unpredictability of who will be responding next.

Category Four processing appears oppressive. It is seemingly overwhelming in the number and nature of demands on the cognitive system. Yet humans have evolved to deal with such demands on most occasions in a near effortless manner. The real challenge to social cognition, then, is to understand how the many components of the information-processing system work together to support human action, especially social interaction.

One important research vector has emerged that directly informs Category Four information processing. The heavy cognitive demands during face-to-face interaction require that social behavior be guided by automatic rather than controlled processes—on on-line rather than retrieval-based processes. Deliberative processes, ones that involve selective retrieval from long-term memory and thoughtful analyses of alternatives, are serial in nature, easily disrupted, and relatively slow in execution. Therefore, such deliberative processes cannot account for most of what guides action in interaction contexts. More needs to be learned about how automatic processes operate in producing the multiple, simultaneous, verbal, and nonverbal behaviors that occur during interaction. More needs to be known about the interface between automatic and controlled processes, especially in regard to controlled override of automatic inclinations.

IS SOCIAL COGNITION SOVEREIGN?

Of course it is. The earlier chapter presented six arguments in support of the sovereignty proposition. They dealt with issues such as the newly achieved relevance of cognitive research to traditional social phenomena, to the priority of social over nonsocial processes, to the capacity of cognitive principles to help understand affective and motivational processes, and to the potential for linking cognitive constructs to the neurological substrate. Not only do those arguments remain valid today, but they have been strengthened by work that has appeared subsequent to the chapter's publication.

The present edition adds a seventh argument supporting the ultimate destiny of social cognition as monarch of social psychology. In its early stages, social cognition was dismissed as the sterile study of memory under laboratory conditions. This shallow caricature was accepted by many scholars in social psychology who were concerned with applying principles of their field to pressing social, organizational, and economic problems. Acceptance of that view led these scholars initially to dismiss social cognition on the grounds that it was irrelevant to their concerns.

A great strength of this second edition is its inclusion of six new chapters that cover many of the ways in which social cognition has contributed to an improved understanding of, and solutions to, such concerns. These chapters cover clinical psychology, close relationships, political psychology, consumer psychology, personnel psychology, and health psychology. The pervasiveness of the cognitive orientation is such that it has permeated all areas of applied social psychology. For example, other chapters could have been included on topics such as law and psychology, the psychology of women, the psychology of ethnic minority issues, and a number of other fields that are now divisions of the American Psychological Association.

It is clear that social cognition is no longer revolutionary. Instead, it has attained the status of "standard science." It no longer can be taught to graduate students as an exciting new conceptual orientation. Students arrive having had broad exposure to the basic principles in their undergraduate curriculum, and therefore are baffled when they encounter fervent advocacy and claims of novelty.

This second edition of the *Handbook* fully conveys the new maturity of social cognition. It amply demonstrates the relevance of information-processing principles to understanding the cognitive dynamics underlying a broad array of traditional domains in social psychology. Indeed, it is easy to envision a future in which there is no longer a need for a separate *Handbook of Social Cognition*. The *Handbook of Social Cognition* will become the *Handbook of Social Psychology*.

—Thomas M. Ostrom
Ohio State University

Preface

When the first edition of the *Handbook of Social Cognition* appeared in 1984, it was a promissory note. The field was then in its infancy, and the areas of research and theory that came to dominate the field during the next decade were only beginning to emerge. The concepts and methods used had frequently been borrowed from cognitive psychology, and had been applied to phenomena in a very limited number of areas. Nevertheless, social cognition promised to develop rapidly into an important area of psychological inquiry that would ultimately have an impact not only on several areas of psychology but on other fields as well.

The promises made by the earlier edition of the *Handbook* have generally been fulfilled. Since the publication of the first edition 10 years ago, social cognition has become one of the most active areas of research in the entire field of psychology, whose influence has extended not only to many other subareas (health psychology, clinical psychology, personality, etc.) but to totally different disciplines (political science, marketing and consumer behavior, organizational behavior, etc.). The impact of social cognition theory and research within a very short period of time is incontrovertible.

The current edition of the *Handbook* clearly conveys the advances that have been made over the years. It is divided into two volumes. Volume 1 is devoted to research and theory pertaining to basic components of social information processing: the encoding of information, its representation in memory, infence processes, and response selection. Although several of these topics were covered in the first edition of the *Handbook* as well, the content of the present chapters is virtually nonoverlapping. For example, John Bargh, who also authored a chapter in the earlier edition on automatic versus controlled information processing, has identified four separate components of automaticity that had not been distinguished at the time the earlier chapter was written, each of which is a distinct focus of current research and theory. Two of the following three chapters, by Robert Wyer and Donal Carlston on the mental representation of people and social events, and by John Kihlstrom and Stanley Klein on the cognitive representation of self, also deal with topics that were discussed in the earlier edition. But, like Bargh's chapter, they cover areas of research and theory that were largely unanticipated by the earlier articles. The fourth chapter, by Eliot Smith, discusses the role of procedural knowledge in social information processing—an exceptionally important topic that had not even been clearly identified at the time the earlier *Handbook* was published.

The next three chapters in Volume 1 also deal with topics that were covered in the first edition but reflect the major advances that have been made in the interim. The chapter on social inference by Denise Beike and Steven Sherman replaces a narrower analysis of cognitive heuristics, incorporating them into a more general discussion of judgment phenomena. Fritz Strack's chapter on response processes reviews research on the cognitive factors that underlie the interpretation of requests for information in a social context that has implications for responses in both laboratory and nonlaboratory situations. Gerald Clore, Norbert Schwarz, and Michael Conway provide a detailed analysis of both the cognitive antecedents of affect and emotion and the impact of affective reactions, once elicited, on the processing of new information. Few, if any, of the issues discussed in either of these chapters had been identified a decade ago.

Volume 2 of the *Handbook* reviews information processing approaches to understanding phenomena in a number of other specific domains of inquiry, none of which was considered in the earlier edition. The research in these domains has often been stimulated by theory and concepts discussed in Volume 1. However, this research has often led to the identification of new theoretical and empirical issues whose implications extend beyond the specific areas in which they were identified. The first chapter, for example, by David Hamilton and Jeffrey Sherman, concerns a phenomenon to which several of the processes discussed in the first volume are relevant. The development and use of stereotypes is nevertheless a fundamental topic in social cognition that was not explicitly considered in the earlier edition at all. Chapter 2, by Richard Petty, Joseph Priester, and Duane Wegener, provides an exceptionally broad and sophisticated review of information processing approaches to understanding communication and persuasion. Shanto Iyengar and Victor Ottati then give an equally penetrating analysis of the cognitive and affective bases of political judgment. This is followed by reviews of cognitive approaches to (a) the dynamics of close relationships, by Margaret Clark and her colleagues, (b) health psychology, by Leslie Clark, and (c) clinical psychology (with a special emphasis on depression) by Gifford Weary and John Edwards. The final two chapters, by Jack Feldman and Frank Kardes, review and evaluate the role of information processing in personnel appraisal and consumer behavior, respectively. The chapters in this volume combine to demonstrate the important influence that social cognition has had not only on other areas of psychology but on other disciplines as well.

There are inevitably limitations to the present volume. As Thomas Ostrom points out in the Foreword, an ultimate objective of social cognition research is to understand the cognitive processing that occurs in social interaction situations of the sort in which information is often exchanged outside the laboratory. At this writing, social cognition research has only begun to examine in detail many of the social contextual factors that underlie the interpretation of information and responses to it more generally. To this extent, the present *Handbook*, like its predecessor, is a promissory note, providing the theoretical and empirical foundations of research to be performed in the future. These future research directions are indicated in virtually all chapters of the *Handbook* in the context of evaluating our current state of knowledge.

The success of a reference volume depends on both the quality of the contributions contained in it and their timeliness. The contributors to the *Handbook* are all among the foremost scholars in the field in the areas to which their chapters pertain. We are greatly indebted to them, not only for the quality of their contributions but also for their cooperation in preparing their chapters under severe time constraints despite numerous other demands and obligations. Many others have also contributed to the success of this project. Most obviously, the editors and staff of Lawrence Erlbaum Associates, and Larry Erlbaum himself, have been constant sources of support since the beginning of the project, and have been instrumental in facilitating its coming to fruition. Our association with LEA on this project, as in the past, has been immensely gratifying, and we cannot imagine a better publisher with whom to work.

Robert S. Wyer, Jr.
Thomas K. Srull

1

The Four Horsemen of Automaticity: Awareness, Intention, Efficiency, and Control in Social Cognition

John A. Bargh
New York University

Contents

> *I do not think, therefore I am.*
> —Jean Cocteau

When the first edition of this *Handbook* appeared in 1984, research on automatic phenomena was just beginning. In the 10 years preceding it, a total of 28 research articles were published on topics directly relevant to the automaticity of a social

1

psychological phenomenon. In the following 10-year-period there have been 123 such research articles.[1] Clearly, that research on automatic phenomena in social psychology has mushroomed in the past decade.

There is now hardly a research domain or topic that has not been analyzed in terms of its automatic features or components. Much attention has been devoted to questions of whether dispositional inferences are made automatically, whether attitudes become activated automatically to influence ongoing behavior, whether accessible social constructs and stereoptypes automatically affect one's judgments of oneself and others, whether people have automatic evaluative and emotional reactions to stimuli, and the degree to which a person is aware or unaware of the influences on his or her judgments and subjective experience.

In deciding how to structure a review of automaticity research, I faced a dilemma: Should it be organized in terms of specific content areas, such as attribution or stereotyping, and describe the extent to which these phenomena are found to be automatic in nature? This would be useful, except that it would miss many of the reasons why so much research attention has been given to questions of automaticity *across* different research domains. Those reasons have to do with the fact that the separate defining qualities of automaticity are important issues in their own right—the extent to which thought and behavior are unintentional, occur outside of awareness, are uncontrollable, and are efficient in their use of attentional resources.

Ten years ago, the consensus view (Johnson & Hasher, 1987) was that a mental process was either automatic—possessing all four of those qualities—or controlled, possessing all the opposite qualities (i.e., intentional, controllable, consumptive of limited attentional resources, and in awareness; see Bargh, 1984; Posner & Snyder, 1975; Shiffrin & Schneider, 1977). If a given process was not a member of one type, then by default it had to be a member of the other. Guided by this prevalent dichotomy, I argued at the time that many claims of automaticity within social psychology were not authentic, because they did not satisfy all four criteria.

---

[1]All of these are included in the Reference section. Because the earlier studies were reviewed in the first edition of this *Handbook* (Bargh, 1984), the present chapter focuses mainly on the post-1983 research. However, mention should be made here of those pioneering studies, and the following is, to my knowledge, a complete list of the pre-1983 research and theory directly relevant to one or more aspects of automaticity (and it is certainly possible that I missed some relevant articles): "top-of-the-head" attributions based on visual salience (Taylor, Crocker, Fiske, Sprinzen, & Winkler, 1979; Taylor & Fiske, 1978), that such salience effects occur automatically at encoding (Smith & Miller, 1979), behavior in routine social interactions (Langer, 1978; Langer, Blank, & Chanowitz, 1978), passive trait category priming effects on social judgment (Higgins, Rholes, & Jones, 1977; Srull & Wyer, 1979, 1980), the application of the self-representation in perceptual selection and encoding (Bargh, 1982; Geller & Shaver, 1976; Hull & Levy, 1979; Markus & Smith, 1981), one's lack of awareness of important influences on one's impressions and judgments (Lewicki, 1982; Nisbett & Wilson, 1977; Wegner & Vallacher, 1977), and one's frequent lack of awareness of the influential stimuli themselves (Bargh, 1982; Bargh & Pietromonaco, 1982; W. Wilson, 1979).

THE DECOMPOSITION OF AUTOMATICITY

It has since become increasingly clear that mental processes at the level of complexity studied by social psychologists are not exclusively automatic or exclusively controlled, but are in fact combinations of the features of each. In cognitive psychology, evidence was accumulating that no process was purely automatic by the four-criteria standard (Kahneman & Treisman, 1984; Logan & Cowan, 1984). For one thing, focal attention allocation seemed to be necessary; even prototypic examples of automaticity such as the Stroop effect did not occur if focal attention was directed just slightly away from the target word (Francolini & Egeth, 1980; Kahneman & Henik, 1981). For another, such automatic phenomena as driving and typing are clearly intentional at some level, in that one intends to drive the car and does not do so otherwise—and also controllable in that the person can stop the automatic activity whenever he or she so desires (Logan & Cowan, 1984). Thus, it seemed that a process can have some qualities of an automatic process (e.g., efficient, autonomous), while simultaneously having qualities of a controlled process as well.

There are abundant social psychological examples of processes that are automatic in some features but not in others (see review in Bargh, 1989). Several studies have examined the efficiency of processes (i.e., the extent to which they occur even when attention is directed elsewhere or when information is coming in at a fast and furious pace). The operation of procedures to classify behaviors as instances of traits (e.g., Smith & Lerner, 1986), gender-stereotypic influences on judgments (Pratto & Bargh, 1991), and the making of dispositional inferences (e.g., Gilbert, Pelham, & Krull, 1988) all have been shown to occur under these attention-overload conditions. However, subjects had the intention in all these cases to form an impression of the target person, or to classify the behaviors in terms of traits. Like driving a car, which requires the intention to drive but also has many automatic components (at least for the skilled and experienced driver), many social judgment phenomena are intentional, but once started they are autonomous and very efficient in their lack of need for attentional guidance.

In summary, no process appeared to satisfy the strict definition of automaticity. At the same time, most interesting mental phenomena are of sufficient complexity to be composed of some automatic and some controlled processing features (a qualification made by Shiffrin & Schneider, 1977, at the outset of automaticity research). Therefore, it was time to get rid of the all-or-none idea of automaticity. It certainly was causing confusion and misunderstanding. For example, discussing one's findings of great efficiency of a process in terms of its automaticity led others to infer (reasonably, given the all-or-none assumption) that the process also was unintentional and uncontrollable. The automaticity of stereotyping affords a good illustration of this problem. Findings of the unintentional and efficient activation of racial and general stereotypes led to the widespread assumption that stereotyping was uncontrollable as well. However, demonstrations of

the possibility of motivational control (see Fiske, 1989), as well as a consideration of the separate stages of the stereotyping process and their differential controllability (Devine, 1989), showed that a process could be simultaneously
unintended and efficient on the one hand, but nonetheless controllable. Therefore, the first moral of the present story is for researchers to be more specific
about the particular qualities of automaticity they are demonstrating and claiming for the process in question—unintentionality, unawareness, uncontrollability, or high efficiency—instead of discussing only its automaticity or relative
automaticity.

Conditional Automaticity

The second and related moral is that the various demonstrations of automatic
processing in social cognition vary as to the conditions that are necessary for the
process to occur. Some of the automatic phenomena that were identified required
the person's intention for their initiation, others required substantial attentional
support, others awareness of the triggering stimulus, and so on. In a previous
analysis of social cognitive phenomena in terms of these conditions (Bargh, 1989),
three general sorts of automaticity could be identified: preconscious, postcon-
conscious, and goal-dependent.

Preconscious Automaticity.   A preconsciously automatic process requires only
that the person notice the presence of the triggering stimulus in the environment.
These processes occur automatically when a stimulus is noticed, as part of the
act of figural synthesis (Neisser, 1967), and do not require a deliberate goal or
intention. Such processes include interpretations, evaluations, and categorizations
that occur prior to and in the absence of conscious or deliberative response to
the stimulus (i.e., during the microgenesis of its perception; Werner, 1956). One
certainly may be aware (and usually is) of the end result of this fast preconscious
construction of the percept. Thus, preconscious is not synonymous with subliminal, although subliminal processes are certainly a subset of preconscious ones.
    Examples of preconscious automaticity include chronically accessible trait con-
struct influences on social perception, because they occur without intention and
even uncontrollably (Bargh & Pratto, 1986), as well as efficiently (Bargh & Thein,
1985). Automatic attitude activation also appears to qualify as a preconscious
phenomenon, because it occurs without intention or controllability (Roskos-
Ewoldsen & Fazio, 1992) and immediately and efficiently (Bargh, Chaiken,
Govender, & Pratto, 1992; Fazio, Sanbonmatsu, Powell, & Kardes, 1986). Attitudes that are strong enough to become active automatically have been discussed
in terms of the "chronic accessibility" of their association to the corresponding
object representation (Fazio et al., 1986); therefore it is not surprising that both chronically accessible trait constructs and attitudes appear to share many preconscious
automatic properties (see Bargh, 1984). Other forms of preconscious automaticity

that have been documented are automatic attention responses to negative stimuli such as trait adjectives (Pratto & John, 1991) and angry faces (Hansen & Hansen, 1988), and physiological reactions to stimuli that are relevant to chronic concerns about the self (Strauman & Higgins, 1987). (It should be noted that many other phenomena ultimately may be found to be as unconditionally automatic as these, but the currently available experimental demonstrations of those phenomena include conditions, such as explicit instructions for subjects to engage in the process, that at the present time preclude conclusions about their unintentional nature [see Bargh, 1992b].)

Postconscious Automaticity. These effects are functionally the same as preconscious effects, except that they require some kind of recent conscious, attentional processing to occur. Priming effects on impression formation (e.g., Higgins, Rholes, & Jones, 1977; Srull & Wyer, 1979) are the best example. Other examples are repeated expression manipulations of attitude accessibility (Herr, Sherman, & Fazio, 1984) and the effect of a recent positive or negative experience (even as mild as having cookies in the subject waiting room) on the accessibility of positive versus negative life experiences (Isen, Shalker, Clark, & Karp, 1978).

Postconscious effects are functionally the same as preconscious ones, except that they are temporary instead of chronic and they result from the residual activation of conscious processing. For example, Fazio and his colleagues obtained the same results of accessible attitudes on behavior and attention whether the attitude was chronically (i.e., a preconscious effect) or temporarily accessible (e.g., Fazio et al., 1986; Roskos-Ewoldsen & Fazio, 1992), and studies comparing chronic and temporary construct accessibility show the same quality of effect for each (Bargh, Bond, Lombardi, & Tota, 1986; Bargh, Lombardi, & Higgins, 1988). The chronic versus temporary distinction between preconscious and postconscious processing is not a trivial one, however. Postconscious effects only occur given recent relevant thought and go away after a short time, preconscious effects are "eternally vigilant" (see Bargh, 1989; Bargh et al., 1988).

Methodologically, the phenomenon of postconscious automaticity — that temporary accessibility can mimic chronic accessibility — is a potential pitfall for researchers who intend to study unconditionally and chronic automatic effects. There have been several recent demonstrations of the effect of having subjects complete questionnaires prior to tests of how they think naturally or "automatically" in the same content domain. Skelton and Strohmetz (1990) showed that having subjects first consider common words for their health connotations resulted in a greater number of symptoms reported on symptom check lists. Mark, Sinclair, and Wellens (1991) showed that giving subjects the Beck Depression Inventory (BDI) at the beginning of the experimental session produced different self-judgments by depressed versus nondepressed subjects compared to the condition in which the BDI was not administered first. Spielman and Bargh (1991) replicated two different studies that had reported automatic thought patterns in depression, but had given subjects the BDI prior to the test of automaticity. In both studies, the original results were replicated only when subjects completed the BDI first.

These findings indicate that one must be careful not to prime or create post-conscious automatic phenomena by having subjects recently engage in a task that causes them to think about the same topics on which one is assessing their chronic or preconscious thought processes (Bargh, 1990). Although similar effects are obtained in studies using priming or some other technique (e.g., repeated atti-tude expression) to create temporary accessibility as in studies of chronic acces-sibility, one cannot conclude that chronic, preconscious automaticity effects exists on the basis of demonstrations of temporary accessibility in that domain. Any mental representation or mode of thinking that is available in memory for use by the subject can be made accessible in an experiment, but this does not mean that every available mental structure or process is chronically accessible (see Hig-gins & King, 1981; Tulving & Pearlstone, 1966) and operates preconsciously.

Goal-Dependent Automaticity.   The third general class of automatic phenome-na only occurs with the person's consent and intent. Examples include the de-velopment of efficient behavior-to-trait judgments through practice (Smith & Branscombe, 1988; Smith & Lerner, 1986) and the evidence that self-concepts or other-concepts become active automatically given the intention to consider the self or another person (Bargh & Tota, 1988; Dovidio, Evans, & Tyler, 1986; Perdue, Dovidio, Gurtman, & Tyler, 1990). For example, in the Bargh and Tota study, negative trait concepts became active automatically (i.e., efficiently and immediately when under attentional load) when depressed subjects were asked to describe the self, but positive concepts were activated automatically when these subjects were trying to think about the average person. The same set of positive trait concepts were activated automatically in nondepressed subjects in both judg-ment contexts (see Paulhaus, Graf, & Van Selst, 1989; and Paulhus & Levitt, 1987, for additional evidence of the increasing positivity of the self-concept in [nondepressed] subjects with increasing attentional load).

The Ecology of Automaticity

Decomposing the concept of automaticity into its component features in this way will also assist one to assess the ecological validity of the phenomenon in ques-tion. For example, suppose the effect requires that subjects be instructed to en-gage in such processing, as when they are given an explicit goal to form an impression or attribution. What is the likelihood that these subjects would spon-taneously have that goal in their natural environment, in the absence of these situ-ational demands? If an effect requires recent conscious thought relevant to the topic in question, how often will subjects normally be thinking along those lines? Clearly, to the extent that an effect does not require such preconditions, it will have a more frequent and important influence on thought, judgment, and behavior (Bargh, 1992b).

One tradition of research in social psychology most closely identified with the work of Zajonc pursues the unconditional, "mere" effects of stimuli in this way. The mere presence theory of social facilitation (Zajonc, 1965), the mere exposure effect on attitude formation (e.g., Zajonc, 1968), the intellectual environment model of birth order effects on intellectual development (Zajonc & Markus, 1975), and the precognitive affective processing system (Zajonc, 1980) were all hypothesized to be unconditional mental phenomena. The exhortation here—to push laboratory phenomena to their limits in exploring the minimum conditions necessary for their occurrence—is in the same tradition (see also McGuire, 1983).

Questions of the awareness, intentionality, controllability, and efficiency of thought and behavior are important in their own right, and transcend specific research domains. The issue of how much one is in control of one's thought and behavior was considered by Posner and Snyder (1975) to be a fundamental question of existence. Fiske (1989) pointed out the importance for the legal system of understanding the role of intentionality, because it strikes at the heart of the issues of responsibility and culpability for one's actions (e.g., in hiring and promotion discrimination cases). Gilbert (1991) argued that differences in how efficiently people accept versus question the validity of what they see and are told matter greatly in determining what they believe and their ability to guard against erroneous beliefs (see also Chanowitz & Langer, 1981). In my opinion, these separate and distinct qualities of automaticity are important matters for study in and of themselves, not only as they are applied to specific research topics. In the following review of the literature on automaticity, I discuss the research in terms of its relevance for these issues of awareness, intentionality, efficiency, and control.

AWARENESS

There are three ways in which a person may be unaware of a mental process:

1. A person may be unaware of the stimulus itself, as in subliminal perception.

2. A person may be unaware of the way in which that stimulus event is interpreted or categorized, as stereotyping and construct accessibility research have demonstrated.

3. The person may be unaware of the determining influences on his or her judgments or subjective feeling states (e.g., the use of felt ease of perceptual categorization or of retrieval from memory as a cue to the validity of the perception or the frequency of the stored event) and thus may misattribute the reason to a plausible and salient possible cause of which he or she is aware.

Consequently, the research literature that is relevant to reviewing the awareness aspect includes stereotyping, construct accessibility, misattribution, perceptual fluency, and subliminality, not to mention mood effects (Erber, 1991; Forgas & Bower, 1987), schematic "capture" effects by knowledge structures sharing representative features with the novel target person or information (Andersen & Cole, 1990; Gilovich, 1981; Lewicki, 1985), and so on. Reviewing the topic of awareness would be a chapter (or a book) in itself; I offer as complete an inventory as possible given the more general purview of this chapter.

Subliminal Perception

Over the past decade, many social psychological studies have demonstrated effects of subliminally presented stimuli. In six of them (Bargh & Pietromonaco, 1982; Bargh et al., 1986; Devine, 1989; Erdley & D'Agostino, 1987; Neuberg, 1988), subliminal trait-related stimuli were presented to activate or prime the corresponding trait concept in memory, making it more accessible and thus more likely to be used subsequently to interpret presented ambiguous but relevant behaviors (see, e.g., Higgins, 1989; Wyer & Srull, 1986). These trait terms were presented outside of the subject's awareness as part of a first experiment that was allegedly unrelated to the second experiment that followed. Subliminality was achieved by brief presentations of the trait terms, their immediate pattern masking without informing subjects as to the nature of the flashes they saw on the tachistoscope or computer screen, and tests of the subjects' momentary awareness and later recognition memory for the stimuli (see Bargh et al., 1986, for a typical procedure). Bargh and Pietromonaco (1982) found that subjects who were exposed subliminally to hostile-relevant stimuli subsequently rated the target person who behaved in an ambiguously hostile manner as possessing more of that trait than did nonprimed subjects. Bargh et al.(1986) replicated the effect for the traits of kindness and shyness, and demonstrated that such priming combined with the subject's chronic accessibility on these traits in an additive fashion. Erdley and D'Agostino (1987) also demonstrated subliminal priming effects. They also showed (in line with the findings of Higgins et al., 1977) that the effect was not due to a general affective (good vs. bad) priming—the target behavior had to be specifically relevant to the primed construct for the priming effect to occur (i.e., the principle of applicability; see Higgins, 1989).

Devine (1989) used subliminal priming to present elements of the African-American stereotype other than hostility (which pretesting had shown was also an element); subjects primed in this manner rated a subsequent target person's ambiguously hostile behavior (Srull & Wyer, 1979) as more hostile than did other subjects. Neuberg (1988) primed subjects subliminally with either competitiveness-related or neutral stimuli, and then had them participate in a Prisoner's Dilemma game on a computer with a fictitious, preprogrammed partner. For dispositionally competitive but not dispositionally cooperative subjects, the subliminal competitive primes increased the competitiveness of their responses to their partner's moves throughout the game.

Perdue et al. (1990) demonstrated a context-dependent automatic activation of generally more positive trait concepts when people think about themselves or their in-group than when they think about others or the out-group. After subliminal presentation of in-group primes such as *us* and *we*, subjects' response times to trait adjectives in a valence classification task (i.e., "Is this a good or a bad trait for someone to possess?" were faster for positive than for negative content. However, this effect was (nonsignificantly) reversed when out-group primes such as *they* and *them* were the subliminal primes. Dovidio et al. (1986) also demonstrated that different sets of concepts become automatically activated depending on whether one is thinking about one's own group or about those outside that group. Importantly, such differential accessibility of positive versus negative constructs occurs with the merest provocation—priming stimuli such as *we* or *they*—suggesting an automatic, cognitive basis for the minimal in-group/out-group effect (e.g., Crocker & Schwartz, 1985; Tajfel, 1970).

Other studies have used subliminal presentation of faces showing a positive or negative emotion to prime affective reactions to a subsequent stimulus (Baldwin, Carrell, & Lopez, 1990; Edwards, 1990; Krosnick, Betz, Jussim, Lynn, & Stephens, 1992; Murphy & Zajonc, 1993; Niedenthal, 1990). Greenwald, Klinger, and Liu (1989) demonstrated subliminal evaluative priming effects in which targets were classified as positive or negative more quickly when a prime of the same valence appeared immediately before it, but more slowly when primes and targets mismatched in valence. Gabrielcik and Fazio (1984) showed that subliminal presentation of words containing the letter *T* resulted in greater frequency estimates for words beginning with that letter, presumably because of the heightened accessibility and ease of recall of memory instances of such words.

A separate line of research using subliminal presentation of stimuli studied mere exposure effects on liking. In an often replicated finding (Kunst-Wilson & Zajonc, 1980), subliminally presenting some novel stimuli more frequently than others results in subjects' greater liking for those stimuli (Bornstein, Leone, & Galley, 1988; Mandler, Nakamura, & Van Zandt, 1987; Seamon, Brody, & Kauff, 1983; Seamon, Marsh, & Brody, 1984). Presumably, the buildup of strength in the representation of the more frequently presented stimuli results in their greater ease or fluency of perception (Gordon & Holyoak, 1983), and this in turn results in a positively valenced feeling of familiarity that is misattributed to qualities of the stimulus (because, of course, the subject has no conscious experience of having seen it before). Bornstein et al. (1988) showed that when subjects experienced repeated subliminal exposure to a photograph of a person with whom they had interacted in a group discussion, they agreed with that person's positions more often than with those of a second confederate.

There is no longer any doubt, given the abundance of evidence, that environmental stimuli processed outside of awareness can have important interpretive and evaluative consequences on subsequent conscious thought and behavior (see also Bornstein & Pittman, 1992; Greenwald, 1992). Moreover, recent research has, through technological and methodological improvements, ensured the subliminality of the triggering stimuli more carefully than did the "New Look" subliminal perception research of 40 years ago (see Erdelyi, 1974, for a review). Skeptics of the existence of subconscious processing phenomena have demanded and received rigorous tests, rather than mere claims, of subliminality. Perhaps this increased experimental rigor has done the most to achieve general acceptance of subliminal phenomena (see Bornstein & Pittman, 1992; Greenwald, 1992). Social cognition researchers have been careful to ensure that subjects are not aware of the content or meaning of the subliminally presented stimuli through the use of sensitive forced-choice recognition measures, momentary awareness (as opposed to later memory) tests, and sophisticated pattern-masking procedures (see Bargh et al., 1986, Greenwald et al., 1989, and Niedenthal, 1990, for additional details).

Still, the greater scientific acceptance of the internal validity of the effects obtained in subliminal presentation experiments has not been matched by an acceptance of their ecological validity. If subliminal perception does not happen very often outside of highly artificial laboratory situations that employ specialized procedures and equipment, says the skeptic, why does it matter for social psychology? Why all this subliminality research?

One reason is that subliminal presentation is a methodological tool that researchers have used to ensure that obtained effects were not due to experimental demand or to some other intentional and strategic processing by the subject. This was the motivation behind the use of subliminal priming by Bargh and Pietromonaco (1982). Similarly, researchers of the affect-cognition interface, or of mere exposure effects, have used subliminal presentation of affective primes to demonstrate evaluative reactions to stimuli that cannot be traced to some conscious computation of liking, based on a consideration of the various qualities of the stimulus (see Zajonc, 1980). Devine (1989) used subliminal presentation to show how racial stereotypes can become active and influence judgments without the person's intention to stereotype.

Thus, social psychological research has used subliminal presentation techniques to investigate the ways in which people are not aware of how they interpret stimuli or of the important influences on their judgments. Lack of awareness of the stimulus event ensures that its subsequent effects were unintended by the subject. Thus, subliminality research can be placed in the context of a larger tradition in social psychology, concerning the extent of awareness and control of influences on a person's judgments and behavior (Bargh, 1992a). Cognitive dissonance paradigms counted on the fact that subjects would not be aware of the powerful influence exerted on their free choice by the experimenter, and so would attribute their decisions to some internal factor (e.g., Festinger & Carlsmith, 1959; Wicklund & Brehm, 1976). Such a lack of access to the causal influences on people's decisions was seized on by self-perception theorists (e.g., Bem, 1972) as a different explanation for dissonance findings. Other attribution research has discovered many other such misattributional tendencies, including those involved in understanding the source of one's internal states such as emotions, arousal, or mood (e.g., Schachter & Singer, 1962; Schwarz & Clore, 1983; Zillman & Bryant, 1974), or one's social and nonsocial judgments (e.g., Nisbett & Bellows, 1977; Nisbett & Wilson, 1977). More recent subliminal presentation studies are direct descendants of this research tradition into the hidden influences on phenomenal experience and social judgment.

In other words, social psychologists have not been studying subliminality per se, but have used subliminal presentation as a tool to study how people can be unaware of many important but unintentional influences over their judgments and behavior. Subjects who are unaware of the stimulus that causes an effect obviously do not intend for the effect to happen, and consequently they are unable to control the effect (Bargh, 1988; Devine, 1989; Fiske, 1989).

Awareness of the Stimulus Versus Awareness of Its Influence.   Perhaps the most important reason why subliminality is not of prime concern for social psychology[2] is that similar results are obtained with supraliminal stimulus presentation as long as subjects are not aware of the influence of that stimulus.[3] Studies using conscious presentation of the critical stimuli have repeatedly produced the same findings as studies using subliminal presentation, provided the relation between those stimuli and subsequent processing tasks has been obscured. Bargh and Pietromonaco (1982), Bargh et al. (1986), Erdley and D'Agostino (1987), and Devine (1989) all obtained assimilative priming effects with subliminal presentation of the primes—the same effect obtained in conscious priming studies when subjects are unaware of the possible influence on their subsequent judgments (see Higgins & King, 1981). Several studies have shown affective reactions to neutral stimuli in line with subliminally presented emotional faces (e.g., Edwards, 1990; Krosnick et al., 1992; Murphy & Zajonc, 1993; Niedenthal, 1990), but other studies have shown similar effects of affect-inducing stimuli of which subjects were consciously aware but did not realize the potential effect (e.g., eye-pupil dilation: Niedenthal & Cantor, 1986; incidental touch: Crusco & Wetzel, 1984). For example, a brief incidental touch by a waitress when returning change increased the size of the tip she received (Crusco & Wetzel, 1984),

---

[2]This is not to say that it does not matter at all; the existence of subliminal phenomena obviously matter for questions such as the nature of consciousness, psychodynamic influences, and its potential for misuse (such as by advertising, governments, etc.; see reviews in Bornstein & Pittman, 1992).

[3]Although, as argued here, the quality of the effect is the same for subliminal and supraliminal presentation, one might suspect that the size of the effect would be greater for stimuli presented supraliminally, given that they impinge on the senses longer and are of greater intensity (that is what makes them supraliminal after all). Although this logic holds for category priming effects, there are nonetheless domains in which subliminal effects are the stronger (e.g., in mere exposure effects; see Bornstein, 1989).

and similar behavior by a librarian when returning a library card resulted in subsequent more positive ratings of the library (Goleman, 1988).

Baldwin and Holmes (1987) showed that prior conscious exposure to a significant other affected subjects' evaluations of themselves, and Baldwin et al. (1990) obtained the same effect using subliminal presentations of the faces of significant others (the Pope to observing Catholics and Bob Zajonc to observing Michigan graduate students). Mere exposure effects of greater liking occurred with both conscious and incidental exposure of the novel stimuli (Moreland & Zajonc, 1977; Zajonc, 1968) and with subliminal presentations (see review by Bornstein, 1989). Devine (1989, Experiment 2) produced stereotypic influences on judgments using stereotype-relevant subliminal priming words, whereas the same stereotypic influences have been produced by consciously perceived target persons or information (e.g., Darley & Gross, 1983; McArthur & Friedman, 1980; Pratto & Bargh, 1991; Rosenfield, Greenberg, Folger, & Borys, 1982; Sagar & Schofield, 1980). In one experiment, Edwards (1990) subliminally presented a positive or negative facial expression as a prime before exposing subjects to the target-attitude objects. In a second experiment, she presented those faces at supraliminal durations. The manipulation induced an affect-based attitude toward the attitude object in both studies, regardless of whether the prime was in or out of awareness.

As a final example, the Greenwald et al. (1989) experiment described earlier found evaluative priming effects for a subliminally presented prime. The same effect has been found repeatedly for supraliminally, but briefly (250 msec), presented evaluative primes in the same evaluative judgment task (Bargh et al., 1992; Fazio et al., 1986).

It is clear from these findings that awareness of the stimulus does not matter to an effect as long as subjects are unaware of the potential influence of that stimulus. When subjects are aware of that potential influence, different effects occur. In category accessibility studies, in which the priming stimuli are still in working memory at the time of the subsequent impression formation task so that subjects could be aware of the potential influence of the priming events on their judgments, contrast rather than assimilation effects are often obtained. The likelihood of the priming stimuli continuing to reside in working memory has been manipulated by the extremity or vividness of the primes (e.g., Dracula as a hostile prime; Herr et al., 1984), by interruption of the priming task (Martin, 1986), and by the subjects processing the priming stimuli with greater effort (Martin, Seta, & Crelia, 1990). Alternatively, Lombardi, Higgins, and Bargh (1987) and Newman and Uleman (1990) assessed whether subjects could recall the primes at the time of the impression-formation task. In all these studies, the residence of the primes in consciousness produced contrast effects in judgment, instead of the assimilative effects obtained when subjects were unaware of the potential influence of the primes.

Other research domains show the same critical role for awareness of a potential influence as opposed to awareness of the critical stimulus. In stereotyping research, in which the subjects are aware of the possible influence of stereotypes on their judgments and descriptions and are motivated to control these influences, they can do so (Devine, 1989, Experiment 3; Pratto & Bargh, 1991). In the Pratto and Bargh (1991) pretesting, between-subjects tests of the existence of gender stereotypes – in which a subject rated either the average male or the average female – were successful in documenting the stereotypes obtained in much previous research (e.g., Ruble & Ruble, 1982), whereas within-subjects tests – in which the same subject rated both the average male and the average female on the same traits – showed no stereotyping at all.

Summary. Subliminal research, then, is important for understanding what kinds of effects occur naturally, immediately, and unintentionally on the part of the subject. What is critical for whether the effect occurs is not subliminality itself but the subject's awareness of the possibility of the influence by that stimulus as well as the subject's values and motivations (see Controllability section) to control that influence.

In this regard, it is important to distinguish between a person's awareness of a stereotype or an accessible construct, and the actual influence of the construct on the person's judgment. One cannot be aware of the actual occurrence of accessibility or stereotypic influences because of the fast, effortless, and immediate (i.e., preconscious) way in which those mental structures capture and interpret relevant environmental input. Nonetheless, through education and other consciousness-raising techniques one can become aware that one might be influenced. For example, one may have no conscious experience of stereotyping an African-American assistant professor applicant, a female engineering graduate school applicant, or a Korean colleague, but might nonetheless take steps in reporting one's judgments and decisions to adjust or counteract these potential influences of the stereotypes. For instance, one could perform a more deliberate and effortful conscious appraisal of the individuating qualities of the person than one would normally (see Fiske, 1989; Fiske & Neuberg, 1990; Thompson, Roman, Moskowitz, Chaiken, & Bargh, 1992). If that is not possible, one might adjust one's opinion somewhat in the direction opposite to the assumed stereotypic influence (Strack, 1992) or consider the opposite conclusion (Lord, Lepper, & Preston, 1984).

Misattribution

As argued previously, a lack of awareness of an influence on thought or behavior matters, because it precludes the possibility of controlling that influence. Another way such unawareness of influence matters is that one might misattribute the cause or source of one's impressions of another or one's own subjective state to more salient potential causes (see Nisbett & Wilson, 1977).

Schwarz and his colleagues (e.g., Schwarz, 1990, Schwarz & Clore, 1983) demonstrated that people often are unaware of the reasons for their current mood (for example, whether it is a sunny or a rainy day) and, unless these true causes are called to their attention in some way, will attribute those moods to whatever is currently salient in their environment—even to a general satisfaction or dissatisfaction with their life if they are being asked to complete such a questionnaire (Schwarz & Clore, 1983).

As Schwarz (1990) argued, current feeling states can serve as a source of information for an individual in making decisions and judgments when the source of those feelings is assumed, correctly or incorrectly, to be the person or topic being judged. Another kind of subjective feeling that has been studied for its nonconscious and misattributional effects is the feeling of ease or fluency in perception that comes from prior experience (Bargh, 1992a; Jacoby, Toth, Lindsay, & Debner, 1992; Smith, chapter 3, Volume 1). Usually, the felt ease of categorizing or perceiving a person or event is a diagnostic cue to the validity of that categorization, either because the person or event unambiguously matches the features of that category or because of the frequency and consistency of mapping that person or event to the category in the past (see Fiske & Neuberg, 1990; Higgins & Bargh, 1987). For example, Anita's victory in the university chess championship is effortlessly understood as an intelligent act. Here the bottom-up strength or diagnosticity of the behavior determines the ease of comprehension; there is no need to engage in a "search after meaning" (see Postman, 1951).

However, suppose that one has a strong expectancy about an individual, a strong stereotype about a group, or a chronically accessible construct concerning people in general. These top-down influences of accessibility can also result in a subjective feeling of ease or effortlessness in perceptual categorization, or perceptual fluency, even with relatively ambiguous and nondiagnostic input (see Higgins, 1989). The consequence is that people often misattribute the source of the fluency caused by the top-down expectancy or accessibility to the diagnosticity of the stimulus. People are quite aware of the stimulus person or behavior; they are less aware of the effect that their own readiness to perceive the person or behavior in certain terms has on the ease of doing so.

Construct Accessibility as Perceptual Fluency.   Recently, several authors argued that such accessibility or readiness effects can be conceptualized as perceptual fluency effects (Bargh, 1992a; Schwarz, Bless, Strack, Klumpp, & Simons, 1991; Sherman, Mackie, & Driscoll, 1990; Smith & Branscombe, 1987, 1988; Spielman & Bargh, 1990). For example, Sherman et al. (1990) primed certain dimensions that were relevant to judgments of a target politician's abilities in either foreign affairs or managing the economy. They hypothesized that subjects would attribute the greater ease of perceiving and categorizing the information with respect to the primed dimensions (relative to the unprimed dimensions) to the validity or diagnosticity of the information. Consistent with the hypothesis, dimensions were given greater weight in subjects' overall judgments. A similar effect of chronically accessible constructs on the weight given by various behaviors in overall liking judgments was obtained by Spielman and Bargh (1990).

Schwarz et al. (1991) also showed that the felt ease of retrieval from memory of relevant information is taken as a cue in memory-based judgments. Although this is the same logic as that of the availability heuristic (Kahneman & Tversky, 1973), it had never been tested directly with an experimental manipulation of felt ease of retrieval while holding the amount of retrieval constant. Schwarz et al. (1991) accomplished this by asking subjects to recall either 8 or 12 instances of times when they behaved in a given trait-like fashion, following which subjects rated themselves on that trait dimension. Pretesting had shown that subjects were able to come up with 8 examples much more easily than 12 examples, so that subjects in the recall-12 condition would experience greater difficulty completing the task than the other subjects. Results showed that although the recall-12 subjects remembered more examples of that trait than did subjects in the recall-8 condition, they nevertheless rated themselves as possessing less of that trait than did the other subjects, in line with the retrieval fluency as cue hypothesis.

Jacoby, Kelley, Brown, and Jasechko (1989) manipulated perceptual fluency by exposing subjects to a series of nonfamous along with famous names. The next day, the previously exposed nonfamous names were more likely than completely novel names to be mistaken as famous. Again, the feeling of familiarity that subjects presumably felt while seeing the name again was misattributed to the fame of the name.

Conclusions

Awareness as an aspect of automaticity is a critical issue for the intentional control of thought and behavior. What matters more than whether one is aware of a stimulus event is whether one is aware of the potential influence of that event on subsequent experience and judgments. All sorts of influences exist of which one does not have conscious knowledge, from immediate and unintended affective reactions to current moods to subjective feelings of familiarity and perceptual fluency. Thus, one attributes these effects to those environmental features one does have conscious knowledge of and that seem plausible causes of one's reactions. This phenomenon was described over 20 years ago when Jones and Nisbett stated, "[One tends] to regard one's reactions to entities as based on accurate perceptions of them. Rather than humbly regarding our impressions of the world as interpretations of it, we see them as understandings or correct apprehensions of it. . . . The distinction between evaluations and primary qualities is never fully made. We never quite get over our initial belief that funniness is a property of the clown and beauty is in the object" (1971, p. 86).

INTENTIONALITY

The intentionality and controllability aspects of automaticity both have to do with how much one is in control of one's own thought and behavior. Intentionality has to do with whether one is in control over the instigation or "start up" of processes, whereas controllability has to do with one's ability to stifle or stop a process once started, or at least to override its influence if so desired. To the extent that perceptual, judgmental, and behavioral processes are triggered by the environment and start up without intention, the environment is more in control (see Bargh & Gollwitzer, in press). To the extent that these processes, once started, can be stopped by an act of will, they are controllable by the individual (see Logan & Cowan, 1984).

Automatic Attention Responses and Perceptual Selection

Two kinds of automatic attention responses (Shiffrin & Schneider, 1977) have been documented in social cognition: (a) responses to information relevant to accessible trait constructs and attitudes, and (b) responses to negatively valenced stimuli. Behaviors clearly relevant to a person's chronically and temporarily accessible trait constructs are more likely to receive attention and be remembered later (Higgins, King, & Mavin, 1982; Sherman et al., 1990), to be noticed and influential in impressions even when attentional processing is severely constrained (Bargh & Thein, 1985), and to draw attention even when the subject is trying to ignore them in a dichotic listening task (Bargh, 1982) or a Stroop color-naming task (Bargh & Pratto, 1986; Higgins, Van Hook, & Dorfman, 1988). For example, Bargh and Pratto (1986) found that subjects took longer to name the color of trait terms corresponding to their chronically accessible than their inaccessible trait constructs. Recently, Roskos-Ewoldsen and Fazio (1992) obtained the same uncontrollable distraction effect for attitude objects when their associated attitude is made temporarily more accessible through its repeated expression by the subject. Therefore, the greater the accessibility in memory, the less subjects are able to prevent devoting processing resources to the corresponding behaviors or attitude objects. As a result, behaviors and objects are more likely to be noticed and be influential in on-line judgments and behavioral decisions.

A second determinant of automatic attention responses is negative social stimuli, in terms of either undesirable behavior (Fiske, 1980), negatively valenced trait terms (Pratto & John, 1991), or faces expressing negative emotions (Hansen & Hansen, 1988). The latter study applied Shiffrin and Schneider's (1977) method of varying the size of the stimulus array through which subjects had to scan to find an angry or happy face. Angry faces seemed to pop out of an array of happy ones; that is, subjects were able to respond quickly when asked whether an angry face was present, and increasing the number of distractor faces did not increase response time (as it would if subjects were engaging in an attentional, serial search process; see Shiffrin & Schneider, 1977).

Pratto and John (1991) used the Stroop task to show longer color-naming latencies (i.e., more uncontrollable distraction) for undesirable than for desirable trait terms, and greater incidental recall of the undesirable trait terms as well. Subsequent experiments ruled out possible artifactual explanations in terms of differences between the desirable and undesirable trait terms in their length, frequency, or the perceived base rates of occurrence for corresponding behaviors. The uncontrollability of this attention response was demonstrated in further studies reported by Pratto (in press), in which the negative trait concepts caused greater distraction even when subjects were informed of the effect and exhorted to overcome it. Pratto and John (1991) couched their predictions in the context of a model of *automatic vigilance*, in which attention is automatically given to stimuli and events that might affect the individual negatively. Taylor (1991) also has described an immediate *mobilization* response in the face of negatively impacting events.

Automatic Evaluation

To be able to immediately notice and attend to negative events, it is necessary to posit an earlier stage of processing in which all incoming stimuli are classified as positive or negative. The results of several recent studies have been consistent with this immediate classification or evaluation stage. Bargh, Litt, Pratto, and Spielman (1989) conducted a replication and extension of Marcel's (1983) study of preconscious analysis of meaning. In that study, a subject answered questions about words presented tachistoscopically for durations that were below his or her individually established recognition threshold. The questions concerned whether a word had been presented at all, the physical characteristics of the word (i.e., whether it was presented in upper- or lower-case letters), and the semantic meaning of the word (i.e., whether another word was a synonym of the target word). Marcel (1983) found that subjects responded at better than chance levels about the semantic meaning of words at presentation durations at which they could not answer the other questions at more than random guessing levels.

Bargh et al. (1989) used trait words as stimuli and added an evaluative question to Marcel's basic design. That is, on any given trial, subjects answered the presence or semantic question about the subliminally presented word, or responded as to whether the word was positive or negative in meaning. Bargh et al. selected the stimuli from Anderson's (1968) normative ratings of traits as to their likability, choosing sets of moderate and extreme and positive and negative adjectives. On successive blocks of trials, words were presented at faster and faster durations.

As predicted, subjects were able to answer the evaluative question at better than chance levels for presentation durations in which they could not answer the semantic question at nonrandom levels. Path analyses confirmed that the subjects' ability to answer the evaluative question correctly was statistically independent of their ability to answer the semantic question correctly. Moreover, the extremity or intensity of the adjectives' evaluative meaning did not matter to these effects. What did matter was whether the stimulus was positive or negative in valence, regardless of its extremity. In other words, subjects had access to the polarity of the trait adjective's valence in the absence of access to other aspects of its meaning, and this knowledge was independent of the extremity of this valence.

This dichotomous preconscious classification of stimuli by valence recalls Neisser's (1967) argument that such preconscious analyses of environmental stimuli are crude and basic, not fine-grained. It also supports the argument of Swann, Hixon, Stein-Seroussi, and Gilbert (1990) concerning the priority of self-enhancement over self-verification responses to self-relevant feedback. These authors posited an initial immediate classification of the feedback as favorable or unfavorable, followed by attention-demanding self-verification only if sufficient resources were available.

Research on the automatic activation of attitudes has also led to the conclusion that there is an initial automatic evaluative classification of stimuli as good or bad that does not vary as a function of the intensity or extremity of the stimulus valence. Fazio et al. (1986) found that a subject's relatively strong attitudes, not his or her relatively weak ones (defined in terms of how quickly subjects could evaluate the attitude object in a previous assessment task), were capable of becoming active automatically in the context of an adjective evaluation task. Attitude objects selected from the assessment phase of the study were employed as priming stimuli in the adjective evaluation task, being presented too briefly (250 msec) to permit intentional, strategic evaluation to occur (see Neely, 1977; Posner & Snyder, 1975). On each trial, one of these strong or weak, good or bad attitude object primes was presented, followed by a target adjective that was clearly positive (e.g., beautiful) or negative (e.g., repulsive) in meaning. Subjects were to classify each adjective, as quickly as possible, as having a positive or negative meaning, by pressing either a "good" or a "bad" button. When the attitude object primes corresponded to the subject's strongly held attitudes, responses were faster when the prime and target evaluations matched than when they mismatched. The effect when primes corresponded to weak attitudes was less evident. Thus, even though subjects were asked to evaluate the adjective targets and not the primes themselves, the strong-attitude primes apparently activated their stored evaluation and consequently facilitated or interfered with evaluating the adjectives with which they were paired. Fazio et al. (1986) concluded that one's strong, relatively accessible attitudes become active automatically at the mere presence of the attitude object in the environment.

Fazio et al. (1986) concluded that the mere presence of the attitude object in the environment was sufficient to activate its associated attitude and, therefore, to influence on-line judgment and behavior concerning the object. However, several aspects of the paradigm they used to assess preconscious automaticity potentially could have activated the attitude through postconscious or goal-dependent means instead. Specifically, subjects were instructed to think about and give their attitudes for each possible prime immediately before testing the automaticity of those attitudes. This procedural step could have increased the temporary accessibility of the relevant attitudes, producing a postconscious automaticity effect that requires recent conscious thought about the attitude object. Moreover, because subjects were intentionally and consciously evaluating the target adjectives while the attitude object primes were being presented, it is possible that the evaluation of the primes depended on subjects' having the evaluative processing goal at the time the primes were presented (see Gollwitzer, Heckhausen, & Steller, 1990; Mandler & Nakamura, 1987).

My colleagues and I (Bargh et al., 1992; Chaiken & Bargh, 1993) found that when the original paradigm was altered to eliminate the possibility of postconscious and goal-dependent activation of attitudes, the automatic activation effect was obtained for all attitude objects, regardless of their relative strengths or accessibilities. For example, in two experiments we inserted a 2-day delay between the attitude assessment phase of the experiment and the adjective evaluation task that assessed automaticity. Because subjects had not evaluated the target consciously, the attitude would not be temporarily more accessible in memory. Nonetheless, the effect identified by Fazio et al. (1986) was maintained. It occurred more generally than it had in the Fazio et al. (1986) studies, however, with even the weakest (i.e., most slowly evaluated) of the subjects' attitudes from among the range of stimuli presented showing the effect.

More recently, we examined the possible goal dependence of the effect by eliminating the adjective evaluation task from the paradigm (Bargh, Chaiken, Raymond, & Hymes, 1993). Specifically, we had subjects pronounce the adjective targets as quickly as possible, and assessed how quickly they could do so under the various prime valence × target valence combinations, as before. Removing this potential condition for the effect and making the experimental situation even more like conditions of mere presence of the attitude object did not eliminate the effect. Rather, the effect again occurred for all attitude object primes, regardless of whether they corresponded to the subject's strongest or weakest attitudes, and was of equivalent strength across the range of attitude strengths. Therefore, under conditions more closely resembling the mere presence of the attitude object in the environment, it appears that nearly everything is preconsciously classified as good or bad,[4] with this effect occurring equally strongly regardless of variations in the underlying strength of the attitude; that is, in the "crude" dichotomous manner demonstrated in the Bargh et al. (1989) and Pratto and John (1991) studies discussed previously.

---

[4]This more general automatic evaluation effect recently has been obtained with complex pictorial stimuli as primes and targets as well as with word stimuli (Giner-Sorolla, Chaiken, Bargh, & Garcia, 1993; Hermans, de Houwer, & Eelen, 1992), so it would appear not to be merely a verbal effect.

A Methodological Caution.   There are important methodological consequences of the existence and ubiquity of this preconscious evaluation effect. The Fazio et al. (1986) and Bargh et al. (1992, 1993) demonstrations of automatic attitude activation used primes and targets that were matched or mismatched randomly on valence alone—they had no other semantic features in common (see also Greenwald et al., 1989). The priming stimuli somehow must have activated all similarly evaluated material in memory, making it immediately and, for at least a short time, more accessible than opposite-valence material in general (see Bargh et al., 1993, for a fuller discussion of mechanism).

Hence, the results of other sequential or context-dependent priming studies that were interpreted in terms of specific features of the primes may have occurred because of correlated differences in the valence of the primes. For example, in a study of age stereotyping by Perdue and Gurtman (1990, Experiment 2), subjects on each trial were subliminally presented with the word *young* or the word *old*, followed immediately by a positive or negative adjective they were to classify as good or bad, following the Fazio et al. (1986) paradigm. Subjects were faster to respond to positive adjectives following *young* and to negative adjectives following *old*, and this was interpreted in terms of the automatic activation of a positive stereotype of young people and a negative stereotype of older people by subjects (who were college students). However, it is likely that *young* is positive and *old* is negative in meaning. Greenwald et al. (1989) showed such priming effects of subliminally presented stimuli based only on the valence match or mismatch between prime and target.

Summary.   Collectively, the evidence in this domain indicates that the automatic, preconscious evaluation of stimuli is a ubiquitous and constant mental process. It leads input to be classified immediately as good or bad, regardless of the intensity, extremity, or strength of that evaluation or affective reaction. At least this is what occurs unconditionally, upon the mere presence of the stimulus in the environment. Following this initial preconscious screening of the environment, there may be differential processing of stimuli based on their self-relevance (e.g., Lazarus, 1991), attitude strength (e.g., Roskos-Ewoldsen & Fazio, 1992), or survival implications (e.g., Pratto & John, 1991). Certainly, the results of the Fazio et al. (1986), Bargh et al. (1992, Experiments 1 and 3), and Roskos-Ewoldsen and Fazio (1992) studies showed variations in the size of the automatic evaluation effect with differences in underlying attitude strength when one has recently thought about one's attitude toward the object. Thus, just because there are no differences in the size or extent of the unconditional automatic evaluation effect does not mean that such differences do not occur given certain conditions.

The ramifications are considerable for a preconscious evaluative process that immediately classifies everything and everyone the individual encounters as either good or bad, because of its potential influence on subsequent judgments (e.g., how one interprets a person's ambiguous behavior) and behavior toward the person or object. The importance of immediate affective reactions for subsequent cognitive processing has already been noted by theorists such as Niedenthal (1990) and Niedenthal and Cantor (1986). Given the automatic evaluation evidence, such reactions may be a more pervasive and constant influence than was previously assumed.

Automatic Stereotype Activation

It has been argued widely that stereotypes are activated automatically by the presence of a group member, as easily identified by physical characteristics such as skin color or gender features, or by accent, dress, and so on (Brewer, 1988; Deaux & Lewis, 1984; Devine, 1989; Fiske, 1989; Perdue & Gurtman, 1990; Pratto & Bargh, 1991; Rothbart, 1981). This activation appears to be unintentional and efficient, at least for the more widely shared stereotypes (within the U.S. culture), such as those for African-Americans and for different genders. Devine (1989, Experiment 2) subliminally presented subjects with words related to the African-American stereotype, both positive (e.g., *musical*) and negative (e.g., *lazy*), but none related to hostility, which her Experiment 1 had shown to be part of the stereotype. Subjects then read about a target person (race unspecified) who acted in an ambiguously hostile manner. Subjects who were primed with the stereotype-related words rated the target person as more hostile than did control subjects. Apparently, the African-American stereotype was activated by the prime words and caused the unprimed trait concept of hostility to become activated and more accessible by virtue of its inclusion in that stereotypic representation (i.e., all-or-none activation; see Fiske & Dyer, 1985; Hayes-Roth, 1977).

Devine's (1989) set of studies was ground breaking conceptually, because of its analysis of the stereotyping process into separate components of stereotype activation and stereotype use, and empirically because it demonstrated the relative controllability of the latter but not the former stage (see next section). However, as a single article, it could not be expected to address and answer each question having to do with stereotype activation.[5] There are intriguing aspects of the findings that call for further study, especially as to the inevitability of stereotype activation in more natural settings.

Most important of these is that the race of the target person whom subjects rated after the subliminal priming task was not specified in the story (subjects read the Donald story used by Srull & Wyer, 1979, in which Donald behaved in ambiguously hostile ways on several occasions). Presumably, most subjects assumed that Donald was White, given base rates and the fact that all subjects in the study were White. In effect, then, the real-world analogue to the results

---

[5]Devine's own subsequent research has been devoted to what is probably the most pressing question springing from her 1989 findings: how to get people to exercise their potential control over their stereotypes (Devine, Monteith, Zuwerink, & Elliot, 1991).

of Experiment 2 would be if the mere presence of an African-American in the current environment caused the perceiver to categorize a White's (or anyone's) ambiguously hostile behavior as more hostile than would a perceiver who had not just encountered an African-American. However, the general assumption about the application of group stereotypes is that they are used in interpreting (or making assumptions about) the behavior of group members, rather than nongroup members who happen to be in their vicinity. Thus, although Devine's (1989, Experiment 2) results were suggestive and provocative, they signaled the need for further research to better understand their implications for automatic stereotype activation and application.

Such additional study is needed all the more in the wake of a recent experiment by Gilbert and Hixon (1991). Subjects watched a videotape in which an Asian-American experimenter held up word-fragment completion items for subjects to complete. Five of these were critical trials (e.g., S __ Y) that had stereotypic (e.g., SHY) as well as nonstereotypic completions (e.g., STY, SPY). (The stereotypicality was determined by pretest assessment of the Asian-American stereotype among the subject population.) With no constraints on attentional capacity, the incidental presence of the Asian-American experimenter did result in a greater number of stereotypic completions compared to the Caucasian experimenter condition. However, in two experiments, giving subjects a simultaneous digit-recall task to constrain attentional processing eliminated the stereotyping effect. Apparently, then, at least for some stereotypes, activation is unintentional, but requires attentional capacity. Further research is needed to determine whether this holds true for other, perhaps more strongly held stereotypic beliefs (as for women or African-Americans). At a minimum, such findings do question the assumption that stereotype activation is inevitable.

Such provisos notwithstanding, Gilbert and Hixon (1991) made an excellent point when attempting to reconcile their findings with those of others (Devine, 1989; Perdue & Gurtman, 1990; Pratto & Bargh, 1991) who have concluded that group stereotypes are automatically activated given the presence of features of a group member. These contrasting findings come from experiments in which the stereotype was primed or activated using verbal labels or descriptions that may force a categorization in terms of the stereotyped group, whereas an actual person displays many other features (height, age, expensiveness of dress, self-confidence, accent, etc.) besides race, gender, or ethnic group membership that also can be used to categorize the person (see also Zarate & Smith, 1990).

For example, if, in an experiment, the subject is told only that the target is elderly, he or she may assume implicitly that the target is passive, needy, and physically weak (see Perdue & Gurtman, 1990); if the subject is told only that the target is an African-American male, he or she may assume implicitly that the target is hostile, athletic, and aggressive (see Devine, 1989). Does this mean that all of these trait expectations are activated automatically in the presence of an elderly African-American? They would seem to be mutually contradictory.

It may be that people have more specific subtypes that become activated automatically (e.g., Taylor, 1981; Weber & Crocker, 1983), or that stronger stereotypes override weaker ones (e.g., the elderly stereotype overrides those for minority group membership). Consistent with this reasoning, Brewer and Lui (1989) examined the priority with which identifying features are used in categorizing people, and found that age and gender are the paramount determinants. Such results call for a more specific and conditional model of automatic stereotype activation than currently exists.

Proceeding down the road suggested by Gilbert and Hixon (1991) and Zarate and Smith (1990; see also Smith & Zarate, 1992), it seems useful to consider real people as collections and combinations of features instead of existing as placements on single dimensions. Thus, stereotypes may not exist at a global abstract level, but rather for specific, concrete exemplars or instances of people with certain combinations of features. For example, instead of a single stereotype triggered by group membership regardless of other features (e.g., African-American, woman), it may require multiple features to become active in the natural environment (e.g., young, male, poorly dressed African-American; middle-aged White female).

Spontaneous Trait Inference

If there is one social–cognitive process that is automatic in all senses of the word, it is the identification or categorization of social behavior in trait terms when that behavior is diagnostic of a trait (i.e., unambiguously relevant to the trait construct; see Higgins, 1989). In their study of priming effects on impression formation, Srull and Wyer (1979) assumed this automatic behavior-to-trait process when they used short sentences indicating hostile or kind behaviors as the priming stimuli. They presented these behavioral examples in scrambled-sentence form (e.g., "the kick he dog"), with subjects instructed simply to make grammatical three-word sentences out of the word string. Although the ostensible purpose of this experiment (i.e., to measure language ability) had nothing to do with personality or impression formation, these behaviors nonetheless primed the corresponding abstract trait construct. In the subsequent, "unrelated" second experiment, subjects formed impressions of a target person whose behavior was ambiguously relevant to the primed trait, and primed subjects considered the target to possess more of that trait than did nonprimed subjects. More recently, Moskowitz and Roman (1992) also showed that trait-implying behavior descriptions have this priming function, although subjects are instructed only to memorize the sentences. Thus, at least with verbal presentation of the behavioral stimuli, behaviors activate corresponding trait concepts unintentionally and without subjects' awareness of such encoding (i.e., "spontaneously"; see Newman, 1991; Newman & Uleman, 1989).

Winter and Uleman (1984) and Winter, Uleman, and Cunniff (1985) used an

encoding-specificity paradigm to test whether this automatic behavior-to-trait encoding proceeded as far as making dispositional inferences about the actor in terms
of that trait. In other words, they asked whether the actor as well as the behavior
was encoded automatically in terms of the relevant trait. To the extent that this
occurs, the trait term (e.g., *kind*) to which the behavior that subjects are trying
to memorize (e.g., "The lawyer took the orphans to the circus") is relevant should
serve as a retrieval cue on the later memory test. However, although the results
of these studies showed that the trait term facilitated retrieval of the behavioral
portion of the sentence, it did not improve recall of the actor (see Hamilton, 1988;
Higgins & Bargh, 1987; Lupfer, Clark, & Hutchinson, 1990). However, using
the same paradigm, when subjects intend to form an impression of the actor in
each sentence, the relevant trait cues do facilitate actor recall (Bassili & Smith,
1986; Moskowitz & Uleman, 1987; see also D'Agostino, 1991). Thus, the evidence at present favors the interpretation that behaviors are encoded automatically in terms of traits they signify, but actors are not encoded by the perceiver
as possessing that trait dispositionally.

Newman (1991) studied the developmental sequence of spontaneous trait inferences across first-grade and fifth-grade children and adults. Interestingly, it
was the fifth-grade children who engaged in the most pervasive use of traits to
encode behavior. Newman concluded that the propensity to think about behavior
in trait terms "covaries with the perceived usefulness of dispositional information for predicting behavior" (p. 221).

Based on such evidence, the assumption that behaviors are identified unintentionally in terms of trait concepts has been incorporated into many models of
person perception (e.g., Hastie & Park, 1986; Pryor, Ostrom, Dukerich, Mitchell, & Herstein, 1983), stereotyping (Brewer, 1988; Pratto & Bargh, 1991), and
especially models of attribution (Gilbert, 1989; Trope, 1986). There is also considerable evidence as to the efficiency of the behavior-to-trait categorization
process, which is discussed in the next section.

EFFICIENCY

The efficiency aspect of automaticity refers to the extent to which the perceptual
or judgmental process demands attentional resources. To the degree that it does,
it may not occur when the attentional demands of the situation are high. Such
conditions of overload are not unusual. As Rothbart (1981), Bargh and Thein
(1985), and Gilbert and Osborne (1989) argued, social interaction routinely requires considerable attention to monitoring one's own appearance and behavior,
preparing one's next responses, comprehending the conversation and gestures of
the people whom one is with, thinking about the content of what they are saying,
figuring out their goals and motives, and so on. Moreover, the information given
off by others during interaction with them comes at its own fast and furious pace,

during which time one does not usually have time to ponder its meaning leisurely.

Consequently, recent research has moved away from self-paced experimental settings, in which only the critical information is present and subjects have plenty of time to consider it, to more ecologically valid conditions of rapid information presentation or attentional load. Take a social interaction out of the laboratory and plump it down onto a busy city sidewalk (or during a walk across a farmyard), and the social perceiver's attention will be divided by many distractions, not the least of which will be a constant monitoring of the environment for signs of potential threat to personal safety (or hygiene).

Many of the phenomena already described in the Awareness or Intentionality (or both) sections also possess the efficiency aspect of automaticity, although they are not discussed further in this section. Subliminal effects of trait primes and emotive faces qualify, of course, as do automatic evaluation effects occurring immediately with appearance of the stimulus word. In addition, automatic attention effects, such as those demonstrated using the Stroop or visual search techniques, are efficient in that they occur despite conscious attention being directed elsewhere (in fact, despite it being a purpose of the attended task to not attend to them; see following section on Controllability).

In this section on efficiency, I focus on the role that efficiency plays in the outcome of intentional processes such as impression formation, self-judgment and other-judgment, and causal attribution. These are examples of goal-dependent automatic processes.

Social Judgment

Bargh and Thein (1985) found that behaviors relevant for a subject's chronically accessible constructs were noticed and influential in impression formation under attentional overload (rapid presentation) conditions: Subjects with a chronically accessible construct for honesty were able to distinguish in their impressions between a mainly honest and a mainly dishonest target, whereas subjects with an inaccessible construct for honesty could not. Moreover, the chronic subjects in the overload condition were equivalent in their behavior recall and impressions to all subjects in the nonoverload condition.

In another study using the rapid presentation manipulation, Pratto and Bargh (1991) found that the effect of gender stereotypes on judgments of a male or female target were equivalent regardless of whether subjects' attention was limited, whereas the effect of other target features (behaviors, trait expectancies) was attenuated by the overload manipulation.

Bargh and Tota (1988) used a concurrent memory load technique to study the efficiency of depressed and nondepressed subjects' self-judgments and other judgments. Half of the subjects had to hold a different six-digit number in working memory on each trial, which consisted of responding "yes" or "no" as to whether a given trait term was true of the self or of the average other person. Depressives made self-judgments on depressed-content traits just as quickly under the load as under the no-load conditions, whereas nondepressed subjects did the same for the nondepressed-content trait, supporting the hypothesis that, when thinking about the self, different content becomes active automatically for depressed versus nondepressed people (both groups of subjects thought about other people most efficiently in terms of nondepressed constructs). Recently, Andersen, Spielman, and Bargh (1992), using the same memory load technique, showed depressed subjects to respond automatically to questions about the likelihood of future events in their lives.

Smith and Lerner (1986; see also Smith, chapter 3, Volume 1) used a response-time measure to show how subjects given the task of judging whether behaviors are instances of specific traits make these judgments more efficiently (faster) with practice, with this procedural knowledge having both specific behavior-to-trait (Smith, Stewart, & Buttram, 1992) and more general skill components (Smith, Branscombe, & Bormann, 1988).

The ways one thinks about oneself or others under attentional stress, and the kinds of information that are picked up about others regardless of concurrent attentional focus or demands, are quite important, because such processes operate (given the goal to do so) much more routinely than do processes that are dependent on the current availability of sufficient attentional capacity for their occurrence.

Dispositional Inference

Winter et al. (1985), Lupfer et al. (1990), and Uleman, Newman, and Winter (1992) examined the efficiency of spontaneous trait inferences using a concurrent memory load technique. Whereas Winter et al. (1985) and Lupfer et al. (1990) found that their secondary task (digit retention) did not interfere with spontaneous trait inferences, indicating their efficiency, Uleman et al. (1992) added a probe reaction-time measure of spare processing capacity, and did obtain interference. Perhaps the Uleman et al. (1992) probe reaction-time task, when added to the other secondary task of digit retention, constituted a greater attentional load than experienced by subjects in the previous two experiments. Thus, it appears that the spontaneous, unintentional encoding of behaviors in trait terms (see Intentionality section) is at least a somewhat efficient process as well.

Gilbert and his colleagues performed a legion of demonstrations of the effect that attention load, or *cognitive busyness* (Gilbert & Osborne, 1989), has on causal attribution processes (Gilbert et al., 1988; Gilbert & Osborne, 1989; Gilbert & Krull, 1988). Gilbert posited a three-stage process of (intentional) person perception: an immediate characterization of behavior in trait terms, a dispositional inference stage, followed by a correction stage in which situational reasons for (or constraints on) the behavior are taken into account.[6] Thus, Gilbert's explanation for the correspondence bias or fundamental attribution error was that dispositional attributions are made first and with great ease and efficiency, with situational attributions possible only if sufficient time and attention are available to the perceiver.

For example, Gilbert et al. (1988) showed subjects a videotape of a woman who was said to be discussing either an intimate, embarrassing topic (e.g., sexual fantasies) or a mundane topic (e.g., hobbies). Thus, there was either a situational reason or not for her somewhat anxious appearance (subjects only saw and did not hear the woman on tape). Some subjects were given a secondary task to load attention while watching the tape, and others did not have this constraint on processing resources. The former group of subjects considered the woman to be more dispositionally anxious than did the nonoverload subjects. Thus, even though all subjects had both the relevant dispositional and situational information available to them, the capacity-limited subjects were unable to use the situational information or to integrate it with the dispositional information to adjust the more efficiently made dispositional inference (see Pratto & Bargh, 1991, for a related finding).

Gilbert (1991) placed this efficient dispositional inference phenomenon in the larger context of a general tendency for people to initially believe or accept propositions as true. This belief or acceptance is said to occur naturally during the process of comprehending the meaning of the incoming information, and only subsequently do people correct or adjust this primary trust in the face of reasons to believe otherwise (e.g., one's own knowledge or experience, the possible motives of the source of the information). If dispositional attributions are made naturally and efficiently in the course of one's attempt to comprehend the meaning of another's behavior, then they too will be accepted as valid if the effortful situational-correction stage is prevented in some way (no time, too much to attend to, etc.).

Conclusions

Perhaps all of these efficient trait categorizations and attributions described in this section are trusted precisely because of their efficiency, in that people experience them as being made effortlessly, as conclusions reached easily (see previous discussion of the use of perceptual fluency as a cue for the validity of the

---

[6]Srull and Wyer (1979) had distinguished earlier between the behavior categorization and the person inference stages. Similarly, Trope's (1986) model of attribution calls for a two-stage process of behavior identification followed by adjustments based on the situational context. Like Gilbert (1989) and others, Trope (1986) argued for the relative automaticity (intended but immediate and efficient) of the identification stage. Trope made the additional hypothesis that situational information can influence behavior identification, not just the adjustment process—a prediction supported by several recent studies (Lupfer et al., 1990; Trope, Cohen, & Alfieri, 1991; Trope, Cohen, & Maoz, 1988).

inference). If so, this is another reason why the relative efficiency of a mental process matters. People's trust in the validity of efficiently reached categorizations, self-judgments, future judgments, and attributions may be of the same cloth as their necessary trust in what their senses are telling them, which also comes to them, not coincidentally, with a subjective experience of effortlessness (see Bargh, 1989).

CONTROLLABILITY

There has been a surge of attention given to studying how the subject's motivations can moderate or even eliminate otherwise automatic (unintended, efficient, unaware) influences on judgments and behavior. As with the Awareness section, it is useful here at the outset to call for some precision in describing what exactly is being controlled in these studies. For example, Devine (1989) was careful to distinguish the process of stereotype activation from that of making stereotypic judgments, and both Trope (1986) and Gilbert (1989) distinguished between a behavior identification and a situational correction stage in their attribution models. In all three of these approaches, the first stage is seen as much less easily controlled than the second. Therefore, such distinctions are important for any discussion of controllability of thought and behavior, because they demonstrate that asking whether stereotyping or dispositional attributions occur automatically are meaningless questions. Just as with other complex mental phenomena, such as those involved in driving a car, social cognitive processes are composed of both automatic and controlled subprocesses.

Thus, what most researchers mean by the question of controllability is not the occurrence of the stereotype's or accessible construct's input into a judgment, but rather whether one is aware of such influences and is both motivated and able to counteract them. In an engaging treatment of this issue of *ultimate control*, Fiske (1989) argued that it is possible to gain control by "making the hard choice" and spending the additional cognitive effort to avoid pigeonholing or stereotyping an individual. Instead, the person can effortfully seek out additional individuating information and integrate it into a coherent impression (see also Brewer, 1988; Fiske & Neuberg, 1990). It may be that all one can do with this extra effort is to adjust one's judgment in the direction opposite to that of the suspected stereotypic influence (see Bargh, 1992a, 1992b; Martin et al., 1990; Schwarz & Bless, 1992; Strack, 1992), but doing so is still an act of control.

Under what conditions will a person go this extra mile? If one processes information about the target person more effortfully, even if there are stereotypic or categorical inputs into one's judgments (as when an influence exists that the perceiver is not aware of and therefore does not engage in an adjustment process; see Bargh, 1989), those judgments will at least be moderated by the additional individuating information collected, and will not be determined solely by the stereotypic input (Fiske & Neuberg, 1990). Many such motivations have now been documented.

Situationally Induced Motivations

Lord et al. (1984) showed that confirmatory biases in hypothesis testing can be overcome by simply instructing subjects to consider alternatives, or the possibility that the opposite conclusion could be correct instead. One will also be more likely to process information about another individual effortfully when that individual has power or control over his or her important outcomes. Such outcome dependency has been shown to increase attention to stereotype- or expectancy-inconsistent information and to result in more individuated impressions (Erber & Fiske, 1984; Fiske & Neuberg, 1990). Similarly, Neuberg (1989) documented how subjects given motivations for greater accuracy in their judgments (through experimental instructions) are more likely to overrule expectations and confirmatory hypothesis testing biases through a more complete gathering of individuating information. In several studies, Tetlock and his colleagues (e.g., Tetlock, 1985; Tetlock & Kim, 1987) showed how making subjects feel accountable for their impressions or judgments – in that they believe they will have to defend and justify those judgments later – results in greater attention to situational constraints on the target's behavior and, in general, more effortful decision making.

Finally, two recent studies showed that motivations can override the influence of passive priming effects on impression formation. Sedikides (1990) found that the *saying is believing* effect (Higgins & Rholes, 1978) – the tendency to shape one's communication to fit the known beliefs or opinions of one's audience, which then causes one's judgments of the target to fall in line with those communications – overrode prior trait construct priming effects on subject's impressions of the target's ambiguous behaviors. Thompson et al. (1992) found that making subjects accountable for their judgments prior to reading about a target person even prevents *subsequent* priming effects on impressions.

Internally Generated Motivations

In the above studies, the source of the motivation to process effortfully resided in the situation, as manipulated by the experimental instructions. However, often the source of the motivation may be within the individual. D'Agostino and Fincher-Kiefer (1992) showed that subjects who were high in need for cognition (Cacioppo & Petty, 1982) are less likely to show the correspondence bias in attribution than other subjects, presumably because they chronically expend greater effort in mental processing and so are more likely to notice and use situational reasons for the target's behavior. In Devine's (1989) Experiment 3, subjects who valued not being prejudiced controlled the stereotypic content of their descriptions of the average African-American, whereas prejudiced subjects did not (producing a more stereotypic description of that group).

Fiske and Von Hendy (1992) and Pittman and D'Agostino (1989) used experimental manipulations to activate motivations within subjects, which then determined how effortfully they formed an impression of a target person. Fiske and Von Hendy (1992) gave subjects who were either high or low self-monitors feedback about their person perception abilities (i.e., that they were good categorizers or individuators) as well as advice on the situational norms or appropriateness of categorizing or individuating people when forming impressions. The dispositional feedback determined whether low self-monitors (who presumably use their internal states, opinions, and abilities as behavioral guides) categorized or individuated the target, whereas the situational norm feedback determined whether high self-monitors (who are presumed to be more likely to use situational cues to guide appropriate behavior) categorized or individuated. Pittman and D'Agostino (1989) increased some subjects' control motivation by depriving them of control over their outcomes in an early part of the experiment. In a subsequent impression formation task, those subjects engaged in more effortful and careful processing of the information. This suggests that a more accurate prediction furnishes the perceiver with better predictive control over his or her environment.

Conclusions

Automated social cognitive processes categorize, evaluate, and impute the meanings of behavior and other social information, and this input is then ready for use by conscious and controlled judgment and decision processes, yet those judgments and decisions are not uncontrollable or predetermined by that automatic input. In the same way, the unintentional and uncontrollable nature of automatic analyses of the environment does not mean they are impossible to control or adjust for when one is aware of them, if one desires. Just as in strong perceptual illusions, one does not have to act in line with what is clearly (but inaccurately) apparent to one's senses when one knows better. The considerable body of research on motivational control over stereotypes and other judgmental biases has shown that, for the most part, the use of automatically supplied input in consciously produced judgmental output is not mandatory (see Bargh, 1988; Fiske, 1989; Jacoby & Kelley, 1990; Thompson et al., 1992).

THE AUTOMATICITY OF EVERYDAY LIFE: AN AGENDA FOR THE NEXT 10 YEARS

Automatic processes are not an unqualified blessing, nor are they an unqualified curse (Higgins & Bargh, 1992). Because of them, people stereotype others and often misunderstand the reasons for their own feelings and behavior. At the same time, automatic affective appraisal of the environment seems to be a ubiquitous and adaptive service (Bargh et al., 1992, 1993; Pratto & John, 1991). For example, Wilson and Schooler (1991) provided evidence that such immediate reactions may be more accurate (in terms of matching experts' opinions) than the preferences one comes up with after additional deliberation.

The automatization of routine thought processes frees one's limited attentional resources for nonroutine matters, and enables a reduction of the massive amount of stimulation and information bombarding one at any given moment into a more manageable subset of important objects, events, and appraisals. But with the increased efficiency of thought also comes a lack of awareness of engaging in that process, leading to a likelihood of misattributing the causes of one's feelings and a loosening of one's intentional grip over decisions and judgments.

Therefore, the recent wave of research demonstrating one's ultimate control over automatic input and judgmental processes is reassuring. In a sense, one is able both to delegate control to these automatized perceptual and judgmental mechanisms through frequent and consistent use of them in the past (Bargh & Gollwitzer, in press), and at the same time largely retain the final say over one's responses to the environment (Bargh, 1990; Logan & Cowan, 1984). Still, whether one exercises this ultimate control is another matter, as to do so one must be aware of the existence of the automatic influence, have the intention to effortfully override it, and also sufficient attentional resources.

The research of the past 10 years has made it clear that the outcomes of social cognitive processes are very different, depending on whether one is aware of influences, whether one has specific intentions or goals within the situation, whether attentional resources are in ample or short supply, and whether one is motivated to take control over one's decisions and behavior. These are distinct and important dimensions on which social situations can vary. The past 10 years of research has been increasingly sensitive to the natural ecology of those situations with regard to a person's awareness, intentions, processing efficiency, and exercise of control within them. Should this trend continue, in the next decade even more will be discovered about the automaticity of everyday life.

ACKNOWLEDGMENTS

Preparation of this chapter was supported in part by Grant MH43265 from the National Institute of Mental Health. My thanks to Dan Gilbert, Roger Giner-Sorolla, Eliot Smith, Thom Srull, Erik Thompson, Jim Uleman, Bob Wyer, and Adam Zuckerman for their extensive comments on a previous version.

REFERENCES

Andersen, S. M., & Cole, S. W. (1990). "Do I know you?": The role of significant others in general social perception. *Journal of Personality and Social Psychology, 59*, 384–399.

Andersen, S. M., Spielman, L. A., & Bargh, J. A. (1992). Future-event schemas and certainty about the future: Automaticity in depressives' future-event predictions. *Journal of Personality and Social Psychology, 63,* 711–723.

Anderson, N. H. (1968). Likableness ratings of 555 personality trait words. *Journal of Personality and Social Psychology, 9,* 272–279.

Baldwin, M. W., Carrell, S. E., & Lopez, D. F. (1990). My advisor and the Pope are watching me from the back of my mind. *Journal of Experimental Social Psychology, 26,* 435–454.

Baldwin, M. W., & Holmes, J. G. (1987). Salient private audiences and awareness of the self. *Journal of Personality and Social Psychology, 53,* 1087–1098.

Bargh, J. A. (1982). Attention and automaticity in the processing of self-relevant information. *Journal of Personality and Social Psychology, 43,* 425–436.

Bargh, J. A. (1984). Automatic and conscious processing of social information. In R. S. Wyer, Jr., & T. K. Srull (Eds.), *Handbook of social cognition* (Vol. 3, pp. 1–43). Hillsdale, NJ: Lawrence Erlbaum Associates.

Bargh, J. A. (1988). Automatic information processing: Implications for communication and affect. In L. Donohew, H. Sypher, & E. T. Higgins (Eds.), *Communication, affect, and social cognition.* Hillsdale, NJ: Lawrence Erlbaum Associates.

Bargh, J. A. (1989). Conditional automaticity: Varieties of automatic influence in social perception and cognition. In J. S. Uleman & J. A. Bargh (Eds.), *Unintended thought.* New York: Guilford.

Bargh, J. A. (1990). Auto-motives: Preconscious determinants of thought and behavior. In E. T. Higgins & R. M. Sorrentino (Eds.), *Handbook of motivation and cognition* (Vol. 2). New York: Guilford.

Bargh, J. A. (1992a). Being unaware of the stimulus versus unaware of its interpretation: Why subliminality per se does not matter to social psychology. In R. Bornstein & T. Pittman (Eds.), *Perception without awareness.* New York: Guilford.

Bargh, J. A. (1992b). The ecology of automaticity: Towards specifying the conditions necessary to produce automatic processing effects. *American Journal of Psychology, 105,* 181–199.

Bargh, J. A., Bond, R. N., Lombardi, W. J., & Tota, M. E. (1986). The additive nature of chronic and temporary sources of construct accessibility. *Journal of Personality and Social Psychology, 50,* 869–878.

Bargh, J. A., Chaiken, S., Govender, R., & Pratto, F. (1992). The generality of the automatic attitude activation effect. *Journal of Personality and Social Psychology, 62,* 893–912.

Bargh, J. A., Chaiken, S., Raymond, P., & Hymes, C. (1993). *Automatic evaluation effects with a pronunciation task: Eliminating potential strategic influences.* Unpublished manuscript, New York University, New York City.

Bargh, J. A., & Gollwitzer, P. M. (in press). Environmental control of goal-directed action: Automatic and strategic contingencies between situations and behavior. *Nebraska Symposium on Motivation, 41.*

Bargh, J. A., Litt, J., Pratto, F., & Spielman, L. A. (1989). On the preconscious evaluation of social stimuli. In A. F. Bennett & K. M. McConkey (Eds.), *Cognition in individual and social contexts.* Amsterdam: Elsevier/North-Holland.

Bargh, J. A., Lombardi, W. J., & Higgins, E. T. (1988). Automaticity of Person x Situation effects on impression formation: It's just a matter of time. *Journal of Personality and Social Psychology, 55,* 599–605.

Bargh, J. A., & Pietromonaco, P. (1982). Automatic information processing and social perception: The influence of trait information presented outside of conscious awareness on impression formation. *Journal of Personality and Social Psychology, 43,* 437–449.

Bargh, J. A., & Pratto, F. (1986). Individual construct accessibility and perceptual selection. *Journal of Experimental and Social Psychology, 22,* 293–311.

Bargh, J. A., & Thein, R. D. (1985). Individual construct accessibility, person memory, and the recall-judgment link: The case of information overload. *Journal of Personality and Social Psychology, 49,* 1129–1146.

Bargh, J. A., & Tota, M. E. (1988). Context-dependent automatic processing in depression: Accessibility of negative constructs with regard to self but not others. *Journal of Personality and Social Psychology, 54,* 925–939.

Bassili, J. N., & Smith, M. C. (1986). On the spontaneity of trait attribution: Converging evidence for the role of cognitive strategy. *Journal of Personality and Social Psychology, 50,* 239–245.

Bem, D. J. (1972). Self-perception theory. *Advances in Experimental Social Psychology, 6,* 1–62.

Bornstein, R. F. (1989). Exposure and affect: Overview and meta-analysis of research, 1968–1987. *Psychological Bulletin, 106,* 265–289.

Bornstein, R. F., Leone, D. R., & Galley, D. J. (1988). The generalization of subliminal mere exposure effects: Influence of stimuli perceived without awareness on social behavior. *Journal of Personality and Social Psychology, 53,* 1070–1079.

Bornstein, R. F., & Pittman, T. S. (Eds.). (1992). *Perception without awareness.* New York: Guilford.

Brewer, M. B. (1988). A dual process model of impression formation. In T. K. Srull & R. S. Wyer, Jr. (Eds.), *Advances in social cognition* (Vol. 1, pp. 1–36). Hillsdale, NJ: Lawrence Erlbaum Associates.

Brewer, M. B., & Lui, L. N. (1989). The primacy of age and sex in the structure of person categories. *Social Cognition, 7,* 262–274.

Cacioppo, J. T., & Petty, R. E. (1982). The need for cognition. *Journal of Personality and Social Psychology, 42,* 116–131.

Chaiken, S., & Bargh, J. A. (1993). Occurrence versus moderation of the automatic attitude activation effect: Reply to Fazio. *Journal of Personality and Social Psychology, 64,* 759–765.

Chanowitz, B., & Langer, E. J. (1981). Premature cognitive commitment. *Journal of Personality and Social Psychology, 41,* 1051–1063.

Crocker, J., & Schwartz, I. (1985). Prejudice and ingroup favoritism in a minimal intergroup situation: Effects of self-esteem. *Personality and Social Psychology Bulletin, 11,* 379–386.

Crusco, A. H., & Wetzel, C. G. (1984). The Midas Touch: The effects of interpersonal touch on restaurant tipping. *Personality and Social Psychology Bulletin, 10,* 512–517.

D'Agostino, P. R. (1991). Spontaneous trait inferences: Effects of recognition instructions and subliminal priming on recognition performance. *Personality and Social Psychology Bulletin, 17,* 70–77.

D'Agostino, P. R., & Fincher-Kiefer, R. (1992). Need for cognition and the correspondence bias. *Social Cognition, 10,* 151–164.

Darley, J. M., & Gross, P. H. (1983). A hypothesis-confirming bias in labeling effects. *Journal of Personality and Social Psychology, 44,* 20–33.

Deaux, K., & Lewis, L. L. (1984). Structure of gender stereotypes: Interrelations among components and gender label. *Journal of Personality and Social Psychology, 46,* 991–1004.

Devine, P. G. (1989). Stereotypes and prejudice: Their automatic and controlled components. *Journal of Personality and Social Psychology, 56,* 680–690.

Devine, P. G., Monteith, M. J., Zuwerink, J. R., & Elliot, A. J. (1991). Prejudice with and without compunction. *Journal of Personality and Social Psychology, 60,* 817–830.

Dovidio, J. F., Evans, N., & Tyler, R. B. (1986). Racial stereotypes: The contents of their cognitive representations. *Journal of Experimental Social Psychology, 22,* 22–37.

Edwards, K. (1990). The interplay of affect and cognition in attitude formation and change. *Journal of Personality and Social Psychology, 59,* 202–216.

Erber, R. (1991). Affective and semantic priming: Effects of mood on category accessibility and inference. *Journal of Experimental Social Psychology, 27,* 480–498.

Erber, R., & Fiske, S. T. (1984). Outcome dependency and attention to inconsistent information. *Journal of Personality and Social Psychology, 47,* 709–726.

Erdelyi, M. H. (1974). A new look at the New Look: Perceptual defense and vigilance. *Psychological Review, 81,* 1–25.

Erdley, C. A., & D'Agostino, P. R. (1987). Cognitive and affective components of automatic priming effects. *Journal of Personality and Social Psychology, 54,* 741–747.

Fazio, R. H., Sanbonmatsu, D. M., Powell, M. C., & Kardes, F. R. (1986). On the automatic activation of attitudes. *Journal of Personality and Social Psychology, 50,* 229–238.

Festinger, L., & Carlsmith, J. M. (1959). Cognitive consequences of forced compliance. *Journal of Abnormal and Social Psychology, 58,* 203–210.

Fiske, S. T. (1980). Attention and weight in person perception: The impact of negative and extreme behavior. *Journal of Personality and Social Psychology, 38,* 889–906.

Fiske, S. T. (1989). Examining the role of intent: Toward understanding its role in stereotyping and prejudice. In J. S. Uleman & J. A. Bargh (Eds.), *Unintended thought.* New York: Guilford.

Fiske, S. T., & Dyer, L. M. (1985). Structure and development of social schemata: Evidence from positive and negative transfer effects. *Journal of Personality and Social Psychology, 48,* 839–852.

Fiske, S. T., & Neuberg, S. E. (1990). A continuum of impression formation, from category-based to individuating processes: Influences of information and motivation on attention and interpretation. *Advances in Experimental Social Psychology, 23,* 1–74.

Fiske, S. T., & Von Hendy, H. M. (1992). Personality feedback and situational norms can control stereotyping processes. *Journal of Personality and Social Psychology, 62,* 577–596.

Forgas, J. P., & Bower, G. H. (1987). Mood effects on person-perception judgments. *Journal of Personality and Social Psychology, 53,* 53–60.

Francolini, C. M., & Egeth, H. E. (1980). On the non-automaticity of "automatic" activation: Evidence of selective seeing. *Perception & Psychophysics, 27,* 331–342.

Gabrielcik, A., & Fazio, R. H. (1984). Priming and frequency estimation: A strict test of the availability heuristic. *Personality and Social Psychology Bulletin, 10,* 85–90.

Geller, V., & Shaver, P. (1976). Cognitive consequences of self-awareness. *Journal of Experimental Social Psychology, 12,* 99–108.

Gilbert, D. T. (1989). Thinking lightly about others: Automatic components of the social inference process. In J. S. Uleman & J. A. Bargh (Eds.), *Unintended thought* (pp. 189–211). New York: Guilford.

Gilbert, D. T. (1991). How mental systems believe. *American Psychologist, 46,* 107–119.

Gilbert, D. T., & Hixon, J. G. (1991). The trouble of thinking: Activation and application of stereotypic beliefs. *Journal of Personality and Social Psychology, 60,* 509–517.

Gilbert, D. T., & Krull, D. S. (1988). Seeing less and knowing more: The benefits of perceptual ignorance. *Journal of Personality and Social Psychology, 54,* 193–202.

Gilbert, D. T., & Osborne, R. E. (1989). Thinking backward: Some curable and incurable consequences of cognitive busyness. *Journal of Personality and Social Psychology, 57,* 940–949.

Gilbert, D. T., Pelham, B. W., & Krull, D. S. (1988). On cognitive busyness: When persons perceivers meet persons perceived. *Journal of Personality and Social Psychology, 54,* 733–740.

Gilovich, T. (1981). Seeing the past in the present: The effect of associations to familiar events on judgments and decisions. *Journal of Personality and Social Psychology, 40,* 797–808.

Giner-Sorolla, R., Chaiken, S., Bargh, J. A., & Garcia, M. (1993). *Automatic evaluation of pictorial stimuli.* Unpublished manuscript, New York University, New York City.

Goleman, D. (1988, February 2). The experience of touch: Research points to a critical role. *New York Times,* pp. C1 ff.

Gollwitzer, P. M., Heckhausen, H., & Steller, B. (1990). Deliberative and implemental mind-sets: Cognitive tuning toward congruous thoughts and information. *Journal of Personality and Social Psychology, 59,* 1119–1127.

Gordon, P. C., & Holyoak, K. J. (1983). Implicit learning and generalization of the "mere exposure" effect. *Journal of Personality and Social Psychology, 45,* 492–500.

Greenwald, A. G. (1992). New Look 3: Unconscious cognition reclaimed. *American Psychologist, 47,* 766–779.

Greenwald, A. G., Klinger, M. R., & Liu, T. J. (1989). Unconscious processing of dichoptically masked words. *Memory & Cognition, 17,* 35–47.

Hamilton, D. L. (1988). Causal attribution viewed from an information-processing perspective. In D. Bar-Tal & A. W. Kruglanski (Eds.), *The social psychology of knowledge* (pp. 359–385). New York: Cambridge University Press.

Hansen, C. H., & Hansen, R. D. (1988). Finding the face in the crowd: An anger superiority effect. *Journal of Personality and Social Psychology, 54*, 917–924.

Hastie, R., & Park, B. (1986). The relationship between memory and judgment depends on whether the judgment task is memory-based or on-line. *Psychological Review, 93*, 258–268.

Hayes-Roth, B. (1977). Evolution of cognitive structure and processes. *Psychological Review, 84*, 260–278.

Hermans, D., de Houwer, J., & Eelen, P. (1992). *Priming and the automatic motivation of affective information in memory*. Manuscript submitted for publication, University of Leuven, Belgium.

Herr, P. M., Sherman, S. J., & Fazio, R. H. (1984). On the consequences of priming: Assimilation and contrast effects. *Journal of Experimental Social Psychology, 19*, 323–340.

Higgins, E. T. (1989). Knowledge accessibility and activation: Subjectivity and suffering from unconscious sources. In J. S. Uleman & J. A. Bargh (Eds.), *Unintended thought*. New York: Guilford.

Higgins, E. T., & Bargh, J. A. (1987). Social perception and social cognition. *Annual Review of Psychology, 38*, 369–425.

Higgins, E. T., & Bargh, J. A. (1992). Unconscious sources of subjectivity and suffering: Is consciousness the solution? In A. Tesser & L. Martin (Eds.), *The construction of social judgments*. Hillsdale, NJ: Lawrence Erlbaum Associates.

Higgins, E. T., & King, G. A. (1981). Accessibility of social constructs: Information-processing consequences of individual and contextual variability. In N. Cantor & J. F. Kihlstrom (Eds.), *Personality, cognition, and social interaction* (pp. 69–122). Hillsdale, NJ: Lawrence Erlbaum Associates.

Higgins, E. T., King, G. A., & Mavin, G. H. (1982). Individual construct accessibility and subjective impressions and recall. *Journal of Personality and Social Psychology, 43*, 35–47.

Higgins, E. T., & Rholes, W. S. (1978). "Saying is believing": Effects of message modification on memory and liking for the person described. *Journal of Experimental Social Psychology, 14*, 363–378.

Higgins, E. T., Rholes, W S., & Jones, C. R. (1977). Category accessibility and impression formation. *Journal of Experimental Social Psychology, 13*, 141–154.

Higgins, E. T., Van Hook, E., & Dorfman, D. (1988). Do self-attributes form a cognitive structure? *Social Cognition, 6*, 177–217.

Hull, J. G., & Levy, A. S. (1979). The organizational function of the self: An alternative to the Duvall and Wicklund model of self-awareness. *Journal of Personality and Social Psychology, 37*, 756–768.

Isen, A. M., Shalker, T., Clark, M. S., & Karp, L. (1978). Affect, accessibility of material in memory, and behavior: A cognitive loop? *Journal of Personality and Social Psychology, 36*, 1–12.

Jacoby, L. L., & Kelley, C. M. (1990). An episodic view of motivation: Unconscious influences of memory. In E. T. Higgins & R. M. Sorrentino (Eds.), *Handbook of motivation and cognition* (Vol. 2, pp. 451–480). New York: Guilford.

Jacoby, L. L., Kelley, C. M., Brown, J., & Jasechko, J. (1989). Becoming famous overnight: Limits on the ability to avoid unconscious influences of the past. *Journal of Personality and Social Psychology, 56*, 326–338.

Jacoby, L. L., Toth, J. P., Lindsay, D. S., & Debner, J. A. (1992). Lectures for a layperson: Methods for revealing unconscious processes. In R. F. Bornstein & Thane S. Pittman (Eds.), *Perception without awareness* (pp. 81–120). New York: Guilford.

Johnson, M. K., & Hasher, L. (1987). Human learning and memory. *Annual Review of Psychology, 38*, 631–668.

Jones, E. E., & Nisbett, R. E. (1971). The actor and the observer: Divergent perceptions of the causes of behavior. In E. E. Jones, D. E. Kanouse, H. H. Kelley, R. E. Nisbett, S. Valins, & B. Weiner (Eds.), *Attribution: Perceiving the causes of behavior* (pp. 79–94). Morristown, NJ: General Learning Press.

Kahneman, D., & Henik, A. (1981). Perceptual organization and attention. In M. Kubovy & J. R. Pomerantz (Eds.), *Perceptual organization*. Hillsdale, NJ: Lawrence Erlbaum Associates.

Kahneman, D., & Treisman, A. (1984). Changing views of attention and automaticity. In R. Parasuraman (Ed.), *Varieties of attention*. New York: Academic Press.

Kahneman, D., & Tversky, A. (1973). On the psychology of prediction. *Psychological Review, 80*, 237–251.

Krosnick, J. A., Betz, A. L., Jussim, L. J., Lynn, A. R., & Stephens, L. (1992). Subliminal conditioning of attitudes. *Personality and Social Psychology Bulletin, 18*, 152–162.

Kunst-Wilson, W. R., & Zajonc, R. B. (1980). Affective discrimination of stimuli that cannot be recognized. *Science, 207*, 557–558.

Langer, E. J. (1978). Rethinking the role of thought in social interaction. In J. H. Harvey, W. I. Ickes, & R. F. Kidd (Eds.), *New directions in attribution research* (Vol. 2, pp. 35–58). Hillsdale, NJ: Lawrence Erlbaum Associates.

Langer, E. J., Blank, A., & Chanowitz, B. (1978). The mindlessness of ostensibly thoughtful action: The role of "placebic" information in interpersonal interaction. *Journal of Personality and Social Psychology, 36*, 635–642.

Lazarus, R. S. (1991). *Emotion and adaptation*. New York: Oxford University Press.

Lewicki, P. (1982). Trait relationships: The nonconscious generalization of social experience. *Personality and Social Psychology Bulletin, 8*, 439–445.

Lewicki, P. (1985). Nonconscious biasing effects of single instances on subsequent judgments. *Journal of Personality and Social Psychology, 48*, 563–574.

Logan, G. D., & Cowan, W. B. (1984). On the ability to inhibit thought and action: A theory of an act of control. *Psychological Review, 91*, 295–327.

Lombardi, W. J., Higgins, E. T., & Bargh, J. A. (1987). The role of consciousness in priming effects on categorization: Assimilation versus contrast as a function of awareness of the priming task. *Personality and Social Psychology Bulletin, 13*, 411–429.

Lord, C. G., Lepper, M. R., & Preston, E. (1984). Considering the opposite: A corrective strategy for social judgment. *Journal of Personality and Social Psychology, 47*, 1231–1243.

Lupfer, M. B., Clark, L. F., & Hutchinson, H. W. (1990). Impact of context on spontaneous trait and situational attributions. *Journal of Personality and Social Psychology, 58*, 239–249.

Mandler, G., & Nakamura, Y. (1987). Aspects of consciousness. *Personality and Social Psychology Bulletin, 13*, 299–313.

Mandler, G., Nakamura, Y., & Van Zandt, B. J. S. (1987). Nonspecific effects of exposure to stimuli that cannot be recognized. *Journal of Experimental Psychology: Learning, Memory, and Cognition, 13*, 646–648.

Marcel, A. J. (1983). Conscious and unconscious perception: Experiments on visual masking and word recognition. *Cognitive Psychology, 15*, 197–237.

Mark, M. M., Sinclair, R. C., & Wellens, T. R. (1991). The effect of completing the Beck Depression Inventory on self-reported mood state: Contrast and assimilation. *Personality and Social Psychology Bulletin, 17*, 457–465.

Markus, H., & Smith, J. (1981). The influence of self-schemas on the perception of others. In N. Cantor & J. F. Kihlstrom (Eds.), *Personality, cognition, and social interaction* (pp. 233–262). Hillsdale, NJ: Lawrence Erlbaum Associates.

Martin, L. L. (1986). Set/reset: Use and disuse of concepts in impression formation. *Journal of Personality and Social Psychology, 51*, 493–504.

Martin, L. L., Seta, J. J., & Crelia, R. (1990). Assimilation and contrast as a function of people's willingness and ability to expend effort in forming an impression. *Journal of Personality and Social Psychology, 59*, 27–37.

McArthur, L. Z., & Friedman, S. (1980). Illusory correlation in impression formation: Variations in the shared distinctiveness effected as a function of the distinctive person's age, race, and sex. *Journal of Personality and Social Psychology, 39*, 615–624.

McGuire, W. (1983). A contextualist theory of knowledge: Its implications for innovation and reform in psychological research. In L. Berkowitz (Ed.), *Advances in experimental social psychology* (Vol. 16). New York: Academic Press.

Moreland, R. L., & Zajonc, R. B. (1977). Is stimulus recognition a necessary condition for the occurrence of exposure effects? *Journal of Personality and Social Psychology, 35*, 191–199.

Moskowitz, G. B., & Roman, R. J. (1992). Spontaneous trait inferences and self-generated primes: Implications for conscious social judgment. *Journal of Personality and Social Psychology, 62,* 728–738.

Moskowitz, G. B., & Uleman, J. S. (1987). *The facilitation and inhibition of spontaneous trait inferences.* Paper presented at the annual convention of the American Psychological Association, New York City.

Murphy, S. T., & Zajonc, R. B. (1993). Affect, cognition, and awareness: Affective priming with optimal and suboptimal stimulus exposures. *Journal of Personality and Social Psychology, 64,* 723–739.

Neely, J. H. (1977). Semantic priming and retrieval from lexical memory: Roles of inhibitionless spreading activation and limited-capacity attention. *Journal of Experimental Psychology: General, 106,* 226–254.

Neisser, U. (1967). *Cognitive psychology.* New York: Appleton-Century-Crofts.

Neuberg, S. L. (1988). Behavioral implications of information presented outside of conscious awareness: The effect of subliminal presentation of trait information on behavior in the Prisoner's Dilemma game. *Social Cognition, 6,* 207–230.

Neuberg, S. L. (1989). The goal of forming accurate impressions during social interactions: Attenuating the impact of negative expectancies. *Journal of Personality and Social Psychology, 56,* 374–386.

Newman, L. S. (1991). Why are traits inferred spontaneously? A developmental approach. *Social Cognition, 9,* 221–253.

Newman, L. S., & Uleman, J. S. (1989). Spontaneous trait inference. In J. S. Uleman & J. A. Bargh (Eds.), *Unintended thought* (pp. 155–188). New York: Guilford.

Newman, L. S., & Uleman, J. S. (1990). Assimilation and contrast effects in spontaneous trait inference. *Personality and Social Psychology Bulletin, 16,* 224–240.

Niedenthal, P. M. (1990). Implicit perception of affective information. *Journal of Experimental Social Psychology, 26,* 505–527.

Niedenthal, P. M., & Cantor, N. (1986). Affective responses as guides to category-based influences. *Motivation and Emotion, 10,* 217–231.

Nisbett, R. E., & Bellows, N. (1977). Verbal reports about causal influences on social judgments: Private access versus public theories. *Journal of Personality and Social Psychology, 35,* 613–624.

Nisbett, R. E., & Wilson, T. D. (1977). Telling more than we can know: Verbal reports on mental processes. *Psychological Review, 84,* 231–259.

Paulhus, D. L., Graf, P., & Van Selst, M. (1989). Attentional load increases the positivity of self-presentation. *Social Cognition, 7,* 389–400.

Paulhus, D. L., & Levitt, K. (1987). Desirable responding triggered by affect: Automatic egotism? *Journal of Personality and Social Psychology, 52,* 245–259.

Perdue, C. W., Dovidio, J. F., Gurtman, M. B., & Tyler, R. B. (1990). Us and them: Social categorization and the process of intergroup bias. *Journal of Personality and Social Psychology, 59,* 475–486.

Perdue, C. W., & Gurtman, M. B. (1990). Evidence for the automaticity of ageism. *Journal of Experimental Social Psychology, 26,* 199–216.

Pittman, T. S., & D'Agostino, P. R. (1989). Motivation and cognition: Control deprivation and the nature of subsequent information processing. *Journal of Experimental Social Psychology, 25,* 456–480.

Posner, M. I., & Snyder, C. R. R. (1975). Attention and cognitive control. In R. L. Solso (Ed.), *Information processing and cognition: The Loyola symposium* (pp. 55–85). Hillsdale, NJ: Lawrence Erlbaum Associates.

Postman, L. (1951). Toward a general theory of cognition. In J. H. Rohrer & M. Sherif (Eds.), *Social psychology at the crossroads* (pp. 242–272). New York: Harper.

Pratto, F. (in press). Consciousness and automatic evaluation. In P. Niedenthal & S. Kitayama (Eds.), *The heart's eye: Emotional influences in perception and attention.* San Diego, CA: Academic Press.

Pratto, F., & Bargh, J. A. (1991). Stereotyping based on apparently individuating information: Trait and global components of sex stereotypes under attention overload. *Journal of Experimental Social Psychology, 27,* 26–47.

Pratto, F., & John, O. P. (1991). Automatic vigilance: The attention-grabbing power of negative social information. *Journal of Personality and Social Psychology, 61,* 380–391.

Pryor, J. B., Ostrom, T. M., Dukerich, J. M., Mitchell, M. L., & Herstein, J. A. (1983). Preintegrative categorization of social information: The role of persons as organizing categories. *Journal of Personality and Social Psychology, 44,* 923–932.

Rosenfield, D., Greenberg, J., Folger, R., & Borys, R. (1982). Effect of an encounter with a Black panhandler on subsequent helping for Blacks: Tokenism or confirming a negative stereotype? *Personality and Social Psychology Bulletin, 8,* 664–671.

Roskos-Ewoldsen, D. R., & Fazio, R. H. (1992). On the orienting value of attitudes: Attitude accessibility as a determinant of an object's attraction of visual attention. *Journal of Personality and Social Psychology, 63,* 198–211.

Rothbart, M. (1981). Memory processes and social beliefs. In D. L. Hamilton (Ed.), *Cognitive processes in stereotyping and intergroup behavior* (pp. 145–181). Hillsdale, NJ: Lawrence Erlbaum Associates.

Ruble, D. N., & Ruble, T. L. (1982). Sex stereotypes. In A. G. Miller (Ed.), *In the eye of the beholder: Contemporary issues in stereotyping* (pp. 188–252). New York: Praeger.

Sagar, H. A., & Schofield, J. W. (1980). Racial and behavioral cues in Black and White children's perceptions of ambiguously aggressive acts. *Journal of Personality and Social Psychology, 39,* 590–598.

Schachter, S., & Singer, J. L. (1962). Cognitive, social, and physiological determinants of emotional state. *Psychological Review, 69,* 379–399.

Schwarz, N. (1990). Feelings as information: Informational and motivational functions of affective states. In E. T. Higgins & R. M. Sorrentino (Eds.), *Handbook of motivation and cognition* (Vol. 2, pp. 527–561). New York: Guilford.

Schwarz, N., & Bless, H. (1992). Constructing reality and its alternatives: An inclusion/exclusion model of assimilation and contrast effects in social judgment. In L. L. Martin & A. Tesser (Eds.), *The construction of social judgments* (pp. 217–245). Hillsdale, NJ: Lawrence Erlbaum Associates.

Schwarz, N., Bless, H., Strack, F., Klumpp, G., & Simons, A. (1991). Ease of retrieval as information: Another look at the availability heuristic. *Journal of Personality and Social Psychology, 61,* 195–202.

Schwarz, N., & Clore, G. L. (1983). Mood, misattribution, and judgments of well-being: Informative and directive functions of affective states. *Journal of Personality and Social Psychology, 45,* 513–523.

Seamon, J. G., Brody, N., & Kauff, D. M. (1983). Affective discrimination of stimuli that are not recognized: Effects of shadowing, masking, and cerebral laterality. *Journal of Experimental Psychology: Learning, Memory, and Cognition, 9,* 544–555.

Seamon, J. G., Marsh, R. L., & Brody, N. (1984). Critical importance of exposure duration for affective discrimination of stimuli that are not recognized. *Journal of Experimental Psychology: Learning, Memory, and Cognition, 10,* 465–469.

Sedikides, C. (1990). Effects of fortuitously activated constructs versus activated communication goals on person impressions. *Journal of Personality and Social Psychology, 58,* 397–408.

Sherman, S. J., Mackie, D. M., & Driscoll, D. M. (1990). Priming and the differential use of dimensions in evaluation. *Personality and Social Psychology Bulletin, 16,* 405–418.

Shiffrin, R. M., & Schneider, W. (1977). Controlled and automatic human information processing: II. Perceptual learning, automatic attending, and a general theory. *Psychological Review, 84,* 127–190.

Skelton, J. A., & Strohmetz, D. B. (1990). Priming symptom reports with health-related cognitive activity. *Personality and Social Psychology Bulletin, 16,* 449–464.

Smith, E. R., & Branscombe, N. (1987). Procedurally mediated social inferences: The case of category accessibility effects. *Journal of Experimental Social Psychology, 23,* 361–382.

Smith, E. R., & Branscombe, N. (1988). Category accessibility as implicit memory. *Journal of Experimental Social Psychology, 24,* 490–504.

Smith, E. R., Branscombe, N., & Bormann, C. (1988). Generality of the effects of practice on social judgment tasks. *Journal of Personality and Social Psychology, 54,* 385–395.

Smith, E. R., & Lerner, M. (1986). Development of automatism of social judgments. *Journal of Personality and Social Psychology, 50,* 246–259.

Smith, E. R., & Miller, F. D. (1979). Salience and the cognitive mediation of attribution. *Journal of Personality and Social Psychology, 37,* 2240–2252.

Smith, E. R., Stewart, T. L., & Buttram, R. T. (1992). Inferring a trait from a behavior has long-term, highly specific effects. *Journal of Personality and Social Psychology, 62,* 753–759.

Smith, E. R., & Zarate, M. A. (1992). Exemplar-based model of social judgment. *Psychological Review, 99,* 3–21.

Spielman, L. A., & Bargh, J. A. (1990). *The influence of immediately prior administration of depression inventories on tests of depressogenic cognition: The "BDI Priming Effect."* Unpublished manuscript, New York University, New York City.

Spielman, L. A., & Bargh, J. A. (1991, May). *The reliance on chronically accessible constructs in global impression formation: The case of conflicting behavioral information.* Paper presented at the annual meetings of the Midwestern Psychological Association, Chicago.

Srull, T. K., & Wyer, R. S., Jr. (1979). The role of category accessibility in the interpretation of information about persons: Some determinants and implications. *Journal of Personality and Social Psychology, 37,* 1660–1672.

Strack, F. (1992). The different routes to social judgments: Experiential versus informational strategies. In L. L. Martin & A. Tesser (Eds.), *The construction of social judgments* (pp. 249–275). Hillsdale, NJ: Lawrence Erlbaum Associates.

Strauman, T. J., & Higgins, E. T. (1987). Automatic activation of self-discrepancies and emotional syndromes: When cognitive structures influence affect. *Journal of Personality and Social Psychology, 53,* 1004–1014.

Swann, W. B., Jr., Hixon, J. G., Stein-Seroussi, A., & Gilbert, D. T. (1990). The fleeting gleam of praise: Cognitive processes underlying behavioral reactions to self-relevant feedback. *Journal of Personality and Social Psychology, 59,* 17–26.

Tajfel, H. (1970). Experiments in intergroup discrimination. *Scientific American, 223,* 96–102.

Taylor, S. E. (1981). A categorization approach to stereotyping. In D. L. Hamilton (Ed.), *Cognitive processes in stereotyping and intergroup behavior* (pp. 88–114). Hillsdale, NJ: Lawrence Erlbaum Associates.

Taylor, S. E. (1991). Asymmetrical effects of positive and negative events: The mobilization-minimization hypothesis. *Psychological Bulletin, 110,* 67–85.

Taylor, S. E., Crocker, J., Fiske, S. T., Sprinzen, M., & Winkler, J. D. (1979). The generalizability of salience effects. *Journal of Personality and Social Psychology, 37,* 357–368.

Taylor, S. E., & Fiske, S. T. (1978). Salience, attention, and attribution: Top of the head phenomena. *Advances in Experimental Social Psychology, 11,* 249–288.

Tetlock, P. E. (1985). Accountability: A social check on the fundamental attribution error. *Social Psychology Quarterly, 48,* 227–236.

Tetlock, P. E., & Kim, J. I. (1987). Accountability and judgment processes in a personality prediction task. *Journal of Personality and Social Psychology, 52,* 700–709.

Thompson, E., Roman, R., Moskowitz, G., Chaiken, S., & Bargh, J. (1992). *Accountability motivation blocks subsequent passive priming effects on impression formation.* Manuscript submitted for publication, New York University, New York City.

Trope, T. (1986). Identification and inferential processes in dispositional attribution. *Psychological Review, 93,* 239–257.

Trope, Y., Cohen, O., & Alfieri, T. (1991). Behavior identification as a mediator of dispositional inference. *Journal of Personality and Social Psychology, 61,* 873–883.

Trope, Y., Cohen, O., & Maoz, Y. (1988). The perceptual and inferential effects of situational inducements on dispositional attributions. *Journal of Personality and Social Psychology, 55*, 165-177.

Tulving, E., & Pearlstone, Z. (1966). Availability versus accessibility of information in memory for words. *Journal of Verbal Learning and Verbal Behavior, 5*, 381-391.

Uleman, J. S., Newman, L., & Winter, L. (1992). Can personality traits be inferred automatically? Spontaneous inferences require cognitive capacity at encoding. *Consciousness and Cognition, 1*, 77-90.

Weber, R., & Crocker, J. (1983). Cognitive processes in the revision of stereotypic beliefs. *Journal of Personality and Social Psychology, 45*, 961-977.

Wegner, D. M., & Vallacher, R. R. (1977). *Implicit psychology*. New York: Oxford.

Werner, H. (1956). Microgenesis and aphasia. *Journal of Abnormal and Social Psychology, 52*, 347-353.

Wicklund, R. A., & Brehm, J. W. (1976). *Perspectives on cognitive dissonance*. Hillsdale, NJ: Lawrence Erlbaum Associates.

Wilson, T. D., & Schooler, J. W. (1991). Thinking too much: Introspection can reduce the quality of preferences and decisions. *Journal of Personality and Social Psychology, 60*, 181-192.

Wilson, W. R. (1979). Feeling more than we can know: Exposure effects without learning. *Journal of Personality and Social Psychology, 9*, 811-821.

Winter, L., & Uleman, J. S. (1984). When are social judgments made? Evidence for the spontaneousness of trait inferences. *Journal of Personality and Social Psychology, 47*, 237-252.

Winter, L., Uleman, J. S., & Cunniff, C. (1985). How automatic are social judgments? *Journal of Personality and Social Psychology, 49*, 904-917.

Wyer, R. S., Jr., & Srull, T. K. (1986). Human cognition in its social context. *Psychological Review, 93*, 322-359.

Zajonc, R. B. (1965). Social facilitation. *Science, 149*, 269-274.

Zajonc, R. B. (1968). Attitudinal effects of mere exposure. *Journal of Personality and Social Psychology, 9* (Suppl. 2, Pt. 2).

Zajonc, R. B., & Markus, G. B. (1975). Birth order and intellectual development. *Psychological Review, 82*, 74-88.

Zajonc, R. B. (1980). Feeling and thinking: Preferences need no inferences. *American Psychologist, 35*, 151-175.

Zarate, M. A., & Smith, E. R. (1990). Person categorization and stereotyping. *Social Cognition, 8*, 161-185.

Zillman, D., & Bryant, J. (1974). Effect of residual excitation on the emotional response to provocation and delayed aggressive behavior. *Journal of Personality and Social Psychology, 30*, 782-791.

2 The Cognitive Representation of Persons and Events

Robert S. Wyer, Jr.
University of Illinois, Urbana-Champaign

Donal E. Carlston
Purdue University

Contents

When people are exposed to information about a social stimulus (a person, object, or event), they often attend to it selectively, focusing on some features while disregarding others. They interpret these features in terms of previously acquired concepts and knowledge. Moreover, they often infer characteristics of the stimulus that were not actually mentioned in the information, and construe relations among these characteristics that were not specified. In short, the cognitive representations that people form of a stimulus differ in a variety of ways from the information on which they were based.

Yet it is ultimately these representations, and not the original stimuli, that govern subsequent thoughts, judgments, and behaviors. Consequently, it is important to understand the nature of these mediating cognitive representations to predict the influence of information on perceivers' judgments or behavioral decisions about the people and objects to which it refers.

Concerns regarding the cognitive representation of social information are reflected in early research and theory on the effects of information relevant to one belief on other, remotely related beliefs (Abelson et al., 1968; Heider, 1958; McGuire, 1960). However, these concerns were rekindled by evidence that there is often very little relation between people's judgments and their recall of the information underlying these judgments (Greenwald, 1968; Hastie & Park, 1986; Lichtenstein & Srull, 1987; Loken, 1984). This latter research indicates that to understand the cognitive determinants of judgments and decisions, one cannot simply rely on people's memory for relevant information. Rather, one must understand the cognitive operations that were performed on this information when it was first received, the mental representations that are formed as a result of these operations, and the manner in which these representations were later used to produce judgments or behaviors.

The cognitive representation of social information has been a central concern in the social cognition area since the mid-1970s (Abelson, 1976, 1981; Hastie et al., 1980; Higgins, Herman, & Zanna, 1981; Newtson, 1976; Wyer & Carlston, 1979). However, theoretical and empirical progress during this period has been uneven. The field has tended to focus on a restricted set of issues, processes, and paradigms, leaving many important aspects of social representation unexplored.

For example, most of the theoretical and empirical work has focused on the mental representations of individual stimulus persons that are formed from trait or behavioral information. Relatively little research has been conducted on the representations that are formed from information acquired in actual social interactions, the representation of groups of individuals, or the representation of oneself (see Kihlstrom & Klein, chapter 4, Volume 1). The cognitive organization of social events has only begun to be investigated (Newtson, 1976; Wyer & Bodenhausen, 1985; Wyer, Shoben, Fuhrman & Bodenhausen, 1985). Finally, with the exception of the impressive program of research presently being conducted by W. McGuire and C. McGuire (1991), the organization in memory of general world knowledge has been virtually ignored since the early work of cognitive consistency theorists (Abelson et al., 1968).

A further limitation of research on the cognition representation of social information is that, with few exceptions, it has proceeded virtually independently of research on social inference (cf. Beike & Sherman, chapter 5, Volume 1). As a result, it is unclear how judgments and decisions are computed on the basis of the mental representations that people form. The manner in which these representations contribute to actual human behavior and interaction is even less clear (see Schneider, 1991).

Finally, the cognitive representation of information has usually been investigated within restricted research paradigms in which the type of information presented and the manner in which it is conveyed are rigorously controlled. This control has been necessary to obtain a clear understanding of the content and structure of the representations that are formed and the processes that underlie their construction. This rigor has been at a cost, however: The conditions investigated often seem only remotely related to those in which people receive information in daily life. Therefore, there is a danger that the empirical findings that have emerged, and the theories that have been developed to account for them, do not apply to the processing of information that is acquired in more natural contexts.

Such criticisms of social cognition research are not uncommon. However, the criticism that laboratory research findings do not generalize to nonlaboratory situations is vacuous unless it is accompanied by a precise statement of the processes engaged by laboratory phenomena that do not occur in other domains, or the processes occurring in other domains that are not engaged in the laboratory. Such statements require a well-developed theory in which the antecedents and consequences of different kinds of cognitive representation are clearly specified. Given such a theory, differences in the results obtained in different situations can be interpreted in terms of specific conditions or processes that characterize one situation but not another. Thus, the development of rigorous theoretical formulations is a necessary first step in assessing the generality of empirical findings obtained within any specific paradigm. Moreover, by bridging the gaps between paradigms, such theoretical formulations ultimately permit a clearer picture of the similarities and differences among different information processing situations, and a more comprehensive and integrative understanding of information processing more generally.

GENERAL THEORIES OF SOCIAL MEMORY

Most theoretical formulations of social memory and judgment have been developed to account for the manner in which a particular type of information is processed under specified conditions. On the surface, the theories and the phenomena to which they apply are often quite different (cf. Brewer, 1988; Fiske

& Neuberg, 1990; Gilbert, Pelham, & Krull, 1988; Higgins & King, 1981; McGuire & McGuire, 1991; Petty & Cacioppo, 1986; Schank & Abelson, 1977; Srull & Wyer, 1989). The formulations are not necessarily incompatible, because each typically pertains to a different type of information that is processed for a particular purpose. However, it will ultimately be desirable to develop a general theoretical framework of social memory within which these more specific formulations can be housed.

Several alternative possibilities are considered in this section. Strengths and weaknesses of each are mentioned, but no attempt is made to select one over the others, despite the (sometimes obvious) preferences of the authors. Each makes some contribution to our understanding of how social information is represented in memory.

Associative Network Conceptualizations

Wyer and Carlston (1979; see also Carlston & Skowronski, 1986) proposed a spreading activation model of social memory. In this model, which was stimulated by Collins and Loftus' (1975) conceptualization of semantic memory, both semantic concepts and referent-specific concepts are represented by nodes in memory. Associations between these concepts, represented by pathways, are formed as a result of thinking about the concepts in relation to one another. When a particular concept is activated (i.e., thought about), excitation spreads along the pathways that connect it to other concept nodes. If sufficient excitation accumulates at these other nodes, these concepts are activated as well.

Once a concept is deactivated, excitation that has accumulated at the node decays gradually over time. Therefore, if a concept has been activated recently or frequently, residual excitation is likely to persist at the corresponding node, and less additional excitation is required to reactivate it. This means that the more recently or frequently a concept has been used in the past, the more likely it is to come to mind and to be used to interpret new information or to make judgments to which it relates.

Variants of a spreading activation model (e.g., Bower, 1981; Carlston & Skowronski, 1986; Higgins, Bargh, & Lombardi, 1985) have been used to account for a number of social phenomena. They have been particularly useful in conceptualizing how the frequency and recency with which concepts are activated affect the later retrieval and use of those concepts (Bargh, 1984; Higgins & King, 1981; Wyer & Srull, 1989). With certain adjustments, such models can readily incorporate a wide variety of different representational forms within a single cognitive structure (e.g., Carlston, 1992). When goal concepts are included, even motivationally driven associations can be accommodated. Finally, other auxiliary assumptions permit a variety of unique predictions concerning memory and inference, some of which have received empirical support (Carlston & Skowronski, 1986).

On the negative side, network models often require additional assumptions to account for commonplace nuances of memory and judgment. Among these nuances, for example, are strategic memory storage and retrieval, the integration of new with old knowledge, and the generation of novel associations or judgments. With such assumptions, network models become increasingly complex and unwieldy.

In addition, associative network models are often vague about whether nodes represent features, concepts, or schemas, and how associations among these different conceptual levels are connected and integrated within the representational structure. As metaphors, associative networks can simply be defined at a level of analysis that is useful in addressing any particular issue. However, as general theories of mental organization, they need to detail the dynamics underlying the spread of excitation within and across such levels.

Associated Systems Theory

Carlston (1992) proposed that people's associative networks encompass a variety of different forms of cognitive representation that are differentially related to the mental systems that govern both (a) the perception and cognitive processing of stimulus inputs and (b) overt responses to these inputs. More specifically, impressions of people are composed of visual appearance, traits, behavioral and affective responses (which relate to the perceptual, verbal, action, and affective systems, respectively), as well as categories, evaluations, orientations, and episodic observations (which relate to pairs of systems, as shown in Fig. 2.1).

Associated systems theory further specifies the interrelations among these different forms of representation (see Fig. 2.1), the factors and processes that underlie their generation and utilization, and their differential contributions to judgments and behaviors. For example, the kinds of representations that people have of an individual are hypothetically influenced by the nature of previous interactions with that person. Passive observation creates representations that are related most closely to sensory systems, such as visual appearance, categorizations, and episodic observations. Behavioral interaction promotes the formation of representations, episodic observations, and relationship orientations. Emotional involvement leads to representations related to the affective system, including affective responses, relationship orientations, and evaluations. Finally, cognitive rumination precipitates representations related to the semantic system, including trait inferences, categorizations, and evaluations. From this perspective, social cognition experiments that permit only passive observation and thought about a stimulus person may encourage the formation of target-referent representations (especially visual appearance, categorizations, and trait inferences), but not perceiver-referent representations (e.g., behavioral and affective responses). On the other hand, these perceiver-referent representations may play a larger role in naturalistic situations that involve actual interaction.

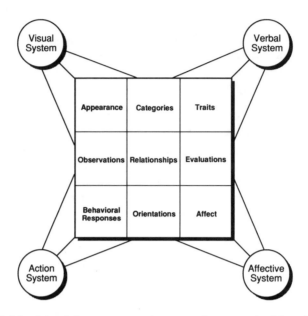

FIG. 2.1.   Interrelations among mental systems and representational forms in associated systems theory.

Associated systems theory makes numerous predictions about the kinds of representations that have the greatest influence on different kinds of judgments and responses. One central hypothesis is that cognitive representations have the greatest impact on the systems to which they are related most closely. For example, trait inferences should have more impact on judgments than on behavior, and response representations should have more impact on behavior than on judgments. However, as an associative network model, associated systems theory also emphasizes the relative salience of different forms of representation, as well as the strength of associations among them. Thus, a particular kind of representation (e.g., behavioral response) may influence a system to which it is not ordinarily related (e.g., the semantic system) by virtue of either its salience or accessibility, or its a priori association with the response. Similarly, an individual may sometimes associate a particular trait, affect, or response with an individual without the kinds of involvements discussed earlier, simply because this representation is strongly related to other material regarding the individual. The generation and utilization of different kinds of representation can be influenced by a variety of other factors as well, including, for example, individual differences in system use and momentary differences in system priming (Carlston, 1992).

At this point, associated systems theory is too new to have established an empirical track record. However, analyses of free descriptions provide initial support for the hypothesized interrelationships among representational forms. Carlston and Sparks (1992) applied multidimensional scaling methods to matrixes of intercorrelations among different kinds of person descriptors that subjects used in writing descriptions of real people. The best-fitting two-dimensional plot of the eight major descriptor types (appearance, traits, affect, etc.) closely corresponded to the pattern of interrelationships shown in Fig. 2.1.

As a theory, the formulation's greatest strengths are its emphasis on the functional nature of representations, its detailing of constraints and influences on the structure of associations among different forms of representations, its specification of the relationship between representation and behavioral responses, and its elaboration of some possible nuances of spreading activation mechanisms. The theory's greatest shortcomings include its complexity, speculative nature, and vulnerability to the criticisms leveled earlier against network models in general.

Schema Models

The term *schema* refers to an organized knowledge structure that embodies important relationships among other concepts (see, e.g., Brewer & Nakamura, 1984). The concept of a schema is widely used in social cognition (Fiske & Linville, 1980). As a general conception of memory, however, schema theory is rather limited. That is, it lacks the processing specifications that are necessary in a fully developed theory of social representation. Moreover, the term is often defined so broadly that it is impossible to know which types of knowledge structures are schematic and which are not. (For attempts to define schemata more precisely and to distinguish between schemata and categories, see Mandler, 1979; Rumelhart, 1984; Wyer & Gordon, 1984.)

Nevertheless, research periodically reminds us that the powerful organizational properties of well-learned knowledge structures have considerable impact on the storage and retrieval of information. For example, consider a recent study by Ritter (1990). Subjects were given facts about different buildings on a college campus. The ability of one such fact to prime retrieval of another was a function of the physical proximity of the buildings to which these facts related. In other words, the underlying structure of these memories did not simply reflect degree of past co-occurrence. Rather, the organizational structure embodied the logical properties of the knowledge involved. Such organizational properties are best represented by schema structures. On the other hand, to provide a useful theory of information processing, schema approaches need to specify more about the mechanics of storage and retrieval, and the nature of interrelations among schemata.

The *Bin* Conceptualization of Social Memory

A quite different conceptualization of memory was proposed by Wyer and Srull (1986, 1989) as part of a general model of social information processing. This conceptualization specifies both the general mechanisms of social memory and the processes that underlie the storage and retrieval of information during the pursuit of different processing objectives.

The model distinguishes between a work space, which contains information and knowledge that is used in the pursuit of immediate processing objectives, and permanent storage. The latter, which is analogous to long-term memory, is conceptualized metaphorically as a set of storage bins. These bins are of three types: (a) a semantic bin, which contains concepts used to interpret individual items of information without regard to their particular referent, (b) a goal bin, which contains schemata or procedures involved in the pursuit of different processing objectives, and (c) referent bins, each of which contains units of knowledge relating to a different referent or domain.

Knowledge units contained in a referent bin can consist of many kinds of information, including (a) a single concept or feature, (b) a configuration of concepts that, in combination, constitute a schema (e.g., a sequence of related events, a visual image, etc.), (c) a judgment or decision, or (d) a nonverbally coded subjective experience or affective reaction (cf. Clore, Schwarz, & Conway, chapter 7, Volume 1). Thus, a bin is assumed to contain many of the types of representations considered by associated systems theory. In the present case, however, each representation is assumed to be stored separately in a bin pertaining to its referent, and any given representation can be retrieved and used independently of other ones.

The model specifies the rules that govern the storage and retrieval of information from any of the different kinds of bins. For example, representations are added to bins in the order they are formed. Moreover, when a unit of knowledge is relevant to a current objective, a copy of it (but not the original) is retrieved and this copy is later returned to the top of the bin from which it was drawn. Because retrieval of information from a bin is based on a probabilistic top-down search, goal-relevant information near the top of the bin is more likely to be retrieved and used. Moreover, frequently used knowledge units also are more likely to be retrieved, because more copies of these are in the bin. Thus, the model often predicts superior recall of both frequently and recently used information, as do associative network models.

The model includes additional assumptions regarding the particular referent bins that will be used to store items, the processes of retrieval, the role of an executor (which guides the flow of information throughout the system, based on procedures or *goal schemata* that are drawn from the goal bin), and so on. Although this gives the model considerable breadth and specificity, it also makes the model vulnerable to the charges of complexity and unwieldiness that we leveled earlier against associative network models. Perhaps theories inevitably tend toward complexity as they attempt to incorporate an expanding base of facts and findings.

Although the bin model has specific implications for the manner in which different units of knowledge are stored and retrieved, it does not specify either (a) the content and structure of the representations that are formed in pursuit of any particular objective, or (b) the manner in which these representations are later used to make judgments and decisions. This openness with regard to content allows the model to incorporate implications of some of the more specific formulations and findings reviewed both in this chapter and elsewhere in this volume.

Smith's Exemplar-Based Model of Social Information Processing

A conceptualization by Smith (1984, 1990a) is unique in its specification of the role of procedural as well as declarative knowledge in processing information. Borrowing from the ACT model developed by Anderson (1976, 1987), Smith makes minimal assumptions about the structure of memory per se, focusing instead on the role of retrieval processes. More generally, he postulates the existence of cognitive procedures, "or productions," that govern the cognitive operations that are performed under a given set of stimulus conditions. Each production has the form of an "IF . . . THEN" rule. The precondition can be conceptualized as a cognitive state that is activated either by the features of the stimulus situation or by internally generated cognitions. The mental actions that result are roughly equivalent to cognitive conditioned responses to the set of features that compose the preconditions. As such, the strength of a production increases with practice (i.e., with the number of times it is employed). The results of a production can be a precondition for a second production, so that an entire sequence of cognitive events can be stimulated by a single precipitating event. However, because the preconditions for a production can include not only the results of previous cognitive operations, but also new experiences that impinge on the cognitive system, the specific sequences that occur can vary considerably over time and situations.

Because the representation of procedural knowledge and its role in social information processing are described in detail elsewhere in the *Handbook* (Smith, chapter 3, Volume 1), we do not elaborate on these matters here. However, one additional component of Smith's conceptualization is of particular importance. That is, both the productions and the cognitive material to which they are applied can be specific to certain stimulus persons or situations. Smith explicitly emphasizes the role of exemplars of concept and categories as a cognitive basis for judgments and decisions (see also Smith & Zarate, 1992). For example, he argues that information about stimulus persons and events is not usually comprehended and organized by comparing the features described with those of a more abstract category or concept (e.g., a prototype). Rather, these features are compared to those of a particular person or event that exemplifies the concept. In other words, the exemplar of a general concept is compared to the representations that have been formed of other, previously encountered exemplars, rather than to the concept.

Smith reports empirical evidence of several types in support of his exemplar-based conceptualization. In addition, he applies the conceptualization to a variety of social inference phenomena, including social categorization, stereotyping, the role of construct accessibility in the interpretation of information, and individual differences in information processing. As with each formulation discussed, several implications of his formulation can be alternatively conceptualized in terms of other models (e.g., Srull & Wyer, 1990; but see Smith, 1990b). Nevertheless, Smith's theory provides a detailed alternative to the processing mechanisms suggested by associative network and bin formulations. Moreover, it readily accommodates behavioral productions, making the linkages between cognition and behavior more explicit than in most other formulations (except, perhaps, associated systems theory). Additional theoretical development is necessary, however, before the production model will represent a full-blown model of social representation and processing.

Comparison of the Formulations

Each of these different general theories of social memory emphasizes a different aspect of memory storage and retrieval. Associative network theories emphasize the importance of past co-occurrence of concepts, as well as the recency and frequency of concept use. Associated systems theory adds an emphasis on the functional role of cognitive representations and, consequently, on the interrelations among different forms of representation. The bin model emphasizes redundancy in the storage of information, recency within referent categories, and a degree of randomness in retrieval mechanisms. Schema theories emphasize the role of past knowledge, and the organization it imposes, in information storage structures. Finally, procedural models call attention to the importance of patterns of information in the instigation of different sorts of cognitive routines, and the importance of specific exemplars in the categorization and interpretation of information.

The specific emphases of each approach have been formalized and extended to account for a broad range of representational phenomena. However, similarities in the assumptions and implications of the various formulations are as important to note as the differences. For example, the construct of schema appears in the bin model and the concept of procedures is incorporated into both the bin model and associated systems theory. Each formulation makes some contribution, and a complete account of social memory will ultimately involve elements of all of them.

We now turn our attention from general models to various specific issues regarding social representation. We begin with the kinds of issues that have preoccupied the field of social cognition: those involving the representation of individual persons, usually in terms of traits. We then progress to some of the other kinds of representational issues (e.g., the use of event representations) that we believe the field needs to explore in more depth.

THE REPRESENTATION OF PERSONS

In the standard social cognition paradigm, subjects are exposed to descriptions of a target person's behavior, generally with instructions to form an impression of the person (e.g., Hastie & Kumar, 1979; Hamilton, Katz, & Leirer, 1980). Stimulus behaviors may vary both in favorableness and the traits they exemplify. In some cases, the behaviors are preceded by a more general trait adjective description of the target actor (alternatively, the target is said to belong to a group whose members typically possess these traits). After exposure to the stimulus, subjects make trait and evaluative judgments of the target and, finally, recall the target's behaviors. The content and structure of the representations that are formed of the target are inferred from the amount, type, and order of the recalled behaviors and, in some instances, from the time required to recall them (Srull, Lichtenstein, & Rothbart, 1985). Minor variants on these procedures have been utilized to explore a variety of issues, some of which are reviewed later.

Trait Encoding Processes

A common assumption in impression formation research is that people encode behaviors in terms of trait concepts. Two more specific questions have been stimulated by this assumption. First, is the encoding of behaviors in terms of trait concepts universal or does it occur only in certain conditions? Second, what determines which of several traits is used to interpret a behavior when several alternatives are applicable?

The Spontaneity of Trait Encodings.   Uleman (1989) and Winter, Uleman, and Cunniff (1985) suggested that trait encodings are made spontaneously (if not automatically) upon exposure to trait-relevant behavior; and, moreover, that such trait encodings are associated with the actor, serving as inferences regarding that individual's attributes. Others have questioned both the inevitability of such trait encodings (Carlston & Skowronski, 1986) and their function as "person inferences," rather than simply as interpretive features of the behavior (Bassili, 1989).

A central issue concerns whether behaviors are inevitably encoded in terms of trait concepts, or whether this occurs only when these encodings are relevant to processing objectives that exist at the time the behaviors are presented. Although Winter et al. (1985) concluded that trait encodings are automatic, more recent research in the same paradigm (Bassili & Smith, 1986) showed that spontaneous trait encodings of behavior occurred only when subjects were instructed to form an impression of a person they described. They were not evident when subjects were given the a priori goal of remembering the behaviors. Results obtained in other paradigms also have mixed implications. Hamilton et al. (1980) found that when subjects read a list of behaviors with the goal of forming an impression of the actor, their later recall of these behaviors was clustered according to the traits each exemplified. Wyer and Gordon (1982) found that, under similar conditions, recall of a trait applying to a person cued the recall of the behavior exemplifying that trait. However, neither of these effects occurred when subjects received the information with instructions to remember it. Thus, these studies suggested that, although subjects spontaneously encode behaviors in terms of a trait concept when their goal is to form an impression, they do not do so automatically in the absence of a goal to which such encoding is relevant.

On the other hand, Carlston and Skowronski (1993) found some evidence for automatic trait encoding using the savings paradigm pioneered by Ebbinghaus a century ago (1885/1964). Carlston and Skowronski asked subjects to learn trait term–person photo pairs. They found that subjects' ability to do so was enhanced by prior exposure to these same photos with behaviors that exemplified the corresponding traits. This was true both when subjects had been told to form an impression of the person described and when they had not. Moreover, this facilitation occurred when subjects showed no recognition of the original behaviors. These results suggested that even uninstructed subjects spontaneously extracted trait implications from the behaviors and associated these traits directly with the photos of the actors. This prior encoding eased their learning of the trait–photo pairs, because they essentially were learning something that they already knew at some level.

The key difference between the savings paradigm and the earlier work on spontaneous trait inference may be in the kind of phenomena being characterized as a trait encoding or inference. The majority of past paradigms on spontaneous trait inference have examined the ability of traits to cue or organize recall about an actor (Hamilton et al., 1980; Winter et al., 1985; Wyer & Gordon, 1982). Thus, the kind of trait encoding being examined is one that shapes the organization and retrieval of stimulus information. It appears that this kind of strong (and probably conscious) trait encoding occurs only when subjects have an explicit impression formation goal. On the other hand, the savings paradigm utilized by Carlston and Skowronski (1986) simply determined whether trait knowledge has been extracted from a stimulus and implicitly associated with the actor. This kind of weak trait encoding can be characterized as a kind of implicit knowledge (Roediger, 1990), which occurs without an explicit learning (or impression) goal, and which is not intentionally retrievable, as explicit memories are.

Thus, a possible resolution of the disparate findings in this area may be that trait concepts are spontaneously associated with an actor, but that this knowledge may not be directly accessible, and may not influence the organization of impressional material unless the perceiver has an impression formation goal. In any case, trait encodings are clearly an integral part of intentional impression formation processes, although their role in unintentional impression formation processes remains somewhat controversial.

Determinants of Concept Accessibility.   Other research has attempted to determine which trait concept will be used to interpret behavioral information when more than one concept is applicable (for reviews see Bargh, 1984; Higgins & King, 1981; Sedikides & Skowronski, 1991; Wyer & Srull, 1989). The likelihood that a concept will be applied can be influenced by its chronic accessibility (Bargh, Bond, Lombardi, & Tota, 1986), and also by situation-specific processing goals that require its use (Higgins & Rholes, 1978; Sedikides, 1990). However, concepts that are activated by events that have nothing to do with a person can also affect the interpretation of a person's behaviors and, as a result, can influence judgments to which those behaviors are relevant (Bargh & Pietromonaco, 1982; Higgins, Rholes, & Jones, 1977; Srull & Wyer, 1979, 1980). Moreover, the effects of these trait encodings on judgments often increase over time (Higgins et al., 1977; Srull & Wyer, 1980; see also Carlston, 1980).

The theoretical explanation of these effects is more controversial than the nature of the effects themselves. Higgins et al. (1987) used a variant of a spreading-activation model to account for the effects of both frequency and recency of concept activation on the accessibility and use of a trait concept to interpret behaviors. For example, their model accounts for the fact that the effects of recency predominate over the effects of frequency when there is only a short time between concept activation and exposure to the stimulus information, whereas frequency effects predominate when the time interval is long. The bin conceptualization proposed by Wyer and Srull (1989) provides a quite different account of these effects, based on the assumption that the frequency and recency of using a concept affects the number of times it is represented in a bin and its proximity to the top, and thus how easily the concept is identified in a top-down search of the bin when the judgment is made.

These conceptualizations assume that priming a stimulus with either trait terms or trait-relevant behaviors activates more general trait concepts that are then used to interpret subsequently encountered behaviors. However, when the prime is a trait-relevant behavior rather than a trait term (e.g., Srull & Wyer, 1979, 1980), Smith's (1990a) exemplar-based formulation provides an alternative interpretation. According to this model, each priming stimulus leaves a memory trace, and its effect on the interpretation of later information depends on the fit between features of those memory traces and features of the stimulus information. However, this fit does not depend on features of any superordinate trait concepts to which the priming behaviors pertain. Smith's alternative account for these effects has received empirical support. That is, behavioral primes seem to affect the interpretation of new behavioral information independently of their trait implications. (However, Smith's findings do not challenge the basic assumption that subjects may often organize behavioral information in terms of trait concepts. Additional evidence regarding this assumption is described later.)

Another finding to emerge from research in this area is that a primed trait concept is more likely to be applied to the encoding of a behavior when the priming is unobtrusive. For example, Lombardi, Higgins, and Bargh (1987) demonstrated that primed trait concepts were more likely to have a positive influence on the interpretation of information when subjects were unable to recall the priming stimuli, and to have a negative effect when subjects could recall them. In a related vein, Skowronski, Carlston, and Isham (1993) found covert priming of a stereotypical category to have positive effects on memory and judgments under conditions in which overt presentation of the category label produced negative or contrast effects.

Martin (1986) and Martin, Seta, and Crelia (1990) suggested that when subjects realize that a salient concept may have been stimulated by factors other than the stimulus being interpreted (e.g., the priming task), they attempt to avoid bias by searching for an alternative concept. If they can identify one, they use it, and so the probability of their adopting the primed concept is actually less than it would have been in the absence of priming. The search for an alternative concept requires cognitive effort, however, so that if subjects are prevented from engaging in such activity, or are not motivated to do so, they are likely to default to the activated concept. In this case, their interpretation of the information will be positively influenced by the prime, just as when the priming was less obtrusive.

Several studies by Martin et al. (1990) provide compelling support for this interpretation. In one study, priming had positive effects on the interpretation of information when subjects were distracted while reading that information, but contrast effects when they were not. In two other studies, motivational factors had similar impact. For example, priming had a positive influence when subjects believed their judgments would be aggregated with others into a group average (a condition that induces "social loafing"; see Petty, Harkins, & Williams, 1980), but had a contrasting effect when subjects believed their judgments would be evaluated individually. In addition, subjects with a low need for cognition (Cacioppo & Petty, 1982) were influenced positively by the primes, whereas those with a high need for cognition were affected negatively. These results all confirm that primed trait concepts are most likely to have a direct influence on the interpretation of behaviors when subjects are either unaware of this potential influence or, if they are aware, when they are unable or unmotivated to search for an alternative concept.

Findings reported by Herr (1986) are also interesting in this light. He found that priming subjects with moderate exemplars of hostility had positive (assimilation) effects on their interpretation of behavioral information, but that priming them with extreme exemplars had negative (contrast) effects. It seems likely that extreme exemplars stimulate more cognitive activity when first considered and are therefore better remembered (Craik & Lockhart, 1972). Consequently, subjects may be more conscious that their interpretation of later behavioral information could be biased by a trait activated by these exemplars, and, therefore, they may suppress their use of this trait.

Organization of Behaviors in Terms of Trait Concepts

Given the evidence that subjects with an impression-formation objective spontaneously encode behaviors in terms of trait concepts, it seems reasonable that they would also organize such behaviors in memory according to the concepts they exemplify. Two sets of studies supported this possibility. Hamilton et al. (1980) found that subjects who read descriptions of trait-related behaviors with the objective of forming an impression of the actor had better recall of these behaviors than subjects who read them with a memory objective. Moreover, the recalled behaviors were clustered in terms of the traits they exemplified.

A more direct test of the organization of behaviors in terms of trait concepts was constructed by Gordon and Wyer (1987). Subjects formed an impression of a person who was described by 18 behaviors, of which 3 exemplified one trait, 6 exemplified a second trait, and 9 exemplified a third. The probability of recalling an item in a given category ordinarily decreases as the number of other items in the category increases (Anderson & Bower, 1979; Rundus, 1971, 1973). Therefore, if subjects in Gordon and Wyer's study organized the behaviors presented by trait category, the probability of recalling a given behavior from the smallest (3-behavior) set should have been greater than the probability of recalling a given behavior from the largest (9-behavior) set. However, if this organization did not occur, the likelihood of recalling each behavior presented should have been the same, regardless of which trait it exemplified.

In fact, set size effects were obtained when the different traits implied by the behaviors were similar in favorableness, suggesting that subjects organized these behaviors by trait category. Moreover, these effects occurred even when subjects were not forewarned that the target possessed these traits, and so there was no explicit demand to think about the behaviors' trait implications. This again suggests that trait encodings of behaviors occur spontaneously when subjects have the goal of forming an impression of the actor (see also Uleman, 1987, 1989).

However, different results occurred when the traits implied by the behaviors differed in favorableness. In this condition, the usual set size effects were only evident if subjects were told explicitly at the outset that the target possessed the traits. When the target's traits were not mentioned, the likelihood of recalling a behavior actually increased with the number of other behaviors that exemplified the same trait. Gordon and Wyer (1987) concluded that, in the latter condition, subjects were uncertain that their trait encodings of the behaviors were correct, so they reviewed the behaviors in each category in relation to one another to confirm the validity of these encodings. This cognitive activity led to the formation of interbehavior associations within each category, the number of which increased with set size. The accessibility of the behaviors and, therefore, the ease of later recalling them, increased correspondingly.

Other research is less supportive of the assertion that subjects with an impression-formation goal spontaneously encode and organize behaviors into trait–behavior clusters. For example, Klein and Loftus (1990) found that subjects with an impression-formation objective had better recall of behaviors than did subjects with a memory objective, even when the clustering of recalled behaviors by trait was very low. In fact, impression-formation objectives increased the recall of behaviors even when each behavior exemplified a different trait, so that no organization of the behaviors in terms of trait concepts was possible. Klein and Loftus concluded that subjects encode behaviors in terms of trait concepts, but do not form trait–behavior clusters. Instead, each trait–behavior pair is stored separately in memory. As a result, a trait concept later can serve as a retrieval cue for behaviors that exemplify it, even though there is no systematic organization of the behaviors around the trait concept.

It is difficult to reconcile this conclusion with Gordon and Wyer's (1987) findings. However, Klein and Loftus' (1990) findings indicated that the previously demonstrated superiority of recall for behaviors under impression formation conditions (Hamilton et al., 1980) is not necessarily due to the behaviors being organized around trait concepts. Rather, it can occur for other reasons of a sort to be indicated presently.

Evaluative Encoding of Behaviors

Srull and Wyer's (1989; Wyer & Srull, 1989) person memory model suggested that subjects with impression-formation goals not only derive trait encodings from presented information, but also extract a general evaluative impression of the actor. General evaluative or likableness inferences play an important role in other impression models as well (e.g., Carlston, 1992; Rosenberg & Olshan, 1970).

Evidence that subjects base these evaluations on the earliest available information was initially provided by Anderson and Hubert (1963). Specifically, these researchers found that evaluations were based disproportionately on trait adjective descriptions that occurred early in the series of information presented. (For more recent evidence of primacy effects in both behaviors and trait descriptions, see Dreben, Fiske, & Hastie, 1979; Lichtenstein & Srull, 1987; Wyer & Gordon, 1982; Wyer & Unverzagt, 1985.)

A more controversial issue involves the extent to which behaviors are organized around an evaluative concept of the actor, rather than a descriptive, trait-based person concept. In principle, these possibilities are not mutually exclusive. That is, information about a person is organized hierarchically, with trait concepts subordinate to an overall evaluative concept of the target, and with the behaviors that exemplify these traits nested within them at a lower level of the hierarchy. However, this latter assumption is inconsistent with several findings. For example, subjects with an impression set typically have better recall of stimulus behaviors than subjects with a memory set (Hamilton et al., 1980; Srull, 1981). If this superior recall were due to the organization of trait and behavioral information into a single, hierarchical representation, this organization should facilitate recall of the trait concepts themselves, as well as of the behaviors that they serve to organize. In fact, however, subjects with an impression objective do not have better recall of the trait adjectives that characterize stimulus behaviors, even though they do have better memory for the behaviors themselves (Wyer & Gordon, 1982).

The role of evaluative factors was evidenced by additional results obtained by Wyer and Gordon (1982). In this study, the behaviors varied independently in both descriptive and evaluative consistency with the target's traits. In other words, if a trait description was *honest*, subjects encountered both honest and dishonest behaviors that were perceived as either favorable (e.g., "returned a wallet to the lost and found," "covered up for a friend who cut class") or unfavorable "turned in a student for cheating on an exam," "picked up the tip a previous customer had left on the table"). Subjects had better recall of behaviors that were descriptively consistent with the target's trait characterization than of behaviors that were descriptively inconsistent with it (presumably because the traits served as retrieval cues for behaviors that were evaluatively inconsistent with the target's traits, not for behaviors that were evaluatively consistent with them). This combination of findings is difficult to explain on the basis of a single, hierarchical representation of the sort described previously.

Other studies (cf. Wyer, Bodenhausen, & Srull, 1984; Wyer & Martin, 1986) showed that describing a target person along one trait dimension (e.g., *kindness*) increases the recall of behaviors that are evaluatively inconsistent with the description, regardless of whether they pertain to the same trait dimension or a different one (e.g., *intelligence*). In general, then, the evidence suggests that a person's behaviors are organized around an evaluative concept of the person, rather than a descriptive one. This evaluative representation may be independent of the trait-based representations that are formed on the basis of the spontaneous trait-encoding described earlier.

Responses to Inconsistency

In the paradigm developed by Hastie and Kumar (1979), subjects are first informed that a target actor possesses some trait, and are then presented with some of that target's behaviors, each presented sequentially for about 6–8 seconds. Characteristically, behaviors are better recalled when they are inconsistent with the trait description than when they are consistent with it. Moreover, as noted earlier, the basis for the inconsistency is typically evaluative rather than descriptive (Wyer & Gordon, 1982; Wyer et al., 1984; Wyer & Martin, 1986). This result is typically attributed to subjects' attempt to reconcile the behaviors' inconsistency with the concept they have formed of the actor (Hastie, 1980; Srull & Wyer, 1989). That is, subjects attempt to understand why a generally nice person would do something undesirable, or why a generally dislikeable person would do something nice. To do this, they think about the inconsistent behavior in relation to other behaviors that have evaluative implications, and this activity produces associative linkages between the inconsistent behaviors and the others. Consequently, there are more retrieval routes to the inconsistent behaviors than to the consistent ones, making the inconsistent ones easier to recall. Srull (1981; Srull et al., 1985) obtained considerable support for this interpretation in a number of studies that examined both the order in which behaviors were recalled and the time required to report them.

At the same time, the conditions that give rise to inconsistency resolution may be more limited than these early studies suggested. For example, inconsistency resolution may not occur if an obvious explanation for the inconsistent behavior is provided that does not require consideration of the other presented behaviors (Crocker, Hannah, & Weber, 1983). It also does not occur if subjects have little time or opportunity to think about the behaviors as they are presented (Bargh & Thein, 1985; Srull, 1981; Srull et al., 1985). On the other hand, if subjects are given a chance to think extensively about the behaviors, either as they are presented or later, their recall of the consistent behaviors increases to a level exceeding that of inconsistent ones (Srull & Wyer, 1989; Wyer, Budesheim, Lambert, & Martin, 1989; Wyer & Martin, 1986).

These latter findings support the thesis that initial reconciliation efforts are often followed by a rather different, bolstering process (Srull & Wyer, 1986; see also Srull & Wyer, 1989). Specifically, subjects who encounter an inconsistent behavior initially engage in inconsistency resolution to comprehend its occurrence. However, given more time, they attempt to marshall support for the central impression that they have formed of the actor by reviewing behaviors that are consistent with it. This bolstering increases the strength of the consistent behaviors' association with the impression, giving them a recall advantage that sometimes overrides the effects of inconsistency resolution.

The generality of incongruity-resolution processes described earlier has been challenged by Hamilton, Driscoll, and Worth (1989). They obtained results similar to those reported by Srull (1981) when the initial description of the target person involved only one trait. However, the recall advantage of inconsistent behaviors disappeared when the description included several different traits. Hamilton et al. concluded that subjects with multiple trait expectations were stimulated to consider and compare consistent as well as inconsistent behaviors. However, their data are equally consistent with the possibility that subjects in the multitrait conditions did not form any interbehavior associations at all. The subjects in their study were given only 6 seconds to think about each behavior, and it is conceivable that the additional cognitive demands involved in considering multiple traits prevented subjects from engaging in the inconsistency resolution that otherwise would have occurred. Several studies, in which subjects had more time to consider each behavior (Wyer & Gordon, 1982; Wyer, Gruenfeld, Lambert, & Budesheim, 1991; Wyer & Martin, 1986), found the usual recall advantage for inconsistent behaviors under multiple-trait expectancy conditions as well as single-trait expectancy conditions.[1]

When initial information about a target person is evaluatively inconsistent, subjects often have difficulty in forming an evaluative impression. However, when the inconsistent items refer to different situations or social roles, subjects are likely to form separate evaluations of the target that are specific to these situations or roles, and to organize the target's behaviors in terms of them. For example, subjects in a study by Wyer and Martin (1986) received information that a person described as kind was also a Nazi or, alternatively, that a person described as dull and unintelligent was also a Nobel Prize winner. Subjects appeared to organize behaviors that referred to the target person by name around an evaluative concept, but to organize behaviors that referred to his or her social role around an evaluative concept of this role. Inconsistency resolution was specific to these different representations. Thus, when the target was a kind Nazi, subjects had better recall of unfavorable behaviors when the target was referred to by name. But they had better recall of favorable behaviors when the target was referred to as a Nazi.

Memory and Judgment

A central issue in the judgment area involves the degree of relationship between people's judgments and their memories for the evidence on which those judgments are presumably based. It seems sensible that evidence and judgments should be related in a straightforward way. Thus, people who remember more positive facts should make positive judgments, and those who remember more negative facts should make negative judgments. Evidence that this straightforward relationship does not obtain (Hastie & Park, 1986) has resulted in several theoretical proposals. For example, in the attitude area, Greenwald (1968) suggested that people's cognitive responses to a stimulus, rather than their memories for it, shape later judgments. Similarly, in the impression domain, Hastie and Park (1986) suggested that when people make initial inferences "on-line," during exposure to a stimulus, judgments are determined by these responses, rather than by memories for the stimulus per se.

However, according to associated systems theory (Carlston, 1992), the mere existence of initial responses or inferences does not necessitate their use in subsequent judgment making. This theory treats both initial responses and more direct,

---

[1]The previous interpretation is strengthened by a comparison of the Hamilton et al. (1989) findings under single- versus multiple-trait expectation conditions. Whereas their interpretation implies that the recall of consistent behaviors should be greater under multiple- than single-trait expectancy conditions, this was not the case. Rather, the recall of inconsistent behaviors was relatively less in multiple-trait expectancy conditions, suggesting that the inconsistency-resolution processes that typically underlie the recall advantage of inconsistent behaviors did not occur.

perceptual representations (such as memories) as associates within a single representational structure. Thus, either the earlier responses or the direct, perceptual representations may be accessed during the construction of either judgments or memories, depending on factors such as the relative salience of these different constructs and the strengths of the pathways that connect them.

For example, Carlston and Skowronski (1986) showed that if the original stimulus behaviors were made particularly salient to subjects, their trait judgments were based on analyses of these behaviors, rather than on earlier inferences. This implies that judgments may be independent of recalled evidence only under very explicit conditions. Specifically, this independence is likely when the judgment task stimulates reliance on prior responses and the memory task stimulates reliance on more direct, perceptual representations. When both tasks stimulate reliance on the same material, evidence and judgments are likely to be related. That is, when both tasks encourage reliance on prior responses, memories will be reconstructed in a way that makes them consistent with judgments (Carlston, 1980; Loftus & Palmer, 1974). When both tasks stimulate reliance on direct perceptual evidence, memory-based (Hastie & Park, 1986) judgments will occur that are consistent with the evidence that subjects can recall. Therefore, memory and judgments are likely to be interdependent in these latter cases.

This account of memory–judgment relationships may seem to imply that social judgments are simply a product of the retrieval of material—either prior inferences about, or perceptual features of, an initial observation. However, explaining judgments in terms of retrieval is an oversimplification. A variety of different approaches (Carlston, 1992; Devine, 1989; Gilbert et al., 1988; Quattrone, 1982; Trope, 1986) suggested that retrieval processes are merely the first stage of a two-stage process, with the second stage being a more controlled screening or editing process.

For example, in Gilbert's model, the initial stage involves accessing a stereotype, and the second stage allows people, with effort, to suppress the implications of that stereotype if they so wish. More generally, when people have the time and inclination, they may engage in a variety of controlled processes that can modify the effects of retrieved information on judgments (Carlston, 1992). However, by minimizing the effects of other mechanisms, lack of effort or capacity can increase the role that the associative memory structure plays in judgment making. Thus, a variety of simple associative effects seem most likely to occur in the absence of deliberate or thoughtful cognitive consideration. This might include, for example, priming effects on the interpretation of stimuli (Higgins et al., 1977; Martin, 1986), mere exposure effects on evaluation (Zajonc, 1968), utilization of availability and representativeness heuristics in judgment making (Nisbett & Ross, 1980; Sherman & Corty, 1984), and stereotyping biases in impression formation (Bodenhausen & Lichtenstein, 1987; Devine, 1989). When more controlled judgment processes are interjected, such effects may be diluted or altered.

Conceptual Integration

Most of the empirical findings concerning the way trait and behavioral information is used to form impressions of a person, and the cognitive representations
that result from this activity, are captured by a general theoretical model of person memory proposed by Srull and Wyer (1989; Wyer & Srull, 1989). The person memory model incorporates many features of earlier conceptualizations
(Hamilton et al., 1980; Hastie, 1981; but see Seta & Seta, 1990, for some divergent evidence). However, it takes into account the different effects of trait and
evaluative encoding of persons' behaviors and the different cognitive responses
that people can have to behaviors that are inconsistent with their concept of what
a person is like. Finally, it has implications for both the recall of information
about a person and judgments of the person.

The model employs an associative network metaphor whereby behaviors, traits,
and evaluative concepts are denoted by nodes in memory, and associations between these concepts, formed as a result of thinking about one concept in relation to another, are denoted by pathways connecting them. The processes it
assumes to occur, and their implications for the representation that results from
these processes, are summarized next.

Encoding and Organization

Suppose subjects with the goal of forming an impression of someone receive
descriptions of the target's behaviors that vary both in favorableness and in the
traits they exemplify. Under these conditions, the following cognitive activities
are postulated.

1. Trait Encoding. Subjects interpret the behavior descriptions in terms of
trait concepts that they exemplify. If two or more concepts are potentially applicable, the concept that comes to mind most quickly is usually used. The encoding of several behaviors in terms of the same trait concept leads to the formation
of trait–behavior clusters.

   a. If subjects already have expectations for the person's traits, only behaviors
      that exemplify these traits are encoded in trait terms.
   b. If subjects do not have a priori expectations for a person's traits at the time
      they learn the person's behaviors, all behaviors with trait implications are
      encoded in trait terms.
   c. If the behaviors exemplify evaluatively different traits (thus making the for-
      mation of a clear person impression difficult), and if subjects have no prior
      indication of the person's attributes, subjects think about the behaviors in
      each cluster in relation to one another or insure that they have interpreted
      them correctly. This cognitive activity establishes associations among the
      behaviors contained in each cluster.

2. Evaluative Encoding. In addition, subjects attempt to extract a general concept of the person as likeable or dislikeable. This is often done on the basis of the initial information presented. Once the concept is formed, subjects' behaviors are encoded evaluatively and thought about with reference to it, leading the behaviors to become associated with the concept. (Consequently, a given behavior can be represented twice: once in a trait–behavior cluster, and once in an evaluative-based representation of the person.)

3. Responses to Inconsistency. If subjects encounter a behavior that is evaluatively inconsistent with their general concept of the person, they engage in two types of cognitive activity:

a. Inconsistency resolution—subjects think about the inconsistent behavior in relation to others that have evaluative implications in an attempt to understand why it occurred. This leads associations to be formed between the inconsistent behavior and others.

b. Bolstering—subjects review the behaviors that are evaluatively consistent with their concept of the person in an attempt to confirm its validity. This activity strengthens the associations of the consistent behaviors with this concept. Inconsistency resolution is usually performed spontaneously upon exposure to an inconsistent behavior. Therefore, it is more likely to occur than bolstering when the time available to think about the information is limited.

4. Storage. The trait–behavior clusters and evaluative person representation that result from these activities are stored in memory independently of one another at a location (bin) pertaining to the person being described.

To see the implications of these assumptions, suppose subjects are told that a target person is both kind and honest. This information is then followed by a series of three favorable kind (k +) behaviors, two unfavorable dishonest (h −) behaviors, and two neutral, trait-irrelevant (O) behaviors. Subjects should encode only the kind behaviors in terms of the trait they exemplify, thus forming a trait–behavior cluster. In addition, they should form a favorable evaluative concept of the person on the basis of the initial trait description, and should consider the behaviors with reference to this concept as well. However, the dishonest behaviors, which are inconsistent with the concept, should stimulate two types of responses. First, subjects should think about the behaviors in relation to others that have evaluative implications, forming associations with these behaviors. Second, they should engage in bolstering, which should increase the association of the consistent (kind) behaviors with the central concept. The representations that are formed should therefore resemble those in Fig. 2.2.[2]

---

[2]If trait descriptions had not been provided, subjects would theoretically form two trait–behavior clusters, one pertaining to each trait. However, because the traits implied by the behaviors are evaluatively inconsistent, no evaluation person concept would be formed, thus an evaluation-based person representation would also not be constructed.

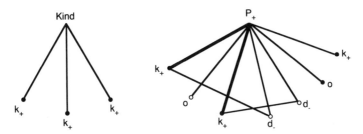

FIG. 2.2.   Cognitive representation implied by person memory model based on (a) initial trait descriptions of the person as kind and intelligent, and (b) a series of kind (k+), dishonest (d−), and neutral (O) behaviors. Behaviors are presented in the order k+,O,k+,d−,d−,O,k+. Wider pathways denote stronger associations. Each inconsistent (d−) behavior is assume·¹ to stimulate the formation of associations of the two evaluatively relevant behaviors that precede it in the sequence.

Retrieval Processes

If subjects are asked later to recall the information they have received, they presumably retrieve these representations one at a time from the bin in which they are stored and, in each case, perform a sequential search of its contents. That is, they start at the central node, progress down a pathway to a behavior node, report this behavior, traverse a pathway from this node to another, report the behavior at the new node, and so on, reinitiating the search from the central node whenever they reach a dead end. When more than one alternative pathway is available, the one that represents the strongest association probably is selected most.

Therefore, suppose subjects form the representations shown in Fig. 2.2. Then, they should retrieve the behaviors in one representation before the behaviors in the second. If they retrieve the trait–behavior cluster first, they should report the kind behaviors before reporting any others; that is, the behaviors should be clustered according to the trait they exemplify (Hamilton et al., 1980). On the other hand, suppose subjects retrieve the general person representation to use as a basis for recall. The first behavior they recall is likely to be a kind (evaluatively consistent) one. However, the next behavior is most likely to be a dishonest (inconsistent) one, because only inconsistent behaviors are linked associatively to consistent ones. The next behavior recalled could be either consistent or inconsistent. However, it is unlikely to be a neutral (O) behavior, because these behaviors are not associated with any others and can only be accessed from the central node. In general, the recall of inconsistent behaviors is primarily a function of the number of pathways leading to them (reflecting the amount of inconsistency resolution that occurred at the time of encoding). However, the recall of consistent behaviors is primarily a function of their association with the central concept (reflecting the amount of bolstering that occurred). Thus, the relative recall advantage of inconsistent and consistent behaviors depends on the relative likelihood that subjects engage in these two kinds of cognitive activity (Wyer & Martin, 1986; Wyer & Srull, 1989).

Judgment Processes

Suppose subjects who have formed representations of a person are asked to make a judgment of this person. Then, subjects are postulated to search for a representation whose central concept has direct implications for the judgments to be made. If they find one, they should use its implications as a basis for judgment without considering the individual behaviors associated with it. Therefore, they will use the central concepts of trait–behavior clusters to make trait judgments, and the concept defining the evaluation person representation to make evaluative (liking) judgments.

If subjects cannot identify a representative whose central concept has direct implications for the judgment, they are assumed to base their judgment on (a) the evaluative implications of the central person concept, and (b) the descriptive implications of behaviors they identify in a partial review of the behaviors associated with the concept.

Thus, suppose subjects in our example are asked to judge the target's kindness, honesty, and likableness. If they have formed the representations shown in Fig. 2.2, they should judge the target to be kind and likable. However, no trait–behavior cluster pertaining to honesty exists. Consequently, subjects must base their judgment of this attribute on the evaluative implications of the central person concept (which are favorable and, therefore, suggest that the person has favorable attributes such as honesty) as well as a partial review of the behaviors associated with the person. Therefore, they should judge the target to be more honest in this case than they would if no initial trait descriptions were provided.

This characterization of the judgment process has several implications that are important in relation to material already discussed. First, judgments of a person are assumed to be typically based on concepts formed at the time the information is presented, rather than computed at the time of judgment. As noted earlier, several other models (see, e.g., Carlston, 1992; Gilbert et al., 1988; Trope, 1986) suggest that subjects who have the time and motivation may engage in judgment processes that alter the implications of simple retrieval for previously formed concepts. However, even when this occurs, judgment processes must necessarily operate on the memory structure created when the information was presented; thus, the concepts and relations generated at input will still have substantial influence.

Second, the person memory model suggests that even though person judgments and recollections of the person's behaviors are based on the same representations, there is no necessary relation between these judgments and the implications of the information that is recalled. This conclusion is consistent with the previously described evidence regarding the independence of memory and judgment (e.g., Hastie & Park, 1986). However, it differs slightly from Carlston's (1992) position, which was described earlier. Carlston similarly assumed that a common representational structure underlies both memory and judgment, but suggested that independence between memory and judgment is likely only when the memory and judgment tasks tap into different aspects of this structure. These views are not inherently contradictory, but they do suggest some uncertainty regarding the conditions and frequency with which memory–judgment dependence will occur.

In summary, the person memory model outlined here accounts for most of the existing evidence bearing on the effects of trait and behavior information on recall and judgments in the domain to which it has been applied. Rather subtle implications of the formation have been confirmed, including the order in which behaviors are recalled, the time required to recall them (Srull, 1981; Srull et al., 1985), and the effects of information that subjects are told to disregard on both recall and judgment (Wyer & Budesheim, 1987; Wyer & Unverzagt, 1985). Nevertheless, there are several limitations to the generality of the model when applied outside the paradigm in which it has been principally evaluated. Several of these limitations are noted next.

The Effects of Social Knowledge and Context on Impression Formation

The general research paradigm described earlier has been used to investigate a variety of questions regarding the nature of person representation. However, the question arises as to whether the conclusions drawn from this research generalize to other situations in which people receive and process information about other people. Three aspects of the paradigm are noteworthy. First, the presented information typically pertains to an unfamiliar person who is either hypothetical or fictitious (e.g., a character in a novel). Second, the information is conveyed under conditions that lead subjects to assume they are supposed to treat it as both accurate and representative of the person it describes. Third, the behaviors that are presented are typically described out of any specific situational context, so the conditions in which they occurred are unclear. All of these factors may predispose subjects to focus their attention on the *semantic* implications of both the trait and the behavioral information, and to form an impression based on their construal of these implications alone.

However, outside the laboratory, information about other people is often acquired under somewhat different conditions.

1. The information often pertains to actual persons about whom recipients have prior knowledge, and to situations with which they are already familiar. Consequently, recipients are likely to interpret the information in relation to this knowledge, rather than in relation to general, semantic concepts.

2. The information is conveyed by a specific source whose knowledge of the target person is often incomplete or biased. Therefore, the source's trait descriptions may be recognized as a matter of opinion, and behavior descriptions may be viewed as nonrepresentative. Moreover, the source may appear to have a communication objective that biases the type of information disclosed.

3. In a similar vein, information communicated in a social context often is directed toward recipients who are thought to have a priori beliefs, attitudes, and expectations. The source may alter his or her communication because of these recipient characteristics (Higgins & McCann, 1984; Higgins & Rholes, 1978). To the extent that recipients are aware of these possibilities, they are likely to base their interpretation of the communication on its *pragmatic* implications (i.e., why the communication was generated, or what it is *intended* to convey) as well as its semantic implications.

4. Communications that are received outside the laboratory are usually conveyed in the context of other types of information (e.g., anecdotes, trait descriptions, expressions of emotion, and nonverbal behaviors). All of these factors are likely to influence the interpretation of communicated items of information.

These considerations suggest that the processing of information acquired in a social context and the mental representations that result from these processes can differ considerably from those that are ordinarily assumed by person memory researchers. Empirical evidence regarding such differences is discussed in the following three sections.

1. The Effects of Real World Knowledge.   When information concerns people and events about which recipients have prior knowledge, it is likely to be interpreted in terms of this specific knowledge, rather than in terms of more general semantic concepts. Comparing new information to what already is known seems likely to produce a spontaneous assessment of the truth or falsity of the new information. Thus, interpreting the statement "George Washington was president of the United States" is likely to involve the spontaneous recognition of the truth of the assertion. Similarly, interpreting "Adolph Hitler was president of the United States" will involve recognition of this statement's falsity.

The comprehension and appraisal of false statements is likely to require more extensive processing than the comprehension and appraisal of true ones. This might be an inherent by-product of the comprehension process (Gilbert, 1991) or a result of subjects' inclination to counterargue with statements deemed to be incorrect. For either or both reasons, the deeper processing of statements that people believe to be false can lead these statements to be better recalled than ones that people believe to be true (cf. Craik & Lockhart, 1972; Wyer & Hartwick, 1980).

The need to take these factors into account in impression formation is reinforced by a series of studies by Wyer, Lambert, Gruenfeld, and Budesheim (1991). In one study, subjects with an impression-formation objective read information about a political candidate that consisted of a variety of different kinds of information. Included were: (a) either favorable or unfavorable personality trait descriptions, (b) a characterization of the candidate as either liberal or conservative in political ideology, (c) favorable and unfavorable overt behaviors the target had performed, and (d) opinion statements that were normatively either liberal or conservative. After receiving the information, subjects evaluated the target, recalled the information they had read, and, finally, reported their own agreement with the opinion statements.

Results were unequivocal. Subjects based their liking for the candidate on the combined implications of the candidate's trait description and political ideology. Moreover, they had better recall of overt behaviors that were inconsistent with their general evaluation of the target than of behaviors that were consistent with it. One might expect subjects' recall of the candidate's opinion statements to be similarly affected, because such statements are essentially verbal behaviors (i.e., subjects who liked the candidate should have better recall for statements with which they personally disagreed, whereas those who disliked the candidate should have better recall for statements with which they personally agreed). These results did not occur. All subjects had better recall of opinion statements with which they disagreed, and this was true regardless of the statements' consistency with either the target's political orientation or subjects' liking for him.

Although there are several possible interpretations of these findings, the important point here is that the opinion statements were not simply thought about in relation to one another or comprehended in terms of general semantic concepts. Rather, they were considered with reference to subjects' personal knowledge and beliefs. The broad implication is that stimulus information may be thought about quite differently when it is comprehended in terms of concepts about known people and events, and that the underlying cognitive representation is therefore likely to differ correspondingly.

2. Impression Formation in Conversations.   Much of the information we acquire about people in everyday life comes from conversations that we overhear or in which we participate. That is, we hear others describe an acquaintance's general characteristics, or we exchange anecdotal descriptions of the person's behavior in various situations. In many ways, these descriptions may resemble the stimuli used in person memory research.

However, conveying information in conversations introduces additional considerations. For example, the descriptions of people that are conveyed in this context are usually subjective and, therefore, potentially inaccurate. Therefore, the process of forming an impression on the basis of these descriptions can require a prior appraisal of the communicator.

Wyer, Budesheim, and Lambert (1990) provided empirical evidence that such descriptions implicate the speaker as well as the person being described. Subjects were first given handwritten trait descriptions of a male target person, ostensibly written by each of two students. Then subjects listened to a tape-recorded conversation between these two students about the target. Each speaker mentioned both favorable and unfavorable things that the target person had done. Finally, subjects guessed the speakers' liking for the target, made evaluations of both the target and the speakers, and recalled the described behaviors.

Both subjects' liking for the speakers and their estimation of the speakers' liking for the target increased with the favorableness of the speakers' initial trait descriptions. However, subjects' own liking for the target did not. If anything, subjects evaluated the target less favorably when the speakers described his traits positively than when they described his traits negatively (a contrast effect). Apparently, subjects attributed each speaker's trait description to his or her general disposition to respond favorably or unfavorably to others. Consequently, they judged speakers who wrote favorable trait descriptions to be more likeable than those who wrote unfavorable descriptions. Then, the subjects used these evaluations as standards of comparison in judging the target, rating him less favorably when the speakers were likeable than when they were dislikable.

Subjects' recall of the behaviors described during the conversation provide further evidence that subjects focused their attention on the speakers but not on the person being discussed. That is, subjects' recall of the target's behaviors was not affected by the behaviors' consistency with the trait description provided by the same speaker. Instead, subjects had better recall of behaviors that were evaluatively inconsistent with the trait description provided by the *other* speaker. Although this result is surprising on first consideration, it has a reasonable explanation. As noted earlier, subjects apparently based their impressions of each speaker on the speaker's trait description of the target. Nevertheless, they were undoubtedly not completely certain of their assumption that this description reflected a general disposition of the speaker, rather than an attribute of the target. Therefore, they might have sought confirmation of this assumption. Behaviors mentioned by one speaker that are inconsistent with the other speaker's trait description of the target suggest that the description is inaccurate and, therefore, confirm the assumption that the description reflects a general disposition of the speaker instead. Therefore, subjects might have thought about these behaviors more extensively with reference to the speaker, and therefore recalled the behaviors better later. If this is so, the representation that is formed when two speakers' trait descriptions differ in favorableness could be modeled (using an associative network metaphor) as shown in Fig. 2.3.[3]

These data suggest that when people hear information about a person in a conversation, they spontaneously focus their attention on the speakers as well as on

---

[3]This representation is applicable when subjects form impressions of both speakers. When subjects are told to form an impression of the target, they appear to form evaluative concepts of both speakers, but think about the behaviors mentioned from the perspective of only one of the speakers. Consequently, one set of pathways connecting the behaviors mentioned by one speaker to the concept of the other speaker would not exist (see Wyer et al., 1990).

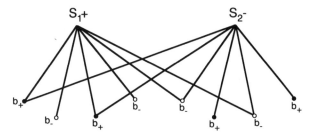

FIG. 2.3.   Cognitive representation formed on the basis of two speakers' descriptions of a third target person. S_1+ and S_2- denote favorable and unfavorable concepts of the speakers based on their initial trait descriptions of the target, respectively. Favorable and unfavorable behaviors are denoted by $b+$ and $b-$, respectively.

the person to whom the information refers. In doing so, they may consider the motivation behind the statements as well as the statements' literal meaning. Further evidence of this possibility was obtained in a second series of studies, where the target of the conversation was actually one of the two speakers whose remarks were overheard (Wyer, Budesheim, Lambert, & Swan, in press). Again, the other speaker's description of the target's traits affected liking for the speaker, but not for the target. Moreover, subjects again had better recall for behaviors described by the target that were inconsistent with the other speaker's trait description of him, and which therefore confirmed the assumption that this description reflected a general disposition of the speaker rather than an attribute of the target.

In contrast, subjects' recall of behaviors that the other speaker mentioned was determined entirely by the favorableness of these behaviors. More specifically, subjects had relatively better recall of unfavorable behaviors the speaker had mentioned; this was true regardless of their consistency with the trait description provided by either this speaker or by the target. The speaker's description of the target's undesirable behaviors presumably violated a conversational norm to be polite, or not to offend the person with whom one is speaking. Therefore, subjects might have thought more extensively about these norm-violating statements in relation to others' statements to understand why they occurred, and the inter-item associations that were formed as a result of this activity may have facilitated later recall of the statements.

Other researchers also have made the case that person impression processes are influenced by characteristics of the conversational situation. For example, Holtgraves, Srull, and Socall (1989) demonstrated that subjects are more sensitive to the forcefulness of conversational statements made by same-status conversationalists than those made by a higher status individual. In the latter case, forceful remarks are normative, whereas in the former, they seem to violate the norm of politeness and therefore attract greater attention.

3. The Informational Context of Person Descriptions. Person-perception paradigms often present items of descriptive information in discreet, isolated units, without the context provided either by the flow of conversation or by the various kinds of interpersonal cues that may accompany descriptive remarks when they are made in social situations. The flow of conversation is centrally important, because communications that respond to particular inquiries or assertions are likely to be interpreted within that context. For example, Holtgraves and Srull (1989) found that self-aggrandizing statements increased liking for the speaker when they were responses to a direct inquiry or to an equivalent self-disclosure by another person. However, self-aggrandizing statements actually decreased liking when they were blurted out of context.

Another kind of context is provided by the kind of information that people often communicate in addition to (or instead of) straightforward trait or behavior descriptions. Imagine the kind of impression you might form if a young woman told you that, "Joe gets this stupid grin on his face whenever he tells a joke." Compare this with the impression you would have if that same woman said, "I just love how Joe gets this stupid grin on his face whenever he tells a joke." An accompanying evaluation or expression of affect can markedly change the meaning of a descriptive remark. People's descriptions of others may encompass a wide variety of different kinds of information (cf. Carlston & Sparks, 1992; Fiske & Cox, 1979), which interact with each other to convey meaning.

Some of the information that accompanies a person description is nonverbal, conveyed by tone of voice, facial expression, body language, and so on. The same descriptive content can take on entirely different meaning when presented with sarcasm, with a smile, or with physical gestures that convey either sincerity or deceit. Although such nonverbal communications have been the source of much study (e.g., DePaulo & Rosenthal, 1982), they have seldom been taken into account in person-perception paradigms.

Future Directions—Pragmatic Implications of Social Information

The experiments described herein confirm that when information is conveyed in a social context, a variety of factors come into play that are generally absent from the paradigms typically used to investigate person memory and impression formation. First, person descriptions are likely to concern real people and events about which subjects already have knowledge. Therefore, these descriptions may be considered in relation to this preexisting knowledge, rather than in relation to other information in the immediate situation. Second, subjects pay attention to the source of the information as well as to the person or object to which the information refers. Third, subjects are sensitive to the social context in which the information is transmitted and its implications for the interpretation of this information. Fourth, the communicated descriptions are likely to encompass a variety of different kinds of information that are interconnected in ways that may influence the audience's interpretations.

One approach to understanding such factors is suggested by research and theory on the principles of communication. For example, Grice (1975; see also Clark & Haviland, 1977; Green, 1989; Higgins, 1981; Sperber & Wilson, 1986) recognized that social communications tend to be guided by certain norms or principles. Four of these were touched on in preceding sections:

1. Informativeness—communications are expected to convey information that adds to the recipient's prior knowledge.
2. Accuracy—communications are expected to convey accurate information about their referents, or about the communicator's attitudes and beliefs concerning them.
3. Relevance—communications are expected to have something to do with the topic being discussed.
4. Politeness—communications are expected to be conveyed in a way that does not unnecessarily offend or embarrass the person to whom they are directed.

These principles are not always independent. For example, a communication cannot always be both polite and accurate. Nevertheless, it is reasonable to suppose that these principles are applied in a large number of social communication situations. They can enter into information processing in two ways. First, communicators attempt to generate messages that are consistent with the principles. (For a discussion of the role of communication objectives in deciding how to respond in interview situations, see Strack, chapter 6, Volume 1; Strack & Martin, 1987.) Moreover, recipients of a communication tend to assume that the message was intended by the communicator to conform to these norms. Therefore, if a message appears to violate one or another of these principles, recipients are stimulated to think about why the violation occurred. This may lead them to reinterpret the message as consistent with the communication objectives they assume to exist.

For example, suppose you heard someone assert that "George Bush is not a member of the Ku Klux Klan." Normally, this might seem to go without saying, or to violate the informativeness principle. However, if you perceive that the remark is intended to be informative, you might infer that the communicator knows of reasons to believe that Bush is a KKK member, but considers these reasons to be invalid. However, if you were previously unaware that such reasons might exist, the remark might actually increase your belief in the proposition being denied.

Evidence for such reasoning was obtained by Wegner, Wenzlaff, Kerker, and Beattie (1981) and, more recently, by Gruenfeld and Wyer (1992). In the latter study, subjects read a news headline that asserted the validity of a proposition that people would ordinarily assume to be true. This headline actually decreased subjects' belief in the validity of the proposition. Moreover, this decrease was comparable to that obtained by a headline that denied the proposition's validity. Furthermore, when the proposition was common knowledge (e.g., "Americans become eligible to vote at the age of 18"), subjects apparently interpreted it as an indirect expression of the communicator's opinion about the desirability of this state of affairs. This interpretation then influenced subjects' own opinions about the situation.

When the statements made during an informal conversation violate communication principles, other considerations arise. Subjects may infer that the literal meaning of a statement does not reflect its intended meaning. For example, an obviously uninformative or inaccurate statement ("You can't beat central Illinois for beautiful scenery") might be interpreted as sarcasm or irony. Moreover, statements that violate the politeness principle might be interpreted as teasing rather than as genuine expressions of hostility. Such effects are integral to a variety of phenomena that occur in informal social interaction, including emotional communications between marriage partners (Scott, Fuhrman, & Wyer, 1991; Watzlawick, Beavin, & Jackson, 1967) and the elicitation of humor (Wyer & Collins, 1992).

A number of factors influence the assignment of pragmatic meaning to statements made in informal conversation (Green, 1989; Sperber & Wilson, 1986). One critical issue concerns the circumstances that lead people to perceive that a conversational norm has been violated. Certainly not all statements that are uninformative, inaccurate, or impolite stimulate recipients to consider their pragmatic implications. In any particular context, there may be thresholds for acceptable levels of informativeness, accuracy, and so on, and only when these thresholds are exceeded is pragmatic information processing likely to occur.

Furthermore, other remarks that are made in a conversation can affect the interpretation of an assertion. For example, the comment "Ronald Reagan was a great president" might be interpreted as sarcasm if it follows a colleague's description of the disastrous consequences of Reagan's economic policies. However, it might be viewed as a true expression of opinion if it follows a colleague's advocacy of a large defense budget. More generally, norm-violating statements are likely to be interpreted in relation to other remarks, creating the sort of interitem associations that facilitate recall according to the person memory model (Wyer & Srull, 1989). Such possibilities will merit further exploration as work on person memory and impression formation increasingly focuses on the processing of information in natural social contexts.

THE REPRESENTATION OF GROUPS

There is a necessary synergy between the cognitive representations of individuals who are members of groups and the representations of the groups themselves. As stereotyping research continually reminds us, people's category memberships are among their most significant features and are among the attributes characteristically composing others' impressions of them (Carlston, 1992). When such categorizations are accessed, they bring with them a host of attributes ordinarily associated with the category (Andersen & Klatzky, 1987). At the same time, individuals also represent the groups of which they are members, and their behavior and characteristics may influence people's perceptions of the group as a whole. Indeed, the group stereotype may actually consist of the attributes of its most salient members (Smith, 1990a). Therefore, impressions of groups and impressions of their constituent members are intertwined.

Researchers have addressed several aspects of this relationship between groups and individuals. In the following sections, we consider the most important of these, including: (a) when a particular individual will be perceived as an individual and when as a representative of a group, (b) how the variability of individuals composing a group is perceived, and (c) how group representations differ from representations of individuals.

Individuals Versus Group Members

A number of factors appear to determine whether a target person is perceived as an individual or as a member of a group. One is the extent to which the target person exemplifies the category. For example, if a graying gentleman wearing spectacles and a sportscoat perfectly fits one's stereotype of a professor, then one should be more likely to view him as a member of that category than as an individual. The role of category fit is emphasized in Fiske and Neuberg's (1990) continuum approach to this issue. An important assumption of this approach is that people may engage in varying degrees of individuation, depending on the initial salience of a label and the consistency of the evidence with that label. Fiske and Neuberg also noted that the perceiver must be motivated to go beyond a readily available label to consideration of the degree of fit.

Category fit and perceiver motivation are also central to Brewer's (1988) formulation, which differed from the continuum model in treating categorization, individuation, and personalization as distinct stages of perceptual processing. If the target person is sufficiently self-involving, perceivers are hypothesized to personalize (treat the target as an individual) rather than to categorize; if a categorized target is a poor fit to the category, perceivers are hypothesized to individuate (treat the target as a specific instance of the category).

Several other perceiver characteristics are also likely to influence the tendency to categorize or individuate another person. One is the a priori salience of the category to the perceiver. Such salience has been studied both as an enduring personality characteristic and as a temporary state (Devine, 1989).

Another pertinent characteristic is the perceiver's own category membership. The importance of this factor was demonstrated by Ostrom, Carpenter, Sedikides, and Li (1991). Subjects learned several facts about each of 8 different individuals,

4 males and 4 females. The facts were relevant to each of four different characteristics (college major, favorite sport, etc.). Later, subjects were asked to recall all of these facts, and the recall data were analyzed to determine which kinds of facts were clustered together. Subjects organized information about members of their own gender according to person, but organized information about members of the opposite gender according to characteristic.

An attempt to individuate group members is also likely to be abandoned when the volume of information presented makes the task too effortful. Rothbart, Fulero, Jensen, Howard, and Birrell (1978) presented subjects with information about the traits of members of a hypothetical group. The complex but elegant design varied the number of different persons who possessed each trait, the number of times each person–trait pairing was presented, and the favorableness of the traits described. When the total amount of information presented was relatively low, subjects based their evaluations of the group on the proportion of persons who had favorable traits, irrespective of the number of times each trait was mentioned. This suggests that subjects organized the presented information around the individuals involved. However, when the amount of information presented was large, subjects based their judgments on the proportion of times each trait was mentioned, regardless of the number of people who possessed it. These results have clear implications for stereotyping. They suggest that when people are confronted with a large amount of information about a group, repeated acts or characteristics of any particular group member will have a disproportionate impact on perceptions of the group as a whole.

Perceived Variability of Individuals in Groups

Subjects typically judge the members of their own groups to be more heterogeneous than members of groups to which they do not belong (Judd & Park, 1988; Park & Judd, 1990; for a detailed discussion of this research, see Hamilton & Sherman, chapter 1, Volume 2). In accounting for this finding, Park and Judd (1990) suggested that subjects spontaneously compare members of their own groups to themselves, but compare members of other groups to a prototypical "average." (This should be true except when one perceives oneself as average.) This could account for the difference in perceptions of ingroup versus outgroup homogeneity.

Park and Judd (1990) provided more direct support for this possibility. They found that subjects' perceptions of the variability of their own groups were positively correlated with the discrepancy between their self-ratings and their ratings of the group as a whole. That is, subjects who rated themselves as average perceived less group variability than those who rated themselves as having relatively extreme attributes. In contrast, subjects' perceptions of the variability of an outgroup were unrelated to their self-perceptions.

The importance of understanding the processes that underlie perceptions of group variability and their representation in memory stems from the assumption that subjects' use of a group stereotype to judge individual members depends on these perceptions. That is, subjects might be more likely to use group-related attributes to judge individuals if the group is believed to be homogeneous with respect to these attributes than if it is not. An alternative possibility is that a person's group membership is used in different ways in these conditions. Lambert and Wyer (1990) found that when subjects believed a group to be heterogeneous with respect to an attribute, information about a target person's membership in the group combined additively with the implications of his or her attribute-related behavior to affect judgments regardless of the typicality of this behavior. When subjects perceived the group to be homogeneous, however, they appeared to use the group as a standard of comparison in judging targets whose behavior was atypical, rating them as less like the group than they would otherwise. These and other results suggested that the influence of perceived group variability on the use of group membership as a basis for judgments is not as straightforward as one might expect.

Differences Between Individual and Group Representations

People often receive information about individuals that is either consistent or inconsistent with the expectations regarding the group to which the person belongs. For example, they may expect members of some group to be quite intelligent, but they may then learn of both smart and dumb acts perpetrated by individual group members. This situation seems quite analogous to the traditional incongruency paradigm, where subjects receive information that is either consistent or inconsistent with either expectations regarding a particular individual. Therefore, one might expect the processes and representations brought to bear in each instance to be quite similar.

This seems likely to be true when the group members know one another and interact frequently. Then, the kind of behavioral homogeneity expected of the group might be similar to that expected of a single individual, and so inconsistency-resolution processes of the sort often identified in person memory research might indeed occur. That is, people might consider the expectancy-inconsistent behavior of one member in relation to the behaviors of other members in an effort to understand why one group member would deviate from the group's behavioral norms.

However, many groups are composed of individuals who do not interact a great deal and may not even know each other. Examples include large categories of people who are commonly grouped together because of their perceived similarity along one or more dimensions (e.g., ethnic, religious, political, and occupational groups). In such cases, there is no need to reconcile the behavior of one deviant group member with the behaviors of others. Consequently, the processes responsible that theoretically enhance the recall of expectancy-inconsistent behaviors of individuals are less apt to occur.

Several studies are consistent with this conclusion. For example, when a group is described as close knit and composed of members who interact frequently, subjects have better recall of individual members' behaviors that are inconsistent with their expectations for the group as a whole (Srull, 1981). In contrast, when the group is composed of members who do not necessarily interact with or know one another, individual members' behaviors are better remembered if they are consistent with group-based expectations (Rothbart, Evans, & Fulero, 1979; Srull, 1981; Wyer et al., 1984).

These findings are important in understanding the effects of group stereotypes. That is, suppose people have a stereotype-based expectation for members of a group as a whole. If they receive information about the behavior of several individual members, they are more likely to remember those behaviors that are consistent with the stereotype than those that are inconsistent with it. On the other hand, when several behaviors of a single group member are conveyed, subjects are more likely to remember those behaviors that are inconsistent with the group stereotype than those that are consistent with it.

THE REPRESENTATION OF SOCIAL EVENTS

With some exceptions (e.g., Berry, 1991; Carlston & Skowronski, 1986; DePaulo, Kenny, Hoover, & Webb, 1987; Ickes, Stinson, Bissonnette, & Garcia, 1990; Rholes & Ruble, 1986), person memory research presents subjects with one-sentence descriptions of behaviors that are mere shadows of the complex social events that people often encounter in their daily lives. Although such one liners are useful, they are not representative of the social situations through which people gain much of their interpersonal knowledge. Written behavioral stimuli primarily tend to engage only subjects' verbal and semantic systems, whereas actual social situations engage visual and behavioral systems as well (Carlston, 1992). Moreover, people who witness a social event observe a great deal more than can be communicated in a written one liner and are either active or passive participants in the proceedings. The consequence is that different kinds of processes tend to be engaged, and different kinds of representations are likely to result.

Whatever their precise form, the importance of event representations in social information processing is undeniable. Such event representations are a fundamental component of people's impressions of other people (Carlston, 1992). According to Bartlett (1932) and his successors (e.g., Black, Galambos, & Read, 1984; Perrig & Kintsch, 1985), event schemas are also essential for interpreting and responding to stories and experiences. We frequently decide whether to participate in a situation, or how to behave in it, by recalling similar situations we have encountered in the past (cf. Abelson, 1976, 1981). Moreover, we often attempt to understand and respond to someone's description of a personal experience by recalling and communicating a similar experience of our own.

In light of the importance of event representations, it is somewhat embarrassing that so little progress has been made in understanding the nature and use of these representations. Initial conceptualizations of how event sequences are represented in memory were inspired by two quite different bodies of research and theory. The first was Newtson's (1976) chunking approach to the coding of behavioral sequences; the second was Schank and Abelson's (1977; see also Abelson, 1976, 1981) conceptualization of the role of cognitive scripts (for alternative formulations, see Bower, Black, & Turner, 1979; Graesser, 1981). Although there have been few new developments in these areas over the past several years, aspects of these approaches merit reiteration.

General Considerations

The representations of event sequence are distinguished from the representations of persons in that they are schematic, rather than categorical (Mandler, 1979; Wyer & Gordon, 1984). That is, many of their features are related to one another according to certain a priori temporal, spatial, or causal rules. Thus, the description of someone as "insensitive, friendly, and intelligent" would make just as much sense as a description of the person as "intelligent, friendly, and insensitive." In contrast, the description of an event as "goes to work, eats breakfast, and gets out of bed" is much more nonsensical than a description of the event as "gets out of bed, eats breakfast, and goes to work." Barsalou and Sewell (1985) demonstrated the schematic character of event representations, as opposed to categorical representations. They showed that whereas features of categories are usually reported in order of typicality, the features of events representations are reported in temporal order, regardless of typicality.

The events that compose an event representation, like those in a person representation, can be at different levels of abstractness. Moreover, they can pertain to a unique event involving particular persons in a specific situation, or to prototypic events that occur frequently with only variations (e.g., eating at a restaurant). The latter representations may often be hierarchical (Abelson, 1981; Wyer & Srull, 1989). That is, "going to dinner at a restaurant" can be conceptualized as a sequence of temporally related event concepts, or frames, such as "entering," "ordering," "eating," and "paying the bill." Each event is essentially a defining feature of the superordinate concept. At the same time, the subordinate events can be conceptualized as event concepts that are defined in terms of more specific ones.

It seems reasonable to suppose that these prototypic representations, which are acquired through learning, are applied in understanding new experiences to which they are related (but see Smith, 1990a). However, life experiences vary considerably in the extent to which they exemplify a prototype and, therefore, in the role of prototypes in comprehending and organizing them. The events that define a prototypic sequence occur with such a high probability that the mention of them provides little new information. For example, people usually assume that a person who ate at a restaurant not only ordered a meal and paid the bill, but did so in a particular order. In contrast, although spilling one's drink is not an unusual occurrence at a restaurant, it is not part of the definition of the event, so it could not be predicted. Moreover, without additional information, one would not know a priori the point during the event sequence at which it occurred. Still other events (e.g., telling one's wife that one wants a divorce) are unrelated to those that typically occur in a restaurant, and yet they might occur in the context of these latter events. Finally, some sequences of events, although recognized as causally related, are not at all predictable on the basis of existing knowledge (e.g., having too many drinks on a flight to San Francisco, forgetting the address of the person one wants to visit, and bursting into tears).

These differences convey the difficulty of developing a general conceptualization of event memory and its role in social information processing. That is, the previously acquired knowledge that is brought to bear on the comprehension of a series of social events, and the representation that is formed from these events, are likely to vary considerably with the type of events involved. Still other considerations arise from the fact that a large proportion of the events we encounter in daily life are ones we directly experience and in which we actively participate. Because the discussion in this section is generally restricted to research on the processing of verbally described sequences of events, its relevance to an understanding of event representations formed outside the laboratory may be questioned. However, similar considerations underlie the representations formed in each case.

In this regard, two alternative conceptualizations have been proposed concerning the representation of observed behavior sequences. Newtson (1973, 1976) hypothesized that observers of a continuous stream of events extract static frames from the sequence that signify breakpoints, or transitions between one conceptually meaningful act and another. Memory for successive breakpoints in the sequence permits the sequence of acts to be reconstructed. The greater the detail with which one wishes to retain the original sequence, the greater the number of breakpoints that are extracted (Newtson, 1973).

In contrast, Ebbesen (1980) postulated that subjects are less inclined to extract frames at breakpoints than at intermediate locations that are each typical of the event in which it occurs, thereby permitting the event to be identified. For example, "walked down the street" would be represented by a single frame, located somewhere in the middle of the event, and encoded in sufficient detail so that the nature of the event can be identified. Note that, to this extent, the representation that is formed would be conceptually analogous to a comic strip, with each frame denoting a different event in the sequence (for a similar analogy, see Abelson, 1976).

The relative merits of the two conceptualizations have been discussed in detail elsewhere (Ebbesen, 1980; Wyer & Srull, 1989). In general, research findings are at least as consistent with Ebbesen's conceptualization as with Newtson's.

Moreover, despite the innovativeness of Newtson's methodology and the impressive empirical work he has reported, it is difficult to apply his conceptualization to some pertinent situations. These include, for example, the representation of event sequences that involve more than one interacting person, or experiences that for other reasons consist of two overlapping sequences of events (e.g., having a discussion about abortion while eating at a restaurant). Ebbesen's formulation circumvented many of these problems.

Ebbesen's (1980) formulation has a further advantage in suggesting an analogy between for representations of observed sequences of events and representations of verbally described events. Both kinds of representations can be viewed as series of symbolically (verbally or visually) coded frames, each of which exemplifies a different event concept. Such analogies are useful in view of the predominant use of verbal event sequences in research on event representation. On the other hand, as noted earlier, the processes and structures involved in first-hand observations and verbal event descriptions may sometimes differ. Therefore, generalization from the verbal research must always be undertaken with caution.

Our discussion is divided into three sections. First, we consider the role of prototypic event representations in the encoding of specific event sequences. Second, we discuss the way that nonprototypic sequences of events are represented in memory. Finally, we note several more general issues that concern the way in which event representations are used in comprehension and inference.

The Role of Prototypic Event Sequences
in the Representation of New Experiences

Suppose subjects are told that John entered a restaurant, was shown to his table, and ordered his meal. As he waited for the food to arrive, he looked at the pictures on the wall. Then, while eating his meal, he accidentally spilled his glass of water and had to clean it up. Finally, he paid his bill and left. Subjects presumably interpret this information in terms of a prototypic restaurant schema. But what aspects of this prototypic schema are actually stored with the episodic representation, and how are the particulars of John's meal integrated with this schematic information? There are several possibilities.

1. Complete Copy Hypothesis. Once the prototypic schema is activated for use in interpreting the information, instantiations of all schema-defining event concepts might be copied into the representation that is formed, regardless of whether the events were mentioned explicitly. Thus, in our example, the representation would include not only the prototypic events that were actually described (entered the restaurant), but also schema-defining events that were not mentioned (e.g., looked at the menu).

2. Partial Copy Hypothesis. According to this hypothesis, only the schema-instantiating events that were actually mentioned are retained in the representation. That is, other unmentioned schema-defining subevents are not added.

3. No Copy Hypothesis. This hypothesis is based on a cognitive efficiency principle. That is, it assumes that information is not represented if it can be inferred on the basis of prior knowledge. Thus, once a prototypic event schema is identified as applicable for understanding what occurred in the situation, events that define the schema (and thus can be predicted on the basis of the schema alone) are not retained. Rather, subjects simply store a "pointer" to the relevant schema, along with a set of equivalence statements that permit specific features of the events to be equated with more general features of the schema (e.g., "restaurant = Timpone's," "customer = John," etc.).

4. Selective Copy Hypothesis. According to this hypothesis, subjects include schema-defining events in the representation they form only if these events are necessary to localize the occurrence of schema-unrelated events that have been mentioned. Thus, in our example, subjects might associate spilling the water with eating the meal, so that the timing of the former event can be reconstructed. As a result of this association, an instantiation of eating would be retained in the representation that is formed. Instantiations of schema-defining events that are not necessary to locate a schema-unrelated event are not retained, however.

The selective copy hypothesis differs from the other three not only in its specification of the conditions, in which schema-defining events become part of the new representation that is formed, but also in the role of schema-unrelated events in the construction of this representation. The first three hypotheses make no provision for the representation of these events. If anything, they assume that the events are simply appended as tags, without being integrated into the representation that is formed (see also Graesser, Gordon, & Sawyer, 1979; Graesser & Nakamura, 1982). In contrast, the selective-copy hypothesis assumes that these events are an integral part of the representation that is formed.

A series of studies (Trafimow & Wyer, 1993) provide support for the selective-copy hypothesis over the three alternatives. Subjects read scenarios that incorporated both schema-defining subevents and schema-unrelated ones. The proportion of schema-defining events that subjects were able to recall later was unrelated to the number of such events presented. However, this proportion increased with the number of schema-unrelated events that were described, as expected if retention of schema-instantiating events is contingent on their association with schema-unrelated events.

In addition, a schema-defining event was more likely to be recalled immediately after an unrelated event than after another schema-defining one. This suggests that the schema-defining events were more strongly associated with schema-unrelated events than with other events in the prototypic sequence. This result is difficult for the other three hypotheses to explain.

An ambiguity concerning the interpretation of Trafimow and Wyer's (1993) findings is worth noting. All four hypotheses described in this section assume that the knowledge structure that is brought to bear on the interpretation of new information is an abstract, prototypic event schema. As Smith (1990a) argued, however, it is quite conceivable that the knowledge structure applied is not the prototypic schema itself, but rather a specific exemplar of the prototype. Such an exemplar could operate in much the same way implied by the selective copy hypothesis. Trafimow and Wyer's findings did not distinguish between these two possibilities.

The Representation of Nonprototypic Events

Trafimow and Wyer's (1993) study concerned the way in which single nonproto-typic events were represented when they occurred in the context of a prototypic event sequence. In many instances, however, entire sequences of events are non-prototypic. Moreover, more than one such sequence might occur, each of which is unrelated to the others. In such cases, thematically related events appear to be organized in a way that reflects the order of their occurrence. However, the sequences appear to be stored independently of one another.

Evidence of this was reported by Wyer and Bodenhausen (1985). Subjects read a story about a person's experiences at a cocktail party, describing events that the person observed or heard being discussed. Several different sequences of events were described. Of these, two were target sequences, consisting of four events each. For example, one sequence contained these events: "Bill saw John reach to get an hors d'oeuvre. As he did so, a guest bumped his arm. He spilled his Bloody Mary on Susan's new white dress. Susan called John an idiot and stalked off to the kitchen."

However, these events were described either in the order they occurred or in the reverse order: "Bill heard Susan call John an idiot and stalk off to the kitchen. John had spilled his Bloody Mary on Susan's new white dress. A guest had bumped John's arm and spilled his drink. John had been reaching to get an hors d'oeuvre at the time."

The events were either described together or separated by other, unrelated events. (This was accomplished by intruding events that distracted the protagonist from attending to or learning about certain events in the sequence until later.) In addition, the order in which the two target sequences were mentioned was counterbalanced. Subjects read the story with instructions to "form an impression of the cocktail party." Later, they were asked to recall the events about which they had read.

Subjects tended to recall the individual events that composed each sequence together, and in chronological order, regardless of where they occurred in the story or the order in which they were mentioned. However, subjects recalled the events that composed the most recently mentioned sequence (i.e., the sequence mentioned nearer the end of the story) before events in the other sequence. This suggests that subjects formed a separate representation of each target sequence. Moreover, the need to comprehend the thematically related events that composed each sequence led subjects to reorganize the events into a mental representation that reflected their actual order of occurrence. However, because the different sequences of events were not related to one another, the representations of these sequences were stored in memory independently of one another, in the order they were constructed. Consequently, the most recent stored representation (pertaining to the event sequence that was mentioned last in the story) was most accessible in memory and was recalled first.

Wyer and Bodenhausen's (1985) findings implied that, although the events in each sequence were spontaneously coded and organized in memory in a way that reflected their temporal order, the sequences themselves were not temporally coded. In this study, however, the two target sequences pertained to totally different persons and situations. In many instances, sequences of events concern the same person or are otherwise related in terms of a more general theme. Subjects are thus likely to encode the events in a way that permits their temporal order to be reconstructed.

Consider the sequence described in Fig. 2.4. This sequence consists of 10 specific events involving Willa. The events define three more general event concepts concerning Willa's learning about her father, the airplane ride, and getting lost in San Francisco, these being subordinate to the still more general event—Willa's trip to San Francisco. In this case, a mental representation of the event sequence that allows the order of the three general event concepts to be recon-

a. The telephone rings
b. Willa gets out of bed
c. Willa learns her father is dying
d. Willa gets on the plane
e. Willa has three drinks
f. Willa feels dizzy
g. The plane lands in San Francisco
h. Willa can't find the hospital
i. Willa breaks into tears

FIG. 2.4.   Theoretical representations of situation-specific event sequence formed from actions a–i. Each square in the diagram denotes a conceptual unit formed from the specific events connected to it.

structed requires that these concepts be coded in a way that denotes their order of occurrence. However, the temporal order of specific events that compose each of the more general ones can be reconstructed on the basis of general world knowledge about the causal relatedness of the type of events described. Consequently, these events do not need to be assigned temporal codes.

Evidence of such differences in temporal coding was obtained by Wyer et al. (1985). Subjects read about a sequence of events of the type described in Fig. 2.4. Afterward, they were given pairs of these events and asked to indicate which occurred earlier (or later). By comparing the times required to make these judgments as a function of the position of the events in the overall sequence, the temporal distance between them, and whether they occurred in the same or different situations, Wyer et al. obtained a coherent picture of both (a) the temporal coding and organization of the items at the time they were read, and (b) the temporal judgment processes that subjects employed later. In particular, as they read the sequence, subjects appeared to divide it into the three conceptual event units of the sort noted earlier, and to assign temporal codes to each. However, they apparently did not assign temporal codes to the specific events that composed each unit, because the order of these events could be reconstructed on the basis of general knowledge. Thus, the representation they formed seems to have resembled that shown at the bottom of Fig. 2.4.

One implication of such a representation is that subjects should be able to reconstruct the temporal order of events more quickly if the events occur in different units than if they occur in the same unit. This is because the first judgment can be made by comparing the temporal codes assigned to the units in which each event is contained, whereas the second judgment requires a computation based on general world knowledge. This was in fact the case. (For additional implications of the conceptualization and empirical support for them, see Wyer et al., 1985.)

Although the studies summarized in this section provide some insight into the way people represent nonprototypic event sequences, they barely scratch the surface in terms of what is needed to develop a conceptualization of how everyday life experiences are interpreted and stored in memory. In addition to the complexities noted at the outset regarding the type and form of the information to be represented, other considerations arise. For one thing, many life experiences consist of two or more overlapping sequences of events, each of which is thematically independent. For example, a couple may begin a discussion of the merits of abortion while ordering their meals at a restaurant. While eating their meals, they might terminate this discussion and begin another, finishing the second discussion while eating dessert. Whether the events that compose each sequence (those pertaining to ordering and eating the meal vs. those that concern the discussions) are represented as a single sequence of events or different sequences is not clear.

A similar situation arises with regard to representations constructed from life events that occur over a long period of time (e.g., the events that led to one's becoming a psychologist) and that are interrupted by others that are totally irrelevant. These event sequences are unlikely to be constructed on-line. Rather, they probably are formed later, after all of the events composing them have occurred. The manner in which these sequences are constructed from the myriad event frames that compose one's life history has yet to be determined. (For one attempt to conceptualize the construction of personal histories, see Ross, 1989.) Thus, although the research described in this section is a step toward understanding the representation of social events, it is a small one, and much more work must be done.

Effects of Event Representations on Comprehension and Inference

Previously formed event representations can be involved in the comprehension of new information in several ways. First, when events are not described in temporal sequence, these event representations can be used to reconstruct their actual order, facilitating comprehension. Second, event representations can be used to infer unmentioned events that may have occurred during the sequence described. They can also be used to infer attributes of the people involved in these events. Each of these possibilities is discussed here.

Reconstruction of Temporal Order.   The order in which we learn about events does not always correspond to the order in which they occur. In such cases, the chronological order must often be reconstructed on the basis of prior knowledge of the types of events described. This knowledge often consists of a previously formed event sequence that relates to the experience. When more than one such event representation is applicable, the one that is activated and applied can have a substantial influence on the comprehension of what occurred.

Read, Druian, and Miller (1985) provide an example. Suppose subjects receive information in the following order:

> John and Mary drove back to the apartment.
> John gave Mary the money.
> They left the apartment.
> John and Mary made love.
> John picked Mary up on the corner near the drugstore.

Two different sequences of these statements make sense. One describes a couple's purchase of a contraceptive device in anticipation of making love ("John gave Mary the money. They left the apartment. John picked up Mary on the corner near the drugstore. They drove back to the apartment. They made love."). The second pertains to an interlude with a prostitute ("John picked up Mary on the corner near the drugstore. They drove back to the apartment. John gave Mary the money. They made love. They left the apartment.").

2. COGNITIVE REPRESENTATION OF PERSONS AND EVENTS

Which sequence a perceiver constructs might be determined by a variety of objectively irrelevant situational factors. For example, the perceiver might be less likely to invoke the prostitute scenario if the actors' names evoke upper-middle-class stereotypes (e.g., John Montague and Mary Dupont) than if they evoke ethnic or working-class stereotypes (John Brown and Maria Sanchez). Moreover, individuals will differ in the extent to which they have such stereotypes, and in the degree to which these are activated and used.

One setting in which events are often learned out of sequence is the courtroom. The order in which crime evidence is presented often bears little relation to the chronological order in which the events actually took place. Jurors' conclusions may depend on how this evidence is conveyed (Pennington & Hastie, 1986, 1988, 1992). In one study (Pennington & Hastie, 1988), subjects listened to the transcript of a murder trial that included both testimony that favored the defense and testimony that favored the prosecution. Sometimes the testimony was organized by witness, much as it was presented in the original trial. At other times, the testimony favoring one or the other verdict was presented in chronological order (e.g., events that preceded the incident were described first, followed by testimony about the incident, then the arrest, the autopsy, etc.). The orders of prosecution evidence and defense evidence were varied independently.

When evidence favoring one verdict was presented chronologically but evidence favoring the alternative was not, 73% of the subjects rendered a verdict consistent with the chronologically presented testimony. When the prosecution and defense testimonies were similarly organized, subjects were as likely to favor one verdict as the other. However, subjects reported greater confidence in their verdict when all testimony was presented in chronological order, rather than in witness order. In other words, increasing the ease with which subjects could construct a temporally ordered representation of events influenced both subjects' judgments and their confidence in these judgments.

In a conceptual replication and extension (Pennington & Hastie, 1992, Experiment 1), subjects heard testimony either in chronological order or organized by evidential issue (i.e., motive, opportunity, etc.). In some conditions, the testimony of three witnesses was contradicted by a fourth who was either high or low in credibility. The preponderance of the evidence had more impact when all testimony was conveyed in chronological order, so that a representation of the event was easy to construct. Additionally, acceptance of the deviant witness' testimony was more dependent on his credibility when the evidence was conveyed in chronological order. In other words, subjects were more sensitive to the failure for the deviant testimony to "fit" when the evidence was conveyed chronologically than when it was organized according to issue.

This interpretation has other implications. For example, consider the credibility of a "majority" witness, whose testimony is consistent with the evidence as a whole. The credibility of such a witness should have less effect when evidence is presented in chronological order than when it is not. Rather, the influence of the testimony should depend on the plausibility of the event representation as a whole. This suggests that a lawyer who has weak witnesses, but can build a convincing story, will be more effective presenting evidence in chronological order. On the other hand, a lawyer who has credible witnesses, but a weak story, will be more effective presenting evidence in witness order.

Inferences of Unmentioned Events.   In jury testimony and in general, the information conveyed about a sequence of events is often incomplete (i.e., some of the events that occurred in the sequence are not mentioned). However, in the course of constructing a mental representation of the event sequence, the missing events may be inferred explicitly or implicitly. If these inferred events become part of the representation that is stored in memory, they may be indistinguishable from the mentioned events when the representation is later recalled. In other words, intrusions are likely to occur.

These sorts of intrusions have been explored by schema theorists for many decades (e.g., Bartlett, 1932). Although a few (e.g., Alba & Hasher, 1983) have been skeptical about the prevalence of such effects, considerable evidence has accumulated to support their existence (Brewer & Namakura, 1984). Research on memory reconstruction (e.g., Loftus & Palmer, 1974), reality monitoring (Johnson & Raye, 1981), and simulation (Anderson & Godfrey, 1987) can also be interpreted as consistent with the argument that extraneous inferences may be difficult to distinguish from reality.

Work on the representation of social events provides examples. In a study of jury decision making (Pennington & Hastie, 1988, Experiment 1), subjects heard courtroom testimony and arrived at a verdict. Later they were given a recognition test that included some unmentioned events that were implied by either a likely "guilt" scenario or a likely "innocence" scenario. Subjects were more likely to falsely recognize those events that supported their earlier verdict than those that opposed it. In other words, they apparently responded to the recognition items by accessing the event representation they had constructed earlier.

A different study by Spiro (1977) had similar implications. Subjects were told that the experiment was concerned with reactions to interpersonal relations, and were asked to read a description of an interaction about an engaged couple. In some versions of the story, the man revealed that he did not want children, the woman became upset, and a bitter argument ensued. Afterward, while subjects were ostensibly engaged in unrelated activities, the experimenter casually mentioned that he knew the couple and that they had eventually married and were still happily together. Subjects who heard this remark might reasonably have tried to imagine how this unexpected outcome came about. They might have speculated that one or the other partner had a change of heart, that the woman found she could not have children, or that some other event led the couple to avoid the conflict that would otherwise have led them to separate. These inferred events might have been added to the representation that subjects constructed and stored in memory. When subjects returned either a few days or several weeks later, they were asked to recall the story they had read in the first session. They were directed to report only things that were mentioned in the original story, and not to include any inferences they might have made. Despite this caution, they made frequent errors, which were even more numerous with the longer delay. The errors typically resulted from attempts to reconcile the experimenter's casual remark with the original story. For example, one subject's rendition of the story included the statement that "the problem was resolved when they found that [the woman] could not have children anyway." Another reported that the man changed his mind. Thus, in trying to reconcile the experimenter's remark with the original story, subjects apparently constructed different event representations that they later retrieved in thinking about the story. In each case, unmentioned events that the subjects inferred were later recalled as having been part of the original story.

Event representations often embody a full sequence of events, including initial antecedents and ultimate consequences. Thus, in applying an event schema to a learned episode, people may infer unmentioned causes or consequences of described events. In one demonstration of such effects (Sedikides & Anderson, in press), subjects read a scenario describing either an American couple's defection to Russia or a Russian couple's defection to the United States. The content of the scenario was identical except for the names of the individuals involved and the direction of the defection. After a short or long delay, subjects were asked to recall the information they had read. Although few intrusion errors occurred when the time delay was short, an appreciable number were evident after a longer period of time had elapsed. Typically, these intrusions were events that would provide explanations for the couple's defection, with the nature of the intrusions dependent on the direction of this defection.

Specifically, when the defectors went from the United States to Russia, the intruded events tended to be idiosyncratic to the individuals involved (i.e., the man was unhappy with his job, the defectors were spies, etc.). In contrast, when the defectors went from Russia to the United States, the intruded events typically referred to situational (country-related) factors that stimulated the move. It is likely that subjects had different event schemata for defectors from Russia and defectors from the United States, and that they spontaneously applied these in interpreting the stimulus information. Then the events that composed those event schemata were erroneously recalled as having been mentioned in the original stimuli.

It seems likely that event sequences provide the bases for many of the attributional phenomenon studied by attribution researchers. Early attribution theories (Jones & Davis, 1965; Kelley, 1967) postulated the existence of general principles that guide the attribution of events to situational or dispositional factors.

However, as others have noted, these principles do not capture the cognitive processes that underlie the explanations that subjects actually generate (Fiske & Taylor, 1991). That is, the event representation that subjects activate to understand an event can sometimes reflect a particular past experience, and the explanation they generate may be based on the antecedents of this specific experience, man who had just broken up with his girlfriend, one might comprehend this event in terms of some similar experience in one's own past. In doing so, one might infer not only the reasons for the breakup, but also the emotions elicited and the likely consequences of this event. Moreover, as discussed in the next section, the likely consequences of this event. Moreover, as discussed in the next section, one might infer trait attributes of the actor or others in the situation. Thus, the utilization of event representations could underlie a variety of different kinds of inferences, including both casual and trait attributions.

The Role of Event Representations in Impression Formation and Judgment. Associated Systems Theory suggests that the representations formed of social events are associatively linked to the individuals involved in these events (see also Wyer & Carlston, 1979; Wyer & Srull, 1989). This may be true whether the individual is the instigator of some action in the event, the recipient of actions instigated by others, or merely a bystander. Moreover, these event representations can embody important information about the individuals with whom they are associated, including, for example, how those individuals look, how they act, how others treat them, and what kinds of events or situations they tend to encounter.

The event representations associated with an individual might be at many different levels of abstractness. For example, they could pertain to either a specific experience involving the person ("He stole Susan's purse on May 1") or to more general behaviors or events ("He steals things"). The representations may be stored separately at a memory location (e.g., bin; see Wyer & Srull, 1986, 1989) pertaining to the person.

Using a reaction-time paradigm, Carlston and Skowronski (1988) demonstrated subjects' utilization of this sort of prototypical event representation in making inferences about a person. In a preliminary session, subjects estimated the likelihood that people who engage in different generic acts possess different trait attributes. Embedded among a number of such items was one asking how likely someone who returned someone's lost money was to be honest. Several weeks later, these subjects returned for an ostensibly unrelated experiment where they viewed a number of videotapes, one of which involved an actor, Dave, trying to convince two co-workers to return money that they all had found while cleaning a professor's lab. Some subjects were led to make immediate inferences about Dave, whereas others were not. Then, after the videotapes were over, some subjects were stimulated to think of Dave's behavior, whereas others were not. Finally, all subjects were asked, "Is Dave honest?" and their response times were recorded.

When subjects had not made immediate inferences, or if they had been primed to think of Dave's behavior, their response times to the question about Dave's honesty were related to the likelihood estimates they had made weeks earlier. More specifically, subjects were quicker to answer the question about Dave's honesty if they had earlier reported a strong relationship between returning money and honesty than if they had reported only a moderate relationship. Presumably, these subjects responded to the question about Dave's traits by bringing their abstract event representations to bear on the specific episode involving Dave. However, this result was not obtained among subjects who had previously been led to make trait inferences and who were not primed to think of Dave's behavior. Presumably these latter subjects merely retrieved their earlier trait attribution, which resulted in a relatively quick response that was unrelated to their likelihood estimates.

As noted earlier, event representations can be used to make inferences about people who are the targets of others' acts, or who are merely present in the situation. No direct information about the individual need be provided, because it may be implied by other, inferred events in the represented sequence. Consider the following three passages (from an example by Schank & Abelson, 1977, which was elaborated by Wyer & Carlston, 1979):

1. John knew his wife's operation would be expensive. There was always Uncle Harry. . . . John reached for the telephone directory.
2. John could not face asking a friend to take out his girlfriend's ugly sister. There was always Uncle Harry. . . . John reached for the telephone directory.
3. John knew his wife's operation would be expensive. There was always Uncle Harry. . . . John reached for the revolver he kept beside his bed.

None of these passages contains any direct information about Uncle Harry. Yet, people reading different passages are likely to generate rather different characterizations of Harry. This is presumably because the event representations invoked by each passage are rather different, as are the roles played by Harry.

FUTURE DIRECTIONS

Mental representations of social events clearly play a central role in the comprehension of new experiences and the assessment of their implications. However, many gaps exist in our understanding of the way these representations are formed, the nature of their content and organization, and the conditions in which they are applied. These gaps may be due, in part, to the idiosyncratic nature of the events that compose each individual's past experience. It will ultimately be necessary to develop research paradigms that are sensitive to these idiosyncrasies, and yet permit the content and structure of people's representations to be examined systematically.

As noted earlier, research on person memory has begun to consider more seriously the cognitive dynamics of impression formation in social sciences. In doing so, it is likely to give substantial attention to the processing of information in informal conversations (cf. Holtgraves et al., 1989; Wyer et al., 1989). Conversations are sequences of events, and representations of conversational sequences may bear a resemblance to other kinds of event representations. At the same time, research on the inferences made from event representations may ultimately take into account the manner in which person inferences and impressions are extracted from these representations (for early efforts in this regard, see Allen & Ebbesen, 1981; Cohen & Ebbesen, 1979). Therefore, it seems likely that future research in social cognition will bring together these presently disparate bodies of theory and research.

Although few empirical paradigms exist that are capable of integrating event memory and person memory, the theoretical formulations introduced at the beginning of this chapter are all capable of providing some theoretical integration. The bin model and associative network models can accommodate person and event representations within the mnemonic structures that they posit, and both make predictions about the kinds of processes and phenomena that may occur due to the commingling of such representations (Wyer & Carlston, 1980; Wyer & Srull, 1989). The procedural mechanisms suggested by Smith (1990a) were similarly applicable to either kinds of cognitive material, and the emphasis this approach placed on utilization of specific exemplars may also be appropriate in both domains. Finally, as noted in the preceding section, associated systems theory suggests that event representations may sometimes be incorporated within person representations (and, perhaps, the other way around). Nonetheless, all of these theories have dealt with the integration of person and event memories in general terms, and many details need to be worked out in future theoretical efforts.

CONCLUDING REMARKS

The past decade of research in social cognition has witnessed many advances in the understanding of the cognitive representation of social information. At the same time, it has begun to reveal potentially serious limitations to the generalizeability of the empirical findings that have emerged and the theoretical formulations developed to account for them. These limitations may be due, in large part, to the paradigms that have been employed. In particular, investigations have focused on the processing of information that is conveyed about unknown persons and events, which is presented out of any social context, and about which subjects have no prior knowledge. The theoretical formulations that have developed seem inadequate to account for the processing of information about familiar people and situation, about which people have prior knowledge, or to account for information that is conveyed by known sources who have particular communication objectives.

New methods must be developed to advance our understanding in this domain. Our review of the literature in both person memory and event memory makes salient the need to understand the role of world knowledge in the processing of new information. The general theoretical formulations discussed at the beginning of this chapter provide some preliminary ways to think about the representations and processes involved. Moreover, some recent work on spontaneous representation (e.g., Carlston & Sparks, 1992; McGuire & McGuire, 1987, 1991) suggested new methodologies for examining the nature and use of cognitive representations. But other new approaches to these issues are needed.

Our skepticism about the adequacy of existing models of person and event memory does not imply that these formulations should be discarded. An incorrect model can still be useful if its assumptions are well stated and have been empirically validated in its domain of application. Failures of the model in other kinds of situations can be localized in specific assumptions that apply in one situation but not another, and a revised formulation can be developed that incorporates this contingency. Perhaps the main contribution of the research and theory discussed in this chapter will ultimately lie in the development of a set of theoretical tools that can be used to conceptualize phenomena in new, more complex social information-processing situations, rather than in the specific research that has been reported. The next decade of research will undoubtedly focus on such situations, and we look forward to the development of social cognition models that will account for the phenomena this research will uncover.

ACKNOWLEDGMENTS

The preparation of this chapter was supported in part by National Institute of Mental Health Grant No. MH-3-8585, BSR. Appreciation is extended to the University of Illinois Social Cognition Group for stimulating comments and advice on many of the ideas expressed.

REFERENCES

Abelson, R. P. (1976). Script processing in attitude formation and decision making. In J. S. Carroll & J. W. Payne (Eds.), *Cognition and social behavior*. Hillsdale, NJ: Lawrence Erlbaum Associates.

Abelson, R. P. (1981). The psychological status of the script concept. *American Psychologist, 36,* 715–729.

Abelson, R. P., Aronson, E., McGuire, W. J., Newcomb, T. N., Rosenberg, M. J., & Tannenbaum, P. (Eds.). (1968). *Theories of cognitive consistency: A sourcebook*. Chicago: Rand McNally.

Alba, J. W., & Hasher, L. (1983). Is memory schematic? *Psychological Bulletin*, *93*, 203–231.

Allen, R. B., & Ebbesen, E. B. (1981). Cognitive processes in person perception: Retrieval of personality trait and behavioral information. *Journal of Experimental Social Psychology*, *17*, 119–141.

Andersen, S. M., & Klatzky, R. L. (1987). Traits and social stereotypes: Levels of categorization in person perception. *Journal of Personality and Social Psychology*, *53*, 234–246.

Anderson, C. A., & Godfrey, S. S. (1987). Thoughts about actions: The effects of specificity and availability of imagined behavioral scripts on expectations about oneself and others. *Social Cognition*, *5*, 238–258.

Anderson, J. R. (1976). *Language, memory and thought*. Hillsdale, NJ: Lawrence Erlbaum Associates.

Anderson, J. R. (1987). Skill acquisition: Compilation of weak-method problem solutions. *Psychological Review*, *94*, 192–210.

Anderson, J. R., & Bower, G. H. (1979). *Human associative memory*. Hillsdale, NJ: Lawrence Erlbaum Associates.

Anderson, N. H., & Hubert, S. (1963). Effects of concomitant verbal recall on order effects in personality impression formation. *Journal of Verbal Learning and Verbal Behavior*, *2*, 379–391.

Bargh, J. A. (1984). Automatic and conscious processing of social information. In R. S. Wyer & T. K. Srull (Eds.), *Handbook of social cognition* (Vol. 3). Hillsdale, NJ: Lawrence Erlbaum Associates.

Bargh, J. A., Bond, R. N., Lombardi, W., & Tota, M. E. (1986). The additive nature of chronic and temporary sources of construct accessibility. *Journal of Personality and Social Psychology*, *50*, 869–878.

Bargh, J. A., & Pietromonaco, P. (1982). Automatic information processing and social perception: The influence of trait information presented outside of conscious awareness on impression formation. *Journal of Personality and Social Psychology*, *43*, 437–449.

Bargh, J. A., & Thein, R. D. (1985). Individual construct accessibility, person memory, and the recall-judgment link: The case of information overload. *Journal of Personality and Social Psychology*, *49*, 1129–1146.

Barsalou, L. W., & Sewell, D. R. (1985). Contrasting the representation of scripts and categories. *Journal of Memory and Language*, *24*, 646–665.

Bartlett, F. C. (1932). *Remembering*. Cambridge: Cambridge University Press.

Bassili, J. N. (1989). Traits as action categories versus traits as person attributes in social cognition. In J. Bassili (Ed.), *On-line cognition in person perception*. Hillsdale, NJ: Lawrence Erlbaum Associates.

Bassili, J. N., & Smith, M. C. (1986). On the spontaneity of trait attribution: Converging evidence for the role of cognitive strategy. *Journal of Personality and Social Psychology*, *50*, 239–245.

Berry, D. S. (1991). Accuracy in social perception: Contributions of facial and vocal information. *Journal of Personality and Social Psychology*, *61*, 298–307.

Black, J. B., Galambos, J. A., & Read, S. (1984). Comprehending stories and social situations. In R. S. Wyer & T. K. Srull (Eds.), *Handbook of social cognition* (Vol. 3, pp. 45–86). Hillsdale, NJ: Lawrence Erlbaum Associates.

Bodenhausen, G. V., & Lichtenstein, M. (1987). Social stereotypes and information-processing strategies: The impact of task complexity. *Journal of Personality and Social Psychology*, *52*, 871–880.

Bower, G. H. (1981). Mood and memory. *American Psychologist*, *36*, 129–148.

Bower, G. H., Black, J. B., & Turner, T. J. (1979). Scripts in memory for text. *Cognitive Psychology*, *11*, 177–220.

Brewer, M. (1988). A dual process of impression formation. In T. K. Srull & R. S. Wyer (Eds.), *Advances in social cognition: Vol. 1. A dual model of impression formation* (pp. 1–36). Hillsdale, NJ: Lawrence Erlbaum Associates.

Brewer, W. F., & Nakamura, G. V. (1984). The nature and functions of schemas. In R. S. Wyer, Jr. & T. K. Srull (Eds.), *Handbook of social cognition* (Vol. 1, pp. 119–160). Hillsdale, NJ: Lawrence Erlbaum Associates.

Cacioppo, J. T., & Petty, R. E. (1982). The need for cognition. *Journal of Personality and Social Psychology, 42*, 116–131.

Carlston, D. E. (1980). Events, inferences and impression formation. In R. Hastie, T. Ostrom, E. Ebbesen, R. Wyer, D. Hamilton, & D. Carlston (Eds.), *Person memory: The cognitive basis of social perception.* Hillsdale, NJ: Lawrence Erlbaum Associates.

Carlston, D. E. (1992). Impression formation and the modular mind: The Associated Systems Theory. In L. L. Martin & A. Tesser (Eds.), *The construction of social judgments* (pp. 301–341). Hillsdale, NJ: Lawrence Erlbaum Associates.

Carlston, D. E., & Skowronski, J. J. (1986). Trait memory and behavior memory: The effects of alternative pathways on impression judgment response times. *Journal of Personality and Social Psychology, 50*, 5–13.

Carlston, D. E., & Skowronski, J. J. (1988). *Trait memory and behavior memory II: The effects of conceptual social knowledge in impression judgment response times.* Unpublished manuscript, University of Iowa, Iowa City.

Carlston, D. E., & Skowronski, J. J. (1993). *Evidence for spontaneous trait inferences using a savings paradigm.* Unpublished manuscript, Purdue University, West Lafayette, Indiana.

Carlston, D. E., & Sparks, C. (1992, May). *A theory-based approach to the analysis of free descriptions of people.* Paper presented at the meeting of the Midwestern Psychological Association, Chicago, IL.

Clark, H., & Haviland, S. (1977). Comprehension and the given-new contract. In R. Freedle (Ed.), *Disclosure production and comprehension.* Norwood, NJ: Ablex.

Cohen, C. E., & Ebbesen, E. B. (1979). Observational goals and schema activation: A theoretical framework for behavior perception. *Journal of Experimental Social Psychology, 15*, 305–339.

Collins, A. M., & Loftus, E. F. (1975). A spreading-activation theory of semantic processing. *Psychological Review, 83*, 407–428.

Craik, F. I. M., & Lockhart, R. S. (1972). Levels of processing: A framework for memory research. *Journal of Verbal Learning and Verbal Behavior, 11*, 671–684.

Crocker, J., Hannah, D. B., & Weber, R. (1983). Person memory and causal attribution. *Journal of Personality and Social Psychology, 44*, 55–66.

DePaulo, B. M., Kenny, D. A., Hoover, C. W., & Webb, W. (1987). Accuracy of person perception: Do people know what kinds of impressions they convey? *Journal of Personality and Social Psychology, 42*, 303–315.

DePaulo, B. M., & Rosenthal, R. (1982). Measuring the development of sensitivity to non-verbal communication. In C. E. Izard (Ed.), *Measuring emotions in infants and children* (pp. 208–247). Cambridge, MA: Cambridge University Press.

Devine, P. G. (1989). Stereotypes and prejudice: Their automatic and controlled components. *Journal of Personality and Social Psychology, 56*, 5–18.

Dreben, E. K., Fiske, S. T., & Hastie, R. (1979). The independence of item and evaluative information: Impression and recall order effects in behavior-based impression formation. *Journal of Personality and Social Psychology, 37*, 1758–1768.

Ebbesen, E. B. (1980). Cognitive processes in understanding ongoing behavior. In R. Hastie, T. Ostrom, E. Ebbesen, R. Wyer, D. Hamilton, & D. Carlston (Eds.), *Person memory: The cognitive basis of social perception.* Hillsdale, NJ: Lawrence Erlbaum Associates.

Ebbinghaus, H. (1964). *Memory: A contribution to experimental psychology.* New York: Dover. (Original work published 1885)

Fiske, S. T., & Cox, M. G. (1979). Person concepts: The effects of target familiarity and descriptive purpose on the process of describing others. *Journal of Personality, 47*, 136–161.

Fiske, S. T., & Linville, P. W. (1980). What does the schema concept buy us? *Personality and Social Psychology Bulletin, 6*, 543–557.

Fiske, S. T., & Neuberg, S. L. (1990). A continuum model of impression formation from category-based to individuating responses: Influence of information and motivation on attention and interpretation. In M. P. Zanna (Ed.), *Advances in experimental social psychology* (Vol. 23, pp. 1–74). San Diego, CA: Academic Press.

Fiske, S. T., & Taylor, S. (1991). *Social cognition* (2nd ed.). New York: McGraw-Hill.

Gilbert, D. T. (1991). How mental systems believe. *American Psychologist, 46,* 107–119.

Gilbert, D. T., Pelham, B. W., & Krull, D. S. (1988). On cognitive busyness: When person perceivers meet persons perceived. *Journal of Personality and Social Psychology, 54,* 733–740.

Gordon, S. E., & Wyer, R. S. (1987). Person memory: Category-set-size effects on the recall of a person's behaviors. *Journal of Personality and Social Psychology, 53,* 648–662.

Graesser, A. C. (1981). *Prose comprehension beyond the word.* New York: Springer-Verlag.

Graesser, A. C., Gordon, S. E., & Sawyer, J. D. (1979). Memory for typical and atypical actions in scripted activities: Test of a script pointer + tag hypothesis. *Journal of Verbal Learning and Verbal Behavior, 18,* 319–332.

Graesser, A. C., & Nakamura, G. V. (1982). The impact of a schema on comprehension and memory. In G. H. Bower (Ed.), *The psychology of learning and motivation: Advances in research and theory* (Vol. 16). New York: Academic Press.

Green, G. M. (1989). *Pragmatics and natural language understanding.* Hillsdale, NJ: Lawrence Erlbaum Associates.

Greenwald, A. G. (1968). Cognitive learning, cognitive responses to persuasion and attitude change. In A. G. Greenwald, T. C. Brock, & T. M. Ostrom (Eds.), *Psychological foundations of attitudes.* New York: Academic Press.

Grice, H. (1975). Logic and conversation. In P. Cole & J. Morgan (Eds.), *Syntax and semantics: Vol. 3. Speech acts* (pp. 68–134). New York: Academic Press.

Gruenfeld, D. H., & Wyer, R. S. (1992). The semantics and pragmatics of social influence: How affirmations and denials affect beliefs in referent propositions. *Journal of Personality and Social Psychology, 62,* 38–49.

Hamilton, D. E., Driscoll, D. M., & Worth, L. (1989). Cognitive organization of impressions: Effects of incongruency in complex representations. *Journal of Personality and Social Psychology, 39,* 1050–1063.

Hamilton, D. L., Katz, L. B., & Leirer, V. O. (1980). Cognitive representation impressions: Organizational processes in first impression formation. *Journal of Personality and Social Psychology, 39,* 1050–1063.

Hastie, R. (1980). Memory for behavioral information that confirms or contradicts a personality impression. In R. Hastie, T. Ostrom, E. Ebbesen, R. Wyer, D. Hamilton, & D. Carlston (Eds.), *Person memory: The cognitive basis of social perception.* Hillsdale, NJ: Lawrence Erlbaum Associates.

Hastie, R. (1981). Schematic principles in human memory. In E. T. Higgins, C. P. Herman, & M. P. Zanna (Eds.), *Social cognition: The Ontario Symposium* (Vol. 1). Hillsdale, NJ: Lawrence Erlbaum Associates.

Hastie, R., & Kumar, P. A. (1979). Person memory: Personality traits as organizing principles in memory for behaviors. *Journal of Personality and Social Psychology, 37,* 25–38.

Hastie, R., Ostrom, T. M., Ebbesen, E. B., Wyer, R. S., Hamilton, D. L., & Carlston, D. E. (1980). *Person memory: The cognitive basis of social perception.* Hillsdale, NJ: Lawrence Erlbaum Associates.

Hastie, R., & Park, B. (1986). The relationship between memory and judgment depends on whether the judgment task is memory-based or on-line. *Psychological Review, 93,* 258–268.

Heider, F. (1958). *The psychology of interpersonal relations.* New York: Wiley.

Herr, P. M. (1986). Consequences of priming: Judgment and behavior. *Journal of Personality and Social Psychology, 51,* 1106–1115.

Higgins, E. T. (1981). The "communication game": Implications for social cognition and persuasion. In E. T. Higgins, C. P. Herman, & M. P. Zanna (Eds.), *Social cognition: The Ontario Symposium* (Vol. 1). Hillsdale, NJ: Lawrence Erlbaum Associates.

Higgins, E. T., Bargh, J. A., & Lombardi, W. (1985). The nature of priming effects on categorization. *Journal of Experimental Psychology: Learning, Memory and Cognition, 11,* 59–69.

Higgins, E. T., Herman, C. P., & Zanna, M. P. (Eds.). (1981). *Social cognition: The Ontario Symposium.* Hillsdale, NJ: Lawrence Erlbaum Associates.

Higgins, E. T., & King, G. (1981). Accessibility of social constructs: Information processing conse-quences of individual and contextual variability. In N. Cantor & J. F. Kihlstrom (Eds.), *Personal-ity, cognition, and social interaction*. Hillsdale, NJ: Lawrence Erlbaum Associates.

Higgins, E. T., & McCann, C. D. (1984). Social encoding and subsequent attitudes, impressions and memory: "Context-driven" and motivational aspects of processing. *Journal of Personality and Social Psychology, 47*, 26–39.

Higgins, E. T., & Rholes, W. S. (1978). "Saying is believing": Effects of message modification on memory and liking for the person described. *Journal of Experimental Social Psychology, 14*, 363–378.

Higgins, E. T., Rholes, W. S., & Jones, C. R. (1977). Category accessibility and impression forma-tion. *Journal of Experimental Social Psychology, 13*, 141–154.

Holtgraves, T., & Srull, T. K. (1989). The effects of positive self-descriptions on impressions: General principles and individual differences. *Personality and Social Psychology Bulletin, 15*, 452–462.

Holtgraves, T., Srull, T. K., & Socall, D. (1989). Conversation memory: The effects of speaker status on memory for the assertiveness of conversation remarks. *Journal of Personality and Social Psychology, 56*, 149–160.

Ickes, W., Stinson, L., Bissonnette, V., & Garcia, S. (1990). Naturalistic social cognition: Empathic accuracy in mixed-sex dyads. *Journal of Personality and Social Psychology, 59*, 730–742.

Johnson, M. K., & Raye, C. L. (1981). Reality monitoring. *Psychological Review, 88*, 67–85.

Jones, E. E., & Davis, K. E. (1965). From acts to dispositions: The attributional process in person perception. In L. Berkowitz (Ed.), *Advances in experimental social psychology* (Vol. 2). New York: Academic Press.

Judd, C. M., & Park, B. (1988). Out-group homogeneity: Judgments of variability at the individual and group level. *Journal of Personality and Social Psychology, 54*, 778–788.

Kelley, H. H. (1967). Attribution theory in social psychology. *Nebraska Symposium on Motivation, 15*, 192–238.

Klein, S. B., & Loftus, J. B. (1990). Rethinking the role of organization in person memory: An independent trace storage model. *Journal of Personality and Social Psychology, 59*, 400–410.

Lambert, A. J., & Wyer, R. S. (1990). Stereotypes and social judgment: The effects of typicality and group heterogeneity. *Journal of Personality and Social Psychology, 59*, 676–691.

Lichtenstein, M., & Srull, T. K. (1987). Processing objectives as a determinant of the relationship between recall and judgment. *Journal of Experimental Social Psychology, 23*, 93–118.

Loftus, E. F., & Palmer, J. C. (1974). Reconstruction of automobile destruction: An example of the interaction between language and memory. *Journal of Verbal Learning and Verbal Behavior, 13*, 585–589.

Loken, B. A. (1984). Attitude processing strategies. *Journal of Experimental Social Psychology, 20*, 272–296.

Lombardi, W., Higgins, E. T., & Bargh, J. A. (1987). The role of consciousness in priming effects on categorization. *Personality and Social Psychology Bulletin, 13*, 411–429.

Mandler, J. (1979). Categorical and schematic organization in memory. In C. R. Puff (Ed.), *Memory organization and structure*. New York: Academic Press.

Martin, L. L. (1986). Set/reset: The use and disuse of concepts in impression formation. *Journal of Personality and Social Psychology, 51*, 493–504.

Martin, L. L., Seta, J. J., & Crelia, R. A. (1990). Assimilation and contrast as a function of people's willingness and ability to expend effort in forming an impression. *Journal of Personality and So-cial Psychology, 59*, 27–37.

McGuire, W. J. (1960). A syllogistic analysis of cognitive relationships. In M. J. Rosenberg, C. I. Hovland, W. J. McGuire, R. P. Abelson, & J. W. Brehm (Eds.), *Attitude organization and change*. New Haven, CT: Yale University Press.

McGuire, W. J., & McGuire, C. V. (1987). Content and process in the experience of self. In L. Berkowitz (Ed.), *Advances in experimental social psychology* (Vol. 20). New York: Academic Press.

McGuire, W. J., & McGuire, C. V. (1991). The content, structure and operation of thought sys-tems. In R. S. Wyer & T. K. Srull (Eds.), *Advances in social cognition: Vol. 4. The content, structure and operation of thought systems*. Hillsdale, NJ: Lawrence Erlbaum Associates.

Newtson, D. A. (1973). Attribution and the unit of perception in ongoing behavior. *Journal of Personality and Social Psychology, 28,* 28–38.

Newtson, D. A. (1976). Foundations of attribution: The perception of ongoing behavior. In J. Harvey, W. Ickes, & R. Kiss (Eds.), *New directions in attribution research* (Vol. 1). Hillsdale, NJ: Lawrence Erlbaum Associates.

Nisbett, R. E., & Ross, L. (1980). *Human inference: Strategies and shortcomings of social judgment.* Englewood Cliffs, NJ: Prentice-Hall.

Ostrom, T. M., Carpenter, S., Sedikides, C., & Li, F. (1991). *Differential processing of in-group and out-group information.* Unpublished manuscript, Ohio State University, Columbus.

Park, B., & Judd, C. M. (1990). Measures and models of perceived group variability. *Journal of Personality and Social Psychology, 59,* 173–191.

Pennington, N., & Hastie, R. (1986). Evidence evaluation in complex decision making. *Journal of Personality and Social Psychology, 51,* 141–158.

Pennington, N., & Hastie, R. (1988). Explanation-based decision making: Effects of memory structure on judgment. *Journal of Experimental Psychology: Learning, Memory and Cognition, 14,* 521–533.

Pennington, N., & Hastie, R. (1992). Explaining the evidence. Tests of the story model for juror decision making. *Journal of Personality and Social Psychology, 62,* 189–206.

Perrig, W., & Kintsch, W. (1985). Propositional and situational representations of text. *Journal of Memory and Language, 24,* 503–518.

Petty, R. E., & Cacioppo, J. T. (1986). *Communication and persuasion: Central and peripheral routes to attitude change.* New York: Springer-Verlag.

Petty, R. E., Harkins, S. G., & Williams, K. D. (1980). The effects of group diffusion of cognitive effort on attitudes: An information-processing view. *Journal of Personality and Social Psychology, 38,* 81–92.

Quattrone, G. A. (1982). Overattribution and unit formation: When behavior engulfs the person. *Journal of Personality and Social Psychology, 42,* 593–607.

Read, S., Druian, P., & Miller, L. (1985). *The role of causal sequence in the meaning of actions.* Unpublished manuscript, University of Southern California, Los Angeles.

Rholes, W. S., & Ruble, D. N. (1986). Children's impressions of other person: The effects of temporal separation of behavioral information. *Child Development, 57,* 872–878.

Ritter, H. (1990). Self-organizing maps for internal representations. *Psychological Research, 52,* 128–136.

Roediger, H. L. (1990). Implicit memory. *American Psychologist, 45,* 1043–1056.

Rosenberg, S., & Olshan, K. (1970). Evaluative and descriptive aspects in personality perception. *Journal of Personality and Social Psychology, 16,* 619–626.

Ross, M. (1989). Relation of implicit theories to the construction of personal histories. *Psychological Review, 96,* 341–357.

Rothbart, M., Evans, M., & Fulero, S. (1979). Recall for confirming events: Memory processes and the maintenance of social stereotypes. *Journal of Experimental Social Psychology, 15,* 343–355.

Rothbart, M., Fulero, S., Jensen, C., Howard, J., & Birrell, P. (1978). From individual to group impressions: Availability heuristics in stereotype formation. *Journal of Experimental Social Psychology, 14,* 237–255.

Rumelhart, D. E. (1984). Schemata and the cognitive system. In R. W. Wyer & T. K. Srull (Eds.), *Handbook of social cognition* (Vol. 1). Hillsdale, NJ: Lawrence Erlbaum Associates.

Rundus, D. (1971). Analysis of rehearsal processes in free recall. *Journal of Experimental Psychology, 89,* 63–77.

Rundus, D. (1973). Negative effects of using list items as recall cues. *Journal of Verbal Learning and Verbal Behavior, 12,* 43–50.

Schank, R. C., & Abelson, R. P. (1977). *Scripts, plans, goals and understanding.* Hillsdale, NJ: Lawrence Erlbaum Associates.

Schneider, D. J. (1991). Social cognition. *Annual Review of Psychology, 42,* 527–561.

Scott, C. K., Fuhrman, R. W., & Wyer, R. S. (1991). Information processing in close relationships. In G. J. O. Fletcher & F. D. Fincham (Eds.), *Cognition in close relationships.* Hillsdale, NJ: Lawrence Erlbaum Associates.

Sedikides, C. (1990). Effects of fortuitously activated constructed versus activated communication goals on person impressions. *Journal of Personality and Social Psychology, 58,* 397–408.

Sedikides, C., & Anderson, C. A. (in press). Causal explanations of defection: A knowledge structure approach. *Personality and Social Psychology Bulletin.*

Sedikides, C., & Skowronski, J. J. (1991). *The law of cognitive structure activation. Psychological Inquiry, 2,* 169–184.

Seta, C., & Seta, J. J. (1990). Identifying the sources of social actions: The role of source cues in person memory. *Journal of Personality and Social Psychology, 58,* 779–790.

Sherman, S. J., & Corty, E. (1984). Cognitive heuristics. In R. S. Wyer & T. K. Srull (Eds.), *Handbook of social cognition* (Vol. 1). Hillsdale, NJ: Lawrence Erlbaum Associates.

Skowronski, J. J., Carlston, D. E., & Isham, J. T. (1993). Implicit vs. explicit impression formation: The differing effects of overt labelling and covert priming on memory and impressions. *Journal of Experimental Social Psychology, 29,* 17–41.

Smith, E. R. (1984). Models of social inference processes. *Psychological Review, 91,* 392–413.

Smith, E. R. (1990a). Content and process specificity in the effects of prior experiences. In T. K. Srull & R. S. Wyer (Eds.), *Advances in social cognition: Vol. 3. Content and process specificity in the effects of prior experiences.* Hillsdale, NJ: Lawrence Erlbaum Associates.

Smith, E. R. (1990b). Reply to commentaries. In T. K. Srull & R. S. Wyer (Eds.), *Advances in social cognition: Vol. 3. Content and process specificity in the effects of prior experiences.* Hillsdale, NJ: Lawrence Erlbaum Associates.

Smith, E. R., & Zarate, M. A. (1992), Exemplar-based model of social judgment. *Psychological Review, 99,* 3–21.

Sperber, D., & Wilson, D. (1986). *Relevance: Communication and cognition.* Oxford: Basil Blackwell.

Spiro, R. J. (1977). Remembering information from text: The "state of schema" approach. In R. C. Anderson, R. J. Spiro, & W. E. Montague (Eds.), *Schooling and the acquisition of knowledge.* Hillsdale, NJ: Lawrence Erlbaum Associates.

Srull, T. K. (1981). Person memory: Some tests of associative storage and retrieval models. *Journal of Experimental Psychology: Human Learning and Memory, 7,* 440–463.

Srull, T. K., Lichtenstein, M., & Rothbart, M. (1985). Associated storage and retrieval processes in person memory. *Journal of Experimental Psychology: Learning, Memory and Cognition, 11,* 316–345.

Srull, T. K., & Wyer, R. S. (1979). The role of category accessibility in the interpretation of information about persons: Some determinants and implications. *Journal of Personality and Social Psychology, 37,* 1660–1672.

Srull, T. K., & Wyer, R. S. (1980). Category accessibility and social perception: Some implications for the study of person memory and interpersonal judgment. *Journal of Personality and Social Psychology, 38,* 841–856.

Srull, T. K., & Wyer, R. S. (1989). Person memory and judgment. *Psychological Review, 96,* 58–83.

Srull, T. K., & Wyer, R. S. (1990). Content and process specificity: Where do we go from here? In T. K. Srull & R. S. Wyer (Eds.), *Advances in social cognition: Vol. 3. Content and process specificity in the effects of prior experiences.* Hillsdale, NJ: Lawrence Erlbaum Associates.

Strack, F., & Martin, L. L. (1987). Thinking, judging and communicating: A process account of context effects in attitude surveys. In H. J. Hippler, N. Schwarz, & S. Sudman (Eds.), *Cognitive aspects of survey methodology.* New York: Springer-Verlag.

Trafimow, D., & Wyer, R. S. (1993). The cognitive representation of mundane social events. *Journal of Personality and Social Psychology, 64,* 365–376.

Trope, Y. (1986). Identification and inferential processes in dispositional attribution. *Psychological Review, 93,* 239–257.

Uleman, J. S. (1987). Consciousness and control: The case of spontaneous trait inferences. *Personality and Social Psychology Bulletin, 13,* 337–354.

Uleman, J. S. (1989). A framework for thinking intentionally about unintended thoughts. In J. S. Uleman & J. A. Bargh (Eds.), *Unintended thought.* New York: Guilford.

Watzlawick, P., Beavin, J. H., & Jackson, D. D. (1967). *Pragmatics of human communication.* New York: Norton.

Wegner, D. M., Wenzlaff, R., Kerker, R. M., & Beattie, A. E. (1981). Incrimination through innuendo: Can media questions become public answers? *Journal of Personality and Social Psychology*, *40*, 822–832.

Winter, L., Uleman, J. S., & Cunniff, C. (1985). How automatic are social judgments? *Journal of Personality and Social Psychology*, *49*, 904–917.

Wyer, R. S., & Bodenhausen, G. V. (1985). Event memory: The effects of processing objectives and time delay on memory for action sequences. *Journal of Personality and Social Psychology*, *49*, 304–316.

Wyer, R. S., Bodenhausen, G. V., & Srull, T. K. (1984). The cognitive representation of persons and groups and its effect on recall and recognition memory. *Journal of Experimental Social Psychology*, *20*, 445–469.

Wyer, R. S., & Budesheim, T. L. (1987). Person memory and judgments: The impact of information that one is told to disregard. *Journal of Personality and Social Psychology*, *53*, 14–29.

Wyer, R. S., Budesheim, T. L., & Lambert, A. J. (1990). The cognitive representation of conversations about persons. *Journal of Personality and Social Psychology*, *58*, 128–218.

Wyer, R. S., Budesheim, T. L., Lambert, A. J., & Martin, L. L. (1989). *Person memory: The priorities that govern the cognitive activities involved in person impression formation.* Unpublished manuscript, University of Illinois, Urbana-Champaign.

Wyer, R. S., Budesheim, T. L., Lambert, A. J., & Swan, S. (in press). Person memory and judgment: Pragmatic influences on impressions formed in a social context. *Journal of Personality and Social Psychology*.

Wyer, R. S., & Carlston, D. E. (1979). *Social cognition, inference and attribution.* Hillsdale, NJ: Lawrence Erlbaum Associates.

Wyer, R. S., & Collins, J. E. (1992). A theory of humor elicitation. *Psychological Review*, *99*, 663–688.

Wyer, R. S., & Gordon, S. E. (1982). The recall of information about persons and groups. *Journal of Experimental Social Psychology*, *18*, 128–164.

Wyer, R. S., & Gordon, S. E. (1984). The cognitive representation of social information. In R. S. Wyer & T. K. Srull (Eds.), *Handbook of social cognition* (Vol. 2). Hillsdale, NJ: Lawrence Erlbaum Associates.

Wyer, R. S., Gruenfeld, D. H., Lambert, A. J., & Budesheim, T. L. (1991). *Political memory: The effects of agreement and ideological inconsistency on the recall of opinion statements and overt behaviors.* Unpublished manuscript, University of Illinois, Urbana-Champaign.

Wyer, R. S., & Hartwick, J. (1980). The role of information retrieval and conditional inference processes in belief formation and change. In L. Berkowitz (Ed.), *Advances in experimental social psychology* (Vol. 13). New York: Academic Press.

Wyer, R. S., Lambert, A. J., Gruenfeld, D. H., & Budesheim, T. L. (1991). *Political memory and judgment: The effects of ideology, opinions, traits and behaviors in the evaluation of politicians.* Unpublished manuscript, University of Illinois, Champaign.

Wyer, R. S., & Martin, L. L. (1986). Person memory: The role of traits, group stereotypes and specific behaviors in the cognitive representation of persons. *Journal of Personality and Social Psychology*, *50*, 661–675.

Wyer, R. S., Shoben, E. J., Fuhrman, R. W., & Bodenhausen, G. V. (1985). Event memory: The cognitive representation of social action sequences. *Journal of Personality and Social Psychology*, *49*, 857–877.

Wyer, R. S., & Srull, T. K. (1986). Human cognition in its social context. *Psychological Review*, *93*, 322–359.

Wyer, R. S., & Srull, T. K. (1989). *Memory and cognition in its social context.* Hillsdale, NJ: Lawrence Erlbaum Associates.

Wyer, R. S., & Unverzagt, W. H. (1985). The effects of instructions to disregard information on its subsequent recall and use in making judgments. *Journal of Personality and Social Psychology*, *48*, 533–549.

Zajonc, R. B. (1968). Cognitive theories in social psychology. In G. Lindzey & E. Aronson (Eds.), *Handbook of social psychology* (2nd ed., Vol. 1). Reading, MA: Addison-Wesley.

3 Procedural Knowledge and Processing Strategies in Social Cognition

Eliot R. Smith
Purdue University

Contents

People not only know things, they know how to do things. The difference between these two types of knowledge – often termed *declarative* and *procedural* – is intuitively compelling. For example, people can often learn a fact after hearing it once. But it is less likely that someone can learn a skill from one-time instruction, without having an opportunity to engage in repeated, often laborious practice (Anderson, 1983).

If one accepts for the moment the common-sense distinction between declarative and procedural knowledge, it immediately becomes apparent that social cognition research vastly underrepresents the procedural side of things. Hundreds of studies have been performed on the content of people's declarative knowledge, their schemas, prototypes, scripts, or stereotypes. Hundreds more deal with the form and organization of declarative knowledge, testing theories involving schemas, associative networks, storage bins, or exemplars. Far fewer studies within social cognition have aimed at formulating explicit models of the way people process information, although process models have been proposed for various types of attributions and judgments (e.g., Smith, 1984; Srull, 1981).

Assumptions about process are implicit in any research, even if the overt goal is to draw conclusions about content or organization. No theory about declarative knowledge can be tested adequately without accompanying assumptions about process. Conversely, testing theories of processing requires assumptions about content (Anderson, 1976). Thus, content-oriented research that fails to make explicit assumptions about procedures is not strengthened by avoiding unnecessary (and perhaps controversial) assumptions, as many appear to believe. Instead, the research is weakened by leaving the assumptions implicit and unclear instead of explicit and open to examination, test, and challenge. My hope is that this chapter, which addresses the nature of procedural knowledge and its role within social cognition, encourages theorists and researchers to devote more thought and attention to explicit models of cognitive processes.

The chapter first covers definitional issues and several different conceptions of the interrelations of procedural and declarative knowledge. Next, it focuses on one of the central properties of procedural knowledge: the way it changes with use, often in the direction of becoming increasingly effortless and automatic. Third, the chapter discusses how people select cognitive processes for use among the many that they have available. As will be seen, a basic distinction must be made between situations in which little cognitive effort is given to the task at hand, and those in which the person is willing and able to expend considerable effort.

For the most part, the chapter discusses specific types of cognitive procedures (such as encoding processes or attributional inferences) only as examples. This chapter does not give much emphasis to specific empirical findings regarding any particular type of procedure, such as the issue of whether perceivers draw attributional inferences automatically when they learn about an actor's behaviors. Chapters in this *Handbook* by Bargh (chapter 1, Volume 1, on automaticity and the role of consciousness), Petty (chapter 2, Volume 2, on persuasion processes), Sherman (chapter 5, Volume 1, on heuristics and social inference), and Strack (chapter 6, Volume 1, response processes), among others, deal with such specifics. Instead, this chapter considers more general properties that are potentially applicable to all types of cognitive procedures regardless of their nature. In the last section, however, I briefly discuss several specific research issues to which ideas about procedural knowledge may be particularly applicable, and I outline some important future research directions.

MODELS OF PROCEDURAL
AND DECLARATIVE KNOWLEDGE

Definitions and Models

Declarative and *procedural knowledge* are not terms that directly describe aspects or systems of the mind. Instead, they have meaning within a particular theoretical model of cognitive structure and function. Existing theories span a wide range of possibilities. Some theories make this distinction in simple and direct form, whereas others entirely lack the distinction. For this reason, it is impossible to give precise definitions that are generally applicable (see Palmer & Kimchi, 1986). Roughly, one can say that within a given theory, declarative knowledge refers to the content of cognition: the nature and organization of information that an individual acquires, processes, stores in memory, and uses in judgment. Procedural knowledge represents the processes that act on declarative knowledge: the sequences of interrelated operations that transform, store, retrieve, or make inferences based on declarative knowledge. (See Ryle, 1945, and Winograd, 1975, for extensive discussion of the declarative–procedural distinction.)

The declarative–procedural distinction has many common-sense correlates, such as the distinction between knowing facts and possessing skills, between data and program in a computer analogy, and between content and process. But common sense alone cannot suffice to classify particular cognitive structures and functions as declarative or procedural, because the distinction has meaning only in the context of an overall theory. This point is underlined by logical demonstrations that different cognitive theories can mimic each other, making identical predictions about observable phenomena (Anderson, 1976; Townsend, 1972). Because empirically indistinguishable theories may draw different boundaries between content and process, the question of whether a particular cognitive function is declarative or procedural is as undecidable as the difference between such theories.

Undecidability is not a remote logical possibility, because there are several examples within social cognition. Hill, Lewicki, Czyzewska, and Schuller (1990) showed that an encounter with a person who possesses two attributes (such as long hair and nastiness) may lead a perceiver to develop a tendency to infer that other long-haired people are also nasty (see also Andersen & Cole, 1990, Experiment 3). Hill et al. described what the perceiver has learned in procedural language as an "implicit processing algorithm" or inference procedure that is applied in person perception. However, under a different theoretical model (Smith & Zárate, 1992), what is learned is assumed to be an exemplar, a cognitive representation of a person. General processes—whose operation is assumed to be unaltered by the addition of a new exemplar—may retrieve the exemplar and use its characteristics when a judgment about another individual is needed. Thus, the effect could be seen as mediated by changes in declarative, rather than procedural, knowledge.

Another example, possibly more familiar, is found in the debate between prototype and exemplar models of category representation. Some models have assumed that people abstract the average characteristics of category members and store them as declarative knowledge—a category prototype (e.g., Reed, 1972). Others account for a similar range of observations by assuming that individual category members are represented in memory, and that averages are not stored, but computed on demand by a process that operates over those mental representations (e.g., Hintzman, 1986). The same observations (e.g., that people can learn central tendencies of categories) can be accounted for by distinct models, which draw the line between declarative and procedural knowledge in fundamentally different places. Such divergent models may make predictions that are empirically indistinguishable (see Barsalou, 1990).

Thus, there is no way to conclude, apart from the details and assumptions of a particular psychological theory, that a phenomenon of interest (e.g., the effect of priming on category accessibility) is declarative or procedural. Explanations of specific empirical phenomena do not (or at least should not) stand in isolation from one another. Instead, theoretical explanations derive plausibility only as the overall models that underlie them are tested in a variety of different contexts. Of course, any realistic model is likely to say that complex phenomena depend on both declarative and procedural knowledge. Trying to clearly separate the two on the phenomenal level (as opposed to the theoretical level) is as fruitless as arguing over whether a fire depends more on the presence of fuel or on a source of ignition.

Because different classes of psychological models suggest different conceptions of procedural knowledge, I describe four basic classes of models that appear in the psychological literature: (a) flowcharts, (b) stored-program models, (c) proceduralization models, and (d) parallel distributed processing models.

Flowchart Models: Fixed Processes Operate on Changing Data

Probably the most familiar visual representation of a small-scale theoretical model in psychology is the flowchart. A series of boxes, arrows, and decision points describes processing steps that are applied to input information. A flowchart model presupposes a fixed processor that handles varying incoming data, much like an industrial machine that sits ready to process and transform raw materials that are dumped into its input hopper. The flowchart is intended to describe the relevant procedural knowledge, whereas the input information is declarative. An example is shown in Fig. 3.1.

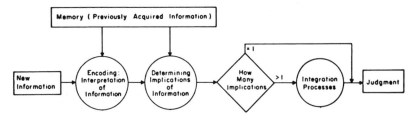

FIG. 3.1.   An example flowchart model (from Wyer & Carlston, 1979, p. 20; reprinted by permission).

Of course, a theorist who presents a flowchart model may or may not assume that processing actually is fixed and unchanging in the larger sense. Developmental changes or past experience may have led the perceiver to construct the particular information-processing path represented in the flowchart. A theorist who is unconcerned with learning or development may use a flowchart to describe a model, without intending to claim that the processing is truly hard wired or fixed in any larger context. Still, by its very nature, flowchart notation deemphasizes change in procedural knowledge and neglects the useful and important constraints on theory that can flow from considerations of development and learning (Anderson, 1987). A flowchart also ignores questions concerning the selection of procedures from a range of alternatives. A flowchart might contain internal decision points that lead processing in one or another direction depending on various conditions. But the selection of one whole process (i.e., one flowchart) versus another is not a question that is within the scope of the flowchart notation. Therefore, such questions tend to be ignored or underemphasized.

Finally, small-scale flowchart models for specific tasks are not well suited for piecing together into larger models of an overall cognitive system (Anderson, 1983; Wyer & Srull, 1989). This is because, in addition to omitting questions of procedural selection, different flowcharts often assume incommensurable processing steps and sequences. Thus, flowcharts are used appropriately by investigators who aim to understand the special-purpose processing sequence that a subject constructs to perform a given task (e.g., human factors researchers, or psychologists studying tasks like reading that are of intrinsic importance). Flowcharts are perhaps less useful when developed for tasks that are arbitrary fabrications of the laboratory, or when the researcher or theorist wishes to contribute to the formulation of an overall, broadly applicable model of cognition in a social context, rather than to understand a particular task.

Von Neumann Models: Stored Programs as Data

A more flexible conception of process draws on a different metaphor: not the industrial machine, but the digital computer. The great mathematician John von Neumann conceived the stored-program computer, in which operating instructions and data are represented identically in memory, the only distinction being the way the information is used. Earlier computers represented programs and data in distinct ways. Readers of a certain age may recall a past generation of punched-card processing machines, which were programmed by inserting wires in a plugboard, but operated on data encoded by holes in cards. In contrast, in a stored-program computer, the same information can be sequentially—or even simultaneously—program and data. Consider that as you write a program on your PC, your word-processing program treats the program text as data. You then compile it: a compiler reads the program text as data and translates it into the form of machine language code—again data. Only when these machine instructions are loaded into memory and executed do they actually direct the operations of the machine's hardware, causing it to carry out the sequence of events specified by the original program.

Of course, the infiltration of computers into everyday life means that one is unamazed by the idea that programs and data files can coexist on the same floppy disk. It also means that psychological theorists have used related ideas in their models (Gigenzerer, 1991). A prominent example is Wyer and Srull's (1980, 1989) storage bin model. In that model, "goal schemas" are retrieved from storage bins (just like any other schemas, which are declarative knowledge structures) and loaded into the "goal specification box" (1989, p. 25). A processing component of the model, the executor, then carries out in sequence each of the processing steps specified by the goal schema. This is a von Neumann architecture: The goal schema is a stored program, accessed from memory as data (declarative knowledge) and then executed as a program (procedural knowledge). Higgins (1989) similarly assumed that procedural knowledge is stored in memory in the same way as declarative knowledge, so that its use follows the same principles of accessibility. Of course, models of this sort require a basic procedural component (like Wyer and Srull's executor) corresponding to a computer's hardware instruction interpretation unit that actually carries out the instructions, using their declarative representation to govern a processing sequence.

A great advantage of stored-program models is their flexibility. A declarative representation of a program or specification of a processing sequence can be modified by experience, like other declarative knowledge representations. Moreover, these models offer a powerful and natural approach to the issue of procedural selection. If procedure-specifying information is incorporated within schemas or other declarative structures, and if the perceiver has available the machinery to select one among many schemata to match input information, then he or she simply can execute procedures attached to a matching schema. The same process that recognizes input information as an instance of a known category (e.g., a police officer) makes relevant procedural information accessible (e.g., if one is lost, ask this person for directions). In this way, the system's ability to operate flexibly on declarative knowledge can also be used to control processing. As the flowchart metaphor could not, the stored-program metaphor can spell out a way for one among many procedures to be selected and executed, depending on the content of incoming information.

There is still one aspect of inflexibility in these models, however. Like a real computer executing a stored program, or an unintelligent clerk following an office procedures manual, the sequence of operations governed by a given program are the same every time. I term this property *procedural invariance*. One might hope, however, that with experience a clerk could eventually learn an office procedure by rote and be able to execute it without referring to the manual, or would even find short cuts or time-saving innovations.

Proceduralization Models: Knowledge Changes with Use

Overturning the assumption of procedural invariance means that the boundary between declarative and procedural knowledge, and the nature of procedural knowledge itself, changes as the knowledge is used. Models with these properties are attractive for several reasons. First, they offer a straightforward account of procedural learning (Fitts, 1964). Initially, someone may learn a description of a processing sequence declaratively. The individual may carry out the process following the stored program, implying a slow, perhaps error-prone, step-by-step operation. But with practice, the process may be proceduralized, or changed into a different form that can be run more directly without repeated reference to the declarative representation of each program step. A computer scientist would speak of the difference between interpretive and compiled execution.

Second, proceduralization models may incorporate mechanisms that produce automatization of procedural knowledge as it is used. An everyday observation is that well-practiced processes become faster and more effortless, and are more likely to be performed spontaneously when appropriate situational conditions are present (Bargh, 1989; Shiffrin & Dumais, 1981). These observations contradict the assumption of procedural invariance, and thereby encourage exploration of models in which knowledge is changed by use. Prominent models involving proceduralization have been proposed by Logan (1988) and Anderson (1983, 1987).

Logan's Memory-Based Automaticity

Logan (1988) studied performance in a domain in which subjects respond to a limited number of stimuli, alphabet arithmetic problems like $E + 5 = $ _____ (the answer is J). As people begin solving these problems, they use a counting algorithm, which is evident in response time (RT) data showing that the time to respond is proportional to the size of the second addend. But with experience, they shift to a different process, where the response is quicker and independent of the problem content. Logan believed that the new process is one of memory retrieval. Solving a problem leaves a memory trace of the problem and the answer.

When the same problem reappears later in the subject's sequence of trials, it automatically triggers a memory retrieval process that goes on in parallel with the subject's algorithmic generation of the solution. If the answer can be retrieved from memory before it can be counted out, the subject can respond on that basis. Extensive experience with the domain leaves large numbers of traces of each problem, assumed to be independently stored in memory. Because the response can be made on the basis of the first memory response that is completed, having more traces (with independent, random retrieval-time distributions) means that the minimum retrieval time, and thus the response, will become faster, on the average.

Logan's (1988) model thus predicts that subjects generally respond to familiar stimuli faster than to new stimuli, because familiar stimuli allow the use of a basically different process — memory retrieval — instead of the algorithmic process that must be used for new stimuli. Logan's published work assumed that the algorithm does not change with practice, and thus that subjects would not speed up when responding to a series of new, nonrepeated stimuli. However, the possibility of algorithmic speedup with practice is not incompatible with the memory-retrieval process that Logan outlined (Logan & Klapp, 1991), and Logan assumed the absence of an algorithmic speedup more for analytic tractability than for substantive reasons (G. Logan, personal communication, November, 1991).

Anderson's Production Compilation

Describing Anderson's (1987) ACT* proceduralization model first requires introducing production systems as a notation for process. A theorist who wishes to describe a fixed and unchanging process has many types of notation to choose from, ranging from flowcharts to statements in a computer programming language. However, these notational systems impose strong interrelations and sequential dependencies into a process. Anyone who has written computer programs knows that one statement generally cannot be added or deleted without corresponding changes being made elsewhere in a program. If the problem to be solved is changed, often many parts throughout the whole program have to change. These observations point to deficiencies of standard procedural computer programming languages or their graphical equivalents, flowcharts, as notations for processes that are assumed to change over time or with experience.

Production systems seem to be a better notation for cognitive processes that are assumed to change (Anderson, 1983, 1987). Production systems are sets of productions, simple if-then or condition–action rules that become candidates for use when their conditions successfully match patterns of available information in memory. Within this basic framework, theories differ on such issues as whether all productions that match are actually applied (fired), and the nature of the conflict-resolution principles that determine what production(s) out of the matching set will be selected to fire.

The virtues of production systems as a process notation include the fact that they tend to be well-structured and homogeneous, and their component productions are relatively independent (Anderson, 1987). These features help assure that production sets generated unsystematically by learning are coherent and free of contradictions. Homogeneity allows the design of learning mechanisms that can generate new productions. Independence means that new productions can be added to the system (or old ones deleted) to change the system's behavior incrementally. These advantages have made production systems an extremely popular language for theorists to use in describing cognitive processes (e.g., Anderson, 1983; Anzai & Simon, 1979; Fox, 1980; Hunt & Lansman, 1986; Kieras & Bovair, 1986; Newell, 1973; Thibadeau, Just, & Carpenter, 1982).

Figure 3.2 shows an example simplified from Fox (1980). This production

```
Symptom rules
     IF (findings (dysphagia present))
     THEN conclude (tonsillitis suspected) and (laryngitis suspected)

     IF (findings (headache present))
     THEN conclude (meningitis suspected) and (tonsillitis suspected) and
          (laryngitis suspected)

Disease rules
     IF (tonsillitis suspected)
     THEN conclude (expect tonsillitis (pyrexia present) (vomiting absent)
          (earache present) (dysphagia present) (headache present))

     IF (laryngitis suspected)
     THEN conclude (expect laryngitis (pyrexia present) (vomiting absent)
          (earache absent) (dysphagia present) (headache present))

Question selection rules
     IF (expect <DISEASE> (<SYMPTOM> present))
     AND NOT (findings (<SYMPTOM> <VALUE>))
     THEN ASK (is <SYMPTOM> present) and conclude (findings (<SYMPTOM>
          present/absent))

     IF (expect <DISEASE1> (<SYMPTOM> present))
     AND (expect <DISEASE2> (<SYMPTOM> absent))
     AND NOT (findings (<SYMPTOM> <VALUE>))
     THEN ASK (is <SYMPTOM> present) and conclude (findings (<SYMPTOM>
          present/absent))

Diagnosis rules
     IF (tonsillitis suspected)
     AND (findings (dysphagia present))
     AND (findings (earache present))
     OR (findings (pyrexia present))
     THEN conclude (diagnosis is tonsillitis) and HALT

     IF (laryngitis suspected)
     AND (findings (dysphagia present))
     AND (findings (earache absent))
     OR (findings (pyrexia absent))
     THEN conclude (diagnosis is laryngitis) and HALT
```

FIG. 3.2.   An example of a production system model for medical diagnosis (adapted from Fox, 1980).

system models behavior in a simulated medical diagnosis situation. A patient presents an initial symptom (e.g., dysphagia [sore throat]), which suggests one or more possible diagnoses via the symptom rules. When a disease is suspected, the configuration of symptoms that would be expected from that diagnosis is deposited into working memory by the disease rules. The question selection rules, which incorporate variables in their patterns, drive the whole process. The first rule asks about a symptom that is expected under a tentative diagnosis, but whose value is currently unknown. The patient responds present or absent, and the symptom value is deposited into memory. The second rule asks specifically about a symptom that can discriminate between two different suspected diseases, but whose value is unknown. Finally, when a confirming pattern of symptom presence and absence is known, a diagnosis is produced by the diagnosis rules. Fox (1980) concluded that this production system offered a good account of humans' performance in this diagnostic task, much better than an alternative Bayesian-probability based model.

Anderson's (1987) ACT* is a prominent example of a model using production notation for procedural knowledge. Productions interact with declarative knowledge in two ways: They are activated when they match activated declarative knowledge, and when fired they can construct or activate declarative knowledge. For example, consider a production like

P1   IF the goal is to form an impression of <person A>
      and <person A> appears to pause and consider
      and then <person A> performs <action>
      THEN conclude <person A> intended to perform <action>

If the impression-formation goal is active and representations encoding the facts that "John hit Jim" and "John appeared to think before hitting Jim" exist in working memory, this production would match. Upon firing, it would deposit a new declarative representation into working memory: "John intended to hit Jim."

In ACT*, procedural knowledge changes with use by general strengthening and through processes of knowledge compilation (Anderson, 1987). First, productions are strengthened when they are used, and this means that they will be quicker to execute in the future. Specifically, the time taken for a production to match available information and fire is an inverse function of its strength (along with some other parameters, such as the complexity of its pattern). Production strengthening generates a speedup of processing that applies even when new information is handled by the strengthened productions.

Second, knowledge compilation processes restructure the sequence of processing steps the person performs, as opposed to speeding up the performance of the same steps like production strengthening. When two productions execute in sequence in the service of the same processing goal, a new production is created that combines the conditions and actions of the original components. In a future situation in which the new, larger production's conditions match, it can apply and fire more quickly than could the original two component productions. For example, assume a perceiver possessed the earlier example production P1 and also

> P2 IF the goal is to form an impression of < person A >
> and < person A > harms < person B >
> and < person A > intended the action
> THEN conclude < person A > is aggressive

P1 would match the initial two facts, resulting in the inference that John's action was intentional. Along with the original fact that "John hit Jim," this new inference now allows P2 to match and fire. The two productions have the same goal, thus a new P3 would be formed by combining their nonredundant conditions and actions:

> P3 IF the goal is to form an impression of < person A >
> and < person A > appears to pause and consider
> and < person A > harms < person B >
> THEN conclude < person A > intended to harm < person B >
> and conclude that < person A > is aggressive

In addition, each time a production is executed with specific declarative contents, a new, more specific version of the production is created (or strengthened if it already exists). Because the specific version has variable references filled in with constants, it may require fewer time-consuming references to long-term memory. Therefore, if the same declarative information is again encountered for processing, it can be handled more quickly by the new, specifically tuned production than it could be by the more general original production. For example,

> P4 IF the goal is to judge whether < behavior > is friendly
> and < behavior > has features 1, 2, and 3
> THEN conclude < behavior > is friendly

might be a general production for judging whether a behavior is friendly. If the person uses P4 to judge a particular behavior B, which possesses the features of friendliness, a new production P5 would be formed as follows:

> P5 IF the goal is to judge whether behavior B is friendly
> THEN conclude behavior B is friendly

The memory retrieval involved in the second condition of P4 has dropped out. Note that this same proceduralization process accounts neatly for the formation of the original production P4 from:

P6   IF the goal is to judge whether <behavior> fits <trait>
and <trait> has features <f1>, <f2>, <f3>
and <behavior> has features <f1>, <f2>, <f3>
THEN conclude <behavior> fits <trait>

This illustrates a general property of Anderson's (1987) proceduralization scheme. It begins with extremely general productions like the highly abstract pattern-match procedure P6, which might be considered to be innate or learned early in life. Productions that are specific to a given task domain are formed as specializations of the original domain-general productions, through experience in that domain.

Because of the effects of production strengthening and production compilation processes, Anderson's (1987) ACT* (like Logan's [1988] theory) predicts that previously encountered information can be processed more quickly than comparable new information. ACT* also predicts that practice will speed the processing of new information, through the general production-strengthening mechanism.

Summary

Models of proceduralization postulate that procedural knowledge changes as it is used. The change is of a more fundamental sort than is allowed by stored-program models, which postulate a knowledge representation that is treated as both declarative and procedural, but which does not change as it is used. Thus, proceduralization models overturn the idea that process is "general and fundamental . . . detached from any particular content," which Schneider (1991, p. 531) called a fundamental assumption of social cognition. Compelling intuitions and everyday observation, as well as research evidence, strongly suggest that procedural invariance does not characterize human information processing, and therefore point theorists toward proceduralization models—or distributed processing models, considered next.

Distributed-Processing Models: Declarative = Procedural

A final class of models eliminates the declarative–procedural distinction in a radical way. Distributed-processing models (Rumelhart & McClelland, 1986), in contrast to traditional information-processing models (e.g., Anderson, 1983; Newell & Simon, 1963), take very seriously the idea that the underlying hardware of the mind is the brain. The brain is composed of tens of billions of individual neurons. Their characteristics vary widely, but compared with modern computers' processing elements, they can be assumed to be quite slow and richly interconnected, to perform rather simple computations, and to operate in parallel. Theorists have constructed models based on general properties like these, rather than on highly specific properties of particular types of neurons, to model an amazingly broad range of behaviors such as reading, visual perception, schema application, syntactic processing, and place recognition (see Rumelhart & McClelland, 1986).

For present purposes, the most important property of distributed-processing models is that they generally maintain no distinction between declarative and procedural knowledge. For example, in the adaptive learning model of Rumelhart, Hinton, and Williams (1986), input information is presented to a distributed-processing network as a pattern of activation across a set of input elements. Activation flows through the network according to the current set of weights on the interconnections, eventually resulting in a pattern of activated output units (see Fig. 3.3). The network can learn to perform various tasks (e.g., to categorize input patterns) as connection weights are modified when its output shows errors or departures from the response deemed correct. Thus, as the weights are modified by experience, they encode both the particular stimulus inputs the network has encountered (declarative knowledge) and the processes the model will carry out on new input (procedural knowledge).

Different cognitive theories make different assumptions about the nature and interrelations of declarative and procedural knowledge. These assumptions vary widely, from the fixed process operating on a stream of input information, which is depicted by a simple flowchart, to the unified representation of distributed-processing models, which do not even make a distinction between declarative and procedural. The most fundamental dividing line among these models may

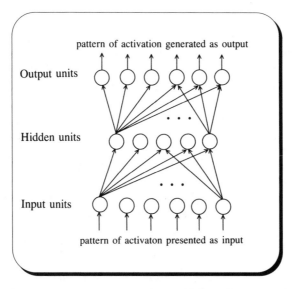

FIG. 3.3.   A parallel distributed processing model. Note: Some connections between units omitted for clarity.

be the issue of procedural invariance. Therefore, I turn next to reviewing evidence relevant to that issue.

DEVELOPMENT OF PROCEDURAL KNOWLEDGE

One key distinction among theories is the assumptions they make about the development of cognitive processes. Flowchart and stored-program models assume procedural invariance, with the limited exception that a whole program could become more or less accessible in some stored-program models. In contrast, proceduralization and distributed-processing models assume that cognitive procedures generally change as they are used. This section reviews empirical evidence on both the existence and the nature of procedural change. Do cognitive processes change as they are used? Are the changes generally toward increased efficiency and automaticity? What is known about the pattern of change that can shed light on its underlying mechanisms?

Initial Interpretive Execution

People can sometimes do something after being instructed once. That is, declarative knowledge, which is relatively easy to acquire, can guide processing. However, this type of processing is generally slow and error-prone. Speed and fluency build up over time as the person gains experience in using the skill (Fitts, 1964). Theoretically, declaratively guided processing is analogous to the computer-science concept of interpretive execution of a program. The person must be assumed to have procedures that can examine the declarative representation of the processing steps and then carry out each step in sequence. Such interpretive execution is part of several models (Anderson, 1983, 1987; Kieras & Bovair, 1986; Neves & Anderson, 1981; Wyer & Srull, 1989). Available evidence supports several conclusions about this process.

1. Declarative Interference. During interpretive execution, the declarative representation of the processing steps to be followed must be held in working memory, along with any data or temporary structures used in the processing. These demands on limited-capacity working memory mean that the process should be susceptible to interference by other simultaneous memory loads. For example, Carlson, Sullivan, and Schneider (1989) showed that a working-memory load slows judgments initially, but has no impact after a small amount of practice making the judgments. Woltz (1988) found that psychometric measures of individuals' working memory capacity correlated with their performance early in the process of skill acquisition, but not later. Anderson (1982) discussed additional research on this issue.

Moreover, interference in declarative memory should be greatest if the other information in memory is similar to the program, so that confusion could result. Singley and Anderson (1985, cited in Anderson, 1987) tested this hypothesis. Subjects learned to use a computer text editor while memorizing facts being presented to them auditorily. If these facts were a description of a different text editor, subjects' memory for them was poor at the beginning of the learning process, but improved over time (as the subjects presumably moved away from interpretive execution to a different type of processing). Memory for facts unrelated to text editing started out better and did not improve as subjects learned the editor.

2. Errors.   A major source of error in the execution of cognitive procedures is the limited capacity of working memory (Anderson, 1987). Therefore, the extra load placed on memory by interpretive execution will lead to more errors. In contrast, as people gain experience with a domain, their capacity to hold domain-related facts in memory increases (e.g., Chase & Ericsson, 1982), thus processing becomes less error-prone.

3. Speed.   Interpretive execution should be slow, because the subject has to refer to and interpret the declarative representation of the processing steps as well as carry them out. Indeed, subjects solving their first problem of a particular type are very slow, as well as error-prone (Anderson, 1982). However, things change quickly: The second problem solution is much faster, because the subject begins to switch away from interpretive execution.

4. Use of Weak Methods.   Interpretive execution depends on the use of weak methods (i.e., methods that are highly general, rather than domain-specific). Such methods include the use of analogy, means–end analysis, and hill-climbing (incremental refinement of a tentative solution by repeatedly seeking small improvements; Newell, 1969). These methods, in turn, are presumed to be innate (Anderson, 1987), or at least to be acquired early in life as an infant interacts with his or her environment. For example, someone may be able to solve a problem without a step-by-step procedure or algorithm by drawing an analogy with a similar problem or example whose solution is known. The analog would guide processing, whereas weak-method procedures would carry out steps such as mapping specific elements of the analog to the new problem. Research on skill domains like computer programming and geometry demonstrates that analogy use is extremely important to novices (Anderson, 1987).

The evidence suggests that purely interpretive execution of a given process need occur only a few times – perhaps only once – before the mode of processing begins to shift. But being able to carry out declaratively guided processing is very useful. An individual can follow instructions that reside in easily changed declarative memory, permitting the learning of novel procedures and flexibility in processing as circumstances change. In social cognition, one might consider therapeutic interventions like Beck's cognitive therapy for depression as involving declaratively guided processing (Beck, Rush, Shaw, & Emery, 1979). The individual learns from the therapist that when negative self-evaluations emerge, he or she should critically examine the underlying self-beliefs and the situational cues that lead to the negative self-evaluations. Conscious, intentional consideration of the situation may lead the individual to conclude that the initial extreme negative reaction was inappropriate. For example, one depressed individual believed that he was not accepted and liked by other people (Moretti & Shaw, 1989). He noted that the receptionist failed to greet him at work in the mornings, taking this as evidence that nobody liked him. Upon reflection, however, he was able to realize that the receptionist actually greeted few employees, and that he had never taken the initiative to greet her first. The hope is that, with practice, such realistic evaluations will eventually be generated more automatically, without intentional, controlled thought.

General Increase in Speed and Efficiency

We have seen that an initial stage of interpretive execution of cognitive procedures, with qualitatively distinct properties, yields within a few trials to a procedural stage. One of the most notable properties of cognitive processes is that they continue to increase in speed and efficiency with practice beyond that point. A seminal paper by Newell and Rosenbloom (1981) described many examples of this general truth, including such diverse tasks as proving geometry theorems, playing card games, recognizing sentences, reading inverted text, and scanning for visual targets. Some of these examples involve data from many thousands of trials. In all cases, the speedup of performance with practice seems to proceed as a power law—graphically, the time per trial plotted against number of trials of practice decreases as a straight line in log-log coordinates. The power law describes a speedup that is rapid at first, but becomes agonizingly slow with extended practice. For example, if the time decreases by a given factor over the first N trials, it will take N* (N-1) more trials to decrease by the same factor again (Newell & Rosenbloom, 1981). If it takes 100 trials to reduce the time per trial from 10 seconds to 7 seconds, 9,900 more trials will be needed to get down to 4.9 seconds.

Properties of Automaticity

Cognitive processes are often described as becoming automatic with practice. Speed or efficiency is obviously one important property of automaticity, but many others have been cited in the literature. Automatic processes are said to be unintentional, effortless, autonomous, and outside of awareness, as well as fast and efficient (Shiffrin & Dumais, 1981). However, recent theory and research have decisively overturned the idea that these intuitively related properties necessarily covary as a unified package (Bargh, 1989; Zbrodoff & Logan, 1986). For example, automatic processes are often subject to tight control, rather than being autonomous and outside of conscious control (Logan & Cowan, 1984).

All cognitive processes, including automatic ones, are conditional: They only occur when certain conditions are in place. However, processes vary in terms of the number and the commonness or scarcity of those conditions. At one extreme, some processes are stimulus-dependent. They will be triggered whenever a particular stimulus is attended to (e.g., literate adults find it impossible to avoid accessing the meaning of a word when they look at its written form). This form of automaticity was labeled *preconscious* by Bargh (1989). Of course, even these processes can be controlled, because people can control they direct spatial attention (Kahneman & Treisman, 1984). Other processes depend not only on a particular stimulus configuration, but also on the perceiver's internal state, such as intentions or processing goals (called *postconscious* and *goal-dependent automaticity* by Bargh, 1989). For example, the common motor processes that are often cited as intuitive examples of automaticity (typing, driving a car) are in reality goal-dependent, because nobody types or drives without meaning to do so.

Thus, one should not expect any sudden, qualitative transition from nonautomatic (or controlled) to automatic processing. Instead, the evidence shows that processes smoothly accumulate speed and efficiency as they are practiced. Although the other putative properties of automaticity do not always covary with speed, speed and efficiency are probably central to all of them. For example, as a process becomes more efficient and less demanding of cognitive resources, it becomes subjectively less effortful, and the individual is less likely to become aware of its occurrence. It also becomes less important to control it. If a process poses few resource demands and will not interfere with other simultaneous processing, one might as well let it run to completion.

Empirical research strategies for distinguishing automatic from nonautomatic processing generally rely heavily on the dimension of speed or efficiency. For example, Gilbert (1989) argued that certain social inferences are more automatic than others, on the grounds that an external cognitive load interferes with some inferences but not others. That is, people generally make inferences about a person's traits that correspond to observed behaviors, regardless of cognitive load. Only when sufficient capacity is available will the perceiver go further to consider whether the inference should be corrected on the basis of situational pressures that might have produced the behavior. Clearly, efficiency (in the sense of minimal resource demands) is the primary cause of this distinction. Similarly, many theorists in social cognition have postulated that inferences that are practiced enough to be highly efficient may eventually occur spontaneously (Bargh, 1984; Carlston, 1992; Smith, 1989a; Winter & Uleman, 1984; Zárate & Smith, 1990). But inferences may occur spontaneously without being fully stimulus controlled (i.e., free from goal-dependence). This will be the case for inferences that serve typical everyday goals (such as to comprehend events or to form impressions of people) that are often in place in an ecological sense.

Mechanisms of Procedural Change: General Speedup

Theoretical models of several different types predict that processing speeds up with practice. However, these models are distinguished by their divergent predictions about the generality of the speedup effect. Thus, the models can be tested competitively by research examining the transfer of practice (see Kolers & Roediger, 1984; Smith, 1990). For example, suppose someone practices a social judgment procedure, making judgments about whether 100 different behaviors imply the trait of friendliness (see Smith, 1989a; Smith, Branscombe, & Bormann, 1988). Different kinds of transfer can then be assessed. Will judging the friendliness of yet another new behavior be faster than judging the first behavior? Can the person now judge one of the previously seen behaviors faster than a new, unseen one? Will the practice on friendliness judgments speed the person on a different task like making intelligence trait judgments or even making judgments about the sounds of words? Different theoretical models differ in their predictions regarding these different types of transfer (Smith 1989a; Smith, Stewart, & Buttram, 1992).

Transfer is of interest not only for testing theoretical hypotheses, but for practical reasons as well (Singley & Anderson, 1989). In education or training, for instance, the learner will ordinarily practice a skill a limited number of times. For example, a student may solve hundreds of physics problems during a college course. The hope is that the learner's application of the skill to new, previously unseen stimuli or situations (e.g., physics problems) will be improved by the training.

Flowchart and Stored-Program Models

Flowchart models have no provision for a speedup of processing with practice at all; processing is fixed and unchanging. The situation is different with stored-program models that treat procedural knowledge as a form of declarative knowledge that can vary in accessibility (e.g., Higgins, 1989; Wyer & Srull, 1989). In these models, using a procedure makes the relevant knowledge more accessible for future use. This applies both to the procedure-specifying information (program) and to declarative information that is accessed from memory by the process. Thus, future uses of a practiced procedure should be faster. The models of Higgins (1989) and Wyer and Srull (1989) can account for a short-term increase in the accessibility of knowledge due to recent use. These models (although not the earlier Wyer & Srull model, 1980) also predict that frequent use over time can lead to a more enduring or chronic change in accessibility. Such a mechanism is necessary to account for the effects of extended practice on procedural speed and efficiency, which are known to be long lasting (e.g., Kolers, 1976).

Thus, stored-program models predict that a perceiver who has made 100 friendliness judgments on different behaviors would be able to judge the 101st more quickly than the 1st. Importantly, however, the prediction would be no different whether the 101st behavior is a new one or is a repetition of one that has already been judged. If the mechanism underlying the speedup with practice is an increase in the accessibility of procedural knowledge (i.e., knowledge about how to make trait judgments) and of declarative knowledge that is used in the judgment (i.e., knowledge about what the construct of friendliness means), a previously judged behavior would not benefit any more than a new one from the speedup. Repeated stimuli derive no special advantage from this mechanism.

Anderson's ACT* Procedural Strengthening

The production strengthening component in Anderson's (1983, 1987) ACT* model yields the same predictions. As already mentioned, ACT* productions accrue strength when they are used, and strength makes productions faster to execute in the future. Hence, production strengthening through use, like the increased accessibility of procedural information in a model like Higgins' or Wyer and Srull's, predicts a speedup of processing that is equal for all information, old or new.

There is much evidence that practice does speed up people's processing of new information. The collection of practice functions cited by Newell and Rosenbloom (1981) has already been mentioned. In the social cognition domain, people speed up as they practice making trait judgments about new behaviors (Smith, 1989a; Smith & Lerner, 1986; Smith et al., 1988, 1992). There is no detectable loss of speed over a delay of as much as 7 days, supporting the idea that practice effects are long lasting. Similar evidence comes from the demonstration by Bargh and Thein (1985) that people for whom a particular trait (such as honesty) is chronically accessible can judge behaviors as honest or dishonest more quickly than other people can. Such observations of what Smith (1989a) termed *general practice effects* can be explained either by the declarative accessibility mechanisms favored by social–cognitive theorists (Higgins, 1989; Wyer & Srull, 1989) or by the procedural-strengthening component of Anderson's model (1983, 1987; see Smith, 1984, 1989a).

Mechanisms of Procedural Change: Item-Specific Facilitation

Proceduralization and parallel distributed-processing models differ from flowcharts and stored-program models in predicting a specific advantage for previously processed information, as well as a general speedup that applies to new information. Thus, a perceiver would be predicted to respond more quickly after 100 judgment trials if the 101st behavior was one that he or she had judged previously, than if the 101st behavior was brand new. This is a *specific practice effect* (Smith, 1989a). The models of Logan (1988) and Anderson (1983, 1987) account for this effect through different mechanisms.

Logan's Memory-Retrieval Model

For Logan (1988), on the first encounter with a stimulus the perceiver must go through a processing algorithm of some sort to compute a response. The response is stored together with the stimulus information in an episodic memory trace. On a future encounter with the same stimulus, the memory trace may be retrieved and used to give a response. Multiple traces, each with its own independent retrieval-time distribution, can be stored by repeated encounters with a particular stimulus. Thus, the expected time to retrieve any one of those traces declines with the number of traces. Logan (1988) demonstrated that this mechanism predicts the well-known power law of practice (Newell & Rosenbloom, 1981). Clearly, it also predicts an advantage for previously processed stimuli over new ones: whereas a previously seen stimulus may quickly cue the retrieval of the appropriate response, a new one can be judged only by going through the (potentially slow) algorithmic process.

Anderson's ACT* Knowledge Compilation

Anderson (1983, 1987) invoked knowledge compilation processes to account for a specific speedup on previously judged stimuli. As described earlier, whenever a general production is executed with specific contents, a specific version of the production is created (or strengthened, if it already exists). The conditions of the more specific production may be simplified as specific information is filled in. Thus, the new production will be able to execute faster when the same information is encountered again later.

For proceduralization models, then, processing a particular stimulus can affect future processing in two distinct ways. It may strengthen a general production, yielding a general practice effect. It may also leave a specific trace (in the form of a stimulus–response trace in memory, or a stimulus-specific production) that can speed up a response if the same stimulus is encountered again in the future.

Parallel Distributed-Processing Models (PDP)

Distributed-processing models such as McClelland and Rumelhart (1985) and Schneider and Detweiler (1988) also predict facilitation of future processing for specific, previously encountered stimuli. In both of these models, encoded stimulus features are presented to the input units of a network, and the flow of activation through the network generates some output. The strengths of the network connections are modified by this process, so that if the same stimulus is presented again, the flow of activation more quickly and precisely matches the desired output. In these models, information about all previously processed stimuli and their associated responses is stored together in the connection weights in a single network. Because processing each stimulus changes the weights, information about older and infrequently encountered stimuli is gradually distorted and eventually lost. Thus, only recent or frequently encountered exemplars would have an advantage over new ones. (Logan's and Anderson's models make this same prediction via incorporating forgetting processes that act on stimulus–response memory traces and newly formed item-specific productions, respectively.)

This is not the place for an extensive disquisition on the relationships of PDP models to more traditional forms of cognitive models. But it appears that, despite their different conceptual bases, terminology, and treatment of the procedural-declarative distinction, Logan's, Anderson's, and these PDP models make similar predictions in this respect: Recently or frequently processed stimuli leave specific traces of some form, which facilitate the repetition of the same processing if the stimuli are encountered again (see Anderson, 1989; Carlson & Schneider, 1989).

Empirical Evidence of Item-Specific Facilitation

Is there evidence for item-specific transfer over and above the well-documented general effect of practice? Yes. Kolers (1976) found that specific pages of inverted text that subjects had read a year earlier could still be read faster than new pages, even if subjects did not recognize them as old. Mitchell and Brown (1988) had subjects name objects depicted in simple drawings, and found that previously named pictures could be named faster than new pictures – even 6 weeks after the initial presentation, and even if the picture was not recognized as having been seen previously. Sloman, Hayman, Ohta, Law, and Tulving (1988) observed that completion of fragmented words subjects had previously read was facilitated for as long as 16 months after the initial study. Subjects had initially spent an average of less than 7 seconds studying each word in a long list. Of course, recognition of the words after more than a year was extremely poor.

One might question whether two distinct theoretical mechanisms are required to explain a general practice effect plus a specific facilitation for processing of previously processed items. But Schwartz and Hashtroudi (1991) demonstrated that speeded processing of repeated items is independent of general skill learning. On some tasks in their studies, subjects processed repeated items more quickly without improving their general skill at the process. These researchers and others (e.g., McAndrews & Moscovitch, 1990) concluded that improvement of general skills and traces of specific repeated items are separate (although usually concurrent) effects of practice.

I noted earlier that the notion of a perceiver's general efficiency in making particular sorts of inferences (e.g., about honesty) is already familiar within social cognition, as chronic accessibility (Higgins, 1989; Wyer & Srull, 1989). Specific facilitation of responses to previously encountered objects has also been invoked in social cognition, for example in Fazio's (1986) model of attitude accessibility. Fazio's theoretical interpretation has much in common with Logan's (1988) instance-memory theory. The key idea is that, once a perceiver has evaluated a particular object, the evaluation may be stored in association with the mental representation of the object. If the association is strong enough, the individual may readily retrieve the evaluation when the object is encountered again. The evaluation may even come to mind spontaneously whenever the perceiver sees or thinks about the object, so that relevant behaviors will be guided by that evaluation or attitude. Fazio's claim is that only attitudes toward previously judged objects—not attitudes toward all objects—can be accessed more quickly. The effect is stimulus specific, rather than general.

In a different area of social cognition, Smith et al. (1992) demonstrated item-specific effects of previous judgments. They had subjects judge whether numerous behaviors implied a particular target trait (intelligent or friendly). Repeated behaviors were judged more quickly than new behaviors, even when 7 days elapsed between the first and second presentations. Some of the behaviors had evaluatively mixed implications for different traits—for example, some were intelligent but unfriendly; others were unintelligent but friendly. When subjects gave overall evaluations of behaviors, those that they had judged previously were rated more in line with their implications for the practiced trait. For example, a subject who had previously rated a friendly but unintelligent behavior as friendly would see it as more positive than a subject who had rated it as unintelligent. This effect occurred even when subjects did not recognize that they had previously seen the behavior, and was equally strong after just a few minutes, after 1 day, and after 7 days.

From the standpoint of a stored-program or construct-accessibility model, it might be argued that item-specific facilitation could arise from an increase in the accessibility of information about the item (e.g., a specific behavior of helping someone push his or her car out of a snowbank), as well as the procedure. Thus, the second time someone judged the friendliness of a behavior, information relevant to comprehending that behavior (e.g., information about helping and about pushing cars), as well as information about the construct of friendliness, would be more accessible. A related idea is that subjects might simply be able to read the behavior description more rapidly if they have previously read it. These suggestions would account for the finding that a repeated behavior can be judged more rapidly on its second presentation. However, they predict an equal facilitation for judgments of a repeated behavior whether it is presented the second time for the same or a different trait judgment. Smith (1989a) tested this hypothesis. Some behaviors were repeated from one block of judgment trials to the next when subjects' task had changed in the interim—for instance, from judging friendliness to judging intelligence. In contrast to the 141 millisecond facilitation of judgments when behaviors were repeated between blocks for the same trait judgment, a trivial and nonsignificant -5 msec facilitation was found for behaviors repeated for a different trait judgment. Thus, facilitation is specific to a behavior–trait pair. It cannot be accounted for in terms of separate increases in accessibility for behavior information and for trait information.

Transfer Appropriate Processing

In fact, this finding is just one illustration of a general principle. Phrased broadly, the issue is whether transfer depends on a previous encounter with a stimulus, or on what process the perceiver previously applied to the stimulus. The process is crucial, as a long line of studies, including Jacoby's (1983), makes plain. Jacoby had subjects either read target words or generate them from conceptual clues. For example, subjects might read the word *cold* or generate it from the clue *hot-*_____ (subjects knew they were to generate opposites). Later, subjects were tested over the target words with either a standard recognition test or a word-fragment completion test. Recognition performance was better for words that the subjects had generated. In contrast, subjects could better complete fragmented words (like c __ __ d) when they had read them. Many others have obtained conceptually similar results (e.g., Roediger & Blaxton, 1987, and in the social cognition domain, Smith & Branscombe, 1988). One might be tempted to assume that simply encountering a word would make its cognitive representation more accessible, so that the subject would be more likely to produce that word later in any kind of test (recognizing it or completing a word fragment). But this is not what is observed. Instead, the type of processing carried out at study determines the effect on various types of tests.

Findings like these are often interpreted using the principle of *transfer appropriate processing* (Morris, Bransford, & Franks, 1977). At study, the perceiver carries out certain processes on the target stimulus (e.g., accessing the word from visual cues in the read condition, or from conceptual cues in the generate condition). Performance on a particular test depends on the degree of overlap of the processes that were carried out at study and those required by the test (Roediger, Srinivas, & Weldon, 1989). For example, recognition performance relies more on conceptual elaboration of the target item, whereas word-fragment completion performance is more strongly facilitated by practice reading the word from visual cues. This is just another way to talk about a specific practice effect. The processes that were applied to a specific item at study are more easily repeated later when the item is re-presented.

The principle of transfer appropriate processing is a leading explanation for implicit memory phenomena, which have recently attracted much research attention (Jacoby & Kelley, 1987; Lewandowsky, Dunn, & Kirsner, 1989; Roediger et al., 1989; Schacter, 1987; Smith & Branscombe, 1988). The term *implicit memory* emphasizes that prior experience with a stimulus can influence the perceiver's judgment or behavior at a later time, without any explicit demand to retrieve and use the prior memory. Thus (in contrast to a recall or recognition test), a word-fragment completion test measures implicit memory: the subject is simply instructed to complete the fragment with an English word, rather than to fill in a word from the list that he or she studied earlier. Initial theorizing about implicit memory stressed its independence from explicit memory measures and leaned toward interpretations in terms of separate memory systems (Squire, 1986; Tulving, 1983). More recently, however, the transfer appropriate processing framework has been applied, based on observations that dissociations are empirically observed not only between explicit and implicit memory tasks, but also among implicit or explicit tasks (Roediger & Blaxton, 1987; Smith & Branscombe, 1988). The entire pattern of findings with regard to implicit memory is best explained by an emphasis on the role of processing. As laid out by Roediger et al. (1989), the fundamental principles are:

> First, we assume that memory tests benefit to the extent that the operations required at test recapitulate or overlap the encoding operations during prior learning (. . . Morris, Bransford, & Franks, 1977; Tulving & Thompson, 1973). This assumption seems relatively uncontroversial at this point.
>
> Second, we assume that explicit and implicit memory tests typically require different retrieval operations . . . and consequently will benefit from different types of processing during learning. (pp. 68–69)

By analyzing the processing demands of various explicit and implicit memory tests (ranging from word-fragment completion to lexical decision, general knowledge, or anagram tests), Roediger and his colleagues organized and interpreted a wide range of experimental results in terms of the overlap between the processes subjects carry out on specific items at study and those required by the tests.

Implications for Models of Procedural Knowledge

The results discussed in this section strongly point in the direction of proceduralization or distributed-processing models over their stored-program or flowchart competitors. Flowchart models provide no mechanisms to account for any changes with processing at all (i.e., they assume procedural invariance). Stored-program models can accommodate a general speedup with practice, by postulating that procedural knowledge (or declarative knowledge used in processing) becomes more accessible with use. However, this mechanism cannot account for the item-specific facilitation or implicit memory effects that have been found in many domains, both social and nonsocial. PDP models, along with proceduralization models like those of Anderson and Logan, incorporate mechanisms that yield item-specific facilitation.

The changes that occur as procedural knowledge is exercised and used imply that an individual's processing repertoire is not fixed for all time. A judgment that is mediated by declarative knowledge at one time may become proceduralized later. Judgments that are slow and effortful at one time may be quick and subjectively effortless later. These changes obviously have profound implications for the individual's selection of cognitive procedures.

SELECTION OF COGNITIVE PROCEDURES

From moment to moment, people select from their vast library of cognitive procedures the ones they will use to process currently available information. Conceptions of this selection process have changed dramatically over the years, particularly in response to changes in theoretical views of automaticity. For example, in the early 1980s, many assumed a clear distinction between automatic and controlled modes of information processing. Automatic processes were considered to be stimulus driven, autonomous, free of resource demands, and not dependent on the perceiver's goals. In contrast, controlled processes were thought to require resources and to be sensitive to the perceiver's goals and other aspects of internal state. Thus, the selection of cognitive processes might have been analyzed as follows: Processes are executed if they are (a) automatically triggered by currently available stimuli, or (b) chosen in a controlled way based on the perceiver's currently active goals. In this conception, automatic processes are not goal dependent.

Today, more is understood about the nature of automatic processing. It is important to note that most automatic processes are goal dependent, rather than triggered autonomously by a mere encounter with a particular stimulus (Bargh, 1989). Even autonomously triggered processes (such as, for adult readers, absorbing the semantic meaning of a visually presented word) became automatic through a lengthy course of development and practice. At many times, these past behaviors must have depended on the perceiver's past goals, such as to earn good grades in reading in elementary school or to read interesting books for pleasure (Bargh, 1990). The old distinction between goal-free automatic processes and goal-dependent controlled processes no longer makes sense.

Fortunately, a newer conceptualization of the way people select cognitive processes has emerged to replace the old. It has arisen more or less independently, but in strikingly parallel form, in diverse substantive areas of research. In the simplest sketch, the notion is as follows. Most of the time, perceivers go through life with a minimal set of default goals—to comprehend their environment, to watch out for threat or danger, to place other people into general social categories (by age, gender, or role), and the like. In the service of these goals, available information is processed to a limited extent without much conscious effort. The results of this processing determine the way people consciously experience the world, and are generally adequate to accomplish the relatively undemanding default goals. Various factors may cause people to question the adequacy of the minimal default processing. They may face a decision in which much is at stake—deciding which automobile to buy or whether to get married. Or they may become aware that they have misperceived or misinterpreted something, perhaps because others disagree with them or because they notice information that is strikingly inconsistent with their prior expectations. Conditions like these may motivate people to devote extensive thought to the issue at hand, if adequate cognitive resources (time, capacity) are available. At times, this effortful processing may correct errors that resulted from the initial, minimal processing. At other times, it may simply confirm and reinforce biases that were inherent in that processing.

Versions of the Dual-Process Model

The reader may recognize that dual-process models fitting this outline have been proposed over the past decade in many domains of social psychology and social cognition.

Attitude Change

Dual-process models have probably been most influential in the field of attitude change. Petty and Cacioppo (1981) and Chaiken (1980) proposed broadly similar models; I emphasize Chaiken's formulation, because it is more process oriented (Eagly & Chaiken, 1993). In its current form (Chaiken, Liberman, & Eagly, 1989), the model assumes that a person may have any of several goals activated in a given situation: to form a valid attitude that will be an accurate guide for thought and action, to defend a currently held attitude, or to create a positive impression on others. Whatever the goal, two types of processing are possible. *Heuristic* processing involves the use of simple, readily accessible decision rules like "experts are always right" or "the majority is correct." Heuristic processing is the default mode; people will process heuristically unless special circumstances intervene. Such circumstances are those that (a) make people feel an unusually great need to be accurate, to defend an attitude, or to create a positive impression, and (b) offer enough time and cognitive capacity to permit more effortful processing. When both of these conditions hold, people will perform *systematic* processing. Systematic processing takes place in addition to but does not replace heuristic processing. It involves the active, effortful scrutiny of all relevant information, and therefore demands considerable cognitive capacity. Many studies support the general assumptions of the heuristic/systematic processing framework in the domain of attitude change and social influence (see Eagly & Chaiken, 1993, for a review). Specific tests of some of its newer aspects, including the postulated attitude-defense and impression-enhancement goals, however, are not yet available (Chaiken et al., 1989).

Chaiken et al. (1989) briefly speculated about the applicability of their framework to social judgment in general, beyond the domain of social influence. For example, they described an imaginary social perceiver who is given information about a target person. The information includes superficial, easily processed cues (like physical attractiveness) and more complex cues (attributionally relevant covariation information) that pertain to the target's degree of sociability. They assume that the perceiver's goal is to form an accurate impression, while noting that the typical focus of the person-perception literature on accuracy may need to be supplemented with consideration of defensive and impression motives. Chaiken et al. predicted that, under ordinary conditions, the perceiver would process heuristically, responding mostly to physical attractiveness and judging that an attractive target is sociable. On the other hand, increased demands for accuracy might spur systematic processing—if capacity is available—and the covariation information might be used to make attributional judgments, which would then be given more weight in the sociability judgments. Thus, Chaiken et al. emphasized that their dual-process framework was applicable outside the domain of social influence and attitude change.

Attitude Access

Fazio (1986) proposed a dual-process model of attitude access and use. If an individual's attitude is strongly associated with the cognitive representation of an attitude object, it may be activated spontaneously upon a mere encounter with the object. Based on several experiments, Fazio argued that access to strong attitudes does not depend on the perceiver's having a particular goal beyond attending to the object. For example, access occurs even when the individual thinks the attitude object is merely a distractor in an experiment (but see Bargh, Chaiken, Govender, & Pratto, 1992, for an alternative view). An association may become strong enough to mediate spontaneous attitude access through repeated expression of the attitude or through extensive direct behavioral experience with the object. On the other hand, when an attitude is associated with an object only weakly or not at all, the individual may still form an attitude if some activated goal demands it. However, this process will be somewhat effortful, involving a search for attitude-relevant information about the object (Fazio, 1986). In either case, whether the attitude is activated quickly and spontaneously or is formed effortfully, it can bias further processing of information about the object, and may shape the individual's actions with regard to the object.

Person Perception

Most of the time, people process information about other people in an extremely superficial manner. People may categorize other people by age, gender, race, or role, but a few minutes after interacting with a shop clerk, people might be unable to answer the simplest questions about that person's appearance. The categorization as a clerk is adequate to guide behaviors directed toward the individual. On the other hand, people may process information about a prospective date, a professor in an important course, or a new next-door neighbor more extensively. Brewer (1988) and Fiske and Neuberg (1988) developed dual-process models of person perception that make slightly different distinctions between low-effort categorical processing and more effortful, individuated processing. They assumed that social categorization goes on all the time, but that more thoughtful processing of person information is triggered by some kind of motivational relevance.

For example, Neuberg and Fiske (1987) demonstrated that perceivers who receive fairly rich information about a target person may simply categorize him or her (e.g., as a former mental patient) and use the category as a basis for judging the person and forming an impression. But if the perceiver expects to interact with the target in an interdependent way, the perceiver will pay more attention to available individuating information about the target, and will use that in preference to the simple categorization.

Correspondent Inference and Attribution

In their program of research, Gilbert and his associates distinguished between less effortful and more effortful processes in the domain of person perception and inference. Consider a perceiver watching a woman who is visibly nervous. The well-known correspondence bias (e.g., Jones & Harris, 1967) means that the perceiver is likely to see the target as a dispositionally anxious person. But what if the perceiver knows that the target is in a situation that would make just about anyone anxious—for example, the target is being interviewed about her sexual fantasies? Presumably, the perceiver should realize that the anxiety might stem from this external source and should discount the dispositional inference appropriately. In a study by Gilbert, Pelham, and Krull (1988), subjects in a control condition did exactly this: They concluded that the target was less dispositionally anxious when they thought the discussion topics were sensitive and anxiety provoking than when they thought the topics were mundane. However, subjects given an extra task that drained their cognitive capacity did not discount, and rated the target as equally dispositionally anxious in both topics conditions. The failure to discount could not stem from a lack of awareness of the topics, for the subjects' extra task was to memorize these topics.

Gilbert's explanation for the results in this and related studies (Gilbert, 1989; Gilbert & Krull, 1988; Gilbert, Krull, & Pelham, 1988), follows the general lines of the other dual-process models discussed here. Minimal effort and processing resources are required to make a correspondent dispositional inference based on observed behavior. Thus, subjects can do this even if their capacity is drained or if they have little reason to think deeply about the target person. On the other hand, considering a range of possible situational causes of the behavior and appropriately discounting the initial correspondent inference requires more processing effort. This second stage is not carried out by subjects who have little cognitive capacity—or, presumably, by subjects who have little reason to devote any effort to the task, although Gilbert's research has not dealt directly with motivation.

Self-Perception and Dissonance

It is striking that current theorizing about self-perception offers a near-exact parallel to the previous models of perception of other people. As Fazio, Zanna, and Cooper (1977) initially suggested, research shows that people's behaviors can alter their self-concepts in two different ways. If the behaviors are within a latitude of acceptance—not too discrepant from the prior self-concept, or in a domain in which the self-concept is weak—then self-perception processes dominate (Bem, 1967). The most accessible behavioral information will be summarized and used to construct or change self-knowledge. For example, subjects who are instructed to make self-enhancing statements in an interview end up with elevated self-esteem. Variables like free choice make little difference; the recent self-statements are highly accessible, regardless of choice (Rhodewalt & Agustsdottir, 1986). This fits with many demonstrations that, spontaneously and without using much capacity, people make correspondent inferences about others based on their immediate observed behaviors and ignoring situational factors like a lack of choice.

On the other hand, behaviors that are outside the latitude of acceptance—that are inconsistent with strongly held self-beliefs—trigger arousal and motivate extensive processing. Of course, this state has been called cognitive dissonance (Festinger, 1957). The outcome of this processing could vary, but when other ways to deal with the inconsistency are blocked, one possible outcome is a change in the self-concept. In contrast to the results obtained within the latitude of acceptance, subjects who make highly inconsistent self-presentations experience dissonance only under conditions of free choice, and the presentations affect self-esteem only in such cases (Rhodewalt & Agustsdottir, 1986). That is, dissonance motivates extensive processing, which includes attributional thinking. As a result, this processing will discount the behavior's implications for the self-concept if it was performed under conditions of no choice, just as in Gilbert's work on the perception of others.

Social Judgment

Finally, the dual-process principle has been formulated in a relatively general way by Martin, Seta, and Crelia (1990). Their experiments focused on trait judgments about another person, but their ideas apply to many types of social judgment. Consider the effect of a priming manipulation that raises the accessibility of a trait construct that is potentially applicable to a target person. As is known, the effect of such priming is usually assimilative: The impression of the target will move closer to the primed trait (Higgins, Rholes, & Jones, 1977). In the Martin et al. work, manipulations varied the perceiver's motivation to correct for the effect of the prime and his or her ability to do so. A perceiver was assumed to be motivated when he or she was aware of the priming and realized that it might contaminate the judgment, whereas ability can be influenced by an external cognitive load or by deadlines. The results clearly indicated that people may correct (and often end up overcorrecting, leading to a contrast effect) when they have both motivation and ability, but otherwise fail to correct and end up using the primed construct.

Toward a Model of Procedural Selection

The dual-process models just discussed share obvious family resemblances. In combination, they suggest several considerations for a general theory of the selection of cognitive processes.

Default Motives

Current thinking about automaticity emphasizes the dependence of automatic, as well as nonautomatic, processes on the perceiver's purposes and goals. Thus, to know what processes people carry out as they walk around all day, one needs to know what goals they typically have in mind. Various theorists have provided lists of needs, goals, or motives (e.g., Baumeister, 1989; Erikson, 1950; Klinger, 1977). The Chaiken et al. (1989) list is useful because it is closely tied to concrete psychological processes. In broad terms, people strive to form accurate impressions of the world and other people, to defend and uphold important existing beliefs and attitudes, and to create and maintain a positive impression on other people. This list is strongly reminiscent of earlier discussions of the knowledge, value-expressive, and utilitarian functions of attitudes, in particular Katz (1960). It is also reassuring that theorists concerned with the self have come up with a similar list of three goals: self-assessment (e.g., Trope, 1983), self-consistency (e.g., Swann, 1983), and self-enhancement (e.g., Taylor & Brown, 1988; Tesser, 1988). In summary, one could say that people strive to comprehend the world, the self, and others; to defend important beliefs, attitudes, and elements of the self-concept; and to ascend in regard and esteem in others' eyes and in their own.

Default Processes

In the service of these typical or default goals, people should typically scan their environment for unexpected events (which signal potential deficiencies in their understanding of what is going on). They should watch out for counterattitudinal messages or other threats to important beliefs or attitudes, and seek to dismiss them as biased or irrelevant. They should seek to meet others' expectations and to emphasize agreement, rather than disagreement, with powerful or attractive others. In all these cases, if especially strong motivations are not brought into play—or if capacity is constrained—people would be expected to use simple, undemanding processes, like Chaiken's (1980) heuristics or simple, efficient decision rules. Examples of heuristics applicable to assessing the validity of persuasive messages include "length means strength" or "experts are always right." A simple heuristic for making judgments about other people is "use your stereotypes" (Bodenhausen & Lichtenstein, 1987). Those applicable to defending attitudes might include "people who disagree with me are ignorant or biased." Useful heuristics for creating positive impressions include "taking moderate attitudinal positions reduces disagreement" and "agreement facilitates liking" (Chaiken et al., 1989).

As Fiske and Taylor (1991) pointed out, the use of heuristics virtually is dictated by people's extremely limited processing capacity and large amount of stored knowledge. Extensive processing is expensive and must be reserved for those rare situations where it is necessary. Further, some kind of accessibility-based selection is required to limit the amount of information drawn from long-term memory and used. Far too much information is potentially relevant to any judgment (this is called the "frame problem" in cognitive science), so people must get along using what is most accessible. On the plus side, use of social knowledge is generally accurate, or at least "close enough for government work" (i.e., close enough to work within the relaxed criteria that we use in much of our everyday life; Fiske, 1993; Higgins & Bargh, 1987). Anderson and Schooler (1991) persuasively demonstrated that the human memory system is tuned quite precisely to the properties of the real world, such that the accessibility of information in memory matches the probability that the information actually will be relevant and useful.

This reasoning suggests that heuristics that are accessible for the particular perceiver are most likely to be used. However, conceptions of accessibility are underdeveloped in most dual-process models. Chaiken and others assumed a stored-program processing model like that of Higgins (1989) or Wyer and Srull (1989), in which a heuristic is a declaratively represented rule that can be made accessible by priming manipulations (Chaiken, 1987). The literature underemphasizes the role of practice in influencing procedural accessibility (perhaps better termed *efficiency* in this context). But it is known that processes often used in the past are especially likely to be evoked by a relevant goal. For example, in a study by Smith (1989a), subjects who had judged many behaviors for their friendliness or intelligence were given some behaviors to evaluate for overall desirability, after they thought the experiment was over. As previously mentioned, their judgments were particularly influenced by the behaviors' implications for the trait they had been practicing. For example, a subject who had judged the friendliness of behaviors might evaluate friendly but unintelligent behaviors relatively positively, compared to a different subject who had been judging intelligence. Because assessing behaviors in terms of their trait implications is part of a general procedure for giving an overall evaluation of the behaviors, the more practiced trait-inference procedure was invoked with a greater probability than alternative, equally applicable, but less practiced trait-inference procedures.

Another consideration is that people's cognitive resources often are limited. Efficiency resulting from practice makes a procedure quicker and less resource demanding. Thus, in a situation where time or processing resources are limited, more efficient procedures have an additional advantage over less efficient ones (Bargh & Thein, 1985; Smith, 1989b). In an on-line processing situation, such as a face-to-face conversation with another person, time is of the essence. Because more input continually becomes available and the perceiver needs to plan his or her own behaviors, an inference that is not made quickly probably will not be made at all. Even if it is made later in retrospect, it cannot influence the course of the interaction.

The effect of practice means that if a perceiver has often used an "agree with experts" heuristic to assess the validity of persuasive messages (e.g., advertisements), the process of applying this heuristic will become more efficient. It will become quicker and less demanding of resources, and applicable even when other tasks draw on cognitive capacity. It also will be more likely to win out over competing heuristics of equal potential applicability, such as "agree with similar others," when an expert who is dissimilar to the perceiver is encountered.

As already shown, practice has specific as well as general effects. Thus, judging behaviors for friendliness (or intelligence) not only tunes the perceiver to be more responsive to the practiced trait dimension in thinking about the desirability of new behaviors, but has a particularly strong impact on evaluations of previously judged behaviors. This specific effect holds up for at least a week, independent of the person's ability to recall the previous exposure to the behavior (Smith et al., 1992). Thus, a perceiver may have a characteristic way of thinking about particular types of stimuli, so that all people tend to be judged on intelligence, honesty, or sociability. But the perceiver may also have particular inferences that readily fall into place for specific stimuli (e.g., "Whenever John gets that knowing smile on his face I think about how intelligent he is"). A perceiver who invokes the expertise heuristic once or twice for a particular message—say a Michael Jordan commercial for athletic footwear—will be much more likely to follow the same processing path on future encounters with the same message.

Thus, both general patterns of processing and specific inferences about particular stimuli can become part of a perceiver's default processing, evoked by typical, everyday social motives to comprehend, defend, and ascend. By making the procedures more efficient and more easily elicited by particular stimuli, previous use of judgment procedures will influence what people do when they encounter those stimuli, or similar ones, in the future. In fact, the effects of procedural efficiency are probably greatest in this default, low-effort condition. When people are systematically processing (i.e., operating with a strong, overriding processing goal, because of some unusual motivational state), the selection of procedures will be controlled largely by their goals and available strategies. But in the absence of systematic processing, the efficiency and ease of use of cognitive procedures that are relevant to typical default goals may play the largest role in what procedures are used.

Conditions Encouraging Systematic Processing

In combination, the dual-process models reviewed earlier point to two factors that are required for systematic processing: motivation and cognitive capacity. Some of the models differentially emphasize these factors. For example, Fiske's (1993) and Brewer's (1988) person-perception models gave more attention to motivation (perhaps on the assumption that capacity will ordinarily be available in the contexts to which their models apply). Gilbert's (1989) model of person perception and inference stressed capacity, whereas the Martin et al. (1990) conceptualization placed equal emphasis on both factors. But it is clear that both capacity and motivation are required for people to engage in extensive, systematic processing.

1. Motivation. Chaiken's (1987) conceptualization is perhaps the most useful framework for thinking about motivation. Chaiken et al. (1989) provided a list of three motives, reviewed earlier: to comprehend the social world, defend strongly held beliefs and attitudes, and ascend in social esteem. In this theoretical model, it is not the presence or absence of these motives that determines whether people will engage in systematic processing, because one or more of the motives are always assumed to be active. Rather, the notion of a variable *sufficiency threshold* is invoked. For example, in many situations, a vague understanding of the social situation or of another person's character will suffice, and systematic processing is unlikely if the perceiver believes that simple heuristics will yield conclusions of adequate validity. But if more subjective confidence or certainty is required (e.g., in forming an impression of an individual with whom one will have extensive interaction), systematic processing will be invoked to increase the subjective validity of conclusions. This is the familiar logic that one would probably want to be more confident that one is making the right product choice when buying an automobile than when buying a toothbrush.

It is important to realize, however, that cognitive interpretive processes operate beneath conscious awareness. Their outputs are given and constitute the world that one phenomenally inhabits (Jacoby & Kelley, 1987). This constructive view of consciousness emphasizes the limited insight that people typically have into the cognitive and social biases that shape their perceptions (Bargh, 1989). Most of the time, people accept the notion that they see the world as it truly is, and thus they generally see little reason to put additional effort into seeking the truth.

2. Capacity. Gilbert's (1989) work on dispositional inference provided the most important empirical insights into the nature and effects of cognitive capacity limitations. In Gilbert's studies, subjects were given a wide range of secondary tasks: to remember numbers or words, to make silly faces, or to plan self-presentations. All these tasks seem to have comparable effects in limiting subjects' ability to systematically process information about situational constraints on behavior, and thus to appropriately discount an initial correspondent inference about a social target. Gilbert argued that social perception often takes place in a context of social interaction, which poses many cognitive demands on the perceiver (i.e., to plan his or her own contributions to a conversation, or to weigh the impression he or she is making on others). Thus, Gilbert suggested, in contrast to the notion implicit in Fiske's (1993) or Brewer's (1988) work, that sufficient capacity to devote systematic thought to other people often will not be available in real-life situations of social interaction.

The combination of motivation and capacity—and thus the use of systematic processing—seems to be unusual in people's everyday lives. But this statement is not intended to derogate people's success in negotiating their lives. Rather, it reflects the success of people's default cognitive processes in accomplishing their default goals to an acceptable level, without much effort, most of the time.

Nature of Systematic Processing

What processing will people carry out when motivation and capacity are present? Unfortunately, this is the situation in which the least can be said in general. The cognitive processes evoked by an activated goal depend on the nature of that goal, and on the particular strategies and subgoals that the individual possesses and uses. All of these factors will be highly variable across perceivers and situations.

For example, suppose that Jane sees Paul, someone she has never met, at a party, and finds him physically attractive. If she considers trying to get to know him better, either of two goals might be put in place: to form an accurate appraisal of his personality and typical behaviors, or to form a positively biased impression (Chaiken et al., 1989). Assuming an accuracy goal, Jane must draw on her repertoire of impression-formation strategies. She might choose to sit back and observe Paul's behavior for a while, to strike up a conversation with him or to question others who know him. If she chooses to interact, she has to decide how to behave with him. If she questions others, she has to choose questions, which might be biased toward confirming the hypothesis that Paul is likable (Klayman & Ha, 1987).

To put this informal example into a broader framework, I present three distinct stages: the activation of goals, the process of planning and elaboration of subgoals, and the choice of strategies to achieve subgoals.

1. Activation of Goals.   Characteristics of social situations may activate goals in social perceivers (Bargh, 1990; Cantor & Kihlstrom, 1989; Sorrentino & Higgins, 1986). Aspects of a situation serve as cues that activate an accessible motivational structure in a perceiver's mind. For example, an opportunity for matching one's performance against standards of excellence may activate an achievement motive in one individual, but might generate fear of failure and a desire to withdraw in another. As this example illustrates, there will be strong individual differences in the mapping between situational cues and goals (Cantor & Kihlstrom, 1989).

2. Planning.   Once a top-level goal is activated, a planning process must take place unless the goal is simple enough to be reached directly in one step. Planning has been considered in the cognitive science literature (e.g., Abelson, 1981;

Schank & Abelson, 1977), but has attracted less attention in social cognition. A plan is a hierarchical tree of subgoals, which furnishes a road map of the sequential steps or alternative pathways that can lead to the ultimate goal. For example, Anderson (1987) considered a person with the overall goal of solving a computer-programming problem by using analogy. This goal would be elaborated into a series of subgoals: Find an appropriate analog (perhaps an example in the textbook), map the parts of the solved example to the parts of the target problem, and use the mapping to produce a solution to the problem. As another example, a hill-climbing search algorithm can be represented as three subgoals: Find the largest difference between the current state and the goal, find a way to eliminate that difference, and find a way (recursively) to move from the resulting state to the goal (Anderson, 1987). The idea of planning as the construction of a hierarchy of subgoals that, in combination, accomplish the overall goal is conceptually attractive, and has had some success in various domains outside of social psychology.

In social psychology, the nature of planning so far has remained little explored. Carver and Scheier (e.g., 1981) described hierarchical relationships among social goals. For example, "be a gracious person" may be a top-level goal dominating a subgoal to "provide guests with refreshments," with lower levels of "measure coffee," "scoop into ground coffee," "move scoop," and so on down to the level of muscle movements. Wyer and Srull (1989) also provided a brief discussion of goal structures, closely related to Schank and Abelson's (1977) treatment. Unlike Carver and Scheier, Wyer and Srull considered not only the vertical hierarchical relations among goals, but also sequential dependencies (e.g., to accomplish A, do B and then C) and alternatives (to accomplish A, do either B or C). Finally, Gollwitzer (1990) characterized planning as involving a special implemental mindset. Research suggested that this mindset, which people adopt following a decision as to what goal to pursue, is characterized by a relatively narrow cognitive focus on plan-related information and by optimistic biases in the evaluation of the previously decided goal.

It is clear that social psychologists have yet to develop a full characterization of the planning process in terms of the retrieval, activation, or construction of behavioral sequences that will accomplish a given goal under various personal and situational constraints. On the other hand, perhaps this is an unrealistic goal. A school of thought has recently emerged in cognitive science (e.g., Agre & Chapman, 1990; Payton, 1990) that rejects traditional approaches to planning. Traditionally, a plan is conceived as analogous to a computer program that is first fully formulated and then passed on to an execution mechanism to be carried out step by step. The new school of thought criticizes this traditional conception, based on experience designing autonomous robots that interact with the real world. This experience shows that it is generally impossible to incorporate enough detail into a plan to make it robust against chance contingencies such as irregularities in the floor, shadows that can be misinterpreted as material objects, and so on. The new school of thought advocates a new view of a plan as a resource that the actor will use along with other knowledge that becomes available. The plan is to be interpreted, rather than directly executed, so the proper analogy is not a computer program but a recipe. A recipe generally guides the behavior of the cook, but leaves open the possibility of substituting for unavailable ingredients, leaving the stove on for a few minutes longer if the cooking appears incomplete, and so on. This revisionist view of planning has yet to have any impact on social psychology, although it is intuitively appealing. Human planning in the service of social goals seems to be opportunistic and readily revisable in the light of new information – in contrast to the fixed stages of goal choice, planning, and execution stressed by current viewpoints (e.g., Gollwitzer, 1990).

3. Strategy Use.   Finally, the perceiver may have specific behavioral or cognitive strategies available to accomplish a current goal or subgoal. Again, these have received only scattered investigation within social psychology. One example is the area of hypothesis testing, where much research was spurred by Snyder and Swann's (1978) provocative proposal that typical hypothesis-testing strategies are biased toward hypothesis confirmation. This idea proved to be an oversimplification (see Klayman & Ha, 1987, for a review). Other examples are the work by Showers and Cantor (1985) on people's strategies for handling achievement situations (see Cantor & Kihlstrom, 1989) and discussion by Linville and Clark (1989) on strategies for coping with stress.

On a first encounter with a new situation, a perceiver may run through all three of these stages: deciding which goal(s) are most important in the situation, which set of subgoals will achieve those top-level goals, and which specific strategies are available. However, the already described research on the development of cognitive processes suggests that this entire process may not be carried through in full more than once because proceduralization may occur (Anderson, 1987; Bargh, 1990; Linville & Clark, 1989). Thus, if the same situation is encountered a second time and the perceiver's default top-level goals remain the same, the perceiver may make the same choices more quickly and with less conscious deliberation than on the first occasion. In this way, the systematic processing that people devote to considering goals and strategies in novel situations turns into the kind of routinized, heuristic processing that people rely on to get them through familiar situations in an adequate and appropriate way (Siegler, 1988). The boundary between systematic and heuristic processing shifts over time: The choices that were once made consciously (when a situation was faced for the first time) become embedded and proceduralized.

Implications of the Dual-Process Model for "Bias" in Processing

It is important to resist the temptation to identify heuristic processing as biased and systematic processing as unbiased. The words *heuristic* and *systematic* may have unfortunate connotations, in that "heuristics and biases" is a well-learned association for many social psychologists, and *systematic* has synonyms like "methodical," "deliberate," and "thorough." In truth, heuristic processing may or may not lead to biased or invalid decisions; heuristics presumably are learned and reinforced in the first place because they work adequately much of the time. The defining characteristic of heuristic processing is not bias, but efficiency and minimal processing demand. Similarly, systematic processing may or may not produce biased conclusions. Sometimes systematic processing is undertaken with the goal of reaching or supporting a specific conclusion—this processing is termed *close-minded* by Chaiken et al. (1989; see also Kunda, 1990). But even when the perceiver is trying to remain open-minded and reach a valid conclusion or judgment, not all biases vanish (Fischhoff, 1982). For example, Smith and Miller (1979) found that the effect of salience on causal attributions, sometimes thought of as reflecting top-of-the-head processing or what is now called a heuristic, was completely unaffected by a blunt manipulation of how much effortful thought subjects gave to their attributional judgments. Rothbart, Dawes, and Park (1984) discussed stereotyping and sampling biases in person perception in intergroup situations, which cannot be avoided (and probably cannot even be reduced) by perceivers' efforts to be fair and unbiased. Fischhoff (1977) demonstrated that forewarning subjects about the hindsight bias and urging them to avoid being influenced by it did not reduce the effects of this bias on their judgments.

Indeed, social psychologists' propensity to conceptualize social judgments primarily in terms of bias may need to be rethought. *Bias* is an intrinsically ambiguous term, used to refer to both properties of a process (e.g., the perceiver considered evidence only on one side of an issue) and properties of an outcome or judgment (e.g., the perceiver made a correspondent dispositional inference that was unwarranted). Confusion caused by this ambiguity pervades much of the literature on social judgment from around 1977 onward, continuing to some extent today. A broader and more process-oriented conceptualization is suggested by the term *mental contamination* (Jacoby, 1991). This term describes a kind of spill-over or cross-talk among processes that are carried out simultaneously, which can occur even when only one process is consciously intended. Some examples illustrate the nature of this contamination and the important fact that it need not reflect any motivational influence. A familiar nonsocial example is the Stroop effect (Cohen, Dunbar, & McClelland, 1990). Given a word printed in colored ink, subjects are asked to name the ink color. If the word is a color name, people are quicker at their task when the word matches the ink color (e.g., "green" printed in green ink) and slower when the word mismatches ("red" printed in green). An unintended process (reading the word) co-occurs with the intended one and measurably influences the subject's response. There are many other examples. In a recent study, Melara and Nairne (1991) had subjects watch a geometric shape move to various positions on a screen and then report on its previous position. The current position of the shape affected these reports; subjects were faster when the current position matched and slower when it mismatched. In the social domain, A. Aron, E. N. Aron, Tudor, and Nelson (1991) timed subjects answering questions about whether various traits described them. On traits where the subjects' self-perceptions and their perceptions of their spouses mismatched, the responses were slow. As Aron et al. suggested, the analogy between this finding and Stroop interference implies that, in a close relationship, cognitive representations of the self and the partner are intimately linked.

The fundamental message from these examples of mental contamination is that multiple, concurrently executing processes may influence people's behavior without their awareness or intention. This can occur even when people are processing as systematically as you like. Subjects in a Stroop experiment focus their efforts on a simple task that they know perfectly well how to do: naming the color of some ink. Compared with color-naming, criteria for important social judgments are generally much fuzzier, subgoals and strategies for performing social judgments and behaviors are usually ill-structured and their adequacy debatable, and strong and conflicting motivations may be present. For these reasons, the effects of mental contamination may be widespread in social life, whether the person processes systematically or heuristically. Trying hard to be accurate is not an infallible remedy for bias and invalidity.

APPLICATIONS AND RESEARCH DIRECTIONS

Procedural Models Within Social Psychology

Several substantive areas within social cognition appear to be particularly suited to analysis in terms of the properties of cognitive procedures. Some already have been mentioned earlier in this chapter, and I review them here only briefly. I also describe a few research programs in social psychology that make particular reference to procedural knowledge.

Higgins' (1989) general model of construct accessibility may be interpretable in procedural terms (Smith & Branscombe, 1987). Higgins and Chaires (1980) had some subjects repeatedly use linguistic constructions involving "and" for a container and its contents (e.g., "jar and cherries" instead of the more natural "of"). This manipulation helped subjects solve the Duncker candle problem, which requires the insight that a box holding tacks can be viewed as a separate object. Higgins and Chaires described this study as demonstrating the priming of interrelational constructs, but Higgins (1989) interpreted the results in terms of procedural accessibility. In addition, work by Bargh and Thein (1985) showed that people can make judgments about their accessible trait constructs more rapidly than they can about other traits, implicating an efficiency dimension. Finally, Smith (1989a; Smith et al., 1992) demonstrated empirically that extensive practice making trait judgments makes people faster and more efficient at that process, for at least 7 days. Practice also tunes subjects to note the implications of a complex, ambiguous behavior for the practiced trait in preference to its implications for other traits. This also is a property of what Higgins (1989) called *trait accessibility*. In summary, it appears possible to identify trait accessibility theoretically with the efficiency of trait-inference procedures, developed through recent or frequent use of those procedures. One novel implication of this reconceptualization is that a half-hour practicing trait judgments in the laboratory has long-lasting effects on accessibility, offering a powerful methodological tool for investigating its properties.

Similarly, I also mentioned earlier that Fazio's (1986) concept of attitude accessibility may be identifiable with an item-specific procedure for accessing an evaluation given the item. On the operational level, Fazio's laboratory manipulations of repeated attitudinal expression closely resemble laboratory manipulations of practice. Theoretically, Fazio's interpretation of his results was similar to Logan's (1988) instance-memory framework, outlined earlier. Thus, as with Higgins' notion of construct accessibility, a reinterpretation of Fazio's model in procedural terms may lead to novel insights.

In addition, researchers in a few areas in social psychology have drawn on procedural notions explicitly. In the area of expertise, Pryor and Merluzzi (1985) and Borgida and DeBono (1989) discussed processing differences between experts and novices in a particular domain. In contrast to the usual treatment of expertise within social psychology as involving a greater amount or organization of knowledge (e.g., Fiske, Kinder, & Larter, 1983), Pryor and Merluzzi (1985) showed that experts and novices on dating share the same knowledge, but that experts can access it more efficiently. Similarly, Borgida and DeBono (1989) demonstrated that people who are experts versus novices with respect to a social stereotype differ in their strategies for testing hypotheses. Other researchers should follow the direction laid out by these two studies. Experts and novices can be expected to differ in procedural efficiency and strategy choice, as well as in the content of their declarative knowledge about the domain.

Judd and Downing (1990) provided fascinating results pointing to an interaction between amount of domain-relevant declarative knowledge (which they labeled expertise) and procedural efficiency produced by practice. In this experiment, subjects who were either expert or nonexpert in the domain of politics underwent a practice manipulation, repeatedly judging the ideological consistency of pairs of issue positions. This practice led to equal increases in the speed of judgments made by experts and novices. Subjects were then given a transfer task: judging the positions of specific political figures on the same set of issues. The procedural practice increased the interissue consistency of these judgments only for expert subjects, not for novices. Judd and Downing (1990) speculated that *both* procedural efficiency and a substantial base of knowledge about politics are required to generate consistent judgments concerning politicians' positions.

Finally, procedural notions have been influential in cognitive approaches to personality, particularly the work of Cantor and Kihlstrom (1989). These theorists attributed procedural as well as declarative knowledge to individuals, and discussed how individual differences in procedures (for activating goals from situational cues, for making self-inferences, or for strategically accomplishing goals) show themselves as personality traits. In a comment on Cantor and Kihlstrom's article, Linville and Clark (1989) took up this procedural focus, applying a production-system model to the domain of coping with stress. On the basis of the properties of ACT* productions, they hypothesized that an individual's use of coping strategies should be quite domain specific. For example, someone who is a defensive pessimist in the academic domain might use quite different coping strategies in social domains. Cantor and Kihlstrom (1989) described evidence for this sort of domain specificity. Observations like these strongly suggest the value of pushing further with analyses of personality based on the fundamental assumption that individuals differ in their procedural knowledge (both its content and efficiency) as well as their declarative knowledge.

Generality or Specificity of Transfer

Suppose someone performs some process on a stimulus item (reading a word, say, or interpreting a behavior as an instance of a trait). The future effects of this experience depend on what information is processed how, and where. Smith (1990) termed these three questions about transfer *content specificity, process specificity,* and *context specificity,* and provided detailed arguments regarding their interpretation. Content specificity gives insights into the generality of the cognitive representation that mediates transfer, for instance, distinguishing between one's general knowledge about a trait construct and a specific episodic memory of a person performing a behavior. If observed, process specificity implicates procedural rather than declarative knowledge in transfer, because only procedural transfer is likely to be specific to the way information is used (Anderson, 1987). Finally, context specificity indicates whether the perceiver processed the focal information in isolation, or integrated with other aspects of the surrounding situation or context. These types of specificity have particular relevance to social categorization processes, which have been studied extensively for their direct relevance to issues of stereotyping and person perception (e.g., Brewer, 1988; Fiske & Neuberg, 1988; Smith & Zárate, 1990; Zárate & Smith, 1990).

Content Specificity

Content specificity has already been discussed in some detail in the Mechanisms of Procedural Change section of this chapter. Briefly, evidence reviewed there shows that performing a process on a particular stimulus has a strong specific effect, facilitating the repetition of the same process on the same stimulus later. In addition, there is a weaker general effect: Future performance of the process on different stimuli will also benefit from this practice (Smith, 1989a). Besides these issues regarding the direct transfer of judgment processes, content specificity has important implications for categorization.

Competing models of categorization postulate that it is based on exemplars, prototypes, or rules (Nosofsky, 1986, 1987). Exemplar-based categorization means that a new stimulus is classified on the basis of its summed similarity to specific known category members (Medin & Schaffer, 1978; Nosofsky, 1987). Prototype-based categorization classifies new stimuli by comparing them to the central tendency (prototype) of the category (Reed, 1972). Rule-based categorization classifies stimuli based on simple rules applied to their attributes, without referring either to known exemplars or prototypes (Nosofsky, Clark, & Shin, 1989).

Although it is not usually considered in these terms, the question of how people categorize is equivalent to a question about content specificity of transfer. That is, suppose the person learns about a number of category exemplars (e.g., a number of Libertarians). Highly specific transfer of the procedures for categorizing those known individuals means that only new individuals who closely resemble known Libertarians will be thought to be category members (i.e., categorization will be exemplar based). On the other hand, more general transfer means that only attributes that are shared by most or all of the known exemplars will be considered. Thus, new individuals will be categorized only when they have those attributes (i.e., when they resemble the category prototype). Rule-based categorization does not fit into this framework. Instead, a categorization rule is most likely the product of a conscious hypothesis formulation and testing process, rather than the result of less analytical, more intuitive similarity judgments (see Jacoby & Kelley, 1987).

In general, research on categorization in both nonsocial domains (Anderson, 1990; Ashby & Perrin, 1988; Nosofsky, 1987; Whittlesea, 1987) and social domains (Medin, Dewey, & Murphy, 1983; Smith & Zárate, 1990) supported exemplar models of categorization. This corresponds well with the evidence reviewed earlier, that transfer from processing a particular stimulus is generally highly specific, applying best to stimuli that closely resemble (or are identical to) the original. However, a crucial qualification must be placed on these statements. Transfer and categorization performance depend on the type of processing applied to a stimulus or exemplar, not just on the objective nature of the stimulus itself.

Process Specificity

The future effect of any experience must be mediated by some type of cognitive representation of that experience. Because the cognitive representation is necessarily a function of how the experience was interpreted, its nature is a joint function of the stimulus content and the processing that was applied (e.g., Smith & Zárate, 1992; Tulving & Thompson, 1973). This principle of transfer appropriate processing already has been reviewed in this paper, and here I briefly sketch some of its implications for categorization.

If people process exemplars in different ways that result in the storage of different types of information, their patterns of categorization will differ (Malt, 1989; Medin, Altom, & Murphy, 1984; Nosofsky et al., 1989; Whittlesea, 1987). For example, under some conditions, perceivers may attend to many individuating attributes of each stimulus (e.g., individual Libertarians), forming individuated representations of each. New individuals who are similar to specific known Libertarian exemplars will then be categorized accordingly. On the other hand, sometimes people only attend to group-typical attributes of each Libertarian exemplar, ignoring all idiosyncratic attributes. They will end up with what is in effect a prototype representation, one that incorporates only typical attributes (Reed, 1972). The categorization decisions of a perceiver who possessed such a representation would be identical with those predicted by a prototype model. For example, a new individual's similarity to specific known exemplars would have no effect, but similarity to the category average would determine categorization.

Thus, if people apply different processes to information about stimulus they encounter, what they store in memory and use for later categorization judgments will change accordingly. In other words, transfer of previous experience depends on how information is processed as well as what information is objectively present.

Context Specificity

Context refers to the aspects of the stimulus situation that are strictly irrelevant to the subject's task. For example, if the person is memorizing words for a later recognition test, the location of a word on the page is an aspect of context. If someone is judging the friendliness of behaviors, the gender or hair length of the person who performs the behavior is context. As this definition makes clear, what is context and what is relevant input to the judgment depends on the nature of the process that is being performed.

The sensitivity of transfer to such aspects of context is an open question. Some research (e.g., Allen & Brooks, 1991) showed strong context sensitivity. In these studies, subjects classified drawings of fictitious animals into different categories according to a simple rule they were taught. The drawings portrayed the animals in various background scenes (e.g., forest or desert), but the backgrounds were irrelevant for categorization. When the subjects were tested later, they performed well with known animals presented against the same background with which they had been learned, and performed poorly when the backgrounds mismatched. Evidently, irrelevant aspects of the background were encoded in memory and influenced later categorization performance. Allen and Brooks argued that context should have such effects if the context and the centrally relevant aspects of the stimulus are processed together as integrated wholes. Thus, subjects might have considered the animal's pictured environment and their physical features together, because they know that real animals' characteristics are adapted to their environments.

On the basis of these results and theory, I might speculate about one type of context specificity suggested earlier. If one sees John tell an off-color joke and concludes that he is sexist, that experience will increase the probability that one will judge a repetition of the same behavior as sexist. But is the transfer limited by the context, in the form of the person who told the joke? That is, will this experience simply increase the likelihood and speed of judging John as sexist when he later repeats this behavior, even if one does not remember the earlier incident? Or will it have an equal effect if one later sees another individual perform the same behavior? To my knowledge, no research is available on this point. But to the extent that the behavior is processed in an integrative fashion with John's personal attributes, transfer should be limited and person specific. For example, if in processing the joke the perceiver thinks that John is the sort of person who would tell a joke like that, or reflects on other possibly sexist acts of his, then transfer to processing other people's jokes would become less likely. On the other hand, if the behavior is processed in isolation from information about John as a person—perhaps because John is a stranger about whom nothing is known— then the transfer should be more context-free, applying even if someone else later repeats the behavior.

The message from considering all three dimensions of transfer—content, process, and context—is that the nature of processing is fundamental. Neither content nor context automatically determines or limits the nature of transfer. Instead, the degree of content and context specificity depends on how information was processed.

Far-Flung Effects of Processing Fluency

The ease, speed, and efficiency with which a person can process a particular stimulus may affect the person's subjective experience. Any such changes, which may stem from previous practice, for example, will often be interpreted as objective properties of the stimulus. This is because interpretive and inferential processes are *preconscious,* operating below the level of conscious awareness. We therefore take their outputs as given, as reflecting the way the world is rather than the way we interpret it. For this reason, people often will misattribute their processing fluency (due to previous experience with a stimulus) as a property of the stimulus itself (Bargh, 1989; Jacoby & Kelley, 1987; Schwarz et al., 1991).

The best-known example of this misattribution process is the effect of mere exposure on liking (Bornstein, Leone, & Galley, 1987; Zajonc, 1968). People say that they like previously encountered stimuli better than new ones. But this effect is not limited to liking; it holds if subjects are asked which stimulus is physically brighter or darker, as well as which one they like better (Mandler, Nakamura, & Van Zandt, 1987). The prior exposure changes subjects' subjective experience of the stimulus, and subjects can interpret this vague feeling in different ways, depending on what question they are asked (see Jacoby & Kelley, 1987).

Jacoby, Kelley, Brown, and Jasechko (1989) provided further evidence of this misattribution process. In one study, they gave subjects a list of names of moderately famous and nonfamous people, and asked them to rate the fame of each one. The subjects had previously studied some of the nonfamous names in a list of names that they knew were all nonfamous. Under conditions where subjects could not recognize a previously seen nonfamous name as having been studied (e.g., after a delay between study and test), they were more likely to rate it as famous (Jacoby et al., 1989). The study exposure led to increased feelings of familiarity for the name, independent of the subject's ability to confidently recollect the circumstances of the prior exposure. If subjects were able to recollect the circumstances, they could have definitely concluded that the name was nonfamous. Subjects misattributed the experience of familiarity as indicating that the name was famous.

In another study (Jacoby, Allan, Collins, & Larwill, 1988), subjects listened to spoken sentences mixed with noise. Some of the sentences had been heard on a previous occasion. The previously heard sentences could be understood more readily when played through noise, but subjects did not attribute this perceptual fluency to the previous exposure. Instead, they said that the noise level was lower for some sentences (the old ones) than for others. Similarly, one might suppose that an argument that one previously has heard might be rated as more persuasive, because it can be easily comprehended and feels familiar, even (or perhaps especially) if one cannot recall the previous exposure. In fact, plausible general knowledge statements that are familiar because of prior presentations are rated subjectively as more valid than comparable novel sentences (Begg, Armour, & Kerr, 1985; Hasher, Goldstein, & Toppino, 1977). Presumably subjects misattribute the familiarity, taking it as evidence of the sentence's truth.

One more example of misattribution of processing fluency is Downing and Judd's (1990, cited in Judd, Drake, Downing, & Krosnick, 1991) work in the attitude domain. Subjects practiced expressing their attitudes toward particular objects and, as a result, became faster in accessing their attitudes. When the subjects later rated their attitudes toward the objects on a continuous scale, the ratings for the practiced objects were more extreme. (Powell & Fazio, 1984, obtained null results in a similar paradigm, but that study may have suffered from low power.) Presumably, subjects who notice that they are evaluating an object particularly quickly may misattribute that processing fluency, reasoning that it reflects confidence or extremity of their evaluation.

In all of these cases, effects of a prior exposure on subjects' subjective reactions to a stimulus are misattributed, mistakenly ascribed to objective qualities of the stimulus rather than to the subject's history of exposure. Of course, such misattribution is more likely under circumstances where the subject cannot consciously recognize the occasion of prior exposure. Thus, procedural efficiency caused by previous exposures can have effects beyond making the process more probable and more likely to be carried out even in the presence of competing resource demands. Efficiency can influence many types of social (and nonsocial) judgment by a process of misattribution, because people conclude that familiar stimuli are more likable, clearer, stronger, brighter, or different in other ways from less familiar stimuli. Misattribution is particularly probable because, as seen repeatedly in this chapter, the effects of procedural knowledge on people's thought, feelings, and actions can exist independent of people's ability to consciously recollect the past experiences that led to the development of the procedural knowledge.

SUMMARY AND CONCLUSIONS

The procedural knowledge that underlies human social behavior is important and worthy of study in its own right. But considering cognitive procedures is essential for generating theoretical predictions, even if a particular theorist's primary interest is in the content or organization of declarative knowledge. Despite their different properties—for instance, in ease of acquisition, accessibility to consciousness and verbal reportability—declarative and procedural knowledge must operate together to generate any overt behavior. Thus, it is important for theorists to understand that no model of declarative knowledge organization or content can be well formulated or testable without a procedural component, and vice versa. Yet procedural and declarative knowledge are often found to be influenced independently by events. That is, a past experience may leave detectable traces in a person's patterns of skill and performance, without any conscious recollection of the past experience being accessible (Jacoby et al., 1989; Smith et al., 1992).

Perhaps the most characteristic property of procedural knowledge is that it changes with use. Practice leads to an overall increase of speed and efficiency. Even this simple observation falsifies flowchart models that predict absolute procedural invariance. This general speedup can be interpreted in terms of stored-program (accessibility) models, which are familiar within social cognition (e.g., Higgins, 1989; Wyer & Srull, 1989) as well as by proceduralization or PDP models. But there are also item-specific effects of practice. I have argued that these are compatible only with proceduralization and PDP models. The increase in procedural efficiency produced by practice makes a previously used procedure more likely to be applied again in the future, particularly when the same stimulus is encountered.

The relative efficiency of alternative procedures can affect the perceiver's thoughts, feelings, and behaviors by influencing how the person processes available information. Thus, it can influence the content of social judgment (Smith et al., 1992). Efficiency presumably will have its greatest impact on procedural selection when (a) time and resources are limited, or (b) the perceiver is unmotivated to go beyond simple default or heuristic processing. These conditions describe most people most of the time, according to the dual-process models that are increasingly popular in various areas of social cognition. When people are willing and able, they use more effortful or systematic processing. Under these conditions, procedural efficiency may not be the main determinant of their judgments and behaviors. But changes in procedural efficiency may still be a consequence of systematic processing, which constitutes practice for goal-selection, planning, strategy-selection, and strategy-use procedures. The practice, in turn, will make the repetition of the same processes less effortful in a future situation (Bargh, 1989).

The properties of procedural knowledge have implications for every area in social cognition. Changes in procedural knowledge may be implicated in such phenomena as Higgins' (1989) or Wyer and Srull's (1989) procedural accessibility and Fazio's (1986) attitude accessibility, although these usually are discussed using different theoretical language. Procedural knowledge may also have a major impact in other, more novel research domains: implicit memory, categorization, and effects of the misattribution of procedural fluency. As researchers continue to explore these and other areas, they should do so with a view to the dynamic interplay of procedural with declarative knowledge.

ACKNOWLEDGMENTS

Preparation of this chapter was facilitated by National Science Foundation grant BNS-9020807 and National Institutes of Mental Health grant 1R01-MH46840. The author is grateful to John Bargh, Donal Carlston, John Kihlstrom, and Robert Wyer for their comments on an earlier version.

REFERENCES

Abelson, R. P. (1981). The psychological status of the script concept. *American Psychologist, 37,* 715–729.

Agre, P. E., & Chapman, D. (1990). What are plans for? In P. Maes (Ed.), *Designing autonomous agents* (pp. 17–34). Cambridge, MA: MIT Press.

Allen, S. W., & Brooks, L. R. (1991). Specializing the operation of an explicit rule. *Journal of Experimental Psychology: General, 120,* 3–19.

Andersen, S. M., & Cole, S. W. (1990). "Do I know you?" The role of significant others in general social perception. *Journal of Personality and Social Psychology, 59,* 384–399.

Anderson, J. R. (1976). *Language, memory, and thought.* Hillsdale, NJ: Lawrence Erlbaum Associates.

Anderson, J. R. (1982). Acquisition of cognitive skill. *Psychological Review, 89,* 369–406.

Anderson, J. R. (1983). *The architecture of cognition.* Cambridge, MA: Harvard University Press.

Anderson, J. R. (1987). Skill acquisition: Compilation of weak-method problem solutions. *Psychological Review, 94,* 192–210.

Anderson, J. R. (1989). Practice, working memory, and the ACT* theory of skill acquisition: A comment on Carlson, Sullivan, and Schneider (1989). *Journal of Experimental Psychology: Learning, Memory, and Cognition, 15,* 527–530.

Anderson, J. R. (1990). *The adaptive character of thought.* Hillsdale, NJ: Lawrence Erlbaum Associates.

Anderson, J. R., & Schooler, L. (1991). Reflections of the environment in memory. *Psychological Science, 2,* 396–408.

Anzai, Y., & Simon, H. A. (1979). The theory of learning by doing. *Psychological Review, 86,* 124–140.

Aron, A., Aron, E. N., Tudor, M., & Nelson, G. (1991). Close relationships as including other in the self. *Journal of Personality and Social Psychology, 60,* 241–253.

Ashby, F. G., & Perrin, N. A. (1988). Toward a unified theory of similarity and recognition. *Psychological Review, 95,* 124–150.

Bargh, J. A. (1984). Automatic and conscious processing of social information. In R. S. Wyer & T. K. Srull (Eds.), *Handbook of social cognition* (Vol. 3, pp. 1–44). Hillsdale, NJ: Lawrence Erlbaum Associates.

Bargh, J. A. (1989). Conditional automaticity: Varieties of automatic influence in social perception and cognition. In J. S. Uleman & J. A. Bargh (Eds.), *Unintended thought* (pp. 3–51). New York: Guilford.

Bargh, J. A. (1990). Auto-motives: Preconscious determinants of social interaction. In E. T. Higgins & R. M. Sorrentino (Eds.), *Handbook of motivation and cognition* (Vol. 2, pp. 93–130). New York: Guilford.

Bargh, J. A., Chaiken, S., Govender, R., & Pratto, F. (1992). The generality of the automatic attitude activation effect. *Journal of Personality and Social Psychology, 62,* 893–912.

Bargh, J. A., & Thein, R. D. (1985). Individual construct accessibility, person memory, and the recall–judgment link: The case of information overload. *Journal of Personality and Social Psychology, 49,* 1129–1146.

Barsalou, L. W. (1990). On the indistinguishability of exemplar memory and abstraction in category representation. In T. K. Srull & R. S. Wyer (Eds.), *Advances in social cognition* (Vol. 3, pp. 61–88). Hillsdale, NJ: Lawrence Erlbaum Associates.

Baumeister, R. F. (1989). Social intelligence and the construction of meaning in life. In R. S. Wyer & T. K. Srull (Eds.), *Advances in social cognition* (Vol. 2, pp. 71–80). Hillsdale, NJ: Lawrence Erlbaum Associates.

Beck, A. T., Rush, A. J., Shaw, B. F., & Emery, G. (1979). *Cognitive therapy of depression.* New York: Guilford.

Begg, I., Armour, V., & Kerr, T. (1985). On believing what we remember. *Canadian Journal of Behavioral Science, 17,* 199–214.

Bem, D. J. (1967). Self-perception: An alternative interpretation of cognitive dissonance phenomena. *Psychological Review, 24,* 183–200.

Bodenhausen, G. V., & Lichtenstein, M. (1987). Social stereotypes and information-processing strategies: The impact of task complexity. *Journal of Personality and Social Psychology, 52,* 871–880.

Borgida, E., & DeBono, K. G. (1989). Social hypothesis testing and the role of expertise. *Personality and Social Psychology Bulletin, 15,* 212–221.

Bornstein, R. F., Leone, D. R., & Galley, D. J. (1987). The generalizability of subliminal mere exposure effects: Influence of stimuli perceived without awareness on social behavior. *Journal of Personality and Social Psychology, 53,* 1070–1079.

Brewer, M. B. (1988). A dual process model of impression formation. In R. S. Wyer & T. K. Srull (Eds.), *Advances in social cognition* (Vol. 1, pp. 1–36). Hillsdale, NJ: Lawrence Erlbaum Associates.

Cantor, N., & Kihlstrom, J. F. (1989). Social intelligence and cognitive assessments of personality. In R. S. Wyer & T. K. Srull (Eds.), *Advances in social cognition* (Vol. 2, pp. 1–60). Hillsdale, NJ: Lawrence Erlbaum Associates.

Carlson, R. A., & Schneider, W. (1989). Practice effects and composition: A reply to Anderson. *Journal of Experimental Psychology: Learning, Memory, and Cognition, 15,* 531–533.

Carlson, R. A., Sullivan, M. A., & Schneider, W. (1989). Practice and working memory effects in building procedural skill. *Journal of Experimental Psychology: Learning, Memory, and Cognition, 15,* 517–526.

Carlston, D. E. (1992). Impression formation and the mind: The associated systems theory. In L. Martin & A. Tesser (Eds.), *Construction of social judgment.* Hillsdale, NJ: Lawrence Erlbaum Associates.

Carver, C. S., & Scheier, M. F. (1981). *Attention and self-regulation: A control-theory approach to human behavior.* New York: Springer-Verlag.

Chaiken, S. (1980). Heuristic versus systematic information processing and the use of source versus message cues in persuasion. *Journal of Personality and Social Psychology, 39,* 752–766.

Chaiken, S. (1987). The heuristic model of persuasion. In M. P. Zanna, J. M. Olson, & C. P. Herman (Eds.), *Social influence: The Ontario Symposium* (Vol. 5, pp. 3–39). Hillsdale, NJ: Lawrence Erlbaum Associates.

Chaiken, S., Liberman, A., & Eagly, A. H. (1989). Heuristic and systematic information processing within and beyond the persuasion context. In J. S. Uleman & J. A. Bargh (Eds.), *Unintended thought* (pp. 212–252). New York: Guilford.

Chase, W. G., & Ericsson, K. A. (1982). Skill and working memory. In G. H. Bower (Ed.), *The psychology of learning and motivation* (Vol. 16). New York: Academic Press.

Cohen, J. D., Dunbar, K., & McClelland, J. L. (1990). On the control of automatic processes: A parallel distributed processing account of the Stroop effect. *Psychological Review, 97,* 332–361.

Eagly, A. H., & Chaiken, S. (1993). *The psychology of attitudes.* Fort Worth, TX: Harcourt Brace Jovanovich.

Erikson, E. H. (1950). *Childhood and society.* New York: Norton.

Fazio, R. H. (1986). How do attitudes guide behavior? In R. M. Sorrentino & E. T. Higgins (Eds.), *Handbook of motivation and cognition* (pp. 204–243). New York: Guilford.

Fazio, R. H., Zanna, M. P., & Cooper, J. (1977). Dissonance and self-perception: An integrative view of each theory's proper domain of application. *Journal of Experimental Social Psychology, 13,* 464–479.

Festinger, L. (1957). *A theory of cognitive dissonance.* Evanston, IL: Row-Peterson.

Fischhoff, B. (1977). Perceived informativeness of facts. *Journal of Experimental Psychology: Human Perception and Performance, 3,* 349–358.

Fischhoff, B. (1982). Debiasing. In D. Kahneman, P. Slovic, & A. Tversky (Eds.), *Judgment under uncertainty: Heuristics and biases* (pp. 422–444). Cambridge: Cambridge University Press.

Fiske, S. T. (1993). Social cognition and social perception. *Annual Review of Psychology, 44,* 155–194.

Fiske, S. T., Kinder, D. R., & Larter, W. M. (1983). The novice and the expert: Knowledge-based strategies in political cognition. *Journal of Experimental Social Psychology, 19,* 381–400.

Fiske, S. T., & Neuberg, S. L. (1988). A continuum model of impression formation: From category-based to individuating processes as a function of information, motivation, and attention. *Advances in Experimental Social Psychology, 23,* 1–108.

Fiske, S. T., & Taylor, S. E. (1991). *Social cognition* (2nd ed.). New York: McGraw-Hill.

Fitts, P. (1964). Perceptual-motor skill learning. In A. W. Melton (Ed.), *Categories of human learning* (pp. 243–285). New York: Academic Press.

Fox, J. (1980). Making decisions under the influence of memory. *Psychological Review, 87,* 190–211.

Gigenzerer, G. (1991). From tools to theories: A heuristic of discovery in cognitive psychology. *Psychological Review, 98,* 254–267.

Gilbert, D. T. (1989). Thinking lightly about others: Automatic components of the social inference process. In J. S. Uleman & J. A. Bargh (Eds.), *Unintended thought* (pp. 189–211). New York: Guilford.

Gilbert, D. T., & Krull, D. S. (1988). Seeing less and knowing more: The benefits of perceptual ignorance. *Journal of Personality and Social Psychology, 54,* 193–202.

Gilbert, D. T., Krull, D. S., & Pelham, B. W. (1988). Of thoughts unspoken: Social inference and the self-regulation of behavior. *Journal of Personality and Social Psychology, 55,* 685–694.

Gilbert, D. T., Pelham, B. W., & Krull, D. S. (1988). On cognitive busyness: When person perceivers meet persons perceived. *Journal of Personality and Social Psychology, 54,* 733–740.

Gollwitzer, P. M. (1990). Action phases and mind-sets. In E. T. Higgins & R. M. Sorrentino (Eds.), *Handbook of motivation and cognition* (Vol. 2, pp. 53–92). New York: Guilford.

Hasher, L., Goldstein, D., & Toppino, T. (1977). Frequency and the conference of referential validity. *Journal of Verbal Learning and Verbal Behavior, 16*, 107–112.

Higgins, E. T. (1989). Knowledge accessibility and activation: Subjectivity and suffering from unconscious sources. In J. S. Uleman & J. A. Bargh (Eds.), *Unintended thought* (pp. 75–123). New York: Guilford.

Higgins, E. T., & Bargh, J. A. (1987). Social perception and social cognition. *Annual Review of Psychology, 38*, 369–425.

Higgins, E. T., & Chaires, W. M. (1980). Accessibility of interrelational constructs: Implications for stimulus encoding and creativity. *Journal of Experimental Social Psychology, 16*, 348–361.

Higgins, E. T., Rholes, W. S., & Jones, C. R. (1977). Category accessibility and impression formation. *Journal of Experimental Social Psychology, 13*, 141–154.

Hill, T., Lewicki, P., Czyzewska, M., & Schuller, G. (1990). The role of learned inferential encoding rules in the perception of faces: Effects of nonconscious self-perpetuation of a bias. *Journal of Experimental Social Psychology, 26*, 350–371.

Hintzman, D. L. (1986). "Schema abstraction" in a multiple-trace memory model. *Psychological Review, 93*, 411–428.

Hunt, E., & Lansman, M. (1986). Unified model of attention and problem solving. *Psychological Review, 93*, 446–461.

Jacoby, L. L. (1983). Perceptual enhancement: Persistent effects of an experience. *Journal of Experimental Psychology: Learning, Memory, and Cognition, 9*, 21–38.

Jacoby, L. L. (1991, October). *Measuring mental contamination (unconscious influences): Process dissociations.* Talk presented at annual meeting of Society of Experimental Social Psychology, Columbus, Ohio.

Jacoby, L. L., Allan, L. G., Collins, J. C., & Larwill, L. K. (1988). Memory influences subjective experience: Noise judgments. *Journal of Experimental Psychology: Learning, Memory, and Cognition, 14*, 240–247.

Jacoby, L. L., & Kelley, C. M. (1987). Unconscious influences of memory for a prior event. *Personality and Social Psychology Bulletin, 13*, 314–336.

Jacoby, L. L., Kelley, C. M., Brown, J., & Jasechko, J. (1989). Becoming famous overnight: Limits on the ability to avoid unconscious influences of the past. *Journal of Personality and Social Psychology, 56*, 326–338.

Jones, E. E., & Harris, V. A. (1967). The attribution of attitudes. *Journal of Experimental Social Psychology, 3*, 1–24.

Judd, C. M., & Downing, J. W. (1990). Political expertise and development of attitude consistency. *Social Cognition, 8*, 104–124.

Judd, C. M., Drake, R. A., Downing, J. W., & Krosnick, J. A. (1991). Some dynamic properties of attitude structures: Context-induced response facilitation and polarization. *Journal of Personality and Social Psychology, 60*, 193–202.

Kahneman, D., & Treisman, A. (1984). Changing views of attention and automaticity. In R. Parasuraman & D. R. Davies (Eds.), *Varieties of attention* (pp. 29–61). New York: Academic Press.

Katz, D. (1960). The functional approach to the study of attitudes. *Public Opinion Quarterly, 24*, 163–204.

Kieras, D. E., & Bovair, S. (1986). The acquisition of procedures from text: A production-system analysis of transfer of training. *Journal of Memory and Language, 25*, 507–524.

Klayman, J., & Ha, Y. (1987). Confirmation, disconfirmation, and information in hypothesis testing. *Psychological Review, 94*, 211–228.

Klinger, E. (1977). *Meaning and void: Inner experience and the incentives in people's lives.* Minneapolis: University of Minnesota Press.

Kolers, P. A. (1976). Reading a year later. *Journal of Experimental Psychology: Human Learning and Memory, 2*, 554–565.

Kolers, P. A., & Roediger, H. L. (1984). Procedures of mind. *Journal of Verbal Learning and Verbal Behavior, 23*, 425–449.

Kunda, Z. (1990). The case for motivated reasoning. *Psychological Bulletin, 108*, 480–498.

Lewandowsky, S., Dunn, J. C., & Kirsner, K. (1989). *Implicit memory: Theoretical issues.* Hillsdale, NJ: Lawrence Erlbaum Associates.

Linville, P. W., & Clark L. F. (1989). Production systems and social problem solving: Specificity, flexibility, and expertise. In R. S. Wyer & T. K. Srull (Eds.), *Advances in social cognition* (Vol. 2, pp. 131–152). Hillsdale, NJ: Lawrence Erlbaum Associates.

Logan, G. D. (1988). Toward an instance theory of automatization. *Psychological Review, 95*, 492–527.

Logan, G. D., & Cowan, W. B. (1984). On the ability to inhibit thought and action: A theory of an act of control. *Psychological Review, 91*, 295–327.

Logan, G. D., & Klapp, S. T. (1991). Automatizing alphabet arithmetic: I. Is extended practice necessary to produce automaticity? *Journal of Experimental Psychology: Learning, Memory, and Cognition, 17*, 179–195.

Malt, B. C. (1989). An on-line investigation of prototype and exemplar strategies in classification. *Journal of Experimental Psychology: Learning, Memory, and Cognition, 15*, 539–555.

Mandler, G., Nakamura, Y., & Van Zandt, B. J. S. (1987). Nonspecific effects of exposure on stimuli that cannot be recognized. *Journal of Experimental Psychology: Learning, Memory, and Cognition, 13*, 646–648.

Martin, L. L., Seta, J. J., & Crelia, R. A. (1990). Assimilation and contrast as a function of people's willingness and ability to expend effort in forming an impression. *Journal of Personality and Social Psychology, 59*, 27–37.

McAndrews, M. P., & Moscovitch, M. (1990). Transfer effects in implicit tests of memory. *Journal of Experimental Psychology: Learning, Memory, and Cognition, 16*, 772–788.

McClelland, J. L., & Rumelhart, D. E. (1985). Distributed memory and the representation of general and specific information. *Journal of Experimental Psychology: General, 114*, 159–188.

Medin, D. L., Altom, M. W., & Murphy, T. D. (1984). Given versus induced category representations: Use of prototype and exemplar information in classification. *Journal of Experimental Psychology: Learning, Memory, and Cognition, 10*, 333–352.

Medin, D. L., Dewey, G. I., & Murphy, T. D. (1983). Relationships between item and category learning: Evidence that abstraction is not automatic. *Journal of Experimental Psychology: Learning, Memory, and Cognition, 9*, 607–625.

Medin, D. L., & Schaffer, M. M. (1978). Context theory of classification learning. *Psychological Review, 85*, 207–238.

Melara, R. D., & Nairne, J. S. (1991). On the nature of interactions between the past and the present. *Journal of Experimental Psychology: Learning, Memory, and Cognition, 17*, 1124–1135.

Mitchell, D. B., & Brown, A. S. (1988). Persistent repetition priming in picture naming and its dissociation from recognition memory. *Journal of Experimental Psychology: Learning, Memory, and Cognition, 14*, 213–222.

Moretti, M. M., & Shaw, B. F. (1989). Automatic dysfunctional cognitive processes in depression. In J. S. Uleman & J. A. Bargh (Eds.), *Unintended thought* (pp. 383–424). New York: Guilford.

Morris, C. D., Bransford, J. D., & Franks, J. J. (1977). Levels of processing versus transfer appropriate processing. *Journal of Verbal Learning and Verbal Behavior, 16*, 519–533.

Neuberg, S., & Fiske, S. T. (1987). Motivational influences on impression formation: Outcome dependency, accuracy-driven attention, and individuating processes. *Journal of Personality and Social Psychology, 53*, 431–444.

Neves, D. M., & Anderson, J. R. (1981). Knowledge compilation : Mechanisms for the automatization of cognitive skills. In J. R. Anderson (Ed.), *Cognitive skills and their acquisition* (pp. 57–84). Hillsdale, NJ: Lawrence Erlbaum Associates.

Newell, A. W. (1969). Heuristic programming: Ill-structured problems. In J. Aronofsky (Ed.), *Progress in operations research* (Vol. 3, pp. 361–414). New York: Wiley.

Newell, A. W. (1973). Production systems: Models of control structures. In W. G. Chase (Ed.), *Visual information processing* (pp. 463–526). New York: Academic Press.

Newell, A. W., & Rosenbloom, P. S. (1981). Mechanisms of skill acquisition and the law of practice. In J. R. Anderson (Ed.), *Cognitive skills and their acquisition* (pp. 1–56). Hillsdale, NJ: Lawrence Erlbaum Associates.

Newell, A. W., & Simon, H. A. (1963). GPS, a program that stimulates human thought. In E. A. Feigenbaum & J. Feldman (Eds.), *Computers and thought* (pp. 279–293). New York: McGraw-Hill.

Nosofsky, R. M. (1986). Attention, similarity, and the identification–categorization relationship. *Journal of Experimental Psychology: General, 115,* 39–57.

Nosofsky, R. M. (1987). Attention and learning processes in the identification and categorization of integral stimuli. *Journal of Experimental Psychology: Learning, Memory, and Cognition, 13,* 87–108.

Nosofsky, R. M., Clark, S. E., & Shin, H. J. (1989). Rules and exemplars in categorization, identification, and recognition. *Journal of Experimental Psychology: Learning, Memory, and Cognition, 15,* 282–304.

Palmer, S. E., & Kimchi, R. (1986). The information processing approach to cognition. In T. J. Knapp & L. C. Robertson (Eds.), *Approaches to cognition* (pp. 37–77). Hillsdale, NJ: Lawrence Erlbaum Associates.

Payton, D. W. (1990). Internalized plans: A representation for action resources. In P. Maes (Ed.), *Designing autonomous agents* (pp. 89–103). Cambridge, MA: MIT Press.

Petty, R. E., & Cacioppo, J. T. (1981). *Attitudes and persuasion: Classic and contemporary approaches.* Dubuque, IA: William C. Brown.

Powell, M. C., & Fazio, R. H. (1984). Attitude accessibility as a function of repeated attitudinal expression. *Personality and Social Psychology Bulletin, 10,* 139–148.

Pryor, J. B., & Merluzzi, T. V. (1985). The role of expertise in processing social interaction scripts. *Journal of Experimental Social Psychology, 21,* 362–379.

Reed, S. K. (1972). Pattern recognition and categorization. *Cognitive Psychology, 3,* 382–407.

Rhodewalt, F., & Agustsdottir, S. (1986). Effects of self-presentation on the phenomenal self. *Journal of Personality and Social Psychology, 50,* 47–55.

Roediger, H. L., & Blaxton, T. A. (1987). Retrieval modes produce dissociations in memory for surface information. In D. S. Gorfein & R. R. Hoffman (Eds.), *Memory and cognitive processes: The Ebbinghaus Centennial Conference* (pp. 349–379). Hillsdale, NJ: Lawrence Erlbaum Associates.

Roediger, H. L., Srinivas, K., & Weldon, M. S. (1989). Dissociations between implicit measures of retention. In S. Lewandowsky, J. C. Dunn, & K. Kirsner (Eds.), *Implicit memory: Theoretical issues.* Hillsdale, NJ: Lawrence Erlbaum Associates.

Rothbart, M., Dawes, R., & Park, B. (1984). Stereotyping and sampling biases in intergroup perception. In J. R. Eiser (Ed.), *Attitudinal judgment* (pp. 109–134). New York: Springer-Verlag.

Rumelhart, D. E., Hinton, G. E., & Williams, R. J. (1986). Learning internal representations by error propagation. In D. E. Rumelhart & J. L. McClelland (Eds.), *Parallel distributed processing: Vol. 1. Foundations.* Cambridge, MA: MIT Press.

Rumelhart, D. E., & McClelland, J. L. (1986). *Parallel distributed processing: Vol. 1. Foundations.* Cambridge, MA: MIT Press.

Ryle, G. (1945). *The concept of mind.* London: Hutchinson.

Schacter, D. (1987). Implicit memory: History and current status. *Journal of Experimental Psychology: Learning, Memory, and Cognition, 13,* 501–518.

Schank, R., & Abelson, R. P. (1977). *Scripts, plans, goals, and understanding.* Hillsdale, NJ: Lawrence Erlbaum Associates.

Schneider, D. J. (1991). Social cognition. *Annual Review of Psychology, 42,* 527–561.

Schneider, W., & Detweiler, M. (1988). A connectionist/control architecture for working memory. In G. H. Bower (Ed.), *The psychology of learning and motivation* (Vol. 21, pp. 54–119). New York: Academic Press.

Schwartz, B. L., & Hashtroudi, S. (1991). Priming is independent of skill learning. *Journal of Experimental Psychology: Learning, Memory, and Cognition, 17,* 1177–1186.

Schwarz, N., Bless, H., Strack, F., Klumpp, G., Rittenauer-Schatka, H., & Simons. A. (1991). Ease of retrieval as information: Another look at the availability heuristic. *Journal of Personality and Social Psychology, 61,* 195–202.

Shiffrin, R. M., & Dumais, S. T. (1981). The development of automatism. In J. R. Anderson (Ed.), *Cognitive skills and their acquisition* (pp. 111–140). Hillsdale, NJ: Lawrence Erlbaum Associates.

Showers, C., & Cantor, N. (1985). Social cognition: A look at motivated strategies. *Annual Review of Psychology, 36,* 275–305.

Siegler, R. S. (1988). Strategy choice procedures and the development of multiplication skill. *Journal of Experimental Psychology: General, 117,* 258–275.

Singley, M. K., & Anderson. J. R. (1989). *The transfer of cognitive skill.* Cambridge, MA: Harvard University Press.

Sloman, S. A., Hayman, C. A. G., Ohta, N., Law, J., & Tulving, E. (1988). Forgetting in primed fragment completion. *Journal of Experimental Psychology: Learning, Memory, and Cognition, 14,* 223–239.

Smith, E. R. (1984). Model of social inference processes. *Psychological Review, 91,* 392–413.

Smith, E. R. (1989a). Procedural efficiency: General and specific components and effects on social judgment. *Journal of Experimental Social Psychology, 25,* 500–523.

Smith, E. R. (1989b). Procedural efficiency and on-line social judgments. In J. N. Bassili (Ed.), *On-line cognition in person perception* (pp. 19–37). Hillsdale, NJ: Lawrence Erlbaum Associates.

Smith, E. R. (1990). Content and process specificity in the effects of prior experiences. In T. K. Srull & R. S. Wyer (Eds.), *Advances in social cognition* (Vol. 3, pp. 1–60). Hillsdale, NJ: Lawrence Erlbaum Associates.

Smith, E. R., & Branscombe, N. R. (1987). Procedurally mediated social inferences: The case of category accessibility effects. *Journal of Experimental Social Psychology, 23,* 361–382.

Smith, E. R., & Branscombe, N. R. (1988). Category accessibility as implicit memory. *Journal of Experimental Social Psychology, 24,* 490–504.

Smith, E. R., Branscombe, N. R., & Bormann, C. (1988). Generality of the effects of practice on social judgment tasks. *Journal of Personality and Social Psychology, 54,* 385–395.

Smith, E. R., & Lerner, M. (1986). Development of automatism of social judgments. *Journal of Personality and Social Psychology, 50,* 246–259.

Smith, E. R., & Miller, F. D. (1979). Salience and the cognitive mediation of attribution. *Journal of Personality and Social Psychology, 37,* 2240–2252.

Smith, E. R., Stewart, T. L., & Buttram, R. T. (1992). Inferring a trait from a behavior has long-term, highly specific effects. *Journal of Personality and Social Psychology, 62,* 753–759.

Smith, E. R., & Zárate, M. A. (1990). Exemplar and prototype use in social categorization. *Social Cognition, 8,* 243–262.

Smith, E. R., & Zárate, M. A. (1992). Exemplar-based model of social judgment. *Psychological Review, 99,* 3–21.

Snyder, M., & Swann, W. B. (1978). Hypothesis testing processes in social interaction. *Journal of Personality and Social Psychology, 36,* 1202–1221.

Sorrentino, R. M., & Higgins, E. T. (1986). Motivation and cognition: Warming up to synergism. In R. Sorrentino & E. T. Higgins (Eds.), *Handbook of motivation and cognition: Foundations of social behavior* (pp. 3–20). New York: Guilford.

Squire, L. (1986). Mechanisms of memory. *Science, 232,* 1612–1619.

Srull, T. K. (1981). Person memory: Some tests of associative storage and retrieval models. *Journal of Experimental Psychology: Human Learning and Memory, 7,* 440–463.

Swann, W. B. (1983). Self-verification: Bringing social reality into harmony with the self. In J. Suls & A. G. Greenwald (Eds.), *Psychological perspectives on the self* (Vol. 2, pp. 33–66). Hillsdale, NJ: Lawrence Erlbaum Associates.

Taylor, S. E., & Brown, J. D. (1988). Illusion and well-being: A social psychological perspective on mental health. *Psychological Bulletin, 103,* 193–210.

Tesser, A. (1988). Toward a self-evaluation maintenance model of social behavior. In L. Berkowitz (Ed.), *Advances in experimental social psychology* (Vol. 21, pp. 181–227). New York: Academic Press.

Thibadeau, R., Just, M. A., & Carpenter, P. A. (1982). A model of the time course and content of reading. *Cognitive Science, 6,* 157–203.

Townsend, J. T. (1972). Some results concerning the identifiability of parallel and serial processes. *British Journal of Mathematical and Statistical Psychology, 25,* 168–199.

Trope, Y. (1983). Self-assessment in achievement behavior. In J. Suls & A. G. Greenwald (Eds.), *Psychological perspectives on the self* (Vol. 2, pp. 93–122). Hillsdale, NJ: Lawrence Erlbaum Associates.

Tulving, E. (1983). *Elements of episodic memory.* Oxford: Clarendon.

Tulving, E., & Thompson, D. M. (1973). Encoding specificity and retrieval processes in episodic memory. *Psychological Review, 80,* 352–373.

Whittlesea, B. W. A. (1987). Preservation of specific experiences in the representation of general knowledge. *Journal of Experimental Psychology: Learning, Memory, and Cognition, 13,* 3–17.

Winograd, T. (1975). Frame representations and the declarative-procedural controversy. In D. Bobrow & A. Collins (Eds.), *Representation and understanding* (pp. 185–210). New York: Academic Press.

Winter, L., & Uleman, J. S. (1984). When are social judgments made? Evidence for the spontaneousness of trait inferences. *Journal of Personality and Social Psychology, 47,* 237–252.

Woltz, D. J. (1988). An investigation of the role of working memory in procedural skill acquisition. *Journal of Experimental Psychology: General, 117,* 319–331.

Wyer, R. S., & Carlston, D. E. (1979). *Social cognition, inference, and attribution.* Hillsdale, NJ: Lawrence Erlbaum Associates.

Wyer, R. S., & Srull, T. K. (1980). The processing of social stimulus information: A conceptual integration. In R. Hastie, T. M. Ostrom, E. B. Ebbesen, R. S. Wyer, D. L. Hamilton, & D. E. Carlston (Eds.), *Person memory: The cognitive basis of social perception* (pp. 227–300). Hillsdale, NJ: Lawrence Erlbaum Associates.

Wyer, R. S., & Srull, T. K. (1989). *Memory and cognition in its social context.* Hillsdale, NJ: Lawrence Erlbaum Associates.

Zajonc, R. B. (1968). Attitudinal effects of mere exposure. *Journal of Personality and Social Psychology Monograph, 9* (Suppl. 2, P. 2), 2–27.

Zárate, M. A., & Smith, E. R. (1990). Person categorization and stereotyping. *Social Cognition, 8,* 161–185.

Zbrodoff, N. J., & Logan, G. D. (1986). On the autonomy of mental processes: A case study of arithmetic. *Journal of Experimental Psychology: General, 115,* 118–130.

4 The Self as a Knowledge Structure

John F. Kihlstrom
University of Arizona

Stanley B. Klein
University of California, Santa Barbara

Contents

> *The fact that man is aware of an ego-concept raises him infinitely*
> *above all other creatures living on earth. Because of this, he is a per-*
> *son; and by virtue of his oneness of consciousness, he remains one*
> *and the same person despite all the vicissitudes which may befall him.*
> —I. Kant (1798/1978)
> *Anthropology From a Pragmatic Point of View*

Social cognition is concerned with how people represent knowledge of people, the situations in which they meet, and the behaviors that they exchange; how that knowledge is acquired through the course of social learning through direct experience, precept, and example; and how that knowledge is used in the course of social interaction. By far the most important of these objects of social cognition, however, is the person doing the cognizing. In this chapter, we discuss the place of the self in social cognition, with special emphasis on the self as a knowledge structure.[1]

THE FACT OF THE SELF

Any psychological analysis of the self must begin with the contribution of James, especially as expressed in chapter 10 of *Principles of Psychology* (1890/1981).[2] In point of fact, the self pervades James' psychology. It is present at the very outset of James' discussion of the mind, when he asserted that "*The first fact for us, then, as psychologists, is that thinking of some sort goes on.* I use the word thinking . . . for every form of consciousness indiscriminately" (pp. 219–220; emphasis original). He then went on to state that

> Every thought tends to be part of a personal consciousness . . . the only states of consciousness that we naturally deal with are found in personal consciousnesses, minds, selves, concrete particular I's and you's [sic]. Each of these minds keeps its own thoughts to itself. . . . It seems as if the elementary psychic fact were not *thought* or *this thought* or *that thought*, but *my thought*, every thought being *owned*. . . . On these terms the personal self rather than the thought might be treated as the immediate datum in psychology. The universal conscious fact is not 'feelings and thoughts exist' but 'I think' and 'I feel.' No psychology, at any rate, can question the *existence* of personal selves. The worst a psychology can do is so to interpret the nature of these selves as to rob them of their worth. (James, 1890/1981, pp. 220–221)

---

[1]For other coverage, see Berkowitz, 1988; Kihlstrom and Hastie, 1990; Markus, 1983; Markus and Cross, 1990; Markus and Sentis, 1982; Markus and Smith, 1981; Markus and Wurf, 1987; Mischel, 1977; Suls, 1982; Suls and Greenwald, 1983, 1986; and Wegner and Vallacher, 1980.

[2]For current appreciations of James on the self, see Markus, 1990; and Myers, 1986; also see Baumgardner, Kaufman, and Cranford, 1990; Cross and Markus, 1990; Knowles and Sibicki, 1990; Lamphere and Leary, 1990; Strube, 1990; and Suls and Marco, 1990.

So there we have it: the self is the unquestionable, elementary, universal fact of mental life, and the fundamental unit of analysis for a science of mental life. It is the problem about which everything else revolves.

James defined the self as "the sum total of all that he CAN call his," and divided the empirical self, or the self as an object of thought, into three constituents. The material self includes the person's body, clothes, family, home, and other personal property, especially that which has come by our own efforts; James argued that these are extensions of the self, part of our identities as individuals. The social self includes the person's understanding of how he or she is viewed by others; it is the person's fame, honor, or reputation. James asserted that we have as many social selves as there are distinct groups of people about whose opinions of us we care; of particular importance is the social self that resides in the mind of the person with whom we are in love. Finally, there is the spiritual self, including the person's understanding of his or her own cognitive, emotional, motivational, and behavioral dispositions.

However, beyond identifying ourselves with our mental faculties, James felt that the spiritual self included "our having become able to think of subjectivity as such, *to think of ourselves as thinkers*" (p. 284). At this more abstract level, the spiritual self is the link to the self as knower, or the central executive. The experience of the spiritual self, of ourselves as thinking, feeling, wanting, doing beings—of the stream of consciousness—is the elementary psychic fact, "I think," that gives rise to psychology in the first place. This elementary psychic fact dispenses with all disputes about whether people have selves at all. James embraced the doctrine of *esse est sentiri*, to be is to be sensed (1890/1980, p. 163; see also Myers, 1986). Because we feel the self, its existence is not to be doubted.

An Ecological Perspective

Almost a century later, and in the same vein, Neisser (1988, 1991, 1992a, 1992c) took a different approach to the constituents of the self, distinguishing among five different kinds of self-knowledge, each having its source in a particular kind of information, and each emerging at a different point in the development of the individual. The *ecological self* refers to the relationship between the person and the physical environment—to be precise, the self as embedded in the physical environment. In large part, it is given by the pattern of optic flow that passes the individual as he or she moves in space, and that, conversely, specifies the position and movement of the person in the environment. It is also given by the correspondence between intentions, or at least agency, and the perceived effects of action on the environment. Similarly, the *interpersonal self* emerges very early in life, as reflected in the subtle choreography of the infant's interactions with his or her caregivers. Partly this is manifest in the baby's appropriate response to others' facial and vocal expressions, partly in the rudiments of turn taking, and partly in making and maintaining eye contact. Just as optic flow locates the individual in physical space, so these kinds of exchanges locate the individual in interpersonal space.

These aspects of the self emerge very early in infancy, within the first year: the looming reflex indicates that babies respond to optical flow almost as soon as it can be measured; and they also imitate their caregivers' facial expressions. They are also, arguably, present in nonhuman animals. But these aspects of the self are not necessarily objects of conscious thought. Mental representation of the self comes somewhat later, in the development of other aspects of selfhood, as the child attends to those things to which his or her caregiver also attends. These include dogs, cows, and cars; they also include the child him- or herself: thus develops the *conceptual self*, or the self-concept proper. Through a regimen of social learning mediated by experience, precept, and example, the child develops a more or less articulated sense of what he or she is like as a person, physically, mentally, and socially.

The conceptual self sets the stage for the emergence of the final two facets of selfhood: the extended (or remembered) self and the private self. The *extended self* extends back into the past and forward into the future. It consists of the individual's record of autobiographical memory (Brewer, 1986), as well as beliefs about the kind of person one might become, for better or for worse (Markus & Nurius, 1986). Logically, having a concept of what one is, and does, is the prerequisite for having memories of what was (or did) in the past, and what might be, and might do, in the future. Infantile and childhood amnesia may reflect the inability of the young child to encode and retain memories of events (Fivush & Hamond, 1990; Neisser, 1992b; Schacter & Kihlstrom, 1989; White & Pillemer, 1979); but it may also reflect the absence of a self-concept on which these memories can be hung. The self is central to episodic memory (Tulving, 1983): to paraphrase James, one might say that the universal memory is not "this happened," but "*I* did this," or "This happened to *me*." Last, but not least in Neisser's account is the *private self*, which develops as the child realizes that some of his or her experiences and thoughts (e.g., hunger, pain, dreams, and secrets) are essentially inaccessible to other people except through the child's own self-reports.

The Social Intelligence Viewpoint

In the course of developing their social intelligence view of personality (Cantor & Kihlstrom, 1987, 1989; Kihlstrom & Cantor, 1989), Kihlstrom and Cantor defined the self as one's mental representation of one's own personality—what his or her characteristic traits, motives, beliefs, attitudes, and values are. Thus:

> We define the self as one's mental representation of oneself, no different in principle from mental representations that a person has concerning other ideas, objects, and events and their attributes and implications. (Kihlstrom & Cantor, 1984, p. 2)

And:

[T]he self may be construed as a person's mental representation of his or her own personality. . . . Formed through both experience and thought, it is encoded in memory alongside mental representations of other objects, real and imagined, in the physical and social world. The mental representation of the self includes both abstract information about the person's attributes (semantic knowledge) and concrete information about the person's experiences, thoughts, and actions (episodic knowledge). (Kihlstrom et al., 1988, p. 146)

This general view also underlies the present work, but we want to expand it in several ways. First, we wish to clarify that the self represents the sociocultural matrix in which the person lives as well as his or her internal cognitive, emotional, motivational, and behavioral attributes. From the social–cognitive perspective, personality is constructed through, and displayed in, social interaction. It is not possible to separate the intrapsychic from the interpersonal. Put another way, it is not possible to view persons as isolated entities, nor can people view themselves in this manner. Second, self-knowledge represents the person's physical as well as psychosocial attributes; it refers to body as well as to mind. We have an idea of what we look like, as well as what we think, feel, want, and do. Third, the self includes the individual's autobiography: a record of his or her actions and experiences (or, at least the important ones), portrayed from his or her subjective point of view. Part of our repertoire of social intelligence is our personal history, on which we can reflect in the course of ongoing experience, thought, and action. Finally, in general, the self-concept is accessible to introspective phenomenal awareness. Examples of a subconscious self-concept may be found in cases of psychogenic fugue and multiple personality disorder (Kihlstrom, 1992); and there are some people who are remarkably obtuse about themselves. But, as a rule, we assume that we know who we are and what we are like.

Within the social intelligence framework, Kihlstrom and Cantor (1984) described two alternative views of the self: as a memory structure, located at a node in an associative memory network representing declarative knowledge about all sorts of things; or as a conceptual structure, embedded in a hierarchy of concepts having to do with the physical and social world. The two construals are not mutually exclusive, of course. Concepts are encoded in declarative memory, and, depending on one's investigative and theoretical purposes, one can think of the self as either a fragment of memory or a concept.

THE SELF AS CONCEPTUAL STRUCTURE

First, let us be quite literal about the idea of the self-concept, and ask what the self looks like from this point of view. For the most part, this inquiry is guided by recent treatises on the structure of concepts in general (Medin & Smith, 1984; Mervis & Rosch, 1981; Neisser, 1987; Oden, 1987; Rosch & Lloyd, 1978; Smith

& Medin, 1981; for developmental perspectives, see Keil, 1989; Markman, 1989; for the perspective of cognitive linguistics, see Lakoff, 1987).

Proper Set View

Historically, of course, concepts were first viewed as *proper sets*, that is, summary descriptions of entire classes of objects whose features are singly necessary and jointly sufficient to identify an object as an instance of a category, and are perfectly nested in subset–superset relations created by adding or subtracting defining features. Thus, the geometrical figure *rectangle* is a plane with four sides and four equal angles; rectangles are subsets of parallelograms, which do not have four equal angles; and squares are subsets of rectangles with the four sides equal. This classical view of concepts began with Aristotle, and was consolidated in the 20th century by Hull (1920) and Bruner, Goodnow, and Austin (1956).

Self and Other Persons Within Proper Sets.   In the domain of personality, the classical proper set view is represented by the classic fourfold typology originally offered by Hippocrates and Galen, and endorsed by Kant (1798/1978). According to this view, there are only four types of people: melancholics, cholerics, sanguines, and phlegmatics, each displaying a unique set of features. In Hippocrates' original formulation, these types were given by the distribution of the four humors of which every animal was composed: black bile, yellow bile, blood, and phlegm. Kant dropped the biology, but retained the conceptual structure. More recently, psychiatric diagnosis, which, after all, is only a special form of social categorization, was construed in terms of proper sets. For example, according to Bleuler (1911/1950), *schizophrenia* was defined by the "4 As"—the fundamental symptoms of associative disturbance, anhedonia, ambivalence, and autism. All schizophrenics displayed these four symptoms, and everyone who displayed them was a schizophrenic. In the ordinary course of everyday living, we often categorize other people this way. Stereotyping, by its very nature, attributes to the individual all the characteristics imputed to the social group of which he or she is a member, and steadfastly refuses to recognize his or her individuality. Now, if we wish, we can think of the self in this way, too. For example, a person's self-concept could consist merely in identifying him- or herself as an example of a particular social category: For example, "I'm a melancholic sort of person, meaning that I share a set of singly necessary and jointly sufficient defining features with all other melancholics."

So, if the self-concept is going to be structured like a proper set, it must have a set of defining features that represents the uniqueness of the individual. Certainly we construe ourselves in terms of characteristics that we share with others. Humans are social animals, and it should not be surprising if our group memberships are represented in our self-concepts. But our individuality has to be represented there as well. Accordingly, suppose that each individual construes him- or herself in terms of a set of features that are singly necessary and jointly sufficient to define ourselves as unique (i.e., as a set of features that is shared with no other person). Suppose further that we identify the self-concept with Allport's (1937) central traits. Allport proposed that each person possessed a unique combination of personal traits, and that some 5 or 10 of these were deemed to be of special importance. If one makes the assumption that these traits are accessible to conscious awareness, then they are candidates for inclusion as defining features of the self-concept.

As a thought experiment, recall that Allport and Odbert (1936) found 17,954 terms in the English language that could be used to distinguish one individual from another (actually, they reported 17,953, but someone miscounted; since that time, of course, many new terms have entered the language). Now, as it happens, there are some $_{17,954}C_5 = 1.55 \times 10^{19}$ possible combinations of 17,954 objects taken 5 at a time, and fully 9.57×10^{35} such combinations when taken 10 at a time. That is far more than enough combinations to uniquely characterize every individual who ever walked the surface of the earth in all its history, and probably everyone who will live from now until Armageddon. So it is possible, at least in principle, to construe the self-concept as a proper set of defining features, with one and only one instance in the self-concept. No particular trait will suffice to distinguish oneself from all others, but the entire package will do so.

Probabilistic View

It is possible for theorists to construe the self as a proper set, but why would they want to do it? The problems with the proper set view of categories are well known, and have been summarized in compelling fashion by Smith and Medin (1981) as follows:

Exclusion of functional features.
Existence of disjunctive concepts.
Existence of unclear cases.
Failure to specify defining features.
Typicality effects.
Family resemblance.
Use of nonnecessary features.
Imperfect nesting.

In response to these sorts of criticisms, Rosch (1975; Rosch, Mervis, Gray, Johnson, & Boyes-Brehm, 1976) and others proposed what has come to be known as the *probabilistic view*, which argues that the summary descriptions of category members take the form of some measure of their central tendency with respect to salient features. Actually, there are at least two different versions of the probabilistic view (Smith & Medin, 1981). According to the *featural version*, the central tendency is represented by a list of features that are present in most members of the category, although these features are not singly necessary nor jointly sufficient to define the concept. Thus, birds tend to fly, sing, and be small, but there are a few large, flightless, songless birds. The category prototype is some instance, real or imagined, that has a large number of these typical features. According to the *dimensional version*, the features in question are represented as continuous dimensions, on which each object has a score. An average score on each dimension is computed for each category member, and the entire set of central tendencies becomes the category prototype. In other words, each member is represented as a point in multidimensional space, and the category prototype lies somewhere in the center of this distribution.

Prototypes of Self and Others.   Of course, the dimensional version of the prototype view has a long history in personality psychology, ever since Wundt noticed that some people only partially fit the criteria for Kant's categories, whereas others fit more than one equally well, and intuited that a shift from discrete types to continuous traits would solve the problem. Whether it succeeded or not, the shift was enormously popular. Many of the classic theories of personality, such as those proposed by Guilford, Cattell, and Eysenck, were couched in terms of individual differences in a finite number of traits. Of course, the entire technology of personality assessment, questionnaires and all, has arisen from the attempt to assess individual differences in terms of trait dimensions. Perhaps the modal model of personality structure is the "Big Five" framework (John, 1990), which holds that individual differences in personality can be summarized in terms of five traits of extraversion, neuroticism, agreeableness, conscientiousness, and intellectance (or, alternatively, openness to experience). In theory, each person can be located as a unique point in a multidimensional space defined by these five dimensions.

Cantor adapted Rosch's approach to the problem of both normal (Cantor & Mischel, 1978; see also Lingle, Altom, & Medin, 1984) and abnormal (Cantor & Genero, 1986; see also Morey & McNamara, 1987) personality. However, it should be understood that Cantor's is an approach to person perception, or impressions of personality, rather than to personality per se, as something that has an existence independent of the observer. It is based on what Allport called the biosocial view of personality, rather than the biophysical view preferred by traditional trait theorists. Cantor was interested in the structure of the categories that guide impression formation, and she argued that concepts of persons—labeled by terms like *wonk, nerd, preppie, hippie*, and *jock*—were fuzzy sets of features, each only probabilistically associated with category membership, their constituent instances linked by family resemblance rather than defining features, and imperfectly nested in tangled hierarchies. She argued that when people formed impressions of others' personalities, they matched their salient features to those of category prototypes, and classified people in terms of the prototype that gave the best match.

Again, on the simple assumption that a person's traits are accessible to introspection, both versions of the probabilistic view can provide models of the self-concept. Thus, people might have a more or less clear idea of their standings on each of the traits comprising the structure of personality — which points are theirs in multidimensional trait space (Breckler, Pratkanis, & McCann, 1991). Or, people might have an idea of which personality prototype they most closely resemble. In fact, shortly after Cantor introduced the prototype approach to person perception, Rogers (1981) argued that the self was also structured as a cognitive prototype, consisting of some set of features that are more or less highly correlated with selfhood.

This interpretation was enormously heuristic, in that it led to a large number of novel, interesting experiments concerned with the problem of self-reference in memory and the nature of judgments concerning the self. On the other hand, this particular interpretation may miss some essential features of both the self-concept and the probabilistic view. To begin with, the self-concept is a concept, not an instance. Further, from the probabilistic view (or the classical view, for that matter), concepts provide summary representations of an entire class of objects. So, if the self-concept is a concept, and conceptual prototypes summarize the features of a number of instances, then of what is the self-concept a prototype? What are the instances summarized by the prototype, if there is only one of each of us?

Context-Specific Selves.   Taking seriously the probabilistic view of the self-concept forces us to recognize that, in some sense, there is more than one of each of us. Perhaps the self-concept is abstracted from random observations of ourselves. It seems more likely, however, that the self-prototypes are abstracted from systematic observations of ourselves in different situational contexts. The assumptions of trait theory notwithstanding, it has been known since the classic study of honesty by Hartshorne and May (1929) that social behavior is remarkably sensitive to the details of the social situation. People who are extraverted or conscientious in one situation may not be so in another, and the degree of similarity in behavior from one situation to another varies with the perceived similarity among the situations in question. There is no reason to think that people fail to represent these relationships mentally. In fact, the self–other difference in causal attribution — the tendency for people to attribute others' behavior to dispositions, but their own behavior to (perceived) situations (Jones & Nisbett, 1972; see also, Goldberg, 1978, 1981; Kelley & Michaela, 1980; Monson & Snyder, 1977) — suggests that we are quite aware of the contextual specificity of our own behavior.

Accordingly, it seems likely that we possess a large set of context-specific selves, as opposed to a monolithic, unitary self, and that these are organized into a kind of hierarchy representing various levels of abstraction (Martindale, 1980). At the very top of the hierarchy is an extremely abstract representation of the self, valid across many contexts, but not particularly informative about what we are like in any particular situation. The hierarchy branches into various subsets and sub-subsets representing the self at ever more concrete situations. Perhaps, as Rosch and Cantor argued, there is some middle level in this scheme that functions as a kind of basic level for self-perception, which optimizes the balance between the richness of the representation and degree to which it is differentiated from other categories at the same level of the hierarchy (Murphy & Smith, 1982; Rosch et al., 1976; Tversky & Hemenway, 1984). If so, the basic level in self-categorization is privileged, in the sense that it represents the ways in which we prefer to think about ourselves, or think about ourselves most readily. If there are context-specific self-concepts, perhaps they are to be found here.

Even without considering multiple, context-specific selves, consideration of person categories as prototypes can help one to understand certain aspects of social decision making. For example, Niedenthal, Cantor, and Kihlstrom (1985) assessed the college housing preferences of freshman undergraduates. These preferences were significantly predicted by the similarity between the subjects' self-ratings on a list of representative trait adjectives, and their ratings of the kind of person who was happy and comfortable in each of the available options—a prototype-matching process similar to what underlies social categorization. Similar findings have been obtained by other investigators in a wide variety of contexts, although they did not explicitly adopt a prototype-matching framework (Burke & Reitzes, 1981; Chassin, Presson, Sherman, Corty, & Olshavsky, 1981; Pervin & Rubin, 1967; Schlenk & Holman, 1980; Solomon, 1983). Interestingly, the reverse phenomenon, prototype distancing, occurs in situations involving threat to self-esteem, such as the choice of a psychotherapist (Niedenthal & Mordkoff, 1991).

Exemplar View

The probabilistic view solves many of the problems of the classical view, but it has problems of its own (Medin, 1989). For example, it can be demonstrated that people use information, such as the variability among category members and the intercorrelations among characteristic features, that are not represented in summary prototypes. In response, Medin and Schaffer (1978) argued that concepts do not provide a summary representation of the features of category members. Instead, they proposed that concepts are represented by the instances; in other words, by concrete exemplars, rather than abstract prototypes. This shift from prototypes to exemplars underscores the appeal of the context-specific self; as in the probabilistic view, the instances represent the self as viewed in different situations. Of course, there is no longer any prototype representing the self in the abstract. Instead, there is just a grouping of particular instances. Moreover, there is no longer any basic level of self-categorization, nor any hierarchy of self-concepts.

If there is no hierarchy, no basic level, no prototype, and no super-abstract superordinate concept, then do any context-specific selves have privileged status, and if so by what right? One hint comes from studies of priming effects, by which structures recently activated through perception and thought remain in a highly accessible state for some period of time (e.g., Meyer & Schvaneveldt, 1971). Another comes from multiple-trace theories of memory (e.g., Hintzman, 1986), which assume that each encounter with an object leaves a separate trace in memory. Thus, frequently encountered objects are represented by multiple traces, and their sheer number makes it more likely that these knowledge structures, as opposed to others, will be accessed during perception and thought—a chronic (as opposed to temporary) state known in the social cognition literature as construct accessibility (Bargh, 1989; Higgins & King, 1981). Taken together, these considerations suggest that those exemplars that have been recently or frequently activated have privileged status in the mental representation of the self.

Perhaps because they retain information that prototypes discard, exemplar models have proved generally superior to prototype models in formal tests (Barsalou & Medin, 1986; Medin & Ross, 1989; Nosofsky, 1988). Nevertheless, it is hard to believe that categories contain no summary information whatsoever. Cantor and Kihlstrom (1987) proposed that people have a mix of exemplar and summary representations of others, shifting between them as needed. The same conclusion might be valid for the self (Klein & Loftus, 1993a, 1993b). Nevertheless, the circumstances under which these shifts might take place are not clear. Perhaps it depends on whether knowledge of the category in question has been acquired directly or vicariously (Lingle et al., 1984). Alternatively, perhaps people shift from exemplar to summary representations as they acquire expertise in a domain (Homa, 1984).

Theory-Based View

Both the prototype and exemplar views, like the classical view that preceded them, explain categorization on the basis of similarity between the features of the object to be categorized and those of the mental representation of the concept. Unfortunately, as Murphy and Medin (1985; Medin, 1989) argued, similarity cannot be the only principle involved in categorization. For one thing, similarity is both extremely flexible and rather arbitrary, and the perception of similarity is distressingly unprincipled (Tversky, 1977). For another, concepts encode information about the relations among features, as well as the features themselves. This fact is not easy to accommodate within similarity-based views of concepts (Armstrong, Gleitman, & Gleitman, 1983). These and similar considerations suggest that similarity is not all there is to categorization.

Accordingly, Murphy and Medin (1985; Medin, 1989) proposed an additional view, the theory-based (or knowledge-based) approach, to explain categorization. According to this view, concepts are organized by theories about the domain they represent, and these theories guide judgments of similarity and define the relationships between concepts and their constituent features. For example, white hair is perceived as more similar to gray hair than to black hair, because of the judge's intuitive theory of aging. On the other hand, gray clouds are perceived as more similar to black clouds than to white clouds, because of the judge's intuitive theory of the weather (Medin & Shoben, 1988). Thus, concepts are represented by a set of attributes that are correlated with each other, as well as with category membership. However, concepts also are defined by one or more principles that explain these relations. Thus, clouds that are heavy with moisture turn dark, whereas aging hair loses pigment. Classification goes beyond feature matching to posit a theory that explains the links between objects, their features, and the categories to which they belong. Theoretical considerations permit instances to be classified together even when they possess no features in common.

The theory view is relatively recent and has not had time to be incorporated into accounts of social categorization. But the addition of theories to similarity judgments is appealing, because it provides a basis for representing both the various features of objects and the exemplars of the categories to which they belong. Thus, to return to the example of psychiatric diagnosis, the Four As in Bleuler's concept of schizophrenia may be the common consequence of an underlying attentional deficit (Chapman & Chapman, 1973); and the conversion disorders (involving functional deficits in perception and voluntary action) and the dissociative disorders (involving functional deficits in memory and identity) belong together because both involve divisions of consciousness (Kihlstrom, 1992). Similarly, in the domain of social cognition, the existence of theory-based concepts helps explain how two individuals, so different superficially, can be perceived as belonging to the same category. The reason is that the concept is represented by a theory of the essence of the category, rather than by a list of characteristic features or exemplars.

Self-Theory.   With respect to the self-concept, the theory view is especially attractive because it provides a way to organize the relations among exemplars and to explain the particular form that a hierarchy of selves takes. More than 20 years ago, Epstein (1973) identified the self-concept with one's intuitive theory of oneself—a theory that explains why we are what we are, think what we think, feel what we feel, want what we want, and do what we do. As he put it then:

> *The self-concept is a self-theory.* It is a theory that the individual has unwittingly constructed about himself as an experiencing, functioning individual, and it is part of a broader theory which he holds with respect to his entire range of significant experience. (p. 407)

In his view, the notion that the self is a theory offers a resolution to the problem, identified by James, that the self is both a knower and an object of knowledge:

after all, theories both represent existing knowledge and guide the acquisition of new knowledge. Like any scientific theory, the self-theory is subject to test, revision, retest, and expansion, although, as is common in science, the theorist may fight valiantly to retain his or her theory.

Epstein believed that the notion of a self-theory should replace that of the self-concept, which he thought suffered from ineffability and tautology. But it is not necessary to abandon the self-concept in favor of the self-theory. Perhaps concepts were ineffable in 1973, but they are less so now. A great deal is known about how natural concepts are structured, and one can see that it makes sense to think of the self-concept as structured in the same manner as other concepts — as a hierarchically arranged set of prototypes, or as a set of exemplars. Furthermore, the prototype and exemplar views of the self-concept help one understand the context specificity of the self. But just as important, recent developments in cognitive theory give another reason not to abandon the self-concept in favor of the self-theory, because concepts *are* theories.

In Epstein's view, the self-concept optimizes the balance of pleasure and pain over the course of the individual's lifetime, maintains self-esteem, and assimilates and organizes experience. But the theory-based view of concepts suggests yet another, more important, function. People appear to have multiple, context-specific selves. The self-concept consists of a mental representation of attributes that are characteristic of ourselves in each of these contexts, as a set of prototypes or exemplars. But it also consists of a self-theory, lying at the core of the self-concept, which links the various attributes to the self and guides the transition between context-specific selves. Moreover, the self-theory explains the variety of context-specific selves, the relations among them, and the narrative of autobiographical memory to which the self is linked.

ASSESSING THE SELF-CONCEPT

How can a person's self-concept, including whatever context-specific selves he or she may possess, be revealed for study? Most assessments of the self-concept rely on some version of the adjective checklist or rating scale. For example, Rogers (1951) developed a version of Stephenson's Q-sort procedure, in which subjects sorted a set of 100 self-referent statements into a forced-normal distribution according to the degree to which they were true of their actual and ideal selves. Of course, such self-descriptions can be collected by means of any adjective rating scale or self-report questionnaire.

Self-Schematics and Aschematics

On the other hand, as Markus (1977) noted, just because an item is self-descriptive does not mean that it is part of the self-concept. Accordingly, after her subjects rate the degree to which each adjective is self-descriptive, they also rate the degree to which it is important to their self-concept. Drawing on Bartlett's concept of the schema as an organized mental structure that guides perception and memory, Markus classified subjects as self-schematic for a particular attribute only if they rate it high in terms of both self-descriptiveness and self-importance. They are classified as aschematic for attributes that are rated as moderate in self-descriptiveness and unimportant to the self-concept. Individuals who are self-schematic and aschematic for particular attributes have been shown to perform differently on a wide variety of tasks (for comprehensive reviews, see Markus & Sentis, 1982; Markus & Smith, 1981; Markus & Wurf, 1987). For example, individuals who are self-schematic for independence and dependence are quicker to make judgments about themselves in these domains, are more likely to remember domain-relevant behavior, are more confident in their predictions about future trait-relevant behavior, and are more resistant to information that contradicts their self-concepts (Markus, 1977). Similar findings have been obtained in domains of gender (Crane & Markus, 1982; Markus, Crane, Bernstein, & Siladi, 1982; Markus, Smith, & Moreland, 1985) and extraversion–introversion (Fong & Markus, 1982).

Although these sorts of experiments have demonstrated interesting differences between self-schematic and aschematic subjects, the classification procedure used in studies of self-schemata necessarily confounds the degree to which a trait is self-descriptive with the degree to which it is important to the self-concept (Burke, Kraut, & Dworkin, 1986; Nystedt, Smari, & Boman, 1991). The problem is that, for some characteristics, it may be important to subjects that they lie somewhere in the middle. In fact, Burke et al. (1986) found that, for eight trait dimensions, measures of self-descriptiveness were only very modestly related to measures of importance to the self-concept. Although the vast majority of personality descriptions are heavily loaded with evaluation, such that most individuals probably prefer to perceive themselves as located near the socially desirable pole, there are obviously some cases in which people prefer to be somewhere in the middle: smart, but not a genius; agreeable, but not obsequious; conscientious, but not fastidious; masculine or feminine, but not to the point of caricature; liberal or conservative, but also moderate. As Jones (1964; Jones & Pittman, 1982) noted, one's self-presentation can be too good to be true, and that self-presentation, and thus self-definition as well, should not be excessive. Thus, the desire to be outstanding is dampened by the desire not to be conspicuous. Because it can be important to people that they be, and be perceived to be, moderate on many trait dimensions, what would seem to be really crucial in Markus' procedure is the rating of self-importance.

Possible Selves

More recently, Markus and Nurius (1986) argued that people possess a number of different self-concepts:

The individual's collection of self-conceptions and self-images can include the good selves (the ones we remember fondly), the bad selves (the ones we would just as soon forget), the hoped-for selves, the feared selves, the not-me selves, the ideal selves, the ought selves. (p. 957)

Thus, in addition to assessing the present self-concept, or what they call the working self-concept, it is also important to consider the individual's *possible selves*, or the specific hopes, fears, and fantasies that the individual has about him or herself (see also Hart, Fegley, & Brengelman, 1993; Markus & Kunda, 1986). As standards against which the current view of self can be evaluated, possible selves have an obvious emotional function; as things to be approached or avoided, their motivation function is also clear. One way in which possible selves can be assessed is with a standard checklist, in terms of which subjects indicate whether each characteristic is part of the present self, whether it was descriptive of them in the past, whether it had ever been considered as a possible self, how probable that possible self was, and how much they would like to possess the attribute in question.

Self-Complexity

Another important aspect of the self-concept is self-complexity, a variant on the cognitive complexity studied in the tradition of Kelly's personal construct theory (Crockett, 1965). Linville (1985, 1987) proposed that there are individual differences in the extent to which people perceive themselves as playing different roles, or behaving in different ways, in different situations. The number of such different selves, and especially the semantic distance between them, is what she means by self-complexity. Self-complexity can be assessed by presenting subjects with a representative set of trait adjectives and asking them to sort them into categories representing different aspects of themselves (traits can be used more than once). Complexity may be quantified by a measure of the dispersion of traits across the categories: a high score indicates that there are many different facets of the self that share relatively few attributes in common. Self-complexity, so measured, is negatively related to the strength of emotional reactions to positive and negative life events (Dixon & Baumeister, 1991; Linville, 1985, 1987). The explanation is that self-complexity prevents emotion elicited in one situation, to which one aspect of the self is related, from spreading to other aspects of the self.

Individual differences in the elaboration of the self-concept also have been studied in the clinical domain. In particular, it has long been speculated that schizophrenics suffer identity confusions and blurring or loss of ego boundaries (for a review, see Gara, Rosenberg, & Cohen, 1987). One empirical approach to this hypothesis has been based on the set theoretic model of self proposed by Rosenberg and Gara (1985). Comparing the self-concept with concepts of other persons, Gara and his colleagues found that the self-concepts of schizophrenics are much less elaborate than those of normal controls (Gara, Rosenberg, & Mueller, 1989; Robey, Cohen, & Gara, 1989). With respect to concepts of other persons, the trend was in the opposite direction, although the differences were not significant due to extremely high variances. Interestingly, and in apparent contradiction to the findings of Linville (1985, 1987), there was no difference between depressed patients and normal controls in terms of elaboration of the self-concept.

Recently, Niedenthal, Setterlund, and Wherry (1992) combined Markus's concept of possible selves with Linville's notion of self-complexity. Interestingly, complexity of the actual self is not strongly related to the complexity of the possible self. Moreover, although actual self-complexity mediates affective responses to success and failure with respect to current goals, possible self-complexity appears to mediate responses to outcomes with respect to future goals. Similarly, Showers (1992) documented individual differences in compartmentalization, or the tendency to sort the positive and negative aspects of self into separate categories. Compartmentalization is positively related to self-esteem in those for whom the positive aspects of self are most important to them, and negatively in those depressed individuals for whom negative aspects of self are most important.

The Spontaneous Self

One problem with checklists and rating scales is that they are somewhat Procrustean: that is, they force people to characterize themselves in terms of a set of categories that are of interest to the researcher, regardless of whether these terms would be chosen by the people themselves. This raises the danger that subjects and investigators might differ in their definitions of the attributes in question, leading to misrepresentations and misperceptions of the self. But even if the attributes in question could be defined with a high degree of consensus, it seems unfair that, in assessing the self-concept, people should be denied the opportunity to define themselves in their own terms. If any aspect of the personality deserves idiographic assessment, it is the self-concept. Accordingly, some investigators have experimented with free-response procedures (see Kendall & Hollon, 1981).

Early examples of this method are the Twenty Statements Test (Kuhn & McPartland, 1954) and the Who Are You? technique (Bugental, 1964). Along the same lines, Jones, Sensenig, and Haley (1974) gave their subjects 20 minutes to list self-descriptive words and phrases. These were then coded into 97 categories (the number reflecting the limitations of computer memory at the time). Multidimensional scaling revealed four broad dimensions, which Jones et al. argued were the central features of the self-concept: evaluation, impulsiveness–inhibition, masculinity–femininity, and communality with others.

A recent variant on Rogers' distinction between real and ideal self was introduced by Higgins (1987, 1989; Higgins, Bond, Klein, & Strauman, 1986; Higgins, Klein, & Strauman, 1985) and his colleagues. Their Selves Questionnaire asks subjects to list traits and attributes comprising their beliefs about themselves in various domains, or self-states. One such domain is the Actual Self, as represented by the following question: "Your beliefs concerning the attributes or characteristics you think you *actually* possess now"; two other facets of the self, known as self-guides, are the Ideal Self (". . . the attributes or characteristics you would *ideally* like to possess; the type of person you wish, desire, or hope to be") and the Ought Self (". . . the attributes or characteristics you believe you *should* or *ought to* possess; the type of person you believe it is your duty, obligation, or responsibility to be"). These self-states can be assessed from the person's own perspective, but they can also be assessed from the standpoint of significant others, such as the respondent's parents and friends. Interestingly, Higgins, Strauman, and their colleagues showed that discrepancies between the actual self and various self-guides are associated with characteristic moods and vulnerability to emotional distress: actual–ideal discrepancies are associated with dysphoria, whereas actual–ought discrepancies are associated with anxiety (Higgins, 1987; Higgins et al., 1985; Strauman, 1989, 1992). In addition, Strauman (1990, 1992) showed that self-guides are particularly effective cues for the retrieval of autobiographical memories from childhood.

Another approach was taken by McGuire (1984; McGuire & McGuire, 1981, 1982, 1988), who simply presented their subjects with a blank sheet of paper (or a tape recorder) and gave them the simple instruction, "Tell me about yourself." A content analysis, based on the responses of a group of sixth graders, yielded the following distribution of categories:

Habitual activities (hobbies, sports, and skills), 24%;
Significant others, 20%;
Attitudes, interests, hopes, and preferences, 17%;
School status, 15%;
Demographic information, 12%;
Self-evaluation, 7%;
Physical characteristics, 5%;
Miscellaneous, 1%.

Note the prominence of significant others in the self-concept: in large part, we define ourselves in relation to other people. Note, too, in contrast to the wealth of literature on self-esteem, that evaluative remarks comprise a relatively small portion of what the McGuires call the "spontaneous self" (although that does not mean that self-esteem is unimportant; see Greenwald, Bellezza, & Banaji, 1988; Showers, 1992).

Salience and Distinctiveness.   In an extensive series of studies, the McGuires showed that the content of the spontaneous self-concept is determined, at least partly, by a principle of salience or distinctiveness. That is, for many attributes, children and adults are more likely to list a particular feature as part of the self-concept if they are different from others on that dimension. This tendency is, in turn, related to a general fact of attentional life, which is that when one cannot encode all the information available, attention is selectively focused on those elements that stand out in some way. In particular, when choosing among all the attributes that could be used to describe themselves, people tend to gravitate toward those that set them apart from other people.

For example, subjects who are left-handed are more likely to mention laterality than are those who are right-handed (McGuire & McGuire, 1980). Similar findings are obtained for other physical and demographic characteristics such as height, weight, hair color, eye color, gender, ethnicity, and birthplace (McGuire & McGuire, 1981; McGuire, McGuire, Child, & Fujioka, 1978; McGuire, McGuire, & Winton, 1979; McGuire & Padawer-Singer, 1976). Perhaps because of difficulties involved in assuring equivalence between subjects' and investigators' constructs, the distinctiveness hypothesis has not been tested with respect to personality attributes. However, even within the domain of physical and demographic attributes, the actual frequency with which distinctive features appear in self-descriptions is rather low. For example, in the report by McGuire and McGuire (1988), only 27% of subjects for whom height was a distinctive characteristic actually mentioned height in their self-descriptions; the comparable figure for birthplace was 10%. Thus, although distinctiveness is an important determinant of the self-concept, it seems likely that the actual content of the self reflects a kind of compromise between assimilation and contrast (Brewer, 1991).

The McGuires' demonstration of distinctiveness effects on the spontaneous self-concept implies that the self-concept varies according to the context in which it is accessed. But it is not clear whether they think that it is the self-concept that varies, or merely the accessibility of its elements. Certainly, the subject's attention to various attributes of the self can be affected by context. What is not known is whether the self-concept varies from context to context, yielding a multiplicity of selves (Markus & Kunda, 1986). Something like this happens in psychogenic fugue and multiple personality. Research on the structure of nonsocial concepts suggests that it is meaningful to think of each individual as possessing a number of different, context-specific selves.

PERSPACE

As part of a project supported by the Program on Conscious and Unconscious Mental Processes of the John D. and Catherine T. MacArthur Foundation (M. J. Horowitz, principal investigator), a computer software system has been developed that may prove useful in the idiographic assessment of the context-specific self-concept (for another approach, see Tunis, Fridhandler, & Horowitz, 1990). The program, known as PERSPACE (now in Version 3.5; Kihlstrom & Cunningham, 1991; Kihlstrom & Olsen, 1992), is inspired by Kelly's (1955) Role Construct Repertory Test for the assessment of personal constructs, and Rosenberg, (1988; Gara & Rosenberg, 1979; Rosenberg & Gara, 1985) set theoretic model for studying the content and organization of the social self (see also Lehrer, 1986).

In one configuration of PERSPACE, the subject begins by typing in a list of targets, such as the important people, situations, or events in his or her life. (For subjects or experimenters who need more concrete cues, PERSPACE also provides a menu of cued-response probes; e.g., the categories of persons used in Kelly's original Rep Test.) After the targets are collected, they are presented individually in random order, and the subject is asked to list features that characterize him- or herself when he or she is with the person or in the situation indicated. These responses provide the basis for assessing context-specific self-concepts, where "context" is defined in terms of the presence of particular people, situations, or events. In the final phase, the attributes listed for each target are merged, edited for redundancy, and collated with the list of targets to form a (potentially rather large) target × descriptor matrix. The cells of this matrix are then randomly presented to the subject, who rates the degree to which the descriptor is characteristic of the target. Thus, for example, if a subject responded "feel nervous" when asked to describe himself in the presence of his grandfather, he would be asked to what extent he feels nervous in the presence of all the other targets on his list. (In the event that the investigator prefers to analyze a particular set of rating scales instead of allowing subjects to generate their own, the descriptor phase can be skipped entirely and the investigator can supply the subject with any of a wide variety of conventional rating schemes.)

After the subject sessions are completed, the target × descriptor matrix is put into a format compatible with the requirements of major data-analysis packages, such as SPSS or BMDP, and submitted to a variety of multivariate statistical analyses, including factor analysis, multidimensional scaling, and cluster analysis. Our preferred mode is cluster analysis, which groups targets together according to similarity of descriptors—or, in the present instance, similarity of self-descriptors. The resulting dendrogram, appropriately partitioned, graphically portrays the conceptual self in context (Kihlstrom & Marchese, in press). For example, it might show that the subject possesses not a unitary, monolithic self-concept, but rather several, each quite different from the others and each tied to the presence of specific people or social situations.

THE DEVELOPMENT OF THE SELF-CONCEPT

The child's understanding of his or her physical world changes over the course of development. This principle applies to the child's understanding of the social world, and of him- or herself as well (for reviews, see Damon, 1983; Damon

& Hart, 1988; Eder, 1989, 1990; Flavell & Ross, 1981; Higgins, Ruble, & Hartup, 1983; Lewis, 1990; for coverage of the literature on self-esteem, see Harter, 1983, 1986, 1988).

Much of the work on the self in infancy has been heavily influenced by psychoanalytic theory, of course, particularly the work of Erik Erikson and Margaret Mahler. Kegan (1982) drew on the theories of Piaget and Kohlberg to produce a cognitive account of the development of selfhood. But there is also empirical work (e.g., Dixon, 1957). First, of course, there is the finding that a majority of infants, by the time they are 18 to 24 months of age, will touch a spot on their faces when it is visible in a mirror (a procedure known as the mark test; see Lewis & Brooks-Gunn, 1979). This suggests that by about 2 years of age, children have acquired a mental representation of themselves that allows them to notice discrepancies between what they see and what they expect to see. This research is particularly interesting, because similar behavior has been observed in chimpanzees or orangutans (Gallup, 1968; Gallup & Suarez, 1986), thus showing some degree of phylogenetic continuity between humans and nonhumans in this respect (for an alternative point of view, see Epstein, Lanza, & Skinner, 1981). Other primate species, including gorillas and pygmy marmosets, appear to fail the mark test, but this does not necessarily mean that they do not have at least rudimentary self-images.

The Self in Language

The ability of children to communicate verbally allows researchers to gather additional evidence concerning the development of the self-concept. For example, by the end of the second year of life, children have begun to make self-descriptive statements (Kagan, 1981). Interview studies by Broughton (1978), Selman (1980), and others indicated that, between ages 2 and 8, children shift their definition of themselves from physical to psychological terms. That is, whereas young children distinguish themselves from others in terms of how they look and what they possess, older children distinguish themselves in terms of what they think and feel. Similarly, Secord and Peevers (1974) found that children's self-descriptions shifted from habitual actions to their comparative action competencies. A focus on psychological constructs shows further development in adolescence (Broughton, 1978; Selman, 1980). Peevers and Secord (1973) noted a number of important changes. First, young adolescents tend to describe themselves in terms of abstract, traitlike qualities; they also speak of themselves in terms of past and future qualities. Later, self-reflection and self-evaluation are added to the repertoire.

Similarly, McGuire and McGuire (1982, 1988; McGuire, McGuire, & Cheever, 1986) analyzed the verbs that appear in self-descriptions. They showed an age shift from verbs of action to verbs of state. Moreover, verbs of state shift from static to dynamic, whereas action verbs shift from overt to covert; overt action verbs shift from physical actions to social interactions; and emotional reactions are replaced by intellectual ones. The McGuires also discovered two other age trends. First, there is a shift from affirmations to negations. Young children make positive statements about what they are, whereas adolescents increasingly talk about what they are not. Second, there is a contraction of the social space within the self, and a shift from affirmation to negation. It will be recalled that significant others (especially kin and friends, but also nonhuman animals who play important roles in the lives of the subjects) make up a relatively large portion of self-descriptions. But the extent to which significant others appear in children's self-descriptions declines systematically between ages 7 and 17.

A comprehensive model of the development of self-understanding has been proposed by Damon and Hart (1988; see also Hart, Fegley, Chan, Fisher, & Mulvey, 1993). First, they adopted the Jamesian distinction between self as object and self as subject. The self as object consists of the physical self, the active self, the social self, and the psychological self. The self as subject embraces issues of continuity, distinctiveness, and agency. Based on a comprehensive literature review, and their own study of children and adolescents from 1st to 10th grade (involving two structured interviews separated by 18 months), they concluded that, from early childhood to late adolescence, the self shows a pattern of regular development in all seven of these domains: from categorical identifications to comparative assessments to interpersonal concerns to systematic beliefs and plans; each new level incorporates and transforms the earlier one(s). For example, in early childhood, the psychological self is defined in terms of an unintegrated list of typical or salient mental states (e.g., "I don't like to stay on the porch"). The older child compares him- or herself with real or imagined others (e.g., "I read and they don't"). In early adolescence, the focus is on interactions with other people (e.g., "I'm the kind of person who loves being with my friends"); the late adolescent integrates his or her characteristics with systematic beliefs and life plans (e.g., "I am somebody who believes that everybody is created equal. . . . I'm going to be a lawyer and take cases and see that everyone gets rights . . ."). These findings were substantially replicated in a follow-up study of 81 students in Grades 5–11.

THE SELF IN CULTURAL CONTEXT

Every person has a self-concept: the ecological and interpersonal distinction between oneself and others is something that belongs to the species, like consciousness and the capacity for language. But just as individuals in different cultures may speak different languages, they may also have different self-concepts, due to differences in socialization regimes imposed on individuals and differing cultural concepts of personhood. As with most of the rest of scientific psychology, research on the self has proceeded in a largely monocultural manner (Kennedy, Scheier, & Rogers, 1984). This strategy has been enormously successful. There is little reason to think that there are important cultural differences in the basic mental processes involved in perceiving, remembering, and thinking. However, there have been a number of cases where cross-cultural comparisons have shed important light on basic processes (e.g., the nature of basic emotions or the structure of the mental lexicon). In any event, a monocultural strategy is probably a mistake for personality and social psychology, which takes as one of its central problems the bidirectional relationship between the mental processes internal to the individual and sociocultural processes operating from outside (Shweder & Levine, 1984; Stigler, Shweder, & Herdt, 1991; Triandis & Brislin, 1980).

For example, Hart, Lucca-Irizarry, and Damon (1986) conducted a study of the development of self-understanding in a Puerto Rican fishing village. Their first finding was that a coding manual developed on a sample of middle-class North American children could be applied, with few revisions, to a sample of Puerto Rican children living in an agrarian, rural setting. Moreover, the levels of self-understanding displayed by the two groups showed comparable patterns of distribution by age. There were some differences. For example, Puerto Rican self-descriptions emphasized social attributes, whereas those from North America emphasized psychological characteristics. Moreover, there were interesting differences observable within developmental levels. For example, comparative assessments by Puerto Rican children were less explicitly comparative and more concerned with the reactions of others. The extent to which these kinds of differences reflect differences between cultures, and differences between classes, is not clear. In a study of children in Iceland, Hart and Edelstein (1992a) found a class difference in the self-attribution of psychological characteristics, but few differences between children dwelling in traditional versus modern communities, independent of class (Hart & Edelstein, 1992b).

Independence and Interdependence

Along much the same line, Markus and Kitayama (1991) identified two rather different construals of self. The independent construal corresponds to a view of the individual "as an independent, self-contained, autonomous entity who (a) comprises a unique configuration of internal attributes (e.g., traits, abilities, motives, and values) and (b) behaves primarily as a consequence of these internal attributes" (p. 224). By contrast, the interdependent construal "entails seeing oneself as part of an encompassing social relationship and recognizing that one's behavior is determined, contingent on, and to a large extent organized by what [one] perceives to be the thoughts, feelings, and actions of *others* in the relationship" (p. 227). The independent self recognizes the social environment, but is primarily concerned with how to be, and express, oneself in social context. Similarly, the interdependent self has a set of internal attributes, but these do not play a powerful role in regulating social behavior.

It is not surprising that the independent construal of self is hypothesized to be characteristic of individuals raised in Northern European and North American cultures, and that the interdependent construal is hypothesized to be characteristic of individuals raised in Asian, African, Latin American, and Southern European cultures. In fact, a large set of studies summarized by Markus and Kitayama (1991) showed that there are substantial differences in the cognitive, emotional, and motivational aspects of selfhood between American college students on the one hand, and their Indian and Japanese counterparts on the other. For example, Cousins (1989) found that, although American students were more responsive to a version of the Twenty Statements Test that asked for abstract, situation-free self-portraits, Japanese students were more responsive to one that asked for context-specific descriptions of themselves.

Of course, there are important differences among subcultures within each of these cultures. For example, many Africans and Asians might bridle at the suggestion that there is a peculiarly African or Asian culture; discussions of Latin American cultures must make, at the very least, distinctions between Iberian and aboriginal traditions; and discussions of differences among European cultures will have to cope with the fact that the notion of the independent self, ostensibly characteristic of Northern Europe, has its origins in the ancient world of Greece and Rome. The development of a global world culture will probably reduce these differences somewhat. At the same time, the emergence of multiculturalism within ethnically diverse societies, like the United States, will certainly make these differences increasingly difficult to assess. Nevertheless, because the self, like the rest of the personality, is constructed within a sociocultural context, the impact of cultural differences on the self-concept cannot be ignored.

THE SELF AS A MEMORY STRUCTURE

Whether explicitly or implicitly, most of the research reviewed so far has adopted the view that the self is a conceptual structure, providing some kind of list of the salient and characteristic attributes of the person. This perspective links personality and social psychology to one of the great traditions in cognitive psychology, the study of concepts and categories. We turn now to another view, not inconsistent with the first, but one that links personality and social psychology to another great tradition — associative network theories of memory.

Effects on Memory: Self-Reference and Self-Generation

In fact, one of the first formal attempts to develop an information-processing view of the self was inspired by both recent advances in memory research and the prototype approach to concepts and categories (Rogers, 1981; see also Greenwald & Pratkanis, 1984; Kuiper & Derry, 1981). For example, in a series of papers, Rogers (1974a, 1974b, 1978) attempted to analyze response to self-referent personality items in terms of Sternberg's (1969) memory-search paradigm. Based on an analysis of response latencies, Rogers decomposed the process of self-reference into four stages: the first two, stimulus encoding and stimulus comprehension, and the fourth, response selection, were familiar from Sternberg's original work; the third, involving a self-referent decision, was somewhat new and underscored the need to understand how the self was represented in memory. To this end, Rogers and his colleagues employed both memory and categorization paradigms.

For example, Rogers, Kuiper, and Kirker (1977) initiated a line of research on the self-reference effect. In a variant on the standard depth of processing paradigm popularized by Craik and Lockhart (1972), subjects studied a list of trait adjectives in one of three orienting tasks: structural, semantic, and self-referent. Self-referent processing produced a large advantage in memory over semantic processing, an effect that has been replicated many times (e.g., Bower & Gilligan, 1979; Keenan & Baillet, 1980; for reviews, see Klein & Kihlstrom, 1986; Klein, Loftus, & Burton, 1989). Based on the idea that depth of processing increases the number of associations between an item and preexisting knowledge, Rogers (1981; Rogers et al., 1977) and others concluded that the self is a highly elaborate knowledge structure containing a great deal of information about the self.

Other effects of self on memory also were uncovered. As summarized by Greenwald (1980, 1981; Greenwald & Banaji, 1989; Greenwald & Pratkanis, 1984), these included the self-generation effect (memory is better for actively generated than for passively perceived material; e.g., Slamecka & Graf, 1978) and the ego-involvement effect (memory is better for persisting than for completed tasks; e.g., Zeigarnik, 1927). Later, Greenwald and Banaji (1989) added a fourth effect, the second-generation effect, in which paired associates containing the names of subjects' friends are better recalled than pairs containing unfamiliar names (but see Bellezza & Hoyt, 1992).

Is the Self Unique?   On the other hand, the status of these effects as uniquely involving the self has been challenged. For example, in the self-reference effect, a number of investigators noted that Rogers et al. failed to control for such potentially confounding variables as evaluation and person reference. For example, the self-reference effect might reflect nothing more than the evaluation that must occur when subjects think about themselves. Alternatively, it might be that memory is enhanced equally when subjects make judgments about people other than themselves. In an extensive series of studies, Klein (Klein & Kihlstrom, 1986; see also Klein & Loftus, 1988) showed that the self-reference effect was a product of organizational activity and had little to do with self-reference per se. That is, the typical self-referent task encourages the subject to sort list items into two categories, those that are and those that are not self-descriptive, whereas the typical semantic task does not encourage categorization of any sort. Klein and Kihlstrom showed that organized semantic and self-referent tasks produced equal advantages in recall, compared with their unorganized counterparts. Moreover, the self-reference effect could be reversed when the semantic task encouraged organization, but the self-referent task did not. Although agreeing that the self might be a highly elaborate memory structure, they discounted the self-reference effect as evidence that this was the case.

More recently, Klein and Loftus (1988) and Klein et al. (1989) provided evidence that both organizational and elaborative processes are involved in self-referent recall enhancement, but which process plays the larger role depends on the type of stimulus material being judged. When the relations between stimulus items are obscure (as typically is the case in self-referent studies), the organizational properties of self-referent encoding are found to promote good recall. By contrast, when the stimulus items share obvious relations, the elaborative properties of self-referent encoding can be shown to mediate self-referent recall enhancement. Thus, the memory-enhancing effects of self-reference can be understood in terms of the same cognitive processes—elaboration and organization—long known to mediate memory performance with tasks not involving self-reference.

Greenwald and Banaji (1989) reached similar conclusions about the second-generation effect. They noted that their experimental procedures represented a close variant of the familiar pegword mnemonic system, and that their results could be duplicated by Shiffrin's SAM model of associative memory (Gillund & Shiffrin, 1984; Raaijmakers & Shiffrin, 1981). Thus, adding the self to a conventional memory experiment appeared to require the addition of no new principles. Moreover, as noted by Klein and Kihlstrom (1986) in a different context, the familiarity of a category is correlated with the strength of category-to-member associations (Barsalou, 1983). Thus, it should not be surprising, in an experiment in which items are associated to personal names, that familiar names are better retrieval cues than unfamiliar ones.

The results of these experiments do not mean that the self is not a memory structure. To the contrary, they seem to indicate that the self can be profitably approached as if it were no different from other knowledge structures stored in memory. The differences between the self and other knowledge structures are quantitative, not qualitative. Thus, to review a second series of studies from Rogers and Kuiper, when the self is construed as a conceptual prototype, it seems to behave like other prototypes stored in semantic memory. For example, memory is enhanced for items that are self-descriptive (Kuiper & Rogers, 1979); subjects who receive a recognition test for a list of previously studied trait adjectives tend to give false alarms to items that are, in fact, self-descriptive (Rogers, Rogers, & Kuiper, 1979); and response latencies in self-rating tasks show an inverted-U effect typical of categorization judgments (Kuiper, 1981).

In yet a third series of studies, Rogers and his colleagues made use of research by Holyoak (1978; Holyoak & Gordon, 1983, 1984; Holyoak & Mah, 1981), Shoben (Shoben, Cech, & Schwanenflugel, 1983), and others on comparative judgment. For example, comparisons of the self-descriptiveness of trait adjectives shows a symbolic distance effect: subjects are faster to judge pairs of traits that are far apart on a dimension of self-descriptiveness than they are those that are close together (Rogers, Kuiper, & Rogers, 1979). Interestingly, however, these investigators did not find a semantic congruity effect in which comparative judgments are faster when the question (e.g., Is X more or less than Y?) matches the magnitudes of the objects in question. This suggested to these investigators that the self is a fixed reference point that cannot be shifted from one point on a judgment scale to another (but see Holyoak & Gordon, 1984). Still, the status of the self as a reference point is confirmed by evidence of asymmetries in comparative judgment (Holyoak & Gordon, 1983; Srull & Gaelick, 1983). Thus, subjects generally judge others to be more similar to themselves than they judge themselves to be similar to others. This difference is reduced when the others are highly familiar, such as one's parents or familiar social stereotypes, but this only means that the self is one among many potential reference points mediating social judgment.

The Taxonomy of Knowledge

There is wide agreement among cognitive psychologists that memory stores two basic types of information: declarative and procedural (Ryle, 1949; Winograd, 1975).[3] Declarative knowledge consists of facts or beliefs about the nature of the world (e.g., that birds have wings and feathers, and that they sing and fly; and that Columbus began the European conquest of the Americas in 1492). Declarative knowledge may be further subdivided into semantic and episodic knowledge (Tulving, 1983). *Semantic knowledge* is the individual's mental lexicon of abstract and categorical information, whereas *episodic knowledge* consists of autobiographical memories. The difference between semantic and episodic knowledge is that episodic memories make reference to events that involve the self and that occurred at a particular (and unique point) in space and time. Thus, one can have semantic knowledge that President Kennedy was assassinated in 1963, and that the space shuttle Challenger blew up in 1986; or one can have episodic memory for the event of learning these facts. The difference between semantic and episodic knowledge is exemplified by the difference between textbook knowledge and flashbulb memories (Brown & Kulik, 1977; Winograd & Neisser, 1992), although not all episodic memories take such dramatic form.

Procedural knowledge consists of the skills, rules, and strategies that are used to manipulate and transform declarative knowledge in the course of perceiving, remembering, thinking, and acting. Procedural knowledge can be further subdivided into cognitive and motor skills: a person can know how to take square

---

[3]More recently, Tulving and Schacter (1990) proposed a third memory system, which holds perceptual information about the structure of objects, rather than their meaning. The perceptual memory system appears to underlie some forms of implicit memory in both normal subjects and brain-damaged patients. Because it is not clearly relevant to the self, the perceptual representation system is not discussed further here.

roots in his or her head, and how to tie square knots with his or her fingers. Some procedural knowledge is innate, but much of it is acquired gradually, through repeated practice—a process known as automatization, routinization, or knowledge compilation (Anderson, 1982). Automatic processes are executed without any intention on the part of the person, cannot be controlled once they are engaged, and consume little or no attentional capacity (Logan, 1988; Schneider & Shiffrin, 1977). Within the domain of social cognition, the processes involved in impression formation and causal attribution may be classified as procedural knowledge (see Smith, chapter 3, Volume 1), as can the processes that generate emotional responses to events (Leventhal, 1984).

Conceptually, the difference between declarative and procedural knowledge is the difference between knowing that and knowing how. But empirically, an important difference between declarative and procedural knowledge is that declarative knowledge is consciously accessible, at least in principle, whereas procedural knowledge is not. We have direct introspective access to what we know and what we believe, but we know our procedural knowledge only by inference (or, perhaps, by slowing the process down and taking note of what we are doing). Thus, from the point of view of memory structures, the self consists exclusively of declarative knowledge. As important as they are to mental life, the individual's repertoire of skills, rules, and strategies are not part of the self. However, metaknowledge (Flavell, 1977; Nelson, 1992) of procedures can be linked to the self. People know that they know how to do such things as take square roots and tie square knots, even if they do not know how they do them, and this sort of declarative knowledge can be an important part of the self.

MEANING-BASED REPRESENTATIONS OF THE SELF

Traditional associative-network theories of memory have focused almost entirely on *meaning-based representations*, which encode information about the semantic relations among objects, events, and their features (Anderson, 1976, 1983; for a historical review, see Anderson & Bower, 1973).[4] In the simplest versions of

---

[4]Although propositions and images represent particular objects, persons, situations, and events, another form of knowledge structure, the schema, is used to represent general categories of things, their characteristic features, and the interrelations among them (for reviews of the schema concept, see Brewer & Nakamura, 1984; Hastie, 1981; Rumelhart, 1984; Taylor & Crocker, 1981). Schemata contain both perception-based and meaning-based information, but this information is more abstract, consisting of a set of slots representing typical attributes and the values that these attributes typically take. Schemata, then, are concepts representing categories. As such, the self-schema may be thought of as a more or less abstract mental representation of the self, representing his or her typical features or attributes and the relations among them. Thus, the self-schema of a certain professor may contain the information that when he is in the office during the academic year he is generally shaved, and wears tweed slacks, shoes and socks, a long-sleeved shirt, and a tie; but that at home, or in the office during the summer, that same person may be found in jeans, a T-shirt, and boat shoes. As such, the self-schema may represent the situation-specific expectations associated with one's repertoire of concept-specific selves.

these theories, like Anderson and Bower's (1973) HAM model, basic concepts are represented by nodes in a graph structure, whereas associative links represent the relations between these concepts. More complex versions of associative network theory, like Anderson's (1983) ACT* model, represent declarative knowledge in terms of abstract propositions, or sentencelike primitive units of meaning consisting of subjects, agents, experiencers, relations, objects, and time, but leaving out much concrete perceptual detail. Such propositions are linked to each other in an extensive, tangled web of factual knowledge known as a propositional network. Network representations make a further distinction between types, or general classes, and tokens, or specific instances, permitting the same verbal label to refer to two different persons, objects, or events. Finally, propositional representations can be organized hierarchically, with one proposition serving as a unit for yet another proposition. Thus, a set of interlocking propositions can specify the spatiotemporal context in which an event occurred, or the causal relationship between two facts, and the like.

Associative-Network Models of Person Memory

Associative networks have served as a popular format for modeling aspects of social cognition, especially person memory, or one's knowledge about particular individuals. Thus, one's knowledge about a particular person (e.g., Jimmy Carter) can be represented as a set of propositions in which that individual serves as either the subject or the object of a number of factual statements.[5] These propositions can represent abstract trait knowledge about the individual (e.g., altruistic, conciliatory), and concrete behavioral information (e.g., renovated slum housing in New York, negotiated with Sadat and Begin at Camp David)— corresponding to semantic and episodic memory, respectively. Within the domain of person memory, research has focused on three general models for the representation of semantic and episodic information about persons (for reviews, see Hastie et al., 1980; Hastie, Park, & Weber, 1984; Kihlstrom & Hastie, in press; Klein & Loftus, 1993a, 1993b; Srull, 1984; Wyer & Gordon, 1984; Wyer & Srull, 1989a, 1989b; see also Wyer & Carlston, chapter 2, Volume 1).

Based on work on categorical organization in verbal learning, Hamilton (1989; Hamilton, Driscoll, & Worth, 1990; Hamilton, Katz, & Leirer, 1980), Ostrom

---

[5]Social memory is not just about persons, and associative networks can represent information about events and behaviors as well as people (and other living things). Moreover, associative networks operating according to a principle of spreading activation are not the only medium in which theories of person memory have been written. For example, Wyer and Carlston (1979) and Wyer and Srull (1989a) proposed that information about persons, including oneself (as well as events and other social objects), is stored in content-addressable bins structured as push-down stacks, and thus operating according to a principle of last in, first out. Each format has its assets and liabilities, discussion of which is far beyond the scope of this chapter. But the two formats are not necessarily incompatible. For example, Wyer and his colleagues indicated that individual items stored in bins may be represented as fragments of a network.

(Ostrom, Lingle, Pryor, & Geva, 1980; Ostrom, Pryor, & Simpson, 1981), and others have proposed a hierarchical model in which episodic information about a person's experiences and behaviors is organized according to semantic information about that person's traits and attitudes. In terms of a generic associative-network model of memory, this situation would be represented by nodes representing traits that fan off a central node representing the person, and in turn collect nodes representing behaviors exemplifying these traits.

An alternative view, stimulated by general computer simulation models of memory such as HAM (Anderson & Bower, 1973) and ACT* (Anderson, 1976, 1983), was proposed by Hastie (1980, 1988; Hastie & Kumar, 1979; Hastie & Park, 1986), Srull (1981; Srull, Lichtenstein, & Rothbart, 1983), and Klein and Loftus (1990a). In general terms, these network models assume that every item of information about a topic has its own link to a central node representing that topic. Once formed, associative links are permanent. When applied to person memory, these models imply that individuals are represented by a content-free, but addressable person node, closely linked to nodes representing the person's name and physical appearance, and also linked to other nodes representing items of semantic (e.g., trait) and episodic (e.g., behavioral) information about that person. Both trait and behavior nodes fan off the central person node, but they are unconnected (or only weakly connected) to each other. Thus, traits and behaviors are represented independently in person memory. Specifically, there is little or no clustering of behaviors by traits, and access to behaviors does not depend on access to the traits they exemplify (nor, for that matter, vice versa).

A third view holds that person memory represents only episodic information (Keenan, 1993; Locksley & Lenauer, 1981). Whereas the trait-based and independent-storage models assume that abstract descriptors are retrieved directly from the memory representation, the pure episodic model asserts that abstract descriptions are inferred from behavioral information retrieved from the representation, in a manner analogous to self-perception theory (Bem, 1967, 1972). Thus, no semantic information pertaining to traits or other generic characteristics is associated directly with the person node.

An alternative representational format has been proposed by Wyer and his colleagues, using a bin metaphor for the organization of memory (Wyer & Srull, 1986, 1989a, 1989b; see also Wyer & Carlston, chapter 2, Volume 1). According to this model, information about people is deposited in permanent, unlimited-capacity, content-addressable storage bins, each labeled by a header that denotes its referent. Bins can contain propositions about a person and his or her traits and behaviors, but they also can contain other kinds of representations, such as images or temporal strings denoting sequences of events. Bins organize information in a push-down stack. That is, representations are stored in bins in the order they are formed and are retrieved by means of a probabilistic, top-down search. Aside from this principle of "last in, first out," bin contents are unorganized. Thus, as in the Hastie-Srull model, each item of information, whether semantic or episodic, might be stored independently of every other item. In addition, several different bins can be formed pertaining to the same individual in different situations or social roles. The contents of one context-specific bin can be stored and retrieved independently of the contents of others.

Associative-Network Models of the Self

Of course, each of these structural models can be applied to the mental representation of one's self in memory. Figure 4.1 shows a schematic representation of each of the three associative-network models. (Wyer & Srull [1986] have also proposed a bin model of the self, which is not depicted here.) Each model is centered on a single node representing the self. In Panel A, derived from the theories of Hamilton and Ostrom, only nodes representing trait information are directly linked to the central self-node; these, in turn, collect information about relevant behaviors. In Panel B, derived from Hastie and Srull, nodes representing trait and behavioral information are independently linked to the self. In Panel C, only nodes representing behaviors are linked to the self, but each behavior is indirectly (i.e., by inference) linked to a node representing the trait it exemplifies.

The question is which one is correct? A series of studies by Klein, Loftus, and their colleagues has shed new light on this question. Their research made use of a priming paradigm (Meyer & Schvaneveldt, 1971), in which processing of a probe facilitates (or, in the case of negative priming, impairs; Roediger & Neely, 1982) processing of a subsequently presented target. The pattern of priming observed serves as the basis for inferences about cognitive structure. Thus, in a lexical decision task, processing of the probe "bread" facilitates subsequent processing of the semantically related target "butter," compared with trials where the probe and target are not related semantically.

Klein and Loftus (1993a, 1993b; see also Klein, Loftus, & Sherman, 1993; Klein, Loftus, Trafton, & Fuhrman, 1992) developed a new priming paradigm comparing three tasks: a descriptive task asked subjects to decide whether a word (e.g., a trait adjective) describes themselves; an autobiographical task required them to retrieve a personal memory associated with the word; and a define task asked the subjects to generate a definition of the word. If self-descriptiveness judgments are mediated by the retrieval of autobiographical memory, then performance of the autobiographical task on a stimulus word should facilitate subsequent performance of the descriptive task on that word. By the same token, if episodes in autobiographical memory are organized by their trait implications, then performance of the descriptive task should facilitate performance on the autobiographical task.

In their first priming study, Klein et al. (1989, Experiment 2) asked subjects to perform two of these tasks successively, generating nine possible task combinations. So, on one trial, a subject might perform the descriptive and autobio-

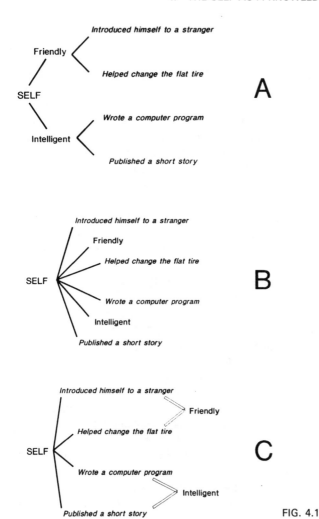

FIG. 4.1

graphical tasks with respect to a particular word; on the next trial, with a new word, he or she might perform the autobiographical and define tasks. Priming was observed in all three cases where the initial and subsequent tasks were of the same type. But the most important results were that, compared with the effects of an initial define task, an initial autobiographical task did not prime performance on a subsequent descriptive task; nor did an initial descriptive task prime performance on a subsequent autobiographical task. Thus, contrary to the trait-based view, descriptive information is not activated in the process of retrieving behavioral information. Contrary to the pure episodic model, retrieving behavioral information has no impact on making descriptive judgments. Apparently, trait (semantic) and behavioral (episodic) knowledge are independent from each other in the mental representation of oneself.

A subsequent experiment (Klein et al., 1992, Experiment 2; see also Experiments 3 and 4) provided a clearer test of these competing hypotheses. It could be that autobiographical retrieval is more important for some trait judgments than others. For example, some theorists have suggested that judgments about traits that are not central to one's self-concept are more likely to depend on autobiographical retrieval than are judgments about traits that are central to one's self-concept (e.g., Bower & Gilligan, 1979; Kihlstrom & Cantor, 1984; Klein & Loftus, 1990b; Wyer & Srull, 1989a). If such a difference exists, it would not be apparent in the data from Klein et al. (1989, Experiment 2), because that study combined all traits without regard to level of self-descriptiveness. Accordingly, subjects in Klein et al. (1992, Experiment 2) rated the self-descriptiveness of each trait presented in the main task. Regardless of the self-descriptiveness of the trait being judged, no priming was observed between the descriptive and autobiographical tasks.

Results from other sorts of studies also support the independent storage of semantic and episodic knowledge about oneself. For example, Klein, Loftus, and Plog (1992) made use of the phenomenon of transfer-appropriate processing (Roediger & Blaxton, 1987; Roediger, Weldon, & Challis, 1989), a variant on the encoding-specificity paradigm of Tulving and Thompson (1973). Basically, the principle of transfer-appropriate processing holds that retention is best when the operations performed at the time of retrieval recapitulate those performed at the time of initial encoding. Thus, retention should be best when subjects perform a descriptive or autobiographical task at both study and test. But if self-description requires autobiographical retrieval, then retention should be relatively good when the subject performs the autobiographical task at encoding, but the descriptive task at retrieval. In a study session, Klein et al. (1992) asked subjects to perform descriptive, autobiographical, or define tasks on a set of trait adjectives. In a test session 2 weeks later, the subjects performed one of the tasks on these same items and a list of distractors, and then were asked to recognize the old items. Recognition was best when the same task was performed at encoding and retrieval, as expected by virtue of transfer-appropriate processing. But, consistent with the notion of independent storage, for trait adjectives subjected to an autobiographical study task, a descriptive task was no more effective as a retrieval context than was a define task.

These conclusions were supported by a study by Klein et al. (1989, Experiment 4), which capitalized on the principle of encoding variability. This principle states that the memorability of an item is a function of the number of different ways it is processed, because each task makes available a different type of trace information (Bower, 1972; Estes, 1959; Martin, 1972). Memory was best when subjects performed both descriptive and autobiographical tasks on items, compared with the single or repeated performance of either task by itself. Thus, the autobiographical and descriptive tasks each make available new information, which is not ordinarily processed in the course of the other.

Neuropsychological Evidence

Perhaps the most dramatic evidence for the independent storage of semantic and episodic self-knowledge comes from the organic and functional disorders of memory. On the organic side, bilateral damage to the medial temporal lobe (including the hippocampus) or the diencephalon (including the mammillary bodies) produces a gross anterograde amnesia, meaning that the person is incapable of remembering events that occurred since the onset of his or her illness, and often premorbid events as well (Kopelman, Wilson, & Baddeley, 1989; Squire, 1987). On the functional side, cases of psychogenic fugue involve a complete loss of autobiographical memory, and sometimes of identity as well (Kihlstrom, 1992; Schacter & Kihlstrom, 1989).

Nevertheless, such patients can describe their personalities accurately. For example, in case of psychogenic fugue, Schacter, Wang, Tulving, and Freedman (1982) asked the patient to complete the Minnesota Multiphasic Personality Inventory (MMPI) both during his fugue and after it was resolved: the two profiles were essentially identical. Assuming that the post-recovery profile was valid, then, it appears that accurate self-description does not require access to autobiographical memories. Most recently, Tulving (1993), testing a speculation by Klein and Loftus (1993a), found that the patient K.C., who lost his entire fund of episodic memory (and underwent a marked personality change) following a motorcycle accident, was able to describe his postmorbid personality with considerable accuracy (with his mother's ratings serving as the criterion). Thus, K.C. was able to acquire accurate knowledge of his new personality without being able to retain information about any of the episodes through which that knowledge was gained.

Results such as these represent a serious challenge to both the trait-based and pure episodic models of self-knowledge. If traits are not automatically activated on the way to behaviors, and if semantic knowledge of self can be accessed without reference to specific episodes, the two types of information must be stored separately. Still, there has to be some connection between semantic and episodic knowledge: Perception of an event is constructed against a background of knowledge stored in semantic memory, and semantic knowledge has its origins in specific learning experiences. Perhaps episodic and semantic knowledge are connected at another level in the tangled network of stored knowledge. For example, episodes may be linked directly to the self and the traits they exemplify. Alternatively, traits associated with an individual may be tokens of more abstract types. These types may be linked to types of characteristic behaviors, with these types linked to tokens representing particular episodes in the lives of specific individuals, self, and others.

PERCEPTION-BASED REPRESENTATIONS
OF THE SELF

In addition to propositional representations based on meaning, more recent state-ments of associative-network theories of memory (e.g., Anderson, 1983, 1990) expanded the list of available forms of mental representation to include perception-based representations. Perception-based representations store one's knowledge of the perceptual structure of objects and events, and they come in at least two forms. *Spatial images* represent information about the configuration, or relative position (with respect to the viewer and each other), of objects or features in mul-tidimensional space. For example, they encode information about whether some-thing is above or below something else, to the left or the right, and in front or behind. Spatial images are involved in such tasks as mental rotation (Shepard & Cooper, 1983) and image scanning (Kosslyn, 1980).

Spatial images need not be visual, because they may preserve information about spatial configuration without also preserving information about visual appearance (the same point applies to other sensory modalities, such as sound and touch). But this information is also preserved, in the form of strictly visual images that contain information on appearance details such as form, color, and perspective. Conceptually, spatial and visual images are quite different. In fact, there is some neuropsychological and brain-imaging evidence that performance on verbal, spa-tial, and visual tasks is mediated by different brain systems (Farah, 1988; Koss-lyn & Koenig, 1992; Sergeant, 1990). Put briefly, it appears that performance on spatial tasks is mediated by the parietal lobes, whereas performance on ex-pressly visual tasks is mediated by the temporal lobes. Although the existence of imagistic as well as propositional codes in memory has been a matter of some debate (Anderson, 1978; Kosslyn & Pomerantz, 1977; Paivio, 1986; Pylyshyn, 1981), the neuropsychological evidence strongly suggests that we make room for a second category of perception-based representation, the visual image.

Images of Others

Perception-based representations have not received much attention in the social cognition literature, but they are clearly important (McArthur & Baron, 1983). For example, we can conjure fairly clear visual and auditory images of the faces and voices of those we know. We can make a wide variety of social judgments based on visual stereotypes: age, from changes in head shape and body propor-tions (Pittenger & Todd, 1983; Shaw & Pittenger, 1977); gender, from gait in walking (Kozlowski & Cutting, 1977); and power, from "babyfacedness" or a receding hairline (McArthur, 1982; Keating, Mazur, & Seagall, 1981). Most of us recognize the voices of our friends when they call on the telephone; we can also recognize them by their gait alone (Kozlowski & Cutting, 1977). Prosopag-nosic patients, who cannot name familiar faces, are able to recognize friends and family by the sound of their voices or their style of walk (Damasio & Damasio, 1986). The symbolic distance effect appears to be mediated by a kind of linear ordering of the people to be compared (Holyoak, 1978). The scripts that guide interpersonal behavior encode the canonical sequence of the various events in a social exchange (Abelson, 1981; Schank & Abelson, 1977).

The Self-Image

Much the same point can be made about perception-based mental representations of the self. We have them, but we have not studied them as much as we have studied verbal knowledge encoded in associative networks. Still, some interesting beginnings have been made. For example, consider the research implications of taking the notion of self-image as literally as the idea of self-concept. Do we really have a mental image of what we look like, in terms of surface features, height, width, depth, posture, and gait? Head (1926) defined the body schema as a postural model of the body by which we maintain stability and adjust to environmental stimulation. It is this body schema that is distorted in prism-adaptation experiments. Similarly, Schilder (1938) referred to the body-image as "the picture of our own body which we form in our mind, that is to say, the way in which the body appears to ourselves" (p. 11), and argued that it was important in maintaining the distinction between self and other. On the other hand, Fisher and Cleveland (1958) argued that the body image is influenced both by the actual perceptual properties of the body surface and the individual's attitudes and expectancies.

A vast amount of clinical evidence has suggested that there is an internal representation of the body and its parts that is independent of immediate sensory stimulation. For example, schizophrenics in the acute stage of their illness often complain of changes in their perceptions of their own bodies (Chapman, Chapman, & Raulin, 1978). Patients with eating disorders such as anorexia and bulimia make it abundantly clear that they have mental images of their own bodies that are widely at variance from objective fact. In body dysmorphic disorder (formerly known as dysmorphophobia), patients with normal physical appearance complain of bodily defects such as wrinkled or spotted skin, enlarged or shrinking hands or feet, excessive facial hair, or misshapen facial features (Phillips, 1991; Rosen, Srebnik, Saltzberg, & Wendt, 1991). In cases of phantom limb, amputees continue to perceive lost arms or legs as if they were still integral parts of their bodies (Melzack, 1989). A similar phenomenon is sometimes observed, albeit temporarily, in cases of spinal anesthesia for orthopedic surgery or caesarian section.

Within clinical psychology, the body image is often studied by means of the Draw-a-Person Test (DAP). Unfortunately, the DAP asks the subject to draw a person, not him or herself. At any rate, the procedure confounds the individuals self-image with his or her ability to draw. However, the more recent literature on eating disorders has provided a set of instruments that can be used to evaluate the person's body-image. For example, Chapman et al. (1978) developed a self-report Body-Image Aberration Scale consisting of a series of questions tapping the feelings of unclear body boundaries, unreality or estrangement of body parts, bodily deterioration, changes in size, proportions, spatial relationships of body parts, and changes in appearance of the body. More recently, Fallon and Rozin (1985; Rozin & Fallon, 1988; see also Zellner, Harner, & Adler, 1989) introduced a set of nine figure drawings of swimsuit-clad males and females which subjects can use to rate their current figure, ideal figure, figure most attractive to the opposite (or, for that matter, the same) gender, and the figure they themselves find most attractive. A related procedure is the Body-Image Assessment (Williamson, Davis, Goreczny, & Blouin, 1989). A common finding is that eating-disordered individuals perceive themselves as heavier or bigger than normal controls, which is indirect evidence that they have inaccurate body images.

In addition, a wide variety of experimental techniques have been adapted to study the self-image and its distortions. In an early line of research, Traub, Orbach, and their colleagues performed a series of experiments with an adjustable body-distorting mirror, not unlike those found in carnival fun houses (Traub & Orbach, 1964; Orbach, Traub, & Olson, 1966; Traub, Olson, Orbach, & Cardone, 1967). In their main experiment, they placed normal subjects in front of a distorting mirror and asked then to adjust the device until their appearance was correct. Based on departures from a perfectly flat mirror, they observed that subjects accepted a wide range of deviations as accurate reflects of their own bodies, suggesting that the self-image is somewhat imprecise. By the same token, a group of chronic schizophrenics showed a much wider range of acceptability than normal controls. However, the patients also showed a wide range of acceptability when viewing distorted reflections of an inanimate object. Thus, although it is fairly clear that normal people have a fairly accurate mental representation of their own appearance, the perceptual distortions shown by schizophrenics may not be unique to the self-image.

Other studies have pursued this question by means of photographs. Thus, Orbach et al. (1966) found that subjects who are shown a range of photographs are able to pick the undistorted one quite reliably, with a small range of acceptance. The difference between this outcome and that obtained in the case of the distorting mirror is that subjects did not have the opportunity to view themselves in an undistorted mirror before making their adjustments. Perhaps, as Orbach et al. (1966) suggested, accurate self-images need to be anchored by an undistorted external reference point. Later research by Yarmey (1979; Yarmey & Johnson, 1982), obtained with photographs the same sort of false alarms effect found by Rogers et al. (1979) in recognition memory for self-descriptive trait adjectives. Perhaps the most compelling evidence for the existence of a memory-based, internal representation of one's own appearance is provided by a study of preferences for photographs of subjects and their friends (Mita, Dermer, & Knight, 1977).

On test trials, subjects were presented with pairs of photographs composed of an original and its mirror reversal. When viewing photos of their friends, subjects preferred the original—how their friends appeared through the lens of a camera. But when viewing photographs of themselves, the same subjects preferred the mirror-reversed version—how they appeared to themselves when they brushed their teeth and combed their hair.

Although these studies comprise a useful beginning to the study of perception-based representations of the self, we are struck by the fact that the field has not yet drawn on the experimental paradigms developed in the study of spatial and visual images (e.g., Kosslyn, 1980; Shepard & Cooper, 1983). For example, we wonder if people show mental rotation effects for depictions of their own bodies, or difficulties in identifying themselves from unusual perspectives, or image scanning effects for landmarks on the surface of their bodies, similar to those found in the domain of nonsocial objects. Furthermore, we wonder if pathologies of body image, such as those found in eating disorders or body dysmorphic disorder, are reflected in individual differences in the performance of such tasks. To take a concrete example, will a bulimic woman who perceives her body to be fatter than it actually is take longer to scan between relevant landmarks (e.g., on the abdomen, arms, or legs) than a normal control?

Linear Orderings and Temporal Strings

Another type of perceptual representation is the *linear ordering*, which contains information about the relative ordering of objects or events along some dimension (e.g., smaller to larger or smaller to bigger). A special case of the linear ordering is the *temporal string*, which marks the progression, sequential order, or temporal succession of a set of objects and events (e.g., first to last, remote to recent, or earlier to later; Underwood, 1977). Although linear orderings and temporal strings do not preserve spatial configuration or sensory detail, they are classified as perception-based, because the linear or temporal relations that they record between objects and events have nothing to do with the meaning of those items.

Temporal Sequencing.   One extremely important aspect of the mental representation of self is the person's set of consciously accessible autobiographical memories.[6] Temporal strings may be especially important in the representation of such knowledge. One's personal experiences have an intrinsic temporal structure. In principle, every episodic memory is associated with a unique temporal marker—at least, every episode in a person's life occurred at a distinct moment

---

[6]Coverage of the extensive literature on autobiographical memory is beyond the scope of this chapter. For comprehensive reviews, see Rubin (1986), Neisser and Winograd (1988), and Cohen (1989).

in time. While we may not remember the precise moments at which events occurred in our lives, we do tend to remember which followed which; the entire set of such memories represents a narrative of the individual's life. Although temporal organization is important to episodic memory, it seems highly unlikely that an individual's entire biography is laid out in a single linear string. Rather, intuitively it seems that one's autobiographical record possesses a kind of phrase structure (Anderson, 1983), in which smaller sequences of memories are recorded as strings within strings; recall of any element in a phrase unit increases the likelihood that all the elements in that unit will be recalled. Within each phrase unit, access is easiest to the first element in the string, and recall proceeds naturally from one item to the next until the end.

An early demonstration of the role of temporal organization in autobiographical memory was a series of studies of posthypnotic amnesia conducted by Kihlstrom and his colleagues (for a review, see Kihlstrom, 1985). In one series of studies, Kihlstrom and Evans (Evans & Kihlstrom, 1973; Kihlstrom & Evans, 1979) examined the order in which subjects recalled the test suggestions administered in the course of a standardized hypnotic procedure. In the absence of suggestions for amnesia, recall tends to be temporally ordered, beginning with the first item and proceeding through to the end. However, when an amnesia suggestion is administered, hypnotizable subjects, who tend to be responsive to such suggestions, show a disruption of temporal sequencing, including a reduced tendency to recall the first item first. Insusceptible subjects who did not experience amnesia showed no such effect. The difference between hypnotizable and insusceptible subjects is observed even when subjects are reminded to recall the items in temporal sequence. Kihlstrom and Wilson (1984) confirmed this effect in a study of serial organization in recall of items in a wordlist. One of the mechanisms for posthypnotic amnesia appears to be a disruption in the temporal tagging of memories and/or the organization of these memories in a temporal sequence, which makes it difficult for the subject to enter the search set and retrieve relevant items.

Temporal organization is also important in memory for other sorts of personal experiences. As noted earlier, people appear to possess scripts for many different types of events, consisting of a set of characteristic events and actions arranged in a sequence that represents the temporal and causal relations among them (Abelson, 1981; Schank & Abelson, 1977). Scripts not only guide the process of categorizing and navigating social interactions; they also help people to remember these interactions later. Thus, when Bower, Black, and Turner (1979) asked subjects to read and recall stories depicting familiar events, they found that the memory reports included (a) intrusions from the generic script that were not in the actual story, (b) confusions among different stories following the same general script, and (c) a tendency to rearrange the events in the story to follow the canonical sequence represented in the script. Similar results were obtained by Wyer and his colleagues (Wyer & Bodenhausen, 1985; Wyer, Shoben, Fuhrman, & Bodenhausen, 1985), who also found a symbolic distance effect in judgments of temporal order.

These findings were obtained in an artificial laboratory situation, but there is good reason to think that memory for actual personal experiences shows the same sort of effects (Fuhrman & Wyer, 1988; Nakamura, Graesser, Zimmerman, & Riha, 1985). In fact, Barsalou (1988) found that chronological order was the highest level of organization observed in autobiographical recall. In describing the events of a particular summer, subjects generally began at the beginning and ended at the end. After describing an extended event (such as a trip to Europe), subjects often returned to the beginning of the epoch in question and recalled another extended event following a parallel time track before turning their attention to another epoch entirely. Barsalou also noted evidence of *pivoting*, or switching from one organizational rubric to another. For example, in the midst of recalling events from a particular time period, subjects switched to recalling memories associated with a particular participant, location, or activity encountered in one of the events.

Temporal Chunking.   Although linear orderings and temporal strings are continuous representations, it is also clear that a hierarchical structure can be superimposed on them, breaking them up into categorical chunks (Huttenlocher, Hedges, & Prohaska, 1988). For example, human height is a continuous dimension, but, by any standard, Danny DeVito and Linda Hunt are short, whereas Magic Johnson and Kareem Abdul Jabar are tall. Similarly, historical time is a continuous dimension, but it is conveniently broken up into chunks such as the Renaissance, the Enlightenment, the 1960s, and the 1970s. Moreover, some means is necessary to represent the causal or enabling relationships among events (Gergen & Gergen, 1988; Mandler, 1984; Pennington & Hastie, 1992; Ross, 1989). The life course of an individual may be conveniently divided into a series of epochs, analogous to Erikson's "eight ages of man": infancy, childhood, adolescence, young adulthood, middle age, old age, and the like; according to one's educational and occupational history; or changes in one's family status. When subjects search autobiographical memory for particular events and experiences, they may enter the time line at the beginning and search forward, or at the end and search backward; or, alternatively, they may begin search at the beginning or end of one of the subordinate epochs.

The temporal organization of autobiographical memory also is revealed by studies of subjects' attempts to date, or judge the relative order of, personal experiences or public events occurring within their own lifetimes. In a series of studies, Brown, Rips, and Shevell (1985; Brown, Shevell, & Rips, 1986) showed that, in the absence of simple fact retrieval, dates are estimated by a means of an accessibility principle: the more easily an event is retrieved and the more knowledge a person has about the event, the more recent it is judged to have occurred. But this is not simply a variant on Tversky & Kahneman's (1973) availability heuristic. Rather, people appear to use whatever information they can remember about the event to locate it in terms of the course of their own lives, and thus produce a valid estimate. Accessibility does bias dating, but it also makes it more likely that subjects will retrieve enough information to permit them to make a decent estimate (Loftus & Marburger, 1983).

Organization of Autobiographical Memory

Barsalou's (1983, 1988) findings showed that autobiographical memory is not organized exclusively according to temporal principles. In an extension of script theory, Schank (1982) proposed that event memory is organized around two higher order conceptual structures: Memory Organization Packets (MOPs) and Thematic Organization Points (TOPs). The mental representation of any particular episode draws on a number of MOPs representing elements that are parts of a number of different scripts, as well as a script containing information peculiar to the class of event in question. Similarly, TOPs are general themes that unite, and give a kind of coherence to, events that might seem wildly different from each other. Interestingly, a study by Reiser, Black, and Abelson (1985) indicated that MOP-like cues are not as effective retrieval cues as script elements, presumably because they relate to too many different memories, producing a kind of fan or cue-overload effect. Kolodner (1984) successfully employed MOP-like structures in CYRUS, a computer simulation of Cyrus Vance's autobiographical memory for his years as secretary of state.

Reiser's results, and the success of Kolodner's model, suggested that autobiographical memory is also organized around activities or event types, although there is some ambiguity about precisely which level of description is the most effective organizer. Similarly, a case study by Wagenaar (1986) found that *what* cues were more effective at retrieving memories than those associated with *where*, *who*, and *when*. However, Barsalou (1988) found that activity cues had no privileged status, compared to participants, locations, or times.

Perhaps reflecting his earlier emphasis on ad-hoc categories, Barsalou (1988) proposed a general scheme for the organization of autobiographical memory that emphasized superordinate temporal structures, but permitted the person to move flexibly among a number of different organizational schemes. The primary organizers of autobiographical memory are *extended time lines*, which are arranged chronologically and hierarchically. Thus, an individual's autobiographical memory may contain a time line representing school, which is a partonomy consisting of elementary school, high school, and college; another representing work, consisting of afterschool jobs, summer employment during college, first job, and present job; and another representing social life, consisting of living at home, dating, first marriage, and second marriage. Each of these local time lines are also partonomies, distinguishing between freshman and senior year, entry-level and final positions, romance and breakup, and the like. These partonomies run in parallel, so that any particular segment of historical time may include aspects of several time lines.

Nested within extended time lines are *summarized events*, which represent events that occurred frequently during a particular period of time. Summarized events are constructed from *specific events*, which are episodic memories in the strict sense. However, this construction process does not require a repetition of a particular event. Rather, it only requires that an event activate a new combination of preexisting generic concepts; if the event activates a conceptual combination that already exists, then it is absorbed into the corresponding summarized event already available in memory.

Extended time lines summarize as well as organize the individual's life history and provide reference points for dating events. They also show interesting developmental trends, in that they are subject to revision at various points in the life cycle. Young children do not have extended time lines, which may account for the difficulty people have in remembering events from early childhood (Crovitz & Quina-Holland, 1976; Kihlstrom & Harackiewicz, 1982; Neisser, 1992b; Wetzler & Sweeney, 1986; White & Pillemer, 1979). However, the elderly, with the benefit of hindsight, may construct extended time lines that are quite different from those they possessed in adolescence or middle age.

In the present context, it is important to note, with Barsalou (1988), that the particular set of time lines represented in an individual's memory may be an important part of his or her self-concept. Viewed objectively, every life is a complex set of overlapping time lines that represent the progress of school, work, personal life, and the like. Which particular time line occupies the highest position in the organization of the individual's memory says a lot about that individual. Adults who become parents often date events around benchmarks in the lives of their children. The man who constantly forgets his wife's birthday and his wedding anniversary does not have his marriage uppermost in his mind. Long ago, Adler (1937) noted that what a person remembers reveals a lot about his or her personality and lifestyle. The same might be said about how people organize their memories. In the final analysis, the organization and content of autobiographical memory may be the clearest expression of oneself (Kihlstrom, 1981).

I AND ME

As James (1890/1981) noted, there is an intimate relationship between the self and consciousness: "The universal conscious fact is . . . 'I think' and 'I feel' " (p. 221). In his view, consciousness comes when we inject ourselves into our thoughts, feelings, and desires; when we take possession of them and own them; and when we experience and acknowledge them as ours. This relation between the self and consciousness raises the issue of the self as knower. Despite Rozin's (1976) photographic evidence of its existence, scientific psychology still disdains the homunculus. Unfortunately, it has proved difficult to know precisely how to construe the self as knower. James grappled with, and ultimately rejected as unsatisfactory, three different approaches: the theory of the soul; the associationistic theories of Locke, Hume, and the Mills; and the transcendentalist theory of Kant. But aside from identifying the I with thought itself, he was unable to make any positive progress.

After struggling with the problem for an entire career, Allport (1943, 1961) simply threw up his hands:

> This puzzling problem arises when we ask, "Who is the I who knows the bodily me, who has an image of myself and sense of identity over time, who knows that I have propriate strivings?" I know all these things and, what is more, I know that I know them. But who is it who has this perspectival grasp? (Allport, 1961, p. 128)

Allport (1961) went on to note that "Philosophers beyond count have racked their brains with this problem. It is beyond our present scope to enter into the argument" (p. 129). We are inclined to agree. But perhaps James was right simply to identify the self as knower with thought itself, and be content. From this point of view, the self as knower is simply the individual mind that is capable of representing the person who embodies it as well as objects and events in the external world. If so, then the self, as both knower and object of knowledge is the point at which cognitive, personality, and social psychology meet.

ACKNOWLEDGMENTS

The point of view represented in this chapter is based on research supported by Grant MH-35856 from the National Institute of Mental Health to J. F. Kihlstrom and a Regents Junior Faculty Fellowship to S. B. Klein. We thank Terrence Barnhardt, Lawrence Couture, Jennifer Dorfman, Elizabeth Glisky, Martha Glisky, Judith Loftus, Lori Marchese, Shelagh Mulvaney, Victor Shames, Allison Titcomb, Michael Valdisseri, and Susan Valdisseri for their comments.

REFERENCES

Abelson, R. P. (1981). Psychological status of the script concept. *American Psychologist, 36*, 715–729.

Adler, A. (1937). The significance of early recollections. *International Journal of Individual Psychology 3*, 283–287.

Allport, G. W. (1937). *Personality: A psychological interpretation.* New York: Holt, Rinehart, & Winston.

Allport, G. W. (1943). The ego in contemporary psychology. *Psychological Review, 50*, 451–478.

Allport, G. W. (1961). *Pattern and growth in personality.* New York: Holt, Rinehart, & Winston.

Allport, G. W., & Odbert, H. S. (1936). Trait-names: A psycho-lexical study. *Psychological Monographs, 47*(No. 211).

Anderson, J. R. (1976). *Language, memory, and thought.* Hillsdale, NJ: Lawrence Erlbaum Associates.

Anderson, J. R. (1978). Arguments concerning representations for mental imagery. *Psychological Review, 85*, 249–277.

Anderson, J. R. (1982). Acquisition of cognitive skill. *Psychological Review, 89*, 369–406.

Anderson, J. R. (1983). *The architecture of cognition*. Cambridge, MA: Harvard University Press.

Anderson, J. R. (1990). *Cognitive psychology and its implications* (3rd ed.). San Francisco: Freeman.

Anderson, J. R., & Bower, G. H. (1973). *Human associative memory*. Washington, DC: Winston.

Armstrong, S. L., Gleitman, L. R., & Gleitman, H. (1983). What some concepts might not be. *Cognition, 13*, 263–308.

Bargh, J. A. (1989). Conditional automaticity: Varieties of automatic influence in social perception and cognition. In J. S. Uleman & J. A. Bargh (Eds.), *Unintended thought* (pp. 3–51). New York: Guilford.

Barsalou, L. W. (1983). Ad hoc categories. *Memory & Cognition, 11*, 211–227.

Barsalou, L. W. (1988). The content and organization of autobiographical memories. In U. Neisser & E. Winograd (Eds.), *Remembering reconsidered: Ecological and traditional approaches to the study of memory* (pp. 193–243). Cambridge: Cambridge University Press.

Barsalou, L. W., & Medin, D. L. (1986). Concepts: Fixed definitions or dynamic context-dependent representations? *Cahiers de Psychologie Cognitive, 6*, 187–202.

Baumgardner, A. H., Kaufman, C. M., & Cranford, J. A. (1990). To be noticed favorably: Links between private self and public self. *Personality & Social Psychology Bulletin, 16*, 705–716.

Bellezza, F. S., & Hoyt, S. K. (1992). The self-reference effect and mental cuing. *Social Cognition, 10*, 51–78.

Bem, D. J. (1967). Self-perception: An alternative interpretation of cognitive-dissonance phenomena. *Psychological Review, 74*, 183–200.

Bem, D. J. (1972). Self-perception theory. In L. Berkowitz (Ed.), *Advances in experimental social psychology* (Vol. 6, pp. 1–62). New York: Academic Press.

Berkowitz, L. (Ed.). (1988). *Advances in experimental social psychology. Vol. 21. Social psychological studies of the self: Perspectives and programs*. San Diego: Academic Press.

Bleuler, E. (1950). *Dementia praecox; or, The group of schizophrenias*. New York: International Universities Press. (Original work published 1911)

Bower, G. H. (1972). Stimulus-sampling theory of encoding variability. In A. W. Melton & E. Martin (Eds.), *Coding processes in human memory* (pp. 85–123). Washington, DC: Winston.

Bower, G. H., Black, J. B., & Turner, T. J. (1979). Scripts in text comprehension and memory. *Cognitive Psychology, 11*, 177–220.

Bower, G. H., & Gilligan, S. G. (1979). Remembering information related to one's self. *Journal of Research in Personality, 13*, 420–432.

Breckler, S. J., Pratkanis, A. R., & McCann, C. D. (1991). The representation of self in multidimensional cognitive space. *British Journal of Social Psychology, 30*, 97–112.

Brewer, M. B. (1991). The social self: On being the same and different at the same time. *Personality & Social Psychology Bulletin, 17*, 475–482.

Brewer, W. F. (1986). What is autobiographical memory? In D. C. Rubin (Ed.), *Autobiographical memory* (pp. 25–49). Cambridge: Cambridge University Press.

Brewer, W. F., & Nakamura, G. V. (1984). The nature and functions of schemas. In R. S. Wyer & T. K. Srull (Eds.), *Handbook of social cognition* (Vol. 1, pp. 119–160). Hillsdale, NJ: Lawrence Erlbaum Associates.

Broughton, J. M. (1978). Development of concepts of self, mind, reality, and knowledge. In W. Damon (Ed.), *Social cognition* (pp. 75–100). San Francisco: Jossey-Bass.

Brown, N. R., Rips, L. J., & Shevell, S. K. (1985). The subjective dates of natural events in very-long-term memory. *Cognitive Psychology, 17*, 139–177.

Brown, N. R., Shevell, S. K., & Rips, L. J. (1986). Public memories and their personal context. In D. C. Rubin (Ed.), *Autobiographical memory* (pp. 137–158). Cambridge: Cambridge University Press.

Brown, R., & Kulik, J. (1977). Flashbulb memories. *Cognition, 5*, 73–99.

Bruner, J. S., Goodnow, J. J., & Austin, G. A. (1956). *A study of thinking*. New York: Wiley.

Bugental, J. F. T. (1964). Investigations into the self-concept: III. Instructions for the W-A-Y method. *Psychological Reports, 15,* 643–650.

Burke, P. A., Kraut, R. E., & Dworkin, R. H. (1986). Traits, consistency, and self-schemata: What do our methods measure? *Journal of Personality & Social Psychology, 47,* 568–579.

Burke, P. J., & Reitzes, D. C. (1981). The link between identity and role performance. *Social Psychology Quarterly, 4,* 83–92.

Cantor, N., & Genero, N. (1986). Psychiatric diagnosis and natural categorization: A close analogy. In T. Millon & G. L. Klerman (Eds.), *Contemporary directions in psychopathology: Towards the DSM-IV* (pp. 233–256). New York: Guilford.

Cantor, N., & Kihlstrom, J. F. (1987). *Personality and social intelligence.* Englewood Cliffs, NJ: Prentice-Hall.

Cantor, N., & Kihlstrom, J. F. (1989). Social intelligence and cognitive assessments of personality. In R. S. Wyer & T. K. Srull (Eds.), *Advances in social cognition* (Vol. 2, pp. 1–59). Hillsdale, NJ: Lawrence Erlbaum Associates.

Cantor, N., & Mischel, W. (1978). Prototypes in person perception. In L. Berkowitz (Ed.), *Advances in experimental social psychology* (Vol. 12, pp. 3–52). New York: Academic Press.

Chapman, L. J., & Chapman, J. P. (1973). *Psychological deficit in schizophrenia.* New York: Appleton-Century-Crofts.

Chapman, L. J., Chapman, J. P., & Raulin, M. L. (1978). Body image aberration in schizophrenia. *Journal of Abnormal Psychology, 87,* 399–407.

Chassin, L., Presson, C. C., Sherman, S. J., Corty, E., & Olshavsky, R. W. (1981). Self-images and cigarette smoking in adolescence. *Personality & Social Psychology Bulletin, 7,* 670–676.

Cohen, G. (1989). *Memory in the real world.* Hillsdale, NJ: Lawrence Erlbaum Associates.

Cousins, S. (1989). Culture and selfhood in Japan and the U.S. *Journal of Personality & Social Psychology, 56,* 124–131.

Craik, F. I. M., & Lockhart, R. S. (1972). Levels of processing: A framework for memory research. *Journal of Verbal Learning & Verbal Behavior, 11,* 671–684.

Crane, M., & Markus, H. (1982). Gender identity: The benefits of a self-schema approach. *Journal of Personality & Social Psychology, 43,* 1195–1197.

Crockett, W. H. (1965). Cognitive complexity and impression formation. In B. H. Maher (Ed.), *Progress in experimental personality research* (Vol. 2, pp. 47–90). New York: Academic Press.

Cross, S. E., & Markus, H. R. (1990). The willful self. *Personality & Social Psychology Bulletin, 16,* 726–742.

Crovitz, H. F., & Quina-Holland, L. (1976). Proportion of episodic memories from early childhood by years of age. *Bulletin of the Psychonomic Society, 7,* 61–62.

Damasio, A. R., & Damasio, H. (1986). The anatomical substrate of prosopagnosia. In R. Bruyer (Ed.), *The neuropsychology of face perception and facial expression* (pp. 31–38). Hillsdale, NJ: Lawrence Erlbaum Associates.

Damon, W. (1983). *Social and personality development.* New York: Norton.

Damon, W., & Hart, D. (1988). *Self-understanding in childhood and adolescence.* New York: Cambridge University Press.

Dixon, J. C. (1957). Development of self-recognition. *Journal of Genetic Psychology, 91,* 251–256.

Dixon, T. M., & Baumeister, R. F. (1991). Escaping the self: The moderating effect of self-complexity. *Personality & Social Psychology Bulletin, 17,* 363–368.

Eder, R. A. (1989). The emergent personologist: The structure and content of 3½-year-olds' and 7½-year-olds' concepts of themselves and other persons. *Child Development, 60,* 1218–1228.

Eder, R. A. (1990). Uncovering young children's psychological selves: Individual and developmental differences. *Child Development, 61,* 849–863.

Epstein, R., Lanza, R. P., & Skinner, B. F. (1981). "Self-awareness" in the pigeon. *Science, 212,* 695–696.

Epstein, S. (1973). The self-concept revisited: Or a theory of a theory. *American Psychologist, 28,* 404–416.

Estes, W. K. (1959). The statistical approach to learning theory. In S. Koch (Ed.), *Psychology: A study of a science* (Vol. 2, pp. 380–491). New York: McGraw-Hill.

Evans, F. J., & Kihlstrom, J. F. (1973). Posthypnotic amnesia as disrupted retrieval. *Journal of Abnormal Psychology, 82*, 317–323.

Fallon, A. E., & Rozin, P. (1985). Sex differences in perceptions of desirable body shape. *Journal of Abnormal Psychology, 94*, 102–105.

Farah, M. J. (1988). Is visual imagery really visual? Overlooked evidence from neuropsychology. *Psychological Review, 95*, 307–317.

Fisher, S., & Cleveland, S. E. (1958). *Body image and personality*. Princeton, NJ: Van Nostrand.

Fivush, R., & Hamond, N. R. (1990). Autobiographical memory across the preschool years: Toward reconceptualizing childhood amnesia. In R. Fivush & J. A. Hudson (Eds.), *Knowing and remembering in young children* (pp. 223–248). Cambridge: Cambridge University Press.

Flavell, J. (1977). Metacognition and cognitive monitoring: A new area of cognitive-developmental inquiry. *American Psychologist, 34*, 906–911.

Flavell, J., & Ross, L. (Eds.). (1981). *Social cognitive development: Frontiers and possible futures*. New York: Cambridge University Press.

Fong, G. T., & Markus, H. (1982). Self-schemas and judgments about others. *Social Cognition, 1*, 191–204.

Fuhrman, R. W., & Wyer, R. S. (1988). Event memory: Temporal-order judgments of personal life experiences. *Journal of Personality & Social Psychology, 54*, 365–384.

Gallup, G. G. (1968). Mirror-image stimulation. *Psychological Bulletin, 70*, 782–793.

Gallup, G. G., & Suarez, S. D. (1986). Self-awareness and the emergence of mind in humans and other primates. In J. Suls & A. G. Greenwald (Eds.), *Psychological perspectives on the self* (Vol. 3, pp. 3–26). Hillsdale, NJ: Lawrence Erlbaum Associates.

Gara, M. A., & Rosenberg, S. (1979). The identification of persons as supersets and subsets in free-response personality descriptions. *Journal of Personality & Social Psychology, 37*, 2161–2170.

Gara, M. A., Rosenberg, S., & Cohen, B. D. (1987). Personal identity and the schizophrenic process. *Psychiatry, 50*, 267–279.

Gara, M. A., Rosenberg, S., & Mueller, D. R. (1989). The perception of self and other in schizophrenia. *International Journal of Personal Construct Psychology, 2*, 253–270.

Gergen, K. J., & Gergen, M. M. (1988). Narrative and the self as relationship. In L. Berkowitz (Ed.), *Advances in experimental social psychology* (Vol. 21, pp. 17–56). San Diego: Academic Press.

Gillund, G., & Shiffrin, R. M. (1984). A retrieval model for both recognition and recall. *Psychological Review, 91*, 1–67.

Goldberg, L. R. (1978). Differential attribution of trait-descriptive terms to oneself as compared to well-liked, neutral, and disliked others: A psychometric analysis. *Journal of Personality & Social Psychology, 36*, 1012–1028.

Goldberg, L. R. (1981). Unconfounding situational attributions from uncertain, neutral, and ambiguous ones: A psychometric analysis of descriptions of oneself and various types of others. *Journal of Personality & Social Psychology, 41*, 517–522.

Greenwald, A. G. (1980). The totalitarian ego: Fabrication and revision of personal history. *American Psychologist, 35*, 603–618.

Greenwald, A. G. (1981). Self and memory. In G. H. Bower (Ed.), *The psychology of learning and motivation* (Vol. 15, pp. 201–236). New York: Academic Press.

Greenwald, A. G., & Banaji, M. R. (1989). The self as a memory system: Powerful, but ordinary. *Journal of Personality & Social Psychology, 57*, 41–54.

Greenwald, A. G., Bellezza, F. S., & Banaji, M. R. (1988). Is self-esteem a central ingredient of the self-concept? *Personality & Social Psychology Bulletin, 14*, 34–45.

Greenwald, A. G., & Pratkanis, A. R. (1984). The self. In R. W. Wyer & T. K. Srull (Eds.), *Handbook of social cognition* (Vol. 3, pp. 129–178). Hillsdale, NJ: Lawrence Erlbaum Associates.

Hamilton, D. L. (1989). Understanding impression formation: What has memory research contributed? In P. R. Solomon, G. R. Goethals, C. M. Kelley, & B. R. Stephens (Eds.), *Memory: Interdisciplinary approaches* (pp. 221–242). New York: Springer-Verlag.

Hamilton, D. L., Driscoll, D. M., & Worth, L. T. (1990). Cognitive organization of impressions: Effects of incongruency in complex representations. *Journal of Personality & Social Psychology, 57*, 925–939.

Hamilton, D. L., Katz, L. B., & Leirer, V. O. (1980). Organizational processes in impression formation. In R. Hastie, T. Ostrom, E. Ebbesen, R. Wyer, D. Hamilton, & D. Carlston (Eds.), *Person memory: The cognitive basis of social perception* (pp. 121–153). Hillsdale, NJ: Lawrence Erlbaum Associates.

Hart, D., & Edelstein, W. (1992a). The relationship of self-understanding in childhood to social class, community type, and teacher-rated intellectual and social competence. *Journal of Cross-Cultural Psychology, 23*, 353–366.

Hart, D., & Edelstein, W. (1992b). Self-understanding development in cross-cultural perspective. In T. Brinthaupt & R. Pilka (Eds.), *The self: Definitional and methodological issues* (pp. 291–322). Albany, NY: State University of New York Press.

Hart, D., Fegley, S., Chan, Y., Fisher, L., & Mulvey, D. (1993). Judgments about personal identity in childhood and adolescence. *Social Development, 2*, 66–81.

Hart, D., Fegley, S., & Brengelman, D. (1993). Perceptions of past, present, and future selves among children and adolescents. *British Journal of Developmental Psychology, 11*, 265–282.

Hart, D., Lucca-Irizarry, N., & Damon, W. (1986). The development of self-understanding in Puerto Rico and the United States. *Journal of Early Adolescence, 8*, 388–407.

Harter, S. (1983). Developmental perspectives on the self-system. In E. M. Hetherington (Ed.), *Handbook of child psychology: Social and personality development. Vol. 4. Socialization* (pp. 275–375). New York: Wiley.

Harter, S. (1986). Processes underlying the construction, maintenance, and enhancement of the self-concept in children. In J. Suls & A. G. Greenwald (Eds.), *Psychological perspectives on the self* (Vol. 3, 136–182). Hillsdale, NJ: Lawrence Erlbaum Associates.

Harter, S. (1988). Developmental and dynamic changes in the nature of the self-concept. In S. R. Shirk (Ed.), *Cognitive development and child psychotherapy* (pp. 119–160). New York: Plenum.

Hartshorne, H., & May, M. A. (1929). *Studies in the nature of character. Vol. 1. Studies in deceit.* New York: Macmillan.

Hastie, R. (1980). Memory for behavioral information that confirms or contradicts a personality impression. In R. Hastie, T. M. Ostrom, E. B. Ebbesen, R. S. Wyer, D. L. Hamilton, & D. E. Carlston (Eds.), *Person memory: The cognitive basis of social perception* (pp. 155–177). Hillsdale, NJ: Lawrence Erlbaum Associates.

Hastie, R. (1981). Schematic principles in human memory. In E. T. Higgins, C. P. Herman, & M. P. Zanna, (Eds.), *Social cognition: The Ontario Symposium* (pp. 39–88). Hillsdale, NJ: Lawrence Erlbaum Associates.

Hastie, R. (1988). A computer simulation model of person memory. *Journal of Experimental Social Psychology, 24*, 423–447.

Hastie, R., & Kumar, P. A. (1979). Person memory: Personality traits as organizing principles in memory. *Journal of Personality & Social Psychology, 37*, 25–38.

Hastie, R., Ostrom, T. B., Ebbesen, E. B., Wyer, R. S., Hamilton, D. L., & Carlston, D. E. (Eds.). (1980). *Person memory: The cognitive basis of social perception.* Hillsdale, NJ: Lawrence Erlbaum Associates.

Hastie, R., & Park, B. (1986). The relationship between memory and judgment depends on whether the judgment task is memory-based or on-line. *Psychological Review, 93*, 258–268.

Hastie, R., Park, B., & Weber, R. (1984). Social memory. In R. W. Wyer & T. K. Srull (Eds.), *Handbook of social cognition* (Vol. 2, pp. 151–212). Hillsdale, NJ: Lawrence Erlbaum Associates.

Head, H. (1926). *Aphasia and kindred disorders of speech.* Cambridge: Cambridge University Press.

Higgins, E. T. (1987). Self-discrepancy: A theory relating self and affect. *Psychological Review, 94*, 319–340.

Higgins, E. T. (1989). Self-discrepancy theory: What patterns of self-beliefs cause people to suffer? In L. Berkowitz (Ed.), *Advances in experimental social psychology* (Vol. 22, pp. 93–136). New York: Academic Press.

Higgins, E. T., Bond, R. N., Klein, R., & Strauman, T. (1986). Self-discrepancies and emotional vulnerability: How magnitude, accessibility and type of discrepancy influence affect. *Journal of Personality & Social Psychology, 51*, 1–15.

Higgins, E. T., & King, G. A. (1981). Accessibility of social constructs: Information-processing consequences of individual and contextual variability. In N. Cantor & J. F. Kihlstrom (Eds.), *Personality, cognition, and social interaction* (pp. 69–122). Hillsdale, NJ: Lawrence Erlbaum Associates.

Higgins, E. T., Klein, R., & Strauman, T. (1985). Self-concept discrepancy theory: A psychological model for distinguishing among different aspects of depression and anxiety. *Social Cognition, 3*, 51–765.

Higgins, E. T., Ruble, D., & Hartup, W. (Eds.). (1983). *Social-cognitive development: A social-cultural perspective.* New York: Cambridge University Press.

Hintzman, D. L. (1986). "Schema abstraction" in a multiple-trace memory model. *Psychological Review, 93*, 411–428.

Holyoak, K. J. (1978). Cognitive reference points in comparative judgment. *Cognitive Psychology, 10*, 203–243.

Holyoak, K. J., & Gordon, P. C. (1983). Social reference points. *Journal of Personality & Social Psychology, 44*, 881–887.

Holyoak, K. J., & Gordon, P. C. (1984). Information processing and social cognition. In R. S. Wyer & T. K. Srull (Eds.), *Handbook of social cognition* (Vol. 1, pp. 39–70). Hillsdale, NJ: Lawrence Erlbaum Associates.

Holyoak, K., & Mah, W. A. (1981). Cognitive reference points in judgments of symbolic magnitude. *Cognitive Psychology, 14*, 228–252.

Homa, D. (1984). On the nature of categories. In G. H. Bower (Ed.), *The psychology of learning and motivation* (Vol. 18, pp. 49–94). Orlando, FL: Academic Press.

Hull, C. L. (1920). Quantitative analysis of the evolution of concepts: An experimental study. *Psychological Monographs, 28* (Whole No. 123).

Huttenlocher, J., Hedges, L., & Prohaska, V. (1988). Hierarchical organization in ordered domains: Estimating the dates of events. *Psychological Review, 95*, 471–484.

James, W. (1981). Principles of psychology. 2 vols. In F. Burkhardt (Ed.), *The works of William James.* Cambridge, MA: Harvard University Press. (Original work published 1890)

John, O. P. (1990). The "Big Five" factor taxonomy: Dimensions of personality in the natural language and in questionnaires. In L. A. Pervin (Ed.), *Handbook of personality: Theory and research* (pp. 66–100). New York: Guilford.

Jones, E. E. (1964). *Ingratiation: A social-psychological analysis.* New York: Appleton-Century-Crofts.

Jones, E. E., & Nisbett, R. E. (1972). The actor and the observer: Divergent perceptions of the causes of behavior. In E. E. Jones, D. E. Kanouse, H. H. Kelley, R. E. Nisbett, S. Valins, & B. Weiner (Eds.), *Attribution: Perceiving the causes of behavior* (pp. 79–94). Morristown, NJ: General Learning Press.

Jones, E. E., & Pittman, T. S. (1982). Toward a general theory of strategic self-presentation. In J. Suls (Ed.), *Psychological perspectives on the self* (Vol. 1, pp. 231–262). Hillsdale, NJ: Lawrence Erlbaum Associates.

Jones, R. A., Sensenig, J., & Haley, J. V. (1974). Self-descriptions: Configurations of content and order effects. *Journal of Personality & Social Psychology, 30*, 36–45.

Kagan, J. (1981). *The second year of life.* Cambridge, MA: Harvard University Press.

Kant, I. (1978). *Anthropology from a pragmatic point of view* (V. L. Dowdell, trans.). Carbondale, IL: Southern Illinois University Press. (Original work published 1798)

Keating, C. F., Mazur, A., & Segall, M. H. (1981). A cross-cultural exploration of physiognomic traits of dominance and happiness. *Ethology & Sociobiology, 2*, 41–48.

Keenan, J. M. (1993). An exemplar model can explain Klein and Loftus' results. In T. K. Srull & R. S. Wyer (Eds.), *Advances in social cognition* (Vol. 5, pp. 69–77). Hillsdale, NJ: Lawrence Erlbaum Associates.

Keenan, J. M., & Baillet, S. D. (1980). Memory for personally and socially significant events. In R. S. Nickerson (Ed.), *Attention and performance VIII* (pp. 651–669). Hillsdale, NJ: Lawrence Erlbaum Associates.

Kegan, R. (1982). *The evolving self: Problem and process in human development.* Cambridge, MA: Harvard University Press.

Keil, F. C. (1989). *Concepts, kinds, and cognitive development.* Cambridge, MA: MIT Press.

Kelley, H. H., & Michaela, J. L. (1980). Attribution theory and research. *Annual Review of Psychology, 31,* 457–501.

Kelly, G. A. (1955). *Personal construct theory. 2 Vols.* New York: Norton.

Kendall, P. C., & Hollon, S. D. (1981). Assessing self-referent speech: Methods in the measurement of self-statements. In P. C. Kendall & S. D. Hollon (Eds.), *Assessment strategies for cognitive-behavioral interventions* (pp. 85–118). San Diego: Academic Press.

Kennedy, S., Scheier, J., & Rogers, A. (1984). The price of success: Our monocultural science. *American Psychologist, 39,* 996–997.

Kihlstrom, J. F. (1981). On personality and memory. In N. Cantor & J. F. Kihlstrom (Eds.), *Personality, cognition, and social interaction* (pp. 123–149). Hillsdale, NJ: Lawrence Erlbaum Associates.

Kihlstrom, J. F. (1985). Posthypnotic amnesia and the dissociation of memory. In G. H. Bower (Ed.), *The psychology of learning and motivation* (Vol. 19, pp. 131–178). New York: Academic Press.

Kihlstrom, J. F. (1992). Dissociative and conversion disorders. In D. J. Stein & J. Young (Eds.), *Cognitive science and clinical disorders* (pp. 247–270). Orlando, FL: Academic Press.

Kihlstrom, J. F., & Cantor, N. (1984). Mental representations of the self. In L. Berkowitz (Ed.), *Advances in experimental social psychology* (Vol. 17, pp. 1–47). New York: Academic Press.

Kihlstrom, J. F., & Cantor, N. (1989). Social intelligence and personality: There's room for growth. In R. S. Wyer & T. K. Srull (Eds.), *Advances in social cognition* (Vol. 2, pp. 197–214). Hillsdale, NJ: Lawrence Erlbaum Associates.

Kihlstrom, J. F., Cantor, N., Albright, J. S., Chew, B. R., Klein, S., & Niedenthal, P. M. (1988). Information processing and the study of the self. In L. Berkowitz (Ed.), *Advances in experimental social psychology* (Vol. 21, pp. 145–177). New York: Academic Press.

Kihlstrom, J. F., & Cunningham, R. L. (1991). Mapping interpersonal space. In M. J. Horowitz (Ed.), *Person schemas and maladaptive interpersonal patterns* (pp. 311–336). Chicago: University of Chicago Press.

Kihlstrom, J. F., & Evans, F. J. (1979). Memory retrieval processes in posthypnotic amnesia. In J. F. Kihlstrom & F. J. Evans (Eds.), *Functional disorders of memory* (pp. 179–218). Hillsdale, NJ: Lawrence Erlbaum Associates.

Kihlstrom, J. F., & Harackiewicz, J. M. (1982). The earliest recollection: A new survey. *Journal of Personality, 50,* 134–148.

Kihlstrom, J. F., & Hastie, R. (in press). Mental representations of self and others. In S. R. Briggs, R. Hogan, & W. H. Jones (Eds.), *Handbook of personality psychology.* Orlando, FL: Academic Press.

Kihlstrom, J. F., & Marchese, L. A. (in press). Situating the self in interpersonal space. In U. Neisser (Ed.), *The conceptual self in context.* Cambridge: Cambridge University Press.

Kihlstrom, J. F., & Olsen, D. (1992). *User manual for the PERSPACE software system, Version 3.5.* Program on Conscious and Unconscious Mental Processes of the John D. and Catherine T. MacArthur Foundation, University of California, San Francisco.

Kihlstrom, J. F., & Wilson, L. (1984). Temporal organization of recall during posthypnotic amnesia. *Journal of Abnormal Psychology, 93,* 200–208.

Klein, S. B., & Kihlstrom, J. F. (1986). Elaboration, organization, and the self-reference effect in memory. *Journal of Experimental Psychology: General, 115,* 26–38.

Klein, S. B., & Loftus, J. (1988). The nature of self-referent encoding: The contributions of elaborative and organizational processes. *Journal of Personality & Social Psychology, 55,* 5–11.

Klein, S. B., & Loftus, J. (1990a). Rethinking the role of organization in person memory: An independent trace storage model. *Journal of Personality & Social Psychology, 59,* 400–410.

Klein, S. B., & Loftus, J. (1990b). The role of abstract and exemplar-based knowledge in self-judgments: Implications for a cognitive model of the self. In T. K. Srull & R. S. Wyer (Eds.), *Advances in social cognition* (Vol. 3, pp. 131–139). Hillsdale, NJ: Lawrence Erlbaum Associates.

Klein, S. B., & Loftus, J. (1993a). The mental representation of trait and autobiographical knowledge about the self. In T. K. Srull & R. S. Wyer (Eds.), *Advances in social cognition* (Vol. 5, pp. 1–49). Hillsdale, NJ: Lawrence Erlbaum Associates.

Klein, S. B., & Loftus, J. (1993b). Some lingering self-doubts: Reply to commentaries. In T. K. Srull & R. S. Wyer (Eds.), *Advances in social cognition* (Vol. 5, pp. 171–180). Hillsdale, NJ: Lawrence Erlbaum Associates.

Klein, S. B., Loftus, J., & Burton, H. (1989). Two self-reference effects: The importance of distinguishing between self-descriptiveness judgments and autobiographical retrieval in self-referent encoding. *Journal of Personality & Social Psychology, 56,* 853–865.

Klein, S. B., Loftus, J., & Plog, A. E. (1992). Trait judgments about the self: Evidence from the encoding specificity paradigm. *Personality & Social Psychology Bulletin, 18,* 730–735.

Klein, S. B., Loftus, J., & Sherman, J. W. (1993). The role of summary and specific behavioral memories in trait judgments about the self. *Personality & Social Psychology Bulletin, 19,* 305–311.

Klein, S. B., Loftus, J., Trafton, R. G., & Fuhrman, R. W. (1992). The use of exemplars and abstractions in trait judgments: A model of trait knowledge about the self and others. *Journal of Personality & Social Psychology, 63,* 739–753.

Knowles, E. S., & Sibicky, M. E. (1990). Continuity and diversity in the stream of selves: Metaphorical resolutions of Williams James's one-in-many-selves paradox. *Personality & Social Psychology Bulletin, 16,* 676–687.

Kolodner, J. (1984). *Retrieval and organizational strategies in conceptual memory: A computer model.* Hillsdale, NJ: Lawrence Erlbaum Associates.

Kopelman, M. D., Wilson, B. A., & Baddeley, A. D. (1989). The autobiographical memory interview: A new assessment of autobiographical and personal semantic memory in amnesic patients. *Journal of Clinical & Experimental Neuropsychology, 11,* 724–744.

Kosslyn, S. M. (1980). *Image and mind.* Cambridge, MA: Harvard University Press.

Kosslyn, S. M., & Koenig, O. (1992). *Wet mind: The new cognitive neuroscience.* New York: Free Press.

Kosslyn, S. M., & Pomerantz, J. P. (1977). Imagery, propositions, and the form of internal representation. *Cognitive Psychology, 9,* 52–76.

Kozlowski, L. T., & Cutting, J. E. (1977). Recognizing the sex of a walker from a dynamic point-light display. *Perception & Psychophysics, 21,* 575–580.

Kuhn, M. H., & McPartland, T. S. (1954). An empirical investigation of self-attitudes. *American Sociological Review, 19,* 68–76.

Kuiper, N. A. (1981). The "inverted-U RT effect" for self and other judgments. *Personality & Social Psychology Bulletin, 7,* 438–443.

Kuiper, N. A., & Derry, P. A. (1981). The self as a cognitive prototype: An application to person perception and depression. In N. Cantor & J. F. Kihlstrom (Eds.), *Personality, cognition, and social interaction* (pp. 215–232). Hillsdale, NJ: Lawrence Erlbaum Associates.

Kuiper, N. A., & Rogers, T. B. (1979). Encoding of personal information: Self-other differences. *Journal of Personality & Social Psychology, 37,* 499–514.

Lakoff, G. (1987). *Women, fire, and other dangerous things: What categories reveal about the mind.* Chicago: University of Chicago Press.

Lamphere, R. A., & Leary, M. R. (1990). Private and public self-processes: A return to James's constituents of the self. *Personality & Social Psychology Bulletin, 16,* 717–725.

Lehrer, R. (1986). Characters in search of an author. In J. C. Mancuso & M. L. G. Shaw (Eds.), *Cognition and personal structure: Computer access and analysis* (pp. 195–228). New York: Praeger.

Leventhal, H. (1984). A perceptual-motor theory of emotion. In L. Berkowitz (Ed.), *Advances in experimental social psychology* (Vol. 17, pp. 117–182). New York: Academic Press.

Lewis, M. (1990). Self-knowledge and social development in early life. In L. Pervin (Ed.), *Handbook of personality: Theory and research* (pp. 277–300). New York: Guilford.

Lewis, M., & Brooks-Gunn, J. (1979). *Social cognition and the acquisition of self.* New York: Plenum.

Lingle, J. H., Altom, M. W., & Medin, D. L. (1984). Of cabbages and kings: Accessing the extensibility of natural object concept models to social things. In R. S. Wyer & T. K. Srull (Eds.), *Handbook of social cognition* (Vol. 1, pp. 71–117). Hillsdale, NJ: Lawrence Erlbaum Associates.

Linville, P. (1985). Self-complexity and affective extremity: Don't put all your eggs into one cognitive basket. *Social Cognition, 3*, 94–120.

Linville, P. (1987). Self-complexity as a cognitive buffer against stress-related illness and depression. *Journal of Personality & Social Psychology, 52*, 663–676.

Locksley, A., & Lenauer, M. (1981). Considerations for a theory of self-inference processes. In N. Cantor & J. F. Kihlstrom (Eds.), *Personality, cognition, and social interaction* (pp. 263–277). Hillsdale, NJ: Lawrence Erlbaum Associates.

Loftus, E. F., & Marburger, W. (1983). Since the eruption of Mount St. Helens has anyone beaten you up? Improving the accuracy of retrospective reports with landmark events. *Memory & Cognition, 11*, 114–120.

Logan, G. D. (1988). Toward an instance theory of automatization. *Psychological Review, 95*, 492–527.

Mandler, J. (1984). *Stories, scripts, and scenes: Aspects of schema theory.* Hillsdale, NJ: Lawrence Erlbaum Associates.

Markman, E. M. (1989). *Categorization and naming in children: Problems of induction.* Cambridge, MA: MIT Press.

Markus, H. (1977). Self-schemata and processing information about the self. *Journal of Social & Personality Psychology, 35*, 63–78.

Markus, H. (1983). Self-knowledge: An expanded view. *Journal of Personality, 51*, 543–565.

Markus, H. (1990). On splitting the universe. *Psychological Science, 1*, 181–185.

Markus, H., Crane, M., Bernstein, S., & Siladi, M. (1982). Self-schemas and gender. *Journal of Personality & Social Psychology, 42*, 38–50.

Markus, H., & Cross, S. (1990). The interpersonal self. In L. A. Pervin (Ed.), *Handbook of personality: Theory and research* (pp. 576–608). New York: Guilford.

Markus, H. R., & Kitayama, S. (1991). Culture and the self: Implications for cognition, emotion, and motivation. *Psychological Review, 98*, 224–253.

Markus, H., & Kunda, Z. (1986). Stability and malleability of the self-concept. *Journal of Personality & Social Psychology, 51*, 858–866.

Markus, H., & Nurius, P. (1986). Possible selves. *American Psychologist, 41*, 954–969.

Markus, H., & Sentis, K. (1982). The self in social information processing. In J. Suls (Ed.), *Psychological perspectives on the self* (Vol. 1, pp. 41–70). Hillsdale, NJ: Lawrence Erlbaum Associates.

Markus, H., & Smith, J. (1981). The influence of self-schemas on the perception of others. In N. Cantor & J. F. Kihlstrom (Eds.), *Personality, cognition, and social interaction* (pp. 233–262). Hillsdale, NJ: Lawrence Erlbaum Associates.

Markus, H., Smith, J., & Moreland, R. L. (1985). Role of the self-concept in the social perception of others. *Journal of Personality & Social Psychology, 49*, 1494–1512.

Markus, H., & Wurf, E. (1987). The dynamic self-concept: A social psychological perspective. *Annual Review of Psychology, 38*, 299–337.

Martin, E. (1972). Stimulus encoding in learning and transfer. In A. W. Melton & E. Martin (Eds.), *Coding processes in human memory* (pp. 59–84). Washington, DC: Winston.

Martindale, C. (1980). Subselves: The internal representation of situational and personal dispositions. In L. Wheeler (Ed.), *Review of personality and social psychology* (Vol. 1, pp. 193–218).
Beverly Hills, CA: Sage.

McArthur, L. Z. (1982). Judging a book by its cover: A cognitive analysis of the relationship between physical appearance and stereotyping. In A. Hastorf & A. Isen (Eds.), *Cognitive social psychology* (pp. 149–211). New York: Elsevier.

McArthur, L. Z., & Baron, R. (1983). Toward an ecological theory of social perception. *Psychological Review, 80*, 252–283.

McGuire, W. J. (1984). Search for the self: Going beyond self-esteem and the reactive self. In
R. A. Zucker, J. Aronoff, & A. I. Rabin (Eds.), *Personality and the prediction of behavior* (pp.
73–120). New York: Academic Press.

McGuire, W. J., & McGuire, C. V. (1980). Salience of handedness in the spontaneous self-concept.
Perceptual & Motor Skills, 50, 3–7.

McGuire, W. J., & McGuire, C. V. (1981). The spontaneous self-concept as affected by personal
distinctiveness. In A. Norem-Hebeisen, M. D. Lynch, & K. Gergen (Eds.), *The self-concept* (pp.
147–171). New York: Ballinger.

McGuire, W. J., & McGuire, C. V. (1982). Significant others in self-space: Sex differences and
developmental trends in the self. In J. Suls (Ed.), *Social psychological perspectives on the self*
(Vol. 1, pp. 71–96). Hillsdale, NJ: Lawrence Erlbaum Associates.

McGuire, W. J., & McGuire, C. V. (1986). Differences in conceptualizing self versus conceptualizing other people as manifested in contrasting verb types used in natural speech. *Journal of Personality & Social Psychology, 51*, 1135–1143.

McGuire, W. J., & McGuire, C. V. (1988). Content and process in the experience of self. In L.
Berkowitz (Ed.), *Advances in experimental social psychology* (Vol. 21, pp. 97–144). San Diego:
Academic Press.

McGuire, W. J., McGuire, C. V., & Cheever, J. (1986). The self in society: Effects of social contexts on the sense of self. *British Journal of Social Psychology, 25*, 259–270.

McGuire, W. J., McGuire, C. V., Child, P., & Fujioka, T. (1978). Salience of ethnicity in the spontaneous self-concept as a function of one's ethnic distinctiveness in the social environment. *Journal
of Personality & Social Psychology, 36*, 511–520.

McGuire, W. J., McGuire, C. V., & Winton, W. (1979). Effects of household sex composition on
the salience of one's gender in the spontaneous self-concept. *Journal of Experimental Social Psychology, 15*, 77–90.

McGuire, W. J., & Padawer-Singer, A. (1976). Trait salience in the spontaneous self-concept. *Journal of Personality & Social Psychology, 33*, 743–754.

Medin, D. L. (1989). Concepts and conceptual structure. *American Psychologist, 44*, 1469–1481.

Medin, D. L., & Ross, B. H. (1989). The specific character of abstract thought: Categorization,
problem-solving, and induction. In R. J. Sternberg (Ed.), *Advances in the psychology of human
intelligence* (Vol. 5, pp. 189–223). Hillsdale, NJ: Lawrence Erlbaum Associates.

Medin, D. L., & Schaffer, M. M. (1978). A context theory of classification learning. *Psychological
Review, 85*, 207–238.

Medin, D. L., & Shoben, E. J. (1988). Context and structure in conceptual combination. *Cognitive
Psychology, 20*, 158–190.

Medin, D. L., & Smith, E. E. (1984). Concepts and concept formation. *Annual Review of Psychology, 35*, 113–138.

Melzack, R. (1989). Phantom limbs, the self, and the brain. *Canadian Psychology, 30*, 1–16.

Mervis, C. B., & Rosch, E. (1981). Categorization of natural objects. *Annual Review of Psychology,
32*, 89–115.

Meyer, D. E., & Schvaneveldt, R. W. (1971). Facilitation in recognizing pairs of words: Evidence
of a dependence between retrieval operations. *Journal of Experimental Psychology, 90*, 227–234.

Mischel, T. (Ed.). (1977). *The self: Psychological and philosophical issues*. Oxford, England: Basil
Blackwell.

Mita, T. H., Dermer, M., & Knight, J. (1977). Reversed facial images and the mere-exposure hypothesis. *Journal of Personality & Social Psychology, 35*, 597–601.

Monson, T. C., & Snyder, M. (1977). Actors, observers, and the attribution process: Toward a reconceptualization. *Journal of Experimental Social Psychology, 13*, 89–111.

Morey, L. C., & McNamara, T. P. (1987). On definitions, diagnosis, and DSM-III. *Journal of Abnormal Psychology, 96*, 283–285.

Murphy, G. L., & Medin, D. L. (1985). The role of theories in conceptual coherence. *Psychological Review, 92*, 289–316.

Murphy, G. L., & Smith, E. E. (1982). Basic-level superiority in picture categorization. *Journal of Verbal Learning & Verbal Behavior, 21*, 1–20.

Myers, G. E. (1986). *William James: His life and thought*. New Haven, CT: Yale University Press.

Nakamura, G. V., Graesser, A. C., Zimmerman, J. A., & Riha, J. (1985). Script processing in a natural situation. *Memory & Cognition, 13*, 140–144.

Neisser, U. (Ed.). (1987). *Concepts and conceptual development*. Cambridge: Cambridge University Press.

Neisser, U. (1988). Five kinds of self knowledge. *Philosophical Psychology, 1*, 35–59.

Neisser, U. (1991). Two perceptually given aspects of the self and their development. *Developmental Review, 11*, 197–209.

Neisser, U. (1992a). The development of consciousness and the acquisition of self. In F. S. Kessel, P. M. Cole, & D. L. Johnson (Eds.), *Self and consciousness: Multiple perspectives* (pp. 1–18). Hillsdale, NJ: Lawrence Erlbaum Associates.

Neisser, U. (1992b). Infantile amnesia. In L. R. Squire (Ed.), *Encyclopedia of Learning & Memory* (pp. 28–30). New York: Macmillan.

Neisser, U. (1992c, May). *The self-concept and its origins*. Paper presented at the Emory Conference on the Conceptual Self in Context, Atlanta,

Neisser, U., & Winograd, E. (Eds.). (1988). *Remembering reconsidered: Ecological and traditional approaches to the study of memory*. Cambridge: Cambridge University Press.

Nelson, T. O. (Ed.). (1992). *Metacognition: Core readings*. Boston: Allyn & Bacon.

Niedenthal, P. M., Cantor, N., & Kihlstrom, J. F. (1985). Prototype matching: A strategy for social decision-making. *Journal of Personality & Social Psychology, 48*, 575–584.

Niedenthal, P. M., & Mordkoff, J. T. (1991). Prototype distancing: A strategy for choosing among threatening situations. *Personality & Social Psychology Bulletin, 17*, 483–493.

Niedenthal, P. M., Setterlund, M. B., & Wherry, M. B. (1992). Possible self-complexity and affective reactions to goal-relevant evaluation. *Journal of Personality and Social Psychology, 63*, 5–16.

Nosofsky, R. M. (1988). Exemplar-based accounts of relations between classification, recognition, and typicality. *Journal of Experimental Psychology: Learning, Memory, & Cognition, 14*, 700–708.

Nystedt, L., Smari, J., & Boman, M. (1991). Self-schemata: Ambiguous operationalizations of an important concept. *European Journal of Personality, 5*, 1–14.

Oden, G. C. (1987). Concept, knowledge, and thought. *Annual Review of Psychology, 38*, 203–227.

Orbach, J., Traub, A. C., & Olson, R. (1966). Psychophysical studies of body image: II. Normative data on the adjustable body-distorting mirror. *Archives of General Psychiatry, 14*, 41–47.

Ostrom, T. M., Lingle, J. H., Pryor, J. B., & Geva, N. (1980). Cognitive organization of person impressions. In R. Hastie, T. M. Ostrom, E. B. Ebbesen, R. S. Wyer, D. L. Hamilton, & D. E. Carlston (Eds.), *Person memory: The cognitive basis of social perception* (pp. 55–88). Hillsdale, NJ: Lawrence Erlbaum Associates.

Ostrom, T. M., Pryor, J. B., & Simpson, D. D. (1981). The organization of social information. In E. T. Higgins, C. P. Herman, & M. P. Zanna (Eds.), *Social cognition: The Ontario Symposium* (pp. 3–38). Hillsdale, NJ: Lawrence Erlbaum Associates.

Paivio, A. (1986). *Mental representations*. Oxford: Oxford University Press.

Peevers, B., & Secord, P. (1973). Developmental changes in attributions of descriptive concepts to persons. *Journal of Personality & Social Psychology, 26*, 120–128.

Pennington, N., & Hastie, R. (1992). Explaining the evidence: Tests of the story model for juror decision making. *Journal of Personality & Social Psychology, 62,* 189–206.

Pervin, L. A., & Rubin, D. B. (1967). Student dissatisfaction with college and the college dropout: A transactional approach. *Journal of Social Psychology, 72,* 285–295.

Phillips, K. A. (1991). Body dysmorphic disorder: The distress or imagined ugliness. *American Journal of Psychiatry, 148,* 1138–1149.

Pittenger, J. B., & Todd, J. T. (1983). Perception of growth from changes in body proportions. *Journal of Experimental Psychology: Human Perception & Performance, 9,* 945–954.

Pylyshyn, Z. W. (1981). The imagery debate: Analogue versus tacit knowledge. *Psychological Review, 86,* 383–394.

Raaijmakers, J. G., & Shiffrin, R. M. (1981). Search of associative memory. *Psychological Review, 88,* 93–134.

Reiser, B. J., Black, J. B., & Abelson, R. P. (1985). Knowledge structures in the organization and retrieval of autobiographical memories. *Cognitive Psychology, 17,* 89–137.

Robey, K. L., Cohen, B. D., & Gara, M. A. (1989). Self-structure in schizophrenia. *Journal of Abnormal Psychology, 98,* 436–442.

Roediger, H. L., & Blaxton, T. A. (1987). Retrieval modes produce dissociations in memory for surface information. In D. Gorfein & R. R. Hoffman (Eds.), *Memory and cognitive processes: The Ebbinghaus Centennial Conference* (pp. 349–379). Hillsdale, NJ: Lawrence Erlbaum Associates.

Roediger, H. L., & Neely, J. H. (1982). Retrieval blocks in episodic and semantic memory. *Canadian Journal of Psychology, 36,* 213–242.

Roediger, H. L., Weldon, M. S., & Challis, B. H. (1989). Explaining dissociations between implicit and explicit measures of retention: A processing account. In H. L. Roediger & F. I. M. Craik (Eds.), *Varieties of memory and consciousness: Essays in honour of Endel Tulving* (pp. 3–41). Hillsdale, NJ: Lawrence Erlbaum Associates.

Rogers, C. (1951). *Client-centered therapy.* Boston, MA: Houghton-Mifflin.

Rogers, T. B. (1974a). An analysis of the stages underlying the process of responding to personality items. *Acta Psychologica, 38,* 204–214.

Rogers, T. B. (1974b). An analysis of two central stages underlying responding to personality items. The self-referent decision and response selection. *Journal of Research in Personality, 8,* 128–138.

Rogers, T. B. (1978). Experimental evidence for the similarity of personality and attitude item responding. *Acta Psychologica, 42,* 21–28.

Rogers, T. B. (1981). A model of the self as an aspect of human information processing. In N. Cantor & J. F. Kihlstrom (Eds.), *Personality, cognition, and social interaction* (pp. 193–214). Hillsdale, NJ: Lawrence Erlbaum Associates.

Rogers, T. B., Kuiper, N. A., & Kirker, W. S. (1977). Self reference and the encoding of personal information. *Journal of Personality & Social Psychology, 35,* 677–678.

Rogers, T. B., Kuiper, N. A., & Rogers, P. J. (1979). Symbolic distance and congruity effects for paired-comparisons judgments of degree of self-reference. *Journal of Research in Personality, 13,* 433–449.

Rogers, T. B., Rogers, P. J., & Kuiper, N. A. (1979). Evidence for the self as a cognitive prototype: The "false alarms effect." *Personality & Social Psychology Bulletin, 5,* 53–56.

Rosch, E. (1975). Cognitive representations of semantic categories. *Journal of Experimental Psychology: General, 104,* 192–223.

Rosch, E., & Lloyd, B. B. (Eds.). (1978). *Cognition and categorization.* New York: Wiley.

Rosch, E., Mervis, C. B., Gray, W., Johnson, D., & Boyes-Brehm, P. (1976). Basic objects in natural categories. *Cognitive Psychology, 8,* 382–439.

Rosen, J. C., Srebnik, D., Saltzberg, E., & Wendt, S. (1991). Development of a body image avoidance questionnaire. *Psychological Assessment: A Journal of Consulting & Clinical Psychology, 3,* 32–37.

Rosenberg, S. (1988). Self and others: Studies in social personality and autobiography. In L. Berkowitz (Ed.), *Advances in experimental social psychology* (Vol. 21, pp. 57–95). San Diego: Academic Press.

Rosenberg, S., & Gara, S. (1985). The multiplicity of personal identity. In L. Wheeler (Ed.), *Review of personality and social psychology* (Vol. 6, pp. 87–113). Beverly Hills, CA: Sage.

Ross, M. (1989). Relation of implicit theories to the construction of personal histories. *Psychological Review, 96*, 341–357.

Rozin, P. (1976). The psychobiological approach to human memory. In M. R. Rosenzweig & E. L. Bennett (Eds.), *Neural mechanisms of learning and memory* (pp. 1–48). Cambridge, MA: MIT Press.

Rozin, P., & Fallon, A. (1988). Body image, attitudes to weight, and misperceptions of figure preferences of the opposite sex: A comparison of men and women in two generations. *Journal of Abnormal Psychology, 97*, 342–345.

Rubin, D. C. (1986). *Autobiographical memory*. Cambridge: Cambridge University Press.

Rumelhart, D. E. (1984). Schemata and the cognitive system. In R. S. Wyer & T. K. Srull (Eds.), *Handbook of social cognition* (Vol. 1, pp. 161–188). Hillsdale, NJ: Lawrence Erlbaum Associates.

Ryle, G. (1949). *The concept of mind*. London: Routledge & Kegan Paul.

Schacter, D. L., & Kihlstrom, J. F. (1989). Functional amnesia. In F. Boller & J. Graffman (Eds.), *Handbook of neuropsychology* (Vol. 3, pp. 209–231). Amsterdam: Elsevier.

Schacter, D. L., Wang, P. L., Tulving, E., & Freedman, M. (1982). Functional retrograde amnesia: A quantitative case study. *Neuropsychologia, 20*, 523–532.

Schank, R. C. (1982). *Dynamic memory*. Cambridge: Cambridge University Press.

Schank, R. C., & Abelson, R. P. (1977). *Scripts, plans, goals, and understanding*. Hillsdale, NJ: Lawrence Erlbaum Associates.

Schilder, P. (1938). *Image and appearance of the human body*. London: Kagan, Paul, Trench, Trubner.

Schlenk, C. T., & Holman, R. H. (1980). A sociological approach to brand choice: The concept of situational self-image. In J. Olson (Ed.), *Advances in consumer research* (Vol. 7, pp. 610–614). Ann Arbor, MI: Association for Consumer Research.

Schneider, W., & Shiffrin, R. M. (1977). Controlled and automatic human information processing: I. Detection, search, and attention. *Psychological Review, 84*, 1–66.

Secord, P., & Peevers, B. (1974). The development and attribution of person concepts. In T. Mischel (Ed.), *Understanding other persons* (pp. 117–142). Oxford: Blackwell.

Selman, R. (1980). *The growth of interpersonal understanding*. New York: Academic Press.

Sergeant, J. (1990). The neuropsychology of visual image generation: Data, method, and theory. *Brain & Cognition, 13*, 98–129.

Shaw, R., & Pittenger, J. (1977). Perceiving the face of change in changing faces: Implications for a theory of object perception. In R. Shaw & J. Bransford (Eds.), *Perceiving, acting, and knowing: Toward an ecological psychology* (pp. 103–132). Hillsdale, NJ: Lawrence Erlbaum Associates.

Shepard, R., & Cooper, L. A. (1983). *Mental images and their transformations*. Cambridge, MA: MIT Press.

Shoben, E. J., Cech, C. G., & Schwanenflugel, P. J. (1983). The role of subtractions and comparisons in comparative judgments involving numerical reference points. *Journal of Experimental Psychology: Human Perception & Performance, 9*, 226–241.

Showers, C. (1992). Compartmentalization of positive and negative self-knowledge: Keeping bad apples out of the bunch. *Journal of Personality & Social Psychology, 62*, 1036–1049.

Shweder, R. A., & Levine, R. A. (Eds.). (1984). *Culture theory: Essays on mind, self, and emotion*. Cambridge: Cambridge University Press.

Slamecka, N. J., & Graf, P. (1978). The generation effect: Delineation of a phenomenon. *Journal of Memory & Language, 26*, 589–607.

Smith, E. E., & Medin, D. L. (1981). *Categories and concepts*. Cambridge, MA: Harvard University Press.

Solomon, M. R. (1983). The role of products as social stimuli: A symbolic interactionism perspective. *Journal of Consumer Research, 10*, 319–329.

Squire, L. R. (1987). *Memory and brain*. Oxford: Oxford University Press.

Srull, T. K. (1981). Person memory: Some tests of associative storage and retrieval models. *Journal of Experimental Psychology: Human Learning & Memory, 7,* 440–463.

Srull, T. K. (1984). Methodological techniques for the study of person memory and social cognition. In R. S. Wyer & T. K. Srull (Eds.), *Handbook of social cognition* (Vol. 2, pp. 1–72). Hillsdale, NJ: Lawrence Erlbaum Associates.

Srull, T. K., & Gaelick, L. (1983). General principles and individual differences in the self as a habitual reference point: An examination of self-other judgments of similarity. *Social Cognition, 2,* 108–121.

Srull, T. K., Lichtenstein, M., & Rothbart, M. (1983). Associative storage and retrieval processes in person memory. *Journal of Experimental Psychology: Learning, Memory, & Cognition, 11,* 316–345.

Sternberg, S. (1969). The discovery of processing stages: Extensions of Donders's methods. *Acta Psychologica, 30,* 276–315.

Stigler, J. W., Shweder, R. A., & Herdt, G. (Eds.). (1991). *Cultural psychology: Essays on comparative human development.* Cambridge: Cambridge University Press.

Strauman, T. J. (1989). Self-discrepancies in clinical depression and social phobia: Cognitive structures that underlie emotional disorders? *Journal of Abnormal Psychology, 98,* 5–14.

Strauman, T. J. (1990). Self-guides and emotionally significant childhood memories: A study of retrieval efficiency and incidental negative emotional content. *Journal of Personality & Social Psychology, 59,* 869–880.

Strauman, T. J. (1992). Self-guides, autobiographical memory, and anxiety and dysphoria: Toward a cognitive model of vulnerability to emotional distress. *Journal of Abnormal Psychology, 101,* 87–95.

Strube, M. J. (1990). In search of self: Balancing the good and the true. *Personality & Social Psychology Bulletin, 16,* 699–706.

Suls, J. (Ed.). (1982). *Psychological perspectives on the self. Vol. 1.* Hillsdale, NJ: Lawrence Erlbaum Associates.

Suls, J., & Greenwald, A. G. (Eds.). (1983). *Psychological perspectives on the self. Vol. 2.* Hillsdale, NJ: Lawrence Erlbaum Associates.

Suls, J., & Greenwald, A. G. (Eds.). (1986). *Psychological perspectives on the self. Vol. 3.* Hillsdale, NJ: Lawrence Erlbaum Associates.

Suls, J., & Marco, C. A. (1990). William James, the self, and the selective industry of the mind. *Personality & Social Psychology Bulletin, 16,* 688–698.

Taylor, S. E., & Crocker, J. (1981). Schematic bases of social information processing. In E. T. Higgins, C. P. Herman, & M. P. Zanna (Eds.), *Social cognition: The Ontario Symposium* (pp. 89–134). Hillsdale, NJ: Lawrence Erlbaum Associates.

Traub, A. C., Olson, R., Orbach, J., & Cardone, S. S. (1967). Psychophysical studies of body image: III. Initial studies of disturbances in a chronic schizophrenic group. *Archives of General Psychiatry, 17,* 664–670.

Traub, A. C., & Orbach, J. (1964). Psychophysical studies of body-image: I. The adjustable body-distorting mirror. *Archives of General Psychiatry, 11,* 53–66.

Triandis, H. C., & Brislin, R. W. (Eds.). (1980). *Handbook of cross-cultural social psychology.* Boston: Allyn & Bacon.

Tulving, E. (1983). *Elements of episodic memory.* Oxford: Oxford University Press.

Tulving, E. (1993). Self-knowledge of an amnesic individual is represented abstractly. In T. K. Srull & R. S. Wyer (Eds.), *Advances in social cognition* (Vol. 5, pp. 147–156). Hillsdale, NJ: Lawrence Erlbaum Associates.

Tulving, E., & Schacter, D. L. (1990). Priming and human memory systems. *Science, 247,* 301–306.

Tulving, E., & Thompson, D. M. (1973). Encoding specificity and retrieval processes in episodic memory. *Psychological Review, 80,* 352–373.

Tunis, S. L., Fridhandler, B. M., & Horowitz, M. J. (1990). Identifying schematized views of self with significant others: Convergence of quantitative and clinical methods. *Journal of Personality & Social Psychology, 59,* 1279–1286.

Tversky, A. (1977). Features of similarity. *Psychological Review, 84*, 327–352.

Tversky, A., & Kahneman, D. (1973). Availability: A heuristic for judging frequency and probability. *Cognitive Psychology, 5*, 207–232.

Tversky, B., & Hemenway, K. (1984). Objects, parts, and categories. *Journal of Experimental Psychology: General, 113*, 169–193.

Underwood, B. J. (1977). *Temporal codes for memories.* Hillsdale, NJ: Lawrence Erlbaum Associates.

Wagenaar, W. A. (1986). My memory: A study of autobiographical memory over six years. *Cognitive Psychology, 18*, 225–252.

Wegner, D. M., & Vallacher, R. R. (Eds.). (1980). *The self in social psychology.* New York: Oxford University Press.

Wetzler, S. E., & Sweeney, J. A. (1986). Childhood amnesia: An empirical demonstration. In D. C. Rubin (Ed.), *Autobiographical memory* (pp. 191–201). Cambridge: Cambridge University Press.

White, S. H., & Pillemer, D. B. (1979). Childhood amnesia and the development of a socially accessible memory system. In J. F. Kihlstrom & F. J. Evans (Eds.), *Functional disorders of memory* (pp. 29–74). Hillsdale, NJ: Lawrence Erlbaum Associates.

Williamson, D. A., Davis, C. J., Goreczny, A. J., & Blouin, D. C. (1989). Body-image disturbances in bulimia nervosa: Influences of actual body size. *Journal of Abnormal Psychology, 98*, 97–99.

Winograd, E., & Neisser, U. (Eds.). (1992). *Flashbulb memories. Emory Symposium on Cognition, Vol. 3.* Cambridge: Cambridge University Press.

Winograd, T. (1975). Frame representations and the declarative-procedural controversy. In D. Bobrow & A. Collins (Eds.), *Representation and understanding* (pp. 185–210). New York: Academic Press.

Wyer, R. S., & Bodenhausen, G. V. (1985). Event memory: The effects of processing objectives and time delay on memory for action sequences. *Journal of Personality & Social Psychology, 49*, 301–316.

Wyer, R. S., & Carlston, D. E. (1979). *Social cognition, inference, and attribution.* Hillsdale, NJ: Lawrence Erlbaum Associates.

Wyer, R. S., & Gordon, S. E. (1984). The cognitive representation of social information. In R. S. Wyer & T. K. Srull (Eds.), *Handbook of social psychology* (Vol. 2, pp. 73–150). Hillsdale, NJ: Lawrence Erlbaum Associates.

Wyer, R. S., Shoben, E. J., Fuhrman, R. W., & Bodenhausen, G. V. (1985). Event memory: The temporal organization of social action sequences. *Journal of Personality & Social Psychology, 49*, 857–877.

Wyer, R. S., & Srull, T. K. (1986). Human cognition in its social context. *Psychological Review, 93*, 322–359.

Wyer, R. S., & Srull, T. K. (1989a). *Memory and cognition in its social context.* Hillsdale, NJ: Lawrence Erlbaum Associates.

Wyer, R. S., & Srull, T. K. (1989b). Person memory and judgment. *Psychological Review, 96*, 58–83.

Yarmey, A. D. (1979). Through the looking glass: Sex differences in memory for self-facial poses. *Journal of Research in Personality, 13*, 450–459.

Yarmey, A. D., & Johnson, J. (1982). Evidence for the self as an imaginal prototype. *Journal of Research in Personality, 16*, 238–246.

Zeigarnik, B. (1927/1935). Uber das Behalten von erledigten und unerledigten Handlungen [On the remembering of completed and uncompleted tasks]. *Psychologische Forschung, 9*, 1–85. Trans. D. K. Adams & K. E. Zener reprinted in K. Lewin, *A dynamic theory of personality* (pp. 243–247). New York: McGraw-Hill.

Zellner, D. A., Harner, D. E., & Adler, R. L. (1989). Effects of eating abnormalities and gender on perceptions of desirable body shape. *Journal of Abnormal Psychology, 98*, 93–96.

5

Social Inference: Inductions, Deductions, and Analogies

Denise R. Beike
Steven J. Sherman
Indiana University

Contents

The term *social inference* refers to drawing conclusions about individuals or social groups based on a set of underlying premises. The inference involves the premises, conclusions, and a set of rules or procedures that connect the premises to the conclusions (Hastie, 1983). From this definition, it is clear that the domain of social inference is extremely broad and complex. It is equally clear that writing

209

a single chapter that embraces the entire domain of social inference is not possible. In the first place, such a chapter would include a tremendous catalog of inferences—causal inferences, category membership inferences, inferences about the attributes or characteristics of individuals and groups, self-relevant inferences, predictive inferences, moral inferences, inferences about sentiment relations, and inferences about the validity of belief propositions.

With this in mind, some decisions about inclusion and exclusion were necessary to limit the scope of this chapter. One choice would have been a superficial coverage of the entire domain. Although such a chapter would have captured the breadth of the field of social inference, it would not have allowed us to do much thinking, speculation, or integration. Thus, we opted for a less than complete coverage of the field of social inference in the hope of achieving depth and integration.

In terms of content, we focus on social inferences concerning the attributes, characteristics, and behaviors of individuals and groups. We are concerned with the processes involved in such inferences, as well as the similarities and differences that characterize these various types of inferences. Our discussion is guided by a two-dimensional taxonomy of this subset of social inferences. Along one dimension, we divide these inferences according to level. At the lowest level are inferences about specific behaviors that might be engaged in by individuals or by members of a group. At an intermediate level, we consider inferences about the personality characteristics of individuals. At the highest level are inferences about the qualities and characteristics of social groups. These three levels roughly correspond to behavioral prediction, impression formation, and stereotype development. Although each of these areas occupies an important place within social psychology, they are rarely examined together in an integrated or cohesive way.

The second dimension of taxonomy involves the direction of inference. We are concerned with how information from each of our three levels (behavioral, individual, and group-level information) is used to make inferences involving social objects from each of these three levels. Information from lower levels may be used to make inferences about higher levels, as when behavioral information is used to form an impression of an individual. Higher level information may be used to make inferences about lower levels, as when group stereotypes are used to draw conclusions about individual members of the group. Finally, information at any level may be used to make inferences at that same level of analysis, as when knowledge about the attributes of one individual is used to form an impression of a different individual. These three directions of inference roughly correspond to induction (low to high level), deduction (high to low level), and analogy (same level). These are, of course, the three basic types of reasoning processes.

We argue that the direction of social inference is a more important determinant of process than the level at which that inference takes place. Thus, the inductive process of learning about an individual from that person's behavior has much in common with the inductive process of learning about a group from the attributes of individual members of the group. On the other hand, the process of inducing group characteristics from individual members' attributes is likely to involve quite different processes from deducing an individual's attributes from perceived group characteristics, although the same two entities are involved in these two inferences.

With this approach, we outline the similarities and differences involved in inferences concerning behavioral prediction, impression formation, and stereotype development. We hope that this endeavor gives a somewhat new and useful organization to the field of social inference.

INDUCTION

On-line Versus Memory-Based Processes

We consider two important kinds of inductive social inference: the formation of stereotypes of groups based on the knowledge of attributes of individual members, and the formation of general impressions of individuals based on the knowledge of specific facts about them. Prior to discussing these kinds of inductive inference, an important distinction must be made between two basic processes of inference making. This is the distinction between on-line and memory-based inferences. According to Hastie and Park (1986), on-line inferences are made and are stored at the time that the relevant information is available. Because these inferences can be directly retrieved for use at a later time, without necessitating the retrieval of component information, correlations between judgments and the recall of specific information are typically low. On the other hand, memory-based inferences involve the retrieval of previously received information as the input for making inferences at a later time. Thus, the inferences are made on the basis of specific evidence previously encoded. Because the inference is based on this retrieved information, correlations between recall and judgment are typically high.

As we shall see, on-line inferences are more likely in the case of inductive inferences about individuals, whereas recall-based inferences are more likely in the case of inductive inferences about groups (Hamilton, 1991). This distinction helps us understand important differences between the processes of impression formation and stereotype development.

Individual Information → Group Inferences

Because we make inferences about group characteristics on the basis of information about individual group members, we clearly use specific information to induce general principles. Many questions arise concerning this type of inference. Which individuals are most important to the inference? What kind of information about these individuals is most important? How is the information about different individuals integrated? What role does the relationship of the perceiver to the group play in the inference drawn? Do errors and biases creep into inferences about groups? How?

The group that is the target of the inference may be very small (billionaires, the Addams family), of a moderate size (a fraternity, nuclear physicists), or quite large (Italians, the Democratic party). In any case, clearly involved in such inferences is the issue of stereotype development—the formation of schematic representations of groups, including expectations about traits, behaviors, preferences, and abilities. Of course, group stereotypes can form in a variety of ways. Because we are concerned with social inference, we consider only one route to stereotype development: global inferences about the group as a function of lower level trait and behavioral information about individual members.

Memory-Based Processes in Group-Level Inferences. The first important point is that inferences about groups are typically memory-based. According to Hamilton (1991), people do not often develop global impressions of groups at the time they receive information about the attributes of individual members. Rather, information about the individuals is processed and stored in long-term memory, and this information is retrieved at a later time when a global judgment of the group is called for. The reason for not developing the stereotype on-line is that perceivers usually do not expect unity and coherence among the attributes of different group members, and thus do not have a tendency to infer any core group qualities.

Such is not always the case, however. Hamilton (1991) makes the important point that on-line inferences of a group are made to the extent that the group is perceived as having unity and meaningfulness. Studies in which the unity of a group is manipulated (e.g., a family vs. a collection of people) indicate that the inference-making process tends to be on-line in the case of coherent groups, but memory-based in the case of loosely connected aggregates of individuals (Coovert & Reeder, 1990; Hilton & von Hippel, 1990; Srull, Lichtenstein, & Rothbart, 1985). In addition, Messick and Mackie (1989) suggest that inferences about one's in-group are more likely to made on-line, whereas inferences about out-groups are typically done in a memory-based fashion.

What are the implications of the fact that inferences about groups on the basis of information about individual members typically are made in a memory-based fashion? One important consequence is group inferences are likely to show illusory correlation effects, the misperception of the association between minority groups and distinctive behaviors (Hamilton & Gifford, 1976). In this paradigm, subjects read about behaviors performed by members of two groups. More statements are read about the members of one of these groups, the "majority group." In addition, there are more positive than negative behaviors that apply to each group, but the overall ratio of positive to negative behaviors is the same for the two groups. Thus, there is no actual association between group membership and the positivity of members' behaviors. After reading all the behavioral information, subjects are asked for their impressions of the two groups. They consistently overestimate the frequency of distinctive (negative) behaviors engaged in by the smaller group, and they hold far more negative impressions of the minority group. On the other hand, when the distinctive behaviors are positive, an illusory correlation develops in which subjects perceive the minority group as more positive (see Hamilton & Sherman, 1989, for a review). Thus, objectively equivalent information about the members of two different groups leads to different impressions and inferences about these groups.

The most popular theoretical account for illusory correlation, the distinctiveness-based account, depends on the fact that inferences about groups are typically memory-based. That is, the behavioral information about group members is processed, but not integrated in an on-line manner, into group impressions. In addition, the most distinctive information (the infrequent type of behavior engaged in by minority group members) is processed most carefully and most deeply. Later, at the time of judgment, long-term memory is searched for relevant information. Not all the original information is accessed. Some has been lost, and time and energy constraints dictate that only a subset of available information will be used. The information that initially has been encoded most deeply is most accessible at the time of judgment, and thus is most likely to be used. This information will be the infrequent behaviors engaged in by minority group members, and thus this information will carry the most weight in inferences about the groups. The deep encoding of these behaviors, combined with a memory-based judgment process, underlies the illusory correlation effect.

In support of this distinctiveness-based process, Hamilton, Dugan, and Trolier (1985) reported the greatest recall for distinctive behaviors engaged in by minority group members. In addition, they found that a summary table of group behavioral information, rather than a presentation of the individual behaviors, eliminated the illusory correlation effect. However, presenting the summary information after the presentation of individual behavior items did not eliminate the illusory correlation, indicating that the illusory correlation bias depends on initial deep encoding of the distinctive information.

However, as we indicated, impressions of groups can also proceed in an on-line fashion, especially when coherence and unity of the group is expected. Because on-line processing would not be subject to encoding and memory biases, the illusory correlation effect should be attenuated under such conditions. In support of this, Pryor (1986) found that when subjects were instructed to form on-line impressions of groups, the illusory correlation effect failed to emerge.

Which Individuals Are Most Important in Developing Group Stereotypes?
Aside from indicating the process that is involved in drawing inferences about groups, the illusory correlation literature tells us what kinds of individuals are most important in developing group stereotypes. With a memory-based impression

process, the most accessible representations of individuals have the greatest impact on stereotypes. Thus, salient and distinctive members should be most important to the group inference process. This issue was directly investigated by Rothbart, Fulero, Jensen, Howard, and Birrell (1978). In a presentation of the attributes of group members, some subjects were exposed to a subset of members who were very extreme with respect to some attribute (e.g., were well over 6 feet tall; committed very serious criminal acts). Other subjects were exposed to a subset of members who were far less extreme (slightly over 6 feet tall; committed mildly criminal acts). The extremity of the members' attributes affected subjects' estimates of the frequency of 6-footers or of criminals. Subjects who were exposed to very extreme group members overestimated this frequency more than those exposed to less extreme exemplars. This indicates that information about salient or extreme members carries a great deal of weight in group stereotypes. In addition, the availability heuristic (Tversky & Kahneman, 1973) plays an important role in stereotype development—members whose representations are most accessible determine inferences about the group as a whole.

In addition to the salience and extremity of the individuals, perceived typicality of group members also determines the importance of individuals in the stereotype development process. Rothbart and John (1985) and Wilder (1986) suggest that attributes of poor or unusual exemplars of a category will not easily generalize to the overall group impression. The attributes of more typical members are more likely to be incorporated into the group stereotype (Rothbart & Lewis, 1988). This is especially important with regard to the possibility of changing negative stereotypes. Atypical positive behaviors by attractive individual members will not be inferred to generalize to the entire group, whereas expected negative attributes of typical members will generalize easily. This idea that attributes of the most typical members are especially important for category inferences receives support from recent work by McKoon and Ratcliff (1989). In their studies of inferences about contextually defined categories, these researchers concluded that the content of an inference is made up of information relating properties of the most typical exemplar to the textual information.

Prior expectations about a group based on the abstracted representation may thus determine the likelihood of drawing inferences about the entire group from the acts or attributes of any particular member. For example, Hamilton and Rose (1980) had subjects read trait descriptions of members of different occupational groups for which prior expectations existed. The traits were either consistent with stereotypes of the groups or unrelated to the group stereotype. No correlation between stereotypic traits and group membership existed in the presentation material. However, subjects believed that traits consistent with the expected occupational stereotype had been presented far more often than they were. Such illusory correlations between group membership and expected attributes will reinforce existing stereotypes and lead to faulty inferences about group level attributes, because expected traits are believed to occur more often than they do.

Not only are people likely to misperceive the qualities of individual members in line with prior expectations and use these biased perceptions in drawing further inferences about the group, but they also may imagine the existence of stereotype-confirming instances and use these imagined instances in forming or strengthening inferences about the entire group. In an elegant demonstration of this effect, Slusher and C. A. Anderson (1987) showed that when subjects imagine members of a stereotyped group, they imagine instances that fit the stereotype. Thus, in imagining a lawyer, a particular individual who is wealthy and verbal is brought to mind. More important, at a later time, it is difficult for subjects to distinguish imagined individuals from actually encountered individuals. Thus, purely imagined individual members (who tend to fulfill prior expectations) can play an important role in the development and maintenance of group level inferences.

What other attributes of individual group members make them likely contributors to group stereotypes? Classic social psychology literature indicates the importance of two such attributes: (a) positivity/negativity, and (b) the order of information presentation. Generally, negative information carries more weight in global impressions than does positive information (Fiske, 1980; Skowronski & Carlston, 1989). In fact, negative social information appears to have special attention-grabbing power and may be attended to automatically (Pratto & John, 1991), perhaps because such information is infrequent or important. Thus, we might expect that, in general, individual group members who display negative behaviors or attributes will attract special attention, will be encoded more deeply, will be more accessible, and will play a greater role in the development of group stereotypes.

With regard to the order of information presented, Hamilton (1991) suggests that with on-line processing, the information first received will play a more important role in the overall impression (primacy effects). However, when information is processed in a memory-based fashion, the more recent information will be more accessible at the time of judgment, and thus play a greater role (recency effects). Because inferences about groups are generally memory-based, we predict that the individual members most recently met will play the greater role in the development of group stereotypes. In support of this contention, Manis and Paskewitz (1987) presented information about group members that was relevant to their level of psychopathology. The subject's task was to judge the overall level of group pathology. A clear recency effect emerged (see also Hilton & von Hippel, 1990). These findings once again indicate that the process of group inference making is likely to be a memory-based process, especially when there is no expected group cohesiveness.

Another aspect of individual member information that plays a role in group-level inferences is the variability of these members. The members of a group may be highly homogeneous in their attributes or may be quite heterogeneous. Park and Hastie (1987) examined the process of instance-based stereotype development by presenting information about the individual group members. This information was either high or low in variability. They found that subjects indeed code this variability, and that it very much affects the degree of generalization to the group as a whole. With low variability information about individuals, subjects generalize to the group more for typical traits, but less for unusual or atypical attributes. With high variability information about members, the opposite is true: Subjects generalize to the group more for unusual attributes. Interestingly, when summary label information about the group is presented prior to the information about individual members, variability of the member information is not perceived and plays no role in group level inferences. This indicates that once expectations exist for a group, subsequent information about individual members plays a far smaller role in shaping or changing the global impressions of the group.

A final interesting question arises about the process of forming group-level inferences on the basis of information about individual members. Is the information about each individual first integrated into a global image of that individual with these individual global images then integrated into an overall group impression? Or is the information about individual members used in an undifferentiated way to develop a group impression without the intervening step of forming and using differentiated impressions of the various individuals? Work by Rothbart et al. (1978) indicates that the answer depends on the cognitive load of the perceiver. Under a low cognitive load, global group impressions are organized around the inferred characteristics of individuals. Under high load, the individual trait information is used in an undifferentiated way, and each piece of information feeds directly into the group impression. Thus, redundant information about an individual member can be ignored for the group impression under low cognitive load, but not under high cognitive load. In the latter case, each piece of individual information is used equally without regard for what is already known about the individual to whom the information is applicable.

Trait and Behavioral Information →
Individual Impression Formation

Piecemeal Processes in Impression Formation. Making inferences about individuals can involve several different kinds of processes. Most recent models of impression formation are dual-process models. Brewer (1988) differentiates category-based impression formation, which involves the application of stereotypes, and personalization, which involves the use of specific and unique behavioral information. Similarly, Fiske and Neuberg (1990) distinguish category-based from piecemeal impression formation. The latter involves the use of behavior and attributes, and is the focus of this section of the chapter—inductions from lower level behaviors or characteristics to general impressions of individuals.

Using behavioral or trait information to form a global impression of an individual is a case of inductive inference. As both individual impression formation and group stereotype development use lower level, more specific information to make higher level generalizations, there should be important similarities between the processes of impression formation and stereotype development. We focus on these similarities and point to certain differences in the processes of making inferences about individuals and groups.

In the area of impression formation, as compared to stereotype development, far more consideration has been given to the process of combining specific information and integrating this information into the global impression. Formal models of information combination and integration have been developed and tested for individual impression formation (N. H. Anderson, 1968, 1981). Nothing comparable has been done concerning inferences at the group level on the basis of information about individual members, although certainly similar kinds of models could be developed.

In any case, it is not the purpose of this chapter to give a detailed presentation of how the specific behavioral and trait information is combined and integrated into an overall impression. Suffice it to say that several general process approaches have been proposed. Early on, Asch (1946) suggested two models of impression formation: (a) a configural model, and (b) an elemental model. The configural, or Gestalt, model assumes that the impression is holistic and that the specific configuration of attributes and their relationships to each other determine the global impression. The elemental model assumes that each attribute enters separately into the impression independently of others, and the evaluations of each element combine in an additive or averaging fashion. N. H. Anderson (1981) championed this latter kind of attribute-based linear model, generally referred to as information integration theory, and proposed and tested important models of impression formation where information about individuals is weighted and combined algebraically into an overall impression. Lopes (1982) extended this kind of model by proposing an anchoring-and-adjustment process, in which the perceiver takes the evaluation of each element and combines it with the current impression, adjusting this impression in one direction or the other. In general, information integration theory includes an analysis of stimulus selection and evaluation, a cognitive algebra of putting the information together, and an analysis of response generation. The main focus has been on the information integration stage, and a set of precise and simple rules involving adding, multiplying, weighting, and averaging provides a general analysis of impression formation and other social inferences (N. H. Anderson, 1968, 1981).

Which Attributes Are Most Important in Developing Impressions of Individuals? Just as we asked what kinds of individuals are most important and most likely to be used in the development of general group stereotypes, we can ask what kinds of characteristics and attributes are most important to the formation of general impressions of individuals. First, there is simple physical appearance information. Different facial features are associated with different trait impressions (Secord, 1958; Secord & Muthard, 1955). Berry and McArthur (1986) and McArthur and R. Baron (1983) focus on several such features, especially "babyfacedness," and suggest that the inferences need not be based on prior stereotypes, but may be made more directly via the perceptual system. That is, a direct link between visual information and impressions is assumed without the intermediate step of categorizing by person type. Other appearance features such as physical attractiveness (Dion, Berscheid, & Walster, 1972) have also been shown to serve as input for general inferences about individuals.

Personality traits are a second category of information that is important to forming global impressions of individuals. Trait information about an individual may be supplied directly in the form of verbal labels (as was done in most of the early studies of impression formation: N. H. Anderson, 1968; Kaplan, 1971; Wyer, 1974) or may be extracted during interaction or on the basis of observation of the individual. Specific behaviors of an individual also clearly serve as input for global impressions. The content of such behaviors and the situational constraints on them have been shown to be very important in the role of these behaviors in inferences about the individual actor (E. E. Jones & Davis, 1965; A. G. Miller, Ashton, & Mishal, 1990; Quattrone, 1982).

Recently, Carlston (1991) developed a multistage processing model that considers the role of appearance, traits, behaviors, and a variety of other information in the formation of impressions. Each type of information is represented in a different form. For example, physical appearance involves the perceptual system and is represented by mental snapshots, videos, and other forms of visual encoding. Traits are represented cognitively by the verbal system, and the form of representation is dictated by the language structure. These forms are partially independent systems that act in parallel and combine into a total aggregation as an associative network, and this aggregation funnels into and determines the overall global impression of an individual.

Of all the various types of information available about individuals, are some types more important than others? The answer is not simple. In general, it is true that the most salient, vivid, and distinctive information about individuals plays the greatest role in global impressions (Nisbett & Ross, 1980). Another aspect of available information that is important in determining the extent to which it is used for inferences about individuals is its diagnostic value. Some information is simply more diagnostic than other information, in that it better distinguishes between types of individuals, and more diagnostic information will generally be used to make stronger global inferences. For example, Skowronski and Carlston (1987) showed that negative behaviors are seen as more diagnostic than positive behaviors when it comes to morality inferences, but positive behaviors are more diagnostic for ability inferences. In addition, extreme behaviors are judged as more diagnostic than moderate behaviors for both morality and ability inferences. General impressions of individuals show biases toward negativity, positivity, and extremity that are in line with the perceived diagnosticity of the behaviors.

Reeder and Brewer (1979) point out that, for certain trait dimensions, behaviors indicative of a standing on one end of the dimension are more diagnostic than behaviors indicative of a standing on the other end. For example, dishonest behaviors are more diagnostic of dishonesty than honest behaviors are of honesty. This is because both honest and dishonest people can and will act honestly, whereas only dishonest people will engage in dishonest acts. This differential diagnosticity is reflected in the strength of trait inferences based on honest versus dishonest behaviors. Just as traits such as these are confirmed differentially based on the diagnosticity of underlying behaviors, they are also differentially disconfirmed. Thus, although it is easy to infer or confirm dishonesty based on one or a few behaviors, it is difficult to disconfirm a prior inference of dishonesty for exactly the same reasons (Rothbart & Park, 1986) — undiagnostic honest behaviors do little to undo the strong inferential impact of previous dishonest behaviors.

Finally, the presence of actions (doing something) will lead to stronger inferences than will the absence of actions (the failure to do something). Occurrences and presences of stimuli are easier to detect and to draw inferences from than are nonoccurrences and absences (J. Newman, Wolff, & Hearst, 1980). Thus, inferences about the global attitudes (Fazio, Sherman, & Herr, 1982) and the moral standing (Spranca, Minsk, & J. Baron, 1991) of individuals are stronger in the case of commission of acts than on the basis of omissions.

As we have seen, the relative importance of inputs for inductive inferences about individuals is, in part, a function of the properties of those inputs such as salience, primacy, and positivity/negativity. However, relative importance is also a function of certain properties of the perceiver. As Markus (1977) points out, different individuals are schematic for different traits. Those attribute dimensions for which one is schematic should carry more weight in the global impressions of another individual. Similarly, Higgins, King, and Mavin (1982) demonstrated that different traits are chronically accessible for different people, and that the highly accessible traits color people's general inferences about other individuals.

In addition to chronic individual differences, recent experiences may affect the kinds of input that guide people's impressions of others. Priming procedures can render certain types of information more accessible, and this information will affect attention to such information (Sherman, Mackie, & Driscoll, 1990) and interpretation of information in a way that affects the overall impression (Higgins, Rholes, & C. R. Jones, 1977; Srull & Wyer, 1979). Priming procedures may affect the interpretation of behaviors either by increasing the accessibility of a general abstract representation that is behavior relevant (Wyer & Srull, 1986) or by adding new exemplars in the form of episodic records (E. R. Smith, 1990).

Moreover, E. R. Smith (1989) investigated the ways in which trait inferences from behavior can be affected by practice and the development of procedural efficiency. That is, practice at making specific kinds of inferences (e.g., "Is finding one's way around a new city indicative of intelligence?") can affect which inferences are made later upon observation of new behaviors. Behaviors are considered relevant to the most practiced trait inference. Thus, an unfriendly but intelligent behavior can lead to a positive or a negative impression of the target, depending on which kind of trait-dimension inference—honesty or intelligence—was practiced more. This facilitation is independent of memory for previously practiced materials and seems to be quite long lasting. Furthermore, these practice effects on inferences appear to be specific to the behavioral items that are practiced (E. R. Smith, Stewart, & Buttram, 1992).

The Importance of Traits Versus Behaviors.   With regard to the overall importance of traits versus behaviors in impression formation, Park (1986) concluded that the impression-formation process is dominated by the use of traits rather than behaviors, and that this tendency increases over time. Moreover, Carlston and Skowronski (1986) found that making previous trait inferences facilitates subsequent judgments about a target person. Once trait inferences are made, relevant behavioral memories are not used for making new inferences. However, if such behavioral memories are activated, these behaviors could once again serve as the input to global inferences. Thus, greater familiarity with an individual leads to greater use of abstract information and less use of behaviors in forming global impressions. Klein and Loftus (in press) presented data in support of this. They measured subjects' latency in retrieving certain past behaviors of an individual. Some subjects were first asked to make a global impression statement about the individual that was relevant to the behaviors; other subjects simply retrieved the behaviors. Savings time (lowered latencies) by the former group indicated the extent to which the behaviors were accessed to make the global impressions. Klein and Loftus found that for judgments of the self, past behavior is not accessed—global impression subjects show no savings in accessing behaviors. This is true even for impressions along nondescriptive dimensions, indicating that a large variety of general trait inferences are made about the self. However, for targets other than the self, subjects clearly access behaviors to make general inferences, as indicated by large savings scores. Even for well-known targets such as "your mother," subjects refer back to behaviors to make inferences.

These findings indicate that trait induction and forming of global impressions is a long-lasting process and that low-level behaviors continue to play a role in social inferences, even after lengthy experience with the target. However, Park (1986) and Klein and Loftus (in press) agree that the use of behaviors in the inference process diminishes with increased acquaintanceship, and over time the impression process is dominated more and more by the use of general traits that have formed. Perhaps it is more accurate to say that traits are inferred from lower level behaviors, appearance, and other kinds of information, and these inferred traits then play a prime role in subsequent impression formation.

Many inferences about individuals may not be based directly on their traits or their behaviors. Rather, a social perceiver may process trait and behavioral information as cognitive representations in the form of stories. These stories are used as narratives for making inferences and decisions about the individual actor. In the area of juror decision making, Pennington and Hastie (1986, 1988) have shown how jurors represent evidence as narratives. These narratives are then matched to verdict categories, and the goodness of fit determines the decision.

One final point should be made concerning the use of low-level behavioral and attribute information in global impression formation. Once the individual target person is categorized and typed as a member of a particular social group, it becomes difficult and less meaningful to attend to and use additional specific information in the inference process. In the first place, it is simply faster and more efficient to use existing category-based inferences about individuals than it is to induce impressions on the basis of low-level information. More important, categorization has the effect of producing category-consistent perceptions, interpretations, and construals of any new lower level behaviors (Darley & Gross, 1983; Kunda & Sherman-Williams, 1993). Thus, these behaviors become "contaminated" inputs to the inference process.

Recent Models of Impression Formation. Recently, there have been several interesting and useful attempts to clarify the components of the social inference process for impression formation. Gilbert (1989) and Gilbert, Pelham, and Krull (1988) focused on two stages in the process of social inferences concerning individuals. The first stage is a characterization process that assigns dispositional inferences to the actor based solely on what the behaviors would imply based on their face value. This process is automatic, requires scant resources, and is difficult to disrupt. The second stage corrects for any situational constraints on the behaviors. This is a conscious and controlled process that takes into account the context in which the behaviors occurred. The interesting implication of this model is that social inferences are likely to be overly dispositional if the inference makers are cognitively busy. In that case, the automatic characterization will occur, but the conscious correction for situational constraints will not occur due to the limited resources available.

Trope (1986, 1989) presented a somewhat different model to account for the fact that social inferences about individuals are often overly dispositional. In his two-stage model, the first stage is an identification stage, in which the characteristics of a behavior and its context are used to identify the behavior. Thus, if a subject is paid to deliver a liberal speech, the content of an ambiguous political statement will be interpreted as liberal during this behavioral identification stage. The same speech might have been interpreted as conservative if the subject had been paid to deliver a conservative speech. The second stage is similar to Gilbert's second stage—a correction that takes into account any situational constraints. Thus, the money offered for the liberal speech diminishes the inference that the speaker is liberal. This model proposes that the result of the identification stage serves as input for the subsequent inference stage. First we categorize the behavior, and then we draw inferences about the strength of implications of that categorization. The biasing effect of the context on the identification of the behavior may be stronger than the subtractive effects of the context on the inference stage. In this case, inferences will be overly dispositional. That is, the inference stage begins from a point where the behavior is already identified as a strong indicator of the disposition that the situation will insufficiently discount. Such effects are most likely to occur when the behavior is ambiguous in nature and thus subject to alternative identifications depending on the context.

Trope's model is similar to an earlier model proposed by Srull and Wyer (1979), who argued that subjects first encode behaviors in terms of activated trait concepts, and then identify the target as a person with the activated trait. In a subsequent stage, other traits are attributed to the target (i.e., traits that are descriptively irrelevant to the activated trait, but associated with the type of person the target is assumed to be).

Inductive Inferences at the Group Versus Individual Level.   We have now seen that both stereotype development of groups and impression formation of individuals involve inductive inferences from low-level information to higher level generalizations. The fact that impression formation and stereotype development proceed through similar processes of inductive inference indicates that there are many similarities between the two, despite the fact that they are generally treated quite separately in social psychology texts. In both cases, specific information is collected and integrated into a global conception. Hamilton (1991) recently argued for such a similarity of basic process and outlined what these mechanisms are.

Nonetheless, there are also important differences between inductive inferences that are made about individuals versus groups. In the former case, low-level diverse behaviors of a single individual are integrated into a global trait for which these behaviors are relevant. In the case of inferences about groups, trait or behavioral information from different individuals are integrated into a global impression of the group. Specific behaviors of individuals represent the lowest level on the hierarchy, individual impressions represent a medium level, and global group inferences represent the highest level. Thus, impression formation involves going from low-level information to medium-level inferences. Group stereotype development involves going from medium-level information to high-level inferences. What differences might we expect in the strength or certainty of these types of inferences? Members of lower level categories share many properties, whereas few properties are shared by the larger number of members of higher level categories (Rosch, 1978). Thus, dogs have more properties in common across all members than do mammals. Lower levels have less variability, whereas higher level categories show great variability and few general attributes. Thus, we might expect that inferences are more likely to be made and can be made with greater strength and certainty in the case of individuals than in the case of groups. In a rough way, behaviors, individual impressions, and group stereotypes can be thought of as representing subordinate, basic, and superordinate category levels. Osherson, E. E. Smith, Wilkie, Lopez, and Shafir (1990) discussed the strength of inferences among category members. Although they did not deal directly with inferences between subordinate, basic, and superordinate category levels, their model is consistent with the prediction that inferences will be made more strongly from low to medium levels than from medium to high levels.

This discussion brings us back to the fundamental difference between individual impression formation and group stereotyping that we raised earlier. In the case of individuals, the perceiver expects a personality that has unity, coherence, and simplicity. With these expectations, the inclination is to take information about an individual and integrate it in an on-line fashion into a coherent impression as that information is received. On the other hand, the same degree of unity, coherence, and organization is not expected in the case of groups. Fewer general qualities are anticipated, and greater variability is expected. Thus, there will be less of a tendency to identify an inherent nature of a group, and on-line processing of information about group members into a global group stereotype is less likely than forming individual impressions. In other words, group impressions are likely to be arrived at through a memory-based process, whereas individual impression formation will generally proceed in an on-line fashion.

What differences might we expect in terms of inferences about groups versus individuals based on the differential predominance of memory-based versus on-line processes? In the first place, there should be differences in the way that inconsistent information is processed. For individuals and on-line processing, information inconsistent with an initial impression will be processed deeply as such information is integrated into the impression. Thus, a perceiver will spend more time processing inconsistent information (Stern, Marrs, Millar, & E. Cole, 1984) and will remember it better (Hastie & Kumar, 1979; Srull et al., 1985). This effect seems to be limited to information that is evaluatively, rather than descriptively, inconsistent with an initial expectation (Wyer, Bodenhausen, & Srull, 1984). In the case of group-level information, the perceiver should be less troubled by any incongruent information because no coherence is expected. Thus, processing time and recall should not be greater for inconsistent information in the case of group-level processing (Srull et al., 1985; Wyer et al., 1984).

Next, we should expect differences in the organization of information about individuals and groups. Information about individual targets should be organized in memory by each individual, whereas information about different groups should not show such organization by group. Stroessner, Hamilton, Acorn, Czyzewska, and Sherman (1989) had subjects read behavior descriptions of four individuals or four groups. Clustering analysis of free-recall data indicated far greater organization by individual than by group.

We have already seen the illusory correlation effect for stereotypes of groups based on the fact that distinctive information is processed deeply and is most accessible at the time of judgment. This effect depends on the fact that information about groups is processed in a memory-based way. For individuals, given the likelihood of on-line processing, the ingredients for illusory correlation are not there, and we should not expect a perceived association between distinctive individuals and distinctive behaviors. In fact, in the case of individuals, the illusory correlation effect is not present (Sanbonmatsu, Sherman, & Hamilton, 1987). Moreover, the usual illusory correlation pattern is reversed, with an unwarranted correlation perceived between the distinctive individual and the more frequent behaviors. This effect is consistent with on-line processing, where the typical kinds of behaviors play the greatest role in forming a coherent impression, and any inconsistent behaviors are assimilated to this impression.

There are also likely to be differences in primacy or recency effects depending on whether the processing is on-line or memory-based. In general, recency effects are predicted when the impression process is memory-based. The most recent information is most accessible at the time of recall-based judgment and will dominate the impression. As seen earlier, recency effects in group stereotypes seem to be the rule (Manis & Paskewitz, 1987). On the other hand, for individuals, where on-line processing is likely, we would expect primacy effects as later information is assimilated to the initial impression (Hilton & von Hippel, 1990; Manis & Paskewitz, 1987).

Park (1986, 1989) studied the development of impressions of individuals and confirmed that such impressions are likely to proceed in an on-line manner. The initial information provides a first impression, and adjustments from this initial position are made. Typically, these adjustments are insufficient, and primacy effects are the consequence. Thus, Park's data support primacy effects in the development of impressions of real people. Park concluded that these primacy effects are of a passive rather than an active nature. That is, the initial information does not override later information. Rather, it turns out that in real-world interactions, much of the important information about people is simply available at early encounters.

We noted earlier that negativity effects should be expected in the case of group stereotype development. That is, negative individuals should carry greater weight than positive individuals in the group impression. This is because negative information draws attention, and this information will thus be encoded deeply and be more available for recall at a later time. Because group impressions are memory-based, such differential accessibility will allow negative information to dominate inferences. Park (1989) suggested that this tendency might be less likely for impressions of individuals because of the on-line nature of the impression formation process.

Although these differences between inferences about individuals and groups are important, we must remember that they are primarily due to the fact that impressions of groups are generally made in a memory-based way, and impressions of individuals are generally made on-line. However, this is clearly not an all-or-none proposition. As Hamilton (1991) pointed out, groups vary in the extent to which unity and coherence is expected. For small, tightly knit groups, assumptions of coherence and low variability may be more likely. In this case, given expectations of group unity, information may be processed on-line; the effects outlined earlier for on-line processing in individuals would also be anticipated. Such groups may be easier to stereotype because of the expected similarity among members.

Just as groups may differ in terms of expectations of unity and consistency, individuals may also differ. We may expect little in the way of personality or coherence from a person known to be moody, irrational, schizophrenic, or manic-depressive. In this case, on-line processing would be less likely, and the impressions of such individuals may hold more in common with the ways in which impressions of groups are generally formed. The basic mechanisms underlying inductive inferences about individuals and groups are similar. Differences arise because of the relative predominance of on-line versus memory-based processes of inference for individuals and groups, respectively. These differences are, in turn, based on the extent to which unity and coherence are expected. Finally, to the extent that the degree of expected coherence is the same for specific individuals or specific groups, the processes and outcomes of the inductive inferences should not be different.

DEDUCTION

Deductive inferences involve the use of higher order generalizations to draw conclusions about specific instances at lower levels of hierarchical representation. We discuss two kinds of deductive social inferences: (a) the use of group level stereotypes to make judgments about individual members, and (b) the use of general impressions of an individual to make predictions about specific characteristics or behaviors of that individual. As in the case of inductive inferences, we point to important similarities and differences in these two levels of deductive inference.

Group Stereotypes → Inferences About Individuals

The direction of inference here is from the general to the more specific. One begins with a global impression or stereotype of a group and makes inferences about an individual member of the group based specifically on that individual's membership in the group. In simplest terms, this process is concerned with the application or use of stereotypes that develop, in part, from the inductive inference processes discussed previously. Thus, information about individuals is used in a bottom-up way to develop a group stereotype, and this stereotype is then used in a top-down manner to draw inferences about other individuals.

Stereotypes are usually conceptualized as abstract knowledge structures that link a social group with a set of trait or behavioral characteristics (Hamilton & Trolier, 1986; S. E. Taylor, 1981). These knowledge structures function as expectations and are applied as people are exposed to new members of the group. A more recent view (E. R. Smith, 1990) proposes that stereotypes are exemplar-based implicit memories of experiences with group members, and that the application of stereotypes is done by retrieving exemplars that are cued by a target individual and the context of exposure.

Category-Based Processes in Impression Formation.   It is quite clear that people use generic social knowledge and feelings about groups to make inferences about individual members. This deductive or top-down inference route for learning about individuals contrasts sharply with the inductive inference route discussed earlier, which uses personalized and low-level behaviors and attributes for individual impression formation. The deductive route is referred to as *category-based processing* (Brewer, 1988; Fiske & Neuberg, 1990) and is viewed as more pervasive than bottom-up processing because it is adaptive, efficient, low cost, and allows for simplification of the information stream (Fiske & Neuberg, 1990). Individualized information processing is far less efficient and requires more time and more cognitive resources. Thus, the deductive or top-down route is preferred for inferences about individuals, especially when there is time pressure or a high cognitive load. The inductive or bottom-up route predominates only when the individual target cannot be easily categorized or when there is strong motivation for an accurate impression.

In general, stereotype application, or category-based impressions, involves a two-stage process. First, it is necessary to identify the individual with some social category. Once category identification is achieved, the attributes of that category can be applied to the individual. We first discuss the process of social category identification. Most theorists agree that social category identification can be a fast and automatic process (Brewer, 1988; Fiske & Pavelchak, 1986; E. R. Smith & Zarate, 1992). An individual will be categorized quickly as a woman, a doctor, or a liberal, and this categorization will then serve as the basis for inferences. Although the process may be fast and is often spontaneous, an understanding of category identification and the outcome of this process can be quite complex. Most people are members of multiple categories (race, gender, occupation). Yet, at any given time, membership in only one of these categories will dominate people's representation or category identification of a person and will be used at that time for making inferences.

Most current models of social categorization are prototype models (Brewer, 1988; Fiske & Neuberg, 1990; see Medin & E. E. Smith, 1984, for a general treatment). That is, a representation of a typical category member for each social category is stored in memory. New individuals are compared to these prototypes and are classified into a social category based on degree of similarity. On the other hand, E. R. Smith (1990) has argued for an exemplar model of categorization in which similarity to individual exemplars is the key to social categorization. The use of exemplars seems greater under impression sets than under memory sets and for in-group rather than out-group members (E. R. Smith & Zarate, 1990).

Social-Category Identification. What factors determine the specific category identification of an individual? In general, people categorize individuals in ways that allow them to make the most inferences and the kinds of inferences that will be most useful. In addition, there are some categories that are no doubt more natural or basic than others and serve as an inescapable basis of category identification. Rothbart and M. Taylor (1992) discussed race and gender as this type of natural category. Natural categories are well-represented in memory because they are familiar, have rich inductive potential, have an essence, and are high in unalterability (Gelman & Coley, 1991). E. R. Smith and Zarate (1992) proposed that age, gender, and race are the best candidates for natural kinds because they are based on physical appearance features and are seen as powerful determinants of important social roles. Thus, people will be categorized automatically according to these attributes, and inferences will be made on the basis of these category memberships—inferences that reflect the stereotypes of these natural categories.

Research has supported the importance of gender and race categories as natural categories that serve as an important basis of social inference. Stangor (1988) examined subjects' tendencies to encode and use gender information. Subjects were simply given the names of four targets in order to activate the gender category of these targets. Various stereotype-consistent and stereotype-inconsistent behaviors by the targets were presented. Then subjects were given a list of behaviors and were directed to recognize them as old or new. Some of the behaviors were associated with a new person who was either of the same or the opposite gender as the original actor. Intrusions (incorrectly saying "old" to new items) clearly favored the stereotype-consistent behaviors. In addition, high gender-accessibility subjects (as determined by the gender-relatedness of their most accessible constructs) showed the strongest tendency to make errors in the direction of gender consistency. These subjects also made the most within-gender false alarms. These results indicate that subjects spontaneously use stereotype knowledge of genders to process information.

More recently, Stangor, Lynch, Duan, and Glass (1992) looked at both race and gender as natural bases of social categorization. Subjects heard a series of statements by various targets whose photographs identified their race and gender. After viewing the entire set of photographs, subjects were asked to match the photos with the set of statements. Within-gender and within-race errors were used as indicators of the extent of natural categorization. Subjects were more likely to categorize targets by their gender (as evidenced by many within-gender errors), but also tended to categorize using a single subordinate category that represented both gender and race. Highly prejudiced subjects showed high levels of categorization by race. Construct accessibility (as manipulated by priming) and processing goals did not affect categorization by race or gender, indicating that such categorization is quite natural and spontaneous. Other equally available information (clothing style and color, physical similarity) was not used as the basis of categorization.

Zarate and E. R. Smith (1990) also investigated the degree of categorization of targets, based on the race and gender of both the target and the subject. Their measure was the speed with which subjects categorized targets according to race or gender. Results indicate generally faster categorization for photographs of Whites and for photographs of males. Male targets are categorized faster by race, and female targets are categorized faster by gender. These results indicate that attention is automatically directed to gender in the case of females, and thus categorization by race is slowed and categorization by gender is speeded up. In addition, subjects classify same-gender photographs faster for both gender and race decisions. Thus, processing information about one's in-group is easier and more efficient.

More important for our purposes, Zarate and E. R. Smith's (1990) subjects showed a strong association between the speed of categorization and the stereotype that they applied. Subjects who were relatively fast on race categorization and slow on gender categorization made a large number of racially related target inferences on a subsequent task. These results show that social categorization goes hand in hand with inferences about individuals and that categorization mediates racial stereotyping. However, no significant relationships emerged for gender-related inferences, perhaps because gender stereotypes are so universally applied.

Although race and gender appear to be natural categories, and individuals are categorized spontaneously into one or the other of these categories, various other social, motivational, and contextual factors affect the way in which individuals may be categorized. E. R. Smith and Zarate (1992) outlined some of the other factors that determine the predominant social categorization of individuals when multiple categories are available. First, the social goal of the perceiver is a strong determinant of categorization. Whether one is interested in dating a target person versus hiring that person affects the social category to which that person is assigned. In addition, easy-to-perceive or salient features (wearing a uniform, solo status) can affect categorization (S. E. Taylor, Fiske, Etcoff, & Ruderman, 1978). Similarly, priming and other external means of altering category accessibility can affect the category to which a person is assigned at any point in time (Higgins et al., 1977; Srull & Wyer, 1979). Practice and the development of categorization procedures along a specific dimension will affect social categorization as well (E. R. Smith, 1989).

Chronic individual differences also play a role in social categorization. Some people are tuned into occupation or social status, whereas others are more concerned with personality typing or marital status. Self-relevant categories are often used chronically (Higgins et al., 1982). Self-status can also affect categorization. People pay greater attention to individuating attributes of the self and the in-group, but greater attention to category-defining attributes of out-group members. Because of these categorization tendencies, stereotypic inferences are more likely to be made for out-group members (Quattrone & E. E. Jones, 1980; Wilder, 1978).

Finally, social categorization depends primarily on the descriptive consistency of the target's relevant attributes for the category, rather than on the evaluative consistency. Thus, a person may be categorized as an extrovert by either positive or negative extrovert characteristics. Interestingly, the overall evaluative response to any person thus categorized should be the same once the categorization occurs. That is, the evaluation should depend only on one's feelings about extroverts, rather than on the evaluation of the specific information used as a basis for the categorization (Fiske & Pavelchak, 1986).

The Application of Category Attributes. Once successful categorization is achieved, top-down or category-based processing is likely to occur. Bottom-up or piecemeal processing will generally occur only when successful social categorization cannot be accomplished or when motivation to form an accurate impression is high. Category-based processing involves the application of category attributes to an individual. Such processing is likely to affect attention to category-relevant features, interpretation of information in a direction that fits category attributes,.and inferences that go beyond the information given in a way that is consistent with the category representation. In fact, once category-based processing is engaged, it becomes difficult to attend to or use specific, individuating attributes of the target person in an overall impression, especially if these attributes are inconsistent with the category stereotype.

Many studies support these effects of category-based processing in impression formation, and it is beyond the scope of this chapter to provide a detailed presentation of this literature. Category-relevant or stereotypic responses seem to be accessible immediately upon the classification of an individual as a category member (Secord, 1959; Tajfel, 1969). Aside from belief inferences, category-based processing is likely to result in affective responses to the target (Fiske & Pavelchak, 1986) as well as in behavior toward the target (Snyder, Tanke, & Berscheid, 1977; Word, Zanna, & Cooper, 1974).

The effects of category-based processing are many. Because the general group stereotype is applied to all group members, the perceiver will minimize the variability of members within the category (Park & Rothbart, 1982). In addition, categorization and the application of category stereotypes will greatly influence interpretations of an individual member's behavior. Thus, identical behaviors of a target individual are interpreted as more aggressive if the target has been categorized as Black rather than White (Duncan, 1976; Sagar & Schofield, 1980). Moreover, construals of incompletely described behaviors will be made in a way that confirms stereotypes. Thus, the phrase "acted aggressively" is likely to be construed as "slapped a child" when applied to a housewife but as "decked a co-worker" when applied to a construction worker. These category-based construals can affect subsequent inferences (Kunda & Sherman-Williams, 1993). Category-based interpretations and construals occur more often when the behavior of the target is ambiguous in nature (Darley & Gross, 1983; Kunda & Sherman-Williams, 1993), and most often when little diagnostic individuating information is available to influence the inference (Krueger & Rothbart, 1988).

Although these effects of category-based, deductive inferences apply to all targets who are categorized as group members, they will not be equally strong for all members. For example, stereotypes will be applied most strongly and with greatest certainty to an individual deemed to be typical of or a good representative of the group, rather than to a fringe member. In support of this, Lord, Lepper, and Mackie (1984) found that subjects act toward a group member in a way that reflects their attitude toward the group only when the member is prototypic. Group stereotypes are not applied to nonprototypic members. Similarly, Glick, Zion, and Nelson (1988) reported that job applicants who are nonprototypic with regard to gender attributes do not have gender stereotypes applied to them. However, the prototypicality of a member may affect the strength of deductive inferences only when the group is perceived as rather homogeneous (Lambert & Wyer, 1990).

Even nondiagnostic information can reduce the prototypicality of a group member, and thus reduce the extent to which a group stereotype will be applied to that member (Fein & Hilton, 1992). This idea assumes that the perceiver has an abstracted representation of the group and that a comparison is made between this representation and the features of individual targets. The more attributes a person has that are inconsistent with group membership, the less strongly the stereotype will be applied. However, the presence of such inconsistent attributes often leads to the creation of a subtype of the overall group. This subtype will often have its own stereotype, and its features will be applied to subtype members (Weber & Crocker, 1983). Thus, we have seen that inductive inferences are more likely to be made from prototypic members, rather than from atypical members, to the group as a whole (Rothbart & Lewis, 1988); deductive inferences are more likely to be made from the group stereotype to prototypic rather than atypical members (Lord et al., 1984).

In short, impressions of individuals depend, to a large extent, on stereotyping – deductive inferences that follow from the categorization of that individual. Which category is applied to an individual (e.g., woman, mother, lawyer, bridge expert) and the goodness of that category's fit to the individual will determine the degree to which category-based inferences will predominate in the overall impression of the individual. The fact that different categories may be applied to an individual at different points in time (depending on priming, motivational factors, etc.) indicates that people's impressions of individuals as inferred from their group membership may be unstable and situation-specific (E. R. Smith, 1990).

Individual Impressions → Behavior Inferences

We now discuss deductive inferences that occur at lower levels in the hierarchy. How does one make inferences about the specific behaviors and attributes of an individual based on the global impression of that individual? Compared with the vast literature on the use of stereotypes and schema-driven processes in impression formation, relatively little work has been done on deductive inferences concerning the specific behaviors and attributes of individuals. Yet, in many ways, these may be among the most important social inferences that are made.

Behavioral Prediction. One kind of behavioral inference is especially critical in people's day-to-day functioning—predictions about their own and others' future behavior and performances. Will my preferred candidate win the election? Am I likely to enjoy living on the West Coast? Answers to questions such as these are key inputs in people's important judgments and decisions, and yet very little is known about how such behavioral inferences are made.

The deductive process that we have outlined suggests that people have well-developed theories about what specific behaviors follow from what general characteristics of individuals. Thus, extroverts are likely to attend parties, talk a lot, be loud, and avoid being alone. Once an individual has been characterized as having a certain personality type, specific behavioral inferences will follow, just as stereotypic trait inferences follow from placing a person in a particular social category. Although this kind of deductive process is common in forming impressions of individuals based on group membership, inferences about specific behaviors from general traits appear to be less common. There are several reasons why it is difficult to draw deductive inferences about specific behaviors from general impressions of an individual:

1. It is generally much easier to draw inferences from specific behaviors to general characteristics than vice versa (Carlston, 1992). Thus, the inductive inference that someone is dishonest, based on the fact that they have lied, is made with more ease and certainty than the deductive inference that someone will lie based on the fact that they are dishonest. This difference may be due to the fact that behavior-to-trait inferences are far more common and more practiced than are trait-to-behavior inferences. Uleman's work (1987, 1989) suggests that trait inferences from behaviors are made rather spontaneously. However, it is unlikely that learning about a general trait of a target individual would lead spontaneously to deductive inferences about specific behaviors in which the individual might engage. Thus, well-practiced procedures might account for the relative ease of inductive as opposed to deductive inferences when it comes to traits and behaviors.

2. As Epstein (1979) and Sherman and Fazio (1983) have pointed out, it is difficult to predict any single behavior from a global attitude or trait. Better pre-

dictive inferences can be made when predicting multiple behaviors. Although this is true—predictions of any single behavior are a dangerous enterprise—it is precisely the accurate prediction of one behavior that is often most necessary. People want to know whether a particular job interview will be successful, not whether a multitude of behaviors over a long period of time will be successful on average.

3. Specific behaviors are a function of the dispositional qualities of the individual, as well as the situational constraints that are present. Thus, deductive inferences about any specific behaviors can be made only with great uncertainty.

Given the difficulty in predicting specific behaviors from global traits, other routes to behavioral inferences often are taken:

1. A person's past behavior is an obvious candidate for use in the prediction of future behavior. In fact, past behavior is generally the best indicator of what a person is likely to do in the future.

2. Alternatively, if no past behaviors of a target individual are available, the behavior of other people, especially similar others, can be used for prediction of behaviors of the target individual. This process would involve analogical reasoning and is discussed more fully in a subsequent section of this chapter. If the behavioral data from enough individuals of known characteristics are available, general principles of prediction can be induced and then used for the prediction of new individuals.

Such actuarial prediction is far superior to prediction based on the uncertain global impressions of a single individual target (Dawes, Faust, & Meehl, 1989). Yet people prefer clinical prediction based on individuating information, rather than more useful and accurate statistical prediction. Thus, people wrongly believe that they can form accurate impressions of individuals and make good predictions from these impressions.

Recently, Karniol (1990) developed a comprehensive model for predictive inferences. She claimed that making predictions about others' thoughts, feelings, and actions involves procedural knowledge in the form of simplifying heuristics (knowing how to make predictions based on a set of general procedures or rules). In addition, one then applies declarative knowledge or content knowledge to make specific predictions. Prototype or stereotype information would be part of one's declarative knowledge. Karniol specified the rules that are used for predictive inferences. These rules are called transformational rules, and they represent procedural knowledge that is independent of declarative knowledge. Examples of such rules include: (a) category instantiation, (b) scripted connections, and (c) stimulus-directed desires. Transformational rules are heuristic devices that are arranged hierarchically, with different hierarchies for different individuals. Predictions are made by applying these rules and choosing a rule based on the fit between the characteristics of the situation and the rule. Once the rule is applied, declarative knowledge is used to make specific predictions. This knowledge may involve specific knowledge about the individual target or general information about the target's category in the form of stereotypes.

Errors in Prediction.   An interesting aspect of predictive inferences is the extent to which these inferences are error-prone. Sherman (1980) demonstrated that people's predictions of their own future behaviors across a variety of activities can be full of errors. For example, whereas 40% of subjects predicted that they would agree to donate an afternoon's time to help a charity if asked to do so, only 2% of a comparable set of subjects actually agreed to such a direct request. Similarly, Greenwald, Carnot, Beach, and Young (1987) reported that subjects greatly overpredicted the likelihood that they would vote in an upcoming election.

Why are these predictive inferences so far off the mark? One possibility is that the predictions are made on a deductive basis from a general self-impression. However, people's self-impressions may be biased in a positive direction. That is, they perceive themselves as more socially desirable, helpful, and conscientious than they really are. Thus, their self-predictions, as deductive inferences from positive global self-images, too often indicate positive thoughts and actions. In fact, the overprediction of positive and normative behaviors is typical (Sherman, 1980). It is also possible that predictive inferences are based not on specific knowledge of the self but on more global schemas of what people generally do or should do in certain situations. People's general theories about how people behave or what factors affect behavior may be quite wrong (Nisbett & Wilson, 1977) and thus lead to errors of prediction.

Just as self-predictions tend to be error-prone, predictions about the behavior of other people are likely to be inaccurate. One example of such inaccuracy involves the overconfidence shown in social prediction. Dunning, Griffin, Milojkovic, and Ross (1990) had subjects predict a friend's responses to a variety of situations and give their level of confidence in their predictions. Regardless of the type of prediction, judgments are overconfident. Interestingly, the degree of knowledge about the target individual has little effect on the level of overconfidence. Thus, overconfidence is equally high for a well-known target, a target who is personally interviewed, or a target about whom little is known. This implies that predictive inferences are not based on deductions from global impressions of the specific target, but are based instead on more general rules about what people are likely to do in what kinds of situations. The overconfidence effect seems to be based on the fact that alternative construals of what people might do in the given situations are not very accessible (Griffin, Dunning, & Ross, 1990). Overconfidence is exhibited to similar degrees for self-predictions (Vallone, Griffin, Lin, & Ross, 1990), again indicating that knowledge of the target and deductive inferences from impressions of the target probably play a minor role in the overconfidence effect.

Behavioral Inferences from Stereotypes Versus Traits. We have seen that deductive inferences about the behavior of an individual may come from two different sources: (a) stereotypes based on group membership and (b) global traits that are part of the impression of the specific individual. Which inferential route is stronger and has more predictive power? There is some discrepancy in the literature. Andersen and Klatzky (1987) reported that trait-defined categories lead to fewer inferences and have less predictive value than do stereotypes. Social stereotypes are described by subjects as richer and more vivid than trait-defined categories, with more idiosyncratic and distinctive features. For this reason, Andersen and Klatzky (1987) maintained that stereotypes lead to more efficient social information processing and to better predictive inferences.

On the other hand, Rothbart (1988) suggested that traits are more informative than general social category membership in predicting social behavior. In support of this, Stangor, Ford, and Duan (1992) found that social category information has a weaker influence on inferences than does trait information.

These inconsistencies in the literature suggest that there are complex differences between traits and stereotypes, especially with regard to their inferential value. Traits are more restrictive and specific than are general social categories. Therefore, inferences and predictions based on traits are likely to be more precise, and the linkages between traits and behaviors are likely to be stronger than the linkages between stereotypes and behaviors. On the other hand, because social stereotypes are broader than trait-defined categories, they suggest a wider range of distinctive behaviors and attributes, and so they may lead to a greater number and variety of inferences. In addition, there are times when a stereotype will activate a trait, and lower level inferences will be made from this trait. At other times, however, a trait can activate a higher level group stereotype, and inferences may be based on the broader social category.

Moreover, there are likely to be individual differences in the use of trait versus stereotype information. Highly prejudiced people are likely to use group stereotype information, whereas low prejudiced people are likely to use impressions of the specific individual. The personal relevance of the particular trait or stereotype in question also will determine the importance of each for the inference process.

Finally, Klatzky and Andersen (1988) suggested that the degree of familiarity with and knowledge about the target person is important in determining whether traits or stereotypes are used more for deductive inference. When targets are moderately familiar, stereotypes will predominate. However, when targets are either unfamiliar (when no group stereotype can be easily applied) or highly familiar (when much individuated information is available), traits will predominate. Understanding the complex relation between trait and stereotype activation will help us better understand the inferential processes involving the use of both trait and social categories for behavioral prediction.

Deductive Inferences at the Individual Versus Behavioral Level.   In our discussion of inductive social inferences, we addressed the question of the likelihood and strength of inferences that are made about individuals as opposed to groups. We pointed out that the individual person level is lower in the social-object hierarchy than are groups. Because lower level categories generally have less variability and share more properties than do higher level categories, we suggested that inductive inferences from behaviors to individual impressions would be made with greater strength and certainty than inferences from individuals to group-level attributes.

We can ask this same kind of question regarding the strength and likelihood of deductive inferences. Are deductive inferences stronger and more likely when made from group stereotypes to impressions of individuals or when made from individual impressions to specific behaviors? The above reasoning suggests that deductions at the lower level (from individual targets to specific behaviors) will be stronger. After all, groups are more heterogeneous and have less coherence than do individual people, who are assumed to have a stable personality. Thus, inferences should be made more easily from the general characteristics of individuals as opposed to the more variable attributes of groups.

However, this conclusion does not fit with our intuitions. We share Carlston's (1991) view that inferences are not made easily from the trait level to the behavior level. On the other hand, stereotypes are employed quite often and quite easily in order to draw inferences about individual group members. Perhaps, as indicated earlier, it is the degree of practice that one has with specific inferences that determines the ease or the likelihood of making such inferences, rather than the hierarchy level at which these inferences are made. Of course, this begs the question of why certain types of inferences are practiced more than others, and future work should be devoted to the issue of which kinds of social inferences are most likely to be made, under what conditions, and why.

ANALOGY

The final major type of social inference is analogical reasoning. The analogical reasoning process involves inferring the characteristics of social objects at one level of the hierarchy from information known about other social objects at that same level in the hierarchy. The characteristics of one person, behavior, or group are inferred by analogy to the characteristics of another person, behavior, or group. Most often, analogical social inferences involve individual people, so most of our examples and discussion concern people rather than groups, traits, or behaviors.

The analogical inference process entails transferring the known characteristics of one person to another. The person about whom the inference is to be made is the *target* of the analogy, and the person from whom information is transferred is the *base*. A moment's introspection may be helpful in understanding how the analogy process works. Imagine meeting a new colleague who is professional and cordial. However, when she smiles, you suddenly are reminded of your mother's smile. Now you find yourself perceiving your colleague's advice as nagging and her compliments as patronizing. Rationally, you may know your colleague is not your mother, but this small bit of similarity between them has struck a psychological chord. Further inferences about your colleague may become colored by your knowledge of your mother's characteristics.

We begin with this intuitive approach to understanding analogical reasoning, because this third type of social inference has not received the enormous empirical and theoretical attention that induction and deduction have received. The process of analogical social inference is not fully understood, nor have a large number of models of the process been proposed. Therefore, the discussion to follow draws on work in cognitive psychology, developmental psychology, and cognitive science, in addition to the relevant social psychological literature. We begin with a description of the analogy process as conceptualized by different researchers.

Read (1984) proposed a five-step model of the analogy process:

1. People search for a well-defined, previously learned deductive rule (as discussed in the previous section) for the inference problem at hand. Finding none, they are likely to look for analogies.
2. People construct or retrieve a mental representation of the target and the general base domain.
3. Individual base instances are retrieved.
4. People map the base instances onto the target instance and search for matching characteristics.
5. The analogy is applied, meaning that some characteristics of a base instance are transferred to the target (see also Gick & Holyoak, 1980, 1983).

In contrast to this rational, step-by-step process, some researchers think of the analogical process as a lower level one. Read's (1984) model fits well with the concept of analogy as an overt, conscious, and effortful reasoning process used in problem solving. A different approach is to consider analogy an automatic, stimulus-triggered, perceptually based process (Hofstadter, 1992). In this view, analogies are not tools sought out and applied by the perceiver to solve particular inference problems, nor do they occur after an exhaustive search for deductive rules has been completed. Rather, analogies are extremely basic; they involve processes such as perception and categorization; they occur in all domains (domain-general); and they cannot be avoided or controlled (nonvolitional) (Gentner, 1992; cf. Gick & Holyoak, 1980, 1983).

In other words, rather than serving as special-purpose, problem-solving modes of thought, analogies are viewed as all-purpose, ubiquitous, unconscious, and undirected processes used in perception and categorization. According to this view, the role of specific instances in shaping inferences is not a planful, strategic use, but generally involves automatic and nonanalytic memory retrieval and use (E. R. Smith, 1990). Analogy making is most likely to be used in this way when the target is ambiguous and requires understanding (Hofstadter, 1992). The outcome of analogical thinking is that stimuli that are actually different are perceived as similar in terms of their relational structures. The essence of one situation is transported to another situation (Mitchell, 1992). The perception of nonidentical objects having similar relational structures affords inferences of further similarities between the two objects, and new knowledge can thus be generated by analogical thinking (Gentner, 1992). Thus, the critical factor affecting analogical thinking in social inference is perceived similarity of the base and target person (Read, 1987). Under most circumstances, transfer on the basis of similarity is a reasonable heuristic principle. The more similar two people are, the more characteristics they are likely to have in common.

The degree of similarity necessary to stimulate analogical reasoning need not be large. Even irrelevant similarities can evoke analogical thinking and can lead one down the garden path to additional but erroneous inferences about the target object (Keil, 1989). As in our previous example, similar smiles can be enough to inspire analogically based inferences. Clearly, focusing on these superficial similarities to infer further similarities cannot always be a rational approach.

Our discussion of similarity, whether it is superficial or deep, focuses on perceived similarity. The similarity need not be objectively verifiable. As long as one believes that one's date has the same eyes as a famous actress, one's inferences about him or her will be affected by this belief. Whether others share one's perception is unimportant to the inference process.

We now explore the issue of similarity and analogy in social inference in more detail. The empirical examples discussed next reveal some of the features of a person that may be involved in analogically based inferences. The following examples, taken together, also help to reveal the nature of the cognitive processes underlying analogical reasoning.

Characteristics of Person A → Characteristics of Person B

One of the earliest demonstrations of the power of similarity between a known individual and a target individual in producing analogical inferences was a study by Berkowitz and Geen (1966). Although this study was originally conducted to test further the validity of Berkowitz's theory of aggression, the findings are relevant to analogical inference as well. Subjects in the Berkowitz and Geen study were introduced to either "Kirk" or "Bob" (an accomplice), who either treated them neutrally or angered them. Subjects then watched either a film about a track race or a film in which Kirk Douglas played a prize fighter who received a severe beating. Afterward, subjects were given the opportunity to administer shocks to the accomplice.

The highest level of aggression was exhibited (not surprisingly) by angry subjects who had watched the Kirk Douglas movie, and (more surprisingly) toward "Kirk" rather than "Bob" (a three-way interaction). Apparently, the similarity of "Kirk" in name alone to Kirk Douglas the prize fighter caused subjects to infer that "Kirk" was more deserving of aggression than "Bob." In this case, name similarity was sufficient to affect subjects' actual behavior toward the confederate.

Although Berkowitz and Geen's (1966) findings seem suggestive of a similarity–analogy link, no direct evidence of similarity was collected. We have simply inferred that "Kirk" was seen as more similar to Kirk Douglas than "Bob" was. Questioning subjects about the similarity among the three persons might have provided better evidence of a similarity-based process. In addition, no direct evidence was garnered to show that subjects were using Kirk Douglas the prize fighter as the specific base for an analogy.

Read (1987) sought to demonstrate the importance of similarity to analogy in a more tightly controlled manner. He gave subjects information about a single member of an obscure (nonexistent) tribe, thus ensuring that this tribe member was the only available base for analogy. He also gave subjects general information about the tribe as a whole. He then asked subjects to make inferences and judgments about a new target tribe member based on this given information.

Read (1987) varied the similarity of the two tribe members (old and new) by varying the number of features they had in common (zero, one, or six). He found that the more similar his subjects judged the two tribe members to be, the more likely they were to use analogy to infer that the newly presented tribe member performed the same behavior as the formerly presented tribe member. That is, the greater the similarity between Individual A and Individual B, the more likely subjects were to infer that B did what A did.

Read (1987) then reasoned that if similarity were indeed mediating the inference process, manipulations (besides number of common features) that were known to affect perceived similarity should also affect subjects' willingness to transfer knowledge about one member to another. One such manipulation was the direction of comparison of Person A and Person B. Tversky (1977) found that the order in which two items are compared affects the degree of perceived similarity between them. Many situations arise in which Item A is perceived as more similar to Item B than Item B is to Item A. Logically, similarity judgments should not show such an asymmetry, but changing the direction of comparison reveals that subjects can and do perceive similarity asymmetrically.

In general, if Object A has more unique features than Object B, A will be seen as less similar to B than B will be to A. This is because the features of the starting object of the comparison are mapped onto the other object, and the shared and unique features of the starting object determine the level of similarity. Thus, when the object with more unique features is the starting point, less similarity is seen. In this way, the former Soviet Union (many unique features) is less similar to Poland (few unique features) than Poland is to the Soviet Union (Tversky, 1977). In short, the direction of comparison of two objects will affect the degree of perceived similarity because the direction determines which item's features are the focus of attention.

With this in mind, Read (1987) compared the effect of direction of comparison and number of unique features on similarity judgments and on the level of analogical social inferences. He predicted that any asymmetries in similarity judgments between two individuals would be paralleled by asymmetries in analogical inferences. That is, if A is seen as more similar to B than B is to A, more analogical inferences should be made when A is compared to B than when B is compared to A. He found that the pattern of inferences indeed paralleled that of the similarity judgments. In other words, if A was judged more similar to B than vice versa, then there was more analogical transfer of A's characteristics to B than vice versa. Thus, similarity seems to mediate the analogical inference process.

The Read (1987) studies point to the importance of similarity to the inference process, and underscore the point that the nature of the similarity need not be relevant to the actual judgment in question. Subjects did not know whether the target and base tribe members' common characteristic(s) were relevant to the to-be-predicted behavior because the behavior was described by a nonsense word (e.g., *tewol*). They only knew that there was a similarity. This does not mean that the similarity was irrelevant, merely that the relevance of the similarity was unknown.

Several studies have documented the sufficiency of completely irrelevant similarity dimensions in inspiring analogical reasoning. For example, Lewicki (1985) found that subjects avoided an experimenter whose hairstyle resembled that of a confederate who had insulted them earlier. In analogical inference terms, if confederate and experimenter have similar hairstyles, one can infer that they are similar enough to share other features (here, nasty disposition). Clearly, few people would claim that hairstyles signal disposition. Indeed, subjects did not make the irrational connection between hair and disposition consciously; rather, the similarity of the two people in terms of hairstyle led in an automatic way to inferences about unrelated features. In support of this, Lewicki (1985) found that no conscious awareness or control was involved in the analogy making demonstrated by his subjects. Subjects were questioned after the experiment about their awareness of the similarity in the two experimenters' hairstyles. None of the subjects reported being aware of the similarity, much less using it as a basis for social inference about the new experimenter. Thus, similarity may be computed and then used to make inferences in some low-level or preconscious manner.

Gilovich (1981) also demonstrated the role of irrelevant similarity in cueing the analogical process. He found that similarity of football jersey number, hometown, and so on caused subjects to infer similar playing abilities in two athletes. For example, if someone has the same jersey number as Michael Jordan, subjects are more likely to infer that he also shoots, jumps, and assists as well. Jersey numbers and hometowns obviously have nothing to do with athletic ability, and yet similarity on these dimensions was sufficient to spur on the analogical inference process.

Another example of the effect of irrelevant similarity on inference is found in White and Shapiro (1987, Study 2). Perceivers had a telephone conversation with a stranger whom they were led to believe either looked like, or did not look like, one of their close friends. The perceivers were more likely to assume that the telephone stranger also resembled the close friend in important personality characteristics when they believed the stranger looked like the friend than when they believed she did not look like the friend, even after conversing with her for 8 minutes. White and Shapiro explained these results in terms of a self-fulfilling prophecy. They suggested that the physical similarity to a friend set up an expectancy of similar personality characteristics, which the subjects went on to confirm behaviorally in the telephone conversation (Snyder et al., 1977). The relevance of this study for the role of similarity in analogical inference is clear: Subjects infer that people share other important features with known individuals if they are similar in some initial way.

Because similarity is so crucial to the analogical inference process, and because similarity among category members varies with the level of category specificity, an interesting question arises: At what level of specificity are analogical inferences most likely to occur? For example, consider the level of specificity at which a person is categorized. Although still falling into the person level of our hierarchy, a person may be labeled in different ways: a man (general or superordinate level), a lawyer (basic level), or a corporate lawyer (specific or subordinate level). Entities at the subordinate level clearly share more characteristics than entities at the basic or superordinate level (i.e., corporate lawyers are more similar to each other than are lawyers or men in general). Thus, it would seem logical to predict that analogical inferences are most likely to occur where similarity among entities is greatest, at the subordinate level of specificity.[1]

However, recent research has cast doubt on such a conclusion. Shipley (1992) found that interindividual inferences were most likely to occur when entities were described by basic-level (rather than subordinate-level) terms. Perhaps the greater

---

[1]We discuss this type of interindividual inference as analogical in nature: moving from the characteristics of one individual to another. However, Shipley (1992) and others (Osherson et al., 1990) have discussed the possibility that such inferences are inductive in nature: moving from the characteristics of one group member to a generalization about the group, and then applying this generalization to another group member. Even so, inferences from one individual to another still seem more likely to occur between individuals at a subordinate level of specificity versus a basic level of specificity. Individuals described at the subordinate level of specificity share more features than individuals described at the basic level, and therefore form a more homogeneous group. As discussed in the previous section on inductive inferences, making generalizations about a group from one member's

accessibility of basic-level entities due to frequent use accounts for this finding, or perhaps perceivers' familiarity with basic-level entities makes them seem more similar to each other. Regardless of the account one prefers, Shipley's findings support our claim that not absolute but perceived similarity is crucial to analogical inference, as similarity judgment is always a dynamic process (e.g., Tversky, 1977).

Analogies and Errors. There is some debate among analogy researchers about the possible benefits of analogy-making, especially those analogies based on the superficial similarities discussed earlier. Some researchers have claimed that reliance on similarity-based analogies leads to errorful, overly simplistic inferences (Keil, 1989; Quine, 1977). Others have argued that analogies are the major source of newly generated information, and that they can be very helpful and informative for the perceiver attempting to understand his or her world (Gentner, 1992). One resolution of this debate is acknowledging that, although superficial similarity may be sufficient to inspire analogically based inferences, it is not always the ideal linkage between target and base. Some kind of causal relationship among the common features will result in the best, most error-free reasoning by analogy (Read, 1984).

In fact, subjects can recognize and prefer to use causally relevant similarity over irrelevant similarity. Read (1984) found that subjects, given similarities among individuals that were either relevant or irrelevant to the judgment in question, prefer to use relevant information as a basis for analogy. Subjects seem to search for and use possible causal linkages between the known features and the feature to be inferred.

The easier it is for subjects to relate the shared feature causally with the to-be-predicted feature, the more likely subjects are to infer that target and base share the to-be-predicted feature. Read's subjects were asked to predict how likely a newly presented target tribe member was to perform a religious ritual. The target tribe member was similar to one tribe member (say, X) in either a causally relevant feature (both behaved similarly in avoiding the medicine man) or a seemingly irrelevant feature (both spent the day weaving). Moreover, Member X had performed the religious ritual. Subjects inferred that the target tribe member was more likely to perform the ritual if he or she had previously read that both the target and Member X had avoided the medicine man than if he or she had read

---

characteristics is more likely to occur when the group is homogeneous than when it is heterogeneous (Park & Hastie, 1987). From this logic, one would predict more inductive interindividual inferences among subordinate-level individuals than among basic-level individuals, just as we predicted from an analogical framework. In any case, in addressing the likelihood of drawing inferences from one individual to another, Osherson et al. (1990) recognized the importance of both interindividual similarity and the likelihood of drawing inductive conclusions on the basis of information about one individual. This issue of whether same-level inferences are analogical (similarity-based) or inductive (based on generalization) arises again later.

that both the target and Member X had spent the day weaving. In other words, subjects were more likely to use an analogy involving Member X if X's features shared with the target were relevant to the inference than if X's shared features were irrelevant. Thus, subjects are sensitive to the potential causal relevance of behavior toward a religious figure and performance of a religious ritual.

One final general point about the role of this fluid similarity in analogical reasoning needs to be made: There are different levels or types of similarity that can influence analogy-making. The specific type of similarity that is most important also changes over time. When perceivers look at a situation only briefly, they focus on local similarities among objects—small and superficial common features. However, after being exposed to the situation for some time, perceivers begin to focus on global similarities among objects—general overall patterns of features (Goldstone, 1992a). For social inferences, this implies that, when first meeting a target person, similarities to a base person in terms of superficial features such as hair color, pitch of voice, or small mannerisms will engage analogical thinking. However, as the perceiver gains more knowledge of the target, the more important global similarities emerge: lifestyle, personality traits, beliefs, and general behavior patterns. Thus, when perceivers have enough time, they will process the deeper, more relevant similarities between the target and base of the analogy. Similarity judgments, then, and the analogical inferences that follow depend on the amount of processing time available. Different objects—those with local overlap of features—will appear similar to a target object early rather than late in one's experience with the target.

Spellman and Holyoak (1992) discussed the differential effects of local versus global similarities, not as a function of processing time but as a result of two different processing stages. They suggest that local, surface similarity is important in the retrieval of appropriate base instances, whereas deeper, global similarity is more important in the mapping or application of the analogy. Spellman and Holyoak seem to prefer the consciously driven, step-by-step conceptualization of the analogy process. Rather than analogical correspondences "popping out" at the perceiver, analogies in their approach are more effortful, time-consuming, and rationally driven. For social inferences, this would imply that, although perceivers might be retrieving base instances through superficial similarity (names, hair color), they eventually see, acknowledge, and use the more important global similarities (traits, beliefs) during the mapping process.

A slightly different effect of causal relevance on the use of analogy was discussed by Tversky and Kahneman (1980). Subjects are more likely to infer that a daughter has blue eyes given that her mother has blue eyes than to infer that a mother has blue eyes given that her daughter has blue eyes. In reality, the probabilities are equal, but subjects perceive a difference in these two judgments. Because of the causal role of the mother in transmitting genes to the daughter, subjects are more confident that daughters have their mother's eye color than that mothers have their daughter's eye color. Tversky and Kahneman argued that, in general, an inference from cause to effect will be made with greater confidence than a prediction from effect to cause. Tversky and Kahneman referred to this rule as an example of a *causal schema*, or a type of causal relationship that seems relevant to the judgment. Taken together, the work on causal schemas and Read's (1984) work on causally relevant features suggest that applying a causal relationship to an analogical social inference can have one of two possible effects:

1. Perceivers will make better judgments when the causal information is important to the judgment, as in Read (1984).
2. Perceivers will make poorer judgments when the causal information is irrelevant to the judgment, as in Tversky and Kahneman (1980).

Exemplar-Based Processes in Analogy. Analogical reasoning involves explicitly or implicitly accessing a similar other and drawing inferences from known information about this other. Unlike induction, analogy does not involve bottom-up generalization from this similar other. General beliefs about the target person's group usually remain unchanged. Unlike deduction, analogy does not involve top-down application of higher level knowledge. The information transferred to the new target person is specific person-level information, not abstracted group-level information. In other words, no stereotype is created or applied during analogical inference. Analogical reasoning is a process that makes use of specific instances rather than generalized abstractions. It is an exemplar-based process.

This distinction between instances (exemplars) and abstractions (prototypes) in long-term memory is a familiar one in social psychology. Although the debate concerning the relative importance of the two rages on (e.g., Homa, Sterling, & Trepel, 1981; Medin, Altom, & Murphy, 1984), E. R. Smith & Zarate (1992) have proposed an entirely exemplar-based analogical mechanism in their model of social judgment.

According to E. R. Smith and Zarate (1992), exemplars are stored as perceived and may be activated when another stimulus is presented. The activated exemplars are used to arrive at a judgment about the target stimulus. The weight that each exemplar carries in this judgment is based on its similarity to the target stimulus on the important (focal) dimensions. The key component of the model is differential attention to stimulus dimensions (Nosofsky, 1987). Each stimulus person has a value on many different dimensions, such as age, gender, skin color, and likability. Situational, contextual, and motivational factors alter attention to the various stimulus dimensions. This differential attention to stimulus dimensions alters perceived similarity of the various stored exemplars to the new stimulus. When attention is directed to one dimension, one set of exemplars may appear highly similar to the target; but when attention is directed to another dimension, an entirely different set of exemplars may appear similar. Differential perceived similarity will affect the weight that each exemplar's value on a given dimension receives in the inference process.

For example, different dimensions are relevant for judging whether a target person would be a good date or a good employee. Evaluations of dates depend on dimensions such as self-confidence, attractiveness, and sense of humor; evaluations of employees are based on other dimensions, such as intelligence, obedience, and creativity. When making judgments about the suitability of a target person as a date, perceivers will attend to the dimensions of confidence, attractiveness, and humor. Exemplars similar to the target on these dimensions will appear most similar overall, and their evaluations as "good dates" will carry the most weight in the judgment of the target. When making judgments about the suitability of the same target person as an employee, different dimensions will be focal and different exemplars will be recruited.

E. R. Smith (1990) maintains that this exemplar-based process captures the flexibility of social inferences. In a schema-based process, the same schema (of an ideal date, good worker, etc.) will be called up on every occasion, and the judgment of the target with respect to any role or category will always be the same. Under an exemplar-based process, different comparison others are recruited, depending on contextual and motivational factors. Thus, the same target may be judged as a potentially good worker on one day and as a poor prospect on another day. This variability in judgment and inference seems typical of social perceivers (Sherman, Judd, & Park, 1989).

However, this flexibility is not the result of different processes. Perceivers in E. R. Smith and Zarate's (1992) model do not choose between inducing an impression of a target from specific behavioral information and deducing an impression from general group information. Instead, impressions and all other judgments are a result of analogy to similar persons. E. R. Smith and Zarate claim that the differential attention mechanism causes judgments to appear to be inductive or deductive, when in fact both kinds of judgments have been made analogically.

For example, assume we have behavioral information about a target person, group-level information about her, and similar other exemplars stored in long-term memory. One of several different impressions potentially results. When our impression of the target is consistent with the behavioral information, most researchers (e.g., Fiske & Neuberg, 1990; Krueger & Rothbart, 1988) assume that the lower level information has been integrated in an inductive manner to arrive at a final impression. That is, attention was directed to the individual's own characteristics. When our impression of the target is consistent with the group-level information, these researchers assume that the higher-level information has been applied in a deductive manner to arrive at a final impression. That is, attention was directed to category information. E. R. Smith and Zarate argued instead that these different impressions result from different dimensions of the target person being focal at the time of judgment and, therefore, different exemplars driving the judgment—but always in an analogical fashion.

E. R. Smith and Zarate proposed that some features of a person are category-defining dimensions (such as skin color and shape of facial features for race), whereas other features are individuating dimensions (such as clothing or weight, which are not definitive of race). When the judgment context causes category-defining dimensions to be the focus of attention, exemplars similar on category-defining dimensions will weigh most heavily in the judgment. To the observer of the outcome of such a process, it appears that the perceiver has applied higher level category information to the target person. In fact, no higher level information is accessed. Only similar exemplars are accessed, and their features are applied to the target.

On the other hand, when individuating dimensions are the focus of attention, exemplars similar on individuating dimensions will weigh most heavily in the judgment. A set of exemplars similar on these dimensions does not form such a neat social category as do exemplars similar on racial characteristics. Instead, it appears that various bits and pieces of the target individual's behaviors and attributes have been integrated into a whole. In reality, according to E. R. Smith and Zarate, the value of various exemplars on the relevant dimensions have been averaged together, weighted by similarity, just as before when the category-defining attributes were focal. In this model, different judgment contexts result in different dimensions being the focus of attention, but there is only one single process of social inference.

Factors Affecting Exemplar Recruitment.   The prototypicality of the exemplar, the familiarity of the exemplar, social defaults, individual differences, and in-group/out-group differences are each considered in turn. A single exemplar can be sufficient to generate inferences about similar others. For example, Hamill, Wilson, and Nisbett (1980) found that observation of a single prison guard was enough to make subjects draw inferences that other prison guards were similar to this prison guard. In fact, subjects made these inferences even when they were told explicitly that the prison guard they observed was atypical of prison guards in general. Thus, subjects seemed to pay no heed to the typicality of the exemplar they used as a base for analogy. However, more recent evidence has suggested that subjects are indeed sensitive to the typicality of the instance being used in analogy. Rothbart and Lewis (1988) found that the most prototypic exemplar is the easiest base to use for social inference. A highly prototypic member of a category is assumed to have all of the category-relevant attributes. Therefore, people are more likely to infer the features of a new category exemplar from an old one if the old exemplar is highly prototypic.

An example should make this clear. Assume that June Cleaver is highly prototypic of television moms, and that Carol Brady is less prototypic. Imagine encountering a new television show featuring a mom whose jewelry preference you do not know. If you are using June Cleaver as the base for analogy, you are quite likely to infer that the new mom prefers pearls (as June does). However, if you are using Carol Brady as the base for analogy, you are not as likely to infer that the new mom prefers bangle bracelets (as Carol does). The prototypicality of the instance seems to facilitate the transfer of knowledge about that instance to a new instance.

Facilitation of analogical inference also occurs when significant, familiar others, as opposed to nonsignificant others or abstract stereotypes, are used as the base for analogy (Andersen & S. W. Cole, 1990). That is, if someone reminds you of your spouse, you are quite likely to infer that they share other characteristics of your spouse; if someone reminds you of your doctor, you are less likely to infer that they share other characteristics of your doctor. Andersen and S. W. Cole explained this effect in terms of the tightness of association in memory of the characteristics of significant versus nonsignificant others. They proposed that significant others are more likely to be represented by organized and coherent schemas than are nonsignificant others.

Perceivers are also affected by the degree to which the base of the analogy is a member of a cultural default group. Expected or default values in our culture include White race, male gender, young age, heterosexuality, and so on (Eagly & Kite, 1987). Perceivers pay more attention to stimulus dimensions on which the target has a nondefault value. That is, perceivers pay more attention to the race of a Black man and the gender of a White woman (Zarate, 1990). Because differential attention leads to differential perceived similarity and differential weighting of exemplars, judgments will be affected by the default status of the target. Inferences about Black males will be chronically overinfluenced by information about Black exemplars on the dimension in question, and inferences about White females will be chronically overinfluenced by information about female exemplars along the dimension in question. This will result in relatively stereotyped inferences about members of nondefault groups.

Individual differences may also operate as a factor affecting attention to stimulus dimensions and perceived similarity. Perceivers become chronically attuned to certain stimulus dimensions by frequently using those dimensions over time (Higgins et al., 1982), or when these dimensions are self-relevant in some way (Fong & Markus, 1982). For instance, some people constantly evaluate others in terms of their honesty, whereas some constantly evaluate others in terms of their attractiveness. More weight should be given to a dimension to which a perceiver is chronically attuned. Exemplars similar to the target in honesty will be overweighted in judgment by honesty schematics, whereas exemplars similar in attractiveness will be overweighted by attractiveness schematics.

In-group/out-group status is another important variable that can determine which exemplars are seen as most similar to the target, and thus which exemplars are most likely to be used for drawing analogical inferences. Characteristics of the target that are distinct from the perceiver's demand attention, whether they are relevant to the judgment or not (Zarate & E. R. Smith, 1990). Thus, features that define out-group membership will demand attention in any judgment because they are distinct from the perceiver's own characteristics. Features that define in-group status will not receive attention because they are shared with the perceiver. That is, a White male perceiver will attend to a Black male's race more than to his gender, whereas a Black female perceiver will attend to a Black male's gender more than to his race (Zarate & E. R. Smith, 1990).

Because differential attention to stimulus dimensions mediates exemplar accessibility, the exemplars that are most similar to an out-group member target will be those that share out-group membership as well as features that are relevant to the inference at hand. However, the exemplars that are most similar to an ingroup member target will be those that share only inference-relevant features. In effect, judgments about an out-group target will be overweighted by the characteristics of out-group members, whereas judgments about an in-group target will be based more on the "proper" individual featural information. E. R. Smith and Zarate (1992) suggested that the differential attention paid to group-defining characteristics for in-groups and out-groups can explain out-group homogeneity effects such as those found by Park and Rothbart (1982). For out-group members, the out-group status demands attention, directing available attention away from any other attributes that might be important to encode. More attention is available to be directed toward the individuating attributes of an in-group member during encoding, resulting in more attributes being encoded overall. Encoding of additional attributes lowers similarity among exemplars. That is, exemplars with two noncommon attributes each are seen as more similar to each other than exemplars with four noncommon attributes each (see E. R. Smith & Zarate, 1992, for a simulation). Thus, out-group members are seen as more similar to each other because fewer attributes of each out-group member are encoded. This novel explanation of the out-group homogeneity effect is but one of the contributions of an analogy-based approach to social inference making.

Characteristics of Group A → Characteristics of Group B

Up to this point, we have discussed only analogical inferences about individuals. Although they do not seem to occur frequently, inferences about one group based on knowledge of another group are certainly possible. Imagine being confronted with the following judgment question: If Fraternity X hazes its pledges, does Fraternity Y?

As with inferences about individuals, we propose that the likelihood of an analogical social inference being generated will depend on the perceived similarity of X to Y, because the inference will be based on analogical processes. Moreover, just as for inferences about individuals, inferences about groups can involve similarity on either relevant or irrelevant dimensions. In terms of the earlier example, if Fraternity X and Fraternity Y are similar on the dimension of number of alcohol violations, this might be a causally relevant dimension for inference. If Fraternity X and Fraternity Y are similar in name (e.g., both have the same Greek letter in their name), this would be an irrelevant dimension for inference. We suspect that relevant similarity will be preferred when both are available, as is the case for individual targets. Common features relevant to the judgment in question are preferred to irrelevant common features as a vehicle for inferences (Read, 1987). However, we also suspect that irrelevant similarity at times will be a sufficient basis for inferring the attributes of one group from those of another.

Trait or Behavior of Individual A → Trait or Behavior of Individual A

Now let us consider inferences about one trait based on our knowledge of a different trait. For analogies involving individuals or groups, we were concerned with inferences between different entities (e.g., from Person A to Person B). In the case of inferring one trait from another, we are concerned with inferences within an entity (e.g., from one characteristic of a person to another characteristic of the same individual). This process is often discussed under the general rubric of implicit personality theories held by the perceiver—theories about which traits go together and why these traits co-occur (D. J. Schneider, 1973). Given information about one trait, perceivers are often willing to assume that certain other traits are also present. For example, given that a person is honest, perceivers may also believe he or she is giving and kind, but not practical. Implicit personality theory researchers explain these effects by proposing that perceivers have theories about various personality types. These types operate as a sort of schema that organizes traits together into a coherent whole. The earlier example might call up a "bleeding-heart liberal" schema, in which the traits are organized around the concepts of integrity and concern for others.

This conceptualization of inferences about one trait leading to inferences of another trait in terms of schemas does not necessarily suggest analogical reasoning. Instead, implicit personality theories are deductive in nature. Perceivers first categorize the trait into a personality type, then apply higher level knowledge about the personality type to infer the presence of other traits.

Alternatively, inferences about one trait based on information about another trait might sometimes proceed through a process akin to analogy. An analogical inference about traits would involve the overlapping similar features of the two traits, just as analogical inferences about people involve the degree of similarity between the two people. For example, if a perceiver learns that a target is punctual, she may use a sort of analogical process to infer that the person is also conscientious. That is, an inference of punctuality may lead to an inference of conscientiousness, due to the number of similar features that the two traits share—being reliable, exacting, true to a standard, and so on.[2]

---

[2]It may be argued that a preliminary categorization must have occurred before the analogy between *conscientious* and *punctual* may be explored. That is, both trait words must be categorized into a person type category (e.g., the consistent person) before similar features will be noticed. Although analogy may proceed without an inductive inference first occurring (e.g., E. R. Smith and Zarate, 1992), we do not argue that all analogical inferences occur without a preliminary categorization step. Induction and analogy may often co-occur, with the output of one process influencing the other process.

C. A. Anderson and Sedikides (1991) investigated the differential roles of deduction based on person types as well as this similarity among traits in trait inference. They contrasted three models of person perception: (a) associationistic, in which persons are perceived in terms of trait covariations; (b) dimensional, in which persons are perceived in a multidimensional similarity space of a limited number of dimensions; and (c) typological, in which persons are perceived in terms of person types with a unique relationship among the traits composing each type. The dimensional model is most similar to a similarity-based analogical inference process of inferences about traits, whereas the typological model is closer to the deductive implicit personality theories we discussed earlier. Anderson and Sedikides found that the typological model made a unique contribution to the person perception process, beyond that of the associationistic and dimensional models. Thus, models of the process of using one trait to make inferences about other traits must include deductive as well as simple analogical components.

The aforementioned process of similarity-based activation of traits also applies to inferences about behaviors. Again, inferences about behaviors based on other known behaviors may proceed either deductively or analogically. Deductive inferences would involve reference to a theory relating the two behaviors: Jogging implies eating granola because both are characteristics of health nuts. Thus, a given behavior, jogging, would lead to an inductive inference about a general characteristic, healthfulness. This general trait would lead in turn to deductive inferences about the presence of other behaviors, such as eating granola. In contrast, analogical inferences, would involve similarity relations between the two behaviors: Playing tennis implies playing baseball, because both are outdoor summer sports involving hitting a ball. The two behaviors share many features and are therefore strongly associated. Just as is the case for inferences about traits, we suspect that inferences about behaviors involve some of these similarity-based analogical components, but necessarily involve deduction as well. Further research may help us understand in which situations, and possibly for which traits, deductive or analogical inferences are preferred.

INFERENCES ABOUT INDIVIDUALS:
INDUCTIVE, DEDUCTIVE, OR ANALOGICAL?

We have discussed three types of social inference—inductive, deductive, and analogical—and examined the operation of each type. We hope some idea of the flexibility and complexity of the task that confronts the social perceiver has been communicated. But within what boundaries is the perceiver flexible? Does the social perceiver simply choose randomly among the three types of social inference for any given judgment? Or do certain judgments and certain contexts seem to call specifically for inductive, deductive, or analogical reasoning?

A general answer to these questions comes from a consideration of the level of specificity of the social inference. Because inductive reasoning moves from the specific to the general, induction is most likely for inferences about social objects higher in the hierarchy, such as groups. Deduction, in moving from the general to the specific, is most likely for inferences about social objects lower in the hierarchy, such as behaviors. Given this, the most interesting possibilities for inferences occur in the middle of the spectrum, at the level of the individual. The individual is often considered the richest, most basic (Rosch, 1978) level of social categorization, in part because individuals fall midway between specific behaviors and general groups in the social hierarchy (Pryor & Ostrom, 1981).

Often, our exposure to individuals involves both specific-level and general-level information. We may know their behaviors as well as their group membership. Here, induction, deduction, and analogy are all available for use. Which inferential process and which information will predominate in judgments about an individual, and what circumstances and factors are likely to affect the choice?

Before we plunge into an in-depth investigation of this issue, one point of clarification is offered. We do not assume that one and only one process can occur for making an inference. That is, we do not assume pure reasoning of one of the three types. Social perceivers can and do use different processes, either sequentially or concurrently, to make the same judgment (Rothbart, 1988).

We break the problem of inductive versus deductive versus analogical inferences about individuals into two questions:

- When is induction used as opposed to deduction?
- When is analogical reasoning used as opposed to the other two types of inference?

Induction Versus Deduction

The issue of the relative importance of induction (bottom-up processing) and deduction (top-down processing) has been a major question for work in social inference. Recently, several researchers have offered models that delineate the conditions under which bottom-up or top-down processing is more likely to be used. These models are useful in part because they offer a theoretical basis for predicting which inferential process subjects are more likely to use under which conditions.

Multiple-Process Models.   The two most relevant and influential models pitting bottom-up against top-down social inference processing are those of Brewer (1988) and Fiske and Neuberg (1990; Fiske & Pavelchak, 1986). Brewer's model offers an explanation of when cognitive representations and impressions will be organized by individual information (*personalized*) and when they will be organized by category information (*category-based*). Personalization is a bottom-up process, whereas categorization is a top-down process. Whether a new target person will be encoded in a category-based or a personalized way is determined by the processing goals and capacities of the perceiver. After the target has been identified, the perceiver chooses to process further information in a personalized way only if some threshold level of self-involvement is present. The perceiver must be motivated to attend to the personal characteristics of the target. Perhaps the perceiver expects future interaction with the target, or the target has some authority over the perceiver. Or perhaps the perceiver is deciding whether to hire the target. If one of these or other motivating factors is not present, the default is category-based processing because of its greater ease and efficiency than personalized processing.

The cognitive representations resulting from these two different processes contain different organizations of information. Category-based representations contain the category or type as the basis for organization. Individual instances of this category (persons) are associated with the category label, with only very distinctive (inconsistent) characteristics associated with the person label. Personalized representations are "flip-flopped"; the individual person is the basis for organization. All characteristics of each person, whether consistent or inconsistent with the category, are associated directly with the person label. In other words, information about the individual is associated more strongly with the category in category-based encoding, whereas information about the individual is associated more strongly with the individual in personalized encoding.

These encoding differences can lead to judgment differences. When information about individuals has been processed in a category-based manner, the specific characteristics of those individuals will be difficult to retrieve. Unless they are category-inconsistent, the characteristics are stored at the category, not the individual, level. Thus, it may be difficult for perceivers to remember later which category-consistent characteristics were present in which individuals. The tendency would be to assume that all category members possessed all of the category-consistent characteristics. Thus, judgments about categorized individuals will be based on category-level rather than individual information (Dull, 1982). That is, the judgment will be made through a top-down, deductive process. When information is encoded in a personalized manner, the specific characteristics of the individual will be easy to retrieve. Therefore, judgments about personalized individuals will be based on a combination of category information and individual information. That is, the judgment will be made through a bottom-up, inductive process. Thus, the cognitive representation of information can partly determine whether an inference is made inductively or deductively.

The main determinant of personalized versus category-based processing in Brewer's (1988) model is the self-involvement of the perceiver, rather than any characteristics of the stimulus person. Brewer discussed several factors that can affect self-involvement and, therefore, the mode of processing chosen. Two main influences are the similarity of the target person to ourselves (Brewer & Lui,

1985) and outcome interdependency between the self and the target (Erber & Fiske, 1984). When the target person is of our own social category, has similar attitudes, or looks like us, we pay special attention to that person and use the more elaborative personalized processing. When the target person is crucial to the achievement of our goals or the fulfillment of our needs, we also pay special attention to that person and process information about the person more carefully. Thus, similar and important others are more likely to receive the elaborated personalized processing that leads to bottom-up inference processes.

A similar distinction between top-down and bottom-up processing is made by Fiske and Neuberg (1990). They proposed a continuum of processes by which perceivers form impressions and make inferences about social objects: from purely categorical processing to elaborate piecemeal processing. Category-based impressions are determined deductively. The object is categorized, and the cognitions, general information, and affective tag associated with the category label are applied to this object in a top-down manner. For example, Betty is a Democrat, and Democrats are self-righteous; therefore Betty is self-righteous.

If the perceiver has any interest in the person being perceived, confirmatory categorization will occur. The perceiver checks to make sure the person has been categorized properly. For example, Betty is pro-life, which does not fit the stereotype of Democrats. Therefore, the perceiver makes sure Betty has been correctly labeled a Democrat. If confirmatory categorization is unsuccessful, the next step is recategorization. The person is categorized into a new category, a subtype, or is encoded as a separate exemplar. Betty may be recategorized as a special type of Democrat, the pro-life Democrat. If recategorization (the third attempt at categorizing the person) fails, then the perceiver finally resorts to piecemeal processing. Until this point, the perceiver's goal has been to categorize the target so that general knowledge about the category may be applied deductively. In addition, the categorization attempts have taken more and more of the individuating information into account as we move down the continuum of processes from initial categorization to confirmatory categorization to recategorization.

Piecemeal processing is the next step. Piecemeal-based impressions are determined inductively. The specific, individuating characteristics of the target person are combined (by averaging or adding) in a bottom-up manner to determine the total impression. For example, Betty is intelligent, pro-life, wealthy, and votes Democratic. All of these attributes are noted and averaged together into a coherent impression of Betty. Piecemeal processing is difficult and demanding for the perceiver; therefore, it is avoided unless absolutely necessary (or unless the perceiver has a great deal of time and attention available to devote to this particular impression). Different impressions of, inferences about, and feelings toward the same person can occur, depending on whether information about that person is processed in a category-based, deductive way or a piecemeal-based, inductive way.

What determines categorical versus piecemeal processing? Like Brewer (1988), Fiske and Neuberg (1990) have assumed that the deductive, category-based process is the path of least resistance. Unless it is necessary to combine information in a piecemeal fashion, category-based processing will be preferred. Any factor that interferes with the ease of categorizing the object will increase the preference for piecemeal-based processing. For example, if the characteristics of the object do not fit or cue any particular social category, piecemeal-based processing will ensue.

Also, outcome dependency determines whether categorical or piecemeal processing is likely to be used. The more the perceiver is dependent on the target for the achievement of some goal, the more likely he or she is to use piecemeal processing of the target's characteristics.

What is meant by characteristics fitting or not fitting a category label? Fiske and Neuberg (1990) stressed that for their model it is descriptive, not evaluative, consistency that affects categorization. As long as the attributes of the object are consistent in meaning with the category label, they need not be consistent in affective valence to engender successful categorization.

To summarize, Brewer (1988) and Fiske and Neuberg (1990) proposed multiple-process models, including a deductive and an inductive component. The deductive component is the default in both models. Special motivations (self-involvement) or aspects of the stimulus (difficulty of categorization) are necessary to engage the inductive process. Perhaps deductive inference is so common because categorization is such an automated process (Fiske & Neuberg, 1990; Gilbert et al., 1988; Trope, 1986). It may be difficult to ignore the category-level information once the category label and its associates in memory have been activated by the categorization process.

In general, we propose that any factors shifting the focus of attention onto the component features of a person, whether motivational, situational, contextual, or mood-related, inspire the more effortful bottom-up processing. We next discuss some of the wide range of factors that can make perceivers more likely to focus on combining lower level behavioral information (induction) or applying higher level group information (deduction).

Top-Down Versus Bottom-Up Processing: Determinants. The issue of using higher level versus lower level information in social inferences has been framed in several different ways over the past two decades. Early investigations by Locksley, Borgida, Brekke, and Hepburn (1980); and Locksley, Hepburn, and Ortiz (1982) demonstrated that subjects, when given specific behavioral information that contradicts a group-level stereotype, neglect the stereotype and make inferences based solely on the individuating information. Locksley et al. (1980) found that even a single specific behavior is sufficient to override the stereotype. On the other hand, Rasinski, Crocker, and Hastie (1985) found that when subjects' own stereotype-based expectancies and assessments of the diagnosticity of the behavioral information are taken into account, subjects' judgments show quite a bit of reliance on the group-level stereotype.

A possible resolution of these two seemingly contradictory findings comes from Krueger and Rothbart (1988). They proposed that whether group-level or behavioral-level information will be preferred in an inference task depends on the relative diagnosticity of the two types of information. When a strong stereotype is available, individuating information may be neglected. On the other hand, when the individuating information is strong, stereotypes may be neglected. Indeed, Krueger and Rothbart found that although a single behavior is never sufficient to override top-down stereotype information, individuating information prevails when it is more diagnostic than stereotype information, and stereotype information prevails when it is more diagnostic than individuating information. Perhaps the Locksley et al. (1980) subjects viewed the behavioral information as more diagnostic for the task at hand, whereas the Rasinski et al. (1985) subjects viewed the stereotype information as more diagnostic.

Overall, predicting whether perceivers will make deductive inferences based on category stereotypes, or inductive inferences based on individuating information, depends on the relative diagnosticity of each type of information. This differential diagnosticity is not veridical but is determined by the perceiver's view and beliefs. In general, the perceived diagnosticity of base rate (stereotype) information is highest when the base rates are concrete, salient, causally relevant to the inference at hand, specific, and valid to the perceiver (Sherman & Corty, 1984).

The collective findings of decision-making and social-inference research point to other factors besides diagnosticity that affect perceivers' tendency to use induction versus deduction. One way to influence decision makers to focus on individual pieces of information and combine them carefully via an inductive inference route is to make them accountable for their decisions. Perceivers who must justify their decisions make more complex (Tetlock, 1983), although not necessarily more accurate (Tetlock, Skitka, & Boettger, 1989), decisions. Accountable perceivers are less likely to rely on initial impressions or simplistic stereotypes.

The complexity of the inference task can also determine processing strategies. Specifically, the more complex the task at hand, the more likely perceivers are to use the simpler deductive process than the more difficult inductive process. Bodenhausen and Lichtenstein (1987) found that subjects were more likely to rely on stereotypes than individuating information when (a) a stereotype was made available by the target's surname, and (b) the judgment task was expected to be complex. Anticipation of a complex task seemed to necessitate reliance on top-down processing. Other cognitive mediators can also make the perceiver's task more difficult, thereby increasing reliance on more simplistic top-down processing. For example, distraction (Petty, Wells, & Brock, 1976) and cognitive load (Pratto & Bargh, 1991) increase stereotype-based responding in judgment tasks. Arousal or mood, which have pervasive effects on cognition, can also affect the tendency to use deduction or induction. High levels of physiological arousal due to exercise alone are sufficient to increase one's tendency to use simplistic processing (Kim & R. S. Baron, 1988). Subjects were more likely to fall prey to stereotyping effects when processing information after strenuous exercise than without exercise. Subjects who had exercised were more likely than control subjects to rely on deductive theories to aid them in recalling which persons and which traits were presented together. Their recall was biased strongly in the direction of preexisting stereotypes. Apparently, physiological arousal distracted subjects from the learning task at hand.

A similar distracting effect of mood was reported recently by Stroessner, Hamilton, and Mackie (1992). They found that only subjects in a neutral mood form illusory correlations. Subjects in either a positive or a negative mood do not show the illusory correlation effect. Stroessner et al. explained these findings in terms of a cognitive, rather than a motivational, account of mood effects. They argued that moods are cognitively distracting and prevent perceivers from devoting attention to other cognitive demands. The Stroessner et al. subjects were indeed less accurate in the positive and negative mood conditions than in the neutral mood condition. Because they have fewer resources available to devote to the sentence-reading task, Stroessner et al. claimed subjects in a positive or a negative mood are unable to devote the extra processing to codistinctive items that would result in an illusory correlation effect in this paradigm. In both the Kim and R. S. Baron (1988) and the Stroessner et al. (1992) studies, arousal interfered with perceivers' ability to perform higher level, more demanding processing.

Anxiety also interferes with perceivers' ability to process information using effortful induction. Anxious subjects process persuasive information less systematically than control subjects, relying on simplistic deductive rules instead of piecing together the information inductively (R. S. Baron, Burgess, Kao, & H. Logan, 1990; a more detailed discussion of the systematic/heuristic distinction follows). The specific arousal patterns of anger, fear, and happiness, but not sadness, also cause an increased reliance on simple deductive stereotyping, rather than an inductive combination of information (Bodenhausen, 1993). Bodenhausen found that subjects are more likely to use ethnic stereotypes of a Hispanic target than to use the given individuating information when they are angry, afraid, or happy (rather than sad or in a neutral mood).

O'Sullivan (1988) made a claim seemingly opposite to that of Bodenhausen. According to Bodenhausen, positive mood will increase reliance on simple deduction, and negative mood (unless it is anger or fear) will decrease reliance on deduction. O'Sullivan agreed that induction is more demanding than deduction but suggested that positive affect will increase the use of inductive personalized processes, whereas negative affect will increase the use of deductive categorical processes.

However, O'Sullivan's definition of affect is slightly different from Bodenhausen's. O'Sullivan described positive and negative affect as feelings directed toward the target. Thus, when the perceiver likes someone, he or she will spend more time processing information effortfully and inductively. This is different from the work of Bodenhausen on general mood states of the perceiver. Essentially, O'Sullivan considered the effects of the evaluation of the target rather than the effects of the perceiver's internal affect or mood. In fact, O'Sullivan's idea of affect toward the perceiver seems more like the concept of outcome dependency in a different guise. A perceiver who likes the target will see his or her fate and future intertwined with the target, more so than if the perceiver does not like the target. Therefore, a positively evaluated target has become important to the perceiver and is more likely to be processed carefully. This idea is not new; as early as 1953, Newcomb pointed out that the balance principle – a cognitive consistency strategy that necessitates some degree of extra processing – applies only for targets whom the perceiver has evaluated positively. In other words, people care about the traits and beliefs of those they like, but are indifferent to the characteristics of disliked others.

Branscombe and Cohen (1990) suggested other influences on the use of top-down versus bottom-up processes in social inferences in their integration of the mood and stereotyping literature. Branscombe and Cohen addressed not the cognitively disruptive effects of mood that Bodenhausen (1992) addressed, but rather mood-congruency effects such as judging ambiguous targets in a manner congruent with one's mood or memory biases toward mood-congruent information. First of all, Branscombe and Cohen conceptualized stereotyping and mood effects as heuristics – simple deductive rules that people use to make a judgment task easier. As such, mood-congruency influences and stereotypes are relatively automatic, and they are preferred whenever perceivers are not inspired to use more complex inductive processes. Branscombe and Cohen proposed that two strong determinants of mood and stereotype use are the perceiver's level of motivation and the complexity of the task. Specifically, the more motivated the perceiver (involved with the target), the less use of stereotypes and mood as heuristics; the more complex the task, the more use of stereotypes and mood as heuristics. That is, only under conditions of high-involvement and low-task complexity are perceivers likely to use complicated inductive processing.

The relative salience of featural versus categorical information can also direct processing. Categories can be primed through frequent or recent activation (Dovidio, Evans, & Tyler, 1986; Higgins, Bargh, & Lombardi, 1985); Higgins et al., 1977; Wyer & Srull, 1981), even without the perceiver's awareness. Once a category has been primed, category-level information that is strongly associated with the category label will also be activated. For example, the word *Blacks* can be used as a subliminal prime. Later judgments about an ambiguously described character will reflect more of the stereotypes associated with Blacks in these primed subjects than in subjects primed with a neutral word (Devine, 1989). Judgments are then biased toward category-level information, such as stereotypes and prototypical characteristics, and less weight is given to individuating characteristics of the target. Because it is possible to prime categories that induce top-down processing, it should also be possible to make individual characteristics more salient and accessible than group-level information, therefore making induction more likely. One way to do this is to emphasize each person's unique characteristics (N. Miller, Brewer, & Edwards, 1985). Presumably, once subjects are focused on individuating information, they will be more likely to combine this information inductively. They may forego attempts at categorization and induce an impression instead. Indeed, Carlston and Skowronski (1986) found that reinstating individuating information after categorization increases subjects' focus on the individuating information, causing impressions to be less category-based.

The perceiver's own group membership can also affect processing strategies. Out-group members are more likely to be judged in stereotypic terms than in-group members. This may be due, in part, to motivation (Tajfel & Turner, 1979) and, in part, to differential accessibility of information about in-group and out-group members. For example, people tend to have more low-level behavioral information encoded about in-group members than about out-group members (Judd & Park, 1988; Linville, Fischer, & Salovey, 1989). Thus, for some out-group categories, only deductive processing may be possible because only group-level (not low-level) information is present, whereas for in-group members, the presence of low-level behavioral information facilitates inductive processing. As Brewer (1988) mentioned, shared group membership is but one of the dimensions of similarity between self and target that can lead to personalized, bottom-up processing of information. Brewer contended that any type of similarity (similar attitudes, preferences, etc.) may be a catalyst toward personalized processing.

In summary, the ease, efficiency, and possible automaticity of deduction will usually be preferred to the complexity and effort involved in induction for most social inference tasks. However, the presence and accessibility of specific versus general information, as well as arousal and motivation, will determine which type of inference will be used in any given situation.

Induction and Deduction Versus Analogy

Having delineated the factors influencing people's tendency to use induction or deduction, we now turn to the third type of inference. When will analogical inference be preferred to either induction or deduction? First, we consider how the nature of the analogical process makes it uniquely suited for certain social situations. Then, we contrast analogy and deduction, specifying more precisely the conditions under which analogy seems particularly likely.

General Situational Pressures Toward Analogy.   Analogical reasoning seems to be a simple, primary process of inference. As we have discussed, recent views of analogical thinking depict it as a basic, all-purpose, ubiquitous, nonvolitional, and undirected process (Gentner, 1992). Deduction, as the application of a general rule to specific cases, is also a rather simple and efficient inference process.

In contrast to deduction, however, experience with the judgment domain is not necessary to use analogy. Perceivers develop deductive rules, heuristics, and stereotypes through experience (Sherman & Corty, 1984). Often the rules and principles (e.g., schemas, scripts, etc.) develop only after a good deal of information integration and extraction of the important principles has taken place. On the other hand, analogy can occur with only a few exemplars encoded and without a general theory linking them together. Indeed, reasoning by comparison to similar exemplars is common among younger children, meaning that it develops early (Kossan, 1981). Deduction is not likely to be used by young children. Moreover, analogy is more likely to be used under heavy cognitive demands and for complex tasks, indicating that it is a low-effort process (Kossan, 1981).

Also, as our earlier example of the colleague who reminds you of your mother illustrates, our intuition is that people often experience this sense of similarity to a known other rather automatically when meeting a new person. If analogical reasoning is a primitive process, it may be one of the earliest sources of social inference about newly met individuals. Perhaps before they have access to category-level information for deduction, or before they have assembled and combined all the behavioral-level information for induction, social perceivers have already generated a few tentative hypotheses about a new person by comparing them to similar others by analogy.

Furthermore, comparison to similar others is more likely to occur under situations of perceived anxiety or threat, which is often involved in meeting a new person. White and Shapiro (1987) found that perceivers were more likely to see newly met persons as similar to familiar others when they expected to be the "bad guy" in a discussion than when they expected to be "one of the crowd." Presumably, the anxiety that the bad guy was experiencing motivated him or her to see unfamiliar others as comfortingly familiar. If others are more likely to be seen as similar to someone people know, then that similarity is more likely to inspire them to use the familiar other as a base for analogy about the unfamiliar stranger. Inference via similar others is also more likely to occur when the similarity is to a significant other (Andersen & S. W. Cole, 1990). Overall, meeting new people who share some common feature with someone people know well seems a likely circumstance for analogical as opposed to inductive or deductive inferences about them.

Analogy Versus Deduction.   Thus far, we have labeled analogy a *primitive* process and deduction a *default* process. Both types of inference seem to be simpler than induction. We do not delve into the issue of analogy versus induction at the level of the individual in further depth. It seems clear that the same factors affecting the use of induction versus deduction also affect the preference for induction versus analogy. Essentially, the choice of induction versus either deduction or analogy is one of employing a complicated and time-consuming process versus a more quick-and-dirty process. In the case of analogical thinking, an involuntary process of similarity judgment and attribute transfer is written over by the inductive process, which takes into account the individuating information about the target.

Can we specify which quick-and-dirty process, analogy or deduction, will be preferred? When will analogy to similar others be used and when will deduction from group-level information be used in inferences about individuals? We have already answered these questions in part by claiming that the use of deduction in social inference necessitates experience with the social domain in question. If the perceiver does not have enough experience with a group of people, or with the world in general, to have developed stereotypes, analogy to similar exemplars may be the only possible route to inference. However, assuming that the perceiver is experienced enough to allow for the potential encoding of either person exemplars and/or higher level group stereotypes, which will be the preferred inference tool?

Some of the important variables have their impact at the time of encoding, whereas others are more important at the time of judgment, so we address each set of factors in turn. First, some definitions are necessary. We assume that knowledge about group categories is stored with the prototype representing that group. The prototype trace contains various types of important general information about the group: its variability, the relevant features, an affective tag. On the other hand, individual members of the group are exemplars of that category. General information is not stored in the exemplar trace. Inference by reference to the group prototype involves application of general group information to the specific person and is therefore deductive. Inference by reference to similar others involves accessing same-level exemplars and is therefore analogical.

E. R. Smith (1990) proposed methodologies for distinguishing exemplar-based from prototype- or category-based inferences. He argued that different inference processes leave cognitive "signatures" that enable one to identify them. Activation and use of general knowledge structures like prototypes and schemas should result in short-lived (a matter of seconds) and general effects on inference. Use of specific traces like exemplars should result in longer lasting and more specific effects on inference. In E. R. Smith's terms, "If a single experience has a notable effect on behavior or judgment on a future occasion, the effect must be mediated by a relatively specific memory of the prior episode" (p. 7).

Thus, exemplar-based processes such as analogical inferences will have long-term effects that are highly specific to the single instance. Prototype-based processes such as deductive inferences will have short-term and more global effects.

Prototypes Versus Exemplars.   The question of analogy versus deduction then becomes: When will group prototypes be used for inference and when will person exemplars be used? Sherman and Corty (1984) reviewed research relevant to this question of prototype versus exemplar use in judgment. They concluded that any manipulation affecting the salience and/or the accessibility of one type of representation over the other will affect which representation influences judgment more. Thus, any factor increasing the salience or accessibility of exemplars will likely result in inference by analogy, and any factor increasing the salience or accessibility of the prototype will likely result in inference by deduction. For example, at encoding, the ease of abstracting a prototype can determine whether information is more likely to be encoded as abstract prototypes or as individual exemplars. Presenting poorly defined categories with much schema-inconsistent information can make the task of abstracting a prototype from a set of information very difficult (Sherman & Corty, 1984). Categories composed of exemplars with many common features facilitate the abstraction of a prototype. Furthermore, this prototype is more meaningful than the prototype of a poorly defined, loose collection of exemplars (e.g., Medin & Schaffer, 1978). Varying subjects' instruction set can also affect the ease of prototype abstraction (Hamilton, Katz, & Leirer, 1980; Hanson, 1982). When subjects are given an impression set, they tend to abstract a prototype from the information given. When given a recall set, subjects tend to store the information in terms of separate exemplars (Hanson, 1982). If a prototype is easily abstracted, it will be available for later inferences about that group. Deductive inferences about individual members of the group seem likely under these circumstances. If a prototype cannot be easily abstracted, analogical inference by reference to similar exemplars seems more likely.[3]

Time pressure or cognitive load during initial encoding also can affect the tendency to encode information in terms of exemplars or prototypes. The fewer cognitive resources available, the more likely information is to be encoded in abstract, prototypic fashion (Rothbart et al., 1978). Thus, only deductive inferences may be possible with information encoded in a purely prototypic manner.

In addition, once a prototype has been formed, exemplars have smaller and smaller effects on judgment as time passes, and prototypic representations dominate judgments (Srull & Wyer, 1980). If a great deal of time has passed between encoding and judgment, then deduction from the group prototype will probably be preferred to analogy to individual exemplars. However, if the information about the group and its members is relatively new, inference by analogy may be more common.

Other factors have their effect at the time of judgment, rather than encoding. Relative salience of exemplars or prototypes can be manipulated through priming (recent and/or frequent activation; Higgins et al., 1977). Also, extreme, very expected, or very unexpected instances are often easily accessible during judgment (Hamilos & Pitz, 1977; Hastie, 1980). There are also individual differences in preferences for instances as opposed to abstractions in various social domains (Tesser & Leone, 1977; Walker, 1976). Finally, the ease of categorizing a person

---

[3]Although inference by analogy to exemplars is a simple process, encoding information in the form of exemplars is cognitively demanding (Fiske & Taylor, 1991).

can determine whether higher level prototypic information is applied to them. People who fit a category well are evaluated in a category-based, deductive manner more often than those who are not a good fit (Fiske & Neuberg, 1990). Therefore, "good" category members would be more likely to be compared to the prototype, whereas "bad" category members would be more likely to be compared to similar exemplars.

In summary, preference for exemplars or prototypes in inferences depends on a variety of variables: the tightness of the category, task set at encoding, resources available for encoding, time passage since encoding, salience, individual difference factors, and goodness of fit to category. E. R. Smith (1990) summarized many of these exemplar-versus-prototype studies as follows: Relatively exemplar-based processing results from trying to form impressions, encountering group members without having a group stereotype, and dealing with in-group members. Relatively prototype-based processing results from trying to remember attributes, having a stereotype before encountering group members, and dealing with out-group members. Furthermore, E. R. Smith stated that "group-level information may almost always be supplemented by individual-level information" (p. 16). Various modes of processing, processing goals, stimulus qualities, and individual differences may affect the amount of attention given to exemplars and prototypes, but exemplars are almost always important. Therefore, analogical inferences seem to predominate. To phrase this less strongly, deductive inference-making interacts with analogical inference-making under many circumstances.

Models of Conscious Analogy and Deduction. Karniol (1990) addressed the issue of analogy versus deduction in the context of behavioral prediction. When predicting the behavior of other people, reasoning by analogy to the self—"What would I feel or think if I were in that situation?"—is one way to predict others' behavior (Higgins, 1981). As discussed earlier, Karniol proposed another possibility: Perceivers have a hierarchy of transformation rules for predicting the behavior of others. These rules are deductive and learned from experience with the world—young children do not use them properly (Karniol, 1990).

An example may be helpful. A perceiver is attempting to predict the behavior of a friend toward a waitress. Assume that the deductive rule the perceiver is attempting to apply is one concerning the target's expectations about the waitress ("stimulus-directed desires-plans-expectations"). The perceiver must access general declarative knowledge about waitresses. If this declarative knowledge is not tagged, the perceiver makes a prediction of the target's behavior based on this knowledge. Perhaps the perceiver will access the fact that waitresses are given tips, so she will predict that her friend will also tip the waitress. But imagine instead that the perceiver has a "self-as-distinct" tag attached to the representation of knowledge about waitresses—perhaps she herself has worked as a waitress and, in her experience, was not always tipped. At this point, the perceiver must compare herself to her friend. If her friend is distinct in the same way (has also been a server who was often stiffed on tips), the perceiver will reason by analogy to herself rather than through application of a general deductive rule. For example, she may predict that the friend, like herself, will not feel obliged to tip the waitress. Notice how unlikely it is for reasoning by analogy to the self to occur: It necessitates accessing a general knowledge structure with a self-as-distinct tag, as well as finding sufficient similarity between the self and the other to use the self as a base for analogy. If any of these factors is not present, deductive rule-based prediction will be used. Karniol (1990) found that sophisticated social decision makers usually prefer these efficient deductive rules to analogy when attempting to predict the behavior of others.

Fiske and Neuberg (1990) agreed with Karniol's (1990) view that all efforts toward deduction must occur before analogy will be adapted. They list comparing a target to the self or to a similar exemplar as a part of the third step in their model. If initial categorization is not sufficient and confirmatory categorization fails, a similar exemplar may be accessed. In general, just as the tendency to use induction versus deduction depends on the relative accessibility of low-level behavioral data versus higher level group stereotype information, the preference for analogy versus deductive inferences about individuals seems to depend on the ease of encoding a prototype and categorizing the person, as well as the accessibility of similar exemplars.

However, Karniol's (1990) and Fiske and Neuberg's (1990) models compare relatively conscious and controlled attempts at using analogy and deduction. Those who view analogy making as ubiquitous, automatic, and virtually perceptual (e.g., Gentner, 1992; Goldstone, 1992b; Hofstadter, 1992) would probably take issue with Karniol's and Fiske and Neuberg's conceptualization of analogical and deductive inferences. If analogy is a ubiquitous and nonvolitional process, E. R. Smith's (1990) proposal that exemplars are involved in virtually every inference is perfectly plausible. That is, all inferences are partly analogical because similar exemplars always impact the inference.

When discussing more controlled, problem-solving strategies and processes, however, we can more readily compare inferences about individual persons that result from combining behavioral information inductively, applying stereotypic knowledge deductively, or inferring the characteristics of similar others analogically. Whenever possible, deduction or analogy is preferred to induction. People will prefer deductive inferences about persons whenever they have prototypic (stereotypic) representations available to them. Deduction is quite simple: Just find an appropriate category for the target and apply general knowledge that is associated with that category in a top-down manner. However, if the person is (a) difficult to categorize, (b) belongs to a category without a strong prototype, (c) readily brings to mind similar others, or (d) belongs to a group with which the perceiver has little experience, analogy will be used instead. Analogy seems to be an inference process that, although distinct from deduction, is similarly nondemanding. The inductive process appears to be the most cognitively demanding, an inference type to be avoided in most situations. Induction will be used only when social perceivers have the luxury of sufficient time, attention, and motivation to devote to the task of assembling bits of data into a coherent whole, or when these individuating bits of data are screaming for attention. Perceivers will attempt to categorize first, or access similar others, before they finally examine the individual characteristics of the target and attempt to assemble them into a coherent whole.

AUTOMATICITY

Although the previous ease-of-use hierarchy generally holds for social inference, it does not apply across the board. For some people in some situations, inductive inferences may be much easier than the other types. One important determinant of which process is likely to be used in any given inference task is the extent to which the various inference processes are spontaneous or automatized. Although many social inferences are made on the basis of a conscious, controlled, and deliberate process, this is not always the case. Throughout this chapter, we have repeatedly discussed social inferences of all three types that appear to be automatic. This is not surprising when one considers the vast number of social inferences about behaviors, person, and groups that a perceiver might make in a single day: "Is Bob playing this game extremely well, or is he cheating?" "Can this acquaintance be trusted with my confidence?" "Are my new neighbors as unfriendly as I've heard?" Clearly social inference processes are common. Perhaps many everyday inferences are made without much thought or attention. After all, if effort and attention were required for every social inference, little cognitive capacity would be left for other necessary information processing.

Automatic processes occur without awareness, require no attention, and cannot be disrupted by concurrent demands. Consequently, they conserve precious cognitive resources (Bargh, 1984; Shiffrin & W. Schneider, 1977). Thus, perceivers often automatize wherever possible. In fact, well-practiced, controlled judgment processes can become automatic fairly quickly (E. R. Smith & Lerner, 1986). Because social inferences appear to be made so frequently, some researchers have suggested that various aspects of the social inference process have become automated (e.g., Devine, 1989; Gilbert, 1989; Trope, 1986; Uleman, 1987, 1989).[4]

---

[4]As the true nature and defining characteristics of automaticity have yet to be determined by cognitive psychologists (see, e.g., Bargh, 1984; Cheng, 1985; Logan, 1988; W. Schneider & Shiffrin, 1977), we do not attempt to apply any single definition. Therefore, an inference process is described as "automatic" or "spontaneous" based solely on the claim of the individual researcher(s) whose work we review. Some inconsistency is inherent in this approach, because different researchers operate under different definitions of automaticity. A resolution of these inconsistent criteria is outside the scope of this chapter (see Bargh, chapter 1, Volume 1, for a more thorough discussion of this issue).

Attitude Activation

Attitude activation, although not an inference, is an automatic initial process that can have wide-ranging effects on later inferences. Fazio's (1990) MODE model of attitudes posits attitudes as object-evaluation associations in long-term memory. The stronger the association between object and evaluation, the stronger the attitude, and the more likely the attitude is to be activated automatically upon mere presence of the attitude object. When an attitude is activated automatically, it causes the object to be construed in attitude-consistent ways. That is, a perceiver might infer that a liked person is adventurous based on knowledge of a particular behavior. However, if the same behavior is performed by a disliked person, it might lead to an inference of recklessness.

The mere presentation of either a positively or a negatively evaluated object can affect this construal of later, unrelated information. When a perceiver is primed with a positively valued object, seeing a target person who performs an ambiguous behavior leads to a positive inference about that person. When a perceiver is primed with a negatively valued object, the same act by the same person can lead to a negative inference (Fazio, Powell, & Herr, 1983). However, this perceptual effect occurs only for subjects with automatically activated attitudes toward the primed object. Automatically activated attitudes guide and direct perception of stimuli in a manner that increases the likelihood of making attitude-consistent social inferences about later information (Fazio, 1990).

Heuristic Processing

The distinction between automatic and controlled processes in social inference making is not a simple one. Rather than conceptualizing cognitive processes as either entirely automated or entirely controlled, most researchers consider cognitive processes to lie somewhere on a continuum between automaticity and control (Bargh, 1984). For example, some processes may occur outside of awareness, but may be affected by concurrent processing demands. Others may occur rapidly and in parallel with other processes, but are subject to some control by the perceiver (see G. D. Logan, 1988). We turn now to a discussion of modes of processing used for social inference that, although not necessarily fully automatic, are less effortful and less thorough than other inference processes.

Heuristic Versus Controlled Processes.   The most extensively researched and heavily debated type of light processing involves cognitive heuristics. In general, *heuristics* are defined as rules or shortcuts that are learned from experience and are applied to various judgment contexts to speed and simplify processing. Tversky and Kahneman (1974) originally specified three such heuristics: (a) availability (easily remembered instances are assumed to occur with high frequency and likelihood), (b) representativeness (the probability that Object A belongs to

Class B depends on the degree to which A resembles B), and (c) anchoring and adjustment (judgments are corrected insufficiently from an initial set point). Although a thorough analysis of cognitive heuristics is outside the scope of this chapter, suffice it to say that judgmental heuristics allow less effortful processing than a thoroughly controlled process and that they lead to more errors than does thoroughly controlled processing. In other words, there are at least two different methods for processing inference-relevant information. One is controlled, conscious, effortful, and thorough; the other (use of heuristics) is more rapid, constrained, and automatic. The interested reader is directed to other reviews of cognitive heuristics for a more detailed analysis (Sherman & Corty, 1984).

Two models dealing with processing persuasive messages make a similar distinction between thorough and light processing. Chaiken (1980), Chaiken, Liberman, and Eagly (1989), and Petty and Cacioppo (1981, 1986), have delineated two different modes of processing persuasive communications. One route to persuasion, the central or systematic route, involves thorough, rational processing of the message content and the argument quality. Central or systematic processing occurs when the perceiver is motivated and has the cognitive capacity to expend the necessary cognitive effort. On the other hand, peripheral or heuristic processing occurs when the perceiver is not motivated, is cognitively busy, or is alerted to various properties of the message form rather than its content. The shortcuts used in peripheral or heuristic processing are learned from experience and require little or no attention for their operation. Persuasion heuristics include rules, such as length of message equals strength of argument, and attractive communicators are credible.

Just like cognitive heuristics, persuasion heuristics allow more superficial processing and are more likely to lead to error. In this case, error cannot be defined objectively but is, instead, a result of attending to unimportant properties of the message or the communicator. Fortunately, however, attitudinal inference accomplished through heuristic processing tends to be shorter lived than attitude change through more thorough processing (Hennigan, Cook, & Gruder, 1982).

To summarize, shortcuts to making social inferences occur when perceivers use heuristics, simplifying rules learned from experience with the decision context, to help them speed processing. These heuristics may or may not be fully automatic (Sherman, 1987). However, all heuristics allow a relatively nondemanding mode of inference making. Note that most heuristics are a form of general knowledge that is learned previously and then applied to a specific new situation. Therefore, these heuristic-based inferences are a form of deduction.

CEST: Two Systems.   Despite the vast amount of research inspired by heuristics in the 1980s, the study of judgmental heuristics has been criticized for being theory poor (Wallsten, 1983). That is, investigators of heuristics have been accused of being overly concerned with demonstrating the errors resulting from these shortcuts, rather than with advancing an integrated theory of how and why judgmental heuristics operate.

A recent theory offers one such integration of research on heuristic processing. Epstein's (1985, 1990, 1991) cognitive-experiential self-theory (CEST) is concerned with how perceivers construe and respond to the world around them. The information that perceivers receive is processed by two separate but interacting conceptual systems: experiential and rational. The experiential system is evolutionarily older than the rational system. It provides a rapid, quick-and-dirty assessment of information. The rational system, on the other hand, is a relatively new system that slowly and dispassionately analyzes information. This distinction between rapid, undemanding, superficial processing and slow, demanding, complex processing parallels the distinctions made by researchers in both judgmental and persuasion heuristics (e.g., Chaiken, 1980; Tversky & Kahneman, 1973). However, Epstein's rational-experiential distinction goes deeper than just the cognitive effort involved in each process.

The experiential system is associationistic; deals with specific representations; is emotional; operates below awareness; and applies deeply ingrained, difficult-to-change rules that are learned from experience. The rational system is concerned with causality rather than associations; deals with abstract symbols; is logical; operates only with awareness and effort; and is highly flexible rather than rule-bound. In terms of our inference taxonomy, the experiential system would be the realm of automatic, default, deductive processes such as heuristics and application of general knowledge, whereas the rational system would be implicated in demanding, complex, inductive processes such as impression formation from low-level behaviors and creative integration of information.

Of course, the distinction between the two systems is much more complex than the distinction between induction and deduction (see Epstein, Lipson, Holstein, & Huh, 1992, for a more complete list of the attributes of each system). However, fitting our taxonomy to Epstein's two systems suggests a reason why social perceivers tend to prefer deduction over induction. That is, deduction can be performed by the more primitive and holistic system. Epstein has argued that people's personal theories of reality reside in the experiential system, and they are more important in everyday affairs than we may realize. Our theories guide everyday perception, inference, and behavioral decisions automatically through the experiential system, and the slower rational system simply cannot keep up.

CEST offers an interesting approach to judgmental heuristics by conceptualizing them as indicators of the experiential system at work. Heuristics in CEST are not shortcuts around regular processing. Rather, they embody the rules of inference used by the experiential system: a focus on immediately available information (availability), the use of representative (representativeness) instances, and staying close to a starting point (anchoring and adjustment). Approaching heuristics as components of a whole system, rather than as isolated decision strategies, has interesting implications. Priming the experiential system prior to inference, as in Epstein et al. (1992), should increase reliance on not just one, but all heuristics, if they are all part of the same system. For example, engaging the emotions of the perceiver should increase reliance on all heuristics because the experiential system is the realm of emotional experience. Similarly, focusing perceivers on cause-and-effect relations rather than on simple associations should increase the influence of the rational system and decrease reliance on the experiential system. Clearly much more research on the implications of CEST for social inference is necessary, but the concept of two conceptual systems holds promise for integrating work on heuristics, affect, and top-down versus bottom-up processing.

Automatic Induction

We now discuss models of each type of social inference that propose truly automatic or spontaneous components. Several models of induction containing automatic components have been offered. Although we have stressed the difficulty of inducing generalities from specific information, some inductive inferences are so well-practiced that they are automatic.

Trait Attribution. Formation of trait impressions from lower level behavioral information, for instance, is proposed to be spontaneous. Uleman (1987, 1989; L. S. Newman & Uleman, 1989; Winter & Uleman, 1984; Winter, Uleman, & Cunniff, 1985) has conceptualized trait attribution as a spontaneous process engaged upon mere comprehension of social information. These researchers have argued that social perceivers automatically assemble information about the trait characteristics of people as they comprehend relevant incoming behavioral information.

In one study (Winter et al., 1985), subjects read sentences about various actors, which were ostensibly fillers between numbers they were to memorize. Later, in a surprise recall task, subjects listed all of the sentences they could remember. One of three types of recall cues was provided for three fourths of the sentences: (a) disposition cues, describing the actor's disposition as implied by the sentence; (b) semantic cues, implying the actor's occupation as described in the sentence; and (c) gist cues, representing the gist of the entire sentence. As an example, for the sentence "The businessman steps on his girlfriend's feet during the foxtrot," the disposition cue was "clumsy," the semantic cue was "three-piece suit," and the gist cue was "dancing." One fourth of the sentences were uncued. Winter et al. found that dispositional cues act as better recall cues than semantic cues or no cues, regardless of the subjects' level of cognitive load during encoding of the sentences. From these findings, Winter et al. concluded that subjects spontaneously infer the traits of the actor during comprehension and encoding of the sentences, without apparent effort.

The idea of spontaneous trait inference has not gone unchallenged. Bassili and M. C. Smith (1986) proposed that cognitive strategies affect whether subjects will form trait inferences on-line comprehension of sentences. They found that the likelihood of spontaneous trait attribution can be increased by instructing subjects to form impressions rather than simply to read and comprehend. They argued that under mere comprehension conditions, spontaneous trait attribution is unlikely. Subjects will tend to make spontaneous trait inferences only if they have some reason to do so.

Further evidence of the spontaneity of trait inferences was provided by Skowronski and Carlston (1992). Subjects in Skowronski and Carlston's study were presented with pictures of target persons during a training phase. Beneath each picture was a description of a behavior. Some of these behavioral statements were indicative of a particular trait (e.g., friendliness) and others were indicative of other traits (e.g., intelligence or dishonesty). Later, during a test phase, subjects were asked to learn the association between these previously seen pictures of target persons and some trait terms. Targets whose pictures had been paired with a behavioral statement during the training phase that was relevant to the trait word to be learned were easier for subjects to associate with the relevant trait. Targets whose pictures had been paired with an irrelevant behavioral statement were more difficult. That is, there was a savings in the number of trials required for pictures previously seen with relevant behavioral statements. Skowronski and Carlston interpreted these results as evidence that subjects make spontaneous trait inferences during the training phase. These trait inferences become associated with the target pictures. When the inferred trait is the same as the trait paired with the picture during the test phase, it acts as a cue. In other words, some of the associative learning has already occurred spontaneously during the training phase, without the subject's volition or awareness.

Causal Attribution. Like trait attribution, elementary causal attribution may also be automatic. We have already mentioned Gilbert's (1989) model, consisting of characterization (which is automatic) and correction (which is attentionally controlled). The first step, characterization, involves automatic induction. Specific behavioral information is combined (without attention, awareness, or effort) into a general inference about the disposition of the target person engaging in these behaviors. Gilbert et al. (1988) found that cognitively busy subjects give overly dispositional attributions about the behavior of actors. Subjects who are not cognitively busy are able to integrate situational information into their attributions. From this finding, Gilbert et al. argued that the cognitively busy subjects do not have sufficient attentional capacity to deal with the situational information, but are able to use dispositional information regardless of available attention. Only with sufficient time and cognitive capacity does it become possible for the perceiver to delve into the many situational peculiarities that can affect behavior. Under these circumstances, the second, corrective step should contribute to the attributional inference.

Both of the previously mentioned automatic inductive processes concern inferring the characteristics of individuals rather than groups, and inferring something internal and constant about the individual rather than something about the unstable situational forces. The process of trying to know another individual and infer constancy in their behavior is apparently a well-practiced one. As Gilbert (1989) argued, the tendency to attribute actions automatically to a person's disposition rather than to situational factors is efficient, practical, more often right than wrong, and therefore adaptive. These models also reinforce our earlier argument that the behavior-to-trait link is stronger than the trait-to-behavior link (Carlston, 1991). People automatically infer that a person who is yelling at a child is nasty, rather than that a nasty person will yell at a child. The latter inference seems to require more cognitive effort. We can conclude from the fact that inference of dispositions is automatic that the behavior-to-trait direction of inference is more practiced or more important to the functioning of the perceiver than the trait-to-behavior direction.

Automatic Deduction

Categorization. We begin our discussion of models of automatic deduction with a discussion of automatic categorization, for the obvious reason that no deductive inference can occur until an object has been categorized (or identified). Throughout this chapter, we have discussed categorization as a necessary, even unavoidable, first step for many social inferences. For impression formation on the basis of group category membership (Brewer, 1988; Fiske & Neuberg, 1990), the target person must first be categorized before the appropriate set of stereotyped general information can be applied to the person. For attribution processes (Gilbert, 1989; Trope, 1986), the target person's behavior must first be categorized before any dispositional inferences can be drawn from it. Here we focus on categorization as a necessary precursor to deductive inferences. However, we first address the issue of categorization as an automated process.

Many social and cognitive psychologists agree that the initial categorization of an object occurs automatically (Fiske & Neuberg, 1990; Fodor, 1983; Nosofsky, 1987; Trope, 1986). Although categorization is not an inference, the way in which an object is categorized can have large effects on further inferences about that object. We have already alluded to the fact that ease of categorization acts as a cue for category-based processing (Fiske & Neuberg, 1990). But it is not just the ease of fitting an object into a category that can direct inferences. Alternative categorizations of the same object can result in different information being encoded and, therefore, being available for later inference.

Certain dimensions are more compelling ones along which to categorize people. Race, gender, and age, as immediately available cues, tend to be the predominant categories into which people place others (Stangor et al., 1992; Zarate & E. R. Smith, 1990). One might say, as Brewer (1988) did, that categorization is more automatic along these dimensions than along any others. But whether people categorize along these physically based dimensions, or there are other dimensions along which people prefer to categorize (e.g., intelligence), how a person, behavior, or object is categorized often occurs outside of awareness and can be extremely difficult to control consciously (Zarate & E. R. Smith, 1990).

How does the way in which a person is automatically categorized affect further inferences about them? Imagine a situation in which a middle-aged, African-American man is applying for a job. He can be categorized by his age, race, or gender, depending on the perceiver's goals, chronic individual preferences for categorizing along one of these dimensions, or priming of one of these dimensions. A perceiver in one context may categorize this job applicant as an African-American. The perceiver may infer that the applicant is lazy by applying group-level stereotypic information in a deductive manner. Thus, the applicant will probably not be hired. A perceiver in another context may categorize the job applicant as middle-aged. From category-level stereotypes, responsibility and emotional maturity may be inferred deductively. Thus, the applicant in this context may be hired. Although context affects the categorization of nonsocial objects as well (Medin & E. E. Smith, 1984; Nosofsky, 1987), social objects—more than nonsocial objects—are what people perceive them to be (i.e., categorize them as). The point is that this perception-altering categorization process may be automatic; therefore, its effects on later inferences can be difficult to control.

Not all theorists agree that categorization of social objects is automatic. Gilbert and Hixon (1991) recently took issue with this notion. They claimed that categorizing a person as a member of a stereotyped group (what Gilbert and Hixon termed *stereotype activation*) is not automatic—mere exposure to a woman or an old person is not sufficient to ensure instant and effortless categorization. Rather, sufficient cognitive resources must be available to be devoted to the categorization task.

In support of their view, Gilbert and Hixon (1991) found that a cognitive busyness manipulation prevents the activation of stereotypes. The presence of an Asian experimenter failed to activate the attributes usually associated with Asians, but only for the subjects who were cognitively busy during exposure to the experimenter. Nonbusy subjects' stereotypes were activated. On the other hand, once a stereotype is activated (i.e., once categorization occurs), application of the stereotype to a relevant target appears automatic. Cognitive busyness did not attenuate the application of the Asian stereotype once it was already activated. In fact, cognitive busyness seems to be necessary for stereotype application to occur; nonbusy subjects whose stereotype was activated did not show any effects of the stereotype biasing their judgments. Gilbert and Hixon suggested that nonbusy subjects can consciously override the stereotype after it has been applied. Bodenhausen and Lichtenstein (1987) provided support for this contention: Subjects whose stereotypes had been previously activated were able to resist the influence of the stereotype only if they were expecting to perform a relatively nondemanding task. Apparently, these subjects could devote additional resources to correcting for the effects of the stereotype on their judgments, whereas subjects expecting a more demanding task could not.

Gilbert and Hixon (1991) attempted to reconcile the seeming inconsistencies between their model and other automatic-categorization findings in the literature. They suggested that merely reading words that describe a stereotyped group (as in Devine, 1989) may automatically activate a stereotype. However, meeting a person (as in Gilbert & Hixon, 1991) does not lead to automatic categorization and activation of a stereotype. In an interpersonal setting, additional cognitive resources may need to be directed at the target person for categorization to ensue. This view opposes Brewer's (1988) contention that the mere presence of a stimulus person automatically and nonvolitionally triggers a social categorization process.

In summary, whether the social categorization of a person is automatic and inescapable remains an open question. However, once a person has been categorized (perceived as a woman, a physicist, a sports fan), the next phase of applying the category attributes appears to be automatic. The following section describes a model based on such automatic initial application.

Stereotyping.   Devine's (1989) model of stereotypes and prejudice involves both automatic and controlled components. Devine proposed that stereotypic, group-level information is automatically activated upon presentation of the stereotype-relevant social object (or perhaps, as Gilbert and Hixon argued, upon reading or hearing the name of the stereotyped group). Indeed, evidence that stereotype information is automatically activated by subconscious primes was found by Dovidio, Evans, and Tyler (1986). Furthermore, Devine found that all subjects, whether low or high in racial prejudice, report the same information when questioned about stereotypes of Blacks. Moreover, when stereotypic information about Blacks is subliminally primed, all subjects evaluate a Black target person more negatively than a White target. Devine argued that negative category-level stereotypes about Blacks are automatically applied to the Black target once activated. This automatic deduction about the Black target occurs outside of awareness or control, because it occurs regardless of the subject's level of prejudice. Thus, Devine concluded that a deductive, top-down inference about the target has occurred automatically.

The second step in Devine's model is a conscious, corrective step in which the perceiver's beliefs check the inferences derived from the first, automatic step. It is only at this step in the process that a difference between low and high-prejudice subjects emerges. When subjects are given sufficient time and attentional capacity to make judgments, high-prejudice subjects make more stereotype-consistent judgments than low-prejudice subjects. From these findings, Devine inferred that stereotypic information is first automatically activated, but then corrected by the perceiver's own personal beliefs, if indeed these beliefs differ from the stereotype.

Of course, the automatic process proposed by Devine (1989) works only if a stereotype has already been formed and stored. But once this stereotype is induced by or provided to the perceiver, it is difficult and attentionally demanding to resist its influence on judgments about people. Automatic deductive inferences may be powerful determinants of people's judgments and behavior, especially when they have insufficient resources to resist their influence.

Automatic Analogy

A model of analogical inference with automatic components already has been discussed: E. R. Smith and Zarate's (1992) exemplar-based model of social judgment. Although this model posits that attention to different stimulus dimensions mediates judgment, attention need not be required for the activation and weighting of similar exemplars in long-term memory. Instead, the process of similarity-based exemplar weighting seems likely to happen below the level of awareness and without effort. Exemplar-based processes tend to require automaticity so that many exemplars can be considered rapidly and in parallel (G. D. Logan, 1988). Furthermore, E. R. Smith and Zarate's model is essentially an extended version of the generalized context model (Medin & Schaffer, 1978; Nosofsky, 1987), which proposes automatic activation of exemplars in long-term memory.

Thus, attention determines only which features of the target will guide the long-term memory search, not whether the search will be conducted. Once the features have been determined, the search and weighting processes seem to be automated and impervious to concurrent processing demands. As discussed earlier, the exemplar retrieval and weighting process is analogical in nature: Information about similar others is averaged and applied to the new target individual. Although attention is an integral step in the model, much of the analogical inference process in E. R. Smith and Zarate's model seems to be automatic. E. R. Smith (1990) emphasized that particular experiences (exemplars) influence the perceiver's judgments in a nonanalytic, automatic process of retrieval and application. The extent to which similar exemplars affect people's inferences about current individuals is, like automatically applied stereotype information, likely to be beyond their control.

Moreover, there is evidence that the very basic and perceptual analogy-making process as discussed in the analogical reasoning section is automatic. For instance, Marks (1989) found that subjects automatically perceive correspondences between pitch and color. These analogical correspondences show Garner interference. That is, subjects were slower to classify pitches when colors were varied orthogonally with the pitches. Stroop interference effects were also found: Subjects classified stimuli faster if they had the same level of intensity on both dimensions (e.g., high and white) than if they had different levels of intensity (e.g., high and black). As Goldstone (1992b) interpreted these findings, subjects could not avoid perceiving the analogy between pitch and color. This could hardly be a planful or analytic analogy, as it actually interfered with the subjects' tasks. Instead, Goldstone argued that subjects automatically perceive the similarity between the two dimensions, and their judgments and behaviors are influenced by this similarity. Social inferences may also be influenced by similarities automatically perceived between social objects. Analogically based inferences then result, without people's awareness (e.g., Lewicki, 1985; E. R. Smith, 1990).

In summary, many influences on people's social inferences occur outside of awareness and without their control. Categorization and attitude activation are two of these automatic influences. Other processes of social inference, such as the application of heuristics, seem to occur with relative ease and spontaneity, although these processes can be controlled by the perceiver. Still other processes seem to be fully automated, occurring instantly and in parallel with concurrent cognitive demands. Despite the fact that perceivers tend to prefer deduction and are ever influenced by analogy, only attempting induction under specific circumstances, any of these three types of inferences can occur through an automatic process. The types of inferences about individuals that people face every day—What is this person like? Why did they do this?—are well-practiced and important enough to have developed into automated processes. Whether inductive, deductive, or analogical, many common, garden-variety social inferences are taken care of by automatic processing, leaving people's conscious minds free to confront the complexities and anomalies of life.

CONCLUSION

In this chapter, we have shown the complexity of the social inference process and provided a framework for getting a handle on this complex set of processes. We have considered social inference making as involving the three fundamental processes of reasoning—induction, deduction, and analogy. Differences among these processes have been stressed in terms of the information used for the inferences and the different psychological structures, functions, and representations that play a role in these types of social inference. In addition, we have speculated about the situational and motivational conditions under which the different inference processes would be adopted, as well as the relative predominance of the three types of reasoning.

Although we have stressed the differences among induction, deduction, and analogy, recent theories have focused more on the similarities among these types of reasoning. For example, Johnson-Laird (1992) claimed that the mental machinery underlying deduction and induction is very similar and depends on the construction of mental models rather than on the use of formal rules of inference. These models make explicit as little information as possible so as to minimize memory load. In using these mental models, inference makers focus on information that is explicit in the models, and they fail to consider alternatives. Thus, they become "satisficers" who do not go beyond a conclusion that at first blush seems to fit the mental model. In this way, both inductive and deductive reasoning can lead to many of the cognitive errors that have been discussed throughout this chapter.

E. R. Smith and Zarate (1992) and Rothbart (1988) also noted similarities among the processes of social inference. For E. R. Smith and Zarate, exemplar-based analogy making is central to inference, and many aspects of social inference previously thought to be based on induction or deduction are, according to these theorists, based on analogical reasoning. Similarly, Kokinov (1992) views analogy making as involving both reasoning and perception. He has argued that analogy, induction, and deduction have far more similarities than differences, because all three involve mapping, transfer, learning, retrieval, and evaluation. Thus, it may not be useful to think of induction, deduction, and analogy as totally separate and independent processes. Rather, these processes are likely to involve similar mechanisms, and to go on together, either simultaneously or sequentially, in social inference making.

Aside from contrasting induction, deduction, and analogy as three processes of social inference, we considered the importance of the different levels at which social inferences are made. At the lowest level were inferences about behaviors, and at the highest level were inferences about groups. Inferences about individuals were in the middle of the hierarchy and were the richest in terms of the potential for involving all three types of social inference processes. We attempted to compare the levels of inference in terms of the processes that were most likely to be involved and in terms of the strength of the conclusions based on these processes. We focused most closely on the direction of social inference at the various levels.

Throughout the chapter, we suggested various ways in which the social inference process might be better understood. We made it clear that there is no single, simple representation that people have of individuals, groups, or behaviors. Rather, social entities are likely to be represented in a variety of ways, and understanding these social representations and their use is a key to understanding the process of social inference. One particularly important aspect of social representation is how the representations of behaviors, traits, individuals, and groups change over time and with experience. Work on changes in cognitive representation as a function of experience with relevant information (Chi, 1991; Hayes-Roth, 1977) will prove to be especially important for understanding changes in social inference that occur over time. Recent work on the development of expertise in both child and adult populations (Chi, 1978, 1988) will also prove useful in this regard.

Like all other social thought and social behavior, social inference making is a function of three kinds of factors: the perceiver, the target, and the situation. We have seen how all three types of factors play a role in social inferences. Target factors include the salience of information, the order of presentation, and the valence of information, among others. Perceiver characteristics such as motivation, involvement, mood, and schematicity were discussed. Finally, situational and contextual factors have their effects on the social inference process. Priming is one such factor, as is the extent to which the situation is cognitively draining. In general, a complete understanding of social inference requires an integration of how perceiver, target, and situational factors interact to affect the process and the outcome of inferences. We hope that some of the ideas in this chapter represent a small step toward achieving this integration.

ACKNOWLEDGMENT

The writing of this chapter was supported by Grant MH40058 from the National Institute of Mental Health.

REFERENCES

Andersen, S. M., & Cole, S. W. (1990). "Do I know you?": The role of significant others in general social perception. *Journal of Personality and Social Psychology, 59*, 384–399.

Andersen, S. M., & Klatzky, R. L. (1987). Traits and social stereotypes: Levels of categorization in person perception. *Journal of Personality and Social Psychology, 53*, 235–246.

Anderson, C. A., & Sedikides, C. (1991). Thinking about people: Contributions of a typological alternative to associationistic and dimensional models of person perception. *Journal of Personality and Social Psychology, 60*, 203–217.

Anderson, N. H. (1968). Application of a linear-serial model to a personality impression task using serial presentation. *Journal of Personality and Social Psychology, 10*, 354–362.

Anderson, N. H. (1981). *Foundations of information integration theory.* New York: Academic Press.

Asch, S. E. (1946). Forming impressions of personality. *Journal of Abnormal and Social Psychology, 41*, 1230–1240.

Bargh, J. A. (1984). Automatic and conscious processing of social information. In R. S. Wyer & T. K. Srull (Eds.), *Handbook of social cognition* (Vol. 3, pp. 1–44). Hillsdale, NJ: Lawrence Erlbaum Associates.

Baron, R. S., Burgess, M. L., Kao, C. F., & Logan, H. (1990, May). *Fear and superficial processing: Evidence of stereotyping and simplistic persuasion.* Paper presented at the annual convention of the Midwestern Psychological Association, Chicago.

Bassili, J. N., & Smith, M. C. (1986). On the spontaneity of trait attribution: Converging evidence for the role of cognitive strategy. *Journal of Personality and Social Psychology, 50*, 239–245.

Berkowitz, L., & Geen, R. G. (1966). Film violence and the cue properties of available targets. *Journal of Personality and Social Psychology, 3*, 525–530.

Berry, D. S., & McArthur, L. Z. (1986). Perceiving character in faces: The impact of age-related craniofacial changes on social perception. *Psychological Bulletin, 100*, 3–18.

Bodenhausen, G. V. (1993). Emotions, arousal, and stereotypic judgments: A heuristic model of affect and stereotyping. In D. M. Mackie & D. L. Hamilton (Eds.), *Affect, cognition, and stereotyping: Interactive processes in group perception* (pp. 13–37). San Diego: Academic Press.

Bodenhausen, G. V., & Lichtenstein, M. (1987). Social stereotypes and information-processing strategies: The impact of task complexity. *Journal of Personality and Social Psychology, 52*, 871–880.

Branscombe, N. R., & Cohen, B. M. (1990). Motivation and complexity levels as determinants of heuristic use in social judgment. In J. Forgas (Ed.), *Emotion and social judgment.* Oxford, England: Pergamon.

Brewer, M. B. (1988). A dual process model of impression formation. In T. K. Srull & R. S. Wyer (Eds.), *Advances in social cognition* (Vol. 1, pp. 1–36). Hillsdale, NJ: Lawrence Erlbaum Associates.

Brewer, M. B., & Lui, L. (1985). Categorization of the elderly by the elderly: Effects of perceiver category membership. *Personality and Social Psychology Bulletin, 10*, 585–595.

Carlston, D. E. (1992). Impression formation and the modular mind: The associated systems theory. In L. L. Martin & A. Tesser (Eds.), *The construction of social judgments* (pp. 301–341). Hillsdale, NJ: Lawrence Erlbaum Associates.

Carlston, D. E., & Skowronski, J. J. (1986). Trait memory and behavior memory: The effects of alternative pathways on impression judgment response times. *Journal of Personality and Social Psychology, 50*, 5–13.

Chaiken, S. (1980). Heuristic versus systematic information processing and the use of source versus message cues in persuasion. *Journal of Personality and Social Psychology, 39*, 752–766.

Chaiken, S., Liberman, A., & Eagly, A. H. (1989). Heuristic and systematic information processing within and beyond the persuasion context. In J. S. Uleman & J. A. Bargh (Eds.), *Unintended thought* (pp. 212–252). New York: Guilford.

Cheng, P. W. (1985). Restructuring versus automaticity: Alternative accounts of skill acquisition. *Psychological Review, 92*, 414–423.

Chi, M. (1978). Knowledge structures and memory development. In R. S. Siegler (Ed.), *Children's thinking: What develops?* Hillsdale, NJ: Lawrence Erlbaum Associates.

Chi, M. (1988). Children's lack of access and knowledge reorganization: An example from the concept of animism. In F. E. Weinert & M. Perlmutter (Eds.), *Memory development: Universal changes and individual differences* (pp. 160–194). Hillsdale, NJ: Lawrence Erlbaum Associates.

Chi, M. (1991). Conceptual change within and across categories: Implications for learning and discovery in science. In R. Giere (Ed.), *Cognitive models of science: Minnesota studies in the philosophy of science* (Vol. 15). Minneapolis, MN: University of Minnesota Press.

Coovert, M. D., & Reeder, G. D. (1990). Negativity effects in impression formation: The role of unit formation and schematic expectations. *Journal of Experimental Social Psychology, 26*, 49–62.

Darley, J. M., & Gross, P. H. (1983). A hypothesis-confirming bias in labeling effects. *Journal of Personality and Social Psychology, 44*, 20–33.

Dawes, R., Faust, D., & Meehl, P. E. (1989). Clinical versus actuarial judgment. *Science, 243*, 1668–1674.

Devine, P. G. (1989). Stereotypes and prejudice: Their automatic and controlled components. *Journal of Personality and Social Psychology, 56*, 5–18.

Dion, K., Berscheid, E., & Walster, E. (1972). What is beautiful is good. *Journal of Personality and Social Psychology, 24*, 285–290.

Dovidio, J. F., Evans, N., & Tyler, R. B. (1986). Racial stereotypes: The contents of their cognitive representations. *Journal of Experimental Social Psychology, 22*, 22–37.

Dull, V. T. (1982). *Two strategies of social classification.* Unpublished dissertation, University of California, Santa Barbara.

Duncan, S. L. (1976). Differential social perception and attribution of intergroup violence: Testing the lower limits of stereotyping of blacks. *Journal of Personality and Social Psychology, 34*, 590–598.

Dunning, D., Griffin, D. W., Milojkovic, J. D., & Ross, L. (1990). The overconfidence effect in social prediction. *Journal of Personality and Social Psychology, 58*, 568–581.

Eagly, A. H., & Kite, M. E. (1987). Are stereotypes of nationalities applied to both women and men? *Journal of Personality and Social Psychology, 53*, 451–462.

Epstein, S. (1979). The stability of behavior: I. On predicting most of the people much of the time. *Journal of Personality and Social Psychology, 7*, 1097–1126.

Epstein, S. (1985). The implications of cognitive-experiential self-theory for research in social psychology and personality. *Journal for the Theory of Social Behavior, 15*, 283–310.

Epstein, S. (1990). Cognitive experiential self-theory. In L. A. Pervin (Ed.), *Handbook of personality: Theory and research* (pp. 165–192). New York: Guilford.

Epstein, S. (1991). Cognitive-experiential self theory: An integrative theory of personality. In R. Curtis (Ed.), *The self with others: Convergences in psychoanalytic, social, and personality psychology* (pp. 111–137). New York: Guilford.

Epstein, S., Lipson, A., Holstein, C., & Huh, E. (1992). Irrational reactions to negative outcomes: Evidence for two conceptual systems. *Journal of Personality and Social Psychology, 62,* 328–339.

Erber, R., & Fiske, S. T. (1984). Outcome dependency and attention to inconsistent information. *Journal of Personality and Social Psychology, 47,* 709–726.

Fazio, R. H. (1990). Multiple processes by which attitudes guide behavior: The MODE model as an integrative framework. In M. P. Zanna (Ed.), *Advances in experimental social psychology* (Vol. 23, pp. 75–110). New York: Academic Press.

Fazio, R. H., Powell, M. C., & Herr, P. M. (1983). Toward a process model of attitude–behavior relation: Accessing one's attitude upon mere observation of the attitude object. *Journal of Personality and Social Psychology, 44,* 723–735.

Fazio, R. H., Sherman, S. J., & Herr, P. M. (1982). The feature-positive effect in the self-perception process: Does not doing matter as much as doing? *Journal of Personality and Social Psychology, 42,* 404–411.

Fein, S., & Hilton, J. L. (1992). Attitudes toward groups and behavioral intentions toward individual group members: The impact of nondiagnostic information. *Journal of Experimental Social Psychology, 28,* 101–124.

Fiske, S. T. (1980). Attention and weight in person perception: The impact of negative and extreme behavior. *Journal of Personality and Social Psychology, 38,* 889–906.

Fiske, S. T., & Neuberg, S. L. (1990). A continuum of impression formation, from category-based to individuating processes: Influences of information and motivation on attention and interpretation. In M. P. Zanna (Ed.), *Advances in experimental social psychology* (Vol. 23, pp. 1–74). New York: Academic Press.

Fiske, S. T., & Pavelchak, M. A. (1986). Category-based versus piecemeal-based affective responses: Developments in schema-triggered affect. In R. M. Sorrentino & E. T. Higgins (Eds.), *Handbook of motivation and cognition: Foundations of social behavior* (pp. 167–203). New York: Guilford.

Fiske, S. T., & Taylor, S. E. (1991). *Social cognition* (2nd edition). New York: McGraw Hill.

Fodor, J. A. (1983). *Modularity of mind: An essay on faculty psychology.* Cambridge, MA: MIT Press.

Fong, G. T., & Markus, H. (1982). Self-schemas and judgments about others. *Social Cognition, 1,* 191–205.

Gelman, S. A., & Coley, J. D. (1991). Language and categorization: The acquisition of natural kind terms. In S. A. Gelman & J. P. Byrnes (Eds.), *Perspectives on language and thought: Interrelations in development* (pp. 146–196). Cambridge: Cambridge University.

Gentner, D. (1992, August). *Analogy, high-level perception, and categorization.* Symposium conducted at the Conference of the Cognitive Science Society, Bloomington, IN.

Gick, M. L., & Holyoak, K. J. (1980). Analogical problem solving. *Cognitive Psychology, 12,* 306–355.

Gick, M. L., & Holyoak, K. J. (1983). Schema induction and analogical transfer. *Cognitive Psychology, 15,* 1–38.

Gilbert, D. T. (1989). Thinking lightly about others: Automatic components of the social inference process. In J. S. Uleman & J. A. Bargh (Eds.), *Unintended thought* (pp. 189–211). New York: Guilford.

Gilbert, D. T., & Hixon, J. G. (1991). The trouble of thinking: Activation and application of stereotypic beliefs. *Journal of Personality and Social Psychology, 60,* 509–517.

Gilbert, D. T., Pelham, B. W., & Krull, D. S. (1988). On cognitive busyness: When person perceivers meet persons perceived. *Journal of Personality and Social Psychology, 54,* 733–739.

Gilovich, T. (1981). Seeing the past in the present: The effect of associations to familiar events on judgments and decisions. *Journal of Personality and Social Psychology, 40,* 797–808.

Glick, P., Zion, C., & Nelson, C. (1988). What mediates sex discrimination in hiring decisions? *Journal of Personality and Social Psychology, 55,* 178–186.

Goldstone, R. (1992a, August). *Locally-to-globally consistent processing in similarity*. Paper presented at the Conference of the Cognitive Science Society, Bloomington, IN.

Goldstone, R. (1992b, August). *Analogy, high-level perception, and categorization*. Symposium conducted at the Conference of the Cognitive Science Society, Bloomington, IN.

Greenwald, A. G., Carnot, C. G., Beach, R., & Young, B. (1987). Increasing voter behavior by asking people if they expect to vote. *Journal of Applied Psychology, 71*, 315–318.

Griffin, D. W., Dunning, D., & Ross, L. (1990). The role of construal processes in overconfident predictions about the self and others. *Journal of Personality and Social Psychology, 59*, 1128–1139.

Hamill, R., Wilson, T. D., & Nisbett, R. E. (1980). Insensitivity to sample bias: Generalizing from atypical cases. *Journal of Personality and Social Psychology, 39*, 578–589.

Hamilos, C. A., & Pitz, G. F. (1977). Encoding and recognition of probabilistic information in a decision task. *Organizational Behavior and Human Performance, 20*, 184–202.

Hamilton, D. L. (1991, August). *Perceiving persons and groups: A social cognitive perspective*. Paper presented at American Psychological Association Convention, San Francisco.

Hamilton, D. L., Dugan, P. M., & Trolier, T. K. (1985). The formation of stereotypic beliefs: Further evidence for distinctiveness-based illusory correlations. *Journal of Personality and Social Psychology, 48*, 5–17.

Hamilton, D. L., & Gifford, R. K. (1976). Illusory correlation in interpersonal perception: A cognitive basis of stereotypic judgments. *Journal of Experimental Social Psychology, 12*, 392–407.

Hamilton, D. L., Katz, L. B., & Leirer, V. O. (1980). Cognitive representation of personality impressions: Organizational processes in first impression formation. *Journal of Personality and Social Psychology, 39*, 1050–1063.

Hamilton, D. L., & Rose, T. L. (1980). Illusory correlation and the maintenance of stereotypic beliefs. *Journal of Personality and Social Psychology, 39*, 832–845.

Hamilton, D. L., & Sherman, S. J. (1989). Illusory correlations: Implications for stereotype theory and research. In D. Bar-Tal, C. F. Graumann, A. W. Kruglanski, & W. Stroebe (Eds.), *Stereotypes and prejudice: Changing conceptions* (pp. 59–82). New York: Springer-Verlag.

Hamilton, D. L., & Trolier, T. K. (1986). Stereotypes and stereotyping: An overview of the cognitive approach. In J. F. Dovidio & S. L. Gaertner (Eds.), *Prejudice, discrimination, and racism* (pp. 127–163). Orlando, FL: Academic Press.

Hanson, C. (1982). *Prototype and exemplar processing in a categorization task*. Unpublished manuscript, Indiana University.

Hastie, R. (1980). Memory for behavioral information that confirms or contradicts a personality impression. In R. Hastie, T. M. Ostrom, E. B. Ebbesen, R. S. Wyer, D. L. Hamilton, & D. E. Carlston (Eds.), *Person memory: The cognitive basis of social perception* (pp. 141–172). Hillsdale, NJ: Lawrence Erlbaum Associates.

Hastie, R. (1983). Social inference. *Annual Review of Psychology, 34*, 511–542.

Hastie, R., & Kumar, P. A. (1979). Person memory: Personality traits as organizing principles in memory for behavior. *Journal of Personality and Social Psychology, 37*, 25–38.

Hastie, R., & Park, B. (1986). The relationship between memory and judgment depends on whether the judgment task is memory-based or on-line. *Psychological Review, 93*, 258–268.

Hayes-Roth, B. (1977). Evolution of cognitive structure and processes. *Psychological Review, 84*, 260–278.

Hennigan, K. M., Cook, T. D., & Gruder, C. L. (1982). Cognitive tuning set, source credibility, and the temporal persistence of attitudinal change. *Journal of Personality and Social Psychology, 42*, 412–425.

Higgins, E. T. (1981). Role taking and social judgment: Alternative developmental perspectives and processes. In J. H. Flavell & L. Ross (Eds.), *Social cognitive development: Frontiers and possible futures* (pp. 119–153). Cambridge: Cambridge University Press.

Higgins, E. T., Bargh, J. A., & Lombardi, W. (1985). The nature of priming effects on categorization. *Journal of Experimental Psychology: Learning, Memory, and Cognition, 11*, 59–69.

Higgins, E. T., King, G. A., & Mavin, G. H. (1982). Individual construct accessibility and subjective impressions and recall. *Journal of Personality and Social Psychology, 43*, 35–47.

Higgins, E. T., Rholes, W. S., & Jones, C. R. (1977). Category accessibility and impression formation. *Journal of Experimental Social Psychology, 13*, 141–154.

Hilton, J. L., & von Hippel, W. (1990). The role of consistency in the judgment of stereotype-relevant behaviors. *Personality and Social Psychology Bulletin, 16*, 430–448.

Hofstadter, D. (1992, August). *The centrality of analogy-making in human cognition.* Paper presented at the Conference of the Cognitive Science Society, Bloomington, IN.

Homa, D., Sterling, S., & Trepel, L. (1981). Limitations of exemplar-based generalization and the abstraction of categorical information. *Journal of Experimental Psychology: Human Learning and Memory, 7*, 418–439.

Johnson-Laird, P. N. (1992). *Human and machine thinking.* Hillsdale, NJ: Lawrence Erlbaum Associates.

Jones, E. E., & Davis, K. E. (1965). From acts to dispositions: The attribution process in person perception. In L. Berkowitz (Ed.), *Advances in experimental social psychology* (Vol. 2, pp. 220–266). New York: Academic Press.

Judd, C. M., & Park, B. (1988). Out-group homogeneity: Judgments of variability at the individual and group levels. *Journal of Personality and Social Psychology, 54*, 778–788.

Kaplan, M. F. (1971). Contextual effects in impression formation: The weighted average versus the meaning-change formulation. *Journal of Personality and Social Psychology, 19*, 92–99.

Karniol, R. (1990). Reading people's minds: A transformational rule model for predicting others' thoughts and feelings. In M. P. Zanna (Ed.), *Advances in experimental social psychology* (Vol. 23, pp. 211–247). New York: Academic Press.

Keil, F. C. (1989). *Concepts, kinds, and cognitive development.* Cambridge, MA: MIT Press.

Kim, H., & Baron, R. S. (1988). Exercise and the illusory correlation: Does arousal heighten stereotypic processing? *Journal of Experimental Social Psychology, 24*, 366–380.

Klatzky, R. L., & Andersen, S. M. (1988). Category-specificity effects in social typing and personalization. In R. S. Wyer & T. K. Srull (Eds.), *Advances in social cognition* (Vol. 1, pp. 91–101). Hillsdale, NJ: Lawrence Erlbaum Associates.

Klein, S. B., & Loftus, J. (in press). The mental representation of trait and autobiographical knowledge about the self. In T. K. Srull & R. S. Wyer (Eds.), *Advances in social cognition* (Vol. 5). Hillsdale, NJ: Lawrence Erlbaum Associates.

Kokinov, B. (1992, August). *Analogy, high-level perception, and categorization.* Symposium conducted at the Conference of the Cognitive Science Society, Bloomington, IN.

Kossan, N. E. (1981). Developmental differences in concept acquisition strategies. *Child Development, 52*, 290–298.

Krueger, J., & Rothbart, M. (1988). Use of categorical and individuating information in making inferences about personality. *Journal of Personality and Social Psychology, 55*, 187–195.

Kunda, Z., & Sherman-Williams, B. (1993). Stereotypes and the construal of individuating information. *Personality and Social Psychology Bulletin, 19*, 90–99.

Lambert, A. J., & Wyer, R. S. (1990). Stereotypes and social judgment: The effects of typicality and group heterogeneity. *Journal of Personality and Social Psychology, 59*, 676–691.

Lewicki, P. (1985). Nonconscious biasing effects of single instances on subsequent judgments. *Journal of Personality and Social Psychology, 48*, 563–574.

Linville, P. W., Fischer, G. W., & Salovey, P. (1989). Perceived distributions of the characteristics of in-group and out-group members: Empirical evidence and a computer simulation. *Journal of Personality and Social Psychology, 57*, 165–188.

Locksley, A., Borgida, E., Brekke, N., & Hepburn, C. (1980). Sex stereotypes and social judgment. *Journal of Personality and Social Psychology, 39*, 821–831.

Locksley, A., Hepburn, C., & Ortiz, V. (1982). Social stereotypes and judgments of individuals: An instance of the base-rate fallacy. *Journal of Experimental Social Psychology, 18*, 23–42.

Logan, G. D. (1988). Toward an instance theory of automatization. *Psychological Review, 95*, 492–527.

Lopes, L. L. (1982). *Towards a procedural theory of judgment.* (Tech. Rep. No. 17, pp. 1–49). Information Processing Program, University of Wisconsin, Madison.

Lord, C. G., Lepper, M. R., & Mackie, D. (1984). Attitude prototypes as determinants of attitude-behavior consistency. *Journal of Personality and Social Psychology, 47*, 751–762.

Manis, M., & Paskewitz, J. R. (1987). Judging psychopathology: Expectation and contrast. *Personality and Social Psychology Bulletin, 13*, 83–94.

Marks, L. E. (1989). On cross-modal similarity: The perceptual structure of pitch, loudness, and brightness. *Journal of Experimental Psychology: Human Perception and Performance, 15*, 586–602.

Markus, H. (1977). Self-schemata and processing information about the self. *Journal of Personality and Social Psychology, 35*, 63–78.

McArthur, L. Z., & Baron, R. (1983). Toward an ecological theory of social perception. *Psychological Review, 90*, 215–238.

McKoon, G., & Ratcliff, R. (1989). Inferences about contextually defined categories. *Journal of Experimental Psychology: Learning, Memory, and Cognition, 15*, 1134–1146.

Medin, D. L., Altom, M. W., & Murphy, T. D. (1984). Given versus induced category representations: Use of prototype and exemplar information in classification. *Journal of Experimental Psychology: Learning, Memory, and Cognition, 10*, 333–352.

Medin, D. L., & Schaffer, M. M. (1978). Context theory of classification learning. *Psychological Review, 85*, 207–238.

Medin, D. L., & Smith, E. E. (1984). Concepts and concept formation. *Annual Review of Psychology, 35*, 113–138.

Messick, D. M., & Mackie, D. M. (1989). Intergroup relations. In M. R. Rosenzweig & L. W. Porter (Eds.), *Annual review of psychology* (Vol. 32, pp. 89–115). Palo Alto, CA: Annual Reviews.

Miller, A. G., Ashton, W., & Mishal, M. (1990). Beliefs concerning the features of constrained behavior: A basis for the fundamental attribution error. *Journal of Personality and Social Psychology, 59*, 635–650.

Miller, N., Brewer, M. B., & Edwards, K. (1985). Cooperative interaction in desegregated settings: A laboratory analogue. *Journal of Social Issues, 41*, 63–79.

Mitchell, M. (1992, August). *Analogy, high-level perception, and categorization.* Symposium conducted at the Conference of the Cognitive Science Society, Bloomington, IN.

Newcomb, T. M. (1953). An approach to the study of communicative acts. *Psychological Review, 60*, 393–402.

Newman, J., Wolff, W. T., & Hearst, E. (1980). The feature-positive effect in adult human subjects. *Journal of Experimental Psychology: Human Learning and Memory, 6*, 630–650.

Newman, L. S., & Uleman, J. S. (1989). Spontaneous trait inference. In J. S. Uleman & J. A. Bargh (Eds.), *Unintended thought* (pp. 155–188). New York: Guilford.

Nisbett, R. E., & Ross, L. (1980). *Human inference: Strategies and shortcomings of social judgment.* Englewood Cliffs, NJ: Prentice-Hall.

Nisbett, R. E., & Wilson, T. D. (1977). Telling more than we can know: Verbal reports on mental processes. *Psychological Review, 84*, 231–259.

Nosofsky, R. M. (1987). Attention and learning processes in the identification and categorization of integral stimuli. *Journal of Experimental Psychology: Learning, Memory, and Cognition, 13*, 87–108.

Osherson, D. N., Smith, E. E., Wilkie, O., Lopez, A., & Shafir, E. (1990). Category-based induction. *Psychological Review, 97*, 185–200.

O'Sullivan, C. S. (1988). Conditional responses in person perception: The categories of our discontent. In T. K. Srull & R. S. Wyer (Eds.), *A dual-process model of impression formation: Advances in social cognition* (Vol. 1, pp. 127–138). Hillsdale, NJ: Lawrence Erlbaum Associates.

Park, B. (1986). A method for studying the development of impressions of real people. *Journal of Personality and Social Psychology, 51*, 907–917.

Park, B. (1989). Trait attributes as on-line organizers in person perception. In J. N. Bassili (Ed.), *On-line cognition in person perception* (pp. 39–59). Hillsdale, NJ: Lawrence Erlbaum Associates.

Park, B., & Hastie, R. (1987). Perception of variability in category development: Instance- versus abstraction-based stereotypes. *Journal of Personality and Social Psychology, 53*, 621–635.

Park, B., & Rothbart, M. (1982). Perception of out-group homogeneity and levels of social categorization: Memory for the subordinate attributes of in-group and out-group members. *Journal of Personality and Social Psychology, 42*, 1051–1068.

Pennington, N., & Hastie, R. (1986). Evidence evaluation in complex decision making. *Journal of Personality and Social Psychology, 51*, 242–258.

Pennington, N., & Hastie, R. (1988). Explanation-based decision making: Effects of memory structure on judgment. *Journal of Experimental Psychology: Learning, Memory, and Cognition, 14*, 521–533.

Petty, R. E., & Cacioppo, J. T. (1981). *Attitudes and persuasion: Classic and contemporary approaches.* Dubuque, IA: W. C. Brown.

Petty, R. E., & Cacioppo, J. T. (1986). *Communication and persuasion: Central and peripheral routes to attitude change.* New York: Springer-Verlag.

Petty, R. E., Wells, G. L., & Brock, T. C. (1976). Distraction can enhance or reduce yielding to propaganda: Thought disruption versus effort justification. *Journal of Personality and Social Psychology, 34*, 874–884.

Pratto, F., & Bargh, J. (1991). Stereotyping based on apparently individuating information: Trait and global components of sex stereotypes under attention overload. *Journal of Experimental Social Psychology, 27*, 26–47.

Pratto, F., & John, O. P. (1991). Automatic vigilance: The attention-grabbing power of negative social information. *Journal of Personality and Social Psychology, 61*, 380–391.

Pryor, J. B. (1986). The influence of different encoding sets upon the formation of illusory correlations and group impressions. *Personality and Social Psychology Bulletin, 12*, 216–226.

Pryor, J. B., & Ostrom, T. M. (1981). The cognitive organization of social information: A converging-operations approach. *Journal of Personality and Social Psychology, 41*, 628–641.

Quattrone, G. A. (1982). Overattribution and unit formation: When behavior engulfs the person. *Journal of Personality and Social Psychology, 42*, 593–607.

Quattrone, G. A., & Jones, E. E. (1980). The perception of variability within ingroups and outgroups: Implications for the Law of Small Numbers. *Journal of Personality and Social Psychology, 38*, 141–152.

Quine, W. V. O. (1977). Natural kinds. In S. P. Schwartz (Ed.), *Naming, necessity, and natural kinds.* Ithaca, NY: Cornell University Press.

Rasinski, K. A., Crocker, J., & Hastie, R. (1985). Another look at sex stereotypes and social judgments: An analysis of the social perceiver's use of subjective probabilities. *Journal of Personality and Social Psychology, 49*, 317–326.

Read, S. (1984). Analogical reasoning in social judgment: The importance of causal theories. *Journal of Personality and Social Psychology, 46*, 14–25.

Read, S. (1987). Similarity and causality in the use of social analogies. *Journal of Experimental Social Psychology, 23*, 189–207.

Reeder, G. D., & Brewer, M. B. (1979). A schematic model of dispositional attribution in interpersonal perception. *Psychological Review, 86*, 61–79.

Rosch, E. H. (1978). Principles of categorization. In E. Rosch & B. B. Lloyd (Eds.), *Cognition and categorization.* Hillsdale, NJ: Lawrence Erlbaum Associates.

Rothbart, M. (1988). Categorization and impression formation: Capturing the mind's flexibility. In R. S. Wyer & T. K. Srull (Eds.), *Advances in social cognition* (Vol. 1, pp. 139–144). Hillsdale, NJ: Lawrence Erlbaum Associates.

Rothbart, M., Fulero, S., Jensen, C., Howard, J., & Birrell, P. (1978). From individual to group impressions: Availability heuristics in stereotype formation. *Journal of Experimental Social Psychology, 14*, 237–255.

Rothbart, M., & John, O. P. (1985). Social categorization and behavioral episodes: A cognitive analysis of the effects of intergroup contact. *Journal of Social Issues, 41,* 81–104.

Rothbart, M., & Lewis, S. (1988). Inferring category attributes from exemplar attributes: Geometric shapes and social categories. *Journal of Personality and Social Psychology, 55,* 861–872.

Rothbart, M., & Park, B. (1986). On the confirmability and disconfirmability of trait concepts. *Journal of Personality and Social Psychology, 50,* 131–142.

Rothbart, M., & Taylor, M. (1992). Category labels and social reality: Do we view social categories as natural kinds? In G. R. Semin & K. Fiedler (Eds.), *Language, interaction, and social cognition* (pp. 11–36). London: Sage.

Sagar, H. A., & Schofield, J. W. (1980). Racial and behavioral cues in black and white children's perceptions of ambiguously aggressive acts. *Journal of Personality and Social Psychology, 39,* 590–598.

Sanbonmatsu, D. M., Sherman, S. J., & Hamilton, D. L. (1987). Illusory correlation in the perception of individuals and groups. *Social Cognition, 5,* 1–25.

Schneider, D. J. (1973). Implicit personality theory: A review. *Psychological Bulletin, 79,* 294–309.

Secord, P. F. (1958). Facial features and inference processes in interpersonal perception. In R. Tagiuri & L. Petrullo (Eds.), *Person perception and interpersonal behavior* (pp. 300–315). Palo Alto, CA: Stanford University Press.

Secord, P. F. (1959). Stereotyping and favorableness in the perception of Negro faces. *Journal of Abnormal and Social Psychology, 59,* 309–321.

Secord, P. F., & Muthard, J. E. (1955). Personalities in faces: IV. A descriptive analysis of the perception of women's faces and the identification of physiognomic determinants. *Journal of Psychology, 39,* 261–278.

Sherman, S. J. (1980). On the self-erasing nature of errors of prediction. *Journal of Personality and Social Psychology, 39,* 211–221.

Sherman, S. J. (1987). Cognitive processes in the formation, change, and expression of attitudes. In M. P. Zanna, J. M. Olson, & C. P. Herman (Eds.), *Social influence: The Ontario Symposium* (Vol. 5, pp. 75–106). Hillsdale, NJ: Lawrence Erlbaum Associates.

Sherman, S. J., & Corty, E. (1984). Cognitive heuristics. In R. S. Wyer, Jr., & T. K. Srull (Eds.), *Handbook of social cognition* (Vol. 1, pp. 189–286). Hillsdale, NJ: Lawrence Erlbaum Associates.

Sherman, S. J., & Fazio, R. H. (1983). Parallels between attitudes and traits as predictors of behavior. *Journal of Personality, 51,* 308–345.

Sherman, S. J., Judd, C. M., & Park, B. (1989). Social cognition. *Annual Review of Psychology, 40,* 281–326.

Sherman, S. J., Mackie, D. M., & Driscoll, D. M. (1990). Priming and the differential use of dimensions in evaluation. *Personality and Social Psychology Bulletin, 16,* 405–418.

Shiffrin, R. M., & Schneider, W. (1977). Controlled and automatic human information processing: II. Perceptual learning, automatic attending and a general theory. *Psychological Review, 84,* 127–190.

Shipley, E. F. (1992, November). *Inductive inferences by preschoolers and level of category label.* Paper presented at the meeting of the Psychonomic Society, St. Louis, MO.

Skowronski, J. J., & Carlston, D. E. (1987). Social judgment and social memory: The role of cue diagnosticity in negativity, positivity, and extremity biases. *Journal of Personality and Social Psychology, 52,* 689–699.

Skowronski, J. J., & Carlston, D. E. (1989). Negativity and extremity biases in impression formation: A review of explanations. *Psychological Bulletin, 105,* 131–142.

Skowronski, J. J., & Carlston, D. E. (1992, June). *Spontaneous trait inferences.* Paper presented at Nags Head Conference on Social Cognition, Nags Head, NC.

Slusher, M. P., & Anderson, C. A. (1987). When reality monitoring fails: The role of imagination in stereotype maintenance. *Journal of Personality and Social Psychology, 52,* 653–662.

Smith, E. R. (1989). Procedural efficiency: General and specific components and effects on social judgment. *Journal of Experimental Social Psychology, 25,* 500–523.

Smith, E. R. (1990). Content and process specificity in the effects of prior experiences. In T. K. Srull & R. S. Wyer (Eds.), *Advances in social cognition* (Vol. 3, pp. 1–59). Hillsdale, NJ: Lawrence Erlbaum Associates.

Smith, E. R., & Lerner, M. (1986). Development of automatism of social judgments. *Journal of Personality and Social Psychology, 50,* 246–259.

Smith, E. R., Stewart, T. L., & Buttram, R. T. (1992). Inferring a trait from a behavior has long-term, highly specific effects. *Journal of Personality and Social Psychology, 62,* 753–759.

Smith, E. R., & Zarate, M. A. (1990). Exemplar and prototype use in social categorization. *Social Cognition, 8,* 243–262.

Smith, E. R., & Zarate, M. A. (1992). Exemplar-based model of social judgment. *Psychological Review, 99,* 3–21.

Snyder, M., Tanke, E. D., & Berscheid, E. (1977). Social perception and interpersonal behavior: On the self-fulfilling nature of social stereotypes. *Journal of Personality and Social Psychology, 35,* 656–666.

Spellman, B. A., & Holyoak, K. J. (1992). If Saddam is Hitler then who is George Bush?: Analogical mapping between systems of social roles. *Journal of Personality and Social Psychology, 45,* 74–83.

Spranca, M., Minsk, E., & Baron, J. (1991). Omission and commission in judgment and choice. *Journal of Experimental Social Psychology, 27,* 76–105.

Srull, T. K., Lichenstein, M., & Rothbart, M. (1985). Associative storage and retrieval processes in person memory. *Journal of Experimental Psychology: Learning, Memory, and Cognition, 11,* 316–345.

Srull, T. K., & Wyer, R. S. (1979). The role of category accessibility in the interpretation of information about persons: Some determinants and implications. *Journal of Personality and Social Psychology, 37,* 1660–1672.

Srull, T. K., & Wyer, R. S. (1980). Category accessibility and social perception: Some implications for the study of person memory and interpersonal judgments. *Journal of Personality and Social Psychology, 38,* 841–856.

Stangor, C. (1988). Stereotype accessibility and information processing. *Personality and Social Psychology Bulletin, 14,* 694–708.

Stangor, C., Ford, T., & Duan, C. (1992). *Influence of social category accessibility and category-associated trait accessibility on judgments of individuals.* Unpublished manuscript, University of Maryland, College Park.

Stangor, C., Lynch, L., Duan, C., & Glass, B. (1992). Categorization of individuals on the basis of multiple social features. *Journal of Personality and Social Psychology, 62,* 207–218.

Stern, L. D., Marrs, S., Millar, M. G., & Cole, E. (1984). Processing time and the recall of inconsistent and consistent behaviors of individuals and groups. *Journal of Personality and Social Psychology, 47,* 253–262.

Stroessner, S. J., Hamilton, D. L., Acorn, D. A., Czyzewska, M., & Sherman, S. J. (1989, August). *Representational differences in impressions of groups and individuals.* Paper presented at American Psychological Association Convention, New Orleans, LA.

Stroessner, S. J., Hamilton, D. L., & Mackie, D. M. (1992). Affect and stereotyping: The effect of induced mood on distinctiveness-based illusory correlations. *Journal of Personality and Social Psychology, 62,* 564–576.

Tajfel, H. (1969). Cognitive aspects of prejudice. *Journal of Social Issues, 25,* 79–97.

Tajfel, H., & Turner, J. C. (1979). An integrative theory of intergroup conflict. In W. G. Austin & S. Worchel (Eds.), *The social psychology of intergroup relations.* Monterey, CA: Brooks/Cole.

Taylor, S. E. (1981). A categorization approach to stereotyping. In D. L. Hamilton (Ed.), *Cognitive processes in stereotyping and intergroup behavior* (pp. 88–114). Hillsdale, NJ: Lawrence Erlbaum Associates.

Taylor, S. E., Fiske, S. T., Etcoff, N. L., & Ruderman, A. (1978). Categorical bases of person memory and stereotyping. *Journal of Personality and Social Psychology, 36,* 778–793.

Tesser, A., & Leone, C. (1977). Cognitive schemas and thought as determinants of attitude change. *Journal of Experimental Social Psychology, 13,* 340–356.

Tetlock, P. E. (1983). Accountability and complexity of thought. *Journal of Personality and Social Psychology, 45,* 74–83.

Tetlock, P. E., Skitka, L., & Boettger, R. (1989). Social and cognitive strategies for coping with accountability: Conformity, complexity, and bolstering. *Journal of Personality and Social Psychology, 57,* 632–640.

Trope, Y. (1986). Identification and inferential processes in dispositional attribution. *Psychological Review, 93,* 239–257.

Trope, Y. (1989). The multiple roles of context in dispositional judgment. In J. N. Bassili (Ed.), *On-line cognition in person perception* (pp. 123–140). Hillsdale, NJ: Lawrence Erlbaum Associates.

Tversky, A. (1977). Features of similarity. *Psychological Review, 84,* 327–352.

Tversky, A., & Kahneman, D. (1973). Availability: A heuristic for judging frequency and probability. *Cognitive Psychology, 5,* 207–232.

Tversky, A., & Kahneman, D. (1974). Judgment under uncertainty: Heuristics and biases. *Science, 185,* 1124–1131.

Tversky, A., & Kahneman, D. (1980). Causal schemata in judgments under uncertainty. In M. Fishbein (Ed.), *Progress in social psychology* (pp. 49–72). Hillsdale, NJ: Lawrence Erlbaum Associates.

Uleman, J. S. (1987). Consciousness and control: The case of spontaneous trait inferences. *Personality and Social Psychology Bulletin, 13,* 337–354.

Uleman, J. S. (1989). A framework for thinking intentionally about unintended thoughts. In J. S. Uleman & J. A. Bargh (Eds.), *Unintended thought* (pp. 425–449). New York: Guilford.

Vallone, R. P., Griffin, D. W., Lin, S., & Ross, L. (1990). Overconfident prediction of future actions and outcomes by self and others. *Journal of Personality and Social Psychology, 58,* 582–592.

Walker, C. J. (1976). The employment of vertical and horizontal social schemata in the learning of a social structure. *Journal of Personality and Social Psychology, 33,* 132–141.

Wallsten, T. S. (1983). The theoretical status of judgmental heuristics. In R. W. Scholz (Ed.), *Decision making under uncertainty* (pp. 21–37). Amsterdam: North-Holland.

Weber, R., & Crocker, J. (1983). Cognitive processes in the revision of stereotypic beliefs. *Journal of Personality and Social Psychology, 45,* 961–977.

White, G. L., & Shapiro, D. (1987). Don't I know you? Antecedents and social consequences of perceived familiarity. *Journal of Experimental Social Psychology, 23,* 75–92.

Wilder, D. A. (1978). Perceiving persons as a group: Effects on attributions of causality and beliefs. *Social Psychology, 1,* 13–23.

Wilder, D. A. (1986). Social categorization: Implications for creation and reduction of intergroup bias. In L. Berkowitz (Ed.), *Advances in experimental social psychology* (Vol. 19, pp. 291–355). New York: Academic Press.

Winter, L., & Uleman, J. S. (1984). When are social judgments made? Evidence for the spontaneousness of trait inferences. *Journal of Personality and Social Psychology, 47,* 237–252.

Winter, L., Uleman, J. S., & Cunniff, C. (1985). How automatic are social judgments? *Journal of Personality and Social Psychology, 49,* 904–917.

Word, C. O., Zanna, M. P., & Cooper, J. (1974). The nonverbal mediation of self-fulfilling prophecies in interracial interaction. *Journal of Experimental Social Psychology, 10,* 109–120.

Wyer, R. S. (1974). Changes in meaning and halo effects in personality impression formation. *Journal of Personality and Social Psychology, 29,* 829–835.

Wyer, R. S., Bodenhausen, G. V., & Srull, T. K. (1984). The cognitive representation of persons and groups and its effect on recall and recognition memory. *Journal of Experimental Social Psychology, 20,* 445–469.

Wyer, R. S., & Srull, T. K. (1981). Category accessibility: Some theoretical and empirical issues concerning the processing of social stimulus information. In E. T. Higgins, C. P. Herman, & M. P. Zanna (Eds.), *Social cognition: The Ontario Symposium* (Vol. 1, pp. 161–198). Hillsdale, NJ: Lawrence Erlbaum Associates.

Wyer, R. S., & Srull, T. K. (1986). Human cognition in its social context. *Psychological Review*, *93*, 322–359.

Zarate, M. A. (1990). *Cultural normality and social perception*. Unpublished doctoral dissertation, Purdue University, West Lafayette, IN.

Zarate, M. A., & Smith, E. R. (1990). Person categorization and stereotyping. *Social Cognition*, *8*, 161–185.

6 Response Processes in Social Judgment

Fritz Strack
Universität Trier, Germany

Contents

OVERVIEW

The title of the present chapter implies that people's overt responses should be treated as a psychological phenomenon in its own right. Specifically, "response processes in social judgment" implies that what people say (or write down) is not necessarily identical to what they think when they are requested to answer a specific question. Therefore, to predict people's responses, it is not sufficient to know their relevant internal representations; rather, one must take other determinants into account.

In the present chapter, I first discuss two conceptual approaches that are related to the distinction between internal representations and overt responses. I then suggest a conversational framework to deal with response effects and apply this view to account for (a) response effects in "standardized question situations" and (b) a series of cognitive biases in social judgment. Finally, I describe some remote consequences that response effects may have for representations in memory and subsequent judgments that are based on these representations.

Responses Versus Representations

The distinction between internal representations and overt responses can be simply illustrated. Assume a respondent who believes a particular politician is rather incompetent has to express her opinion in a survey. In one condition, a bipolar response scale of competence ranging from −3 to +3 is provided and the respondent may select "−2" to express her opinion. In another condition, a unipolar competence scale from 0 to 6 is provided and the respondent may choose "1" to communicate the same attitude. Although they are different by any objective standards, both responses can be assumed to be manifestations of the same internal representation (Jöreskog, 1971; Upshaw, 1978; see also Eiser, 1990). In a trivial way, the different responses do not reflect different representations, but are a function of the particular answer format that has been provided.

However, the distinction between overt response and internal representation is less clear when it is not the specific format that influences a response, but the wider context in which the answer must be given. The following example may serve as an illustration. In my survey, respondents have to communicate the presumed competence of the same politician after reporting their opinion about an extremely incompetent political figure on the same response scale. Under such a condition, respondents typically report a value that is more positive than if the extreme exemplar had not been rated. Under these circumstances, it is not clear whether the differences exist merely on the response dimension or whether they reflect divergent internal representations. In fact, both positions on this issue have been advocated in the literature (e.g., Helson, 1964; Upshaw, 1965).

CONCEPTUAL BASES FOR DIFFERENTIATING
BETWEEN OVERT RESPONSES
AND INTERNAL REPRESENTATIONS

Psychometric Test Theory

Differentiating between responses and internal representations resembles the distinction between true value and error in psychometric test theory (e.g., Lord & Novick, 1968; see also Upshaw, 1984). In theories of psychological measurement, an observed response is made up of two components: a true score, which reflects the actual psychological property; and an error score, which is determined by contextual influences. Psychometric test theory further assumes that the error is a random variable and normally distributed around the true value. Thus, multiple measurement (i.e., several questions tapping the same underlying representation) is used to approach the true value. Moreover, such test theories do not make assumptions about the psychological representation of the true value. Specifically, they do not assume that respondents know their true values and can report them on request. For example, the assessment of a respondent's extraversion does not require the respondent to know the meaning of this characteristic when answering a question that pertains to the attribute.

Introspection Theory

However, theories of social judgment often are based on the assumption that individuals do know their true values and can describe them "with candor and accuracy" (Campbell, 1981). This position has been advocated by survey researchers for whom "subjective phenomena" (Turner & Martin, 1984; see also Strack & Schwarz, 1992) were the targets of assessment. For example, social scientists have assumed that "respondents can give valid reports of their own subjective states" (Martin, 1984, p. 298). Thus, individuals' true attitudes and opinions were seen to be assessable simply by asking the appropriate questions.

The mechanism that guarantees such privileged, unbiased, and immediate access to one's subjective characteristics is the method of introspection (Martin, 1984). As a consequence of this alleged introspective capability, errors are caused solely by the motivation not to tell the truth. That is, if respondents' competence is ruled out as a source of error, their motivation must be held responsible for deviations from the truth. Specifically, the desire to make a positive impression by giving a socially desirable answer (e.g., DeMaio, 1984; Paulhus, 1991) is considered the prime source of error. Thus, the introspection theory of generating self-reports admits that there may exist discrepancies between internal representations and open responses, and that such incongruities suggest that respondents are lying to pursue personal goals other than telling the truth.

Obviously, this theory has serious problems in dealing with contextual influences on judgment. It seems unlikely that the effects of rather innocuous variations in question order (e.g., Strack, Martin, & Schwarz, 1988), question wording, or the response scale are the result of differences in the motivation to tell the truth. Moreover, there is no empirical evidence that contextual influences (for examples, see also Schuman & Presser, 1981) have such motivational consequences. Therefore, an introspection theory that focuses exclusively on motivational dete minants is of limited use in explaining response processes. To be sure, the goal to behave in a socially desirable manner may, under specific conditions, override the goal to tell the truth. However, such a conflict of motives is incapable of accounting for the myriad of contextual influences that have been documented as determinants of observed responses (e.g., Schuman & Presser, 1981).

Conversation Theory

Facing these limitations, an alternative conceptual framework for response processes seems warranted. This conceptualization is based on the assumption that to understand response processes, one must recognize that asking and answering questions is a type of conversation and has properties of a natural discourse in which two (or more) people engage in a purposeful verbal interaction.

As linguist Grice (1975) put it: "Our talk exchanges do not normally consist of a succession of disconnected remarks, and would not be rational if they did. They are . . . cooperative efforts; and each participant recognizes in them . . . a common purpose or set of purposes, or at least a mutually accepted direction" (p. 45).

The conversational nature of this exchange tends to be overlooked, because contributions are often restrained by certain formats in which questions and answers have to be provided. Such "standardized question situations" (Strack, in press; Strack & Schwarz, 1992; see also Clark & Schober, 1992) often arise when data are collected on the basis of individuals' self-reports. Examples include attitude surveys (see Schwarz & Strack, 1991) and experiments in the social and psychological sciences in which questions are standardized and answers have to be given in a format provided by the researcher (see Bless, Strack, & Schwarz, 1993). Because of those restrictions, standardized questioning in the social sciences is often considered to be equivalent to measurement in the natural sciences.

However, to understand response processes, it is useful to recognize the conversational nature of such interactions. As indicated before, communications in natural settings give participants a large degree of freedom to generate messages in a format of their choosing. In most situations, questioners and respondents can decide to be more or less specific, to be elliptical or redundant, or to ask for feedback about an earlier comment. This lack of restriction serves an important function in the conversation process (see Clark & Clark, 1977). Specifically, it has become apparent that to identify the intended meaning of a communication, a collaborative interaction between conversants plays a crucial role.

Quite some time ago, Krauss and Weinheimer (1964, 1966) found that in the course of an interaction, respondents became more accurate and efficient in identifying ambiguous objects that the questioner had selected if the respondent received feedback from the questioner. On the basis of these observations, Clark and his collaborators (e.g., Clark & Wilkes-Gibbs, 1986) developed a "collaborative theory of reference" (Schober & Clark, 1989) to explain the process of understanding in natural discourse. In this collaborative perspective, speakers and listeners give each other feedback to ensure that a communication's intended meaning is understood.

The studies that were conducted within this perspective (Garrod & Anderson, 1987) convincingly demonstrated that to understand what is meant, deciphering the semantic meaning of a particular word or sentence is not sufficient. Rather, the respondent must go beyond the linguistic units to identify the intended meaning of an utterance (i.e., the questioner's communicative intention). In the endeavor, the unrestricted interaction between participants plays a crucial role.

Obviously, standardized questioning lacks this type of unconstrained exchange. Typically, respondents do not receive feedback if their interpretation of a question corresponds to what the questioner had in mind. Furthermore, the questioner has no indication of whether a response that is provided in a given format is based on the intended meaning of the question. In such situations, the standardized context of questions and answers may serve as a substitute for the unrestricted feedback that occurs in natural situations. Specifically, respondents are likely to rely on contextual features to a greater degree than participants in natural settings (Bless et al., 1993). In other words, the principles of natural conversations should be applicable to standardized situations as well, with respondents using whatever cues are available to infer the communicative intention of the questioner.

At this point, another difference between natural discourses and standardized situations becomes apparent. In natural communications, the communicative intentions of both the questioner and the respondent are often ambiguous. That is, a person who asks a question may not necessarily request information in natural settings. Rather, questions may represent "indirect speech acts" (Searle, 1975, 1976) that express or imply behavioral requests (e.g., "Can you open a window?"), threats (e.g., "Do you want me to lock away your bicycle again?"), assertions (e.g., "Don't you think the play was awful?"), and other actions. Similarly, in natural discourses, responses may not be intended merely to inform the questioner. However, in standardized situations, respondents can (or at least should[1]) assume that questioners want information. This intention can be conveyed by a direct request or a question. In turn, respondents in standardized situations most likely will try to obey this request and provide the desired information. To be

---

[1] Of course, in a psychological experiment, a question may be asked to influence cognitive processes. However, it is important that this intention is not recognized by the respondent (see Bless et al., 1993).

sure, in specific situations, respondents may strive for alternative goals, particularly the goal to make a good impression. But, as mentioned before, this goal will be activated only under very specific circumstances. Thus, it can be assumed that respondents can recognize the questioner's intention and are motivated to cooperate.

The Cooperative Principle. Determination of the motivation to cooperate is necessary, but not sufficient, to understand response effects. One must also identify the mechanisms of cooperation once the motivation is established. The principles best known and studied as rules for communicating in natural situations are those identified by Grice (1975), whose central postulates were subsumed under the "cooperative principle." This consisted of four rules that are described shortly.

The "Maxim of Quantity" requires participants in a discourse to provide the right amount of information. That is, a contribution should convey not more and not less information than is necessary to understand what is meant. The "Maxim of Quality" demands that the conversants tell the truth, the "Maxim of Relevance" requests that contributions should relate to one another, and the "Maxim of Manner" requires them to be clear and without obscurity (for a more detailed discussion of the Gricean principles, see Levinson, 1983). The assumption that speakers adhere to these rules (Higgins, 1981; McCann & Higgins, 1992) is important for the listener to (a) infer the intended meaning of an utterance and (b) generate a response that meets the expectations of the speaker.

However, the implementation of these rules can require additional information from the speaker. An example is the application of the Maxim of Quantity. To determine the appropriate amount of information, a respondent may ask the questioner for further specification. Thus, the question "Where do you live?" could be countered with whether the request for information refers to the country, the city, or the neighborhood. Instead of bothering the questioner, however, the respondent may infer what would be new information to the questioner and what would not. Such an inference may be based on the larger context in which the question is posed. Thus, if the information is requested by a foreign colleague, the response "Lower East Side" would violate the Maxim of Quantity, whereas "New York" would be appropriate. The reverse would be true if the same question were asked by a colleague at a New York university. Who asks a question under what circumstances allows inferences about the state of knowledge and what would be new to the questioner. According to which participants in a discourse add information to what they assume the partner already knows, this "given-new contract" (Clark, 1985; Clark & Haviland, 1977) also may be realized by monitoring the course of a conversation. That is, an answer should go beyond the information that already has been provided.

Cooperation Under Natural and Standardized Conditions. In natural situations, it is the context at large that helps interpret people's communicative intentions. For example, the question "Can you open a window?" will only be interpreted as a request for information if the respondent's pertinent capability is, in fact, questionable and the Maxim of Quantity is observed. If it is not, the respondent will take it as a request for action. Thus, a child may cooperate by answering "Yes, I can," whereas a cooperative adult may respond with "Just a second."

Although such indirect speech acts rarely occur in standardized situations, this example shows how pragmatic characteristics that are external to the question proper determine the response under natural conditions. In standardized situations, the respondent cannot expect the questioner to take his or her specific situation (e.g., his or her capability) into account. Therefore, contextual cues that help determine the communicative intention of the questioner are sought. The particular response format, the order in which questions are asked, and the wording of questions can provide these cues.

In the following paragraphs, I describe how such different aspects of standardized question situations determine the generation of responses as a function of inferences about what information the questioner wants to have. In other words, the respondents who can safely assume that their task is to provide information must decide how they can be informative.

CONVERSATIONAL ASPECTS OF RESPONDING IN STANDARDIZED SETTING: CONTEXTUAL RESPONSE DETERMINANTS

Suppose a stranger asks a person if it is expensive to eat in a certain restaurant that was awarded a Michelin star. The person might well respond, "Yes, quite expensive." However, this response might be misleading if the questioner is looking for a gourmet restaurant. In this case, it might be more appropriate to respond "No, not very expensive." Thus, two responses that contradict each other semantically may be both appropriate; each might be an informative contribution to a conversation, depending on the presumed topic of discourse or the range of targets that the respondent must take into account.

Natural contexts often provide valuable cues for inferences that disambiguate the question. In the previous example, the questioner's appearance (dinner jacket vs. jeans and sweater) may be sufficient to infer what type of restaurant he or she has in mind. Alternatively, the respondent may explicitly request more information ("It depends on what you are looking for"). Finally, the respondent may offer several interpretations spontaneously ("For a regular restaurant, it would be very expensive; for a gourmet place, however, it is cheap").

These overt collaborative attempts at being informative (i.e., obeying the Maxim of Quantity) are not possible in standardized situations. However, in these situations, the context of the question can provide the necessary cues and respondents are likely to rely on such cues to a much greater extent than they would in natural discourse.

The Response Scale

Standardized situations typically require the reporting of judgments in a predetermined format. For example, respondents often receive a scale whose endpoints are verbally described. To judge a restaurant, for example, the scale endpoints might be labelled "not at all expensive" and "very expensive." The distance between those poles may be divided by categories that are or are not connected with verbal descriptions or numbers. Thus, a category above the midpoint of a scale with seven categories might be designated "4," "+1," or "moderately expensive." Although questions that are framed within such response scales are constructed as instruments of measurement that project an objective stimulus array on a subjective continuum (e.g., Thurstone, 1928), they also provide cues for inferences about the questioner's communicative intention.

Response Categories.   It was demonstrated that respondents may use the categories of a scale to infer the intended meaning of a question in two studies by Schwarz and his associates. In one experiment conducted by Schwarz, Strack, Müller, and Chassein (1988), respondents were asked how often they felt really irritated. Of course, real irritations ranged from minor events (e.g., having to wait for service in a restaurant) to major problems (e.g., a fight with one's spouse). The reported frequencies of occurrence were a consequence of the interpretation. In such cases, respondents used the range of the provided response alternatives as the basis for inferences. In their study, Schwarz et al. (1988) used the frequency range as an experimental variation. Specifically, half of the subjects reported the frequency of their irritation on a scale from "several times daily" to "less than once a week," whereas the remaining respondents were given a scale from "several times a year" to "less than once every 3 months." Not surprisingly, the respondents' ratings were a function of the provided range, such that scale values reflecting higher frequencies were obtained in the low-frequency scale condition and lower frequencies were observed in the high-frequency scale condition. This response difference could not be explained sufficiently by the assumption that respondents computed a subjective estimate in both conditions that they mapped onto the divergent scales. Rather, the provided scale alternatives led to different interpretations of the question being asked. When later asked to describe the experiences on which their ratings were based, subjects under the high-frequency scale condition reported less annoying incidents than subjects under the low-frequency scale condition. Thus, it was not only the wording of the question per se that determined subjects' response to it. The response scale also influenced subjects' inferences about the intended meaning of the question. The additional clarification that a participant in a natural discourse might have requested explicitly was provided by a contextual cue, the use of which was possible, because the question and the response scale belonged to the same conversational context.

Inferences can also be drawn from the numeric values of a rating scale. Given an 11-point rating scale, the values may range from "−5" to "+5" or from "1" to "10." Although such scales are often considered equivalent, recent findings suggest that valence of the numbers may provide a contextual cue. This was demonstrated by Schwarz, Knäuper, Hippler, Noelle-Neumann, and Clark (1991), who asked German adults "How successful would you say you have been in life?" Although the poles of both response scales were labeled "unsuccessful" and "successful," one scale had "0" as its midpoint and ranged from "−5" to "+5," whereas the other reached from "0" to "10." The numeric labels showed a dramatic impact on the responses. Whereas 34% of the respondents endorsed a value that was equal or less than the midpoint of the 0–10 scale, only 13% did so on the −5−+5 scale. This difference indicated different interpretations of the word *unsuccessful*. When the term was combined with the numeric value "0," respondents interpreted it as an absence of success. However, when combined with the numeric value "−5," *unsuccessful* was understood as the presence of failure. The interpretation of this scale effect was supported by independent evidence. For example, a fictitious student who rated his academic success as "−4" on the bipolar scale was assumed by observers to fail twice as often as a student who reported a rating of "2" on the unipolar scale. This was true, although both values were formally equivalent along 11-point rating scales of the type previously described.

These findings show that respondents in standardized situations infer the intended meaning of a question by using the labels of the response scale as contextual cues.

Range of Targets.   Alternatively, the same goal of identifying the intended meaning of a question and determining the requested information also can be reached if several stimuli have to be judged using a response scale. Thus, the range of targets may serve as a conversational cue. Assume two possibilities. In the first case, the restaurants to be assessed include Joe's Pizza Parlor and The Golden Goose, a restaurant that has been awarded a Michelin star. In the second case, the targets are confined to restaurants that have the Michelin distinction. The first possibility suggests that the questioner refers to restaurants in general; the second possibility allows the inference that gourmet restaurants are the topic of discourse. As a consequence, the same target is rated as more expensive in the first case than in the second.

This prediction corresponds to explanations that construe the response scale as a flexible rubber band (Postman & Miller, 1945; Volkmann, 1951), rather than a rigid yardstick. In this view, the respondent "anchors" the scale so that its endpoint corresponds to the most extreme stimulus in the range. In my example, the lower anchor would be Joe's, and all the gourmet restaurants would be assembled at the upper end of the scale. Therefore, the latter restaurants would be rated as more expensive along the scale than they would if Joe's was not among the set of those considered. In other words, the introduction of the pizza parlor as an anchor would produce a contrast effect on ratings of the other stimuli.

Technically, the rubber band notion does not imply an identification of the topic of discourse. It merely requires that the most extreme values be identified for use in anchoring the scale. However, this presupposes that all stimuli are simultaneously available at the time of judgment. This is not always the case. That is, the targets are often presented sequentially and have to be assessed in a consecutive manner. Thus, judges have to infer the possible range of the stimuli. Of course, such an inference can be drawn if the topic of discourse is identified. When a scale applies to attitudinal judgments, one stimulus that might be considered in construing the range of values to which the scale is relevant is one's own position (Upshaw, 1965). For example, suppose several persons' attitudes toward the legalization of drugs have to be rated on a scale from *liberal* to *conservative*. If the judge favors the legalization of heroin and all of the attitude statements considered are less extreme than this position, the judge's attitude might be used to anchor the scale. Thus, a statement advocating the legalization of marijuana would be judged as more conservative than it would if the judge's attitude was moderate (i.e., within the range of alternatives considered). In other words, the judge's attitude has a contrast effect on the ratings of others' attitudes. More generally, if a respondent's perspective (Upshaw, 1965; Upshaw & Ostrom, 1984) changes as a function of one's own attitude on an issue, one's judgments of other stimuli on the relevant dimension change as well.

The fact that people include their own attitudes into the range of stimuli has consequences for communication. For example, the way a friend who is extremely conservative will be described to a third person will depend on the recipient's own political stand. That is, if the recipient is liberal, a description implying a higher degree of conservatism (e.g., very conservative) will be provided than if the recipient leans toward conservatism (e.g., rather conservative). At the expense of being inconsistent by using different categories to describe the same stimulus, respondents are more informative if they take the presumed interpretation of the receivers into account, which is determined by their stand on the issue.

Ordinal Versus Distance Information.   Respondents who are required to rate several stimuli on a relevant dimension can provide two types of information. On the one hand, they furnish comparative information that is reflected by the ordinal position of the stimuli on the scale. In my example, if The Golden Goose is placed closer to the "expensive" pole than to Joe's Pizza Parlor, the questioner knows that the gourmet restaurant is more expensive than the fast-food place. However, the distance between the two stimuli on the scale also provides information about the degree to which the two eating houses differ. Thus, the questioner may assume that they are more different if they are assigned to the most extreme categories along the scale than if they are assigned to adjacent categories.

However, under certain circumstances respondents only provide one type of information at the expense of the other. Suppose again that the stimuli being considered include six gourmet restaurants and Joe's Pizza Parlor. Confined to a 7-point scale, a judge cannot communicate both the rank order of the restaurants and the degree to which they differ with respect to price of their entrees. Judges have a choice. First, although they are not identical on the judgmental dimension, all the gourmet restaurants could be assigned to the top category and Joe's to the bottom one. Then, the distance information would be conveyed at the expense of the ordinal information. That is, the recipient would not learn anything about the relative costliness of the top restaurants. Alternatively, the judge might convey the relative position of the gourmet restaurants and assign them to different categories on the scale. As a consequence, Joe's Pizza Parlor and a gourmet eating house might end up in adjacent categories and the distance from the least expensive connoisseur place to Joe's will be the same as to the next more expensive top restaurant.

Parducci (1965) provided a model that captured this conflict. Guided by his "range-frequency" theory, he found that if the distribution of the stimuli is skewed, judges tend to equalize the original dispersion by distributing their judgments evenly over the available categories. That is, respondents give priority to information about the relative position of the stimuli over information about their distance on the response dimension. In my example, the questioner will learn about the relative costliness of all restaurants, but not about how much they differ from each other.

However, this conflict can simply be solved by providing more categories. Assume that instead of 7 categories, my response scale had 70 categories. Then, a judge may communicate both the minor differences between the six gourmet restaurants and the much greater distance of the top places from Joe's Pizza Parlor. In fact, Parducci and Wedell (1986) found that the importance of the frequency principle (i.e., the tendency toward an equal distribution over the response scale) was diminished greatly if the number of categories available was increased.

Wording of the Question

Not surprisingly, how a question is worded determines its interpretation. The semantic meaning can obviously vary as a function of the words that are used and thus influence responses. However, different wordings of questions that seem semantically equivalent can also have response effects.

For example, semantically, to "forbid" and to "allow" are antonyms and "not allow" seems equivalent to "forbid." However, the proportion of survey respondents who answered "yes" when asked if an activity (e.g., smoking marijuana) should be "forbidden" was consistently lower than the proportion who answered "no" when asked if this same activity should be "allowed" (Rugg & Cantril, 1944; Schuman & Presser, 1981). This asymmetry suggested that "not forbidding" was not "allowing." As Hippler and Schwarz (1986) demonstrated, many respondents considered the possibility that they would not actively oppose the activity, but would not support it either. Those respondents neither wanted to "allow" nor to "forbid."

The *type* of article is another example of how the wording of a question can affect responses. Most prominently, consequences of the use of the definite versus indefinite article was investigated by Loftus (1975). In a series of studies, part of the subjects in a witness situation who had previously seen a videotape of a car accident were asked if they had seen "*the* broken headlight," whereas other participants were asked if they had seen "*a* broken headlight." This manipulation typically resulted in more affirmative responses if the definite article was employed.

The explanation of this phenomenon has been primarily memorial in nature. It is assumed that the presupposition semantically implied by the use of the definite article (i.e., "there *was* a broken headlight") distorted the memory representation of the event, which, in turn, caused an erroneous recall. Despite some dissenting opinions (Lindsay & Johnson, 1989; McCloskey & Zaragoza, 1985; Tversky & Tuchin, 1989), memory mechanisms are still widely held responsible for the phenomenon (Loftus & Hoffman, 1989).

However, there is evidence that the wording of the question is not sufficient to produce the effect (e.g., Dodd & Bradshaw, 1980; Smith & Ellsworth, 1987). In these studies, inferences based on the communicator's credibility or expertise determined whether the differential use of the article had an effect. Moreover, Strack and Bless (in press) found that the presupposition implied by use of the definite article was only used as a base for an inference when other strategies were not applicable. Specifically, part of the experimental conditions allowed subjects to base their answers to the question of whether they had previously seen a certain object both on the conversationally conveyed presupposition that the object had been presented ("Did you see *the* screwdriver?") and on their own metacognitive knowledge (i.e., the belief they *would* have remembered the particular object had it been presented). The applicability of this metacognitive strategy was manipulated by varying the salience of the items in the recognition set. The differential use of judgmental strategies was observed when subjects were asked if they had seen an item that was not presented. Then, the use of the direct versus the indirect article only increased false alarms if the object was not salient. If the object was salient, almost all subjects correctly rejected the item as "not seen before."

These findings suggest that, in the absence of a memory trace, judgmental strategies may come into play and judges may prefer one strategy over the other. These findings also suggest that the surface structure of a task does not fix the mental mechanisms used to solve it. Thus, a memory task may be solved by inferential strategies that are applicable in a given situation. In this perspective, leading questions do not influence responses by altering what has been encoded about the target, but by allowing the respondent to infer what was probably the case. If better alternatives are not available, respondents may use those cues to generate a required response.

Preceding Questions

Questions that were previously asked and answered provide information about the questioner's current state of knowledge. This information is important, because it allows the respondent to obey the maxim of quantity by making his or her answer as informative as required. This is the case if an answer adds to what the recipient already knows. However, the respondent's knowledge changes as a function of the ongoing discourse. As a consequence, the informativeness of a statement depends on communications that have preceded it in the conversation. In other words, a contribution should build on the "common ground" (Clark, 1985) that has been established between participants of the discourse. Syntactically, switching from the indirect to the direct article symbolizes that a target has become a given and allows for new information to be added. Clark and Haviland (1977) described this application of Grice's Maxim of Quantity to a natural discourse the "given-new contract."

The fact that the new value of a contribution is determined by one's previous contributions requires participants in a discourse to keep track of what one has said before. In a natural situation, this type of monitoring occurs automatically; a conversant would normally not repeat a previous contribution unless there were reason to assume that the recipient has not understood its content. For example, suppose a person is first asked the question "How is your wife?" followed by "And how is your family?" He is unlikely to take his wife's well-being into consideration in answering the second question, because, given his previous answer, it would not be informative. Note that this is not the case if the questions had been asked in the reverse order.

The given-new contract should be obeyed in standardized situations when two questions overlap in their content. This is the case if a general question follows a more specific one and their contents are in a subset–superset relation or if their content intersects. In addition, the two (or more) questions must be related to each other. In natural contexts, the speaker guarantees that the rule of relation is observed. In standardized situations, however, this rule is not always obeyed. On the contrary, such a perception is actively avoided by placing related questions at different positions in a questionnaire, separating them by several filler items. Thus, a respondent may or may not see a series of questions as belonging together. More generally, a respondent's application of the Maxim of Quantity depends on his or her perception of the relatedness of the items involved (Strack, 1992).

This hypothesis was tested in a study by Strack et al. (1988; cf. Tourangeau, Rasinski, & Bradburn, 1991), in which the conversational context was manipulated experimentally. Subjects were given a questionnaire that included two questions whose content stood in a subset–superset relationship. The more specific question addressed respondents' happiness with their dating, whereas the more general one concerned their happiness with life as a whole. If the two questions are perceived to belong to the same context of discourse, the given-new contract should be applied and the respondents should avoid being redundant. In analogy to the previous example, they should not base the judgments of happiness with life in general on their happiness with dating if they have already reported their dating happiness. However, if the questions are not perceived to belong together, answering the specific question should render the relevant content more accessible and should increase the probability that the answer to the general question is based on the content of the specific one (see Higgins, Rholes, & Jones, 1977; Srull & Wyer, 1979, 1980). Thus, correlations between the answers should be high in the specific-general order if no conversational context is established. However, under the conversational-context condition, the correlation should be reduced, because the same contents should not be communicated twice. To establish the conversational context, the two questions were introduced with the following statement: "We are now asking two questions about your life, a) happiness with dating, b) happiness with life in general." No such introduction was employed in the no-context condition. Moreover, to further avoid the perception of relatedness, the questions in the latter condition were printed on different pages of the questionnaire. The pattern of correlations corresponded to the predictions. Compared with the control conditions, in which the general question preceded the specific one, the correlation decreased when a conversational context was introduced ($r = .16$), but increased when it was not ($r = .55$).

The assumption that the decreased correlation under the latter condition was caused by an exclusion of the activated content requires a more diagnostic test. Therefore, a conceptual replication was conducted by Schwarz, Strack, and Mai (1991). German adults who had either a spouse or a partner were asked how satisfied they were with both their current relationship and their lives. Both the order of the questions and the conversational context were varied. Two new conditions were added, in which respondents were explicitly instructed either to include or exclude the redundant content of the specific question when they rated their satisfaction with their lives in general.

The previous pattern of correlation coefficients clearly was replicated. That is, the correlation between the answers decreased if the conversational context was introduced. Moreover, the correlations under conditions where respondents were explicitly instructed to include or exclude the specific content matched exactly the conditions under which the given-new contract was expected to implicitly require respondents to consider the specific information or not. Taken together, this set of findings suggests that respondents in standardized situations comply with the Gricean Maxim of Quantity when they answer questions whose content is related in a part–whole fashion.

In extension of this logic, Strack, Schwarz, and Wänke (1991) applied the same procedure to questions whose contents were semantically similar. Specifically, they asked subjects how happy and satisfied they were with their lives. It was assumed that respondents who observed the given-new contract would be more likely to differentiate between the similar concepts of happiness and satisfaction than would respondents who were not concerned about avoiding redundance. To foster the perception of relatedness, a box was drawn around the questions "Here are two questions about your life." To prevent such a perception, the two questions were presented as being part of two different questionnaires that used different scales, colors, and type face and were described as serving different purposes. "Happiness" was the last item of survey one, "satisfaction" the opening question of the second questionnaire.

In contrast to many cognitive theories (e.g., Wyer & Srull, 1989), the conversational logic predicted that the correlation between the two answers would be higher if the questions were separated and lower if they were presented as conversationally related. These predictions were born out by the data. The correlation between the similar dimensions of subjective well-being was almost perfect ($r = .96$) if the questions belonged to different surveys. In contrast, if they were perceived as related, the correlation of the answers dropped dramatically ($r = .65$).

These results provide further evidence that conversational principles are often relevant in standardized question situations. However, this is true only if the standardized exchange has features of a natural discourse. That is, the questions must represent an ongoing dialogue in which both the questions and answers to them are perceived as part of the same exchange. However, this is often ambiguous in standardized situations.

However, it is not necessary to establish a conversational context explicitly. The immediate sequence of questions may be sufficient to elicit such a perception. This was the case in a study by Ottati, Riggle, Wyer, Schwarz, and Kuklinski (1989), who found that respondents expressed a more positive attitude toward the general topic of free speech if a preceding question about the same issue referred to a specific group that was positively evaluated (e.g., the American Civil Liberties Union [ACLU]) than if it referred to a group that was negatively evaluated (e.g., the American Nazi Party). However, this assimilation effect was found only when the two questions were separated in the questionnaire. If the specific question immediately preceded the general one, a contrast effect was found such that the positive content produced a more negative attitude and vice versa.

Another aspect of informativeness concerns the required accuracy of a response. Respondents are often uncertain as to how exact their answer has to be. This is particularly relevant if they are requested to report past occurrences and their frequencies. For example, suppose subjects are asked to report if or how often they went to see a movie or a doctor during the last 6 months. They may not interpret the interviewer's request as a demand to engage in an exhaustive memory search. Rather, they may infer that their communication goal will be attained by providing an estimate that is only approximate. Given the constraints of most question situations, such an interpretation seems to comply with the cooperative principle.

To make such frequency estimates, subjects may first recall the number of instances that occurred during a shorter period of time and extrapolate. Thus, in the previous example, they might recall the number of movies they have seen during the last month and extrapolate from that database to the requested time period (Bradburn, Rips, & Shevell, 1987). This strategy could result in overestimations or underestimations of the actual frequency.

To induce respondents to provide a more precise answer, Loftus, Klinger, Smith, and Fiedler (1990) suggested a "two-time frame questioning procedure." Specifically, these authors recommended asking for the frequency of the same behavior in different time periods. For example, to increase the accuracy of subjects' estimates of how often they had a physical examination within the last 2 months, they first might be asked to indicate the number of physicals they had during a different period (e.g., the last 6 months). Loftus et al. compared respondents' medical records with their reports of doctors' visits and found more accurate responses under such conditions than under conditions in which the initial question had not been asked.

The effectiveness of this procedure apparently results from an inference that respondents draw about the level of accuracy they are expected to attain. That is, the fact that two questions are asked pertaining to the same content in slightly different temporal frames suggests to respondents that the questioner has a specific interest in possibly different frequencies of occurrence of the event at different points in time, and therefore make a greater effort to compute the frequency accurately. Thus, as in experimental situations where repeated measures draw subjects' attention to what the experimenter wants to know (see Bless et al., 1993), the repeated posing of similar survey questions can be used to communicate this interest (see also Strack et al., 1988).

Summary

The studies summarized in this section demonstrated that conversational principles are not only applied in responding to questions in natural situations, but also come into play when both questions and answers are confined to specific formats that prevent the type of unrestricted collaboration that is important for effective understanding (Krauss & Weinheimer, 1964, 1966). Moreover, because respondents in standardized question situations typically receive neither clarification of questions they do not understand nor feedback about the appropriateness of their responses, they rely heavily on contextual cues in construing what information they are supposed to provide (Strack & Schwarz, 1992). The significance of these cues, however, can only be grasped if they are embedded an appropriate communication framework that is guided by principles of conversation of the sort identified by Grice (1975).

JUDGMENTAL BIASES

The veridicality of judgments are often evaluated by the degree to which they obey acknowledged norms. Deviations from such norms are considered illusions, errors, or biases (e.g., Nisbett & Ross, 1980), and have attracted researchers' attention ever since visual illusions became a central topic in the psychology of perception (e.g., Helmholtz, 1903).

Judgmental biases have been investigated under different theoretical perspectives. On the one hand, motivational processes have been postulated to account for such distortions of judgments. For example, research stimulated by the theory of cognitive dissonance (Festinger, 1957) assumed that such biases were caused by an unpleasant feeling evoked by the awareness of inconsistent cognitions. Therefore, judgments were seen as achieving or maintaining cognitive harmony.

Alternatively, Tversky and Kahneman (1974) proposed that attempts to simplify difficult cognitive tasks underly judgmental biases. Several heuristics have been identified that, under specified conditions, lead to results that deviate from accepted norms.

In some cases, however, the conversational aspects of the situation can account for the effect. Researchers on judgmental bias tended to overlook the determinants of the experimental situation in which judgments were generated. To be sure, "experimental demands" (Orne, 1962) have been the topic of previous investigations. However, this research focused primarily on subjects' motivations to comply (or not to comply) with the experimenter's hypotheses. In contrast, from a conversational perspective, subjects' motivation to cooperate with the experimenter is taken for granted. It is the implementation of this motivation that needs to be explained.

Specifically, subjects' biased judgments may be the result of interpreting the experimenter's intention as consistent with conversational principles. That is, biases might not reflect deficits in subjects' reasoning. Rather, they result from the social nature of judgment tasks and from subjects' sensitivity to cues that help them cooperate in the exchange. The following discussion provides examples of biases that are the results of conversational influences. These examples are taken from research on causal attributions – the tendency to confirm preexisting beliefs and on judgmental heuristics.

Biased and Unbiased Causal Attributions

The influence of conversational norms on responses also has been identified in the context of causal explanations (Hilton, 1990; Hilton & Slugoski, 1986). More specifically, a respondent who is asked to explain why a certain event has occurred must take the recipient's presumed state of knowledge into account to render the explanation informative. Thus, among the many necessary conditions of an event, the respondent must select one determinant as the cause, and that selection must fulfill the Maxim of Quantity. To use Hilton's (1990; also see Wyer, 1981) example, suppose a doctor diagnoses a drinking problem in a patient and is asked by a colleague who does not know the patient's history why this person has become an alcoholic. The doctor may refer to the fact that the patient was among a group of workers who was laid off recently. If asked by the patient's wife, however, the doctor may offer a genetic predisposition as an explanation of why her husband, but not his unemployed co-workers, became addicted.

Hilton (1990) argued that causal explanations imply a "rather than" as a contrast case that has to be identified in the conversational situation. In the previous example, the doctor asked by the patient's wife infers the co-workers' nonaddiction as the contrast case. To specify her request for causal information, the wife could have explicitly added a "rather than" clause to her question. However, more frequently, the respondent must draw an inference on the basis of the context in which the question is asked. Often respondents may draw on their own background knowledge and infer that what was new to them is likely to be informative to the questioner. Thus, the generic contrast case is the norm from which the incident deviates (Kahneman & Miller, 1986). Thus, if a person is asked why he or she is taking a shower, the answer "because the water is running" would be a somewhat surprising explanation. Conversely, it would be entirely appropriate to explain the fact of *not* taking a shower by mentioning the lack of water. In the first case, the supplied cause does not go beyond the generic norm implying that water runs through showers. However, in the second variant, the explanation consists of the deviation from the supposed norm, and therefore is accepted readily. In fact, the first explanation is appropriate if the norm is reversed. Assume there is a draught and the water is only running for a short time; in this case, the first explanation would be entirely acceptable. If no specific knowledge about the normal situation is available, the questioner who trusts the respondent obeys the conversational principles may infer the particular contrast case to render the explanation appropriate.

This conversational analysis is not only a necessary supplement to any theory of causal attribution (for a more detailed application, see Hilton, 1990; Hilton & Slugoski, 1986), it also sheds new light on some of the biases that have been frequently identified. To the extent that such strategies can account for attributional or judgmental response tendencies, the identified bias must be seen as a reaction to specific conversational requirements, rather than as the product of faulty thinking.

In the realm of attribution research, causal attributions appear to depend on whether one's own or another person's behavior is being explained (Jones & Nisbett, 1972). Specifically, actors are more likely to find situational causes, whereas observers are more likely to identify causes in the person (Nisbett, Caputo, Legant, & Maracek, 1973). This difference has usually been explained in terms of attentional mechanisms (Storms, 1973; Taylor & Fiske, 1978). However, McGill (1989) pointed out that requests for explanations of one's own or another's behavior may be ambiguous about the implied contrast case. In standardized situations where no feedback is provided by the questioner, respondents may disambiguate questions about one's own and another's behavior differently. If this is so, actor and observer attributions should be eliminated if this ambiguity is removed. McGill (1989) added the adjunct "in particular" to either the person or the course of action (e.g., "Why did you/your best friend [in particular] choose this major [in particular]?"). When this was done, the difference between actor and observer attributions disappeared. These findings suggest that, in addition to an attentional focus that is affected by the perspective of a judge, the particular question may imply a conversational focus on either the person or the situation. This difference in focus can lead to divergent responses that are not simply a function of biased thinking.

Confirmation Bias

Individuals' responses are often slanted toward a confirmation of their initial hypotheses. This "confirmation bias" has been attributed to a tendency to select and process information in a biased fashion (e.g., Skov & Sherman, 1986; for a critical analysis, see also Higgins & Bargh, 1987). In one seminal study about this topic, Snyder and Swann (1978) introduced a paradigm in which the selection of questions served as an indicator of a confirmatory strategy. Specifically, Snyder and Swann supplied a pool of questions from which subjects had to choose a certain number to determine from the answers if a target person was either extroverted or introverted. As Snyder and Swann pointed out, the questions provided were of the type that typically are asked of people already known to possess the attribute in question, such as "In what situations are you most talkative?" The authors found that the "hypothesis" that subjects were asked to test determined the type of question selected. Thus, if a participant had to find out if the target person was an extravert, he or she would select questions that one would typically ask if one already knows that the target person is extraverted (e.g., "What do you like about loud parties?"). This selective search for relevant information was taken as evidence of a confirmation bias in hypothesis testing.

Semin and Strack (1980) found that this bias was solely a function of the particular task that subjects had been assigned (i.e., which hypothesis they were asked to test), independently of their personal belief in the validity of the hypothesis. Specifically, because subjects had to choose among questions that were not ideally suited to test the hypothesis in question, they selected the ones that were most relevant to the task at hand. These were the questions that presupposed the attribute that was the target of the hypothesis. For example, a question that asked what a person liked about loud parties implied the person to be an extravert. Thus, the observed confirmation bias was primarily determined by subjects' attempts to provide relevant contributions in an interaction constrained, such that the most relevant choices were also biased toward a confirmation of the hypothesis.

However, this finding is hardly a phenomenon that generalizes to natural situations, because in nonlaboratory situations people formulate questions spontaneously, rather than selecting them from a list of alternatives. Under such conditions, they will be much less likely to construct questions that presuppose the presence of the attribute being evaluated (Trope & Bassok, 1982; Wyer, Strack, & Fuhrman, 1988).

Judgments by Representativeness

Judgmental heuristics are known to simplify complex cognitive processes under suboptimal conditions (Kahneman, Slovic, & Tversky, 1982; Sherman & Corty, 1984). This simplification is achieved by using judgmental cues that typically are correlated with features of the target. For instance, the "availability heuristic" (Tversky & Kahneman, 1973) uses the experienced ease with which certain information can be retrieved from memory as the basis for judgments of frequency and probability, as well as for trait ascriptions (Schwarz et al., 1991). The "representativeness heuristic" (Kahneman & Tversky, 1972) uses the degree of similarity between a target and the typical member of a category as the primary basis of judgments of category membership.

Correspondence Bias.   The representativeness heuristic is often applied when the task requires the categorization of people on the basis of characteristics. For example, in a study by Kahneman and Tversky (1973), subjects received information about a person's attributes that were typical of either engineers or lawyers. Along with this individuating information, subjects received base-rate information conveying the a priori probability that a person belonged to one group or the other. The base-rate information had little effect on subjects' predictions of the target's category membership, whereas the individuating information had a substantial effect. Thus, a person who resembled the typical engineer was classified as such, although base-rate information blatantly contradicted this categorization (Kahneman & Tversky, 1973).

However, faulty reasoning is not the only factor that is responsible for subjects' failure to take base-rate information into account (Gigerenzer, 1991). In addition, subjects' responses are influenced by their interpretation of what the experimenter wants them to consider.

Specifically, Schwarz, Strack, Hilton, and Naderer (1991) investigated this possibility using a situation analogous to that constructed by Kahneman and Tversky (1973). They argued that subjects in the original study might have framed the situation as a task that required them to base their judgment on the individuating characteristics of the target person and not on information about the statistical distribution. Specifically, the original instructions to subjects mentioned that psychologists had administered personality tests to determine the characteristics of the target person. In addition, subjects were informed that (a) experts (presumably psychologists) who were highly accurate had done the same task, (b) subjects' judgments would be compared with those expert judgments, and (c) a bonus would be paid for estimates coming close to the expert panel.

These characteristics of the experimental task might have suggested to subjects that responses should be based on information that a psychologist would find useful (i.e., individuating information about the target person). To investigate this possibility, Schwarz et al. (1991) varied the instructions so that half of the subjects were told that researchers had collected the information and that statisticians had been the experts. Thus, the judgment task was either framed as a problem of psychology or of statistics.

Moreover, dependent on the framing, it should matter if the individuating information deliberately was provided to describe one particular person or if it has been drawn randomly by a computer. If the task is framed as a psychology problem, the deliberately selected information should be more relevant than if the task is described as statistical in nature. Conversely, the randomly drawn information should have more impact if the task is framed statistically, because the random drawing suggests representativeness of this information for the population.

The results were consistent with these expectations. The individuating information exerted the strongest effect if Kahneman and Tversky's (1973) original instructions were used (i.e., the task was framed as psychology problem and the individuating information appeared to be deliberately provided). If the task was framed as a statistical problem, the deliberately selected individuating information had little effect. In contrast, the same information had a strong effect on judgments if it appeared to be drawn randomly by a computer. This interaction between the framing of the task and perceived intentionality of providing the information suggests that the use of individuating information depends, in part, on the communicational context. In other words, the observed overreliance on individuating information may not reflect an inherent cognitive bias, but a strategy whose application depends on the framing of the task.

Conjunction Fallacy. Tversky and Kahneman (1983) found that, under specific conditions, the estimated probability of the conjunction of two events will exceed the probability of the component events. This "conjunction fallacy" probably occurs, because the joint occurrence is more representative than the isolated occurrence of the constituent. For example, Tversky and Kahneman gave subjects the description of a person named Linda, who was portrayed as an activist concerned with feminist, social, and ecological issues. Such a person does not fit the stereotype of a bank teller. Subjects were asked to determine, on the basis of the personality sketch, which of the two alternatives was more probable: "Linda is a bank teller" or "Linda is a bank teller and active in the feminist movement." Most subjects judged the second event to be more probable than the first.

This apparent violation of the basic axioms of probability and set theory is attributed to the application of the representativeness heuristic. Specifically, it is assumed that the conjunctive event is more typical of Linda than one of the component events. That is, Linda the feminist bank teller appears to be more representative of her personality than Linda the mere bank teller. If, in this case, the judgment is based on the typicality of the incident, the logic of probability is clearly violated.

However, there are alternative interpretations of the conjunction effect. For instance, Fiedler (1988) replicated the original results when subjects were asked to assess the probability of the conjunctive event, but this tendency was dramatically reduced when the word *frequency* was used instead. As one possibility, the semantic connotations of *frequency* and *probability* seemed to be more divergent in everyday understanding than in probability theory. More generally, it may be inappropriate (for an extensive discussion of this argument, see Gigerenzer, 1991) to extend principles of probability theory that have been formulated to describe relative frequencies in a series of events to single occurrences. Gigerenzer demonstrated that presumable effects of the representativeness heuristic disappeared if the problem was framed as a frequency judgment. This suggests that subjects' biased responses often may not be a function of a particular heuristic, but the result of an interpretation of the task that deviates from the experimenter's construal.

One such interpretation has been suggested by Dulany and Hilton (1991) as an alternative explanation of the conjunction fallacy. These authors pointed out that the question subjects were asked in the original experimental task was somewhat anomalous, because it implied comparing events that stand in a set–superset relationship. Just as it is odd to ask a child to indicate if a particular plant is a flower or a daffodil – a critique advanced by Adler (1984) toward some of Piaget's studies – it is peculiar to ask if a person belongs to a superordinate or a subordinate category. Respondents might reject the question as meaningless or reinterpret it in a way that remedies the anomaly under the assumption that the questioner attempted to be cooperative. Such a reinterpretation might consist of adding the negation of the subordinate category to the superordinate category, and thus partitioning the subordinate category. For Tversky and Kahneman's (1973) example, the superordinate case "Linda is a bank teller" will be reinterpreted as "Linda is a bank teller and *not* active in the feminist movement" if the comparison case is "Linda is a bank teller and active in the feminist movement" (Agnoli & Krantz, 1989).

In a more systematic treatment, Dulany and Hilton (1991) contrasted several interpretational possibilities and found that the conjunction effect was frequently associated with interpretations that deviated from a simple comparison of the conjunction with one of its components. Although these authors were not able to explain the entire variance of the effect, a large proportion was due to interpretations that consisted of specific additions to the components.

THE ROLE OF POLITENESS

So far, response effects as a function of communicative influences were explained as attempts to convey the information that a questioner presumably is seeking. However, in social communications, participants may pursue goals that go beyond the requirement of being informative. Goals that focus on the relation between communicators, rather than the communicative task, also may determine the generation of responses. For example, people might want to maintain a relationship beyond the current interaction, and may therefore avoid utterances that would endanger this goal. Many such " 'social relationship' goals" (Higgins, 1981) can be summarized under the principle of politeness (see Wyer & Srull, 1989).

According to Brown and Levinson (1987), *politeness* refers to behaviors that address face concerns of the interactants. Specifically, people want to have their positive self-images acknowledged by others (positive face), and they want their actions to be unimpeded by others (negative face). As one possibility, politeness concerns arise when actors anticipate that their actions might pose a threat to one of those face needs. They may then adjust their verbal (and nonverbal) behaviors to be more polite (see Holtgraves & Joong-nam, 1990). Alternatively, politeness concerns may arise after the fact if a person's face needs have already been threatened. Then, the person who caused the face-threatening act (or a third person) might offer mitigating accounts to restore the victim's face (see Gonzales, Pederson, Manning, & Wetter, 1990).

Based on these considerations, politeness as a response determinant may manifest itself in at least four ways. Participants in a communication should (a) abstain from negative characterizations of a recipient, (b) avoid information that may serve as a standard for downward comparisons, (c) not disagree in their expressed opinions from the recipients' attitudes, and (d) provide mitigating accounts for face-threatening acts.

Avoiding Negative Characterizations of a Recipient

The most blatant violation of a person's positive face is a negative evaluation. To express one's dislike to another person is normally the end of a relationship. Although such utterances may be used intentionally to terminate personal ties, people tend to maintain relationships and avoid uttering negative assessments. Compliments may be more frequent than criticisms; and if the situation requires communicating such information, people try to appear as positive as possible (e.g., by using euphemisms) or to soften the negative implications (for specific strategies, see Brown & Levinson, 1987).

Avoiding Being a Positive Comparison Standard

Negative evaluations not only may be communicated in a direct fashion, but they also may be elicited by positive self-descriptions. In this case, concerns for one's face may be in conflict with face needs of a recipient. On the one hand, people want to make a positive impression (Schlenker, 1980; Tedeschi, 1981) and tend to present themselves to others in a positive light. For example, a meta-analysis of surveys on subjective well-being suggested that respondents reported being happier with their lives when they were asked in a personal interview than when the same question was part of a self-administered questionnaire (Smith, 1979). However, experimental evidence by Strack, Schwarz, Chassein, Kern, and Wagner (1990) found that respondents reported less happiness in a public situation than under private conditions. This was the case when the interviewer was physically disabled and sitting in a wheelchair, conceivably due to the anticipated negative self-evaluation that their positive report might elicit in the interviewer. Recognizing the recipient's face needs, subjects seem to have adjusted their public self-reports in a negative direction. More generally, positive self-descriptions may lead to negative evaluations if they are made without being justified by the course of the communication (Holtgraves & Srull, 1989).

Avoiding Disagreements

The third caveat is about disagreements. People who share similar opinions tend to like each other (Heider, 1958; Newcomb, 1961). Conversely, disagreements may strain a positive relationship. Within politeness theory, they are face-threatening acts that should be avoided. Brown and Levinson (1987) described several strategies to avoid or camouflage open disagreement. For example, a person might use a white lie ("Yes, I do like your new hat!"). Alternatively, polite persons might hedge their opinions by using vague expressions ("looks *interesting*," "I *kind of* like it," etc.).

Manis, Cornell, and Moore (1974) conducted a study in which subjects had to relay a previously heard message that either favored or opposed the legalization of marijuana to an audience that favored one of the two sides of the issue. Not only were the transmitted messages tailored to the attitude of the recipients, but subjects' memory for the original message was distorted in the direction of these attitudes.

In a related vein, Higgins and Rholes (1978) had subjects summarize information about a target person to an audience who either liked or disliked this person. Moreover, the effect of these descriptions on subjects' memory for the original information and their liking for the target increased over time. That is, the implications of the information that subjects recalled were distorted in the direction of the audience's attitude, and their own liking for the person became increasingly more consistent with these implications. Similar results were obtained by

Higgins and McCann (1984), who found that such effects may be increased further if the audience has a high social status and the communicator is a high authoritarian.

These results suggest that context-driven communications may persevere and result in changes of cognitive representations (a more detailed discussion of such effects is provided next).

Accounts

If a face-threatening act occurs unintendedly, politeness requires that the agent provides an explanation to help restore the victim's face. For example, if the actor accepts responsibility for a mishap or transgression, the victim may be more likely to continue the relationship than if the actor denies any responsibility. However, the first option is not without costs, because it implies a threat to the offender's claim to a desirable social identity. In the light of politeness theory (Brown & Levinson, 1987), subjects' accounts can be seen as reflecting individuals' concerns about protecting their own face needs and those of others. Thus, the politeness of their explanations is a function of those concerns.

In a series of experiments, Gonzales, Manning, and Haugen (1992), and Gonzales, Pederson, Manning, and Wetter (1990) investigated the determinants of different accounts. In one study, Gonzales et al. (1990) created a situation in which subjects were led to believe that they committed a gaffe (spilling cola) with either mild or severe consequences (affecting computer printout or a camera) for a victim. In addition, the status relation between offender and victim was manipulated.

The authors found that when the consequences of the gaffe were mild, offenders differed in their explanations as a function of their status. That is, less effortful accounts were provided if the offender's status was higher than that of the victim than if the status relationship was reversed.

To assess the quality of the provided accounts, the authors classified subjects' spontaneous utterances into four categories: concessions, excuses, justifications, and refusals. These responses were ordered on a mitigation-aggravation dimension, such that concessions and excuses contained mitigating elements that reduced conflict, whereas justifications and refusals contained aggravating elements that tended to escalate conflict. The authors found that women offenders were more likely to use concessions and excuses to account for the alleged mishap than were men.

In a related simulation study, Gonzales et al. (1992) found that subjects who had to imagine being asked by a victim to "explain what happened" were more likely to use concessions if the described predicament was highly blameworthy than if it was only moderately blameworthy.

Such divergent types of explanations influenced victims' evaluations of the offenders. For nonintentional offenses, victims' assessments were found to be less negative if concessions or excuses were offered to explain the incident (Gonzales et al., 1992).

PSYCHOLOGICAL CONSEQUENCES

Although response effects are primarily adaptations to the requirements of a particular response situation, they nevertheless can have consequences for memory and judgment. Several examples are given next.

Comparative Judgments

Frequently, subjects believe they are expected to compare a target stimulus with other stimuli along a given dimension. This expectation could be induced by either the request to make an explicit rating of the target and the context stimuli along the response scale, or simply by providing relevant information about other potential targets. Suppose one is asked to evaluate the harshness or leniency of a group of judges. If a specific record of sentencing decisions of a particular judge is presented along with information about other judges' sentencing history, respondents may anchor the response scale at the judges with the most extreme sentences and assign leniency/harshness values to the remaining judges according to the relative position of their sentences (Upshaw, 1965; Upshaw & Ostrom, 1984). Thus, the properties of the task induces respondents to engage in comparative judgments. This is particularly likely if the context stimuli, as well as the target, must be positioned along the response scale. Then, for reasons noted earlier, the values of the context stimuli should have a contrast effect on ratings of the target.

However, the comparative nature of the judgment is likely to be preserved in memory only if the context stimuli are stored along with the target rating. This often is not the case and the context-related response gets stored in memory independently of the context. Later, it is retrieved out of context and interpreted with reference to a new standard, with decisions and judgments being formed on the basis of this new interpretation (Wyer & Srull, 1989). Thus, the contextually induced response may eventually result in a change of the cognitive representation of the target stimulus, and the recall may be distorted in the direction of the new context information.

Sherman, Ahlm, Berman, and Lynn (1978) demonstrated that subjects' judgments of recycling as a target issue were influenced by their prior rating of other social issues. Specifically, a contrast effect was obtained, such that their ratings were more positive if the context issues were trivial than if they were highly important. Moreover, when subjects' attention was directed on their target judgments, subsequent behavioral decisions supporting a recycling project were in line with the contextually influenced ratings. Specifically, subjects were more willing to distribute pamphlets if the judgment of the importance of recycling was made in the context trivial issues. This study demonstrates that context-affected judgments may become autonomous and determine behaviors decisions when the subjects' attention is directed toward the judgment by itself.

Similarly, it is conceivable that the context may change over time and that a new context may suggest inferences that contradict the original information about the target. This was demonstrated in a series of studies by Higgins and his collaborators (Higgins & Lurie, 1983; Higgins & Stangor, 1988a; for a more general perspective, see also Higgins & Stangor, 1988b) who provided students with information about several judges' sentencing decisions, such that a target judge's record was either at the upper or lower end of the sentencing distribution. As a result, the target judges' sentencing was categorized as either "harsh" or "lenient" when subjects had to rate the judges' decisions along a response scale. More interestingly, a week later, subjects learned about the sentencing decisions of some additional judges who also had a record of either higher or lower sentencing decisions. When subjects were asked to recall the target judge's original sentences, they were influenced by the new context. The results suggest that subjects remembered their original harshness rating and entered the scale with this rating and inferred judge Jones' sentencing from the corresponding values of the new context. Thus, subjects seem to have reconstructed their memory by drawing inferences using both the original rating on the harshness scale and the new context information.

How such reconstructive processes may be relevant in autobiographical-memory tasks frequently has been demonstrated by Ross and his colleagues (e.g., Ross, 1989; Ross & Conway, 1986). These authors have shown that subjects may use knowledge about their present states, along with subjective theories of stability and change, to assess previous states of themselves. In one study (Conway & Ross, 1984), subjects had to assess their study skills both before and after participating in a "skills program." Despite the program's actual ineffectiveness, participants "recalled" their previous skills as poorer than they actually were. That is, subjects used their present skills as a standard for a comparative rating of their past skills. Although alternative interpretations are possible, these findings illustrate for a different domain how contextually generated assessments may be used for further inferences—in this case, to reconstruct one's autobiography.

Although contextual information often is provided by the situation, it may be elicited by the target stimulus. As Kahneman and Miller (1986) argued, stimuli may "recruit their own alternatives" and thus provide a default context for a comparative assessment.

Comparisons with Presumed Population Averages

Rating tasks not only may induce comparisons with other specific stimuli, but also with the average of the population. Schwarz and his associates (for an overview, see Schwarz, 1990) argued that when respondents are asked to provide self-reports about the frequency of some behavior, they assume that the mean of a response scale corresponds to the mean of the population. Consequently, respondents may draw inferences about the population from the response scale they are given, and may use this information both to reconstruct their memory and to engage in social comparison (Festinger, 1954).

Schwarz and colleagues demonstrated this phenomenon in several studies. In one experiment (Schwarz, Hippler, Deutsch, & Strack, 1985), a sample of German adults reported how many hours they spend watching TV. For half of the sample, the response scale ranged from "up to ½ hour" to "more than 2½ hours," whereas the other half received a scale ranging from "up to 2½ hours" to "more than 4½ hours." If the autobiographical information is accessible in memory, respondents can retrieve this information to compute their TV consumption, and then can compare this consumption to that of the population at large, as inferred from the scale midpoint. However, in some cases, respondents are either unable or unmotivated to draw on their episodic memory, and instead may retrieve a previously formed belief about their relative position ("I am an average TV watcher"). Then, they infer their absolute frequency of watching TV from the value along the scale that they assume reflects this position, without further search of memory for specific instances. Schwarz et al. obtained evidence of such mechanisms. First, respondents reported spending more time watching TV if the high-frequency response categories were provided. This suggests that respondents used beliefs about their relative position in the population to answer the question. On the other hand, respondents assigned more importance to the role that TV watching played in their life under the low-frequency condition. This would be predicted if subjects computed their TV watching on the basis of episodic self-knowledge and then evaluated this typicality by comparing it to the population average (as inferred from the scale midpoint). That is, respondents who were given the low-frequency scale inferred that they watched more TV than average, whereas those who were given the high-frequency scale inferred that they were below average. To the extent that subjects believed that watching TV is a waste of time, subjects should then report being less "satisfied with the variety of things they do in their leisure time" in the former condition than in the latter. This was in fact the case.

A related effect was obtained by Schwarz and Scheuring (1988). In this study, subjects were asked to indicate either the frequency of their sexual intercourse or the frequency with which they masturbated. Again, the scale was varied such that subjects' frequency estimates were likely to be either above or below the scale midpoint, and thus to be seen as either above or below average. However, the consequences of such perceptions depend on the implications of the activities for the assessment of one's sexual relationships. Although frequent intercourse reflects positive aspects of sexual relationships, frequent masturbation is more likely to be indicative of deficits. Consistent with these expectations, subjects reported less satisfaction with their sex life if they had reported their intercourse along a high-frequency scale than if they had reported their masturbation along such a scale. Correspondingly, subjects reported greater satisfaction if they had reported their masturbation along the low-frequency scale than if they had reported their intercourse along it.

However, such straightforward variations of the response scale not only might affect comparisons with presumed population parameters, but they also could induce intraindividual comparisons on different dimensions. Schwarz and Scheuring (1988) conducted a second study in which the same subjects had to indicate the frequencies of both intercourse and masturbation. By using the previously described scale manipulation, the authors were able to control the relative position of the two activities. Thus, by using either high or low scale frequencies, subjects were induced to report engaging in one activity relatively more often than in the other. In this case, relationship satisfaction depended on the relative frequencies of the two activities that the subjects reported, regardless of the relation of these estimates to the population average. That is, subjects reported the highest relationship satisfaction when they used the low-frequency masturbation scale and the high-frequency intercourse scale (which led them to report a low frequency of masturbation, but a high frequency of intercourse). Conversely, subjects who reported their behavior on the reversed combination of scales expressed the lowest relationship satisfaction.

These findings suggest that responses that are controlled by technical characteristics of the response scale can elicit psychological processes, like comparisons, that have far-reaching implications for judgments and evaluations in different domains. As a result, seemingly "innocuous" features of questions and their frames are only effective in determining the behavioral aspects of a specific response. They may also change the psychological representation of the issue, and consequently may have emotional and behavioral consequences.

CONCLUSIONS

In the present chapter, I demonstrated that the specific conditions under which people are required to generate a response have systematic effects on the outcome. I described how contextual variables like the range of the response scale, previous questions, or innocuous aspects of their wording may determine the overt response.

However, such response effects cannot be understood sufficiently if one focuses merely on the stimulus characteristics of the situation. Although such influences are effective, an explanation that is based solely on features of the task does not account for the psychological processes underlying response effects. Therefore, a theoretical perspective is warranted that allows a common view of different response phenomena. In the present chapter, I construed responses as acts of communication and invoked Grice's conversational principles as an explanatory framework. These rules guiding communicational interaction proved useful to account for a wide variety of contextual influences, including a series of judgmental biases.

However, this perspective raises some questions about the separation between the generation of judgments and that of responses. For example, Strack et al.

(1988) found that the correlation between the previously elicited specific happiness judgments and subsequent general ones was lower if the two questions were asked in the same conversational context. This result can be explained as a response effect. That is, subjects were assumed to obey the "given-new contract" (Clark & Haviland, 1977) and edited the overt expression of their judgment by basing their new response on aspects that were not included in their previous answer.

This finding by itself, however, does not guarantee that the onset of conversational influence occurs only after the judgment was formed. It is conceivable that subjects in our study generated their judgments of general happiness by selectively including information that was new for the recipient. Thus, in order to obey the "given-new contract" subjects may have asked *themselves* how happy they were with aspects of their life other than the ones that they had previously communicated. In this interpretation, the conversational influences do not create mere response effect but determine the generation of the underlying judgment.

The distinction between judgmental and response processes is reminiscent of the conceptual separation between "true value" and "error" in the theory of survey responding (Turner & E. Martin, 1984). In this view, response effects (Schuman & Presser, 1981) are deviations from the true value. An expressed attitude, for example, that is influenced by a preceding question is not identical with the person's "actual" attitude. However, as thinking and judging does not occur in a vacuum, contextual influences are present even if they are not detected by an appropriate variation of conditions. Moreover, they are part and parcel of the judgmental process in standardized situations (Strack & L. Martin, 1987). Thus, the criterion of contextual influences cannot be used to distinguish between true value and error.

The difficulty to conceptualize response processes by assuming structural differences between the generation of judgments and responses has similar reasons. This view implies that the judgment is recalled or formed before it is translated into the response format. However, this clear-cut succession appears to be an idealized situation. Often, it cannot be ruled out that the contextual requirements of the task determine judgmental processes. This is particularly likely if the judgment cannot be recalled from memory, but must be formed on the spot. Thus, the conversational framework that I used to account for response processes directs attention to a potential ambiguity in assumptions about the role of response processes in the processing of social information that needs to be addressed in future research.

ACKNOWLEDGMENTS

Writing of this chapter was supported by grants from the Deutsche Forschungsgemeinschaft (Str 264/6-1 and Str 264/8-1). The chapter has profited from many discussions with Norbert Schwarz, Herbert Bless, and Bettina Hannover.

Special thanks go to Robert S. Wyer, who perused an earlier version of the manuscript and provided valuable suggestions.

REFERENCES

Adler, J. F. (1984). Abstraction is uncooperative. *Journal for the Theory of Social Behavior, 14*, 165–181.

Agnoli, F., & Krantz, D. H. (1989). Suppressing natural heuristics by formal instruction: The case of the conjunction fallacy. *Cognitive Psychology, 21*, 515–550.

Bless, H., Strack, F., & Schwarz, N. (1993). The informative functions of research procedures: Bias and the logic of conversation. *European Journal of Social Psychology, 23*, 149–165.

Bradburn, N. M., Rips, L. J., & Shevell, S. K. (1987). Answering autobiographical questions: The impact of memory and inference on surveys. *Science, 236*, 157–161.

Brown, P., & Levinson, S. C. (1987). *Politeness. Some universals in language usage*. Cambridge: Cambridge University Press.

Campbell, A. (1981). *The sense of well-being in America*. New York: Russell Sage.

Clark, H. H. (1985). Language use and language users. In G. Lindzey & E. Aronson (Eds.), *Handbook of social psychology* (Vol. 2, pp. 179–232). New York: Random House.

Clark, H. H., & Clark, E. V. (1977). *Psychology and language. An introduction to psycholinguistics*. New York: Harcourt Brace Jovanovich.

Clark, H. H., & Haviland, S. E. (1977). Comprehension and the given-new contract. In R. O. Freedle (Ed.), *Discourse production and comprehension* (pp. 1–40). Hillsdale, NJ: Lawrence Erlbaum Associates.

Clark, H. H., & Schober, M. F. (1992). Asking questions and influencing answers. In J. M. Tanur (Ed.), *Questions about questions. Inquiries into the cognitive bases of surveys* (pp. 15–47). New York: Russell Sage.

Clark, H. H., & Wilkes-Gibbs, D. (1986). Referring as a collaborative process. *Cognition, 22*, 1–39.

Conway, M., & Ross, M. (1984). Getting what you want by revising what you had. *Journal of Personality and Social Psychology, 47*, 738–748.

DeMaio, T. J. (1984). Social desirability and survey measurement: A review. In C. F. Turner & E. Martin (Eds.), *Surveying subjective phenomena* (Vol. 2, pp. 257–282). New York: Russell Sage.

Dodd, D. H., & Bradshaw, J. M. (1980). Leading questions and memory: Pragmatic constraints. *Journal of Verbal Learning and Verbal Behavior, 19*, 695–704.

Dulany, D. E., & Hilton, D. J. (1991). Conversational implicature, conscious representation, and the conjunction fallacy. *Social Cognition, 9*, 85–110.

Eiser, J. R. (1990). *Social judgment*. Milton Keynes: Open University Press.

Festinger, L. (1954). A theory of social comparison processes. *Human Relations, 7*, 117–140.

Festinger, L. (1957). *A theory of cognitive dissonance*. Stanford: Stanford University Press.

Fiedler, K. (1988). The dependence of the conjunction fallacy on subtle linguistic factors. *Psychological Research, 50*, 123–129.

Garrod, S., & Anderson, A. (1987). Saying what you mean in a dialogue: A study in conceptual and semantic co-ordination. *Cognition, 27*, 181–218.

Gigerenzer, G. (1991). How to make cognitive illusions disappear: Beyond "heuristics and biases." In W. Stroebe & M. Hewstone (Eds.), *European review of social psychology* (Vol. 2, pp. 83–115). Chichester: Wiley.

Gonzales, M. H., Manning, D. J., & Haugen, J. A. (1992). Explaining our sins: Factors influencing offender accounts and anticipated victim responses. *Journal of Personality and Social Psychology, 62*, 958–971.

Gonzales, M. H., Pederson, J. H., Manning, D. J., & Wetter, D. W. (1990). Pardon my gaffe: Effects of sex, status, and consequence severity on accounts. *Journal of Personality and Social Psychology, 58*, 610–621.

Grice, H. P. (1975). Logic and conversation. In P. Cole & J. L. Morgan (Eds.), *Syntax and semantics 3: Speech acts* (pp. 41–58). New York: Academic Press.

Heider, F. (1958). *The psychology of interpersonal relations.* New York: Wiley.

Helmholtz, H. (1903). Optisches über Malerei [optical aspects of painting]. In H. Helmholtz (Ed.), *Vorträge und Reden. Zweiter Band* (pp. 93–135). Braunschweig: Vieweg und Sohn.

Helson, H. (1964). *Adaptation-level theory.* New York: Harper & Row.

Higgins, E. T. (1981). The "communication game": Implications for social cognition and persuasion. In E. T. Higgins, C. P. Herman, & M. P. Zanna (Eds.), *Social cognition: The Ontario Symposium* (Vol. 1, pp. 343–392). Hillsdale, NJ: Lawrence Erlbaum Associates.

Higgins, E. T., & Bargh, J. A. (1987). Social cognition and social perception. In M. R. Rosenzweig & L. W. Porter (Eds.), *Annual review of psychology* (Vol. 38, pp. 369–425). Palo Alto, CA: Annual Reviews.

Higgins, E. T., & Lurie, L. (1983). Context, categorization, and memory: The "change-of-standard" effect. *Cognitive Psychology, 15,* 525–547.

Higgins, E. T., & McCann, C. D. (1984). Social encoding and subsequent attitudes, impressions, and memory: "Context-driven" and motivational aspects of processing. *Journal of Personality and Social Psychology, 47,* 26–39.

Higgins, E. T., & Rholes, W. S. (1978). "Saying is believing": Effects of message modification on memory and liking for the person described. *Journal of Experimental Social Psychology, 14,* 363–378.

Higgins, E. T., Rholes, W. S., & Jones, C. R. (1977). Category accessibility and impression formation. *Journal of Experimental Social Psychology, 13,* 141–154.

Higgins, E. T., & Stangor, C. (1988a). A "change-of-standard" perspective on the relations among context, judgment, and memory. *Journal of Personality and Social Psychology, 54,* 181–192.

Higgins, E. T., & Stangor, C. (1988b). Context-driven social judgment and memory: When "behavior engulfs the field" in reconstructive memory. In D. Bar-Tal & A. W. Kruglanski (Eds.), *The social psychology of knowledge* (pp. 262–298). Cambridge: Cambridge University Press.

Hilton, D. J. (1990). Conversational processes and causal explanation. *Psychological Bulletin, 107,* 65–81.

Hilton, D. J., & Slugoski, B. R. (1986). Knowledge-based causal attribution: The abnormal conditions focus model. *Psychological Review, 93,* 75–88.

Hippler, H. J., & Schwarz, N. (1986). Not forbidding isn't allowing: The cognitive basis of the forbid-allow asymmetry. *Public Opinion Quarterly, 50,* 87–96.

Holtgraves, T., & Joong-nam, Y. (1990). Politeness as universal: Cross-cultural perceptions of request strategies and inferences based on their use. *Journal of Personality and Social Psychology, 59,* 719–729.

Holtgraves, T., & Srull, T. K. (1989). The effects of positive self-descriptions on impressions: General principles and individual differences. *Personality and Social Psychology Bulletin, 15,* 452–462.

Jones, E. E., & Nisbett, R. E. (1972). The actor and the observer: Divergent perceptions of the causes of behavior. In E. E. Jones, D. E. Kanouse, H. H. Kelley, R. E. Nisbett, S. Valins, & B. Weiner (Eds.), *Attribution: Perceiving the causes of behavior.* Morristown, NJ: General Learning Press.

Jöreskog, K. G. (1971). Statistical analysis of sets of congeneric tests. *Psychometrika, 36,* 109–133.

Kahneman, D., & Miller, D. T. (1986). Norm theory: Comparing reality to its alternatives. *Psychological Review, 93,* 136–153.

Kahneman, D., Slovic, P., & Tversky, A. (Eds.). (1982). *Judgment under uncertainty: Heuristics and biases.* New York: Cambridge University Press.

Kahneman, D., & Tversky, A. (1972). Subjective probability: A judgment of representativeness. *Cognitive Psychology, 3,* 430–454.

Kahneman, D., & Tversky, A. (1973). On the psychology of prediction. *Psychological Review, 80,* 237–251.

Krauss, R. M., & Weinheimer, S. (1964). Changes in reference phrases as a function of frequency of usage in social interaction: A preliminary study. *Psychonomic Science, 1,* 113–114.

Krauss, R. M., & Weinheimer, S. (1966). Concurrent feedback, confirmation, and the encoding of referents in verbal communication. *Journal of Personality and Social Psychology, 4*, 343–346.

Levinson, S. (1983). *Pragmatics.* Cambridge: Cambridge University Press.

Lindsay, D. S., & Johnson, M. K. (1989). The eyewitness suggestibility effect and memory for source. *Memory & Cognition, 17*, 349–358.

Loftus, E. F. (1975). Leading questions and the eyewitness report. *Cognitive Psychology, 7*, 560–572.

Loftus, E. F., & Hoffman, H. G. (1989). Misinformation and memory: The creation of new memories. *Journal of Experimental Psychology: General, 118*, 100–104.

Loftus, E. F., Klinger, M. R., Smith, K. F., & Fiedler, J. (1990). A tale of two questions: Benefits of asking more than one question. *Public Opinion Quarterly, 54*, 330–345.

Lord, F. M., & Novick, M. R. (1974). *Statistical theories of mental test scores.* Reading, MA: Addison-Wesley.

Manis, M., Cornell, S. D., & Moore, J. C. (1974). Transmission of attitude-relevant information through a communication chain. *Journal of Personality and Social Psychology, 30*, 81–94.

Martin, E. (1984). The task posed by survey questions. In C. F. Turner & E. Martin (Eds.), *Surveying subjective phenomena* (Vol. 1, pp. 295–300). New York: Russell Sage.

McCann, C. D., & Higgins, E. T. (1992). Personal and contextual factors in communication: A review of the "communication game." In G. R. Semin & K. Fiedler (Eds.), *Language, interaction and social cognition* (pp. 144–172). London: Sage.

McCloskey, M., & Zaragoza, M. (1985). Misleading postevent information and memory for events: Arguments and evidence against the memory impairment hypothesis. *Journal of Experimental Psychology: General, 114*, 1–16.

McGill, A. (1989). Context effects in judgments of causation. *Journal of Personality and Social Psychology, 57*, 189–200.

Newcomb, T. (1961). *The acquaintance process.* New York: Holt, Rinehart & Winston.

Nisbett, R. E., Caputo, C., Legant, P., & Maracek, J. (1973). Behavior as seen by the actor and as seen by the observer. *Journal of Personality and Social Psychology, 27*, 154–164.

Nisbett, R. E., & Ross, L. (1980). *Human inference: Strategies and shortcomings of social judgment.* Englewood Cliffs, NJ: Prentice Hall.

Orne, M. (1962). On the psychology of the psychological experiment: With particular reference to demand characteristics and their implications. *American Psychologist, 17*, 776–783.

Ottati, V. C., Riggle, E., Wyer, R. S., Schwarz, N., & Kuklinski, J. (1989). Cognitive and affective bases of opinion survey responses. *Journal of Personality and Social Psychology, 57*, 404–415.

Parducci, A. (1965). Category judgment: A range-frequency model. *Psychological Review, 72*, 407–418.

Parducci, A., & Wedell, D. H. (1986). The category effect with rating scales: Number of categories, number of stimuli, and method of presentation. *Journal of Experimental Psychology: Human Perception and Performance, 12*, 496–516.

Paulhus, D. L. (1991). Measurement and control of response bias. In J. P. Robinson, P. R. Shaver, & L. S. Wrightsman (Eds.), *Measures of personality and social psychological attitudes* (pp. 17–59). San Diego: Academic Press.

Postman, L., & Miller, G. A. (1945). Anchoring of temporal judgments. *American Journal of Psychology, 58*, 43–53.

Ross, M. (1989). Relation of implicit theories to the construction of personal histories. *Psychological Review, 96*, 315–340.

Ross, M., & Conway, M. (1986). Remembering one's own past: The construction of personal histories. In R. M. Sorrentino & E. T. Higgins (Eds.), *Handbook of motivation and cognition* (Vol. I, pp. 122–144). New York: Guilford.

Rugg, D., & Cantril, H. (1944). The wording of questions. In H. Cantril (Ed.), *Gauging public opinion* (pp. 23–50). Princeton: University Press.

Schlenker, B. R. (1980). *Impression management. The self-concept, social identity, and interpersonal relations.* Monterey, CA: Brooks-Cole.

Schober, M. F., & Clark, H. H. (1989). Understanding by addressees and overhearers. *Cognitive Psychology, 21,* 211–232.

Schuman, H., & Presser, S. (1981). *Questions and answers in attitude surveys.* Orlando, FL: Academic Press.

Schwarz, N. (1990). Assessing frequency reports of mundane behaviors: Contributions of cognitive psychology to questionnaire construction. In C. Hendrick & M. Clark (Eds.), *Review of personality and social psychology* (Vol. 11, pp. 98–119). Beverly Hills, CA: Sage.

Schwarz, N., Bless, H., Strack, F., Klumpp, G., Rittenauer-Schatka, H., & Simons, A. (1991). Ease of retrieval as information: Another look at the availability heuristic. *Journal of Personality and Social Psychology, 61,* 195–202.

Schwarz, N., Hippler, H. J., Deutsch, B., & Strack, F. (1985). Response scales: Effects of category range on reported behavior and comparative judgments. *Public Opinion Quarterly, 49,* 388–495.

Schwarz, N., Knäuper, B., Hippler, H. J., Noelle-Neumann, E., & Clark, L. (1991). Rating scales: Numeric values may change the meaning of scale labels. *Public Opinion Quarterly, 55,* 570–582.

Schwarz, N., & Scheuring, B. (1988). Judgments of relationship satisfaction: Inter- and intraindividual comparisons as a function of questionnaire structure. *European Journal of Social Psychology, 18,* 485–496.

Schwarz, N., & Strack, F. (1991). Context effects in attitude surveys: Applying cognitive theory to social research. In W. Stroebe & M. Hewstone (Eds.), *European review of social psychology* (Vol. 2, pp. 31–50). Chichester: Wiley.

Schwarz, N., Strack, F., Hilton, D., & Naderer, G. (1991). Base rates, representativeness, and the logic of conversation: The contextual relevance of "irrelevant" information. *Social Cognition, 9,* 67–84.

Schwarz, N., Strack, F., & Mai, H. P. (1991). Assimilation and contrast effects in part-whole question sequences: A conversational-logic analysis. *Public Opinion Quarterly, 55,* 3–23.

Schwarz, N., Strack, F. Müller, G., & Chassein, B. (1988). The range of response alternatives may determine the meaning of the question: Further evidence on informative functions of response alternatives. *Social Cognition, 6,* 107–117.

Searle, J. R. (1975). Indirect speech acts. In P. Cole & J. L. Morgan (Eds.), *Syntax and semantics, Vol. 3: Speech acts* (pp. 59–82). New York: Seminar Press.

Searle, J. R. (1976). The classification of illocutionary acts. *Language in Society, 5,* 1–24.

Semin, G. R., & Strack F. (1980). The plausibility of the implausible: A critique of Snyder & Swann. *European Journal of Social Psychology, 10,* 379–388.

Sherman, S. J., Ahlm, K., Berman, L., & Lynn, S. (1978). Contrast effects and the relationship to subsequent behavior. *Journal of Experimental Social Psychology, 14,* 340–350.

Sherman, S. J., & Corty, E. (1984). Cognitive heuristics. In R. S. Wyer & T. K. Srull (Eds.), *Handbook of social cognition* (Vol. 1, pp. 189–286). Hillsdale, NJ: Lawrence Erlbaum Associates.

Skov, R. B., & Sherman, S. J. (1986). Information gathering processes: Diagnosticity, hypothesis-confirmatory strategies, and perceived hypothesis confirmation. *Journal of Experimental Social Psychology, 22,* 93–121.

Smith, T. W. (1979). Happiness: Time trends, seasonal variations, inter-survey differences, and other mysteries. *Social Psychology Quarterly, 42,* 18–30.

Smith, V. L., & Ellsworth, P. C. (1987). The social psychology of eyewitness accuracy: Misleading questions and communicator expertise. *Journal of Applied Psychology, 72,* 294–300.

Snyder, M., & Swann, W. B. (1978). Hypothesis-testing processes in social interaction. *Journal of Personality and Social Psychology, 36,* 1202–1212.

Srull, T. K., & Wyer, R. S. (1979). The role of category accessibility in the interpretation of information about persons: Some determinants and implications. *Journal of Personality and Social Psychology, 37,* 1660–1672.

Srull, T. K., & Wyer, R. S. (1980). Category accessibility and social perception: Some implications for the study of person memory and interpersonal judgments. *Journal of Personality and Social Psychology, 38,* 841–856.

Storms, M. D. (1973). Videotape and the attribution process: Reversing actors' and observers' point of view. *Journal of Personality and Social Psychology, 27,* 165–175.

Strack, F. (in press). *Kognitive und kommunikative Einflüsse in standardisierten Befragungssituationen* [Cognitive and communicative influences in standardized question situations]. Heidelberg: Springer.

Strack, F. (1992). "Order effects" in survey research: Activative and informative functions of preceding questions. In N. Schwarz & S. Sudman (Eds.), *Order effects in survey research* (pp. 23–34). New York: Springer.

Strack, F., & Bless, H. (in press). Memory for non-occurrences: Metacognitive and presuppositional strategies. *Journal of Memory and Language.*

Strack, F., & Martin, L. L. (1987). Thinking, judging, and communicating: A process account of context effects in attitude surveys. In H. J. Hippler, N. Schwarz, & S. Sudman (Eds.), *Social information processing and survey methodology* (pp. 123–148). New York: Springer.

Strack, F., Martin, L. L., & Schwarz, N. (1988). Priming and communication: Social determinants of information use in judgments of life satisfaction. *European Journal of Social Psychology, 18,* 429–442.

Strack, F., Schwarz, N. (1992). Communicative influences in standardized question situations: The case of implicit collaboration. In G. Semin & K. Fiedler (Eds.), *Language and social cognition* (pp. 173–193). London: Sage.

Strack, F., Schwarz, N., Chassein, B., Kern, D., & Wagner, D. (1990). The salience of comparison standards and the activation of social norms: Consequences for judgments of happiness and their communication. *British Journal of Social Psychology, 29,* 303–314.

Strack, F., Schwarz, N., & Wänke, M. (1991). Semantic and pragmatic aspects of context effects in social and psychological research. *Social Cognition, 9,* 111–125.

Taylor, S. E., & Fiske, S. T. (1978). Salience, attention, and attribution: Top-of-the-head phenomena. In L. Berkowitz (Ed.), *Advances in experimental social psychology* (Vol. 11, pp. 249–288). New York: Academic Press.

Tedeschi, J. T. (1981). *Impression management. Theory and social psychological research.* New York: Academic Press.

Thurstone, L. L. (1928). Attitudes can be measured. *American Journal of Sociology, 33,* 529–554.

Tourangeau, R., Rasinski, K. A., & Bradburn, N. (1991). Measuring happiness in surveys: A test of the subtraction hypothesis. *Public Opinion Quarterly, 55,* 255–266.

Trope, Y., & Bassok, M. (1982). Confirmatory and diagnosing strategies in hypothesis testing. *Journal of Personality and Social Psychology, 43,* 22–34.

Turner, C. F., & Martin, E. (Eds.). (1984). *Surveying subjective phenomena (Vols. 1 and 2).* New York: Russell Sage.

Tversky, A., & Kahneman, D. (1973). Availability: A heuristic for judging frequency and probability. *Cognitive Psychology, 4,* 207–232.

Tversky, A., & Kahneman, D. (1974). Judgment under uncertainty: Heuristics and biases. *Science, 185,* 1124–1131.

Tversky, A., & Kahneman, D. (1983). Extensional versus intuitive reasoning: The conjunction fallacy in probability judgment. *Psychological Review, 90,* 293–315.

Tversky, B., & Tuchin, M. (1989). A reconciliation of the evidence on eyewitness testimony: Comments on McCloskey and Zaragoza (1985). *Journal of Experimental Psychology: General, 118,* 86–91.

Upshaw, H. S. (1965). The effect of variable perspectives on judgments of opinion statements for Thurstone scales: Equal-appearing intervals. *Journal of Personality and Social Psychology, 2,* 60–69.

Upshaw, H. S. (1978). Social influence on attitudes and on anchoring of congeneric attitude scales. *Journal of Experimental Social Psychology, 14,* 327–339.

Upshaw, H. S. (1984). Output processes in judgment. In R. S. Wyer & T. K. Srull (Eds.), *Handbook of social cognition* (Vol. 3, pp. 237–256). Hillsdale, NJ: Lawrence Erlbaum Associates.

Upshaw, H. S., & Ostrom, T. M. (1984). Psychological perspective in attitude research. In J. R. Eiser (Ed.), *Attitudinal judgment* (pp. 23–41). New York: Springer-Verlag.

Volkmann, J. (1951). Scales of judgment and their implications for social psychology. In J. H. Rohrer & M. Sherif (Eds.), *Social psychology at the crossroads* (pp. 273–294). New York: Harper.

Wyer, R. S. (1981). An information-processing perspective on social attribution. In J. H. Harvey, W. Ickes, & R. F. Kidd (Eds.), *New directions in attribution research* (Vol. 3, pp. 359–404). Hillsdale, NJ: Lawrence Erlbaum Associates.

Wyer, R. S., & Srull, T. K. (1989). *Memory and cognition in its social context*. Hillsdale, NJ: Lawrence Erlbaum Associates.

Wyer, R. S., Strack, F., & Fuhrman, R. (1988). Der Erwerb von Informationen über Personen: Einflüsse von Aufgabenstellung und persönlichen Erwartungen [The acquisition of information about persons: Task influences and personal expectations]. *Zeitschrift für Experimentelle und Angewandte Psychologie, 35*, 657–688.

7 Affective Causes and Consequences of Social Information Processing

Gerald L. Clore
University of Illinois

Norbert Schwarz
University of Michigan

Michael Conway
Concordia University

Contents

The study of affect is as old as scientific psychology. One hundred years ago, two of the most influential psychologists were Wilhelm Wundt and William James. Both were centrally concerned with affect but in different ways—Wundt was a structuralist and James was a functionalist. Wundt (1874) was concerned with the underlying structure of emotions, and his conclusions were similar to those of recent investigators concerning the dimensions of emotional quality (e.g., Russell, 1980). But James was more concerned with function than structure. When it came to questions of structure and classification, James believed that the number of emotions was infinite, and hence not susceptible to systematic treatment. He said that he "should as lief read verbal descriptions of the shapes of the rocks on a New Hampshire farm as toil through the literature of emotion . . ." (1890, p. 448).

Emotion is again a central problem in psychology, and the distinction between structure and function is still important. This distinction is reflected in the organization of this chapter. Before reviewing work on structure and function, however, we need to establish what we mean by *emotion*. Hence, the first section asks, "What Is an Emotion?" Issues of terminology turn out to be important because there is not broad agreement on certain key issues in the study of emotion. This is followed by the second section, "The Cognitive Causes of Emotion," which takes a cognitive approach to Wundt's question about the structure of emotion. The third and final section, "The Cognitive Consequences of Emotion," takes a cognitive approach to James's question about the function of emotion.

WHAT IS AN EMOTION?

A central issue about emotion that social psychologists have addressed recently concerns whether the concept of emotion can be defined. Russell (1991) argued that it cannot be defined in classical terms, and that the best one can do is specify the features that tend to occur in prototypical examples (see also Fehr & Russell, 1984). Russell proposed that prototypes are required for understanding lay concepts of emotion, but necessary and sufficient conditions still might be sought for arriving at a technical definition.

In response, Clore and Ortony (1991) argued that these two approaches to definition serve different functions. Prototypes contain typical attributes and are used to identify instances of emotion, but concepts, whether lay concepts or technical ones, contain more than a list of typical attributes. They specify the relations among the attributes, and are therefore useful for reasoning about emotion. That is, concepts contain theoretical information that can be used to support reasoning about emotion. They also provide back-up criteria for identifying emotions when the matching-to-prototype heuristic fails.

As an alternative, Clore and Ortony suggested a combined approach. They argued that if people had only prototypes of emotion, they would be able to identify an emotion, but they would have no understanding of why emotions have the attributes they do or how a deviant example still could be a category member. Conversely, if people had only classically represented concepts, they would have a hard time identifying emotions. They suggest combining the best aspect of prototype theory, namely, that category membership often can be determined by similarity to a prototype, with the best aspect of the classical view, namely, that members of the same category often share properties that are not perceptually available.

How Do Emotions Differ from Nonemotions?

To assess theories of emotion, it is important to be able to distinguish emotions from nonemotions. Several investigators have focused on the problem, including Shields (1984), Mees (1985), and Ortony, Clore, and Foss (1987). Although much of the research concerns emotion words, the focus is on the attributes of the psychological conditions referred to by the words that make them emotional or nonemotional. Emotions are not primarily linguistic phenomena, of course, but the best access we have to the variety of emotions is through language. The power of words to distinguish many emotions, and to do so with precision, greatly exceeds what can be done in terms of physiology, expression, or behavior.

The need to distinguish emotions from nonemotions is evident in approaches in which dimensions are derived from judgments of the similarity among words denoting emotions. For example, the sample of states on which Russell's (1980) well-known dimensions are based includes a number, such as, sleepy, tired, and calm, that may not be good examples of emotions (Morgan & Heise, 1988). One of the reasons for disagreement among empirically derived lists of emotions is that no effort is usually made to control whether subjects consider the candidate terms in the context of "feeling something" or "being something." Clore and Ortony (1988) argued that, in English, good examples of emotion terms seem equally emotional in both feeling and being contexts. For example, "being angry" sounds just as emotional as "feeling angry," but this is not the case for such conditions as "neglected." "Feeling neglected" is emotional, but "being neglected" is not. If one were aware of being neglected and one cared about being neglected, then "being neglected" might cause an emotion, but "being neglected" is clearly not itself an emotion.

Ortony et al. (1987) conducted an analysis of 600 words taken from frequently used lists of emotions. The goal was to arrive at a principled basis on which to determine which ones were emotions and why. They concluded that emotion terms refer to *internal mental states that are focused primarily on affect* (where *affect* simply refers to the perceived goodness or badness of something). Terms judged to be poor examples fail to satisfy one or more critical conditions. For example, some of the rejected terms refer to what they called *external conditions* (e.g., abandoned), rather than *internal conditions*; some refer to *bodily states* (e.g., tired), rather than *mental states*; and some to *nonstates* (e.g., faithful), rather than *states*. Some terms that did refer to states did not qualify as emotions, because they were *behavioral states* (e.g., cowering) or *cognitive states* (e.g., confused), rather than *affective states* (e.g., happy). About 200 affective terms were isolated that were good candidates for emotions. The 600 words then were analyzed in a scaling study (Clore, Ortony, & Foss, 1987). The results showed that this characterization embodies the same distinctions as those made implicitly by subjects rating the terms. It became clear that good examples of emotion terms (e.g., *adore, afraid, aggravated, angry, anguished, annoyed, anxious, apprehensive, ashamed, awe-struck,* etc.) do not refer directly to events, bodily reactions, feelings, or behavior, but to the mental events that ties these things together.

How Do Emotions, Moods, and Affect Differ?

In our usage, affect refers simply to valence—the positive and negative aspect of things. All emotions are affective, but not all affective things are emotions. For example, preferences and attitudes are affective, but they are not emotions. Emotions are states, whereas preferences and attitudes are dispositions. This distinction is reflected in the characterization of emotion noted earlier as "internal mental states that are primarily focused on affect." However, that characterization did not distinguish emotions from moods. Moods are also affective states.

The distinction between emotions and moods has recently attracted considerable attention. For example, they have been distinguished in terms of external versus internal concerns, present versus future orientation, and object versus objectless focus. For Morris (1992), emotions concern appraisals of external circumstances, whereas moods concern the state of internal resources. Batson, Shaw, and Oleson (1992) suggested that emotion concerns the present, whereas mood concerns anticipation of the future. Schwarz and Clore (1988) and Frijda (1986) discussed emotions as having a specific focus, whereas moods are nonspecific. A related emphasis of Averill's (1980) was that emotions have an object that moods may not have. We shall emphasize this distinction. Thus, one might experience the emotion of sadness over the death of one's pet, and this event might also leave one in a sad mood that would no longer be specifically about the loss of the pet, but would involve a general gloomy perspective along with dysphoric feelings. But moods need not be caused by emotions. One can have a series of quite minor setbacks, none of which give rise to an emotion, but which collectively leave a residue of depression or irritability. In our usage, then, *mood* refers to the feeling state, which need not be about anything, whereas *emotion* refers to how one feels in combination with what the feeling is about. These characteristics are reflected in our use of language that implies specific referents for emotions, but not for moods. Thus, we say that we are afraid "of" something and angry "about" something, but that we are "in" a happy or sad mood.

One consequence of this stance is that cognitive causes may be essential for emotion, but not for mood (Clore, Ortony, Dienes, & Fujita, 1993). Thus, a person can be in a depressed mood on a cold, dreary morning simply because the absence of sunlight inhibited the release of a particular hormone, rather than as a result of having appraised the day's opportunities as unpromising. Similarly, antidepressants may change the mood of depressed individuals by acting directly on their neurochemistry. These changes tend to alter moods, rather than emotions, although they may change the likelihood of positive or negative emotions.

The basic cognitive model is that emotions result from ongoing, automatic, but implicit appraisals of situations with respect to whether they are positive or negative for one's goals and concerns (e.g., Arnold, 1960). Moods may have other causes as well. The experience of emotion serves as internal communication (Oatley & Johnson-Laird, 1987), feedback (Carver & Scheier, 1990), or information (Schwarz & Clore, 1983) about the nature and urgency of the situation. The output of this process has control precedence (Frijda, 1986), serving to reorder information processing priorities (Simon, 1967).

A cognitive view in no way implies that emotion is not also a set of neurochemical, physiological, and muscular changes; a set of universal social signals; and a set of motivational and perhaps behavioral inclinations that have some commonality across species. The idea that emotions are caused by cognitive appraisals of situations does not imply that people are rational, nor is it implied that people cannot be surprised by their own emotions, or that people necessarily know why they are happy or upset. It does imply that there is order to emotions, that emotions serve specific identifiable functions for the organism, and that they can be studied to advantage by the methods currently available to investigators of social cognition.

What Are the Necessary Conditions for Emotion?

Emotions are multifaceted phenomena, and it seems unlikely that any one feature can be said to be a sufficient basis for deciding that a psychological state is an emotion. But are there conditions that are necessary? For example, much work has been done on facial expressions, and expressions often serve as reliable signals of the presence of a particular emotion, but clearly they are not sufficient, because actors routinely pose expressions without necessarily being emotional first. Indeed, Ekman (1992b), one of the chief proponents of expression as a central aspect of emotion, now says that a distinctive facial expression is not a requirement for an emotion.

However, feeling often is used synonymously with emotion. Is feeling either a necessary or a sufficient condition? That feeling is probably not a sufficient condition can be seen by considering instances in which the feelings are produced directly in the laboratory without an emotional cause. For example, stimulation of the posterior hypothalamus in the cat produces what is called "sham rage" (Bard, 1928). If such a procedure in humans gave rise to reports of anger-like feelings or angry behavior, most people would agree that "sham anger" would be a better label for the state than "anger," because part of what we mean by anger is that one is angry about something (see Oatley & Johnson-Laird, 1987, for an alternative view).

Is feeling a necessary condition? Linguistic tests suggest it might be. For example, it is odd to say "I was angry but I did not feel anything," but quite acceptable to say "I was angry but I did not do or say anything." On such grounds, feeling might be a good candidate for a necessary condition for emotion. However, this requires that one deal satisfactorily with situations in which the person acts emotional and perhaps can be shown to have relevant physiological activity, but reports no emotional feelings (Lang, 1988).

If one decides that feelings are necessary, is the appropriate physiology to support such feelings also necessary? It may be a mistake to assume, as often is done, that emotional feelings amount to nothing more than sensing particular patterns of autonomic activity. Some emotional feelings, such as contempt (Niewenhuyse, Offenberg, & Frijda, 1987) or pride, can be experienced without perceiving any physiological changes (Mees, 1990). Conversely, emotional feelings may include distinctive thoughts. For example, Parrott (1988) pointed out that the experience of jealousy is more than a dull ache in the stomach or other bodily symptoms. The jealous person also experiences troubling thoughts and images of his or her loved one in the arms of another and so on. From this view, the concept of emotional feelings might include all of the experiential aspects of emotion, including the subjective experience of thoughts, bodily sensations, awareness of desires, and the feedback from posture, expressions, and anticipated or actual behavior.

What about cognitive processes—the largely unconscious appraisal activity that gives rise to emotional thoughts and feelings? A coherent argument can be made that a necessary condition for a state to be an emotion is that it is caused by a cognitive evaluation or appraisal of something as positive or negative. In a review of current definitions of emotion, Strongman (1987) suggested that of the various components of emotion sometimes mentioned in definitions, the cognitive component may be the only necessary one. Ortony and Clore (1989) argued for the necessity of appraisal processes in emotion by considering the relation of feelings to emotions as analogous to the relation between symptoms and diseases. For example, feelings function as a symptom of emotion just as temperature is a symptom of disease. But before we conclude that a person has a particular disease, we must be able to make a good case that the symptom has the right kind of cause. It is not the presence of symptoms, but the presence of symptoms that are assumed to be appropriately caused that result in diagnoses. Similarly, with respect to emotions, it is not feelings however they are caused that are important, but feelings that are assumed to arise from an emotional source (Ortony & Clore, 1989).

What Is Basic About Basic Emotions?

In chemistry, the scientific strategy that turned out to be best involved searching for basic elements. Particular chemical elements were found that are irreducible, meaning that there are no more primitive entities at the same level of analysis. It became possible to characterize all physical matter as combinations of basic chemical elements. A similar path was pursued in the study of color vision. All possible colors turned out to be combinations of two or three basic colors. In the study of emotion, too, the concept of basic emotions has been popular for over a hundred years (e.g., Ekman, 1992a; James, 1884).

However, Ortony and Turner (1990) argued that the concept is too ill defined to anchor emotion research on a firm footing. As a result, there is little agreement on such issues as how many basic emotions exist. The possibilities include two (Weiner & Graham, 1984), three (Watson, 1930), four (Gray, 1982), five (Oatley & Johnson-Laird, 1987), six (Ekman, Friesen, & Ellsworth, 1982), seven (McDougall, 1926), eight (Plutchik, 1980), nine (Tomkins, 1984), ten (Izard, 1971), or perhaps eleven (Arnold, 1960). In addition, some of the emotions that are called basic by some investigators are questionable as examples of emotions. For example, it has been argued that interest (Izard, 1971) and surprise (Plutchik, 1980) fail to meet reasonable criteria for being emotions at all, let alone basic emotions (Clore & Ortony, 1988). Ortony and Turner argued convincingly that the usual logical criteria for basicness in other fields have not been addressed by emotion theorists. For example, basic emotion theorists have not shown that emotions believed to be basic are irreducible (for a relevant exchange, see Frijda, 1987; Oatley & Johnson-Laird, 1987). Also, they have not specified how basic emotions combine to form nonbasic emotions.

In reply, defenders of the idea (Ekman, 1992a; Izard, 1992; Panksepp, 1992) pointed out that, despite uncertainty about the total number of basic emotions, good agreement exists on the basicness of some emotions (e.g., anger, fear, joy). They also indicate that their idea of basicness mainly concerns whether an emotion has an identifiable biological substrate. Such emotions are believed to occur more often across cultures and across species, whereas nonbasic emotions are more likely to show cross-cultural variability and species specificity. Some of the evidence for basicness comes from the extensive research by Ekman and his colleagues, who have isolated distinctive facial expressions for emotions believed to be basic (Ekman et al., 1982). They have also shown that these emotions are recognized reliably even in culturally remote societies (Levenson, Ekman, Heider, & Friesen, in press), and that some of them have distinctive physiological markers (Ekman, Levenson, & Friesen, 1983).

Ortony and Turner (1990) suggested that one might develop an alternative, component model, in which basicness resides not in the emotional expressions, but in some components of them. For example, furrowing the brows, a component of anger expression, may indicate effort. They may occur in expressions of anger, not because anger expressions operate as a functional whole, but because angry situations are likely to involve effortful responding. However, Shaver, Wu, and Schwartz (1992) argued that the existence of subcomponents that are basic does not argue against the basicness of the whole.

Some emotion theorists (e.g., Plutchik, 1980) use a palette metaphor when discussing how basic emotions (like colors) combine. Scherer (1984), reflecting the view that there are basic components of emotion rather than basic emotions, prefers the metaphor of a kaleidoscope, whereby any number of emotions can emerge from combinations of components. At the same time, Scherer suggests that a degree of prewiring probably constrains the possible combinations. Thus, the organism may be prepared for various kinds of emotional syndromes without there being a small set of basic emotions.

Firm conclusions about basic emotions would be premature at this time. It is not clear whether the concept will turn out to be critical to the study of emotion. However, Ortony and Turner's (1990) challenge has encouraged investigators to be more specific about what they mean, so that the utility of the basic emotions concept can be assessed.

Distinguishing Emotions

Emotions have many facets. Some emotions are characterized by distinctive patterns of thought (Parrott, 1988) and feeling (Davitz, 1969; De Rivera, 1977; Russell, 1980). A fair number have distinctive facial expressions (Darwin, 1872; Ekman, Friesen, & Ellsworth, 1972; Izard, 1971) and perhaps vocal properties (Scherer, 1986). Some emotions emerge developmentally before others (Campos & Barrett, 1984). A few also can be distinguished in terms of the patterns of autonomic (Ekman et al., 1983), and neurological activity (Panksepp, 1992). Some emotions are represented by many words, and some may not be represented at all in certain cultures and languages (Lutz & White, 1986). Much effort has been invested on the faith that some emotions have distinctive motor programs or action tendencies (Berkowitz, in press; Frijda, 1986; Leventhal, 1982; Plutchik, 1980). Clearly a number of features might differentiate one emotion from another. There are at least four major approaches to the question of how specific emotions differ from each other. These include psychometric, physiological, expressive, and cognitive approaches.

Psychometric. Investigators taking the psychometric approach have generally collected ratings of emotional words, faces, or experiences. These are usually analyzed using factor analytic or multidimensional scaling techniques (Russell, 1980). Following in the footsteps of Wundt, the object is to determine the underlying perceptual dimensions. These are usually characterized as a dimension of valence (e.g., positive vs. negative) and a dimension of arousal (e.g., excited vs. relaxed). The facet of emotion that is focused on in this approach is presumably how the various emotions feel when experienced.

Physiological. Because the experience of emotion often has strong bodily components, many investigators have sought to distinguish among individual emotions physiologically. However, this has proved surprisingly difficult. Lack of progress in this endeavor was an important argument in favor of Schachter and Singer's (1962) popular view that the physiological component of emotion could be reduced to nonspecific autonomic arousal. Their view was that distinctions among emotions depend on the interpretations that people place on their experience of nonspecific autonomic arousal. Although this view contributed to the perceived viability of a cognitive approach to emotion, the theory is no longer a strong contender, in part, because most investigators believe that different emotions must have some distinctive physiology. Modest success has been reported by Ekman et al. (1983) in differentiating emotions in terms of patterns of heart rate and skin conductance. Despite the scarcity of systematic data, the effort to map emotions physiologically still seems promising, because it jibes with one's personal experience (e.g., that the feeling of being flushed when embarrassed is quite different from feeling a pit in one's stomach when anxious).

Expressive. Investigators have been much more successful at distinguishing emotions in terms of facial expressions (Ekman et al., 1972). For example, the wide-eyed look of fear is easily discriminable from the glare of anger. By painstakingly mapping the muscles of the human face, a reliable coding system has been developed for facial expressions (Ekman & Friesen, 1975). Despite the demanding requirements for using the system, it has achieved wide currency among emotion researchers. In addition, facial electromyographic activity (EMG) that is too subtle to be socially perceptible has been shown to vary as a function of the pleasant versus unpleasant nature of visual stimuli (e.g., Caccioppo, Bush, & Tassinary, 1992).

Cognitive. In addition to the fact that emotions differ in terms of how they feel, in their physiology, and in the facial expressions that make them known, emotions also differ from each other in terms of the situations that give rise to them or, more exactly, the cognitive representations of those situations. For example, the situations in which fear arises are different from those in which disappointment or nostalgia arise. The second section of the chapter focuses on recent work on the cognitive contribution to emotion variation.

THE COGNITIVE CAUSES OF EMOTION

Having discussed some general issues about the nature of emotion, we shift focus to Wundt's question concerning the structure of emotional differentiation. Turning aside James' implied admonition to avoid such problems, we review some recent attempts to classify emotions. Agreement with James that the number of possible emotions may be infinite need not imply that they have no order. Although a merely descriptive approach might be endless and pointless, recent attempts to classify emotions with respect to their causal components appear more promising. As indicated in subsequent sections, there is a lot of convergence on the important cognitive causes of the emotions, and this is a notable advance in an area that has seen little agreement over the last century.

Central Concepts for a Cognitive Analysis: Goals and Standards

Goals

People's behavior is not random and is not driven solely by momentary external forces, but in addition reflects some internal structure of goals, interests, and beliefs. These kinds of mental structures are central concepts in cognitive analyses of emotion. It is generally assumed that positive emotions result from goal satisfaction and negative emotions from goal thwarting. By themselves, these assertions seen noncontroversial, but they require some qualification. For example, is it the case that goal satisfaction is required for a positive emotion? Probably not. One may be pleased, for example, simply at progress toward a goal or displeased at making what seems like insufficient progress. Indeed, Carver and Scheier (1990) maintain that it is rate of progress that triggers emotion, regardless of whether the goal is ever achieved. Positive emotion occurs when the rate of progress toward a goal is greater than expected and negative emotion when it is less than expected.

At first glance, some emotional events may seem to fall outside of an analysis based on goals. Pleasant emotions experienced while walking on a beach or in response to a beautiful sunset would seem to occur precisely because one is not pursuing a goal at the time. However, emotion theorists use the concept of goal in quite a broad way. For example, Schank and Abelson (1977) distinguished achievement goals, satisfaction goals, entertainment goals, preservation goals, crisis goals, and so on. Ortony, Clore, and Collins (1988) simplified these to three kinds of goals—*active pursuit goals* (things one wants to get done), *interest goals* (things one wants to see happen), and *replenishment goals* (things that recur on a regular basis). The active pursuit goals are intended to include many of Schank and Abelson's more specialized goals. High level, active pursuit goals may be quite implicit and may endure for a long time (e.g., achieving a sense of fulfillment in one's work, getting married and having a large family). Lower level active pursuit goals may be more explicit and last less long. They are more likely to be the immediate conscious reasons for action. Interest goals differ in that they involve things one wants to see happen, but that one is not normally able to influence (e.g., to see one's favorite team win). These include Schank and Abelson's preservation goals, where the object is to maintain some status quo (e.g., maintain one's health). A threat to interest goals can also lead to active pursuit goals (e.g., one may react to illness with instrumental action). Interest goals may last forever, such as one's perpetual interest in one's own well-being. Different from either active pursuit or interest goals are replenishment goals, which include many biological needs. These are goals that cannot be discarded when fulfilled, because they have a cyclical character (e.g., sleeping, putting gas in one's car).

Is it the case that any goal achievement (or any rapid progress toward goal achievement) results in positive emotion? Again, probably not, because some instances may be too trivial and may give rise to *emotional potential* but not to an emotion as such (Ortony et al., 1988). According to Wyer and Srull (1989), goal importance and other variables affect intensity. They concluded from prior research that one should be more upset at an interruption the greater the goal importance, the greater the investment, and the less the distance to the goal. Thus, if one planned to go to the theater, but was prevented from doing so, one should be more upset if the play was of special interest than if it was of only mild interest (goal importance). One should be more upset if someone just ahead in line got the last ticket than if the last ticket had been sold months before (distance to goal). One should be more upset if one had gone to a lot of trouble to get to the ticket office than if one had invested little effort (investment). These factors are formalized in the following equation:

$$\text{Negative affect} = V(k_1 I - k_2 D)$$

where V is goal importance, I is investment or sum of the weights (W) of the goals that will have to be retraced, and D is the distance to the goal. The distance, D, equals the difference between the total time and effort required to reach the goal and the sum of the weights of the subgoals already reached. The ks refer to constants.

The ticket example refers to an active pursuit goal, but the same analysis applies to other goals. For example, negative emotions based on thwarting of a preservation goal involve something one already had that is taken away. Because the thwarting occurs when one already has reached the goal, the distance from the point of interruption to the goal (D) would be zero. Because intensity is greater the less the distance to the goal, this scheme predicts that people should react intensely to the disruption of their preferred states of affairs, at least assuming the implicit goal is important (V) and one had made some investment (I) in attaining it.

For positive emotions, Wyer and Srull (1989) have given a similar analysis. Emotions such as pride, satisfaction, and joy resulting from goal accomplishment should be more intense the more effort and time one expended in the achievement, and also the less the a priori likelihood or expectation of achieving the goal. Thus, the intensity of positive affect experienced at any point along the path to a goal is given by:

$$\text{Positive affect} = V(1 - P)D^b$$

where V is the subjective value of the goal, P is the subjective likelihood of attaining it, and D^b is simply the sum of the weights of the various subgoals involved in attaining it. This formulation has the advantage that the same general set of parameters that predict intensity of negative emotions also predicts the intensity of positive emotions.

Such formalisms are useful, because they force one to be explicit about how the relevant factors are interrelated. However, it would be wrong to infer from them that precise predictions can be made. For example, there is no way to know which of many possibly relevant goals a particular person will think of when a certain event occurs, just as one cannot know which path a particular leaf might take when falling from a tree. In addition, it would be wrong to assume that such a formalism includes all of the relevant variables. For example, Kahneman and Tversky (1982) suggested that how upset the person would be about the theater tickets would depend on rather different factors. They suggested that one's response would depend on the experiential outcomes of mental simulations of scenarios in which one acted differently. One would be more upset, for example, if it were easy to imagine a scenario in which one could have succeeded in getting tickets by doing something slightly different.

Goal Importance.   In cognitive accounts of emotion (Ortony et al., 1988; Wyer & Srull, 1989), goals are assumed to exist in a hierarchy. Goals that are higher in a hierarchy are more important than goals lower in a hierarchy, because they carry more implications. High-level goals of surviving, maintaining one's health, and so on are necessary conditions for satisfying most other goals. Although important, such goals are often not particularly salient. For example, the ultimate goal of eating may be survival, but this goal is not usually salient as one tucks into one's dinner. Therefore, it seems likely that the impact of a goal on emotional intensity may depend less on its abstract importance in the entire goal structure than on its salience in the moment.

In one recent study of sports fans, for example, college basketball fans indicated their emotional reactions to their team's performance during each game of a championship season (Clore, Ortony, & Brand, in preparation; Ortony, 1990). At the start of the season, the fans had indicated that, in the context of their life goals in general, the success of the team was not very important; but during the actual games, many of these fans became highly emotional. Apparently, the importance or salience of a goal is context specific. During a sports event such as a basketball game, a fan gets to live in a simplified world in which only a few well-defined goals are salient. With respect to these goals, the positivity and negativity of each event is defined clearly. In the heat of the moment, the fan's belief that the referee has called a blocking foul for what was obviously a charging foul can take on inordinate importance. For the moment, such concerns as marriage, death, and taxes can become irrelevant. Indeed, this is presumably part of the appeal of sports events and entertainment more generally: to allow one to take a mental vacation from one's everyday goals and concerns.

Goal Conflict.   We argue that the importance or weighting of a given goal varies with the situation. This is not at all surprising, given that a primary function of emotion is to reorder the processing priorities as situations change (Simon, 1967). This process goes a long way toward explaining the extraordinary ability of people to be flexible and adapt to changing circumstances. But the same process sometimes leads people to sacrifice more important goals for less important ones, often resulting in regret. Indeed, such emotional short-sightedness is a common theme in literature and drama. The supreme example is perhaps that of Faust selling his eternal soul to the devil and then living to regret it. The results of a program of research on goal conflict by Emmons and King (e.g., 1988) presumably would be no surprise to Faust. They found that conflicting goals affect moods and emotions, as well as the propensity to become physically ill.

Standards

Cognitive theories of emotion generally focus on goals as the primary basis for appraisals and on events as the object of those appraisals. But some appraisals may be based on standards, principles, or norms, rather than goals. For example, Higgins (1987) distinguishes emotions based on oughts from those based on ideals, and Ortony et al. (1988) distinguish emotions based on standards from those based on goals. These concepts become useful when considering such emotions as pride and shame. In some accounts (e.g., Shaver, Schwartz, Kirson, & O'Connor, 1987), pride is considered a form of happiness and shame a form of fear. That view implicitly assumes that all emotions are based on the relevance of situations for goals. An alternate view is that pride and shame do not concern the satisfaction or thwarting of goals, but rather the meeting or falling short of oughts (Higgins, 1987) or standards (Ortony et al., 1988).

Virtual Cognitive Structure

The assumption that appraisals are made with respect to some sort of enduring cognitive structures, such as goals, is basic to most cognitive accounts of emotion. But a close inspection of that assumption raises some questions. Is it reasonable, for example, to assume that one carries around in one's head a representation of everything to which one aspires, no matter how trivial? An alternative possibility is that we construct them as we need them, and that one's goal hierarchy is a virtual, rather than an actual, structure. Although people behave as if there were such a representation, many goals may be constructed as required from a combination of general aspirations and momentary, local considerations. One may have a variety of abstract goals, standards, values, and attitudes that represent what generally matters to the person. But the specific goals with respect to which a situation elicits an emotion may not exist before the appraisal is made. Ortony et al. (1988) proposed that:

> Presumably most of what we have stored are high-level, relatively nonspecific goals, standards, and attitudes, all of which have powerful generative capabilities. For example, if one has as a standard that people ought not to inflict needless pain, one presumably has implicitly (or sometimes explicitly) a host of instantiations of this standard such as that one ought not to harm animals and so on. (p. 47)

People continually propagate inferences about the implications of the specific situations in which they find themselves or imagine they might find themselves. If these inferences make contact with elements in the appraisal structure, then goals, standards, or attitudes are activated. When this happens, the situation is seen by the person as relevant to his or her concerns and the possibility of emotional reactions that will impinge on conscious experience arise.

The concept of virtual cognitive structure comes from the computer science literature. Few psychologists have been concerned with the nature of appraisal processes at this level. Exceptions include Carver and Scheier (1990), Mandler (1984), Oatley and Johnson-Laird (1987), and Ortony et al. (1988). But in the artificial intelligence literature, some models of simplified situations with goals and affective reactions built into them are beginning to appear (for a review see Pfeifer, 1988). Many of these do not make substantive predictions of special interest to investigators of social cognition, but the general idea of asking questions about emotion from the point of view of system design would seem to have a lot to recommend it. This approach contrasts with the more microscopic concerns of traditional psychology, in which questions about the function of particular processes in the larger cognitive system often remain unasked.

Methods

Before detailing specific theories of emotion, a brief discussion of method is in order. There are at least four different methods that have commonly been used, including those focused on emotion vignettes, emotion prototypes, on-line emotions, and recalled emotions. Some investigators (e.g., Weiner, Graham, & Chandler, 1982) have employed standard vignettes in which one or more situational feature is varied. Subjects read the vignettes and imagine how they would respond emotionally in each situation. A related method is one in which subjects essentially serve as cultural informants (e.g., Shaver et al., 1987). They are asked to draw on their general knowledge to indicate for a particular emotion what eliciting conditions, responses, feelings, and so on are typical. A third method involves studying emotions on-line, as they occur. Typically a standard questionnaire about subjects' experiences is administered during or soon after an emotionally relevant event, such as taking a final exam (e.g., Smith & Ellsworth, 1987).

Recall, one of the most common methods (e.g., Roseman, Spindel, & Jose, 1990), involves asking subjects to recall when a given emotion was felt, to tell what happened, and to rate aspects of the situation believed to be cause the emotion. To measure subjects' perceptions of their own responsibility, Roseman et al. had subjects make ratings on a 9-point scale ranging from "Thinking that I was not at all responsible for the event" to "Thinking that I was very much responsible for the event." Similar items measured perceptions of the responsibility of other people and of the circumstances.

There are potential problems with each method, but we focus briefly on the recall method. One problem concerns the degree to which subjects have access to the critical information. Use of this approach assumes that whatever appraisal dimensions were active at the time were encoded by individuals in a way that would allow them to be recalled and rated. A second problem concerns the influence of folk theories about emotions on subjects' responses. As they attempt to understand their own experiences, subjects' memories may become assimilated to conventional beliefs about emotion (Parkinson & Manstead, 1992).

A third problem concerns the potentially confounding effects of intensity. Emotional episodes vary both qualitatively and quantitatively. For example, depending on the terms used, a request for an anger event might yield a memory of a relatively intense situation, such as a serious argument with a spouse, whereas questions about feeling guilty might elicit a less intense event, such as failing to send a birthday card to one's grandmother. The problem, of course, is that the variables found to differentiate such episodes are as likely to reflect the differences between strong and weak states as the differences between anger and guilt (see Frijda, Ortony, Sonnemans, & Clore, 1992, for an analysis of the concept of emotional intensity and the problem of equating the intensity of different emotions).

Despite these problems, the methods that have been used appear generally appropriate to the task at hand, which is primarily to make rough cuts among cognitive and perceptual variables with respect to their general relevance to large numbers of common emotions. Given the number of emotions of interest in these general theories, it would be difficult to devise multiple measures for each emotion, to attempt to capture in vivo instances, or to devise laboratory inductions for each. However, such efforts might be useful and appropriate for in-depth studies of particular emotions.

Much more might be said about method in the study of emotion (see Scherer, 1988, for a brief review), but we turn to the main concern of this section—a review of some current psychological models of the cognitive bases of emotional variety.

Cognitive Accounts of Emotional Variety

The work of Arnold (1960) provided an important early statement of the cognitive approach to emotion. Her concept of appraisal has been particularly influential. She proposed that people implicitly evaluate everything they encounter, and that such evaluations occur immediately and automatically. The sources of evaluation come from the immediate experiences of pleasure and pain, from memory of the affect associated with previous experiences, and from imagining possible good and bad consequences so that, according to Arnold, appraisal depends on memory plus expectation. Others whose research has been especially important in defining a cognitive approach to emotion include Schachter and Singer (1962), Lazarus (1966), and Mandler (1975). However, this early work tended not to include overall schemes for categorizing emotions, therefore they are not reviewed in depth in this chapter.

The effort to provide a comprehensive cognitive account of emotion variation is a relatively recent enterprise; most of the theories have been published within the last 10 years. Hence, few studies allow direct comparisons among theories. Still, as we see, there is considerable convergence on some important issues. In the following section, we outline the basic idea behind several recent theories and compare them using the relatively comprehensive account proposed by Ortony et al. (1988) as a common reference point. Some of the theories in this section focus on a particular principle or concept, such as attribution (Weiner, 1985), self-discrepancy (Higgins, 1987), or prototypes (Shaver et al., 1987). Some have a unique focus that sets them apart, such as a focus on action readiness (Frijda, 1986) or the temporal sequence of cognitive processes (Scherer, 1984). Still others are eclectic and focus primarily on the variables that predict various emotions, rather than theorizing about the cognitive processes involved (Roseman, 1984; Smith & Ellsworth, 1985). However, for the most part, the theories are based on similar principles.

A Hierarchical Theory

An account proposed by Ortony, Clore, and Collins (1988) (**herein referred to as the OCC account**) maintains that the emotions one experiences depends on the aspect of a situation to which one attends. There are three things on which one can focus, including events, actions, or objects. In particular, one can focus on the outcomes of events, the agency of actions, the attributes of objects, or on some combinations of these. In this view, all emotions involve positive or negative (affective) reactions to something. In the case of events, the basic affective reaction is to be *pleased or displeased about the outcomes of events*. Hope, fear, relief, disappointment, happiness, and sadness are some of the ways of being pleased or displeased at the outcomes of events or, in the case of hope and fear, the possible outcomes of events. These emotions appear in the left branch of Fig. 7.1. When focusing on actions rather than events, the basic affective reaction is to *approve or disapprove of the actions of an agent*. Pride, shame, admiration, and reproach are some of the ways to approve or disapprove of the actions of agents. These emotions appear in the middle branch of Fig. 7.1. Finally, when focusing on objects, the relevant affective reaction is to *like or dislike the attributes of an object*. Love, hate, and disgust are common emotions that involve liking or disliking the attributes of objects. These emotions appear in the rightmost branch of the figure. Finally, in addition to the possibility of focusing on one of these three possible aspects, one can also focus on two aspects of a situation at once. For example, gratitude involves both being pleased about the outcome of an event and approving of relevant actions at the same time. Similarly, anger involves both being displeased and disapproving at the same time.

ORTONY, CLORE, AND COLLINS' TYPOLOGY OF EMOTIONS

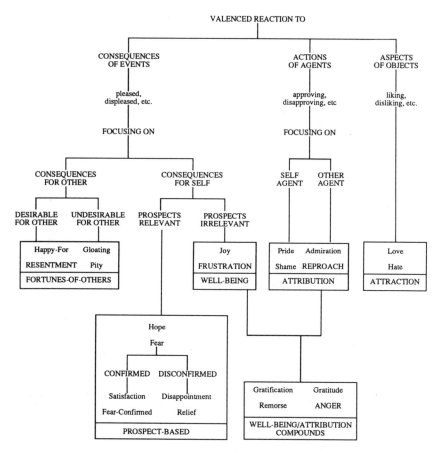

FIG. 7.1.   The cognitive structure of emotions. Cognitive factors that differentiate three kinds of affective reactions into 22 emotion types (Ortony, Clore, & Collins, 1988).

As in all cognitive models of emotion, it is assumed that the positive or negative nature of affective reactions depends on appraisals of a situation in terms of personal concerns. In the OCC account, the nature of the goodness or badness depends on one's cognitive focus. In the case of events, one has the affective reaction of being pleased only if one sees the outcome of events as *desirable*. In the case of actions, one has the affective reaction of approval only if one sees someone's action as *praiseworthy*. In the case of objects, one has the affective reaction of liking only if one finds the attributes of an object *appealing*. These perceptions arise from a process of appraising the implications of the situation for one's personal concerns. The kind of personal concern also varies with the focus. The outcomes of events are appraised relative to one's *goals*, the actions of agents are appraised relative to one's *standards*, and the attributes of objects are appraised relative to one's *attitudes or tastes*.

According to the OCC account, then, three affective reactions (e.g., *pleased, approving, liking*) are based on three kinds of appraisals (e.g., *desirability, praiseworthiness, appealingness*) of three kinds of things (*events, actions, objects*). And these three kinds of appraisals are made with respect to three kinds of cognitive structures (*goals, standards, attitudes*). According to the OCC account, all emotions are differentiated forms of these three general affective reactions: (a) *being pleased or displeased at the outcome of events appraised as desirable or undesirable with respect to one's goals*, (b) *approving or disapproving of the actions of agents appraised as praiseworthy or blameworthy with respect to one's standards*, and (c) *liking or disliking the attributes of objects appraised as appealing or unappealing with respect to one's tastes or attitudes*.

A major aim of the theory is to use a consistent set of terms in a clear and precise way. To do this, some terms such as *being pleased/displeased* or *desirable and undesirable event* take on specialized meanings. Because emotions are states, the terms *liking* and *disliking* refer to the momentary experience of liking or disliking, rather than to a disposition or attitude of liking toward something.

One virtue of proposing multiple bases for emotional appraisals is the ease with which it allows one to account for multiple reactions to the same situation. For example, suppose that one were to learn that one's neighbor beats his or her children. How might one go about predicting which emotion is most likely? One possibility is that it depends on the aspect to which one attends. One might feel pity, sympathy, and sadness if one focuses on the outcomes for the children, but one might feel reproachful, indignant, and outraged if one focuses on the neighbor's actions. Anger might occur if one focuses on both the outcomes and the action at the same time. Or one might feel dislike, disgust, and contempt if one focuses on the neighbor as a person. The hypothesis that different emotions result from taking different perspectives on a situation might be tested using a priming methodology, but no such study has been reported in the literature. If one were actually exposed to such a situation, all of these feelings might be experienced in succession. Because emotional states can linger, more than one might be active at the same time.

Cognitive Prerequisites of Specific Emotions.   According to the OCC account, affective reactions often involve an appraisal that implicates one's goals, standards, or attitudes. Specific differentiated emotions, such as anger, fear, pity, or shame, require that certain cognitive distinctions also be made. These include such distinctions as whether the implications for one's goals already have been realized or are only possibilities, whether the person responsible is oneself or another person, and so on. Thus, the emotion of *fear* is a differentiated form of the affective reaction of *being displeased*. The formal specification of fear in this system is *being displeased at the prospect of an undesirable event*. To see what this means in the context of Fig. 7.1, follow the *event-based branch*. Assume one is focusing on the *consequences* for *self* (rather than for another), on the *prospect* of an event happening (rather than on an event that has definitely occurred), and on the possible outcomes that are *undesirable* (rather than desirable). When these cognitive conditions exist, the resulting affective reaction, if any, is a kind of *fear* emotion. It is important to note that Fig. 7.1 is intended to emphasize a logical, not a temporal, structure. The cognitive distinctions that are involved in particular emotions often occur simultaneously as features of a single perception.

The eliciting conditions for 22 emotion types are given in Fig. 7.1. Emotions sharing common eliciting conditions form groups (fortunes-of-others emotions, well-being emotions, prospect emotions, attribution emotions, attraction emotions, well-being-attribution compounds). The number of emotions that can be distinguished on some basis is presumably large. For example, these 22 emotion types each may encompass several tokens—terms denoting specific states within the same type. The states denoted by these tokens may differ in a number of ways from others in the same type, but they all share the same general eliciting conditions. A couple of examples of the emotion specifications given for each of the 22 emotions can be seen in Table 7.1.

The well-being emotions form a particularly large category, including all states in which one focuses on events and is pleased or displeased at the desirable or undesirable outcomes for oneself. Many of the emotions in the distress type differ from each other mainly in the specific goal that is thwarted, including grief

TABLE 7.1
Sample Emotion Specifications
from Ortony, Clore, and Collins (1988)

Fear Emotions

Type Specification	(displeased about) the prospect of an undesirable event
Tokens	apprehensive, anxious, cowering, dread, fear, fright, nervous, petrified, scared, terrified, timid, worried, etc.
Variables Affecting Intensity	(1) the degree to which the event is desirable (2) the likelihood of the event
Example	The employee, suspecting he was no longer needed, feared that he would be fired.

Distress Emotions

Type Specification	(displeased about) an undesirable event
Tokens	depressed, distressed, displeased, dissatisfied, distraught, feeling bad, feeling uncomfortable, grief, homesick, lonely, lovesick, miserable, regret, sad, shock, uneasy, unhappy, upset, etc.
Variables Affecting Intensity	the degree to which the event is desirable
Example	The driver was upset about running out of gas on the freeway.

(distress at the loss of a loved one), lonesomeness (distress at being alone), homesickness (distress at not being home), or lovesickness (distress at not being with a lover). Some may involve seemingly irrevocable losses, as in sadness, and some may involve the interruption of subgoals on the way toward a larger goal, as in frustration. These emotions may each have unique implications, but all share the same general eliciting conditions. Consequently, all are considered examples of the same emotion type, labelled "distress" in the figure. In the lower half of Table 7.1, the formal specification of the distress emotions can be seen.

The emotions toward the bottom of Fig. 7.1 are cognitively differentiated forms of the three affective reactions at the top of the figure (e.g., being pleased, approving, liking). They achieve their distinctiveness as they are cognitively constrained. The least cognitively differentiated are some of the object-based (attraction) emotions. For example, disgust at the prospect of eating a cockroach (Rozin & Fallon, 1987) is probably one of the less cognitively involved of emotional reactions. Similarly, liking and disliking are often relatively undifferentiated reactions, and people can be quite inarticulate about why they like or dislike something.

Evidence for the proposed scheme comes from a study of 120 college basketball fans who recorded their reactions before, during, and after the games that they watched (Clore et al., in preparation; Ortony, 1990). The data were analyzed separately for wins and losses, and in both, cluster analyses showed that the emotions grouped themselves into the predicted categories of goal-based, standard-based, and attitude-based emotions.

The data also allowed a number of other hypotheses to be tested. For example, the distinction between goal-based and standard-based emotions could be seen in fans' reports of disappointment. It turned out that when fans said they were disappointed, some were disappointed *about* the outcome of the game and some were disappointed *in* the actions of the team. The difference between these two states was apparent in the fact that some instances of disappointment clustered together with such emotions as sad and frustrated (which are clearly goal based), whereas others clustered with such emotions as ashamed and embarrassed (which are hypothesized to be standard based). A second form of evidence concerned the variables that governed the intensity of emotion. The disappointment of subjects who appeared to be disappointed about the outcome was made more intense by beliefs that the game was an important one, and expectations that the outcome would be different—factors concerned with goals and outcomes. The disappointment of those that appeared to be disappointed in the performance of the team was made more intense by perceptions that the players had "not played well," that they had "not hustled," and that they did "not deserve to win"—all concerned with standards of play. Although both sets of fans were distressed, some were focused on the outcome and some on the quality of play.

A Motivation-Plus-Cognition Theory

Roseman (1984) proposed a structural theory of emotion in which combinations of five appraisals determine which of 14 emotions will be experienced. The important dimensions of appraisal include whether something is *event caused or person caused*, whether the outcome is *positive or negative*, *certain or uncertain*, whether the motivation is *appetitive* (reward seeking) or *aversive* (punishment avoiding), and whether the self is *strong or weak*. The emotions covered include hope–fear, joy–sadness, liking–disliking, pride–shame, relief–distress, and also disgust, frustration, anger, and regret. For example, Roseman, Antoniou, and Jose (1992) proposed that, ". . . sadness results from an event that is inconsistent with an appetitive (reward-seeking) motive, is certain to occur, and is caused by circumstances, when the self is weak. In contrast, anger results from an event that is inconsistent with either an appetitive or an aversive (punishment-avoiding) motive, and is caused by other persons, when the self is strong" (p. 3).

Supported Hypotheses

The most recent version of Roseman's theory (Roseman et al., 1992) is shown in Fig. 7.2. Evidence from Roseman's research and the research of others provides support for many of the proposed factors, as follows:

1. Motive Consistency.   Events appraised as motive consistent elicit positive emotions, and events appraised as motive inconsistent elicit negative emotions (Roseman et al., 1990). The idea that the valence of emotions comes from the extent to which events are motive consistent is implicit or explicit in all cognitive accounts.

2. Appetitive Versus Aversive Motivation.   Events related to appetitive motives elicit joy or sadness, and events related to aversive motives elicit relief, distress, or disgust (Roseman, 1991; Roseman et al., 1992). The notion that one feels sad after failing to achieve pleasure, but distress after failing to avoid pain, represents an interesting distinction that has not been made by others, except for Higgins (1987), who makes this observation the centerpiece of his theory.

3. Certainty.   Positive events appraised as uncertain elicit hope rather than joy or relief, and negative events appraised as uncertain yield fear rather than sadness, distress, or disgust (Frijda, 1986; Roseman et al., 1992; Smith & Ellsworth, 1985; Tesser, 1990). Certainty is also a variable in Smith and Ellsworth's theory to be discussed next, as well as in Scherer's (1984) theory. In the OCC account, hope and fear are isolated from other similar emotions through the "Prospect relevant vs. non-prospect relevant" distinction. Certainty is considered primarily as a variable that influences the intensity, rather than the kind, of emotion.

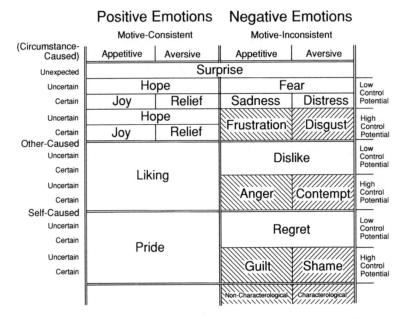

FIG. 7.2. Roseman's (1992) revised emotion theory (from Roseman, Antoniou, & Jose, 1992, reprinted by permission).

4. Self Versus Other Caused. Positive events caused by self yield pride, whereas those caused by others might yield love. Negative events caused by self yield shame, guilt, or regret, whereas those caused by others might yield dislike or anger (Frijda, 1986; Smith & Ellsworth, 1985; Tesser, 1990; Weiner et al., 1982). The self–other distinction is common to most cognitive theories and does similar work in separating self-focused versus other-focused emotions.

Changes from 1984 Theory

In addition, Roseman et al. (1992) reported research in which subjects recalled events in their lives that triggered one of several emotions. They described the events and then made a series of ratings on the proposed appraisal dimensions. On the basis of their own results and those of others, they made several alterations in the original 1984 theory, including replacing two of the original dimensions, adding a new dimension, and dropping an old one, as described next:

1. Unexpectedness. Because it predicts surprise, unexpectedness replaces uncertainty. Neither novelty (Scherer, 1984), unfamiliarity, nor uncertainty (Roseman, 1984) was successful in predicting surprise (Roseman et al., 1992). In the OCC account, surprise is not considered an emotion (because it is not inherently good or bad), but unexpectedness (surprisingness) is included as a global intensity variable for all emotions.

2. Control Potential.   Control potential is introduced as a replacement for power. Predictions concerning power have not been supported, because people do not see themselves as more powerful in situations that lead to frustration, anger, and regret (Roseman et al., 1990). Neither own power (Roseman, 1984; Scherer, 1988), stimulus power (Arnold, 1960), nor stimulus controllability (Frijda, 1986) were predictive. In the new version, negative events that one can, in principle, do something about (high control potential) are seen as frustrating, whereas events that can not be controlled at all should simply make one sad.

Roseman also interprets a perception of illegitimacy as conferring control potential on a situation. The idea is that perceiving injustice gives one a sense of control potential. Predictions about legitimacy on its own were not supported.

3. Characterological Versus Noncharacterological.   This factor is added, because some results (Roseman et al., 1992) suggest that shame and guilt might be distinguished by whether the problem is with the person as object (characterological) or merely with the behavior or noncentral attribute of the person (noncharacterological). When others are the object, this distinction yields contempt versus anger. Also, disgust may be felt for an object that is bad in itself, whereas frustration will be felt if only its effect is bad. Here Roseman seems to be making the same distinction as the object versus event focus distinction in the OCC account. Reviewing inconsistencies across several studies, Roseman also implicitly arrives at the event versus agency distinction found in the OCC account, saying:

> "Circumstance-caused" emotions (Roseman, 1984a) can also be elicited when no cause is specified for an event (Weiner, 1985), or when a causal agent is identified but the agency information is disregarded in a person's focus on the event itself (cf. Ortony et al., 1988). If subjects disregard agency information and focus on events (e.g., focus on the fact of an unreasonable delay, disregarding who or what caused it), the event-directed emotion (e.g., frustration) would be experienced regardless of whether the agent was self, other, or circumstance. (Roseman et al., 1992, pp. 28–29)

4. Attribution to Circumstances.   Roseman et al. (1992) eliminated attribution to circumstances as a necessary determinant for circumstance-caused emotions such as fear, frustration, joy, and sadness. The idea was that for many emotions causal attribution simply is not a consideration. For example, one may feel sad about an event that clearly was caused by someone if one's focus is not on causation or blame, but simply on the unfortunate nature of the outcomes. The major feature of the OCC account is that it is built around this variation in focus. According to that view, of the many characteristics of a situation, only some are salient within a given focus, and the emotions triggered will depend on those features.

Convergence with the OCC Account

The proposed changes increase the convergence between Roseman's theory and the OCC account. In particular, there are three changes that make the two theories similar. Roseman's theory accomplishes certain goals by introducing new variables, and the OCC account does so by hypothesizing different points of attentional focus:

1. One change was the new emphasis on the fact that causal attribution is only sometimes the focus. At other times, one may focus on outcomes without regard to causation. In a similar way, a central feature of the OCC account is that eliciting conditions are arranged hierarchically, such that some variables are relevant for one effective focus, but not another.

2. The characterological versus noncharacterological (behavioral) distinction allows Roseman to separate disgust from frustration, contempt from anger, and shame from guilt. Similar distinctions are made in the OCC account (except for the distinction between shame and guilt). Rather than a local "characterological versus noncharacterological" variable, however, the OCC account achieves the same end with the hierarchical structure in which some emotions involve a focus on outcomes, some on actions, and some on the objects themselves. Thus, disgust, contempt, and shame involve a focus on the object, whereas frustration, anger, and guilt involve a focus on either outcomes or actions.

3. The effect of the new control potential variable also is similar to the effect of OCC's focus variable. In Roseman's theory, control potential distinguishes anger from dislike and also guilt and shame from regret. The OCC account distinguishes among them by assuming that sometimes one focuses on actions and sometimes on outcomes. When focused on actions and appraising them relative to standards, some are seen as blameworthy, so that anger rather than dislike is felt or guilt and shame rather than regret. Some of the same explanatory power can be achieved either by adding new variables (Roseman) or by capitalizing on the fact that one can focus on some aspects of a situation to the exclusion of others (OCC).

The Theory as a Hierarchy

Roseman's theory is diagrammed in Fig. 7.2. This representation (Roseman et al., 1992) looks like an ANOVA design with some missing cells. The missing cells reflect the fact that the variables are not completely crossed (i.e., some play a role under some conditions, but not under others). In other words, the structure is actually hierarchical, as can be seen in Fig. 7.3. The figure shows the same information as Fig. 7.2, only rearranged as a hierarchy. If one views the Roseman et al. "Circumstance-Caused" category as equivalent to the "Event Focus" category in the OCC account, and the Roseman et al. "Other-Caused" and "Self-Caused" categories as reflecting an "Action Focus," the two theories look very much the same. As discussed earlier, Roseman's "Certain" versus "Uncer-

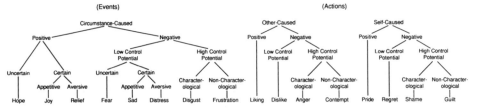

FIG. 7.3.   Roseman's (1992) revised emotion theory represented as a hierarchy.

tain" distinction reflects the "Prospects Relevant" versus "Prospects Irrelevant" distinction in the OCC account. Also, the characterological–noncharacterological distinction in Roseman's theory mirrors the "Object Focus" versus the other two possible foci ("Events" and "Actions") in the OCC theory.

However, Roseman makes one distinction that Ortony et al. did not, concerning appetitive versus aversive motivation. This distinction allows Roseman to account for relief as distinct from joy, and distress as distinct from sadness. The OCC account distinguishes relief from joy in a slightly different way by making a hierarchy under hope and fear (uncertainty or prospect emotions), in which the hope or fear either is confirmed (yielding satisfaction or disappointment) or disconfirmed (yielding fears confirmed or disappointment). But the sadness versus distress distinction (also seen in Higgins) is not included in the OCC account.

Individual Differences

Roseman et al. (1992) proposed that a motivation-plus-cognition theory is needed, rather than simply a cognitive theory of emotion. They suggested that emotions may be influenced by what one wants as well as by what one thinks. Although motivation is clearly already present in goal-based cognitive theories, they see this as a way to incorporate into emotion theory individual differences in motivation, such as an elevated need for intimacy or power and so on. They predicted that differences in motive could produce differences in emotion, even when cognitions about a situation are the same.

The question of how differences in temperament or chronic motivation affect the emotion process is an interesting one. Within the OCC account, chronic motives should change the intensity of emotions via changes in the desirability of relevant outcomes, the praise or blameworthiness of relevant actions, or the appealingness of relevant objects. So, a person with a heightened motivation for power might feel worse than someone else when he or she fails to be elected to office, because more of a person's goal hierarchy is involved in the goal for power. Alternatively, heightened motivation might lower the threshold for emotion, making relevant emotions more likely or more intense. The same analysis also might handle differences in temperament. Thus, for hostile persons, less added frustration would be necessary to trigger anger. Similarly, for anxious persons, less added threat would be needed for fear; and, perhaps, for happy people, less added humor would be required to burst into laughter.

A Dimensional Theory

A related account was proposed by Smith and Ellsworth (1985). These authors have not proposed a distinctive view of the processes involved in emotion production. Instead, they have taken an eclectic approach, in which they reviewed previous research and abstracted eight dimensions proposed by various other writers as important in differentiating emotions. These included *pleasantness, effort, attention, certainty, responsibility, control, legitimacy,* and *obstacles*.

It is clear from even a causal reading of these first three theories that there is considerable convergence of view. Table 7.2 summarizes the similarities and differences among these approaches by listing the common and unique cognitive distinctions hypothesized to account for emotional variety.

Smith and Ellsworth (1985) asked subjects to recall situations in which they felt each of 15 different emotions (happiness, sadness, anger, fear, disgust, surprise, challenge, boredom, hope, interest, contempt, frustration, pride, shame, and guilt). These situations were rated on the eight proposed appraisal dimensions. The results showed that six dimensions were useful in distinguishing among subjects' emotions, including the proposed dimensions of pleasantness, anticipated effort, attentional activity, and two dimensions that were combinations of the originally proposed responsibility and control dimensions. These were *human agency* (whether self or other was responsible and in control of the situation) and *situational control* (whether the situation was being controlled by a human agent

TABLE 7.2
Some Appraisal Dimensions

Roseman, Antoniou, and Jose (1992)	Smith and Ellsworth (1985)	Ortony, Clore, and Collins (OCC; 1988)
Common Factors		
Event caused versus person caused	Impersonal versus human control	Outcome versus agent focused
Self- versus other agency	Self- versus other agency	Self- versus other agency
Positive versus negative	Pleasantness	Positive versus negative
Certain versus uncertain	Certainty	Prospect relevant versus irrelevant
Characterological versus non-characterological		Object focused versus outcome or action focused
Unique Factors		
Appetitive/aversive motivation	Attention	Self- versus other outcomes
Hi versus low control potential	Anticipated effort	
Expectedness		

or by impersonal circumstances). The proposed dimensions of legitimacy and perceived obstacle did not turn out to stand on their own.

Smith and Ellsworth (1985) found a unique pattern of cognitive appraisals for each emotion except that shame and guilt were not distinct, nor were anger and contempt. The roles played by the dimensions are summarized next:

1. Pleasantness. Not surprisingly, the pleasantness variable accounted for a sizable amount of variance (20%–25%).

2. Anticipated Effort. With respect to the anticipated effort to remove an obstacle to a goal, most negative emotions were high, as was challenge, whereas happiness and boredom were rated as involving little effort. In the OCC account, neither challenge nor boredom are considered emotions, and effort is included as an intensity variable, rather than as an eliciting condition. In Smith and Ellsworth's data, effort differentiated annoyance and rage, although these too may differ primarily in intensity.

3. Certainty. Uncertainty about whether something will or will not happen distinguished fear, hope, and surprise from other emotions. In our OCC account, too, fear and hope are characterized by uncertainty. As indicated earlier, however, surprise is not considered an emotion, but as an intensity variable in the OCC account.

4. Attentional Activity. According to Smith and Ellsworth (1985), the first appraisal that is made is whether to attend to, ignore, or avoid a stimulus. No similar variable is included in the OCC or Roseman accounts, but in Scherer's account, considered next, a novelty check serves the same function. Smith and Ellsworth found that frustration, interest, challenge, and most positive emotions were associated with a desire to attend, whereas boredom and disgust were associated with a desire to avoid attending.

5. Responsibility and Control. Subjects' perception of causes differentiated the emotions of sadness (chance), shame or guilt (self-caused), and anger (other caused). This is generally compatible with the OCC account, although the latter begins at a somewhat different point. In the OCC account, attribution of cause is also a feature of shame and anger, but sadness involves focusing primarily on the undesirability of the outcomes, rather than on the causes. Thus, although attributions to chance might sometimes be involved in sadness, it seems unlikely that sadness generally involves a focus on chance. Indeed, a common reaction to reading about horrible crimes that clearly were caused by a person is not so much anger as sadness that such events happen. As discussed earlier, an emotion like sadness is not (according to the OCC and new Roseman accounts) an emotion that achieves its distinctive character by virtue of a causal attribution. Such emotions are simply not about responsibility, but about the undesirability of outcomes.

In a follow-up study, Smith and Ellsworth (1987) obtained cognitive appraisals and reports of emotional states both before students took a midterm examination and immediately after they received their grades. At both times, most students reported feeling more than one emotion. The study is interesting, because subjects were actively experiencing emotions as opposed to simply recalling earlier situations. They assessed their experience of six emotions, including anger, happiness, hope, challenge, apathy, fear, and guilt. Most were associated with a characteristic appraisal. Anger was associated with appraisals of unfairness, apathy with appraisals of other agency, fear with unpleasantness, hope/challenge with anticipated effort, and happiness with appraisals of pleasantness. Sadness did not emerge in the exam situation as an independent emotion, and guilt, although present, was not predicted by the appraisal dimensions assessed.

Smith and Ellsworth (1987) focused on the dynamic nature of emotional life, noting that most of the emotions occurred along with other emotions, rather than by themselves. Moreover, subjects often reported contradictory emotions. For example, most subjects (60%) who felt guilty also felt angry, although attributing the negative action to another person is a prerequisite for anger and attributing it to oneself is a prerequisite for guilt. Presumably they felt they had not studied as much as they should have (self-agency), but also that the test had too many picky, unfair, multiple-choice questions (other agency). In other research from this perspective, Smith (1989) used an imagery task to explore the links between the appraisal dimensions and both physiological activity (e.g., heart rate and skin conductance) and expressive behavior (e.g., EMG's indicating eyebrow frowns and smile).

Tesser (1990) reported a conceptual replication of Smith and Ellsworth (1985). He interviewed subjects and asked them to recall eight different situations, indicating the degree to which they had experienced each of 18 emotions (the 15 studied by Smith and Ellsworth plus jealousy, envy, and pride in other). The patterns of the emotions, along the appraisal dimensions, were highly correlated with those reported by Smith and Ellsworth. In fact, the average correlation of the location of the 15 emotions on each of the six dimensions with the earlier patterns was $r = .85$, with only situational control correlating less than $r = .50$. Among the new emotions studied, the dimensions were not related to pride in other, but accounted for about 40% of the variance in reports of jealousy and envy.

Manstead and Tetlock (1989) conducted a similar study of some of the appraisal dimensions and emotions examined by Smith and Ellsworth (1985), and also added some new ones. The results were generally compatible. They found evidence for the usefulness of new factors they called "unexpectedness," "own and others benefit," and "inconsistency with behavioral standards." These new variables, except for unexpectedness, are also part of the OCC account.

What Is an Appraisal?   The use of the term *appraisal* by Roseman (1984), Smith and Ellsworth (1985), and Frijda (1986) differs from the usage in some other models. For example, they include whether an action is caused by self or other as an example of an appraisal. In some other theories, such as the OCC account, appraisals must be affective; they must concern the goodness or badness of something. Appraisals can include whether something is desirable, praiseworthy, or appealing, but not whether an action is one's own or someone else's. Appraisals are differentiated into specific emotions when modified by whether an action is one's own or someone else's, whether an outcome is known or unknown, and so on. However, we are inclined to view these factors as descriptive features of the situation, rather than as appraisals. They are perceptual constituents of emotion, whereas appraisals concern the ways in which a situation is positive or negative.

Correlates Versus Causes.   Smith and Ellsworth (1985) think of the cognitive conditions of emotion elicitation as a set of dimensions with continuous variation. The more one feels that another person is responsible for a negative event, for example, the more one's emotional reaction will be characterized by angry, rather than sad, feelings. This dimensional approach contrasts somewhat with a discrete emotions view, but Smith and Ellsworth suggest that continuous dimensions are not necessarily incompatible with discrete emotions. One can think of common discrete emotions as representing regions of the dimensional space that frequently co-occur or that are subjectively salient. Alternatively, within a discrete emotions view, the dimensions may be useful for describing differences among the emotions. By contrast, the cognitive variables in the OCC account are seen as the necessary conditions for the elicitation of a particular emotion, rather than variables that are simply descriptive of or associated with the emotion.

A Sequential Process Theory

A number of cognitive-emotion theorists have focused on the order in which cognitive operations occur in the appraisal process (e.g., Arnold, 1960; Lazarus, 1966; Schachter & Singer, 1962; Weiner, 1985). However, the most detailed proposals about the sequence of processes in emotion elicitation come from Scherer (1984, 1988). Scherer's component process model of emotion uses the logic of facet theory as a framework for thinking about all aspects of emotion, including their cognitive elicitation. He assumes that the various component processes can combine to form any number of emotions. Scherer proposes that emotions result from a sequence of *stimulus evaluation checks* that all organisms go through.

Novelty Check.   The first of these checks is an evaluation of the novelty or unexpectedness of the stimulus. This stage includes such precognitive operations as the startle reflex or the orienting response, as well as more extended processing. Boredom and surprise, which he considers emotions, emerge at this stage. Also, in the case of a stimulus that is unexpected, subsequent stimulus checks may be speeded up.

Intrinsic Pleasantness or Unpleasantness Check.   The second check involves evaluating the intrinsic pleasantness of the stimulus, as opposed to its potential for goal satisfaction. Disgust would be an example of an emotion based principally on the inherent unpleasantness of a stimulus. Scherer's intrinsic pleasantness–unpleasantness check is comparable in the OCC account to the experience of momentary liking or disliking based on tastes or attitudes.

Goal/Need Conduciveness Check.   The third stimulus evaluation check is the assessment of the goal/need conduciveness of the stimulus. To show the difference between the value of a stimulus based on inherent pleasantness and goal conduciveness, Scherer pointed out that even intrinsically pleasant stimuli can interrupt ongoing plans and be evaluated negatively in terms of goal attainment. In the OCC account, too, an appraisal based on goals can conflict with an appraisal of the same stimulus based on inherent pleasantness. Going to the dentist may facilitate health maintenance goals, but is often inherently unpleasant.

Coping Potential.   The fourth stimulus evaluation check determines the coping potential of the organism with regard to a past or future event. It includes four subchecks, including checks for cause (who or what caused the event), control (whether the consequences can be controlled), power (one's relative power with respect to obstacles), and adjustment (the ease of adjusting to uncontrollable events). Sadness is expected to result from events judged both negative and uncontrollable. Anger might result when, after negative events, one judges oneself to have high power; whereas fear might result from judgments of low power.

Norm/Self-Compatibility Check.   Scherer suggests that although all species should show the first four stimulus checks, perhaps only humans (and their close mammalian relatives) engage in a norm/self-compatibility check. This check involves comparing the actions of oneself and others against applicable standards, such as social norms or one's self-concept. As in the case of the OCC account and of Higgins' theory, this check is relevant to such emotions as embarrassment, shame, and guilt. Theories that include only motives or goals and not standards as sources of value (e.g., Roseman, 1984) may be less able to treat these emotions satisfactorily.

The stimulus evaluation process is a continuous loop, and although some of the steps may be skipped as when one reevaluates stimuli, Scherer says that they will always occur in the same hierarchical order. Each stimulus check further differentiates the emerging emotional state. For example, surprise may result from the first stimulus check (the novelty check) and then may become a more specific emotion after subsequent checks. The inherent pleasantness check or the goal conduciveness check might turn the neutral or ambiguous surprise response into a positive emotion. As indicated earlier, Clore and Ortony (1987) have argued that surprise is not a good example of an emotion for precisely this reason. To be an emotion, a state must be positive or negative, but one can be surprised about either positive or negative events. Hence, surprise may modify an emotion (e.g., make it more intense) without being a good example of an emotion by itself.

The elicitation variables proposed by Scherer, although anchored in a somewhat different theory, are comparable to those suggested in the OCC account, in Roseman's account, and in Smith and Ellsworth's account (Table 7.2). These approaches depend on such factors as whether the event is caused by personal or impersonal forces, whether the personal agent is self or other, how probable or expected the event was, the implications for one's goals, whether standards are relevant, and the potential for control.

Cross-Cultural Research. An issue that arises is the degree to which these appraisal factors are universal and the degree to which they are local to the countries of the investigators. There appear to be some unique emotions or emotion concepts in some cultures (Lutz & White, 1986), but the most common emotions seem quite universal, and systematic studies in diverse countries consistently show that the cross-cultural variation in the relations between the cognitive appraisal dimensions and particular emotions show little systematic variation across cultures (Mauro, Sato, & Tucker, 1992; Wallbott & Scherer, 1988). Mauro et al. (1992) found evidence for the role of pleasantness, certainty, attentional activity, coping ability, and need/goal conduciveness with little or no effect of culture. Similarly, the roles of norm/self-compatibility and legitimacy in emotion elicitation also showed little cultural variation.

An Action Readiness Theory

The most distinctive feature of Frijda's (1986) theory, however, is the fact that he distinguishes emotions in terms of the actions for which they prepare one as well as patterns of cognitive appraisals. According to Frijda, emotions involve states of action readiness elicited by events appraised as emotionally relevant. He considers action readiness as part of the emotion, rather than being an outcome of the emotion. The action readiness concept includes both minute facial muscle changes and gross motor behavior, and also both automatic fight/flight reactions and learned behavior. He views the physiological components of emotion as serving the patterns of action readiness, which in turn are reflected in feelings of action readiness, facial expressions, and, of course, actual behavior.

Frijda, Kuipers, and ter Schure (1989) examined the role of 17 action tendencies and 13 appraisal factors to determine how well they were related to self-reports of 32 emotional states. Subjects recalled instances of several emotions and indicated the relevance of a variety of appraisal dimensions and action readiness modes to each. The action readiness modes were:

moving toward, against, or away
disappear from view
exuberance, inhibition
in command, submitting
helping, rejecting

hyperactivation, helplessness
attending, disinterest
excited, rest
interruption
don't want

The appraisal dimensions included:

valence
certainty
expectedness
effort
controllability

*importance
agency
fairness
*familiarity

modifiability
interestingness
*changes in self-esteem
affecting someone else

By now these dimensions should look familiar. Except where indicated with an asterisk, they overlap those suggested by Roseman, Smith and Ellsworth, and OCC (see Table 7.2). In addition, familiarity is included in Scherer's account.

The results showed that appraisal cues led to 40% correct prediction of emotions and action readiness cues to 46%. Together they yielded almost 60% correct predictions. The largest appraisal factor was valence or pleasant–unpleasant, and the largest action readiness factor revolved around the item "don't want." All of the negative emotions studied were associated with the appraisal dimensions of "unpleasantness" and "importance" and with the action tendency modes of "don't want." In addition, a sample of the results shows that:

1. Anger (anger, contempt, annoyance, rage) was related to the appraisal dimensions of "certainty" and "agency other" and to the action tendency mode of "moving against."
2. Disgust (disgust, aversion) was not distinct from anger in appraisal dimensions, but was associated with action tendencies of "moving away" rather than "moving against."
3. Fear (fear, anxiety, startled) was associated with appraisal dimensions of "uncertain," "unexpected," "controllable," and "familiar" and to action tendencies to "move away" but also to "approach."
4. Shame (shame, regret, guilt) was related to appraisals of "certainty," and "self-agency." Shame, but not regret and guilt, was associated with "disappear from view."

With few exceptions, the appraisal results are similar to those reported by others. As in studies by Roseman, fairness did not show up as a general factor of appraisal. But it did differentiate several negative emotions, again suggesting a hierarchical, rather than a dimensional, structure. No action readiness modes differentiated such complex emotions as jealousy, regret, distrust, and disappointment apart from the general "don't want" and, in some cases, "attending."

A great deal of attention has been devoted in recent years to the cognitive eliciting conditions of emotions. By contrast, work is just beginning on the output of emotions, and Frijda's work, along with that of Shaver and Schwartz (Shaver et al. 1987), is an important beginning. One problem with the theory at the present stage of development is that there is no principled criterion for deciding what counts as an action readiness. Some of the action readiness items (e.g., "Boiling inwardly") seem to be better examples of feelings than of action readiness. Others (e.g., "I felt I was in command") seem like what others include as an appraisal, and some (e.g., "crying," "blushing") seem to be expressions.

An Attribution Theory

Weiner (1985) has proposed an account focused on emotions that involve attribution. He conceptualizes emotion as a more or less automatic response of pleasure or displeasure concerning the outcome of an event. Then, especially if the emotion is negative and unexpected, one is believed to engage in a search for causes. The causal attribution that is made varies in terms of whether the cause is internal versus external, stable versus unstable, and controllable versus uncontrollable. These dimensions are important, because they have strong implications for motivation and emotion. For example, a tennis player who believes his or her failure in a match was caused by a lack of talent should have low motivation to continue, because lack of talent is a stable and uncontrollable cause. He or she also might feel shame, because lack of talent is an internal, as opposed to an external, cause.

Weiner is concerned primarily with emotions that are relevant to achievement situations. He proposes that one first responds with outcome-related emotions of happiness or frustration, which are attribution independent. Then, one of seven emotions might occur, depending on how this first reaction is explained. These include pride, anger, pity, guilt, shame, gratitude, and hopelessness. For example, whether one feels anger, pity, guilt, or gratitude depends on the controllability and internality of the attribution. In a 2 × 2 matrix varying controllability (controllable vs. not) and locus of causation (failure of self vs. other), guilt, shame, anger, and pity fall into the four cells. Both guilt and shame are reactions to failures of the self, guilt being felt when the failure is controllable and shame when it is not. Anger and pity concern the failures of others, anger being felt when the failure is controllable and pity when it is not. Wiener (1985) said, "We feel anger toward the lazy and therefore punish lack of effort, but we feel pity toward the unable and therefore do not punish lack of ability" (p. 562). The proposed eliciting conditions for anger parallel those proposed in the OCC account. "The attributional antecedent for anger is an ascription of a negative self-related outcome or event to factors controllable by others" (Weiner, 1985, p. 562). Thus, attributions to lack of effort elicit guilt from self and anger from others. On the other hand, shame concerns failures seen as self-relevant and uncontrollable, such as lack of ability.

A 2 × 2 matrix can also be made for positive outcomes by varying stable versus unstable and internal versus external causes. The matrix includes pride, relief, gratitude, and surprise. Pride and belief both concern internally caused successes—pride occurring when the cause is assumed to be stable and relief when unstable. Gratitude and surprise are reactions to externally caused successes— gratitude occurring when the cause is assumed to be another person who intend- ed to help (stable cause) and surprise occurring when the cause is unstable (e.g., good luck).

Weiner points out that socially shared knowledge about the emotional effects of various attributions underlies the practice of giving excuses that will help the other person avoid an internal attribution. For example, saying one is ill protects the self-esteem of others more than saying one does not enjoy being with them.

When Do Attributions Occur? An issue that arises in attributional accounts concerns the timing of attributions and emotions. As indicated above, Weiner (1985) shares with Arnold (1960) and Lazarus (1966) a two-stage model, in which emotional reactions typically involve a primary and then a secondary appraisal. The primary appraisal establishes the goodness or badness of the event, and the secondary appraisal establishes the cause. Success or failure is believed to first produce primitive reactions of happiness or frustration, which then stimulate a search for a cause. Depending on the attributions made, new emotions result.

The idea that attributions involve a separable stage of the emotion process was also characteristic of Schachter and Singer's (1962) attributional approach. They induced in subjects a state of undifferentiated arousal by injecting them with epinepherin and then arranged for a confederate in the same room to act either angry or playful to influence subjects' interpretations of their experience of arousal. This method was dictated by the Schachter-Singer model that the physiological component of emotion was a state of undifferentiated arousal, and that the emo- tional quality depended on cognitive interpretations of that arousal. Although Schachter and Singer made it clear that perceptions of arousal and attributions were often simultaneous, their method encouraged the idea that attributions usually come later.

A somewhat different emphasis can be seen in the writing of Heider (1958), the originator of attribution theory. Heider is a gestalt psychologist for whom attributions are often an inseparable part of perception, not something that occurs after perception. When one sees one billiard ball strike another, and the second begins to move immediately, one perceives the first ball as having caused the second to move. One does not see motion first and then ask oneself why; the causal attribution is part of the perceived event.

Weiner's (1985) model is not intended to be a comprehensive theory of emotion, but the eliciting conditions it specifies for the attribution emotions are generally similar to those proposed in the OCC account. In the OCC account, if one perceives an action as praiseworthy, one might feel admiration if the actor is another person and pride if the actor is one's self. Admiration and pride are differentiations of the affective reaction of approval, but it is not the case that one first experiences approval and then has to ask what caused the action of which one is approving. Rather, as in Heider's account, the self versus other attribution is often part of the initial perception.

Liu, Karasawa, and Weiner (1992) recently extended the attributional approach. They noted that dispositional attributions are more likely for negative than for positive emotions. They inferred that this is a consequence of the functional difference between positive and negative emotions. Following Schwarz (1990), the underlying notion is that negative emotions require action, and action requires one specific target of effort, whereas positive emotions generally signal that things are fine, and that one can continue doing the same thing. In addition, happiness may generally require that many things fall into place so that one can reach one's goal, whereas unhappiness can result when a single link in the chain fails. In three scenario experiments, Liu et al. showed that scenarios depicting negative emotions are more likely to be followed by attributions to one and only one sufficient cause, whereas positive emotions evoke inferences of multiple causality.

Learned Helplessness.   Weiner (1985) has distinguished a variety of emotions using attributions, but the majority of research on attribution and emotion has concerned a single emotional state—depression. For example, the work of Seligman (e.g., Seligman, Abramson, Semmel, & Von Baeyer, 1979) and Alloy and Abramson (e.g., 1979) focuses on the fact that attributions of negative outcomes to internal, stable, and uncontrollable causes produce feelings of hopelessness, helplessness, and depression. Stemming from the original demonstration of learned helplessness in dogs (e.g., Seligman, Maier, & Solomon, 1971), these investigators have explored the consequences of learned helpless beliefs for depression and the role of individual differences in attributional style in the risk of depression.

Implicit Theories of Ability.   In a related line of work, Dweck and Leggett (1988) proposed that the power of attributions flow from a person's implicit theory of the domain in question. They showed how individual differences in implicit theories of intelligence affect a person's goals, emotions, and behavior. Dweck and Leggett referred to individuals who believe ability to be fixed and unchanging as "entity theorists" and those who believe ability to be malleable and controllable as "incremental theorists." Even though entity theorists do not differ in ability, they are prone to helplessness in the face of failure. Consequently, they appear to avoid situations where they might fail and adopt performance goals (to look good), rather than learning goals. In contrast, incremental theorists have a mastery orientation and are challenged by failure. Thus, they appear to seek out challenge and adopt a goal to learn.

In terms of the OCC account, entity theorists are focused on themselves as objects and on ability as fixed. On the other hand, incremental theorists do not have a preoccupation with themselves as fixed entities — success and failure conveys information about the world and about their strategy, rather than about themselves. With respect to their achievement goals, entity-oriented theorists would be likely to experience self-as-object emotions such as self-disgust or contempt when they fail, whereas incremental theorists would be more likely to experience outcome-based emotions such as frustration. With respect to their performance goals, entity-oriented subjects would experience fear, but incremental theorists would experience hopefulness. To the incremental theorist, failure can serve as an incentive, because it is a sign that learning can take place. Indeed, Diener and Dweck (1978) showed that after failure, mastery-oriented children often become more rather than less motivated. On the other hand, entity theorists find in failure evidence of personal flaws and are motivated to cover up and avoid disclosing their inadequacy (performance goals), rather than risking failure to learn. One of the most interesting aspects of Dweck and Leggett's work is their generalization of their theory from success and failure in academic pursuits to other domains, including reactions to social rejection and moral failure.

A Prototype Theory

For the appraisal theorist, the important part of reality is in the mind of the perceiver. For the prototype theorist, the important part of emotion is also in the mind of the perceiver. Although most investigators of emotion use subjects' concepts of emotion as a proxy for studying emotions, investigators of emotion prototypes study such concepts for their own sake. For example, Shaver et al. (1987) obtained similarity ratings on 250 emotion terms and then conducted a hierarchical cluster analysis. They isolated three levels corresponding to (a) general positive and negative affective reactions, (b) middle level concepts consisting of five basic emotions (love, anger, happiness, sadness, fear), and (c) subordinate emotions (e.g., liking, hope, disgust, shame, anxiety). The authors envisioned the emotional process as one in which eliciting conditions give rise to a basic emotion that might then be differentiated on the basis of the situational context into one of the subordinate forms.

In common with other cognitive accounts, Shaver et al. (1987) assumed that the elicitation of an emotion ultimately depends on a person having appraised a situation as relevant to his or her goals. Of most interest, however, are data collected on the content of people's prototypes about the basic emotions. They solicited open-ended answers to questions about the antecedents, responses, and self-control procedures for each of the basic emotions. For example, subjects mentioned that fear was elicited by threat of social rejection, threat of harm or death, being in the dark, and so on. They mentioned that responses to fear include feeling nervous, having a trembling voice, whimpering, and fleeing, and that coping with fear can involve trying to keep calm and hiding the fear from others. On the basis of these kinds of responses, Shaver et al. provided maps of the content of common emotion prototypes.

The approach taken by Shaver and Schwartz and their colleagues is both similar to and different from that taken in the OCC account. The approaches are similar in that emotions are seen as hierarchically structured in both. Also, in both approaches some emotional reactions are considered to be cognitive differentiations of other emotions. However, Shaver and Schwartz take a strong stand on the issue that there are five basic emotions from which all other emotions emerge. Ortony et al. (1988) recognized that some emotions can serve as a basis for others, but expressed doubt that there is a single set of irreducible emotions that combine to account for all others. Of course the concept of a basic level category in a conceptual system is not necessarily the same thing as a basic emotion in a biological sense.

The most fundamental difference between the Shaver and Schwartz approach and the others discussed here lies in the prototype approach they have adopted. As indicated earlier, Shaver and Schwartz focus on the conditions for the use of emotion concepts, rather than the eliciting conditions for emotions. Thus, one is more likely to apply the concept of anger in a situation that resembles one's prototype of anger. If someone sees a person who is red in the face hit another person who has just insulted him or her, one is likely to infer the presence of anger. This prototype approach concerns beliefs about eliciting conditions, which may or may not encompass the actual elicitation conditions for emotions. However, a strong argument in favor of this approach came from a recent study by Shaver et al. (1992), who compared the categories of emotion terms used by Chinese, Italian, and U.S. subjects and found strong agreement. On the basis of these results, they argued that certain emotions are universal; and they saw evidence for a biological basis for these emotions in this universality.

As discussed earlier, the basis of a prototype position is the belief that it is impossible to specify the necessary and sufficient conditions for the concept of emotion, and perhaps for emotions themselves (Fehr & Russell, 1984; Russell, 1991). To the extent that other cognitive theories are attempts to specify the necessary and sufficient conditions for emotions, then the Shaver et al. (1987) view is fundamentally at odds with them. On the other hand, progress can be made by studying the various facets of emotion specifying the conditions of emotions without taking a position on whether emotion is definable.

A Self-Discrepancy Theory

Higgins (1987) proposed a hypothesis that focuses on self-schemas and the emotional consequences of self-discrepancy. The idea is that one has a general schema for one's self (actual self) that can be more or less discrepant from schemas about the way one would like to be (ideal self) or the way one thinks one should be (ought self). Moreover, each of these viewpoints on the self can be from one's own standpoint or from the standpoint of one or more others. The basic possibilities are that an actual self-schema (from own or other's standpoint) may be compared with either an ideal or an ought self-schema (also from own or other's standpoint). The ideal and ought selves are believed to function as *self-guides*, and comparisons between these self-guides and one's actual self are believed to have emotional consequences.

The formulation does not attempt to explain the usual set of specific emotions. It focuses instead on two general kinds of emotional outcomes—feeling dejected and feeling agitated. The hypothesis is that self-ideal discrepancy should induce feelings of dejection, self-ought discrepancy, and feelings of agitation. For example, if Pauline is a movie reviewer whose *ideal* is to be a writer of snappy prose, but who finds instead that her writing puts people to sleep, she should feel dejected, sad, and discouraged. If she also thinks she ought to formulate her own opinion, but on occasion gets her material from other reviewers, she might feel agitated and experience emotions of shame, worry, and fear.

A study by Strauman and Higgins (1988) provided supporting data. They found that actual–ideal self-discrepancies were associated with reports of disappointment and dissatisfaction, whereas actual–ought discrepancies were associated with reports of fear and restlessness. A second study also found that actual–ought discrepancies were related to social anxiety (agitation), whereas actual–ideal discrepancies were associated with depression (dejection). Strauman and Higgins (1987) also showed that these emotional consequences could be triggered by priming material in memory relevant to ideal or ought selves. In a clinical population, Strauman (1989) found an association between clinical depression and actual–ideal discrepancies and between social anxiety and actual–ought discrepancies. Further supporting data came from nonclinical populations (e.g., Higgins, Bond, Klein, & Strauman, 1986; Higgins, Klein, & Strauman, 1985).

A recent study found a relationship between these processes and birth order (Newman, Higgins, & Vookles, 1992). It was reasoned that, because of the more intense parenting styles experienced by first-born children, parental ideals and oughts should have a bigger impact on first-borns. As expected, first-borns had smaller discrepancies between their actual self and parental ideals and oughts than did later-borns, and the discrepancies that did exist were correlated more highly with their emotions than was the case with later-borns.

Method. The method that Higgins and Strauman have used involves having subjects list, in an open-ended fashion, traits or other attributes describing themselves and their self-guides. Subjects list up to 10 attributes describing their actual selves and up to 8 attributes for each self-guide. Each attribute is rated on a 4-point scale in terms of the degree to which it applies. Dejection is the sum of ratings on 9 emotions, including depressed, disappointed, discouraged, hopeless, low, sad, not happy, not optimistic, and not satisfied. Agitation is the sum of ratings on the emotions of agitated, dread, guilty, irritable, on-edge, restless, tense, threatened, and uneasy. Recent research by Ahadi (1993) and by Gohm (1992) defining the various selves using more traditional personality measures failed to find the relationships hypothesized by Higgins. It may be that Higgins and Strauman's practice of obtaining depictions of the self in subjects' own words is an important step in tapping active cognitive construals of the self.

In the most recent version of the theory (Higgins, 1990), several new concepts and comparisons have been added. The concept "can" has been added in recognition that sometimes one's ideal is within reach and sometimes it is not. Thus, although discrepant from one's ideal, one's actual self may or may not be all that one can do. An expectation factor concerning what one thinks one will be in the future also has been added. Although discrepant from one's ideal, one's actual self may or may not be discrepant from what one expects to do in the future.

Self-Discrepancy Theory and the OCC Account

Higgins (1990) couches his predictions in terms of general feeling tones of dejection and agitation, rather than in terms of specific emotions. Dejection might appear as sadness, depression, or disappointment, and Higgins includes both anxiety and shame as examples of agitation emotions. The process by which a failure to meet one's goals results in sadness seems straightforward, but the inclusion of anxiety along with shame as a reaction to a failure to meet standards implies a more complex process. Presumably one would feel shame about the action, but also would be anxious about rejection from others as an outcome. To relate the Higgins' and OCC accounts requires looking separately at the predictions of sadness and anxiety and the prediction of sadness and shame.

Consider first the prediction of sadness and anxiety. One's ideal self concerns what one wants to be like and is based on approach goals and possible rewards. The loss of such rewards should result in sadness (dejection). On the other hand, the ought self concerns avoidance of possible punishment. The threat of such negative outcomes should result in anxiety (agitation). Roseman (1984) also distinguishes approach motivation from avoidance motivation. He hypothesized that thwarted approach motivation leads to sadness and thwarted avoidance motivation to distress. The approach–avoidance variable is not part of the OCC account, but the distinction concerning whether prospects are relevant or not makes the same sadness versus anxiety prediction. That is, sadness would reflect current goal failure, whereas anxiety would reflect the prospect of future punishment.

Now consider the prediction of sadness and shame. In the OCC (1988) account, sadness reflects a focus on outcomes, whereas shame and guilt reflect a focus on the blameworthiness of actions. A joint consideration of situations relevant to both goals and standards is illustrated in Fig. 7.4. The figure shows (around

FIG. 7.4.   In situations varying in ought versus ideal consistency, Higgins (1987) predicts dejection versus agitation. When considered as standard versus goal consistency, Ortony, Clore, and Collins (1988) predict pride, gratification, happy, happy/shame, shame, self-anger, sad, and pride/sad.

the outside of the circle) the OCC predictions for situations varying in standard versus goal consistency. It shows along the axes (on the inside of the circle) Higgins' predictions (agitation vs. dejection) for the same situations considered as varying in ought versus ideal consistency. The OCC account specifies pride versus shame when focusing on standards (oughts) and joy versus sadness when focusing on goals (ideals). Higgins makes predictions at the discrepant ends of the dimensions, but not at the consistent ends. The figure raises interesting questions about what happens in situations in which ideal and ought selves are salient at the same time. In situations that are both goal discrepant and standard discrepant, the OCC account predicts the occurrence of self-anger (self-reproach, remorse, penitent, etc.), and Higgins (1990) would presumably predict the occurrence of dejection and agitation at the same time. In situations that are both goal consistent and standard consistent, the OCC account predicts the occurrence of gratification (pleased with oneself, self-satisfaction, smug, etc.), and Higgins does not address positive states.

Neither theory has anything to say about the remaining possibilities, where ought and ideal are in conflict. How do students feel after cheating on an exam to achieve their ideal grade versus passing up an opportunity to do so and condemning themselves to a lower grade? These are approach-avoidance situations in which people might experience multiple emotions, rather than a single hybrid emotion. Presumably the emotion experienced in the moment coincides with the focus of attention, so that choosing to abstain makes one feel proud of the act but sad about the grade, whereas giving in to temptation makes one feel happy about the grade but ashamed of the act. As indicated in the figure, things that one ought to do but does not want to do might be thought of as *duties*, whereas things that one wants to do but ought not do might be thoughts of as *sins*.

Criteria for Emotion Theories

There are many theories of emotion, some of which were described previously. It should be apparent that all can account for at least some of the known facts about emotion elicitation. Many of the theories make similar predictions, but they nevertheless differ in a variety of ways. One way to compare the theories is with respect to how well they deal with certain enduring problems, including the problem of positive emotions, the relation between emotions and emotion words, whether the theory is testable, how the theory relates emotion to behavior, and the degree to which the theory can be formalized.

Accounting for Positive Emotions.   One criterion for assessing emotion theories is whether they accommodate positive emotions as something more than the mere absence of negative emotion. In goal-based theories, the valence of an emotional state reflects whether goals are satisfied or thwarted. As a result, goal-based theories can, at least in principle, handle positive and negative emotions equally well. These would include such theories as that of Abelson (1983), Frijda (1986), Oatley and Johnson-Laird (1987), the OCC (1988) account, Roseman (1984), Scherer (1984), Smith and Ellsworth (1985), Wyer and Srull (1989), and others. However, theories that rely specifically on the interruption of goal-directed activity as the trigger for emotion, such as Mandler's (1975, 1984) and Berscheid's (1982), have a more difficult time handling the positive emotions and seem limited for that reason.

The work of Lazarus and his colleagues was not reviewed, because they have not focused on emotional structure as such. Nevertheless, they have done a more thorough job than most of analyzing how positive emotions function in the coping process. Lazarus, Kanner, and Folkman (1980), for example, discussed how positive emotions make the act of "taking a breather" from stressful activity an effective way to cope. They also discussed how positive emotions act as "sustainers" that energize coping efforts, and as "restorers" during the later stages of coping, when healing and recovery take place.

Ellsworth and Smith (1988) made a point of studying the positive emotions. They concluded that the positive emotions (and their associated appraisals) are somewhat less differentiated than the negative emotions. They nevertheless found considerable differentiation among six states that they considered positive emotions, including interest, hope/confidence, challenge, tranquility, playfulness, and love. Each had a distinctive pattern of appraisal.

One of the salient facts about the emotion lexicon is that there are more emotion terms for negative than for positive emotions. However, this fact is not necessarily a reliable guide to the emotion types that exist. The disproportionate number of negative terms may indicate that negative events are more frequent or that there is greater survival value in precise communication about negative states. Most theorists also focus their explanations on negative emotions. For example, in most lists of so-called "basic emotions," joy is usually the only positive emotion that is listed. The OCC account is unusual in that it includes an equal number of positive and negative emotion types. It assumes that variables that have negative implications for one's goals also can have positive implications, creating the possibility of a positive state that parallels each kind of negative state. For example, anticipation gives some emotions a distinctive character, but, in addition to anticipation of threat, as in fear, there is also anticipation of opportunity, as in hope. It is easier for events to have a negative, rather than a positive, effect with respect to certain kinds of goals (e.g., preserving one's health). Although this might increase the incidence of negative emotions, it would not seem to require the postulation of different kinds of elicitation factors or emotions.

Emotions and Emotion Words. A related issue concerns the role of natural language terms for emotion in theory construction. Because the object is to construct theories of emotions, rather than theories of emotion terms, this is an important issue. Some have argued that new emotion concepts should be developed based solely on covariances established by psychological research. Such a position was championed in personality by Cattell (1946) and in the developmental study of emotion by Kagan (1984). We, on the other hand, see no prospect of developing a system of emotion that ignores the concepts provided by language. Although emotions are not linguistic phenomena, they are represented richly in language by emotion words and phrases.

Still, although it offers a useful starting place, the emotion lexicon does not provide a perfect map of emotions. For example, it is not the case that there is one term for every emotion, and one emotion for every emotion term. Do *annoyed, furious, peeved,* or *enraged* refer to four different kinds of emotion or to different forms and intensities of the same kind of emotion? In addition to such redundancy, there are also linguistic gaps. But, does the failure of a language to have a single lexical entry for an emotion mean that members of that culture do not experience the emotion? Despite the obviousness of this problem, almost all of the systems that we have reviewed equate the emotions in their theories with single English language emotion terms. The shortcoming of this approach is that it may be difficult to achieve any more order in one's theory than is found in the rather disorderly language of emotions.

Rather than focusing on emotion words, the OCC account characterizes types of emotions that share cognitive eliciting conditions. Therefore, the terms of the theory are not particular English words (e.g., fear), but specifications of these emotion types. As was shown in Table 7.1, the emotion type of which the English term *fear* would be a token, for example, is "being displeased at the prospect of an undesirable event." Because such terms as *displeased* and *undesirable* have particular meanings in the theory, one can know more precisely what is and is not being explained than if a term such as *fear* were used.

A related problem is that it is often unclear how the emotion terms that are included in a theory are related to other emotion terms that are not included. Shaver et al. (1992) related them empirically. They used similarity ratings of emotion terms by speakers of different languages, and the terms were then reduced to groups of terms by hierarchical cluster analyses. The OCC theory also focuses on emotion types as specified in terms of cognitive eliciting conditions. For each type there are multiple emotion tokens (specific emotion terms).

Testability. An important criterion for a good emotion theory is that it be testable and that it generate empirical research. Frijda's, Higgins', Roseman's, Scherer's, Smith and Ellsworth's, and Weiner's theories have been especially generative. Many of the approaches have attempted to establish the elicitation variables completely empirically by computing correlations between potentially important factors and reported emotions. However, when reviewing studies that take this approach, one cannot help but feel that it is a blunt instrument for attempting to cut nature at its joints. For example, in a large-scale study by Wallbott and Scherer (1988), all of the appraisal factors were to a greater or lesser extent correlated, however minimally, with all of the emotions studied, and it is not clear how to separate variables that merely covary with the emotions from those that are important in the elicitation of the emotions. Within a correlational approach, what would be needed is a multivariate analysis focused on latent variables with multiple measures for each variable, and it is not clear whether that is feasible.

In the absence of the ability to discover emotional structure empirically from the ground up, it might be useful to start with a logical analysis of the meaning of the emotion concepts to be studied. This was the approach taken in the OCC account. It has been argued by Smedslund (in press) that many of the propositions of cognitive emotion theories have no empirical content. In the OCC account, in particular, the proposed eliciting conditions are essentially analyses of what the emotion terms mean. Thus, what one means when one says that someone is fearful, for example, is something like their *being displeased at the prospect of an undesirable outcome.* Hence, conducting a study to see if people report being afraid when they are displeased about the possibility of an undesirable event is a bit like testing to see if all bachelors are unmarried. A failure to confirm the hypothesis would reflect only on the procedure and measures and might never lead one to change one's definition of *fearful.*

On the other hand, the empirical enterprise involves more than testing hypotheses. It also includes establishing measures and procedures within which to study emotional phenomena. Moreover, failures of predictions do lead to changes in the way specific emotions are characterized (e.g., Roseman et al., 1992). Indeed, even the adequacy of statements that are intended as nothing more than definitions can be challenged by finding examples that should be accommodated but are not. Thus, there may not be as sharp a dividing line between analytic and synthetic truth as one might assume, at least in psychology.

One of the limitations of research aimed at testing the cognitive factors in emotion elicitation is that it often requires subjects to agree on the qualitative distinctions between such states as resentment versus anger or sympathy versus pity. An alternative is to focus research on emotional intensity (Frijda et al., 1992). A unique characteristic of the OCC account is that it includes proposals about the cognitive variables governing the intensity of emotions in addition to those that elicit them. In addition, the theory hypothesizes that emotions sharing the same set of eliciting conditions should also share a common set of intensity variables. These intensity hypotheses put empirical meat on the definitional bones of the OCC account, affording a strong quantitative basis for testing hypotheses not only about the intensity variables themselves, but also hypotheses about the relations among the emotions and hypotheses about the proposed structure as a whole. One of the advantages of using intensity predictions as a way to assess the proposed structure is that quantitative comparisons can be made. That is, there is less opportunity for ambiguity in the quantitative tests of hypotheses about whether more or less of a given emotion was experienced than in research attempting to make qualitative tests of whether subjects felt anxious or guilty.

Accounting for Behavior.   The theories on which we have focused concern emotion elicitation, but a comprehensive theory also might be expected to indicate how emotions are related to behavior. However, only Frijda's (1986) theory offers a systematic treatment of the action implications of emotion. Frijda suggests that emotions are characterized by particular patterns of action readiness, as discussed earlier, and that these patterns are responsible for the distinctive experience of each emotion. An alternative possibility, however, is that the effects on behavior may be indirect, stemming from changes in goals. Indeed, almost all of Frijda's action readiness modes are statements beginning with "I wanted," implying that they concern not so much motor programs, but desired states or goals. For example, the action readiness found in shame, "I wanted not to be noticed by anyone," may not refer so much to an action tendency as to a goal.

The structures responsible for emotions in humans presumably evolved out of systems that were dominated by automatic response patterns. It seems likely, as Frijda argues, that part of the experience of emotion reflects these impulses. But one of the chief advantages of emotions appears to be that they allow the organism to go beyond the limitations of reflexes and fixed action patterns (see Scherer, 1984, for a discussion of this point). What does it mean to suggest, as often is done, that fear involves behavioral tendencies to escape, that anger involves activation of aggressive responses, that shame involves tendencies to hide, and so on? Words such as *behavior*, *response*, and *action*, even when qualified by words such as *tendencies*, *readinesses*, or *inclinations*, imply that specific large muscle groups and motor circuits are activated when angry, fearful, or ashamed. Are one's legs automatically programmed to run when afraid, one's arm programmed to hit when angry, or one's hands programmed to cover one's face when ashamed? It might be interesting to see EMG studies aimed at testing such hypotheses. An emotion such as fear presumably involves a redistribution of blood from the viscera to the large muscles, and such effects presumably would enable one to engage in rapid action or extreme exertion. But such general activation is not the same thing as a specific action tendency or a motor program.

As indicated earlier, perhaps similar advantages can be had if one assumes that the direct effects of emotions are motivational, rather than behavioral. One probably can achieve more agreement about the likely goals of angry, fearful, or ashamed persons than about their likely behavior. For example, it seems clear enough that fear involves a heightened desire to avoid harm or loss, but it is not at all clear whether the attainment of this goal would necessitate selling one's stocks, listening to the weather report, or running fast. Therefore, the immediate effects of emotion may be as much mental as behavioral. Indeed, in the final section of this chapter, we review the growing body of research investigating the implications of emotions for styles of cognitive processing. The data suggest that negative affect creates an analytic, detail-oriented mental set, whereas positive affect fosters global, heuristic processing.

A position that sees emotion as relevant to behavior, but that avoids assuming a direct link to behavior is proposed by Carver and Scheier (1990). They suggest that behavior is guided by a hierarchy of control mechanisms in which the output of one often serves as the input to another at a higher level. They propose that emotion is a signal to pursue a particular superordinate goal. For example, a person who is about to touch a snake as part of a treatment for snake phobia is likely to experience fear. They suggest that the function of the fear is to inform the system that a superordinate goal that is highly relevant to this situation is being thwarted—in this case, the goal of safety.

Degree of Formalization.   Few of the theories reviewed here attempt much in the way of formalization. Exceptions can be found in the work of Wyer and Srull (1989), Carver and Scheier (1990), and the OCC (1988) account. Wyer and Srull proposed mathematical formalizations aimed at quantifying the likely intensity of emotional responses when goals in a goal hierarchy are satisfied or thwarted. The formulas are an aid to systematic exploration of the implications of assumptions about goals and their relation to emotion. It is less clear how meaningful the actual numbers are, because of the serious assumptions required (e.g., such as that all of the goals and their interrelationships in a system are known). Still, this is an encouraging beginning and a practical aid to making at least ordinal predictions.

Carver and Scheier (1990) see emotion elicitation as a function of the process of monitoring one's progress toward goals. They suggest that what is important is not one's discrepancy from the goal, but the rate at which this discrepancy is being reduced. In this formulation, behavior is analogous to distance, and what the monitoring system responsible for emotion is sensitive to is a quantity analogous to velocity. In formal terms, velocity is the first derivative of distance over time. To the extent that this physical analogy is meaningful, the perceptual input responsible for emotion is the first derivative over time of the input information used by the action monitoring loop. They suggest that the process functions as a feedback loop, in which the rate of discrepancy reduction is compared with some reference value, which is an acceptable or desired rate of behavioral discrepancy reduction. One kind of output of the comparison process they propose is experiential. The comparison produces both a hazy sense of outcome expectancy and a feeling of positiveness or negativeness. Positiveness reflects a faster than satisfactory progress toward a goal, and negativeness reflects a less than satisfactory rate of progress. Among the implications of this model is the observation that the kinds of actual–ought and actual–ideal discrepancies focused on by Higgins (1987) should not be as important as the rate at which such discrepancies are being reduced relative to expectations.

A different kind of formalization has been undertaken by the OCC account. With an eye to AI applications, they have attempted to write a system of rules and representations about the elicitation of emotions, a first step toward building AI programs that can reason about emotion. The eliciting conditions that were shown earlier in Fig. 7.1 have been written as production rules of the kind also found in Anderson's (1983) ACT theory. For example, for the emotion of joy, one of these rules might be as follows (Ortony et al., 1988, p. 182):

(1) IF *DESIRE* $(p,e,t) > 0$
THEN set *JOY-POTENTIAL* $(p,e,t) =$
$f_j[/ DESIRE (p,e,t)/,I_g (p,e,t)]$

This formalism says that if the computed desirability (*DESIRE*) of an event is positive, then the amount of joy potential (*JOY-POTENTIAL*) is a function both of how desirable the event (*e*) is for this person (*p*) at this time (*t*) and also of the combined effects of the intensity variables (I_g).

Whether one feels joy would depend on the outcome of a rule such as Rule 2 (Ortony et al., 1988, p. 183):

IF *JOY-POTENTIAL* $(p,e,t) > JOY THRESHOLD (p,t)$
THEN set *JOY-INTENSITY* $(p,e,t) =$
JOY-POTENTIAL $(p,e,t) - JOY-THRESHOLD (p,t)$
ELSE set *JOY-INTENSITY* $(p,e,t) = 0$

This rule simply checks to see whether joy potential exceeds the threshold required to have a joy emotion. There are benefits of distinguishing emotions and emotion potentials. For example, it would allow a natural-language understanding system to deal with sentences like: "John was in a wonderful mood that morning. When his children were obnoxious at breakfast, it didn't bother him at all" (Ortony et al., 1988, p. 184). In such an example, a good mood might be thought of as raising the threshold for anger, such that factors producing anger potential might not produce an anger emotion.

One goal of the theory is to produce specifications of emotions and their intensity variables of the kinds that could enter into successful AI programming. The goal is not to produce a computer that feels, but one that can reason about emotions or understand text that requires emotion concepts, such as stories or narratives of everyday behavior. Success in such an endeavor requires a system of rules and representations about the elicitation of emotions. Although interesting and potentially useful, such rules deal mainly with emotion identification. Modeling emotion generation will involve modeling the appraisal process, in which the desirability or goal conduciveness values are computed (see Pfeifer, 1988, for a review of existing AI models of emotion). Regardless of whether computers can be made to reason about emotion, the kind of preliminary formalization seen in the OCC account is desirable as a way to foster more precise and systematic theory.

In summary, we have focused on two of our three topics. The first section, "What Is an Emotion?", included a discussion of various definitional and conceptual issues in the study of emotion. The second section, "The Cognitive Causes of Emotion," concerned proposals about the cognitive causes of emotions. This material addressed questions about the structure of emotion, which we referred to initially as Wundt's question. We turn now to the third section, "The Cognitive Consequences of Emotion." This material addresses questions about the function of emotion, which we referred to initially as James's question. It is divided into three parts, corresponding to research on the role of affect in memory, judgment, and cognitive processing.

THE COGNITIVE CONSEQUENCES OF EMOTION

An individual's affective state may influence each and every step of the information processing sequence, from selective attention to information, to the encoding of information and its subsequent retrieval from memory. In addition, affective states may influence evaluative judgments and individuals' choice of heuristic or systematic processing strategies. Although there is little disagreement that affective states may have these influences, there are differing views regarding underlying processes and the specific conditions under which various effects may emerge. More than other areas of social cognition research, current thinking about the interplay of affect and cognition is characterized by a considerable number of distinct theoretical models that are formulated in terms of different constructs and assumptions, and that frequently lead to different and sometimes opposite predictions. The area is rich for debate, as data seem available to lend support to the various positions advanced.

In this section of the chapter, we summarize what we consider key theoretical positions, identifying major and distinctive predictions, inconsistent findings, and issues for future research. We first review models that bear on the impact of affective states on the encoding, storage, and recall of information. Next, we turn to the impact of affective states on evaluative judgments. Finally, we return to many of the issues raised in these sections and cast them in the broader framework of affective influences on the spontaneous use of heuristic or systematic processing strategies. In reviewing empirical work, we do not strive for comprehensiveness, but limit ourselves to exemplary studies bearing on key theoretical issues. Moreover, we focus more on experimental mood induction research than on studies using clinical populations, given the interpretive difficulties that may arise in the latter case. A more comprehensive review of empirical findings, including studies based on clinical populations, is provided by Morris (1989).

Mood and Memory

Recent theorizing about the impact of affective states on memory has been dominated by two distinct approaches. One line of research (see Ellis & Ashbrook, 1988, for a review) explored the impact of affective states on individuals' attentional resources and emphasized disruptive effects of affective states on memory performance. The other line of research conceptualized affective states in terms of units in memory representation and emphasized facilitative as well as inhibiting effects on memory performance, depending on the match between affect at learning and affect at recall, or the match between affect at recall and the valence of the material to be recalled (see Blaney, 1986, for a review).

Disruptive Effects of Affective States

The Resource Allocation Model. In general, the amount of attentional resources people can invest is assumed to be limited and variable, being influenced by factors such as age, arousal, and emotional states (Hasher & Zacks, 1979). Although one may assume that any affective state, if sufficiently intense, may capture attention, and therefore decrease attention to other external stimuli, most researchers focused on the impact of negative affect on attentional resources (Ellis & Ashbrook, 1988; Roy-Byrne, Weingartner, Bierer, Thompson, & Post, 1986; Sullivan & Conway, 1989). According to Ellis and Ashbrook's resource allocation model, negative affective states are likely to reduce the resources that can be allocated to a given task because mood-congruent thoughts intrude into consciousness; these thoughts may include reflections about one's current mood state, one's bodily sensations, or the sources of one's mood. In line with this assumption, several studies indicated that people in an induced or chronic negative mood have difficulty suppressing mood-congruent material when instructed to do so (Howell & Conway, 1992; Wenzlaff, Wegner, & Roper, 1988). Moreover, induced and chronic negative affect are associated with greater self-focused attention (e.g., Conway, Giannopoulos, Csank, & Mendelson, 1993; Ingram, 1990; Wood, Saltzberg, & Goldsamt, 1990), which may involve attempts at self-understanding that require the investment of attentional resources. As a result of these intruding thoughts and ruminations, negative affective states may interfere with information processing that requires more than minimal amounts of attentional resources. Accordingly, depressed individuals are expected to engage in less processing and/or more simple processing of information; they are likely to evidence a different amount or type of elaboration and organization in the encoding of information. Several studies support this position (see Ellis & Ashbrook, 1988).

For example, Ellis, Thomas, and Rodriguez (1984) explored the impact of depressed moods on the recall of words presented in contexts that varied the amount of required elaboration. Previous work demonstrated that, in the absence of mood inductions, recall is greater for words presented in a context that requires more elaboration at the encoding stage relative to words presented in low-elaboration contexts (Stein & Bransford, 1979). However, being in a depressed mood eliminated this elaboration effect, suggesting that negative affective states may interfere with elaboration. These findings have been replicated with naturally depressed subjects identified on the basis of self-report measures such as the Beck Depression Inventory (BDI; Potts, Camp, & Coyne, 1989).

Induced negative affect also has been shown to limit people's tendency to impose organization on information they are trying to learn. In perceptual grouping tasks that involve the repeated presentation of letter strings that are identical in sequence but differ in grouping (e.g., CA DM ET and C ADME T), learning typically is facilitated by reorganizing the material into more meaningful units (e.g., CAD MET). Leight and Ellis (1981) observed that induced negative affect interfered with such reorganization and led to reduced recall. Related evidence for less organization under negative affect has been obtained with clinically depressed subjects. For example, Watts and Cooper (1989) asked depressed and control subjects to memorize a story. Usually, people better remember the central aspects than the peripheral aspects of a story (Mandler, 1984). However, this effect relies on people organizing the presented material in terms of the story structure. In contrast, depressed subjects did not show a recall advantage for central material, which suggested that they did not organize the presented material. They did, however, show greater recall of highly imageable items, a recall advantage that is not considered resource dependent.

In addition to interfering with elaboration and organization at encoding, dysphoric affective states also may reduce performance at retrieval (Ellis, Thomas, McFarland, & Lane, 1985). After being presented the same sentence stimulus as used in Ellis et al. (1984), mood was induced and recall assessed. Subjects experiencing negative affect recalled fewer words than neutral mood control subjects, regardless of whether the words had been encoded in high- or low-elaboration contexts. In general, the negative impact of dysphoric mood states on recall performance is more evident for less structured, less organized material (Ellis & Ashbrook, 1989).

These and related findings suggest that dysphoric affective states can interfere not only with the elaboration and organization of information at encoding, but also with retrieval. Overall, recall performance can be expected to be worse. Whereas Ellis and Ashbrook's (1988) resource allocation model attributed these effects to reduced attentional resources, Hertel and colleagues (Hertel & Hardin, 1990; Hertel & Rude, 1991; for a similar position, see Fiedler, 1991) suggested that these findings reflect a deficit in initiative. According to this assumption, depressed individuals are less likely to instigate strategies or to generate appropriate hypotheses when performing unstructured tasks. However, when they are provided instructions that enable them to structure their tasks, they reveal fewer or no performance deficits, suggesting that they have sufficient resources to complete tasks effectively if they are guided to use appropriate strategies. Of course, one may argue (see Ellis, 1990, 1991) that an examination of various possible strategies and the initiation of one of them requires attentional resources. Hence, guiding subjects' choice of strategies reduces resource demands, rendering Hertel's findings compatible with the resource allocation model. According to this model, the negative impact of dysphoric states should decrease as the demand on attentional resources decreases.

In summary, negative affective states have been found to reduce the elaboration and organization of material at the encoding stage and to interfere with retrieval, much as the assumption that negative affective states reduce attentional resources would lead us to expect. However, the most compelling evidence has been provided by studies that used material not affective in nature, as the studies reviewed illustrate. When the to-be-learned material is strongly valenced, affective states may inhibit, as well as facilitate, encoding and recall. Moreover, Mackie and Worth (1989) have suggested that positive affective states also can limit attentional resources, and may do so to a higher degree than dysphoric states, although, to our knowledge, this hypothesis has not been tested in the memory domain. Finally, research into affective influences on other aspects of cognitive performance has produced a large number of findings that are incompatible with the predictions of the resource allocation model. We review these findings in the context of our discussion of affective influences on processing strategies.

Affective States and Information Valance

The Associative Network Model.   Whereas the resource allocation model focuses on affective influences on attentional resources, a second line of research conceptualizes affect in terms of units in memory representation. Extending Anderson and Bower's (1973) human associative memory model, Bower (1981) proposed an associative network model in which emotions are represented by emotion nodes (see also Bower, 1991; Bower & Cohen, 1982; Gilligan & Bower, 1984). According to this model, emotions function in an associative network as central nodes, which are linked to related ideas, events of corresponding valence, autonomic activity, and muscular and expressive patterns. When new material is learned, it is associated with the nodes that are active at the time of learning. Accordingly, material that is learned in a particular affective state is linked to the respective emotion node. When an emotion node is stimulated, activation spreads along the pathways, increasing the activation of other nodes connected to the emotion node. Activation of a node above a certain threshold brings the represented material into consciousness.

These assumptions lead to four key predictions that have received considerable attention in recent research (see Blaney, 1986; Forgas & Bower, 1988; Singer & Salovey, 1988, for reviews). First, the model predicts state-dependent recall as a function of matching moods at the time of learning and at the time of recall. In general, any contextual factor may serve as a discriminatory cue facilitating memory when the context at recall matches the context at learning (e.g., Godden & Baddeley, 1975); context can refer both to the state of the learning environment and the state of the person. According to the associative network model, affective states also may serve as discriminatory cues, facilitating recall of material learned in the same mood. Presumably, material that is learned while in a certain mood is associated with the respective mood node. If this, rather than another, mood node is activated at the time of recall, the excitation spreading from the mood node increases the likelihood that the excitation of the node that represents the learned material exceeds threshold, thus bringing the material into consciousness. This state-dependent recall prediction is based on matching moods at learning and recall. In contrast, a second prediction is based on matching valences of mood at the time of recall and of the to-be-recalled material, independent of the mood at time of learning. This prediction is referred to as mood-congruent recall. Again, the activation spreading from an emotion node may increase the activation of related nodes above threshold, resulting in increased recall of material that matches the valence of the current mood. Although state dependency and mood congruency can be clearly distinguished conceptually, they are often difficult to separate empirically, as is seen later. A third prediction from the model concerns mood-congruent encoding of new material. The spreading of activation from a mood node may prime mood congruent concepts, and hence may result in mood congruent encoding of ambiguous information. In addition, the activation of mood congruent concepts and associations may facilitate the elaboration of new information that may be related to these concepts, resulting in a richer network of associations for material that is congruent, rather than incongruent, with mood at encoding. Finally, the assumption of mood congruent encoding and recall processes leads to the prediction of judgmental biases, independent of whether the judgments are made on-line or off-line (Hastie & Park, 1986). As is seen later, it is often difficult to determine which of these distinct effects is reflected in a particular finding, and the model fares best under conditions where several of these effects are likely to combine.

A similar model has been proposed by Spies and Hesse (1986) on the basis of Anderson's (1983) ACT model. In addition, Wyer and Srull (1989) offered a related conceptualization in the framework of their storage unit ("bin") model of memory. Aside from using a different model of memory structure, Wyer and Srull's account also differed with regard to the representation of emotions in memory. Bower (1991) assumed that "about six (plus or minus a few) basic emotions are *biologically wired into the brain*, and that a number of innate as well as learned environmental situations can turn on a particular emotion node. When a particular emotion node is turned on . . . it spreads activation to a variety of indicators, such as characteristic physiological and facial expressions" (p. 32, emphasis added), as well as to nodes that represent associated semantic material. In this biological conceptualization, the activation of the emotion node drives the corresponding physiological and expressive reactions. In contrast, Wyer and Srull (1989) assume that what is represented in memory are "*concepts* of different emotions or affective states" and that these concepts "can be retrieved and used to process information . . . in much the same way as other concepts" (p. 352, emphasis added). According to their model, what drives affective influences on recall is not the affective experience per se, but the activation of the appropriate emotion concept, which is essentially semantic knowledge. "If emotion concepts happen to be in the work space at the time information . . . is sought, these concepts and their associated features may fortuitously be included among the probe cues that are compiled" to search memory for relevant material (Wyer & Srull, 1989, p. 377). This conceptualization allows that mood congruent recall may be observed in the absence of affective experiences, provided that the appropriate emotion concept is activated. Moreover, mood congruent recall may not be observed, despite affective experiences, if these experiences are not labeled with the corresponding emotion concept (see our discussion of Parrott & Sabini, 1990; Wyer & Srull, 1989).

In a closely related vein, Isen, Shalker, Clark, and Karp (1978) suggested for positive mood that "thoughts associated with or responsible for the good mood or mood inducing event may serve to cue us to positive material in memory in much the same way that a category name has been found to cue material of that category that was previously learned" (p. 2; for a more extended discussion of this view, see Isen, 1987). Reflecting the attention that these different models received in recent research, however, our discussion focuses on Bower's (1981, 1991) network theory.

Mood-Congruent Exposure and Encoding.   Several studies have indicated mood effects on the exposure to and encoding of valenced information (C. Kelley, cited in Bower, 1983; Forgas & Bower, 1987; Mischel, Ebbesen, & Zeiss, 1973). For example, Forgas and Bower observed in an impression formation task that happy subjects spent more time examining positive rather than negative information about the target person, whereas sad subjects dwelt longer on the target's negative rather than positive characteristics. According to the associative network model, these differential exposure times reflect that mood-congruent material evokes more associations than mood-incongruent material and hence results in richer elaboration, which takes more time (Bower, 1991). Consistent with this elaboration interpretation, longer exposure times were associated with better recall (Forgas & Bower, 1987). In a similar vein, Bower, Gilligan, and Monteiro (1981, Experiments 1 and 5), using hypnotic mood inductions, had subjects read a story describing positive and negative events and characters. As predicted, subjects tended to recall information about story characters whose affect was congruent with their mood at the time of encoding, again suggesting that this material received more elaboration. Findings of this type suggest that the disruptive effects of affective states on the encoding and organization of information hypothesized by the resource allocation model (Ellis & Ashbrook, 1988) may be limited to material that is affectively neutral and hence does not lend itself to mood-congruent elaboration.

State-Dependent Recall. In general, recall is facilitated when the context at the time of recall matches the context at the time of learning (Eich, 1980; Godden & Baddeley, 1975; see Tulving, 1983, pp. 226–238, for a review). Several studies employing different kinds of mood manipulations indicated that affective states may serve as relevant discriminatory cues, much as has been shown for other contextual cues (see Singer & Salovey, 1988, for a review). Not surprisingly, the impact of affective states and of other contextual cues is reduced, as the need for retrieval cues declines. For example, state-dependent learning effects are more likely to be observed in free recall than in recognition tasks and in a two-list interference paradigm than in a single-list paradigm.

In the single-list paradigm, subjects learn one list of material while in a certain mood and recall the material while in the same or a different mood. Although superior recall under matching than under mismatching moods has occasionally been observed in a single-list paradigm (e.g., Bartlett, Burleson, & Santrock, 1982, Experiment 2; Bartlett & Santrock, 1979), many studies failed to obtain strong evidence for state-dependent recall effects under this condition (e.g., Bartlett et al., 1982, Experiments 1 and 2; Bower, Monteiro, & Gilligan, 1978, Experiments 1 and 2; Leight & Ellis, 1981). In contrast, more consistent results initially were obtained in a two-list interference paradigm: List A was learned while in a happy mood, and List B was learned while in a sad mood. In this case, being in the same mood at the time of recall facilitated recall in several studies, whereas being in the opposite mood led to reduced recall (e.g., Bower et al., 1978, Experiment 3; Schare, Lisman, & Spear, 1984, Experiment 3). For manic-depressive patients, Weingartner, Miller, and Murphy (1977) assessed free associations at different times of their manic-depressive cycle, and later asked them to recall these associations during a similar or dissimilar phase of the cycle. Again, superior recall was observed under conditions of matching affective states. However, subsequent studies (e.g., Bower & Mayer, 1985; Marshall-Garcia & Beck, 1985; Wetzler, 1985) failed to replicate state-dependent recall in a two-list paradigm. Of these studies, Bower and Mayer's presents the most problematic failure to replicate, because these authors used the materials employed in the successful Bower et al. (1978) study and induced moods of comparable intensity. At present, a theoretical rationale that would account for the inconsistent findings seems lacking. Indeed, Bower and Mayer (1985) concluded that "mood-dependent retrieval is an evanescent will-o'-the-wisp, and not the robust outcome suggested by earlier reports" (p. 42).

Mood-Congruent Recall.   Whereas state-dependent recall requires matching moods at the time of encoding and recall, independent of the valence of the to-be-learned material, mood-congruent recall refers to match of mood at recall with the valence of the recalled material, independent of mood at learning. However, the distinction between the valence of the material and mood at learning is problematic. Most importantly, mood-congruent recall has been demonstrated most convincingly for autobiographical memory. In several studies (for reviews see Blaney, 1986; Morris, 1989; Singer & Salovey, 1988), subjects were more likely to recall happy memories when in a happy rather than sad mood, or sad memories when in a sad rather than happy mood (Bower, 1981; Madigan & Bollenbach, 1982; Mathews & Bradley, 1983; Natale & Hantas, 1982; Snyder & White, 1982; Teasdale & Taylor, 1981; Teasdale, Taylor, & Fogarty, 1980).

It seems reasonable to assume, however, that happy events induce a happy mood at the time of their occurrence, whereas sad events induce a sad mood. If so, the valence of the event is inherently confounded with the experiencer's mood at the time of encoding. Accordingly, facilitative effects of mood on the recall of autobiographical memories may reflect state-dependent recall, rather than mood congruency per se. In light of the inconsistent findings obtained in the state-dependent recall studies reviewed earlier, which have typically used neutral rather than strongly valenced material, mood effects on recall may be most reliable under conditions where (a) the valence of the to-be-recalled material matches the mood at recall, and (b) the material was initially learned in a matching mood state. Thus, mood-congruent selectivity in recall may be most likely under conditions that simultaneously satisfy the criteria for state dependency and mood congruency.

As Morris (1989) observed, although mood congruency and state dependency are "conceptually distinguishable, in practice it is virtually impossible to tell which one might be accounting for any given set of results" (p. 72). In fact, several authors (Blaney, 1986; Teasdale & Russell, 1983) pointed out that even the repeatedly observed impact of moods on word associations or the recall of valenced words (e.g., Isen et al., 1978; Madigan & Bollenbach, 1982, Experiment 2; Laird,

Wagener, Halal, & Szegda, 1982) may involve a component of state dependence. To the extent that words of a given hedonic tone are more likely to be used in contexts characterized by a similar hedonic tone, they may be associated differentially with the user's affective state.

Finally, the recall of autobiographical memories shows an interesting asymmetry, as noted by Blaney (1986) and Singer and Salovey (1988). In several studies (e.g., Natale & Hantas, 1982; Salovey & Singer, 1985), happy moods reliably facilitated the recall of happy memories and inhibited the recall of sad memories, relative to neutral moods. In contrast, although sad moods inhibited the recall of happy memories, they did not facilitate the recall of sad ones, relative to neutral moods. Hence, selectivity in recall under sad mood is often restricted to less recall of happy memories, in contrast to what the associative network model would predict.

Several accounts for this asymmetry have been offered. Most frequently, the asymmetric impact of positive and depressed mood has been attributed to mood repair efforts (e.g., Isen, 1984; Singer & Salovey, 1988). According to this account, individuals in a depressed mood may attempt to repair their mood by avoiding further negative memories. In fact, considerable evidence indicates that individuals in a depressed mood engage in a variety of mood repair efforts, including self-reward, helping behavior, or distracting activities (see Morris & Reilly, 1987, for a review). Such controlled processes presumably may override the automatic impact of mood congruent accessibility. Although this assumption is in line with the observation that sad moods are not associated with increased recall of sad memories, it also suggests that individuals in a sad mood deliberately may try to recall happy memories, resulting in mood-incongruent recall. However, the evidence bearing on this implication is mixed. As noted, most studies observed that subjects in a depressed mood recalled less positive events than subjects in an elated mood. However, control conditions in which moods are not manipulated are typically missing (see Blaney, 1986; Morris, 1989; Salovey & Singer, 1988, for reviews). Hence, it is conceivable that depressed subjects recall more positive material than subjects in a neutral mood, as the mood repair hypothesis suggested, although less positive material than subjects in an elated mood. More important, Parrott and Sabini (1990) noted that

standard laboratory procedures may discourage this activity (i.e., mood repair) while encouraging mood congruent recall. Cooperative subjects may inhibit their attempts at mood repair if the mood instructions, mood measures, or cover story causes them to suspect that such attempts would interfere with the experiment. At the same time, many laboratory procedures may expose subjects to stimuli that semantically prime mood congruent concepts and memories, thus augmenting any tendencies toward mood congruent recall that are produced by mood alone. (p. 321)

Consistent with these arguments, studies that did obtain symmetrical effects of happy and sad moods on recall typically used hypnotic mood inductions, along with instructions to maintain the induced mood throughout the experimental session.

However, a direct test of the hypothesis that standard laboratory procedures inhibit mood repair yielded mixed results. In a provocative set of studies, Parrott and Sabini (1990) observed mood-congruent recall when subjects were instructed to get themselves into a happy or sad mood while listening to appropriate music (Experiment 3). Under this condition, depressed subjects recalled events from their high school days that were more negative than the events recalled by elated subjects. Moreover, this result was obtained independent of whether subjects were told to sustain their mood after the mood induction. However, mood congruency was not observed when subjects were unaware that the music played to them might alter their mood (Experiment 4). Under this condition, the first high school event recalled by depressed subjects was a happy one, whereas the first event recalled by elated subjects was a sad one, indicating that the events that were most accessible in memory, and hence recalled first, were mood incongruent. Identical findings were obtained in two additional studies that used naturally occurring events, such as the return of a graded exam (Experiment 1) or sunny versus cloudy days (Experiment 2), as quasi-experimental mood manipulations. In both cases, the first event recalled was again mood incongruent. In all three studies, however, the observed mood incongruency was limited to the first event recalled, whereas the subsequent events tended to reflect mood congruency.

How are we to interpret this set of findings? That subjects recalled mood congruent events when instructed to get themselves into a certain mood, but initially recalled mood incongruent events when they were unaware of the mood related nature of the study, indicates that standard laboratory procedures facilitate mood congruent recall, as Parrott and Sabini (1990) suggested. In contrast to their interpretation, however, it seems questionable that this reflects an inhibition of mood repair efforts under standard laboratory conditions. Although the observation that sad subjects initially recalled a happy event is in line with the mood repair notion, the parallel observation that happy subjects initially recalled a sad event is not. To account for this unexpected pattern, Wyer and Srull (1989) suggested that, when asked to recall a past event, individuals may think about the past in relation to the present. When they are in a good (bad) mood, they may feel that "things aren't always that good (bad)," prompting the recall of a mood incongruent event. Having recalled a mood incongruent event, however, they may notice that "things aren't always that bad (good) either" (p. 383), again prompting the recall of an event of opposite valence, resulting in mood congruency on the second event recalled, as observed in Parrott and Sabini's (1990) studies.

However, if it is not mood repair, what drives the differences between standard laboratory procedures and less obtrusive mood inductions? One possibility was suggested by Wyer and Srull (1989). As discussed, Wyer and Srull assumed that mood congruent recall does not result from the affective state, but from the label attached to it. According to their model, what is represented in memory is not the emotion, but a semantic emotion concept. This concept is always activated when subjects are explicitly told to get themselves into a particular affective state. Under more natural conditions, however, this concept is activated only when subjects use it spontaneously to interpret their current feelings. If the appropriate emotion concept is activated, it may serve as a search cue, resulting in the recall of other material to which the label has been attached. As a result, mood congruent recall would be more likely to be obtained when the appropriate concept is activated explicitly by the mood induction procedure than when it is not.

However, Wyer and Srull's (1989) assumptions provide no obvious mechanism to account for the frequently observed asymmetric impact of happy and sad moods on recall, although their model does account for the differential effects of obtrusive and unobtrusive mood inductions observed by Parrott and Sabini (1990). But Parrott and Sabini's findings also did not provide consistent support for a mood repair explanation of asymmetric recall effects, since mood-incongruent recall was not limited to sad subjects.

As an alternative account, the observation that happy moods facilitate the recall of mood-congruent material, whereas sad moods primarily inhibit the recall of mood-incongruent material, has been traced to structural differences in the storage of positive and negative material. Cramer (1968), Isen (1984), and Matlin and Stang (1979) all suggested that positive material is more interconnected in memory than negative material. If so, a two-step process may account for the observed asymmetry. Specifically, being in a good mood may facilitate the recall of some positive event, which in turn may facilitate the recall of other positive events, assuming that they are connected in memory. In contrast, being in a bad mood may also facilitate the recall of a congruent, negative event. However, this event would not facilitate the recall of other negative events, assuming that negative events are less likely to be interconnected. As a result, mood-congruent recall would be more pronounced under a good mood than under a bad mood, but only part of this facilitation effect would be due directly to the impact of mood per se. Unfortunately, the available data do not allow an evaluation of this possibility. Moreover, it seems unclear why memories of positive events should be more interconnected in memory, given that negative events are more likely to trigger explanatory efforts (e.g., Bohner, Bless, Schwarz, & Strack, 1988), which should establish pathways between negative memories.

Although it is difficult to separate the relative contributions of state dependency and mood congruency in studies using autobiographical recall, it is also difficult to separate the relative contributions of mood congruent recall and mood congruent encoding in many studies that used nonautobiographical material. As Morris (1989) noted, many studies that obtained selective recall of mood congruent material have allowed subjects to control the length of exposure to the to-be-remembered material (e.g., Derry & Kuiper, 1981; Forgas & Bower, 1987). In this case, the obtained selectivity in recall may reflect mood-congruent elaboration of the presented material at encoding, as discussed earlier, as well as the facilitating effect of mood at the recall stage.

In summary, mood-congruent recall has been found to be a rather fragile phenomenon that is sometimes difficult to obtain in empirical studies (cf. Blaney, 1986; Bower & Mayer, 1985; Morris, 1989). Most importantly, mood-congruent recall is most likely to be obtained for self-referenced material, such as autobiographical memories, and it is "impossible or difficult to demonstrate when stimulus exposure occurs under sets that are explicitly antithetical to self-referencing" (Blaney, 1986, p. 232). Moreover, mood congruency may be limited to relatively unstructured material, and tends to be difficult to find when material is presented in narrative form, such that positive and negative elements clearly are interconnected (Hasher, Rose, Zacks, Sanft, & Doren, 1985; Mecklenbräuker & Hager, 1984) or otherwise well organized (Fiedler, Pampe, & Scherf, 1986). Finally, the relative contributions of mood congruency, state dependency, and mood-congruent encoding are difficult to disentangle in many studies, and mood-congruent selectivity in recall may be most likely to be obtained when several of these processes operate in combination. In addition, the notion of mood congruency in recall predicts mood effects on evaluative judgments, a possibility that we address in more detail next.

Mood and Evaluative Judgments

One of the most reliable findings regarding the interplay of affect and cognition concerns the impact of moods on evaluative judgments. In general, a target is likely to be evaluated more favorably when the judge is in a positive, rather than a negative, mood (see Forgas, 1992; Morris, 1989; Schwarz, 1990; Schwarz & Clore, 1988, for reviews). Experimental demonstrations of this basic finding cover a wide variety of evaluative judgments, ranging from satisfaction with consumer goods (Isen et al., 1978) and the evaluation of other persons (e.g., Forgas & Bower, 1987), selected activities (Carson & Adams, 1980) or past life events (e.g., Clark & Teasdale, 1982), to reports of happiness and satisfaction with one's life as a whole (Schwarz & Clore, 1983). According to models of mood-congruent memory (e.g., Bower, 1981; Isen et al., 1978), these findings reflect biased recall of valenced information from memory. As an alternative account, Schwarz and Clore (1983, 1988) suggested that mood effects on evaluative judgments can reflect the use of affective states as a source of information. Next, we address both of these accounts in light of the available data, speculating on the conditions under which one or the other process may mediate mood congruency in evaluation.

In addition, affective states may influence judgments by eliciting different processing strategies, which, in turn, may result in a differential use of information. This possibility is addressed in the next section of this chapter, bearing on moods and processing strategies.

Mood Congruent Recall and Evaluative Judgments.   Assuming that judgments are based on the information that is most accessible at the time (see Higgins, 1989; Higgins & Bargh, 1987, for reviews), the associative network model reviewed earlier predicts mood-congruent biases for on-line as well as off-line (Hastie & Park, 1986) judgments. In the case of memory-based (offline) judgments, this presumably reflects the mood-congruent recall of valenced material from memory. In the case of online judgments, this presumably reflects the impact of mood-congruent associations in response to the stimulus. According to these assumptions, mood effects on evaluative judgments are mediated by affective influences on the accessibility of mood-congruent valenced information and this information is used in forming a judgment.

Consistent with these assumptions, a significant relationship between mood-congruent recall and evaluative judgments has been observed in some studies (Forgas, in press). However, numerous other studies generated data patterns that are inconsistent with the predictions of the associative network model. Hence, we first introduce the competing feelings-as-information model and evaluate the evidence by contrasting the predictions derived from both models.

Feelings as Information: The "How-Do-I-Feel-About-It?" Heuristic.   Emotion researchers have long assumed that moods reflect the general state of the organism, an assumption that prompted Jacobsen (1957) to refer to moods as "barometers of the ego." Similarly, Nowlis and Nowlis (1956) suggested that moods are "a source of information or discriminable stimuli to the organism about the current functioning characteristics of the organism" (p. 352). Extending these assumptions, Wyer and Carlston (1979) suggested that individuals' affective states may serve as information in making judgments, a possibility that was systematically explored by Schwarz and Clore (1983, 1988; see also Clore, 1992; Clore & Parrott, 1991; Schwarz, 1987, 1990).

According to this feelings-as-information hypothesis, individuals may use their apparent affective reactions to a target as a basis of judgment. In fact, by definition, some evaluative judgments refer to one's affective reaction to the stimulus. For example, when asked how "likeable" a person is, one may base one's judgment on one's own feelings toward the person, rather than on a review of the person's features. Other evaluative judgments may not refer directly to one's feelings about the target, but may pose a task that is complex and demanding. Again, the judgmental task may be simplified by assessing one's own feelings about the target. Rather than computing a judgment on the basis of recalled features of the target, an individual may ask him or herself, "How do I feel about it?" In doing so, he or she may mistake feelings due to a preexisting state as a reaction to the target stimulus, resulting in more positive evaluations under pleasant than under unpleasant moods. This assumption generates a number of predictions that cannot be derived from the assumption that mood effects on evaluative judgments are mediated by mood-congruent recall or encoding, of which we review only two (see Schwarz & Clore, 1988; Schwarz, 1990, for more detailed discussions).

Perceived Informational Value. The most crucial prediction is that the impact of affective states on evaluative judgments is a function of the states' perceived informational value. If individuals attribute their current feelings to a source that is irrelevant to the evaluation of a target stimulus, the informational value of their affective state should be discredited and their feelings should not influence the evaluative judgment. On the other hand, according to models of mood-congruent recall, the impact of affective states should depend only on the evaluative implications of the information retrieved from memory, rather than on information provided by the affective state. Therefore, models of mood-congruent recall predict that manipulations of the informational value of one's current affective state will not influence its impact on evaluative judgments.

In line with the feelings-as-information hypothesis, Schwarz and Clore (1983) observed that the impact of mood on judgments of life satisfaction was eliminated when subjects attributed their current feelings either correctly (Experiment 2) or incorrectly (Experiment 1) to a transient source. For example, subjects reported higher life satisfaction and a more elated current mood in telephone interviews when called on sunny rather than rainy days. However, this difference was eliminated when the interviewer mentioned the weather as part of a private aside, thus directing subjects' attention to this source of their elated or depressed state (Experiment 2). Similarly, recalling a sad life event did not influence subjects' judgments of life satisfaction when they could misattribute the resulting sad feelings to the alleged impact of the experimental room (Experiment 1). In addition, current mood, as assessed at the end of the experiment, was more strongly correlated with judgments of life satisfaction when subjects' attention was not directed to a transient source of their feelings than when it was. Conceptual replications of these findings have been reported by Keltner, Locke, and Audrain (1993), Schwarz, Servay, and Kumpf (1985), and Siemer and Reisenzein (1992).

In combination, these findings indicate that individuals may use their current feelings as a basis of judgment unless the diagnostic value of their feelings for the judgment at hand is called into question. This discounting effect (Kelley, 1972) is incompatible with predictions based on mood-congruent recall, because the attributional manipulations discredit only the implications of one's current feelings, but not the implications of valenced information about one's life recalled from memory. Given these findings, it is not surprising that mood effects on evaluative judgments have been observed in the absence of any evidence for mood effects on the recall of relevant information from memory (e.g., Fiedler et al., 1986).

Relative Contributions of Mood and Thought Content. In addition, the predictions of both models differ with regard to the contributions of mood at the time of judgment and the specific content by which the mood is induced. From the perspective of an associative network model of memory, judgments should be most consistent with current mood when mood is induced by a technique that itself increases the accessibility of mood-congruent material that is relevant to the judgment at hand. For example, a depressed mood that is induced through thoughts about a serious disease should affect judgments about diseases more strongly than a depressed mood that is induced by other thoughts, because information about diseases would be activated by both the content of one's thoughts and one's depressed mood. On the other hand, according to the feelings-as-information hypothesis, the nonemotional content of the mood-inducing stimulus should be irrelevant, unless it influences the apparent informational value of the accompanying feelings.

In line with the latter hypothesis, several studies indicate that mood effects on evaluative judgments are largely independent of the specific content by which the mood was induced (e.g., Johnson & Tversky, 1983; Mayer, Gaschke, Braverman, & Evans, 1992; see Schwarz & Clore, 1988, for a review). For example, Johnson and Tversky observed that reading descriptions of negative events, which presumably induced a depressed and slightly anxious mood, increased judgments of risk across a wide set of targets. Most importantly, the impact of mood was independent of the object of judgment or the content by which the mood was induced. For example, reading about cancer affected judgments of the risk of cancer, but had equally strong effects on judgments of the risk of accidents and divorce. Such thoroughly generalized effects, undiminished over dissimilar content domains, are incompatible with models of mood-congruent recall. However, they are consistent with the feelings-as-information hypothesis. According to this hypothesis, individuals may simplify the difficult task of evaluating unknown risks by consulting the feelings that the stimulus apparently elicits. If they feel depressed and anxious, they may conclude that the risk they are asked to evaluate is indeed depressing and threatening, and may then evaluate it as being more severe than they would under a more positive mood. This assumption leads to the prediction that the impact of mood is independent of the content by which it was induced, unless its informational value is discredited.

In combination, these and related findings (see Clore, 1992; Schwarz, 1990; Schwarz & Clore, 1988, for reviews) demonstrate that individuals may use their perceived affective state as a basis of judgment, according to what one might call a "How-do-I-feel-about-it?" heuristic. Although these findings are incompatible with the assumption that mood effects on evaluative judgments are necessarily mediated by mood-congruent recall, they obviously do not preclude that mood-congruent recall may result in biased judgments as well, an issue to which we return later.

The Informational Value of Moods and Specific Emotions. Although the preceding discussion, and most of the empirical evidence currently available, focused on the impact of global moods, the same general logic holds for specific emotions. In applying the feelings-as-information model to specific emotions, however, it is important to consider the different informational values of moods and emotions. Specifically, a central characteristic of mood states is their diffuse and unfocused quality (Clore, 1985; Ewert, 1983), which sets them apart from specific emotions. In contrast to moods, emotions are specific reactions to particular events, reflecting specific appraisal patterns as discussed in the first section of this chapter. Moods do not always have easily identifiable causes. They may come about gradually, and they tend to last longer than emotions. Moreover, moods may develop as the residual of a specific emotion once the emotion's intensity dissipates and its cause is no longer in focal attention (Bollnow, 1956). Thus, the cause of a mood tends to be more remote in time than the cause of an emotion and tends to be less clearly defined for the experiencer.

It is this undifferentiated and unfocused nature of mood states that leads them to be used as information in making a wide variety of different judgments. In fact, when subjects are induced to attribute their moods to specific causes—as in the Schwarz and Clore (1983) experiments reviewed earlier—its impact on judgments that are unrelated to that source vanishes. These considerations suggest that the informational value of specific emotions is more restricted than the informational value of global moods. Given that the source of an emotion is more likely to be in the focus of attention, one's emotional feelings may be more likely to be attributed (correctly) to a specific event. This should reduce their potentially biasing role in judgments that are unrelated to this event.

This hypothesis was supported by research by Keltner et al. (1993). These authors induced a sad mood by having subjects vividly imagine a negative life event. Subsequently, some subjects were asked to describe "what emotions" they currently felt, whereas others indicated where and when the negative event took place. Compared to the latter group, those subjects who labeled their current feelings with specific emotion terms were considerably less affected by the mood manipulation and reported significantly higher life satisfaction, despite being in a depressed mood. In fact, describing one's current emotions was as effective in reducing the impact of an imagined sad event on life-satisfaction judgments as misattributing one's sad feelings to the experimental room. In combination, these studies suggests that labeling their current feelings with specific emotion terms induced subjects to identify specific causes for their current feelings, thus leading subjects to consider them as uninformative for subsequent evaluative judgments that did not pertain to these specific causes. A particularly interesting implication of this analysis holds that specific emotions may be unlikely to affect unrelated judgments shortly after their onset, when the event that elicited them is still salient. Rather, their more general impact may be expected after the emotion dissipates, leaving the individual in a diffuse mood as described by Bollnow (1956).

However, these considerations do not imply that specific emotions would not serve informative functions—they only emphasize that their informational value is likely to be more restricted and specific. On theoretical grounds, this specification likely reflects the implications of the appraisal pattern that underlies the respective emotion. In line with this hypothesis, Gallagher and Clore (1985) observed that feelings of fear affected judgments of risk but not of blame, whereas feelings of anger affected judgments of blame but not of risk. Similarly, Keltner, Ellsworth, and Edwards (1993) observed in several experiments that angry subjects assigned more responsibility to human agents than to impersonal circumstances, whereas sad subjects assigned more responsibility to impersonal circumstances than to human agents, reflecting the appraisal patterns of anger and sadness. In combination, these findings illustrate that, unlike global mood states, specific emotions have very localized effects on judgment. However, as in the case of moods, these effects are eliminated when the informational value of the emotion is called into question by misattribution procedures (e.g., Schwarz et al., 1985).

Similarly, the impact of arousal states (e.g., Zillman, Johnson, & Day, 1972; see Zillman, 1978 for a review) and bodily sensations (e.g., Martin, Harlow, & Strack, 1992; Strack, Martin, & Stepper, 1988; Adelmann & Zajonc, 1989 for a review; see Clore, 1992, for a review) has been found to depend on their perceived causes, consistent with the logic of the feelings-as-information model. For example, in Zillman's (1978) excitation transfer paradigm, effects of physical arousal induced by vigorous exercise on judgment and behavior have been observed only under conditions where subjects were unlikely to attribute their feelings to the impact of the exercise. Extending this line of work, Martin et al. (1992) observed that induced facial expressions affected the interpretation of an ambiguous social situation, and that these effects were more pronounced when subjects were aroused. However, the impact of arousal as well as facial expression was largely eliminated when subjects (correctly) attributed their arousal to physical exercise, thus rendering subjective experience uninformative for the judgment at hand.

Finally, the impact of nonaffective phenomenal experiences, such as the ease with which information comes to mind, follows the same pattern (see Clore, 1992, for a review). For example, one study explored the role of the phenomenal experience of ease of recall, which is central to Tversky and Kahneman's (1973) availability heuristic (Schwarz et al., 1991). Subjects were found to rely on the ease with which some information came to mind only when the informational value of this phenomenal experience was not discredited by misattribution manipulations. In related work (Clore & Parrott, in press), feelings of uncertainty were induced in subjects who later read a poem and rated their ability to understand it. They were more likely to believe that they understood the poem when the feelings of uncertainty they experienced were attributed to the experimental manipulation than when they saw them as part of their reaction to the poem (see Clore, 1992; Clore & Parrott, 1991; Schwarz et al., 1991; Strack, 1992, for a more extended discussion of the informational value of nonaffective experiences).

In summary, the reviewed findings indicate that individuals may use phenomenal experiences of an affective as well as nonaffective nature as a source of information in making a judgment. However, they will rely on these experiences only if they consider them to reflect their reaction to the target. If the experiences are attributed, either correctly or incorrectly, to some other source, their informational value for the judgment at hand is called into question, eliminating the otherwise observed impact.

What Determines the Use of One's Feelings as a Basis of Judgment? The reviewed findings indicate that mood effects on evaluative judgments often reflect the use of one's affective state as a source of information, rather than any impact of mood-congruent recall of information from memory. However, these findings do not preclude that mood-congruent recall may produce evaluative biases as well. Next, we consider the conditions that may determine if judgments are based directly on the informational implications of one's mood or on recalled information.

Consistent with what one would expect on theoretical grounds, the currently available evidence suggests that the use of the "How-do-I-feel-about-it?" heuristic is particularly likely under the following four conditions: (a) when the judgment at hand is affective in nature (e.g., liking for another person); (b) when little other information is available; (c) when the judgment is overly complex and cumbersome to make on the basis of a piecemeal information processing strategy; and, (d) when time constraints or competing task demands limit the attentional resources that may be devoted to forming a judgment. Recall mediated effects, on the other hand, should be particularly likely when individuals engage in an effortful piecemeal judgmental strategy, have sufficient time and attentional resources to do so, and when the somewhat tricky prerequisites for mood-congruent recall, are met (see Forgas, 1992, for a related discussion). We discuss each of these aspects in turn.

A judgment that refers explicitly to how one feels about the object of judgment renders one's feelings highly relevant. Accordingly, it is not surprising that judgments of liking and preference have been found to be influenced strongly by respondents' feelings (e.g., Clore & Byrne, 1974; Zajonc, 1980). Moreover, one's feelings are sometimes the only source of information available to form a judgment. For example, in one study Murphy and Zajonc (1993) asked subjects to judge the evaluative meaning of unknown Chinese ideographs. Subjects based their judgments on their apparent affective response to the target, unaware that this response was elicited by the subliminal presentation of happy or frowning faces that preceded the ideograph (e.g., Murphy & Zajonc, 1993). Findings of this type suggest that individuals are likely to consult their feelings about the target when little other information is available.

Complementing these findings, other studies indicate that the impact of feelings decreases as the amount or salience of competing information increases. For example, Srull (1983, 1984) reported that subjects' moods influenced their evaluations of unfamiliar, but not of familiar, products. In addition, Strack, Schwarz, and Gschneidinger (1985, Experiments 2 and 3) observed that subjects who provided short, nonemotional reports of a past life event used this event as a standard of comparison, resulting in contrast effects on judgments of current life satisfaction. On the other hand, subjects who had to report a past life event in an emotionally involving style relied on the elicited mood state in evaluating their current life satisfaction, resulting in assimilation effects (see Clark & Collins, in press; Clark, Collins, & Henry, in press, for conceptual replications). Findings of this type suggest that individuals may rely either on thought content or on the feelings elicited, depending on which source of information is more salient. In general, other sources of relevant information may be increasingly ignored as the salience or intensity of the affective state increases.

Although the preceding findings suggest that individuals may consult their feelings due to a lack of other relevant information, they may also do so because too much information is available or because limited attentional resources do not allow for the systematic use of available information. In either case, asking oneself how one feels about the target may provide an efficient heuristic that greatly simplifies the judgmental task and limits the demands on attentional resources. For example, Schwarz, Strack, Kommer, and Wagner (1987, Experiment 1) observed pronounced mood effects on judgments of general life satisfaction, but not on judgments of satisfaction with specific life domains, such as one's income. This presumably reflects that evaluative criteria for specific life domains are well defined and that comparison information is easily available, whereas the evaluation of one's life-as-a-whole requires a multitude of comparisons along many dimensions with ill-defined criteria (see Schwarz & Strack, 1991, for a more detailed discussion). Consistent with this assumption, subjects who were put into a bad mood by being in an overheated, dirty room with an offensive odor reported lower general life satisfaction, but higher satisfaction with their own apartment than subjects in a more pleasant room (Schwarz et al., 1987, Experiment 2). Thus, they used their affective state to evaluate their overall well-being but easily accessible descriptive information to evaluate their apartment. In a similar vein, Levine, Wyer, and Schwarz (in press) observed mood effects on judgments of global self-esteem, but not on judgments of domain specific self-esteem, providing that relevant descriptive information was accessible. In each of these studies, subjects were more likely to rely on their feelings at the time of judgment when the judgmental task was more complex. Finally, Siemer and Reisenzein (1992) found that mood effects on judgments of life satisfaction were more pronounced when subjects were under time pressure, or worked on a secondary task, while forming the judgment. In other words, subjects' use of their feelings as a basis of judgment increased as attentional resources decreased.

In combination, these findings suggested that the use of one's feelings as a basis of judgment reflects a simplifying heuristic strategy. On the other hand, mood effects on evaluative judgment that are mediated by mood-congruent recall may be expected only if subjects engage in a more effortful piecemeal strategy (see Forgas, 1992). However, in the absence of (mis)attribution manipulations that discredit the informational value of subjects' current feelings, it is difficult to determine whether the use of feelings as information or mood-congruent recall drives any particular observed effect of moods on evaluative judgments. At the present stage of research, we can only conclude that moods may influence evaluative judgments either directly, by serving as a basis of judgment, or indirectly, by influencing what comes to mind (Clore, 1992). However, given the robustness of mood effects on evaluative judgments on the one hand, and the fragility of mood congruent recall on the other hand, the former seems more likely than the latter.

Affective States and Spontaneous Processing Strategies

Although most of the empirical work reviewed earlier explicitly addressed the impact of affect on memory or judgment, many of the obtained findings may be conceptualized as reflecting influences of affective states on individuals' spontaneous adoption of a heuristic or systematic strategy of information processing. Although this proposal seems uncontroversial, there is little agreement as to which affective state may be associated with which type of processing strategy, let alone any consensus about underlying mechanisms. Affect induced differences in processing strategy have been attributed to differences in attentional resources, differences in the accessibility of procedural knowledge, and differences in motivation, or some combination of these factors. In the present section, we review key proposals and resultant predictions before we turn to relevant research. As becomes evident, there are findings that support, as well as contradict, each of the key proposals, and the specific impact of affect cannot be predicted without considering the specific processing requirements presented by the specific task for which mood effects are being examined.

Theoretical Approaches

Affective States and Attentional Resources. Ellis and Ashbrook (1988) proposed that, because dysphoric affective states elicit intrusive thoughts, they limit attentional resources. Consistent with this model, research reviewed earlier indicates limited elaboration and organization of new information under dysphoric moods. The model predicts that dysphoric individuals may use less information in forming judgments and may prefer simple over complex judgmental procedures. The derivative model proposed by Hertel and colleagues (e.g., Hertel & Hardin, 1990) suggests that depressed mood leads to deficits only in initiative, which is expected to be reflected in poorer performance on tasks that require the generation of complex hypotheses or of organizational schemes; deficits for depression are not expected for well-structured tasks.

Other researchers argued that elated affective states can limit attentional resources (Isen, 1987; Mackie & Worth, 1989). For example, Isen hypothesized that positive material in memory "is more extensive and at the same time better integrated, so that positive affect is able to cue a wide range of thoughts" (p. 217). If so, the material brought to mind by positive affect could limit the resources available for task performance.

The Tuning Function of Affective States: Feelings as Information.   As discussed earlier, different situations elicit different affective reactions. Extending Schwarz and Clore's (1988) feelings-as-information model, Schwarz (1990) and Schwarz and Bless (1991) suggested that this relationship is bidirectional, which has been argued by emotion theorists who assume that "emotions exist for the sake of signaling states of the world that have to be responded to, or that no longer need response and action" (Frijda, 1988, p. 354). Thus, although different situational appraisals elicit different emotions, the experience of a certain emotion also informs the individual about the nature of the current psychological situation. Positive affective states inform individuals that their situation is safe and does not threaten current goals; positive outcomes are not lacking, and there is no threat of negative outcomes. In contrast, negative affective states inform individuals that the current situation is problematic; positive outcomes are lacking or negative outcomes threaten.

The model further assumes that people are motivated to obtain positive and avoid negative outcomes. Accordingly, negative emotions inform individuals that action needs to be taken. However, effective action requires understanding, and attempts at change are likely to be facilitated by a systematic, detail-oriented, resource-dependent processing style. Attention may be directed to acts at a lower level of abstraction (Wegner & Vallacher, 1986). Moreover, individuals may be unlikely to take risks in a situation perceived as problematic; simple heuristics and novel solutions may be avoided. In contrast, positive affective states inform individuals of a benign situation, and, consequently, they may not readily invest attentional resources unless it is required in the pursuit of current goals. In pursuing these goals, individuals may take risks, given that the situation is considered safe. Hence, simplifying heuristics may be favored, novel procedures and possibilities may be explored, and unusual, creative associations may be elaborated (see Schwarz, 1990, for a more detailed discussion, and Fiedler, 1988; Kuhl, 1983, for related hypotheses). The assumed impact of affective states on individuals' spontaneously adopted processing style may be overridden by currently active processing goals (e.g., Bless, Bohner, Schwarz, & Strack, 1990; Bless, Mackie, & Schwarz, 1992). However, this flexibility should be more likely under elated than under depressed moods, because paying less systematic attention to a possibly problematic environment may not be adaptive.

In addition to these motivational assumptions, the model posits that negative affective states may increase the accessibility of procedural knowledge that has been shown to be effective for dealing with similar affect-related situations in the past, thereby facilitating the required action signaled by the affective state. Activated procedural knowledge would involve a range of cognitive and behavioral components that are oriented to situational requirements, as reflected in the observation that different emotions are associated with different states of action readiness that are evident in physiological changes (Lacey & Lacey, 1970; Obrist, 1981) and overt behavior (Ekman, 1982; Izard, 1977), as well as in introspective reports (Davitz, 1969; Frijda, 1986, 1987). Although the activated procedural knowledge is presumably tuned to meet the situational action requirements signaled by the affective state, the primed procedure may be applied to unrelated tasks that the individual works on while in the respective state, provided that the procedure is applicable (Higgins, 1989). In contrast, positive emotions, having in the past been elicited in situations that did not call for particular action, may not prime any specific procedure, thereby contributing to a higher cognitive flexibility under elated affect.

Although the assumption that certain affective states may prime procedural knowledge is admittedly speculative and difficult to test empirically, the hypothesized motivational implications of affective states have received qualified support. Martin, Ward, Achée, and Wyer (1993) induced happy or sad moods and assessed the time subjects spent studying behavioral descriptions to form judgments (Experiment 1) or the number of examples generated on a creativity task (Experiment 2). On the basis that feelings may serve informative functions, they assumed that subjects consult their current feelings in deciding how much effort to invest in the task. To explore this possibility, Martin et al. varied the decision rule offered to subjects. Some subjects were told to stop when they no longer enjoyed the task, whereas others were told to stop when they felt they had enough information to form a judgment or had generated enough examples. Under "enjoyment" instructions, subjects invested more effort when they felt good rather than bad, suggesting that they interpreted their positive or negative feelings as indicating that they were, or were not, enjoying the task. Conversely, under "task" instructions, subjects invested more effort when they felt bad rather than good. In this case, positive feelings were apparently interpreted as an indication of satisfactory performance, which allowed termination, whereas negative feelings indicated dissatisfactory performance, which motivated subjects to continue on the task. These findings indicate that the motivational effects of affective states are mediated by their informational implications. They also demonstrate that the impact of these states depends on the specific decision rule that underlies subjects' motivation to engage in behavior. In the Martin et al. study, the decision rules were provided by the experimenter. Without experimenter intervention, which rule is adopted may be influenced by affective states. If negative feelings signal a problematic situation, depressed individuals may generally adopt a performance-related decision rule, rather than an enjoyment rule. If so, they should invest substantial effort, as did the negative mood subjects under "task" instructions in the Martin et al. study. If positive feelings signal no particular requirements, elated individuals may adopt either enjoyment or performance rules, again suggesting greater cognitive flexibility under elated mood.

In summary, the core assumption is that thought processes are tuned to meet the requirements signaled by one's affective state. Negative affective states are likely to foster the use of detail-oriented systematic processing strategies, whereas positive affective states are likely to foster the use of more simplifying heuristic processing strategies, for the reasons outlined earlier. An increased use of simplifying heuristic strategies under elated affect also has been proposed by Isen and colleagues (Isen, Means, Patrick, & Nowicki, 1982; see Isen, 1987, for a review). However, their analysis has not traced the hypothesized effects to the informational functions of affective states, nor have they addressed the impact of negative moods. As noted earlier, Isen (1987) argued that positive material is extensive and well interconnected in memory, giving individuals in elated moods access to a wide variety of material, with a possible consequence that "this larger amount of material in mind might also result in a defocusing of attention" (p. 237). Moreover, Isen suggested that positive affect may promote reliance on intuitive decision strategies and judgmental heuristics. These hypotheses can be subsumed under the cognitive tuning model, which has the advantage of providing a coherent conceptualization of the impact of positive as well as negative affective states that is compatible with a long history of psychological theorizing on the signaling functions of emotions (see Frijda, 1986, 1988).

The Impact of Loss of Control. Control motivation is relevant to the issue of affect induced differences in information processing. Temporary exposure to uncontrollable events has been shown to elicit increased attributional activity, more careful and deliberate processing of available information, and increased information search (Pittman & D'Agostino, 1985, 1989; Pittman & Pittman, 1980). In line with helplessness formulations of depression (Seligman, 1975), Weary and her colleagues (see Weary, Marsh, Gleicher, & Edwards, 1993, for a review) proposed that depression is characterized by uncertainty about one's ability to understand, predict, and control one's social environment and to produce desired outcomes. At least at mild and moderate levels of depression, this uncertainty is supposed to give rise to control motivation, leading to the adoption of an accuracy goal. This in turn results in a systematic style of information processing that can be characterized as highly resource dependent, vigilant, and complex, with more extensive processing of and search for relevant information.

Although focusing on chronic depression, rather than on the effects of transient moods, the Weary et al. model is compatible with the assumption that temporary negative moods signal a problematic environment. From the latter perspective, information conveyed by transient negative moods may also give rise to control motivation. Finally, both models predict less systematic information processing under severe chronic depression, although for different reasons. According to Weary et al., severely depressed individuals have expectations of extreme uncontrollability, which undermine the elicitation of control motivation. From the feelings-as-information perspective, it is noteworthy that phenomenological studies of severe depression indicate that the experience of "sadness" or of "being in a bad mood" typically is not part of the melancholic state of severe depression (see Tölle, 1982, p. 232 ff., for a review). Hence, the information conveyed by chronic melancholy may differ from that conveyed by milder dysphoric states.

Empirical Findings

Numerous empirical findings can be accounted for by the resource and process assumptions discussed earlier. As is evident from a review of recent research, however, many reliably observed effects are compatible with more than one set of assumptions. Moreover, direct evidence for underlying processes is typically missing, rendering theoretical implications difficult to draw.

Focus of Attention.   A large body of literature indicates a narrowed focus of attention under negative affect, although this narrowing of attention has typically been observed for information related to the affect inducing event (Broadbent, 1971; Bruner, Matter, & Papanek, 1955; Easterbrook, 1959; Eysenck, 1976). Moreover, Wegner and Vallacher (1986) observed that, compared with successes, failures to obtain a desired outcome, which are often associated with negative affective reactions, are more likely to foster attention to details of one's action strategy.

Depressed affective states may also promote greater attention to details that are unrelated to the affect inducing event. For example, using Newtson's (1973) unitization task, Lassiter and Koenig (1991) observed that naturally depressed individuals unitized behavioral sequences at a finer rate than nondepressed individuals, in particular when the target's behavior conveyed positive affect. Moreover, studies of affective influences on persuasion (e.g., Bless et al., 1990; Bless et al., 1992) and stereotyping (Edwards & Weary, 1993), which we review in more detail later, consistently indicate that depressed affect is associated with more attention to details of the presented arguments or the described behaviors of the target person. In sum, research on focus of attention is consistent with the cognitive tuning and control motivation models.

Degree of Elaboration of Presented Information.   To date, affective influences on the elaboration of information have been explored most systematically in the domain of persuasion, in part because the cognitive dynamics underlying the processing of persuasive communications are well understood (Eagly & Chaiken,

1993; Petty & Cacioppo, 1986). In general, a message that presents strong arguments is more persuasive than a message that presents weak arguments, provided recipients are motivated and able to process the content of the message. If recipients do not engage in elaborative processing of message content, the advantage of strong over weak arguments is eliminated.

A consistent finding is that individuals in an elated mood are less likely to engage in systematic message elaboration than individuals in a nonmanipulated, neutral, or depressed mood (Bless et al., 1990; Bless et al., 1992; Bohner, Crow, Erb, & Schwarz, 1992; Mackie & Worth, 1989; see Schwarz, Bless, & Bohner, 1991, for a review; Worth & Mackie, 1987). Specifically, elated individuals are persuaded moderately by weak as well as strong arguments, indicating that they do not engage in systematic message elaboration. In contrast, individuals in a depressed mood are persuaded strongly by strong arguments, but not by weak arguments, indicating that they engage in systematic message elaboration. These differences in message elaboration also are reflected in cognitive response data. Whereas depressed recipients report more disagreeing thoughts in response to weak and more agreeing thoughts in response to strong messages, elated recipients' cognitive responses show no differences as a function of message strength.

The cognitive tuning model proposes that positive mood leads people to favor a heuristic processing style, yet that this style can be overridden by current processing goals. Addressing this, Bless et al. (1990, Experiment 1) explicitly instructed some of their subjects to pay attention to message quality. Under this instruction, elated subjects differentiated between strong and weak arguments, suggesting that elated individuals have sufficient attentional resources to engage in systematic message processing. In contrast, Mackie and Worth (1989) argued that the reduced elaboration of persuasive messages under positive mood is due to reduced resources. Some of their subjects were told that they could take all the time they wanted to read, repeatedly if they wished, the persuasive message. Under this condition, elated subjects differentiated between strong and weak arguments. For Mackie and Worth, this demonstrated that increased processing time compensated for reduced resources under elated mood. However, it is conceivable that informing subjects that they may take their time and reread the message may convey to them that a carefully considered response to the message is asked for. If so, Mackie and Worth's findings would parallel the impact of processing instructions obtained in the Bless et al. (1990) study. On the other hand, the Bless et al. instruction to pay attention to message quality may have provided subjects a more focused task, and hence may have reduced resource demands, rendering their findings compatible with a reduced resources account. To distinguish between these two accounts, future research needs to manipulate subjects' processing capacity or processing goals in ways that are not open to reinterpretation in terms of the respective other concept. In any case, elated subjects' ability to process message content on instruction suggests that any constraints on processing capacity under elated moods are not severe. Consistent with this view, elated subjects do not show less recall of presented arguments than depressed subjects (Bless et al., 1990), in contrast to what a reduced resources account might predict.

In sum, the persuasion findings are most consistent with the cognitive tuning and control motivation accounts. Whether some of the findings for positive mood can be attributed to reduced resources remains unclear. Finally, the findings for negative mood are clearly incompatible with what would be expected from persons reduced resources.

Amount of Presented Information Used.   Affective influences on the amount of information used have been addressed in interpersonal judgment and impression formation, decision making, and problem solving. In the domain of interpersonal judgment, induced positive mood has been associated with reliance on the sole item of category membership, whereas induced depressed mood has been associated with reliance on a wider range of individuating information (e.g., Bless, 1992; Bodenhausen, 1993; Edwards & Weary, 1993). Assuming that reliance on category membership information reflects a heuristic use of stereotypes that simplifies the judgment process (Bodenhausen, 1993; Fiske & Neuberg, 1990), these findings are consistent with the cognitive tuning model. Similarly, Sinclair (1988) observed that subjects in an elated mood made less use of detailed performance information and showed more halo effects and lower accuracy in a performance appraisal task than subjects in a depressed mood, with neutral mood subjects falling in between. Moreover, subjects in an induced elated mood showed more primacy effects in impression formation than subjects in a depressed mood (Sinclair & Mark, 1992). These patterns of results are generally consistent with the cognitive tuning model. On the other hand, resource restriction assumptions can account only for the findings obtained under positive mood, but not under negative mood.

In contrast, there is some evidence of decreased information use under chronic depressed affect in the domain of decision making. For example, Conway and Giannopoulos (1993) observed that chronically depressed individuals used a smaller amount of available, relevant information in a complex decision making task. Depressed subjects used fewer of the dimensions of information that were available for the evaluation of part-time jobs. This effect was not due to depressed subjects systematically ignoring certain dimensions, suggesting that their affective state did not induce a particular focus, but simply limited the amount of information considered. In addition, depressed subjects did not simplify the information they used, nor did they combine the information they used in a more simple manner than nondepressed subjects. This revealed a degree of specificity in their limited information use that is not readily accountable in terms of motivational deficits. Other research on chronic depression and problem solving also suggests that depressed individuals make less use of available information. For example, they maintain faulty hypotheses in the face of feedback that indicates a revision is in order (Dobson & Dobson, 1981; Silberman, Weingartner, & Post, 1983).

In sum, the available findings indicate increased information use under depressed affect in the domain of social judgment, but decreased information use on nonsocial tasks. Although the latter finding is restricted to naturally depressed subjects, research by Weary et al. (1993) suggests that the temporary versus chronic nature of depressed affect is not the crucial variable that drives the emerging differences. Rather, the observed effects may be domain specific, an issue to which we return later.

Amount and Diagnosticity of Information Searched For. Research that addressed chronically depressed subjects' search for social information consistently observed increased information search under mild to moderate depression (see Weary et al., 1993, for a review). For example, Hildebrandt-Saints and Weary (1989) observed that nondepressed individuals sought more diagnostic information about a target person when they expected to interact with that person than when they did not. In contrast, depressed individuals generally sought more diagnostic information about the target than nondepressed individuals, regardless of whether future interaction was expected. This pattern of findings is consistent with control motivation and cognitive tuning accounts, but not with the view that negative affect is associated with reduced resources. On the other hand, the results were obtained for items selected from a provided list, and one might argue that limited information use for negative affect may be more apparent on tasks that require subjects to generate possible topics or issues that need be addressed by social interactants.

Attributional Complexity. In correlational work, Marsh and Weary (1989) observed that mild and moderate chronic depression are associated with higher attributional complexity, as assessed by the Attributional Complexity Scale (Fletcher, Danilovics, Fernandez, Peterson, & Reeder, 1986). Extending this research, Conway et al. (1993) reported correlational evidence that depressed individuals' higher attributional complexity scores are due to their tendency to engage in attempts at self-understanding. Some experimental findings also suggest increased attributional complexity under negative affect. McCaul (1983) observed that mildly depressed subjects were less likely than nondepressed subjects to infer a corresponding attitude from the content of an essay that was written for money, thus revealing greater sensitivity to situational constraint. In contrast, Sullivan and Conway (1989) obtained evidence for increased dispositional inferences under induced depressed moods. In their studies, subjects were asked to write several causes for each behavior described to them. In this case, subjects in a depressed mood generated more correspondent dispositional attributions than subjects in a neutral mood. Such attributions require little information and few resources. Finally, Bohner, Marz, Bless, Schwarz, and Strack (1992) observed that induced elated moods consistently led to dispositional inferences about a target person shown on a videotape, whereas induced depressed moods did so on some but not all of the assessed judgments. As these mixed findings indicate, strong conclusions concerning the impact of affective states on attributional complexity cannot be drawn at this time.

A more reliable finding is that depressed individuals make internal attributions for their own successes and failures, whereas nondepressed individuals show a self-serving attributional pattern (see Sweeney, Anderson, & Bailey, 1986, for a review). However, this evenhandedness under depression remains poorly understood. These findings may either reflect differences in self-schemata, an issue not addressed by any of the assumptions discussed here, or limited attentional resources associated with negative mood. Perhaps depressed individuals make more internal attributions because these attributions require fewer resources than attributions involving a consideration of situational factors.

Categorization Breadth. Initial studies on emotion and categorization breadth were conducted by Isen and her colleagues. For example, Isen and Daubman (1984) found that happy subjects categorized information more broadly than did neutral mood control subjects. Happy subjects created fewer and more inclusive categories on a category-creation task, were more likely to include nonprototypical exemplars in a given category (e.g., "cane" in the category *clothing*), and rated nonprototypical exemplars as being more prototypical. These findings were taken to reflect that positive affect either (a) promotes heuristic use; (b) draws attention to affective aspects of material that are not typically seen as affective in nature, thus creating otherwise unnoticed shared features; or (c) brings a more diverse range of material to mind.

These findings were replicated and extended by Murray, Sujan, Hirt, and Sujan (1990). They observed that elated subjects categorized more broadly than neutral subjects when they were not provided with an explicit categorization goal, whereas depressed subjects formed narrower categories in this condition. In addition, the Murray et al. (1990, Experiment 1) data indicated that explicit processing instructions influenced the performance of happy subjects but not of sad ones. Specifically, subjects were asked to categorize a number of television programs, focusing on either similarities or differences among the various programs. As expected, happy subjects formed more distinct categories when asked to focus on differences, rather than on similarities. Moreover, happy subjects' performance under similarity instructions did not differ from their spontaneous performance, suggesting that they used similar strategies under both conditions. In contrast, sad subjects spontaneously formed more distinct categories than happy subjects under no instruction conditions, and their performance was not influenced by either difference or similarity instructions. This asymmetry in responsiveness to externally provided processing goals was replicated by Sinclair, Mark, and Weisbrod (reported in Sinclair & Marks, 1992), using a somewhat different categorization task.

These various findings are compatible with the cognitive tuning model that posits a preference for more heuristic processing in positive mood, but one that can be overridden by specific task demands. Negative mood is shown to be associated with a more rigid preference for more systematic, detail-oriented processing. These findings cannot be interpreted in a straightforward manner in terms of reduced resources for either positive or negative mood, because the relation of breadth of categorization to availability of attentional resources is unclear. In any case, the findings do not suggest similarly reduced resources for both positive and negative mood, because the effects of these mood states on categorization differ.

Heuristic Use.   To our knowledge, only one study has directly addressed the question of increased heuristic use under positive mood. This work concerned reliance on Tversky and Kahneman's (1973) availability heuristic. In a pioneering experiment, Isen et al. (1982) observed that subjects in an induced happy mood were more likely to rely on the ease with which exemplars came to mind in making frequency judgments than subjects in a neutral mood. This increased use of the availability heuristic may reflect that positive affect promotes heuristic use, or reduces attentional resources, thus forcing subjects to rely on a simpler judgmental strategy.

Creative Problem Solving.   The available findings indicate better performance on creative problem-solving tasks for people in a positive mood. For example, Isen and colleagues observed that happy subjects were more likely to solve Duncker's (1945) candle task and provided more unusual associations on the Remote Associations Test (see Isen, 1987; Isen, Daubman, & Nowicki, 1987; Isen, Johnson, Mertz, & Robinson, 1985). Similarly, Murray et al. (1990) observed that happy subjects listed more unique features of television programs than subjects in a neutral mood. In other research, subjects induced to experience positive affect performed better on the Means-Ends Problem Solving Test (Platt & Spivack, 1975) than neutral mood control subjects (Mitchell & Madigan, 1984). This test calls for the generation of means by which certain specified endings can be achieved in unstructured, ambiguous situations.

The available research has generally been consistent with the cognitive tuning model that predicts a greater readiness to explore novel and unusual solutions under positive mood. In addition, many creativity tasks are of a rather playful nature and lend themselves to the adoption of an "enjoyment" rule, whereby people continue to work on a task as long as they enjoy it (cf. Martin et al., 1993). Hence, individuals in a good mood may work longer on a task because their positive feelings suggest continued enjoyment, whereas individuals in a negative mood may terminate task because they interpret it as a lack of enjoyment. The findings on creative problem solving are not consistent with a resource constraint model.

Logical Problem Solving. A consistent finding is that negative affect facilitates performance on tasks that require the detection of covariation (see Alloy, 1988, for a review). In general, nondysphoric subjects are likely to overestimate the degree of contingency between their actions and their outcomes, whereas subjects experiencing induced or chronic negative affect are not as prone to exhibit this illusion of control (e.g., Alloy & Abramson, 1979). Furthermore, the illusion of control typically observed under neutral mood increases under good mood (Alloy, Abramson, & Viscusi, 1981). These findings are consistent with the cognitive tuning model. Depressed affective states may tune cognitive processes in a way that facilitates covariation detection. On the other hand, reliance on heuristics under positive affect should impair covariation detection. Furthermore, the informational implications of negative affect in regard to the nature of the current situation may already convey a certain lack of control, in contrast to the implications of positive affect.

Depressed individuals' more accurate covariation judgments can also be accounted for in terms of limited attentional resources. It seems that the illusion of control is mediated by the generation and faulty, subjective verification of complex hypotheses concerning patterns of responses and outcomes (Alloy & Abramson, 1979, Study 2). In this case, dysphoric individuals' more realistic estimates of control may be due to their limited resources interfering with the generation of complex hypotheses. Indeed, dysphoric subjects provided with complex hypotheses exhibited the same illusion of control as nondysphoric subjects (Abramson, Alloy, & Rosoff, 1981). Although the latter finding may simply indicate that subjects may be led astray by an experimenter's provision of misleading information (see Bless, Strack, & Schwarz, 1993, for a more general discussion), the possibility that the generation of complex hypotheses is important deserves further exploration.

Findings for positive and negative mood are less consistent for other logical problem-solving tasks. Positive mood has been shown to be associated with improved performance for a number of tasks. Young children induced to a positive mood performed better than neutral affect control subjects on discrimination problems that required the identification of which stimulus in a set of three was correct. Subjects were repeatedly presented with the set of stimuli in varying order; they were asked to indicate which was correct and were given feedback on their responses (Masters, Barden, & Ford, 1979). Positive mood induction has also been shown to improve performance on mathematical problem-solving tasks (Kirschenbaum, Tomarken, & Humphrey, 1985).

For negative affect, increased as well as decreased performance has been reported. For example, Fiedler and Fladung (1986, reported in Fiedler, 1988) observed that subjects in an induced bad mood produced fewer logical inconsistencies in a multiattribute decision task than subjects in a good mood. Specifically, the latter were twice as likely to violate transitivity of preference as the former, by producing inconsistent triads of the form $A > B$, and $B > C$, but $A < C$.

However, other studies indicated poorer performance for subjects in a negative mood. In the research conducted with children by Masters et al. (1979), induced negative mood led to poorer performance on discrimination problems. Logical problem-solving research with depressed subjects selected on the basis of self-report measures, peer nomination (for children), or clinical criteria also revealed performance deficits for negative affect (Dobson & Dobson, 1981; Perkins, Meyers, & Cohen, 1988; Silberman et al., 1983).

In fact, such mixed findings are to be expected in the problem-solving domain because none of the processes hypothesized will necessarily result in improved performance. For example, the cognitive tuning and control motivation models generally predict increased systematic processing under negative affect. However, systematic processing may not result in improved performance if subjects do not have access to appropriate algorithms. Similarly, any priming of procedural knowledge under negative affect should facilitate performance only to the extent that it is applicable to the current task. If inapplicable, the primed procedure may actually interfere with performance. Similarly, positive affect may either facilitate or interfere with logical problem solving, depending on whether spontaneously adopted heuristics are applicable to the current task. Furthermore, such heuristics may be discarded in the face of task demands or instructions, rendering it difficult to make strong predictions concerning the effects of positive mood. Finally, if one assumes that logical problem-solving tasks lend themselves more easily to a task-oriented decision rule (i.e., one that focuses on task persistence until performance is satisfactory), the Martin et al. (1993) results suggest that individuals will invest more effort under negative rather than positive affect. Whether such effort would lead to improved performance would again depend on the algorithms required and employed.

Conclusions. The findings for positive affect reviewed earlier seem generally consistent with the assumption of the cognitive tuning model that positive affect promotes the spontaneous adoption of less detail-oriented heuristic processing strategies (Fiedler, 1988; Kuhl, 1983; Schwarz, 1990). The findings do not suggest that positive affect is associated with severe constraints on attentional resources, because elated subjects seem quite able to engage in resource-dependent, systematic processing if called on to do so by task demands or explicit instruction. Elated subjects seem to exhibit a degree of flexibility in their processing style that is relatively absent for depressed subjects.

The findings for negative affect, however, are quite inconsistent. On the one hand, being in a negative mood has been found to increase elaboration of the content of persuasive messages, the use of individuating information in studies of stereotyping, and the accuracy of person perception. However, temporary as well as chronic negative affect has been found to facilitate but also to impair attributional complexity, logical problem solving, and information use. Although some of these findings suggest that negative affect promotes the spontaneous adoption of a resource-dependent, detail-oriented, and systematic style of information processing (see Fiedler, 1988; Kuhl, 1983; Schwarz, 1990), other findings support the view that attentional resources are constrained under negative affect (see Ellis & Ashbrook, 1988).

Theoretical Gaps, Ignored Contingencies, and Issues for Future Research

Attentional Resources. The key assumption of attentional resource models holds that affective states may limit available attentional resources due to intruding thoughts. Although such intrusions have been documented for negative affect, as discussed previously, it seems implausible that every induction of negative affect in the laboratory or negative experience in daily life should result in intrusive thoughts. Suppose, for example, that negative affect is induced by sad memories of an event long passed or by failure on some experimental task that the subject may never have to face again. In these cases, intrusions may be minimal and subjects may be more than willing to focus on some other task to put the unpleasant experience behind them. On the other hand, if the memory bears on current concerns, or if subjects may be able to make up for the failure by repeating the task later on, rumination about the negative experience seems more likely. In fact, recent theorizing about the nature of ruminative thought (see Martin & Tesser, 1989) may help specify the conditions under which diverse mood inductions may or may not be likely to elicit intruding thoughts. From this perspective, it is not surprising that restrictions in attentional resources have been documented most consistently for chronically depressed individuals, who presumably deal with negative current concerns. Clearly, evidence about the emergence of intruding thoughts during task performance would be helpful, although such evidence is admittedly difficult to obtain.

There is some evidence that people in a positive mood may suffer more intrusions of positive material than people in a negative mood (Howell & Conway, 1992). This is consistent with the view that positive affect may bring a large amount of material to mind (see Isen, 1987), yet it is unclear if the sheer accessibility of positive material is intrusive and reduces attentional resources in a way that seems plausible for negative material, which may elicit rumination and may be generally more difficult to suppress (Howell & Conway, 1992; Wenzlaff et al., 1989). In fact, it has been suggested that positive affect may be associated with increased attentional resources, in light of the beneficial effects of positive mood inductions on subjects' performance on logical and creative problem-solving tasks (Sullivan & Conway, 1988).

The amount of attentional resources invested in and required of a particular task can depend on various factors. For example, if subjects are more highly motivated, perhaps due to an emphasis on accountability or responsibility (cf. Kunda, 1990), they may invest more attentional resources. Increased motivation could also presumably lead a person to adopt compensatory strategies if limited resources seem to hinder performance. In addition, the degree to which subjects are provided either structure for a task or information that limits the need to generate hypotheses may render less apparent the effects of any reduction in attentional resources (cf. Ellis, 1990, 1991).

More generally, it is often difficult to specify how much attentional resources a task actually requires, or how resource constraints might affect performance. For example, as noted earlier, it is unclear how breadth of categorization relates to available attentional resources. Does broader categorization require more attentional resources as it involves the integration of diverse material, or less attentional resources because of less attention to detail? The answer is unclear. In fact, the attentional resource requirements of a task may depend on the strategy chosen. For example, assume that an apparent insufficiency in attentional resources prompts a person to rely on some heuristic. If the heuristic is applicable, this could result in improved performance; if the heuristic is inapplicable, performance would be impaired, but not directly due to reduced resources. Even in the absence of possible differences in heuristic use, the relation of attentional resources to performance is not always straightforward. Reduced resources may hinder performance in many cases, whereas in others, increased investment of attentional resources leads to poorer performance (see Tetlock & Boettger, 1989). In summary, drawing strong performance predictions for a task from resource limitation assumptions requires extensive knowledge concerning the processes that subjects might invoke, the resource requirements of such processes, and the relation of these processes to level of performance. These are conditions that cannot be met in a wide range of information-processing domains. Finally, it is often difficult to disentangle reduced attentional resources from limited motivation (cf. Hertel & Hardin, 1990).

Cognitive Tuning.   Ambiguities also arise with regard to the cognitive tuning model that assumes that different affective states signal different psychological situations. These may in turn influence individuals' motivation to engage in effortful systematic processing as well as the accessibility of procedural knowledge (Schwarz, 1990). On the one hand, the basic assumption that affective states serve informative functions is consistent with a history of psychological theorizing about emotions and is supported by research on affective influences on evaluative judgments. On the other hand, the impact of affective states on processing preference seems conditional. In general, the model predicts that, *ceteris paribus*, negative affect is more likely than positive affect to instigate resource-dependent, systematic processing, reflecting that the former signals a problematic situation that requires action, whereas the latter does not. However, depending on the affect inducing event, individuals in a negative affective state may focus on dealing with the source of their unpleasant affect, rather than engaging in systematic processing of information on an unrelated task. Moreover, individuals in a positive affective state may also engage in resource-dependent, systematic processing if required by current goals. Finally, as observed by Martin et al. (1993), the impact of affective states on persistence may depend on the specific decision rule adopted, which may be affected by the nature of the task, by instructions provided by the experimenter, and by the affective state itself. As a result of these contingencies, one cannot expect that particular affective states will have the same type of impact on performance across mood manipulations and tasks.

Moreover, whether increased effort results in improved performance depends on whether the person is able to use appropriate algorithms. For example, subjects in a bad mood may be willing to invest more effort. But this should only result in superior performance if the relevant procedure for solving the task is available to them in the first place. Hence, facilitatory effects should be limited to tasks for which subjects know the appropriate algorithm. On the other hand, inhibiting effects due to a lack of effort should be quite general, given that knowing the relevant algorithm does not facilitate performance if it is not applied. If so, it is not surprising that the cognitive tuning model is most consistently supported by research into affective influences on persuasion, stereotyping, and person perception. These content domains require the application of procedures with which subjects are well familiar, and hence may be most likely to show improved performance under negative and impaired performance under positive affect. In contrast, many logical problem-solving tasks require the application of less familiar procedures, which may not be readily available. As a result, expending more effort under negative affect is unlikely to improve performance, whereas expending little effort under positive affect is likely to impair performance even for subjects who may know the appropriate algorithm. An additional factor that must be taken into account is that increased effort for certain tasks may actually be associated with poorer performance, as Tetlock and Boetger (1989) demonstrated with regard to Nisbett, Zukier, and Lemley's (1981) *dilution effect*.

Finally, we know little about the specific nature of procedural knowledge that may be primed by different affective states. Moreover, direct evidence bearing on this assumption of the model is missing, although it is generally consistent with research that indicates that different emotions are associated with different states of action readiness (see Frijda, 1986, 1987; Tooby & Cosmides, 1990). As many emotion theorists assume, emotions have evolved over the course of human evolution as adaptive mechanisms that respond to key features of recurrent situations. If one of their adaptive effects is that they increase the likelihood that we use strategies that are adequate for handling these situations by eliciting the appropriate action readiness, their effects may actually be quite specific. Suppose for example, that a depressed mood indicates an absence of positive outcomes. If so, understanding the covariation of actions and outcomes would seem to be an important prerequisite for handling the respective situation. Hence, it would be quite adaptive if a depressed affective state increased the accessibility of procedures that facilitate covariation detection. The empirical findings consistently suggest that this is the case. On the other hand, it is less clear that modus ponem or other rules of logical inference would help much in that situation. Indeed, studies that explored mood effects on the application of logical rules did not find inconsistent facilitatory effects of depressed affect. Again, it is perhaps not surprising that the more reliable effects have been obtained in the domain of persuasion and person perception. Monitoring what others want one to do, or determining what kind of person the other is, bears on the outcomes that may be expected and hence may be very adaptive responses to any situation that is characterized as "problematic." If this analysis is correct, appropriate predictions of the type of performance that will be facilitated or inhibited by a specific affective state demand careful analyses of the information-processing requirements that were associated with different adaptation problems in ancestral environments to which emotions developed as adaptive responses (see Tooby & Cosmides, 1990). Presumably, the procedures that were helpful in meeting these requirements will be the ones that are primed by the respective affective state. If so, we may have much to learn from evolutionary analyses of emotions and the appraisal patterns that underlie them.

On the methodological side, this implies that researchers need to pay more attention to the specific nature of the affective experience they induce in their subjects by a given mood manipulation. We certainly will have to go beyond the positive–negative dichotomy that characterizes most work in this area, although we acknowledge that inducing specific, distinct moods is a difficult task (e.g., Polivy, 1981). At a more general level, these concerns bear on a key issue in recent discussions of evolutionary cognitive psychology (e.g., Cosmides & Tooby, 1989; Tooby & Cosmides, 1989). Whereas cognitive psychologists have typically assumed that humans use a limited set of general reasoning mechanisms that can be applied to a large variety of problems, evolutionary psychology has maintained that human reasoning is probably not characterized by the application of a few general purpose tools. Rather, humans seem to use a large variety of specialized tools appropriate for different tasks (see Cosmides & Tooby, 1989, and Smith, Langston, & Nisbett, 1992, for detailed discussions). If so, disentangling the effects of affect on cognitive processes will be even more challenging.

SUMMARY

We have reviewed current psychological theory and research on several topics, including the nature of emotion, the cognitive causes of specific emotions, and the cognitive consequences of mood and emotion. Moods and emotions were distinguished and the basic emotions concept was considered. Emotion was viewed as a multifaceted phenomenon for which no single aspect appears to be a sufficient condition. The roles of feelings and cognitive appraisals as necessary conditions within certain views were discussed.

In the cognitive causes section, the role in the appraisal process of virtual cognitive structures such as goals and standards was considered. Eight current theories were reviewed, all of which focus on the cognitive eliciting conditions for specific emotions. These included theories advanced by Ortony, Clore, and Collins; Roseman; Smith and Ellsworth; Scherer; Frijda; Shaver and Schwartz; Weiner; and Higgins. They were considered using the Ortony et al. account as a basis of comparison. Criteria for evaluation of theories was suggested, including: (a) how theories handled positive emotions; (b) how they distinguished emotions from emotion words; (c) the degree to which they lent themselves to empirical test; (d) how their proposed cognitive structure was linked to behavior; and (e) the degree to which they had been formalized into quantitative, symbolic, or computational forms.

The cognitive consequences section covered theory and research in three related literatures focusing mainly on mood. These included mood and memory, mood and evaluative judgments, and mood and spontaneous processing strategies. Theoretical accounts of mood and memory phenomena included models based on resource allocation and on associative networks. Research was reviewed suggesting that negative affective states may reduce attentional resources for some material, and that mood-congruent memory is a rather fragile phenomenon.

A more robust phenomenon is the effect of mood on evaluative judgment. The primary explanations for this effect include models based on mood-congruent recall and the informational value of affective feelings. Research was reviewed supporting hypotheses that moods may influence judgment directly by serving as a basis for judgment, and indirectly by influencing what comes to mind.

Finally, recent research on the effects of mood on processing strategies was reviewed. The primary explanations considered include the limited cognitive resource model and a version of the feeling-as-information model. The latter assumes that one's thought processes become tuned to meet the requirements signaled by affective states. The research indicates that positive affect is associated with more spontaneous and heuristic informational processing strategies, but evidence on the processing consequences of negative affect is less consistent. The presence of gaps between the assumptions made by the major explanations and evidence relevant to the hypothesized intervening processes was discussed.

REFERENCES

Abelson, R. P. (1983). Whatever became of consistency theory? *Personality and Social Psychology Bulletin, 9,* 37–54.

Abramson, L. Y., Alloy, L. B., & Rosoff, R. (1981). Depression and the generation of complex hypotheses in the judgment of contingency. *Behaviour Research and Therapy, 19,* 35–45.

Adelmann, P. K., & Zajonc, R. B. (1989). Facial efference and the experience of emotion. *Annual Review of Psychology, 40,* 249–280.

Ahadi, S. (1993). *Self-guides and the big five.* Unpublished manuscript, University of Oregon, Eugene.

Alloy, L. B. (1988). *Cognitive processes in depression.* New York: Guilford.

Alloy, L. B., & Abramson, L. Y. (1979). Judgment of contingency in depressed and nondepressed students: Sadder but wiser? *Journal of Experimental Psychology: General, 108,* 441–485.

Alloy, L. B., Abramson, L. Y., & Viscusi, D. (1981). Induced mood and the illusion of control. *Journal of Personality and Social Psychology, 41,* 1129–1140.

Anderson, J. R. (1983). *The architecture of cognition.* Cambridge, MA: Harvard University Press.

Anderson, J. R., & Bower, G. H. (1973). *Human associative memory.* Washington, DC: Winston.

Arnold, M. B. (1960). *Emotion and personality.* New York: Columbia University Press.

Averill, J. R. (1980). A constructivist view of emotions. In R. Plutchik & H. Kellerman (Eds.), *Emotions: Theory, research, and experience* (Vol. 1, pp. 305–339). New York: Academic Press.

Bard, P. A. (1928). A diencephalic mechanism for the expression of rage with special reference to the sympathetic nervous system. *American Journal of Physiology, 84,* 490–515.

Bartlett, J. C., Burleson, G., & Santrock, J. W. (1982). Emotional mood and memory in young children. *Journal of Experimental Child Psychology, 34,* 59–76.

Bartlett, J. C., & Santrock, J. W. (1979). Affect dependent episodic memory in young children. *Child Development, 50,* 513–518.

Batson, C. D., Shaw, L. L., & Oleson, K. C. (1992). Differentiating affect, mood, and emotion. In M. S. Clark (Ed.), *Review of Personality and Social Psychology* (Vol. 11, pp. 294–326). Beverly Hills, CA: Sage.

Berkowitz, L. (in press). Towards a general theory of anger and emotional aggression: Implications of the cognitive-neoassociationistic perspective for the analysis of anger and other emotions. In T. K. Srull & R. S. Wyer (Eds.), *Advances in social cognition* (Vol. 5). Hillsdale, NJ: Lawrence Erlbaum Associates.

Berscheid, E. (1982). Attraction and emotion in interpersonal relations. In M. S. Clark & S. T. Fiske (Eds.), *Affect and cognition* (pp. 37–54). Hillsdale, NJ: Lawrence Erlbaum Associates.

Blaney, P. H. (1986). Affect and memory: A review. *Psychological Bulletin, 99,* 229–246.

Bless, H. (1992, September). *Stimmungseinflüsse und die Nutzung kognitiver Repräsentationen in der sozialen Urteilsbildung* [Mood effects on the use of cognitive representations]. Paper presented at the convention of the Deutsche Gesellschaft für Psychologie, Trier, Germany.

Bless, H., Bohner, G., Schwarz, N., & Strack, F. (1990). Mood and persuasion: A cognitive response analysis. *Personality and Social Psychology Bulletin, 16,* 331–345.

Bless, H., Mackie, D. M., & Schwarz, N. (1992). Mood effects on encoding and judgmental processes in persuasion. *Journal of Personality and Social Psychology, 63,* 585–595.

Bless, H., Strack, F., & Schwarz, N. (1993). The informative functions of research procedures: Bias and the logic of conversation. *European Journal of Social Psychology, 23,* 149–165.

Bodenhausen, G. V. (1993). Emotions, arousal, and stereotypic judgments: A heuristic model of affect and stereotyping. In D. M. Mackie & D. L. Hamilton (Eds.), *Affect, cognition, and stereotyping: Interactive processes in group perception* (pp. 13–37). San Diego: Academic Press.

Bohner, G., Bless, H., Schwarz, N., & Strack, F. (1988). What triggers causal attributions? The impact of valence and subjective probability. *European Journal of Social Psychology, 18,* 335–345.

Bohner, G., Crow, K., Erb, H. P., & Schwarz, N. (1992). Affect and persuasion: Mood effects on the processing of message content and context cues and on subsequent behavior. *European Journal of Social Psychology, 22,* 511–530.

Bohner, G., Marz, P., Bless, H., Schwarz, N., & Strack, F. (1992). Zum Einflug von Stimmungen auf Attributionsprozesse in der Personenwahrnehmung [Mood effects in person perception]. *Zeitschrift für Sozialpsychologie, 23,* 194–205.

Bollnow, O. F. (1956). *Das Wesen der Stimmungen.* Frankfurt: Klostermann.

Bower, G. H. (1981). Mood and memory. *American Psychologist, 36,* 129–148.

Bower, G. H. (1983). Affect and cognition. *Transactions of the Royal Philosophical Society of London, Series B, 302,* 387–402.

Bower, G. H. (1991). Mood congruity of social judgments. In J. P. Forgas (Ed.), *Emotion and social judgments* (pp. 31–53). Oxford, England: Pergamon.

Bower, G. H., & Cohen, P. R. (1982). Emotional influences in memory and thinking: Data and theory. In M. S. Clark & S. T. Fiske (Eds.), *Affect and cognition* (pp. 291–332). Hillsdale, NJ: Lawrence Erlbaum Associates.

Bower, G. H., Gilligan, S. G., & Monteiro, K. P. (1981). Selectivity of learning caused by affective states. *Journal of Experimental Psychology: General, 110*, 451–473.

Bower, G. H., & Mayer, J. D. (1985). Failure to replicate mood congruent retrieval. *Bulletin of the Psychonomic Society, 23*, 39–42.

Bower, G. H., Monteiro, K. P., & Gilligan, S. G. (1978). Emotional mood as a context of learning and recall. *Journal of Verbal Learning and Verbal Behavior, 17*, 573–585.

Broadbent, D. E. (1971). *Decision and stress*. London: Academic Press.

Bruner, J. S., Matter, J., & Papanek, M. L. (1955). Breadth of learning as a function of drive-level and maintenance. *Psychological Review, 62*, 1–10.

Caccioppo, J. T., Bush, L. K., & Tassinary, L. G. (1992). Microexpressive facial actions as a function of affective stimuli: Replication and extension. *Personality and Social Psychology Bulletin, 18*, 515–526.

Campos, J. J., & Barrett, K. C. (1984). Toward an understanding of emotions and their development. In C. E. Izard, J. Kagan, & R. B. Zajonc (Eds.), *Emotions, cognition, and behavior* (pp. 229–263). New York: Cambridge University Press.

Carson, T. P., & Adams, H. E. (1980). Activity valence as a function of mood change. *Journal of Abnormal Psychology, 89*, 368–377.

Carver, C. S., & Scheier, M. F. (1990). Origins and functions of positive and negative affect: A control-process view. *Psychological Review, 97*, 19–35.

Cattell, R. B. (1946). *The description and measurement of personality*. New York: Harcourt Brace Jovanovich.

Clark, D. M., & Teasdale, J. D. (1982). Diurnal variation in clinical depression and accessibility of memories of positive and negative experiences. *Journal of Abnormal Psychology, 91*, 87–95.

Clark, L. F., & Collins, J. E. (in press). Remembering old flames: How the past affects assessments of the present. *Personality and Social Psychology Bulletin*.

Clark, L. F., Collins, J. E., & Henry, S. M. (in press). Biasing effects of retrospective reports on current self-assessments. In N. Schwarz & S. Sudman (Eds.), *Autobiographical memory and the validity of retrospective reports*. New York: Springer Verlag.

Clore, G. L. (1985, August). *The cognitive consequences of emotions and feelings*. Paper presented at the meeting of the American Psychological Association, Los Angeles.

Clore, G. L. (1992). Cognitive phenomenology: Feelings and the construction of judgment. In L. L. Martin & A. Tesser (Eds.), *The construction of social judgments* (pp. 133–164). Hillsdale, NJ: Lawrence Erlbaum Associates.

Clore, G. L., & Byrne, D. (1974). A reinforcement affect model of attraction. In T. L. Huston (Ed.), *Foundations of interpersonal attraction* (pp. 173–170). New York: Academic Press.

Clore, G. L., & Ortony, A. (1988). Semantics of the affective lexicon. In V. Hamilton, G. Bower, & N. Frijda (Eds.), *Cognitive science perspectives on emotion and motivation* (pp. 367–398). Amsterdam: Martinus Nijhoff.

Clore, G. L., & Ortony, A. (1991). What more is there to emotion concepts than prototypes. *Journal of Personality and Social Psychology, 60*, 48–50.

Clore, G. L., Ortony, A., & Brand, S. (in preparation). *The joy of victory and the agony of defeat: The emotions of sports fans*. Champaign: University of Illinois.

Clore, G. L., Ortony, A., Dienes, B., & Fujita, F. (1993). Where does anger dwell? In T. K. Srull & R. S. Wyer (Eds.), *Advances in social cognition* (Vol. 5, pp. 57–87). Hillsdale, NJ: Lawrence Erlbaum Associates.

Clore, G. L., Ortony, A., & Foss, M. (1987). The psychological foundations of the affective lexicon. *Journal of Personality and Social Psychology, 53*, 751–766.

Clore, G. L., & Parrott, W. G. (1991). Moods and their vicissitudes: Thoughts and feelings as information. In J. Forgas (Ed.), *Emotion and social judgment* (pp. 107–123). Oxford: Pergamon.

Clore, G. L., & Parrott, W. G. (in press). Cognitive feelings and metacognitive judgments. *European Journal of Social Psychology.*

Conway, M., & Giannopoulos, C. (1993). Dysphoria and decision making: Limited information use in the evaluation of multiattribute targets. *Journal of Personality and Social Psychology, 64,* 613–623.

Conway, M., Giannopoulos, C., Csank, P., & Mendelson, M. (1993). Dysphoria and specificity in self-focused attention. *Personality and Social Psychology Bulletin, 19,* 265–268.

Cosmides, L., & Tooby, J. (1989). Evolutionary psychology and the generation of culture, Part II. *Ethology and Sociobiology, 10,* 51–97.

Cramer, P. (1968). *Word association.* New York: Academic Press.

Darwin, C. (1872). *The expression of the emotions in man and animals.* London: J. Murray.

Davitz, J. R. (1969). *The language of emotion.* New York: Academic Press.

De Rivera, J. (1977). A structural theory of the emotions [Monograph]. *Psychological Issues, 10,* 227–275.

Derry, P. A., & Kuiper, N. A. (1981). Schematic processing and self-reference in clinical depression. *Journal of Abnormal Psychology, 90,* 286–297.

Diener, C. I., & Dweck, C. S. (1978). An analysis of learned helplessness: Continuous changes in performance, strategy, and achievement cognitions following failure. *Journal of Personality and Social Psychology, 36,* 451–462.

Dobson, D. J. G., & Dobson, K. S. (1981). Problem-solving strategies in depressed and nondepressed students. *Cognitive Therapy and Research, 5,* 237–249.

Duncker, K. (1945). On problem-solving. *Psychological Monographs, 58,* Whole # 5.

Dweck, C. S., & Leggett, E. L. (1988). A social-cognitive approach to motivation and personality. *Psychological Review, 95,* 256–273.

Eagly, A. H., & Chaiken, S. (1993). *The psychology of attitudes.* Fort Worth, TX: Harcourt Brace Jovanovich.

Easterbrook, J. A. (1959). The effect of emotion on cue utilization and the organization of behavior. *Psychological Review, 66,* 183–201.

Edwards, J. A., & Weary, G. (1993). Depression and the impression formation continuum: From piecemeal to category-based processing. *Journal of Personality and Social Psychology, 64,* 636–645.

Eich, J. E. (1980). The cue-dependent nature of state-dependent retrieval. *Memory and Cognition, 8,* 157–173.

Ekman, P. (1982). *Emotion in the human face.* New York: Cambridge University Press.

Ekman, P. (1992a). Are there basic emotions? *Psychological Review, 99,* 550–553.

Ekman, P. (1992b, August). *Role of facial expression in the experience of emotion.* Paper presented at the meeting of the American Psychological Association, Washington, DC.

Ekman, P., & Friesen, W. V. (1975). *Unmasking the face: A guide to recognizing emotions from facial clues.* Englewood Cliffs, NJ: Prentice-Hall.

Ekman, P., Friesen, W. V., & Ellsworth, P. (1972). *Emotion in the human face.* New York: Pergamon.

Ekman, P., Friesen, W. V., & Ellsworth, P. (1982). What emotion categories or dimensions can observers judge from facial behavior? In P. Ekman (Ed.), *Emotion in the human face* (pp. 39–55). New York: Cambridge University Press.

Ekman, P., Levenson, R. W., & Friesen, W. V. (1983). Autonomic nervous system activity distinguishes among emotions. *Science, 221,* 1208–1210.

Ellis, H. C. (1990). Depressive deficits in memory: Processing initiative and resource allocation. *Journal of Experimental Psychology: General, 119,* 606–626.

Ellis, H. C. (1991). Focused attention and depressive deficits in memory. *Journal of Experimental Psychology: General, 120,* 310–312.

Ellis, H. C., & Ashbrook, P. W. (1988). Resource allocation model of the effects of depressed mood states on memory. In K. Fiedler & J. Forgas (Eds.), *Affect, cognition, and social behavior* (pp. 25–43). Toronto: C. J. Hogrefe.

Ellis, H. C., & Ashbrook, P. W. (1989). The "state" of mood and memory research: A selective review. *Journal of Social Behavior and Personality, 4,* 1–21.

Ellis, H. C., Thomas, R. L., McFarland, A. D., & Lane, J. W. (1985). Emotional mood states and retrieval in episodic memory. *Journal of Experimental Psychology: Learning, Memory, and Cognition, 11*, 363–370.

Ellis, H. C., Thomas, R. L., & Rodriguez, I. A. (1984). Emotional mood states and memory: Elaborative encoding, semantic processing, and cognitive effort. *Journal of Experimental Psychology: Learning, Memory, and Cognition, 10*, 470–482.

Ellsworth, P. C., & Smith, C. A. (1988). Shades of joy: Patterns of appraisal differentiating pleasant emotions. *Cognition and Emotion, 2*, 301–331.

Emmons, R. A., & King, L. A. (1988). Conflict among personal strivings: Immediate and long-term implications for psychological and physical well-being. *Journal of Personality and Social Psychology, 54*, 1040–1048.

Ewert, O. (1983). Ergebnisse und Probleme der Emotionsforschung [Findings and problems of emotion research]. In H. Thomae (Ed.), *Theorien und Formen der Motivation. Enzyklopadie der Psychologie* (Vol. 1). Göttingen: Hogrefe.

Eysenck, M. W. (1976). Arousal, learning, and memory. *Psychological Bulletin, 83*, 389–404.

Fehr, B., & Russell, J. A. (1984). Concept of emotion viewed from a prototype perspective. *Journal of Experimental Psychology: General, 113*, 464–486.

Fiedler, K. (1988). Emotional mood, cognitive style, and behavior regulation. In K. Fiedler & J. Forgas (Eds.), *Affect, cognition, and social behavior* (pp. 100–119). Toronto: Hogrefe International.

Fiedler, K. (1991). On the task, the measure, and the mood in research on affect and social cognition. In J. Forgas (Ed.), *Emotion and social judgment* (pp. 83–104). Oxford: Pergamon.

Fiedler, K., Pampe, H., & Scherf, U. (1986). Mood an memory for tightly organized social information. *European Journal of Social Psychology, 16*, 149–164.

Fiske, S. T., & Neuberg, S. L. (1990). A continuum of impression formation, from category-based to individuating processes: Influences of information and motivation on attention and interpretation. In M. P. Zanna (Ed.), *Advances in experimental social psychology* (Vol. 23, pp. 1–74). San Diego, CA: Academic Press.

Fletcher, G. J. D., Danilovics, P., Fernandez, G., Peterson, D., & Reeder, G. D. (1986). Attributional complexity: An individual difference measure. *Journal of Personality and Social Psychology, 56*, 757–764.

Forgas, J. P. (1992). Affect in social judgments and decisions: A multi-process model. In M. P. Zanna (Ed.), *Advances in experimental social psychology* (Vol. 25, pp. 227–275). San Diego: Academic Press.

Forgas, J. P. (in press). Affective influences on the perception of atypical people. *Journal of Personality and Social Psychology.*

Forgas, J. P., & Bower, G. H. (1987). Mood effects on person perception judgments. *Journal of Personality and Social Psychology, 53*, 53–60.

Forgas, J. P., & Bower, G. H. (1988). Affect in social and personal judgments. In K. Fiedler & J. Forgas (Eds.), *Affect, cognition, and social behavior* (pp. 183–207). Toronto: Hogrefe International.

Frijda, N. H. (1986). *The emotions.* New York: Cambridge University Press.

Frijda, N. H. (1987). Emotions, cognitive structure, and action tendency. *Cognition and Emotion, 1*, 235–258.

Frijda, N. H. (1988). The laws of emotion. *American Psychologist, 43*, 349–358.

Frijda, N. H., Kuipers, P., & ter Schure, E. (1989). The relationships between emotion, appraisal, and emotional action readiness. *Journal of Personality and Social Psychology, 57*, 212–228.

Frijda, N., Ortony, A., Sonnemans, J., & Clore, G. (1992). The complexity of intensity: issues concerning the structure of emotion intensity. In M. S. Clark (Ed.), *Review of Personality and Social Psychology* (Vol. 11, pp. 60–89). Beverly Hills, CA: Sage.

Gallagher, D., & Clore, G. L. (1985, May). *Effects of fear and anger on judgments of risk and blame.* Paper presented at the meeting of the Midwestern Psychological Association, Chicago.

Gilligan, S. G., & Bower, G. H. (1984). Cognitive consequences of emotional arousal. In C. Izard, J. Kagen, & R. Zajonc (Eds.), *Emotions, cognition, and behavior* (pp. 547–588). Cambridge, England: Cambridge University Press.

Godden, D. R., & Baddeley, A. D. (1975). Context dependent memory in two natural environments: On land and under water. *British Journal of Psychology, 66*, 325–331.

Gohm, C. L. (1992). *Self-discrepancy theory and cultural gender stereotypes.* Unpublished master's thesis, Central Michigan University.

Gray, J. A. (1982). *The neuropsychology of anxiety.* Oxford: Oxford University Press.

Hasher, L., Rose, K. C., Zacks, R. T., Sanft, H., & Doren, B. (1985). Mood, recall, and selectivity in normal college students. *Journal of Experimental Psychology: General, 114*, 104–118.

Hasher, L., & Zacks, R. T. (1979). Automatic and effortful processes in memory. *Journal of Experimental Psychology: General, 108*, 356–388.

Hastie, R., & Park, B. (1986). The relationship between memory and judgment depends on whether the judgment task is memory-based or on-line. *Psychological Review, 93*, 258–268.

Heider, F. (1958). *The psychology of interpersonal relations.* New York: Wiley.

Hertel, P. T., & Hardin, T. S. (1990). Remembering with and without awareness in a depressed mood: Evidence of deficits in initiative. *Journal of Experimental Psychology, General, 119*, 45–59.

Hertel, P. T. & Rude, S. S. (1991). Depressive deficits in memory: Focusing attention improves subsequent recall. *Journal of Experimental Psychology: General, 120*, 301–309.

Higgins, E. T. (1987). Self-discrepancy theory: A theory relating self and affect. *Psychological Review, 94*, 319–340.

Higgins, E. T. (1989a). Knowledge accessibility and activation: Subjectivity and suffering from unconscious sources. In J. S. Uleman & J. A. Bargh (Eds.), *Unintended thought* (pp. 75–123). New York: Guilford.

Higgins, E. T. (1989b). Self-discrepancy theory: What patterns of self-beliefs cause people to suffer. In L. Berkowitz (Ed.), *Advances in experimental social psychology* (Vol. 2, pp. 93–136). New York: Academic Press.

Higgins, E. T. (1990). Personality, social psychology, and person-situation relations: Standards and knowledge activation as a common language. In L. A. Pervin (Ed.), *Handbook of personality: Theory and research* (pp. 301–338). New York: Guilford.

Higgins, E. T., & Bargh, J. A. (1987). Social cognition and social perception. *Annual Review of Psychology, 38*, 369–425.

Higgins, E. T., Bond, R. N., Klein, R., & Strauman, T. J. (1986). Self-discrepancies and emotional vulnerability: How magnitude, accessibility, and type of discrepancy influence affect. *Journal of Personality and Social Psychology, 51*, 5–15.

Higgins, E. T., Klein, R., & Strauman, T. J. (1985). Self-concept discrepancy theory: A psychological model for distinguishing among different aspects of depression and anxiety. *Social Cognition, 3*, 51–76.

Hildebrand-Saints, L., & Weary, G. (1989). Depression and social information gathering. *Personality and Social Psychology Bulletin, 15*, 150–160.

Howell, A., & Conway, M. (1992). Mood and the suppression of positive and negative self-referent thoughts. *Cognitive Therapy and Research, 16*, 1–21.

Ingram, R. E. (1990). Self-focused attention in clinical disorders: Review and a conceptual model. *Psychological Bulletin, 107*, 156–176.

Isen, A. M. (1984). Toward understanding the role of affect in cognition. In R. S. Wyer, Jr. & T. K. Srull (Eds.), *Handbook of social cognition* (Vol. 3, pp. 179–236). Hillsdale, NJ: Lawrence Erlbaum Associates.

Isen, A. M. (1987). Positive affect, cognitive processes, and social behavior. In L. Berkowitz (Ed.), *Advances in experimental social psychology* (Vol. 20, pp. 203–253). New York: Academic Press.

Isen, A. M., & Daubman, K. A. (1984). The influence of affect on categorization. *Journal of Personality and Social Psychology, 47*, 1206–1217.

Isen, A. M., Daubman, K. A., & Nowicki, G. P. (1987). Positive affect facilitates creative problem solving. *Journal of Personality and Social Psychology, 52*, 1122–1131.

Isen, A. M., Johnson, M., Mertz, E., & Robinson, G. (1985). Positive affect and the uniqueness of word association. *Journal of Personality and Social Psychology, 48,* 1413–1426.

Isen, A. M., Means, B., Patrick, R., & Nowicky, G. (1982). Some factors influencing decision making strategy and risk-taking. In M. S. Clark & S. T. Fiske (Eds.), *Affect and cognition: The 17th Annual Carnegie Mellon Symposium on Cognition* (pp. 243–261). Hillsdale, NJ: Lawrence Erlbaum Associates.

Isen, A. M., Shalker, T. E., Clark, M. S., & Karp, L. (1978). Affect, accessibility of material in memory, and behavior: A cognitive loop? *Journal of Personality and Social Psychology, 36,* 1–12.

Izard, C. E. (1971). *The face of emotion.* New York: Appleton-Century-Crofts.

Izard, C. E. (1977). *Human emotions.* New York: Plenum.

Izard, C. E. (1992). Basic emotions, relations among emotions, and emotion-cognition relations. *Psychological Review, 99,* 561–565.

Jacobsen, E. (1957). Normal and pathological moods: Their nature and function. In R. S. Eisler, A. F. Freud, H. Hartman, & E. Kris (Eds.), *The psychoanalytic study of the child* (pp. 73–113). New York: International University Press.

James, W. (1884). What is an emotion? *Mind, 9,* 188–205.

James, W. (1890). *Principles of psychology.* New York: Holt.

Johnson, E., & Tversky, A. (1983). Affect, generalization, and the perception of risk. *Journal of Personality and Social Psychology, 45,* 20–31.

Kagan, J. (1984). The idea of emotion in human development. In C. E. Izard, J. Kagan, & R. B. Zajonc (Eds.), *Emotions, cognition, and behavior* (pp. 38–72). New York: Cambridge University Press.

Kahneman, D., & Tversky, A. (1982). The simulation heuristic. In D. Kahneman, P. Slovic, & A. Tversky (Eds.), *Judgment under uncertainty: Heuristics and biases.* New York: Cambridge University Press.

Kelley, H. H. (1972). *Causal schemata and the attribution process.* Morristown, NJ: General Learning Press.

Keltner, D., Ellsworth, P., & Edwards, K. (1993). Beyond simple pessimism: Effects of sadness and anger on social perception. *Journal of Personality and Social Psychology, 64,* 740–752.

Keltner, D., Locke, K. D., & Audrain, P. C. (1993). The influence of attributions on the relevance of negative feelings to satisfaction. *Personality and Social Psychology Bulletin, 19,* 21–30.

Kirschenbaum, D. S., Tomarken, A. J., & Humphrey, L. L. (1985). Affect and adult self-regulation. *Journal of Personality and Social Psychology, 48,* 509–523.

Kuhl, J. (1983). Emotion, Kognition und Motivation, II [Emotion, cognition, and motivation]. *Sprache und Kognition, 4,* 228–253.

Kunda, Z. (1990). The case for motivated reasoning. *Psychological Bulletin, 108,* 480–498.

Lacey, J. I., & Lacey, B. C. (1970). Some autonomic nervous system relationships. In P. Black (Ed.), *Physiological correlates of emotion* (pp. 205–227). New York: Academic Press.

Laird, J. D., Wagener, J., Halal, M., & Szegda, M. (1982). Remembering what you feel: Effects of emotion on memory. *Journal of Personality and Social Psychology, 42,* 646–657.

Lang, P. J. (1988). What are the data of emotion? In V. Hamilton, G. Bower, & N. Frijda (Eds.), *Cognitive science perspectives on emotion and motivation* (pp. 367–398). Amsterdam: Martinus Nijhoff.

Lassiter, G. D., & Koenig, L. J. (1991). *Depression and the unitization of behavior.* Manuscript submitted for publication.

Lazarus, R. S. (1966). *Psychological stress and the coping process.* New York: McGraw-Hill.

Lazarus, R. S., Kanner, A. D., & Folkman, S. (1980). Emotions: A cognitive-phenomenological analysis. In R. Plutchik & H. Kellerman (Eds.), *Emotion: Theory, research, and experience: Vol. 1. Theories of emotion* (pp. 189–217). New York: Academic Press.

Leight, K. A., & Ellis, H. C. (1981). Emotional mood states, strategies, and state-dependency in memory. *Journal of Verbal Learning and Verbal Behavior, 20,* 251–266.

Levenson, R. W., Ekman, P., Heider, K., & Friesen, W. V. (in press). Emotion and autonomic nervous system activity in an Indonesian culture. *Journal of Personality and Social Psychology*.

Leventhal, H. (1982). The integration of emotion and cognition: A view from the perceptual-motor theory of emotion. In M. S. Clark & S. T. Fiske (Eds.), *Affect and cognition* (pp. 121–156). Hillsdale, NJ: Lawrence Erlbaum Associates.

Levine, S., Wyer, R. S., & Schwarz, N. (in press). Are you what you feel? The affective and cognitive determinants of self-esteem. *European Journal of Social Psychology*.

Liu, J. H., Karasawa, K., & Weiner, B. (1992). Inferences about the causes of positive and negative emotions. *Personality and Social Psychology Bulletin, 18*, 603–615.

Lutz, C., & White, G. M. (1986). The anthropology of emotions. *Annual Review of Anthropology, 15*, 405–436.

Mackie, D. M., & Worth, L. T. (1989). Processing deficits and the mediation of positive affect in persuasion. *Journal of Personality and Social Psychology, 57*, 27–40.

Madigan, R. J., & Bollenbach, A. K. (1982). Effects of induced mood on retrieval of personal episodic and semantic memories. *Psychological Reports, 50*, 147–158.

Mandler, G. (1975). *Mind and emotion*. New York: Wiley.

Mandler, G. (1984). *Mind and body*. New York: Norton.

Mandler, J. M. (1984). *Stories, scripts, and scenes: Aspects of schema theory*. Hillsdale, NJ: Lawrence Erlbaum Associates.

Manstead, A. S. R., & Tetlock, P. E. (1989). Cognitive appraisals and emotional experience: Further evidence. *Cognition and Emotion, 3*, 225–240.

Marsh, K. L., & Weary, G. (1989). Depression and attributional complexity. *Personality and Social Psychology Bulletin, 15*, 325–336.

Marshall-Garcia, K. A., & Beck, R. C. (1985). Mood and recognition memory: A comparison of two procedures. *Bulletin of the Psychonomic Society, 23*, 450–452.

Martin, L. L., Harlow, T. F., & Strack, F. (1992). The role of bodily sensations in the evaluation of social events. *Personality and Social Psychology Bulletin, 18*, 412–419.

Martin, L. L., & Tesser, A. (1989). Toward a motivational and structural theory of ruminative thought. In J. S. Uleman & J. A. Bargh (Eds.), *Unintended thought* (pp. 306–326). New York: Guilford.

Martin, L. L., Ward, D. W., Achée, J. W., & Wyer, R. S. (1993). Mood as input: People have to interpret the motivational implications of their moods. *Journal of Personality and Social Psychology, 64*, 317–326.

Masters, J. C., Barden, R. C., & Ford, M. E. (1979). Affective states, expressive behavior, and learning in children. *Journal of Personality and Social Psychology, 37*, 380–390.

Mathews, A., & Bradley, B. (1983). Mood and the self-reference bias in recall. *Behavior Research and Therapy, 21*, 233–239.

Matlin, M. W., & Stang, D. (1979). *The Pollyanna Principle: Selectivity in language, memory, and thought*. Cambridge, MA: Shenkman.

Mauro, R., Sato, K., & Tucker, J. (1992). The role of appraisal in human emotions: A cross-cultural study. *Journal of Personality and Social Psychology, 62*, 301–317.

Mayer, J. D., Gaschke, Y. N., Braverman, D. L., & Evans, T. W. (1992). Mood-congruent recall is a general effect. *Journal of Personality and Social Psychology, 63*, 119–132.

McCaul, K. D. (1983). Observer attributions of depressed subjects. *Personality and Social Psychology Bulletin, 9*, 74–82.

McDougall, W. (1926). *An introduction to social psychology*. Boston: Luce.

Mecklenbräuker, S., & Hager, W. (1984). Effects of mood on memory: Experimental tests of a mood-state-dependent retrieval hypothesis and of a mood-congruity hypothesis. *Psychological Research, 46*, 335–376.

Mees, U. (1985). What do we mean when we speak of feelings? On the psychological texture of words denoting emotions. *Sprache und Kognition, 4*, 2–20.

Mees, U. (1990). *The criteria and intensity indicators of emotions*. Unpublished manuscript, Universitat Oldenburg, Germany.

Mischel, W., Ebbesen, E., & Zeiss, A. (1973). Selective attention to the self: Situational and dispositional determinants. *Journal of Personality and Social Psychology, 27*, 204–218.

Mitchell, J. E., & Madigan, R. J. (1984). The effects of induced elation and depression on interpersonal problem solving. *Cognitive Therapy and Research, 8*, 277–285.

Morgan, R. L., & Heise, D. (1988). The structure of emotions. *Social Science Quarterly, 51*, 19–31.

Morris, W. N. (1989). *Mood: The frame of mind.* New York: Springer-Verlag.

Morris, W. N. (1992). A functional analysis of the role of mood in affective systems. *Review of Personality and Social Psychology* (Vol. 11, pp. 256–293). Beverly Hills, CA: Sage.

Morris, W. N., & Reilly, N. P. (1987). Toward the self-regulation of mood: Theory and research. *Motivation and Emotion, 11*, 215–249.

Murphy, S. T., & Zajonc, R. B. (1993). Affect, cognition, and awareness: Priming with optimal and suboptimal stimulus exposures. *Journal of Personality and Social Psychology, 64*, 723–739.

Murray, N., Sujan, H., Hirt, E. R., & Sujan, M. (1990). The influence of mood on categorization: A cognitive flexibility interpretation. *Journal of Personality and Social Psychology, 59*, 411–425.

Natale, M., & Hantas, M. (1982). Effect of temporary mood states on selective memory about the self. *Journal of Personality and Social Psychology, 42*, 927–934.

Newman, L. S., Higgins, E. T., & Vookles, J. (1992). Self-guide strength and emotional vulnerability: Birth order as a moderator of self-affect relations. *Personality and Social Psychology Bulletin, 18*, 402–411.

Newtson, D. (1973). Attribution and the unit of perception of ongoing behavior. *Journal of Personality and Social Psychology, 28*, 28–38.

Niewenhuyse, B., Offenberg, L., & Frijda, N. H. (1987). Subjective emotion and reported body experience. *Motivation and Emotion, 11*, 169–182.

Nisbett, R. E., Zukier, H., & Lemley, R. H. (1981). The dilution effect. *Cognitive Psychology, 13*, 248–277.

Nowlis, V., & Nowlis, H. H. (1956). The description and analysis of mood. *Annals of the New York Academy of Sciences, 65*, 345–355.

Oatley, K., & Johnson-Laird, P. N. (1987). Towards a cognitive theory of the emotions. *Cognition and Emotion, 1*, 29–50.

Obrist, P. A. (1981). *Cardiovascular psychophysiology.* New York: Plenum.

Ortony, A. (1990, August). *The cognition-emotion connection.* Paper presented at the meeting of the American Psychological Association, Boston.

Ortony, A., & Clore, G. L. (1989). Emotion, mood, and conscious awareness. *Cognition and Emotion, 3*, 125–137.

Ortony, A., Clore, G. L., & Collins, A. (1988). *The cognitive structure of emotions.* New York: Cambridge University Press.

Ortony, A., Clore, G. L., & Foss, M. (1987). The referential structure of the affective lexicon. *Cognitive Science, 11*, 361–384.

Ortony, A., & Turner, T. J. (1990). What's basic about basic emotions? *Psychological Review, 97*, 315–331.

Panksepp, J. (1992). A critical role for "affective neuroscience" in resolving what is basic about basic emotions. *Psychological Review, 99*, 554–560.

Parkinson, B., & Manstead, A. S. R. (1992). Appraisal as a cause of emotion. In M. S. Clark (Ed.), *Review of personality and social psychology* (Vol. 11, pp. 122–149). Beverly Hills, CA: Sage.

Parrott, W. G. (1988). The role of cognition in emotional experience. In W. J. Baker, L. P. Mos, H. V. Rappard, & H. J. Stam (Eds.), *Recent trends in theoretical psychology* (pp. 327–337). New York: Springer-Verlag.

Parrott, W. G., & Sabini, J. (1990). Mood and memory under natural conditions: Evidence for mood incongruent recall. *Journal of Personality and Social Psychology, 59*, 321–336.

Perkins, S. C., Meyers, A. W., & Cohen, R. (1988). Problem-solving ability and response to feedback in peer-nominated mildly depressed children. *Cognitive Therapy and Research, 12*, 89–102.

Petty, R. E., & Cacioppo, J. T. (1986). *Communication and persuasion: Central and peripheral routes to attitude change.* New York: Springer-Verlag.

Pfeifer, R. (1988). Artificial intelligence models of emotion. In V. Hamilton, G. Bower, & N. Frijda (Eds.), *Cognitive science perspectives on emotion and motivation* (pp. 287–320). Amsterdam: Martinus Nijhoff.

Pittman, N. L., & Pittman, T. S. (1980). Deprivation of control and the attribution process. *Journal of Personality and Social Psychology, 39,* 377–389.

Pittman, T. S., & D'Agostino, P. R. (1985). Motivation and attribution: The effects of control deprivation on subsequent information processing. In J. H. Harvey & G. Weary (Eds.), *Attribution: Basic and applied issues* (pp. 117–142). San Diego, CA: Academic Press.

Pittman, T. S., & D'Agostino, P. R. (1989). Motivation and cognition: Control deprivation and the nature of subsequent information processing. *Journal of Experimental Social Psychology, 25,* 465–480.

Platt, J. J., & Spivack, G. (1975). *Manual for the means–ends problem solving procedure.* Philadelphia: Hahnemann Community Mental Health/Mental Retardation Center, Department of Medical Health Sciences, Hahnemann Medical College and Hospital.

Plutchik, R. (1980). A general psychoevolutionary theory of emotion. In R. Plutchik & H. Kellerman (Eds.), *Emotion: Theory, research, and experience: Vol. 1. Theories of emotion* (pp. 3–31). New York: Academic Press.

Polivy, J. (1981). On the induction of emotion in the laboratory: Discrete moods or multiple affect states. *Journal of Personality and Social Psychology, 41,* 803–817.

Potts, R., Camp, C., & Coyne, C. (1989). The relationship between naturally occurring dysphoric moods, elaborative encoding, and recall performance. *Cognition and Emotion, 3,* 197–205.

Roseman, I. J. (1984). Cognitive determinants of emotion: A structural theory. In P. Shaver (Ed.), *Review of personality and social psychology: Vol. 5. Emotions, relationships, and health* (pp. 11–36). Beverly Hills, CA: Sage.

Roseman, I. J. (1991). Appraisal determinants of discrete emotions. *Cognition and Emotion, 5,* 161–200.

Roseman, I. J., Antoniou, A. A., & Jose, P. E. (1992). *Appraisal determinants of emotions: Revising current theories.* Unpublished manuscript, University of California, Los Angeles.

Roseman, I. J., Spindel, M. S., & Jose, P. E. (1990). Appraisals of emotion-eliciting events: Testing a theory of discrete emotions. *Journal of Personality and Social Psychology, 59,* 899–915.

Roy-Byrne, P. P., Weingartner, H., Bierer, L. M., Thompson, K., & Post, R. M. (1986). Effortful and automatic processes in depression. *Archives of General Psychiatry, 43,* 265–267.

Rozin, P., & Fallon, A. E. (1987). A perspective on disgust. *Psychological Review, 94,* 23–41.

Russell, J. A. (1980). A circumplex model of affect. *Journal of Personality and Social Psychology, 39,* 1161–1178.

Russell, J. A. (1991). In defense of a prototype approach to emotion concepts. *Journal of Personality and Social Psychology, 60,* 37–47.

Salovey, P., & Singer, J. A. (1985, August). *The effects of mood on the recall of childhood and recent autobiographical memories.* Paper presented at the annual convention of the American Psychological Association, Los Angeles, CA.

Schachter, S., & Singer, J. E. (1962). Cognitive, social, and physiological determinants of emotional state. *Psychological Review, 69,* 379–399.

Schank, R. C., & Abelson, R. (1977). *Scripts, plans, goals, and understanding.* Hillsdale, NJ: Lawrence Erlbaum Associates.

Schare, M. L., Lisman, S. A., & Spear, N. E. (1984). The effects of mood variation on state-dependent retention. *Cognitive Therapy and Research, 8,* 387–408.

Scherer, K. R. (1984). On the nature and function of emotion: A component process approach. In K. R. Scherer & P. Ekman (Eds.), *Approaches to emotion* (pp. 293–317). Hillsdale, NJ: Lawrence Erlbaum Associates.

Scherer, K. R. (1986). Vocal affect expression: A review and model for future research. *Psychological Bulletin, 99,* 143–165.

Scherer, K. R. (1988). Criteria for emotion-antecedent appraisal: A review. In V. Hamilton, G. Bower, & N. Frijda (Eds.), *Cognitive science perspectives on emotion and motivation* (pp. 89–126). Amsterdam: Martinus Nijhoff.

Schwarz, N. (1987). *Stimmung als Information: Untersuchungen zum Einflu von Stimmungen auf die Bewertung des eigenen Lebens* [Mood as information]. Heidelberg, Germany: Springer Verlag.

Schwarz, N. (1990). Feelings as information: Informational and motivational functions of affective states. In E. T. Higgins & R. Sorrentino (Eds.), *Handbook of motivation and cognition: Foundations of social behavior* (Vol. 2, pp. 527–561). New York: Guilford.

Schwarz, N., & Bless, B. (1991). Happy and mindless, but sad and smart? The impact of affective states on analytic reasoning. In J. Forgas (Ed.), *Emotion and social judgment* (pp. 55–71). Oxford: Pergamon.

Schwarz, N., Bless, H., & Bohner, G. (1991). Mood and persuasion: Affective states influence the processing of persuasive communications. In M. Zanna (Ed.), *Advances in experimental social psychology* (Vol. 24, pp. 161–199). San Diego, CA: Academic Press.

Schwarz, N., Bless, H., Strack, F., Klumpp, G., Rittenauer-Schatka, H., & Simons, A. (1991). Ease of retrieval as information: Another look at the availability heuristic. *Journal of Personality and Social Psychology, 61*, 195–202.

Schwarz, N., & Clore, G. L. (1983). Mood, misattribution, and judgments of well-being: Informative and directive functions of affective states. *Journal of Personality and Social Psychology, 45*, 513–523.

Schwarz, N., & Clore, G. L. (1988). How do I feel about it? Informative functions of affective states. In K. Fiedler & J. Forgas (Eds.), *Affect, cognition, and social behavior* (pp. 44–62). Toronto: Hogrefe International.

Schwarz, N., Servay, W., & Kumpf, M. (1985). Attribution of arousal as a mediator of the effectiveness of fear-arousing communications. *Journal of Applied Social Psychology, 15*, 74–78.

Schwarz, N., & Strack, F. (1991). Evaluating one's life: A judgment model of subjective well-being. In F. Strack, M. Argyle, & N. Schwarz (Eds.), *Subjective well-being: An interdisciplinary perspective* (pp. 27–47). Oxford: Pergamon.

Schwarz, N., Strack, F., Kommer, D., & Wagner, D. (1987). Soccer, rooms and the quality of your life: Mood effects on judgments of satisfaction with life in general and with specific life-domains. *European Journal of Social Psychology, 17*, 69–79.

Seligman, M. E. P. (1975). *Helplessness: On depression, development, and death*. San Francisco, CA: Freeman.

Seligman, M. E. P., Abramson, L. Y., Semmel, A., & Von Baeyer, C. (1979). Depressive attributional style. *Journal of Abnormal Psychology, 88*, 242–247.

Seligman, M. E. P., Maier, S. F., & Solomon, R. L. (1971). Unpredictable and uncontrollable aversive events. In F. R. Brush (Ed.), *Aversive conditioning and learning* (pp. 347–400). New York: Academic Press.

Shaver, P., Schwartz, J., Kirson, D., & O'Connor, C. (1987). Emotion knowledge: Further exploration of a prototype approach. *Journal of Personality and Social Psychology, 52*, 1–11.

Shaver, P., Wu, S., & Schwartz, J. C. (1992). Cross-cultural similarities and differences in emotion and its representation: A prototype approach. In M. S. Clark (Ed.), *Review of personality and social psychology* (Vol. 11, pp. 175–212). Beverly Hills, CA: Sage.

Shields, S. A. (1984). Distinguishing between emotion and nonemotion: Judgments about experience. *Motivation and Emotion, 8*, 355–369.

Siemer, M., & Reisenzein, R. (1992). *Effects of mood on evaluative judgments: Influence of reduced processing capacity and mood salience*. Manuscript submitted for publication.

Silberman, E. K., Weingartner, H., & Post, R. M. (1983). Thinking disorder in depression. *Archives of General Psychiatry, 40*, 775–780.

Simon, H. (1967). Motivational and emotional controls of cognition. *Psychological Review, 74*, 29–39.

Sinclair, R. C. (1988). Mood, categorization breadth, and performance appraisal: The effects of order of information acquisition and affective state on halo, accuracy, information retrieval, and evaluations. *Organizational Behavior and Human Decision Processes, 42*, 22–46.

Sinclair, R. C., & Mark, M. M. (1992). The influence of mood state on judgment and action: Effects on persuasion, categorization, social justice, person perception, and judgmental accuracy. In L. L. Martin & A. Tesser (Eds.), *The construction of social judgments* (pp. 165–193). Hillsdale, NJ: Lawrence Erlbaum Associates.

Singer, J. A., & Salovey, P. (1988). Mood and memory: Evaluating the network theory of affect. *Clinical Psychology Review, 8*, 211–251.

Smedslund, J. (in press). The pseudo empirical in psychology and the case for psychologic. *Psychological Inquiry.*

Smith, C. A. (1989). Dimensions of appraisal and physiological response in emotion. *Journal of Personality and Social Psychology, 56*, 339–353.

Smith, C. A., & Ellsworth, P. C. (1985). Patterns of cognitive appraisal. *Journal of Personality and Social Psychology, 48*, 813–838.

Smith, C. A., & Ellsworth, P. C. (1987). Patterns of appraisal and emotion related to taking an exam. *Journal of Personality and Social Psychology, 52*, 475–488.

Smith, E. E., Langston, C., & Nisbett, R. (1992). *Rules and reasoning.* Unpublished manuscript, University of Michigan, Ann Arbor.

Snyder, M., & White, P. (1982). Moods and memories: Elation, depression, and remembering the events of one's life. *Journal of Personality, 50*, 139–167.

Spies, K., & Hesse, F. W. (1986). Interaktion von Emotion und Kognition [Interaction of emotion and cognition]. *Psychologische Rundschau, 37*, 75–90.

Srull, T. K. (1983). Affect and memory: The impact of affective reactions in advertising on the representation of product information in memory. In R. Bagozzi & A. Tybout (Eds.), *Advances in consumer research* (Vol. 10). Ann Arbor, MI: Association for Consumer Research.

Srull, T. K. (1984). The effects of subjective affective states on memory and judgment. In T. Kinnear (Ed.), *Advances in consumer research* (Vol. 11, pp. 530–533). Provo, UT: Association for Consumer Research.

Stein, B. S., & Bransford, J. D. (1979). Constraints on effective elaboration: Effects of precision and subject generation. *Journal of Verbal Learning and Verbal Behavior, 18*, 769–777.

Strack, F. (1992). The different routes to social judgments: Experiential versus informational strategies. In L. L. Martin & A. Tesser (Eds.), *The construction of social judgments* (pp. 249–276). Hillsdale, NJ: Lawrence Erlbaum Associates.

Strack, F., Martin, L. L., & Stepper, S. (1988). Inhibiting and facilitating conditions of the human smile: A non-obtrusive test of the facial feedback hypothesis. *Journal of Personality and Social Psychology, 53*, 768–777.

Strack, F., Schwarz, N., & Gschneidinger, E. (1985). Happiness and reminiscing: The role of time perspective, mood, and mode of thinking. *Journal of Personality and Social Psychology, 49*, 1460–1469.

Strauman, T. J. (1989). Self discrepancies in clinical depression and social phobia: Cognitive structures that underlie emotional disorders. *Journal of Abnormal Psychology, 98*, 14–22.

Strauman, T. J., & Higgins, E. T. (1987). Automatic activation of self-discrepancies and emotional syndromes: When cognitive structure influence affect. *Journal of Personality and Social Psychology, 53*, 1004–1014.

Strauman, T. J., & Higgins, E. T. (1988). Self-discrepancies as predictors of vulnerability to distinct syndromes of chronic emotional distress. *Journal of Personality, 56*, 685–707.

Strongman, K. T. (1987). *The psychology of emotion.* New York: Wiley.

Sullivan, M. J. L., & Conway, M. (1989). Negative affect leads to low-effort cognition: Attributional processing for observed social behavior. *Social Cognition, 7*, 315–337.

Sweeney, P. D., Anderson, K., & Bailey, S. (1986). Attributional style in depression: A meta-analytic review. *Journal of Personality and Social Psychology, 50*, 974–991.

Teasdale, J. D., & Russell, M. (1983). Differential effects of induced mood on the recall of positive, negative, and neutral words. *British Journal of Clinical Psychology, 22,* 163–171.

Teasdale, J. D., & Taylor, R. (1981). Induced mood and accessibility of memories: An effect of mood state or induction procedure? *British Journal of Clinical Psychology, 20,* 39–48.

Teasdale, J. D., Taylor, R., & Fogarty, S. J. (1980). Effects of induced elation-depression on the accessibility of memories of happy and unhappy experiences. *Behavior Research and Therapy, 18,* 339–346.

Tesser, A. (1990). Smith and Ellsworth's appraisal model of emotion: A replication, extension, and test. *Personality and Social Psychology Bulletin, 16,* 210–223.

Tetlock, P. E., & Boettger, R. (1989). Accountability: A social magnifier of the dilution effect. *Journal of Personality and Social Psychology, 57,* 388–398.

Tomkins, S. S. (1984). Affect theory. In K. R. Scherer & P. Ekman (Eds.), *Approaches to emotion* (pp. 163–195). Hillsdale, NJ: Lawrence Erlbaum Associates.

Tölle, R. (1982). *Psychiatrie* [Psychiatry] (6th ed.). Heidelberg, Germany: Springer Verlag.

Tooby, J., & Cosmides, L. (1989). Evolutionary psychology and the generation of culture, Part I. *Ethology and Sociobiology, 10,* 29–49.

Tooby, J., & Cosmides, L. (1990). The past explains the present. Emotional adaptations and the structure of ancestral environments. *Ethology and Sociobiology, 11,* 375–424.

Tulving, E. (1983). *Elements of episodic memory.* Oxford, England: Oxford University Press.

Tversky, A., & Kahneman, D. (1973). Availability: A heuristic for judging frequency and probability. *Cognitive Psychology, 5,* 207–232.

Wallbott, H. G., & Scherer, K. R. (1988). How universal and specific is emotional experience? Evidence from 27 countries and five continents. In K. R. Scherer (Ed.), *Facets of emotion* (pp. 31–56). Hillsdale, NJ: Lawrence Erlbaum Associates.

Watson, J. B. (1930). *Behaviorism.* Chicago: University of Chicago Press.

Watts, F. N., & Cooper, Z. (1989). The effects of depression on structural aspects of the recall of prose. *Journal of Abnormal Psychology, 98,* 150–153.

Weary, G., Marsh, K. L., Gleicher, F., & Edwards, J. A. (1993). Depression, control motivation, and the processing of information about others. In G. Weary, F. Gleicher, & K. L. Marsh (Eds.), *Control motivation and social cognition* (pp. 255–287). New York: Springer Verlag.

Wegner, D. M., & Vallacher, R. R. (1986). Action identification. In R. M. Sorrentino & E. T. Higgins (Eds.), *Handbook of motivation and cognition: Foundations of social behavior* (Vol. 1, pp. 550–582). New York: Guilford.

Weiner, B. (1985). An attributional theory of achievement motivation and emotion. *Psychological Review, 92,* 548–573.

Weiner, B., & Graham, S. (1984). An attributional approach to emotional development. In C. Izard, J. Kagan, & R. Zajonc (Eds.), *Emotion, cognition, and behavior* (pp. 167–191). New York: Cambridge University Press.

Weiner, B., Graham, S., & Chandler, C. C. (1982). Pity, anger, and guilt: An attributional analysis. *Personality and Social Psychology Bulletin, 8,* 226–232.

Weingartner, H., Miller, H., & Murphy, D. L. (1977). Mood state-dependent retrieval of verbal associations. *Journal of Abnormal Psychology, 86,* 276–284.

Wenzlaff, R. M., Wegner, D. M., & Roper, D. (1988). Depression and mental control: The resurgence of unwanted negative thoughts. *Journal of Personality and Social Psychology, 55,* 882–892.

Wetzler, S. (1985). Mood state-dependent retrieval: A failure to replicate. *Psychological Reports, 56,* 759–765.

Wood, J. V., Saltzberg, J. A., & Goldsamt, L. A. (1990). Does affect induce self-focused attention? *Journal of Personality and Social Psychology, 58,* 899–908.

Worth, L. T., & Mackie, D. M. (1987). Cognitive mediation of positive mood in persuasion. *Social Cognition, 5,* 76–94.

Wundt, W. (1897). *Outlines of psychology.* (C. H. Judd, Trans.) Leipzig: William Englemann.

Wyer, R. S., & Carlston, D. (1979). *Social cognition, inference, and attribution.* Hillsdale, NJ: Lawrence Erlbaum Associates.

Wyer, R. S., & Srull, T. K. (1989). *Memory and cognition in its social context.* Hillsdale, NJ: Lawrence Erlbaum Associates.

Zajonc, R. B. (1980). Feeling and thinking. Preferences need no inferences. *American Psychologist, 35,* 151–175.

Zillman, D. (1978). Attribution and misattribution of excitatory reactions. In J. H. Harvey, W. I. Ickes, & R. F. Kidd (Eds.), *New directions in attribution research* (Vol. 2, pp. 335–368). Hillsdale, NJ: Lawrence Erlbaum Associates.

Zillman, D., Johnson, R. C., & Day, K. D. (1972). Attribution of apparent arousal and proficiency of recovery from sympathetic activation affecting excitation transfer to aggressive behavior. *Journal of Experimental Social Psychology, 10,* 503–515.

Author Index

Note: This index refers the reader to pages in both volumes of this *Handbook*. Volume numbers (1), (2) are given in parentheses. Page numbers in *italics* indicate the location of full bibliographical references.

Subject Index

Note: This index refers the reader to pages in both volumes of this *Handbook*. Volume numbers **(1)**, **(2)** are given in parentheses.

DATE DUE